BEST PRACTICES IN ADOLESCENT LITERACY INSTRUCTION

D0979817

Also from Kathleen A. Hinchman

Tutoring Adolescent Literacy Learners:
A Guide for Volunteers
Kelly Chandler-Olcott and Kathleen A. Hinchman

Best Practices in Adolescent Literacy Instruction

SECOND EDITION

Edited by

Kathleen A. Hinchman
Heather K. Sheridan-Thomas

Foreword by Donna E. Alvermann

THE GUILFORD PRESS
New York   London

© 2014 The Guilford Press
A Division of Guilford Publications, Inc.
72 Spring Street, New York, NY 10012
www.guilford.com

Printed in the United States of America

This book is printed on acid-free paper.

Last digit is print number: 9 8 7 6 5 4 3 2 1

Library of Congress Cataloging-in-Publication Data

Best practices in adolescent literacy instruction, second edition / edited by
Kathleen A. Hinchman, Heather K. Sheridan-Thomas; foreword by Donna E.
Alvermann.—Second edition.
    pages cm
   Includes bibliographical references and index.
   ISBN 978-1-4625-1534-9 (paperback)—ISBN 978-1-4625-1538-7 (cloth)
   1. Language arts (Secondary)—United States.   2. Language arts (Middle
school)—United States.   3. Language experience approach in education—United
States.   I. Hinchman, Kathleen A.   II. Sheridan-Thomas, Heather K.
   LB1631.B44 2014
   372.47′5—dc23
                                                                2014002162

About the Editors

Kathleen A. Hinchman, PhD, is Professor of Reading and Language Arts at Syracuse University. A former middle school teacher, she is coauthor or coeditor of several books, including *Teaching Adolescents Who Struggle with Reading* and *Reconceptualizing the Literacies in Adolescents' Lives.* Her current work is concerned with secondary school implementation of the Common Core State Standards for English Language Arts.

Heather K. Sheridan-Thomas, EdD, is Assistant Superintendent for Instructional Services at the Tompkins–Seneca–Tioga Board of Cooperative Educational Services in Ithaca, New York. Formerly a teacher education professor, public school administrator, and secondary school teacher, her current focus is on implementing the Common Core State Standards in a way that honors the professionalism and expertise of teachers while preparing adolescents to be literate, thoughtful stewards of this planet in the 21st century.

Contributors

Donna E. Alvermann, PhD, is Distinguished Research Professor of Language and Literacy Education at the University of Georgia. A former classroom teacher in Texas and New York, she teaches classes and seminars in adolescent literacy. Her research interests include adolescents' online literacies, popular culture in K–12 classrooms, digital media and learning, multimodal texts, and professional development in content-area/disciplinary literacy.

Randy Bomer, PhD, is Professor and Chair in the Department of Curriculum and Instruction at the University of Texas at Austin. He is a past president of the National Council of Teachers of English. His research investigates the ways teachers leverage the knowledge and interests that children and youth bring to school in order to grow as readers and writers.

Fenice B. Boyd, PhD, is Associate Professor of Literacy Education at the University at Buffalo, The State University of New York. She is a former music and reading teacher at the middle school level. Her research interests include the Common Core State Standards, writing genres, topics of diversity writ large, and adolescents' literacy learning and practices in and out of school.

Karen Bromley, PhD, is SUNY Distinguished Teaching Professor in the School of Education at Binghamton University, The State University of New York, where she teaches courses in literacy instruction and assessment, children's literature, and writing. She is a former third-grade teacher and a K–8 reading specialist in New York and Maryland.

William G. Brozo, PhD, is Professor of Literacy in the Graduate School of Education at George Mason University. A former secondary school literacy teacher, his research focuses on adolescent and content literacy, secondary school literacy reform, struggling learners, and closing the literacy achievement gap for boys. He is the author of *Supporting Content Area Literacy with Technology* and the *Adolescent Literacy Inventory*.

Kelly Chandler-Olcott, EdD, is Professor and Chair of the Reading and Language Arts Center at Syracuse University. A former secondary English and social studies teacher, she has conducted research on content-area literacy, teachers' classroom-based inquiry, and adolescents' technology-mediated literacy practices.

Aubrey Comperatore, MA, is a doctoral student in Teacher Education and Literacy Studies at the University of North Carolina at Chapel Hill.

Deborah R. Dillon, PhD, is Associate Dean for Professional, Graduate, and International Programs and the Guy Bond Chair in Reading at the University of Minnesota. Her research focuses on the role of motivation in engaged literacy practices, and the ways in which teachers and students can collaborate to create experiences in which learners feel self-efficacious and find learning meaningful.

Douglas Fisher, PhD, is Professor of Educational Leadership at San Diego State University. A former staff development specialist, he has written many journal articles and books, including *Teaching Students to Read Like Detectives* and *Better Learning through Structured Teaching.* He is a teacher–leader at Health Sciences High and Middle College in San Diego, California.

Michelle Fowler-Amato, MA, is a doctoral candidate at the University of Texas at Austin. She has taught both middle school and high school language arts and has served as a literacy coach. Her research interests include adolescent literacy, the teaching of writing, and sociocultural influences on teaching and learning.

Nancy Frey, PhD, is Professor in the Department of Educational Leadership at San Diego State University. She is a credentialed special educator, reading specialist, and administrator, and a frequent coauthor with Douglas Fisher on books about literacy and leadership, including *Rigorous Reading: 5 Access Points for Comprehending Complex Texts.* She is a teacher–leader at Health Sciences High and Middle College in San Diego, California.

Cynthia Greenleaf, PhD, is codirector of the Strategic Literacy Initiative at WestEd in San Francisco, where she leads the agency's research and development efforts focused on promoting higher-level literacy for diverse youth. Her research has been integral to the development of the Reading Apprenticeship framework, the central organizing principle of the Strategic Literacy Initiative.

Margaret C. Hagood, PhD, is Associate Professor at the College of Charleston, where she teaches undergraduate and graduate courses in literacy. Her research explores how teachers and students understand new literacies and use out-of-school literacies to improve performance in teaching and learning with literacies in schools. She is a coeditor of the *Journal of Adolescent and Adult Literacy.*

Leigh A. Hall, PhD, is on the faculty at the University of North Carolina at Chapel Hill, where she teaches literacy courses. Her research addresses issues relevant to literacy and middle school and teacher education, and includes how students' identities as readers influence the decisions they make when reading and how teachers can use information about students' identities to inform practice and improve their reading comprehension.

Kathleen A. Hinchman, PhD (see "About the Editors").

David R. Krauter, MA, is a literacy coach, former elementary school teacher, and doctoral candidate in Curriculum and Instruction at Arizona State University. His research interests include classroom discourse, teacher and student identities, and the development of collaborative networks in education.

Alisa G. Leckie, PhD, is Assistant Professor at Georgia Southern University. She cofounded a dual language program and has extensive teaching experience with English language learners (ELLs). Her research interests include how rigorous grade-level content can be made accessible to ELLs and how language policy influences educational practice.

Cindy Litman, MS, is Senior Research Associate at WestEd's Strategic Literacy Initiative in San Francisco. She has performed multiple research and development roles for elementary, secondary, and after-school literacy initiatives for more than 20 years, with a special focus on the relationship between social, emotional, and intellectual literacy development.

Josephine Peyton Marsh, PhD, is Professor in Residence at Arizona State University Preparatory Academy and Associate Professor of Literacy Education at Arizona State University. A former adolescent literacy teacher, her research interests include collaborative professional development, school change, and student engagement in literacy learning.

Elizabeth Birr Moje, PhD, is Associate Dean for Research and Community Engagement and the Arthur F. Thurnau Professor of Literacy, Language, and Culture in Educational Studies at the University of Michigan. Her research interests revolve around the intersection between the literacies and texts youth are asked to learn in the academic disciplines and those they experience outside of school.

Kristen A. Munger, PhD, is Assistant Professor of Counseling and Psychological Services at the State University of New York at Oswego, where she teaches graduate courses in research methods and school psychology. Her research explores the cognitive processes of early reading and spelling, early literacy assessments, and the types of texts used for reading instruction.

Maria S. Murray, PhD, is Assistant Professor of Literacy Education at the State University of New York at Oswego. Her research interests include the invented spellings of young students, the types of texts used for reading instruction, and early reading intervention for students most at risk for reading difficulty.

David G. O'Brien, PhD, is Professor of Literacy Education at the University of Minnesota. His areas of research include adolescent literacy, academic literacies, and motivation and engagement related to the use of multimodal texts and digital learning spaces. His most recent project focuses on how affordances of digital tools combined with literacy practices support learning across the curriculum.

Lettice Pelotte, MEd, is a high school English teacher and a doctoral student in Curriculum and Instruction at Arizona State University. Her research interests include discourse within online fan cultures, young adult literature, and public pedagogy.

Todd F. Reynolds, EdS, is a doctoral student and graduate assistant in Literacy Education at the University of Wyoming, where he also teaches English language arts methods classes for preservice teachers. An experienced high school English teacher, elementary literacy coach, and fifth-grade teacher, his research interests include dialogue and discourse in the classroom, disciplinary literacy, and preservice teacher education.

Zaline Roy-Campbell, PhD, is on the faculty of the Reading and Language Arts Center at Syracuse University and director of the Teaching English Language Learners (TELL) M.S. Program. Her research interests include language and literacy issues in education; preparing effective teachers of English language learners; and the intersections between knowledge production, culture, and language of instruction.

Eliane Rubinstein-Ávila, EdD, is Associate Professor at the University of Arizona. Formerly a bilingual teacher in California, her research focuses on immigrant and nondominant youth, and how biliteracy, race, ethnicity, class, gender, and culture intersect with in-school and out-of-school contexts. She has published articles across a range of academic journals.

Leslie S. Rush, PhD, is Associate Dean for Undergraduate Programs in the College of Education at the University of Wyoming, where she has long served as an English teacher educator. Her research interests include literacy coaching in secondary schools and disciplinary literacy. She is the coeditor of *English Education,* the journal of the Conference on English Education, and is a consultant for the Southern Regional Education Board's college and career readiness curriculum development project.

Cynthia Shanahan, PhD, is Professor Emerita of Literacy, Language, and Culture at the University of Illinois at Chicago. She is a researcher on Project READI, a reading comprehension study funded by the Institute of Education Sciences that studies argumentation in history, science, and literature. She also is working on a college and career readiness curriculum project with the Southern Regional Education Board.

Timothy Shanahan, PhD, is Distinguished Professor Emeritus at the University of Illinois at Chicago, where he was founding director of the Center for Literacy. Previously he was director of reading for the Chicago Public Schools, and is past president of the International Reading Association. He has authored more than 200 publications on literacy education and was inducted into the Reading Hall of Fame in 2007.

Heather K. Sheridan-Thomas, EdD (see "About the Editors").

Jennifer Speyer, BA, is a history teacher at the Detroit Institute of Technology and a master's student at the University of Michigan.

Alfred W. Tatum, PhD, is Professor and Interim Dean of the College of Education at the University of Illinois at Chicago. His research focuses on improving the literacy achievement of African American males and on using texts as tools to preserve one's humanity. He has authored three books, including *Fearless Voices: Engaging a New Generation of African American Adolescent Male Writers.*

Codruta Temple, PhD, is on the faculty at the State University of New York at Cortland, where she teaches courses in foreign language methods and bilingual and multicultural education. Her research focuses primarily on adolescents' acquisition of subject-specific discourses.

Andrea L. Tochelli, MS, is a former elementary and middle school teacher and a doctoral candidate in Reading Education at the University at Buffalo, The State University of New York. Her research interests include the use of digital technologies for multimodal composing as well as the use of video as a mediation tool in teacher professional development.

Foreword

An invitation to write the foreword to the second edition of *Best Practices in Adolescent Literacy Instruction* comes at a particularly apt time. Issues surrounding the Common Core State Standards and their assessment are on the radar of most adolescent literacy educators. So, too, are the consequences of Race to the Top funding and an ever-escalating media interest in teacher accountability, including program accountability in teacher education at the postsecondary level.

Rising above the storm of claims, critiques, and countercritiques, the second edition is an authoritative voice of reason and calm. The book's chapter authors are well versed in the issues that potentially threaten the morale of adolescent literacy educators everywhere. With steady precision and exciting insights, these authors offer a way out of any crisis, whether manufactured or real. To their credit, they do so without dodging the complexities of or minimizing the difficulties involved in teaching adolescent learners at a time when powerful influences both in and out of school compete for their attention.

The editors of this edition have demonstrated once again a keen sense of the field and where it is headed. They know the value of having timely updates for touchstone chapters and of adding new chapters on topics that are increasingly visible, such as disciplinary literacies and discourse studies. At the same time, they have a knack for providing just the right balance between time-tested methods and innovative approaches. The bottom line is that the editors keep it real, in the sense of being true to themselves while embracing the unknowable.

A feature that I greatly admired in the first edition has found its way into the current edition as well. Here I'm referring to what some have called the book's "dippability" factor. Briefly, it involves choosing a focal topic (e.g., youth identity, assessment, or motivation) pertinent to adolescent literacy instruction and then following that topic without regard for linear restrictions or moving through the various "dressings" that different chapter authors have given it. A "dippable" book invites purposeful searching and sense making about topics that interest a reader in ways an author may not have anticipated.

For example, when I set out to read the nearly finalized chapters on my computer, I was searching for information on assessment practices in a range of classroom contexts as described by those authors with unique perspectives on the topic. Much to my delight, the storyline that I discovered by dipping first here and then there was quite different from the one I would have discovered had I decided to read whole chapters with "assessment" in their titles at a time.

But however one reads *Best Practices in Adolescent Literacy Instruction* is immaterial when compared to what one will take from the book and use. Between the covers (whether paper or digital) of this second edition lie powerful ideas capable of generating change from within the profession rather than from without—the kind of change that puts young people and their literacy needs front and center.

DONNA E. ALVERMANN, PhD
University of Georgia

Preface

We, like many of our authors, squeezed our work on this second edition into our other Race to the Top–related work in U.S. schools and institutions of higher education. The widespread adoption—and critique—of the Common Core State Standards for English Language Arts, along with response to intervention and other aspects of new teacher and teacher education evaluation systems, make it clear that we have entered a new era in adolescent literacy education, one of heightened accountability to the literacies of all students in grades 5–12. We are also acutely aware of our obligation to attend to what is not so easily measured—the identity work, evolving use of texts, and engagement with social media that portend the literacies to come. The second edition of *Best Practices in Adolescent Literacy Instruction* is a comprehensive edited volume with revised chapters that help teachers address the college and career readiness aspirations of Race to the Top, and, importantly, students' lifelong success and fulfillment.

As with the first edition of this book, we note with irony that one phrase in our title, *best practices*, is contentious in adolescent literacy scholarship. It hints at instructional practices suited to all youth, even though youths' literacies are about who they are as individuals. They sample affinity groups and enact their many differences in strengths, backgrounds, and needs, and their individual preferences in music, film, gaming, social media, and so on. Even so, research on literacy instruction does indeed suggest tools that responsive teachers can modify to scaffold students' development of self-regulated reading, writing, and alternative communication. Our references to best practices are intended to invoke such tools.

The term *adolescent literacy* can also carry the pejorative connotation of a not-yet-fully-formed ability to read and write. Yet the label can also focus educators' gaze on youths' full complement of in-school and out-of-school literacy practices instead of on the narrower concerns of other, now dated, descriptors, such as secondary school or content-area reading or literacy (Alvermann, Jonas, Steele, & Washington, 2006). We refer to adolescent literacy to align ourselves with efforts that respect youths' insights that help them to develop a full array of literacy practices and that prepare them for the literacies that will come next in our rapidly changing world.

Part I of this edition, *Valuing Adolescence,* encourages us to embrace and enhance youths' literacies with attention to their various social alignments. In "Texts and Adolescents: Embracing Connections and Connectedness," Alfred W. Tatum explains the value of culturally grounded text lineages. Eliane Rubenstein-Ávila and Alisa G. Leckie suggest the importance of instruction that starts with adolescents' existing linguistic strengths in "Meaningful Discipline-Specific Language Instruction for Middle School Students for Whom English Is an *Additional* Language." David G. O'Brien and Deborah R. Dillon's chapter, "The Role of Motivation in Engaged Reading of Adolescents," answers many teachers' most important questions about their work with older, seemingly unmotivated youth. Engaging youth in rhetorical critique is the focus of Margaret C. Hagood's chapter, "Using Discourse Study as an Instructional Practice with Adolescents to Develop 21st-Century Literacies of Critically Conscious Citizens." Responding to youth who struggle with academic literacies is Leigh A. Hall and Aubrey Comperatore's important terrain in "Teaching Literacy to Youth Who Struggle with Academic Literacies."

Part II, *Developing Literacy Strategies,* contains recommendations for teaching students strategies for reading and writing. Kristen A. Munger and Maria S. Murray explain how teachers can help students utilize a wide array of complex texts in "Text Complexity and Deliberate Practice: Common Cores of Learning." In "Active Engagement with Words," Karen Bromley focuses on vocabulary development teaching strategies that encourage students' independence. Douglas Fisher and Nancy Frey explain that new insights about developing skills in reading disciplinary content necessitate strategic reading comprehension instruction in "Comprehension in Secondary Schools." Building on youths' existing writing strategies is the focus of Randy Bomer and Michelle Fowler-Amato's chapter, "Expanding Adolescent Writing: Building upon Youths' Practices, Purposes, Relationships, and Thoughtfulness." Cynthia Shanahan leads us to consider multiple strategies in "Reading and Writing across Multiple Texts."

Part III, *Developing Disciplinary Literacies,* contains a variety of new ideas for subject area–focused literacy instruction. Codruta Temple and Kathleen A. Hinchman help us invite youth to learn the nuances of mathematics-specific language in "Fostering Acquisition of Mathematics Language." Elizabeth Birr Moje and Jennifer Speyer discuss practices and strategies for teachers in their chapter "Reading Challenging Texts in High School: How Teachers Can Scaffold and Build Close Reading for Real Purposes in the Subject Areas." "Teaching History and Literacy" is the focus of Timothy Shanahan and Cynthia Shanahan's chapter. Leslie S. Rush and

Todd F. Reynolds add to our insights regarding literacy instruction in English classes in "Literacy Support in English/Language Arts Classrooms: Motivation, Dialogue, and Strategy Instruction." Heather K. Sheridan-Thomas concludes Part III with "Assisting Struggling Readers with Textbook Comprehension," which reminds us that students who struggle with academic literacies require extra guidance to access their textbooks.

Part IV, *Addressing Program and Policy Issues*, explains the issues involved in organizing systems to provide literacy instruction for all youth. For instance, Fenice B. Boyd and Andrea L. Tochelli delineate methods for integrating multimodal texts in discipline-specific study in "Multimodality and Literacy Learning: Integrating the Common Core State Standards for English Language Arts." Cindy Litman and Cynthia Greenleaf show us how apprenticeship can yield literacy success in "Traveling Together over Difficult Ground: Negotiating Success with a Profoundly Inexperienced Reader in an Introduction to Chemistry Class." Zaline Roy-Campbell and Kelly Chandler-Olcott challenge us to organize classroom literacy work that addresses each student's needs in "Differentiating Literacy Instruction for Adolescents." "Assessment for Literacy Growth and Content Learning in Secondary Schools," William G. Brozo's chapter, explains how to gather information for data-driven adolescent literacy instruction. "Coaching and Growing Literacy Communities of Practice," by Josephine Peyton Marsh, David R. Krauter, and Lettice Pelotte, explains how to organize responsive schoolwide literacy improvement.

We began the first edition of this book by inviting authors to share their ideas for literacy instruction that cognitive and sociocultural research suggested as engaging and effective for youth in grades 5–12. We asked the second edition's authors to consider the implications of this research for addressing school reform initiatives since 2008. We are most pleased with the result; their contributions represent the most significant ideas of our era for tackling adolescent literacy instruction and program development. Some of this research may seem more applicable to discipline-specific study, whereas other research may seem more relevant to academic literacy classes. Some of these ideas may appear more suitable for upper elementary and middle schools, whereas others may work better in high schools. We urge you to consider all the principles and examples presented and to design literacy instruction that engages, challenges, and embraces our youth as they prepare for life in these quickly changing times. We wish you good luck with these important efforts.

ACKNOWLEDGMENTS

With special thanks to Craig Thomas, Louise Farkas, and Mary Beth Anderson at The Guilford Press, we dedicate this second edition to our colleagues and friends for their thoughtful contributions, feedback, and encouragement, and, as always, to Bill and Sloan, for their patience, support, and affection.

KATHLEEN A. HINCHMAN
HEATHER K. SHERIDAN-THOMAS

REFERENCE

Alvermann, D. E., Jonas, S., Steele, A., & Washington, E. (2006). Introduction. In D. E. Alvermann, K. A. Hinchman, D. W. Moore, S. F. Phelps, & D. Waff (Eds.), *Reconceptualizing the literacies in adolescents' lives* (2nd ed., pp. xxi–xxxii). New York: Erlbaum.

Contents

PART I

Valuing Adolescence

CHAPTER 1

Texts and Adolescents

Embracing Connections and Connectedness

Alfred W. Tatum

The tenets of this chapter are:

- Examining adolescents' meaningful relationships with texts is central to selecting and discussing texts with high- and low-performing readers.
- Understanding which adolescents are finding texts meaningful and why is central to shaping curricular practices.
- Recognizing that adolescents can relate to texts yet fail to find the texts meaningful after reading them is useful for rethinking the roles of texts for adolescents.

Engaging students with texts by honoring their multiple identities has been a focus of adolescent literacy for more than two decades. However, it is still unclear whether adolescents who read texts that connect to their multiple identities find the texts meaningful. In addition, it is unclear whether high academically performing readers experience more meaningful relationships with texts than low academically performing readers. I decided to expand the chapter from the first edition of this book by adding findings from a more recent study that examined adolescents' meaningful relationships with texts, looking at adolescents across ethnicities and academic performance by grades.

An examination of this issue is warranted because students' relationships with texts are constantly changing in relationship to evolving technologies inside and outside of schools. Also, curricular shifts for U.S.

secondary school students are being implemented to align instruction with the Common Core State Standards (CCSS). Examining adolescents' meaningful relationships with texts is an initial step toward identifying ways educators can select and discuss texts to nurture resilience in high and low academically performing adolescents. As I mentioned in the first edition of this text, students generally participate in superficial discussions of characters and content in classrooms without gaining a deeper understanding of the text's meaning as it relates to who they are and what they can become. Or students are disengaged from texts because they assess the texts as being irrelevant, teacher-driven selections mandated by school curricula that are more exclusive than inclusive to students with varying cultural and linguistic histories and experiences.

Classroom environments and curricula are not often structured to shape students' lives by engaging them with texts that they find meaningful. This absence of meaningful texts is problematic because middle and high school students are striving to find their place in the world as they bump against academic, cultural, emotional, gender, historical, linguistic, and social forces that inform their existence. I am especially concerned that students are being deprived of textual lineages, that is, texts that they will remember years into the future as being meaningful and central to their human development.

Curricular decisions continue to be made in high schools without the benefit of data about students' relationships with texts to govern these decisions for all students across ethnicities and achievement levels. This is problematic because curricular and pedagogical choices could be inadvertently affecting adolescents' relationships with text, thereby contributing to their disengagement with reading in and out of schools.

Classroom environments and the teaching occurring within these environments may not be responding adequately to students' multiple literacy needs. As a result, the meaningful encounters that adolescents could experience with books, poems, and essays in schools during an optimal period of their development may be severely compromised in middle and high school classrooms. Teachers need to foster students' partnership with texts.

Classrooms are ideal settings in which to introduce and engage adolescents with texts connected to some larger ideological focus of literacy instruction (e.g., functioning in a global society, improving the human condition). Classrooms are also ideal settings in which educators can use texts to broker positive relationships with adolescents and connect students to something important that will lead to different actions and thinking beyond the reading event.

This chapter is grounded in the work of other researchers who have explored how gender and social class influence students' discussion of texts (Clark, 2006; Smith & Wilhelm, 2006; Sprague & Keeling, 2007) and the potential of text to be transformative for students (Lalik & Oliver, 2007;

Mosenthal, 1998; Tatum, 2005). It also aligns with Glenn's (2012) work on touchstone texts. These are texts in adolescents' lives that are woven into their school and social behavior. These are also texts that move adolescents to feel differently about themselves, affect their views of themselves and others, and move them to some action in their current time and space because of ethnic, gender, personal, or other connections with texts (Tatum, 2008). These texts become part of one's textual lineage (Tatum, 2009).

EXAMINING TEXTUAL LINEAGES

Concerned about engaging African American adolescent males with texts, I began examining why, from a historical perspective, African American males engaged with texts. As a data collection tool, I began to construct textual lineages (see Figure 1.1). I was aiming to use the historical relationship African American males had with text to identify implications for engaging young men with text in today's classrooms. The examination yielded a rich history between African American males and texts. Historically, texts have been central in their literacy development, with the connection among reading, writing, speaking, and action eminently clear. African American males gravitated toward texts connected to larger ideals such as cultural uplift, economic advancement, resistance to oppression, and intellectual development. Characteristically, these texts were "enabling" texts. An enabling text is one that moves beyond a sole cognitive focus—such as skill and strategy development—to include a social, cultural, political, spiritual, or economic focus (Tatum, 2006).

Subsequent to my historical analysis of African American males' interaction with texts, I began to collect the textual lineages of middle and high school students in schools where I provide professional development for teachers. The goal was to use students' textual lineages, along with their voices, to shape how teachers and administrators select reading materials that speak to, inform, shape, and contribute to the intellectual and emotional development of adolescents, as well as to how teachers plan instruction for adolescents (see Figure 1.2).

During the academic school year 2006–2007, I collected more than 3,126 textual lineages from middle and high school students. They were asked to identify texts (i.e., books, essays, or poems) that they thought that they would always remember and explain why the texts were meaningful to them (see Figure 1.3). In 2012 I used these students' textual lineages to identify patterns of meaningful relationships for an additional survey study of teens and texts. These patterns yielded an 18-item questionnaire completed by 1,194 adolescents across nine high schools. This chapter is based on these two data sets.

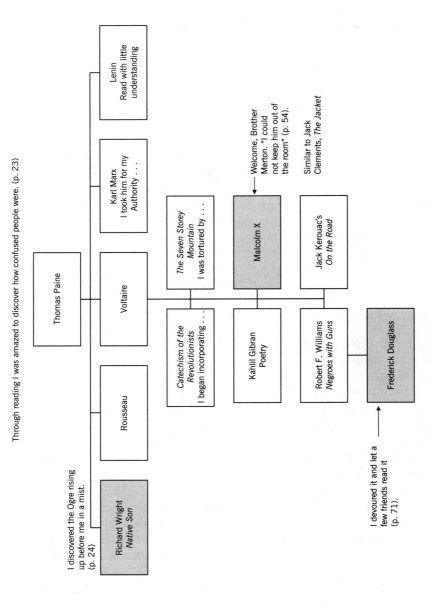

FIGURE 1.1. Eldridge Cleaver's textual lineage, constructed from reading *Soul on Ice* (1968).

Directions: In each box below, place the title of a text (i.e., book, essay, or poem) that you think you will always remember. Place only one title in a box. Explain why you think you will always remember the text or explain why the text was meaningful to you. Look at the example.

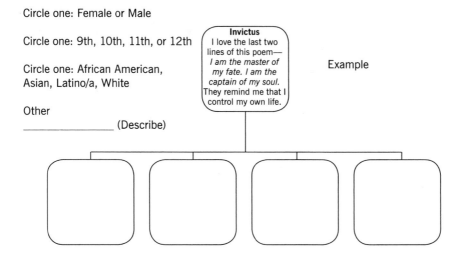

Circle one: Female or Male

Circle one: 9th, 10th, 11th, or 12th

Circle one: African American, Asian, Latino/a, White

Other

_____ (Describe)

> **Invictus**
> I love the last two lines of this poem—
> *I am the master of my fate. I am the captain of my soul.*
> They remind me that I control my own life.

Example

FIGURE 1.2. Textual lineage chart completed by students.

Identified Texts from Students' Textual Lineages

According to the survey, 3,126 middle and high school students identified a wide range of texts that they believe they will always remember. Among the texts are classic literature (e.g., *The Scarlet Letter* [Hawthorne, 1850/2000]), young adult literature (e.g., *Bang* [Flake, 2005], *Forged by Fire* [Draper, 1998], *No Turning Back* [Naidoo, 1995], *The Contender* [Lipsyte, 1996]), nonfiction and memoirs (e.g., *A Child Called It* [Pelzer, 1993], *Angela's Ashes* [McCourt, 1999], *I Know Why the Caged Bird Sings* [Angelou, 1983], *An Inconvenient Truth* [Gore, 2006], *My Bloody Life* [Sanchez, 2000], *Tuesdays with Morrie* [Albom, 1997]), and adult fiction (e.g., *My Skin Is My Skin* [Dejon, 2007], *The Body* [Kureishi, 2004]). However, if the aim is discussing texts in culturally responsive ways, then the explanations the students provide are far more important than the titles and genres, because the explanations provide implications for teaching and curricula.

The students' comments suggest that texts that move them to feel differently about themselves, affect their views of themselves, or move them to some action in their current time and space are the ones they remember or find meaningful. The following student quotations illustrate this point:

1. Considering the texts that were assigned to you **in school** during the past year, how often did you find the texts to be meaningful to you? Circle **one.**
   (1) Never   (2) Rarely   (3) Sometimes   (4) Frequently   (5) Always

I read a text that . . .	Strongly Disagree (1)	Disagree (2)	Agree (3)	Strongly Agree (4)
1. Had a **lasting** effect on me	1	2	3	4
2. Made me want to do something for someone **else**	1	2	3	4
3. I **continued** to think about after I finished it	1	2	3	4
4. Started me on a new **path**	1	2	3	4
5. I **reread** several times on my own	1	2	3	4
6. **Stayed** in my mind	1	2	3	4
7. I felt a **connection** with	1	2	3	4
8. **Shaped** who I am	1	2	3	4
9. Changed the way I **behaved** toward other people	1	2	3	4
10. **Opened** my mind	1	2	3	4
11. I chose to **talk** about it with others	1	2	3	4
12. I **recommend**ed to others	1	2	3	4
13. Made me feel **connect**ed to something important	1	2	3	4
14. Made me think about **moments** in my life	1	2	3	4
15. That was **important** to me	1	2	3	4
16. **Caused** me to think the way I think today	1	2	3	4
17. **Changed** me	1	2	3	4

FIGURE 1.3. Adolescents and texts survey.

1. "*The text teaches me* that I am beautiful."
2. "*The text inspires me* in so many ways, especially in embracing life."
3. "*The text made me realize* that my life was not as bad as I thought."
4. "*The text shows me* that I can make something out of my life."
5. "[The text] was important because *it helped me change my life.*"

In addition to the "enabling qualities" of the texts (Tatum, 2006), the students identified texts that led them to become reflective and introspective. They mentioned:

1. "It made my life look narrow."
2. "It is based on real-life experiences."
3. "It resembled a part of my life."

4. "Reminds me how lucky I am."
5. " . . . I shouldn't let . . . my kid be abandoned on the street even if [others] tell me that it will mess up my life.

The texts the students identified and the explanations they provided mesh with other research that found that readers interrogate texts for their authenticity in terms of cultural representations of students' local contexts in school and larger cultural contexts outside of school (Clark, 2006; Galda & Beach, 2004). The students also made varying connections to the texts.

Ethnic and Gender Connections

Some of the students' comments make it clear that ethnic and gender connections are paramount to their remembering of texts. For example, one African American eighth-grade male, commenting on *No Turning Back* (Naidoo, 1995), stated, "'Cause black people did it," as part of his explanation for remembering the text. A white ninth-grade female student shared, "Reading about how a woman was outcast from her society because [of] a decision really made me think about my choices."

Another eighth-grade African American male makes a similar gender connection to the text *Bang* (Flake, 2005). He wrote, "It has been influential because *boys* do drugs in here, and I can see how it affects you so I will be strong and smart." He had the option of making the connection to the main character's African American identity; instead, he chose to focus on the gender identity.

Personal Connections

Several students made personal connections without mentioning ethnicity or gender. In explaining *The Body* (Kurieshi, 2004), a ninth-grade Asian American female offered:

> " 'The most important things are the hardest things to say. They are the things you get ashamed of, because words diminish them—words shrink that seem limitless when they were in your head to no more than a living size when they are brought out.' I love this quote because it is very honest. There are a million things that I want to say to people, but I am always afraid to do so."

This student used the text to think about a personal goal of wanting to use her voice to communicate with people, but she was reticent because of an internal fear. In this case, the text resonated with the student as she thought about her personal identity, not necessarily related to ethnicity or gender.

More personal connections emerge from several other students. An eighth-grade African American male shared that "I like this book because

I need this book. I feel it." This is similar to a ninth-grade white male, who offered, "I can't afford to forget one word in the book. But honestly, it's a great self-help book." Both students are suggesting that they favor texts that are personally significant to them. This position is also captured by the ninth-grade white female who found life lessons in *Tuesdays with Morrie* (Albom, 1997), and the ninth-grade Asian American student who found the strength to believe in herself after reading the *Naruto* (Kishimoto, 2003–2014) manga series.

Adolescent Connections

Several adolescents identified books that had central characters in the same age range for a significant part of the text. They were able to relate to, or peep into, the experience of an age peer who influenced their views or emotions in some way. For example, a ninth-grade Latino male, sharing his thoughts on *A Child Called It* (Pelzer, 1993), stated, "I love books based on real life especially if it is on childhood." He suggested that books about adolescents resonated with him. An Asian American girl reflected on her life through a male character, similar in age, in the text, *Among the Hidden* (Haddix, 2006). She shared, "It was one of the first books that made me realize that my life wasn't as bad as I thought it was." Luke, the main character, has to spend 12 years in hiding because his family had him illegally during a period of government-enforced legislation that prevented parents from having more than two children. Luke eventually comes out from hiding to find that he must suppress his personal opinions because they are considered dangerous and threatening to the government. The young man in the story has to determine what he is willing to sacrifice to live. The whole notion of suppression of freedoms resonates with adolescents, and I am assuming this to be the case with this student.

The adolescent connections cross ethnic lines, as illustrated by a ninth-grade Latino male who finds instruction from the 17-year-old African American main character from Harlem in the novel *The Contender* (Lipsyte, 1996). The student shared, "This book shows me that I can make something out of my life from nothing." He is referring to the main character, who learns how to become a man after dropping out of high school. This character overcomes his personal fears and triumphs in the end. This student does not refer to the main character's ethnicity or gender, but suggests that he can learn from someone in his peer group.

BEING CULTURALLY RESPONSIVE

Although more research is needed to ensure that the topic of culturally responsive literacy teaching is discussed responsibly and critically, the students who constructed textual lineages suggest that there are multiple

dimensions of being culturally responsive. They suggest that being culturally responsive:

1. Encourages adolescents to reflect on and become introspective
   about their own lived experiences and histories.
2. Encourages adolescents to make connections across their multiple
   identities—adolescent, ethnic, gender, and personal.
3. Encourages adolescents to become enabled in some way to be different or do or think differently as a result of the texts.
4. Avoids pigeonholing adolescents by selecting texts based solely on
   ethnicity or gender; students find value in texts across ethnic and
   gender lines.
5. Recognizes the need to identify a wide range of texts that are
   aligned to the needs of adolescents, and not limiting text selection
   to standards-driven or achievement-driven imperatives shaped by
   potentially stifling public policy and school mandates.
6. Honors the voices of adolescents, who can provide valuable insights
   on the types of text they find meaningful and significant.
7. Includes a wide variety of texts to expand what is generally allowed
   in stagnant, age-old traditions of high school English curriculum or
   packaged curricula in middle schools.

The suggestions emerging from the students' voices align neatly with
advice from Gay (2000), who suggests that "Culturally responsive teaching has many different shapes, forms, and effects" (p. 2). She, too, recognizes the multidimensionality of culturally responsive teaching. This
form of teaching encompasses curriculum content, learning context, classroom climate, student–teacher relationships, instructional techniques, and
assessments. Gay also warns against the absence of caring in a culturally responsive approach to literacy teaching. She states, "Caring teachers
are distinguished by their high performance expectations, advocacy, and
empowerment of students as well as by their use of pedagogical practices
that facilitate school success" (p. 62).

Culturally Responsive Pedagogy and Curricula

Texts that provide knowledge about historical and modern-day contexts
can be powerful for adolescents. Commenting on Gore's (2006) *An Inconvenient Truth*, a ninth-grade white male wrote, "I loved this book because
it was extremely straightforward about the issue of global warming and
what we can do about it." Other adolescents identified Weisel's (2006)
Night as a book that they found meaningful because of the new knowledge
they gained about the Holocaust. This text also provides a straightforward,
compelling account of a major historical event.

Both nonfiction and fiction texts can be used to give students knowledge about historical modern-day contexts. This is true of Iweala's (2007) *Beasts of No Nation*. This debut novel is a gripping account of a young boy who becomes a guerilla fighter in his nation's civil war. The content is quite disturbing: there is murder and man-on-boy rape. In his description of a disturbing rape of a young boy by the commandant, the author writes: "[B]ut me I was not struggling because I know that he will be killing me if I am struggling and since I am wanting to vomit and die" (p. 83).

This text is eerily similar to Jack London's (1903/2003) *Call of the Wild*, in which the author describes the transformation of a civilized dog into a beast of the wild with no moral consideration. He writes:

> He must be master or mastered; while to show mercy was a weakness. Mercy did not exist in the primordial life. It was misunderstood for fear, and such misunderstandings made for death. Kill or be killed, eat or be eaten, was the law; and this mandate, down out of the depths of Time, he obeyed. (p. 54)

By page 47 of *Beasts of No Nation*, the young boy becomes a ruthless killer. The author writes:

> Under the bed there is a woman and her daughter just hiding. She is looking at us and worrying so much it is looking like somebody is cutting her face with a knife. She is smelling like goat and we are wanting to kill her so we are dragging her out, all of us soldier, but she is holding her daughter. They are holding each other and shaking like they are having fever. They are so thin more than us and the skin is hanging down like elephant skin so I am know she is fat before the war is coming and making rich and fat like poor and thin. The girl is so shrinking, she is almost like unborn baby—I am knowing because I have been taking them from their mother's belly to be seeing who is girl and who is boy. Are you my mother, I am saying. Are you my sister? But they are only screaming like Devil is coming for them. I am not Devil. I am not bad boy. I am not bad boy. Devil is not blessing me and I am not going to hell. But still I am thinking maybe Devil born me and that is why I am doing all of this. . . . But it is not Devil that is borning me. I am having father and mother and I am coming from them. (pp. 47–48)

This text will lead students to question why is this atrocity allowed to happen in our world. Some students may even ask whether the content is true. These types of thought-provoking texts must be selected with care. I used the examples above to illustrate the types of controversial texts that adolescents favor, but that are often not part of the curricula. The costs and benefits of text selections should be weighed carefully to avoid alienating teachers, students, or parents.

Texts can be selected that lead students to discuss the conditions that enable human beings to treat their fellow humans inhumanely or enable people to deal with inhumane conditioning. Jane Yolen's (1990) *The Devil's Arithmetic*, Lois Lowry's (1989) *Number the Stars*, and Julius Lester's (1968) *To Be a Slave* come to mind. Lester offers testimonies of the enslaved and their "ability to retain humanity under the most inhuman conditions" (p. 111). I am struck by the words during each reading, particularly when a slave owner, who professed Christianity, told an enslaved man, "If I catch you here servin' God, I'll beat you. You ain't got no time to serve God, We bought you to serve us" (p. 105). Or when a son recalls, "They whipped my father 'cause he looked at a slave they killed and cried" (p. 33). He also writes, "Yet it is all the more remarkable that even two hundred years of slavery are looked upon matter-of-factly and not as a time of unrelieved horror" (p. 74). Lester's novel, as well as the others, if mediated effectively, will stand the reader in his or her tracks.

The goal is not to depress adolescents with "heavy" texts but to structure curricula by "considering what issues are worth exploring and understanding when composing essential questions" to engage adolescents (Smith & Wilhelm, 2006, p. 62). Unfortunately, we live in a country that does not have a clear definition of the role of literacy instruction for adolescents. Therefore, little discussion during curriculum conversations focuses on essential questions that young adolescents should or want to address. The discussions of 21st-century literacy skills in public policy documents and the exploration of new literacies primarily in colleges and universities have not influenced the widespread selection and discussion of texts in middle and high school classrooms. I think again about the words of Eldridge Cleaver (1968), who intimated that some texts are difficult to block out; no matter what you try, they penetrate your thinking. Yet it is easy for many adolescents to block out texts in schools because most do not allow students to navigate cultural communities, or they do not reflect cultural expectations (Galda & Beach, 2004; Moje & Hinchman, 2004) connected to essential questions that are cognitively challenging for students (Smith & Wilhelm, 2006).

Responsive teaching and curricula focus on powerful and authentic texts for adolescents that help them bridge in-school and out-of-school discontinuities that exist for many students across ethnicity, gender, and language. Walter Mosley's (2005) *47* begs for consideration of a middle school audience. This text blends historical and speculative fiction. An excerpt that promotes visual imagery follows:

> It smelled bad in there and it was too hot in the summer and freezing in the winter. And every night they chained your feet to an eyebolt in the floor. The men out there were mostly angry and so they were always fighting or crying or just plain sad. But the worst thing they said about the slave quarters was that once you were there you stayed there for the rest of your life. (p. 12)

Students can use this text to wrestle with an essential question related to breaking the chains that secure one to the floor. This focus is not too different from the students who completed the textual lineages. They shared:

- "I love this book because this book teaches you to be strong, and always believe in yourself."—Ninth-grade Asian American female
- "Reading about how a woman was outcast from her society because of a decision really made me think about my choices."—Ninth-grade white female
- "The book shows me that I can make something of my life from nothing."—Ninth-grade Latino male
- "I will always remember this book because it taught me that being in gangs can mess up your life. It was important because it helped me change my life."—Ninth-grade Latina female

Figuratively speaking, all of the students expressed an interest in breaking chains either by becoming strong, making appropriate decisions, making something out of nothing, or by avoiding circumstances that shape a negative life outcome trajectory. Roadmap texts explored in caring, supportive classroom environments that honor students' voices, aligned with pedagogical practices focused on academic excellence and identity development, serve adolescents well. Adolescents respond positively to powerful texts in tandem with powerful literacy instruction. Teachers must integrate the two in order to respond to students' needs. This may require teachers to rebuild their textual lineages with adolescents in mind, or to be willing to explore a wide range of texts with their students.

FROM CONNECTIONS TO CONNECTEDNESS: FINDINGS FROM THE SURVEY

While the need for culturally responsive pedagogy and curricula as discussed in this chapter holds true, my current work suggests that being culturally responsive does not necessarily lead to meaningful reading experiences during and after the reading event for low and high academically performing students. For example, students can find connections to the texts during the reading event, but the texts fail to connect them to something important beyond the literacy event. This finding emerged from a survey study that was conducted to learn more about adolescents' meaningful relationships with texts. I end this chapter with a description of the survey study conducted in 2012.

The 1,194 adolescent students surveyed provided responses indicating their meaningful relationships with texts. Students from six urban schools, one suburban school, and one rural school completed the survey: 76.5% were ages 14–17, 51.6% were white, 76% were first-language English speakers, 62% lived in a two-parent home, 97% were from a class size between 20 and 30 students, and 83.6% were between A to C students in terms of overall school performance. Findings of the survey indicated that high academically performing adolescents and low-performing adolescents are "rarely" or "sometimes" reading texts they find meaningful. The survey data also indicated that adolescents read texts that they continue to think about or feel connections with, that they talk about with others, that lead them to think about important moments in their lives and open their minds, and that they view as important. However, the data also indicated that adolescents disagree that they are reading texts that start them on a new path, shape who they are, change the way they behave toward other people, make them feel connected to something important, cause them to think the way they think, or change them (See Table 1.1).

While it is clear that adolescents are finding connections with texts in school, it is unclear why the texts are not connecting them to something important. The connections make sense in light of the attention that has been given over the years to paying attention to the identities of adolescents during literacy instruction. It is now time to strive toward having these meaningful connections students are having with texts translate into actions beyond the texts. Understanding adolescents' connections with texts and working to have the texts connect them to something meaningful offers a new lens for teaching and mediating texts that extends the varying connections adolescents make. This understanding adds a new dimension to culturally responsive pedagogy, and it could be useful for thinking about

TABLE 1.1. Median Ratings with Questionnaire Items

Median rating of 2 = Disagree	Median rating of 3 = Agree
Started me on a new path (item 5)	Had a lasting effect on me (item 2)
I reread several times on my own (item 6)	Made me want to do something for someone else (item 3)
Shaped who I am (item 9)	I continued to think about after I finished it (item 4)
Changed the way I behaved toward other people (item 10)	Stayed in my mind (item 7)
Made me feel connected to something important (item 14)	I felt a connection with (item 8)
Caused me to think the way I think today (item 17)	Opened my mind (item 11)
Changed me (item 18)	I chose to talk about it with others (item 12)
	I recommended to others (item 13)
	Made me think about moments in my life (item 14)
	That was important to me (item 16)

the roles of texts in relationship to evolving technologies, proposed curricular changes influenced by the CCSS, and the shift toward informational and disciplinary texts. Each can be strengthened by embracing connections and connectedness.

CONCLUSIONS

In this chapter I discussed the need for examining students' textual lineages; for understanding texts, students, and contexts; for structuring pedagogy and curricula to discuss texts with students in culturally responsive ways; and for connecting adolescents to something meaningful beyond the reading event. Students' voices were used to help define cultural responsiveness and its multiple dimensions. It was also made evident that students connect to texts in a variety of ways: adolescent connections, ethnic connections, gender connections, and personal connections. Also, survey data were used to identify patterns of meaningful relationships adolescents have with texts. These student voices helped provide a dynamic blueprint for discussing texts with adolescents in culturally responsive ways.

However, there is still a divide between what we know and what happens in classrooms. Several factors contributing to this divide were offered: structural and curricular handicaps influenced by tradition, public policy, low levels of reading achievement, lack of research on discussing texts with adolescents in culturally responsive ways, and the absence of a clear definition of literacy instruction for adolescents. Fortunately, more attention is being given to adolescent literacy and best practices to address some of the challenges and demands for advancing the literacy development of students who are increasingly attending more diverse schools. This is being accelerated by evolving technologies that are shifting adolescents' relationships with texts and policies affecting curricular offerings.

Classroom contexts are changing. Out-of-school contexts are complicated by issues of race, social class, and language. Literacy instruction cannot afford to ignore either context. I have suggested that we can begin to discuss texts with adolescents in culturally responsive ways by honoring what we learn from their growing textual lineages and by building the textual lineages of students who are without them in relation to the in-school and out-of-school contexts that influence their lived experiences and histories. Becoming culturally responsive must be less of a cliché and more of a clarion call. In addition, I have suggested that we move from connections to connectedness. I offer the following to strengthen the call. We need to:

1. Define the role of literacy instruction for adolescents in a way that honors students' multiple identities and is connected to a large ideological focus.

2. Identify texts that allow students to make connections across their multiple identities.
3. Connect texts to essential questions.
4. Build the textual lineages of all students to help ensure that they can identify texts that are meaningful and significant to them.
5. Structure pedagogy and curricula that aim to strengthen students' academic, ethnic, gender, linguistic, and personal competencies.
6. Tap into students' voices to become smarter about teaching them.
7. Focus on the translation of ideas emerging from the text that aim to connect adolescents to something meaningful.

This clarion call can help us move culturally responsive literacy teaching from the sidelines, where it is marginalized, to the core of instruction. It can also help us rethink the roles of text within and beyond the reading event. These shifts in focus allow us to respond to the needs of all of students as they appear in our classrooms, each wrapped in different experiences and histories.

DISCUSSION AND ACTIVITIES

1. Discuss your own and your students' textual lineages and the insights this information provides on discussing texts in culturally responsive ways. Ask your students to identify texts that have been influential to them, and why, and compare what they say to the texts you identified.

2. Administer the adolescents and texts survey to identify your students' meaningful relationships with texts.

3. What recently published texts have you encountered that might resonate in culturally responsive ways with the adolescents you teach? Do keep in mind that there may be considerable differences between the texts that younger and older adolescents, and varying communities, find engaging. How do the texts compare to the texts adolescents are assigned in schools?

4. How might classroom pedagogy and curriculum selections align with and help to develop students' lived experiences and histories in culturally responsive ways that they recognize and value?

REFERENCES

Albom, M. (1997). *Tuesdays with Morrie: An old man, a young man, and life's greatest lesson.* New York: Doubleday.
Angelou, M. (1983). *I know why the caged bird sings.* New York: Bantam.
Clark, L. W. (2006). Power through voicing others: Girls' positioning of boys in literature circle discussion. *Journal of Literacy Research, 38,* 53–79.
Cleaver, E. (1968). *Soul on ice.* New York: Delta.

Dejon. (2007). *My skin is my skin.* Urbanbooks.net: Urban Books.

Draper, S. (1998). *Forged by fire.* New York: Aladdin.

Flake, S. (2005). *Bang.* New York: Hyperion.

Galda, L., & Beach, R. (2004). Response to literature as a cultural activity. In R. Ruddell & N. Unrau (Eds.), *Theoretical models and processes of reading* (5th ed., pp. 852–869). Newark, DE: International Reading Association.

Gay, G. (2000). *Culturally responsive teaching: Theory, research, and practice.* New York: Teachers College Press.

Glenn, L. N. (2012). Playing for real: Texts and the performance of identity. In D. Alvermann & K. Hinchman (Eds.), *Reconceptualizing the literacies in adolescents' lives* (3rd ed., pp. 3–28). New York: Routledge.

Gore, A. (2006). *An inconvenient truth: The planetary emergence of global warming and what we can do about it.* New York: Rodale.

Haddix, M. P. (2006). *Among the hidden.* New York: Aladdin.

Hawthorne, N. (2000). *The scarlet letter.* New York: Modern Library Edition. (Original work published 1850)

Iweala, U. (2007). *Beasts of no nation.* New York: HarperCollins.

Kishimoto, M. (2003–2014). *Naruto* (series). San Francisco: Viz Media.

Kureishi, H. (2004). *The body.* New York: Scribner.

Lalik, R., & Oliver, K. L. (2007). Differences and tensions in implementing a pedagogy of critical literacy with adolescent girls. *Reading Research Quarterly, 42*(1), 46–70.

Lester, J. (1968). *To be a slave.* New York: Puffin.

Lipsyte, R. (1996). *The contender.* New York: HarperCollins.

London, J. (2003). *Call of the wild.* New York: Scholastic. (Original work published 1903)

Lowry, L. (1989). *Number the stars.* New York: Bantam.

McCourt, F. (1999). *Angela's ashes.* New York: Simon & Schuster.

Moje, E. B., & Hinchman, K. (2004). Culturally responsive practices for youth literacy learning. In T. L.Jetton & J. A. Dole (Eds.), *Adolescent literacy research and practice* (pp. 321–350). New York: Guilford Press.

Mosenthal, P. (1998). Reframing the problem of adolescence and adolescent literacy: A dilemma-management perspective. In D. E. Alvermann, K. A. Hinchman, D. W. Moore, S. F. Phelps, & D. R. Waff (Eds.), *Reconceptualizing the literacies in adolescents' lives* (pp. 325–352). Mahwah, NJ: Erlbaum.

Mosley, W. (2005). *47.* New York: Little, Brown.

Naidoo, B. (1995). *No turning back: A novel of South Africa:* New York: HarperTrophy.

Pelzer, D. (1993). *A child called "it": One child's courage to survive.* Omaha, NE: Omaha Press.

Sanchez, R. (2000). *My bloody life: The making of a Latin King.* Chicago: Chicago Review Press.

Smith, M., & Wilhelm, J. (2006). *Going with the flow: How to engage boys (and girls) in their literacy learning.* Portsmouth, NH: Heinemann.

Sprague, M., & Keeling, K. (2007). *Discovering their voices: Engaging adolescent girls with young adult literature*. Newark, DE: International Reading Association.

Tatum, A. W. (2005). *Teaching reading to black adolescent males: Closing the achievement gap*. Portland, ME: Stenhouse.

Tatum, A. W. (2006). Engaging African American males in reading. *Educational Leadership, 63*(5), 44–49.

Tatum, A. W. (2008). Discussing texts with adolescents in culturally responsive ways. In K. Hinchman & H. Sheridan-Thomas (Eds.), *Best practices in adolescent literacy instruction* (pp. 3–19). New York: Guilford Press.

Tatum, A. W. (2009). *Reading for their life: (Re)building the textual lineages of African American adolescent males*. Portsmouth, NH: Heinemann.

Weisel, E. (2005). *Night*. New York: Hill & Wang.

Yolen, J. (1990). *The devil's arithmetic*. New York: Puffin.

CHAPTER 2

Meaningful Discipline-Specific Language Instruction for Middle School Students for Whom English Is an *Additional* Language

Eliane Rubinstein-Ávila
Alisa G. Leckie

The main purpose of this chapter is to convey the many ways middle school can make content-area concepts comprehensible to students for whom English is an additional language, by intentionally including opportunities for language and literacy development to scaffold content knowledge. At the secondary level, English language learners are likely to be in mainstream content-area classes. This trend, in addition to the advent of the Common Core State Standards that emphasize discipline-specific literacy and exposure to complex texts for all students, calls for instruction that scaffolds the academic language demands of the content being taught. The following are the points on which we expanded throughout the chapter:

- We posit a rationale for using the term *students for whom English is an additional language*.
- We explain the heterogeneity among secondary students for whom English is an additional language in the United States.
- We convey the importance and advantages of bringing language to the forefront of content instruction (connection to the Common Core State Standards).

- We present several strategies across the four language domains (listening, speaking, reading, and writing) that are likely to enhance students' learning across content areas, with examples of strategies in each of the four main academic subject areas (language arts, mathematics, natural and social sciences).

- We provide instructional vignettes that illustrate the incorporation of language development while working to develop students' content-area concepts.

- Last, we summarize, raise some concerns, and highlight a few issues for future reflection.

WHAT DIFFERENCE DOES A TERM MAKE?: A RATIONALE FOR USING ENGLISH AS AN <u>ADDITIONAL</u> LANGUAGE

Although English language learners (ELLs) is the term most commonly used in the United States to describe students who are not native English speakers and who are in the process of developing English competencies, throughout this chapter we will adopt *the term students for whom English is an additional language* (EAL), which is more commonly used by scholars in the European Union (EU). EAL expresses a more holistic profile of such students, for it acknowledges that students who are learning English as a new language are developing linguistic competencies *in addition to* the linguistic competencies they already use in another or other languages or dialects (Rubinstein-Ávila & Johnson, 2008). Thus EAL acknowledges what learners know—not only the competencies they are in the process of developing, as was explained in the first author's coauthored chapter in the first edition of this volume. We hope that more school districts and teachers recognize that secondary ELLs are already competent users of one or more languages or dialects and acknowledge that their existing linguistic repertoires function as resources for developing competencies in English.

Bilingualism and multilingualism are viewed as social, cultural, and economic resources across most of the globe. In fact, it is important to keep in mind that most children around the world grow up in bilingual or multilingual environments (Grosjean, 2010). Just as some children in India, especially in the southern part of the country, may be speakers of Tamil, Urdu, and Hindi before arriving to the United States, indigenous children in rural Mexico or Central America may already be bilingual in their indigenous home language in addition to Spanish, before they develop English proficiency (Rubinstein-Ávila & Johnson, 2008). Therefore, in this chapter we continue to underscore that secondary students who are in the process of developing English competencies are likely to be proficient users of at least one other language (regardless of their prior formal education levels).

HETEROGENEITY AMONG EAL SECONDARY STUDENTS

Most teachers are well aware that EALs not only come in all shapes and sizes, but that they are different in many other ways. Spanish-speaking students (referred to commonly as Hispanics or Latin@s) are the largest language minority group across U.S. schools. We want to remind readers that Spanish is spoken in over 23 countries worldwide; thus Latin@s are a highly heterogeneous student population who are likely to use different varieties of Spanish. Also, speakers of the same language do not necessary share common values, religious beliefs, political ideologies and/or immigration histories. Although officially most Latin Americans are Roman Catholics, these students may have been socialized in a variety of religious beliefs and cultural practices. It is important to keep in mind, for example, that although students from the Dominican Republic and Mexico share Spanish as a common language, they do not share the same history or ancestry, and they are unlikely to share cultural practices or immigration status and experiences (Rubinstein-Ávila & Johnson, 2008). Moreover, EAL students vary in family socioeconomic status (SES), or class, which is likely to influence the educational experiences (formal and informal) to which they have been exposed (Rubinstein-Ávila, 2003).

Also, not all secondary EALs are immigrants. Many have been born on U.S. soil but may have lived transnational lives between the United States and their parents' countries of origin. It is important to note that although Puerto Rican students are not "immigrants" per se, they may face many of the language and adaptation challenges other immigrant students face. In fact, in some schools refugee students from many parts of the globe (e.g., Sudan, Somalia Iraq, Syria), whose families have been granted political asylum as a result of our government's far-reaching diplomatic and military involvement, may outnumber immigrant students.

Consequently, the range of prior educational experiences among secondary EALs may be vast—from refugee camps, rural areas, multigrade, one-room schools taught by a teacher who have only completed the eighth grade, to exclusive, state-of-the-art, private bilingual (or multilingual) schools, where teachers may hold graduate degrees. Another common assumption to avoid is the assessment of EALs' parental education by the current jobs they hold. Parents who may have been certified teachers, nurses, or even lawyers and doctors, in their countries of origin may be employed in the service sector in the United States because of language barriers and a lack of reciprocity of professional certification (Rubinstein-Ávila & Johnson, 2008).

The degree to which EALs have attained English proficiency ranges on a continuum from emergent to advanced. This range in competencies also necessitates a range of scaffolding to build on individual needs and strengths. The instructional scaffolds required for an emergent EAL to experience academic success across subjects will be different from the scaffolds needed for students who have already developed some of the more complex English language competencies. Furthermore, in addition to students' levels of English language competencies, content-area teachers' expectations need to take into account factors such as students' prior formal schooling experiences and the academic and linguistic supports available at individual schools.

Although many students classified as ELLs can actively engage with content-area texts and participate in academic classroom discussions, some may be at the emergent stages of proficiency and may need a (bilingual) partner and intensive language support in order to benefit fully from classroom instruction. Regardless of where they are, students need to be both supported and challenged in order to continue to grow as language and as content learners. Moreover, they need to be provided ample opportunities (and modes) to demonstrate their knowledge and understanding of content-area concepts.

In addition to knowing who one's students are and understanding their academic strengths and needs, scholars such as Gándara and Contreras (2009) and Moschkovich (2012), remind us that viewing all languages as resources for learning, and focusing on students' academic achievement—as opposed to a narrow emphasis on English language proficiency—are two of the most important characteristics of high-quality instruction for this population.

DISCIPLINE-SPECIFIC LANGUAGE: IMPLICATIONS OF THE COMMON CORE STATE STANDARDS FOR ENGLISH LANGUAGE ARTS FOR <u>ALL</u> SECONDARY TEACHERS

Recent scholarship on the language use within specific disciplines conveys a rich, complex, and much broader view of language—a view that extends beyond specialized vocabulary, embracing various registers as well as discourse practices. In fact, Moschkovich (2012), a math and language educator/scholar, uses the phrase "the language of mathematics" to refer to the (complex) communicative competencies students need to participate in the discourse of mathematics, as opposed to simply defining a vocabulary list of mathematical terms.

Thus discipline-specific language (DSL) includes both the oral and written aspects of language that are required for secondary students to communicate concepts, information, and ideas particular to a discipline, be it mathematics, science, or social studies. Although the CCSS is a *fait accompli*, it does not provide pedagogical suggestions. Rather they affirm that their use in the creation of state English language proficiency (ELP) standards will have "significant implications" (National Governors Association Center for Best Practices & Council of Chief State School Officers, 2010, p. 3) for instruction, primarily across secondary classrooms.

The CCSS highlight a new role for secondary teachers. As pointed out in the Common Core ELPD Booklet, up until now, the language development of EALs was the purveyor of the ESL (English as a second language) teachers. However, with the implementation of CCSS, all content-area teachers will be expected to utilize strategies in their discipline-specific classes to render the content knowledge they teach comprehensible for EALs. This puts discipline-specific language development *through* content knowledge at the forefront of instruction.

Discipline-specific teachers will need to be able to recognize, and make explicit to their students, the language and literacy practices that are embedded in their discipline. ESL teachers will be expected to "cultivate a deeper knowledge of the discipline-specific language and literacy practices that ELLs need in order to perform the activities germane to those disciplines" (National Governors Association Center for Best Practices & Council of Chief State School Officers, 2010, p. 4).

ADVANTAGES TO BRINGING LANGUAGE TO THE FOREFRONT OF INSTRUCTION

Emphasizing the structures of language and texts can facilitate the literacy and language development and access to complex content knowledge for EALs and, at the same time, all other students. In altering instructional routines just slightly to include explicit discussions about and practice with language, teachers can promote second language acquisition and academic literacy. Many of the content-area literacy practices that benefit the literacy development of native English speakers are also beneficial to EALs (August & Shanahan, 2010).

Integrating explicit instruction regarding text structures, word study, and comprehension strategies facilitates understanding of content while developing language and literacy skills. With the advent of the CCSS and their emphasis on disciplinary literacy, it is essential that teachers expose all students to complex texts with sufficient scaffolding to make those texts comprehensible. Highlighting vocabulary, language patterns, and text structures, in addition to incorporating reading strategies and opportunities to discuss texts and concepts, is the type of scaffolding that can result in academic success for ELLs.

THE IMPACT OF THE CCSS ON INSTRUCTION FOR EALs

Because the CCSS emphasize language practices and stress the importance of exposing all students to complex texts, in essence all single-subject, content-area teachers will be expected to know how to convey and develop content knowledge by engaging students in language practices such as saying, doing, listening, and being that facilitate the conveyance of ideas and information. We are reminded by Moschkovich (2012) that teachers who have had proven success with students from nondominant communities (including EALs/bilinguals) are highly committed to student–home communication, believe in their students' academic potential, and reject deficit-oriented models of their students. Such teachers are likely to hold high expectations and often are agentive about modifying instruction to meet their students' specific linguistic and academic needs.

These demands on secondary teachers are great; nevertheless, so are the many demands on EAL students. They are expected to closely read complex text, construct oral and written arguments, elaborate on ideas collaboratively, and determine key points of oral discourse or written text. All secondary students are expected to analyze both primary and secondary sources related to a topic and to incorporate that analysis into argumentative and explanatory texts, according to CCSS. This level of discipline-specific literacy is challenging for most students, and even more so for EALs.

There are many strategies that educators can utilize to help bring language to the forefront of instruction in ways that build on the learning of content. In fact, including language practices in the content areas is likely to enhance all secondary students' learning because it provides opportunities to use the language of the discipline in multiple ways. As students receive a wider range of academic language use in their classrooms, their engagement with the content will likely be deeper and more meaningful.

In summary, all secondary teachers, not only ESL teachers, will be expected to place language at the forefront of content instruction, which means explicitly underscoring the structures of language and using strategies that promote the close and careful reading of texts. This includes the scaffolding of high-quality content-area conversations (Fisher, Frey, & Rothenberg, 2008) and incorporating opportunities for students to process their learning through oral presentations and writing.

An example of instructional strategies that promote language in the content areas is the deconstruction of "juicy sentences" (Wong-Fillmore & Fillmore, 2012) to deepen EALs' understanding of linguistic structures, which they are likely to encounter in their academic texts. This strategy involves emphasizing a single sentence, or focal sentences, and analyzing them both for linguistic and conceptual reasons during instruction. The authors state that the "juicy sentence" should be worthy of extended analysis. The sentence ought to be "so complex it begs for explication, is grammatically interesting, and is focused on an important point in the passage" (p. 6). Also drawing students' attention to the parallel structures, first and final sentences of paragraphs, the strategic uses of the dashes, and facilitating students' understanding of authors' arguments appear multiple times in the CCSS.

It may not seem prudent, or even seem counterintuitive, for content-area teachers to spend so much time carefully studying a single sentence or a paragraph (not at the expense of context, of course); however, being able to deconstruct and label such linguistic patterns and structures provide EALs the necessary scaffolds to access complex academic texts. Furthermore, it provides EALs the opportunity to engage with the same texts as their English-proficient peers. Thus in this sense, less (coverage) is more. Helping EALs to deconstruct small portions of challenging texts can be more linguistically and academically beneficial than having them read longer texts that have been simplified for use with EALs. Linguistic minority students need to be exposed to a range of complex texts, and need to acquire the tools to comprehend those complex texts.

THE CLOSE READING OF CONTENT-AREA TEXTS THROUGH TEXT ANNOTATION

Similarly, the use of text annotations can facilitate EALs' text comprehension and bring language to the forefront of instruction. Close reading can be defined as an examination of the deep structures of a text through repeated readings (Fisher & Frey, 2012), and text annotations are a way for students to track their own thinking while reading. When used in conjunction, close reading and text annotations can help EAL students comprehend complex content-area texts. One way to join the two strategies is for the teacher to read a passage from a text to the students while they follow along and then explain to students the aspects of the text they should focus on and annotate (model) during independent reading. For example, a science teacher might have students circle the words that indicate the steps in a process, such as photosynthesis, and then have them jot down questions they have as they read or connections they make in the margins. Finally, the teacher has students work through the text again with a partner and compare their respective annotations and make collaborative meaning of the text.

In this type of instruction, students have the opportunity to read the same text three times, each with a distinctive purpose. The first oral reading by the teacher can help students make the spelling/pronunciation connections of academic vocabulary and get a sense of the content concepts. Through verbal emphasis, teachers can also indicate which words and phrases warrant attention during students' independent annotations.

The second reading, with the inclusion of the annotating process, directs students to specific aspects of the text and provides information to teachers regarding students' comprehension. As in the previous example, if students are to circle words and phrases that show the steps in the process of photosynthesis, teachers can easily see whether students have marked key concepts as they are circulating around the room. This provides teachers an opportunity to walk around the classroom and work with particular students who are having difficulty (not only EALs). The final reading of the text with a partner provides students, especially EALs, the opportunity to discuss the text and clarify concepts with a peer. We elaborate on this strategy further in the next section.

THE IMPORTANCE OF STUDENTS' ORAL LANGUAGE

Several studies have shown that the majority of talk in classrooms is done by the teacher, not the students—particularly in classrooms with low-achieving students and language-minority students (Guan Eng Ho, 2005; Lingard, Hayes, & Mills, 2003). Instead, EALs need multiple and varied opportunities to engage in classroom conversations in which they produce the language of schooling and express their learning. Learning cannot be a passive endeavor for EALs; they cannot simply be recipients of written and spoken information. They need to be the speakers and the writers so they can process content concepts, improve their academic language fluency, and practice what they learn. One way to do this is through "content-area conversations" (Fisher et al., 2008). Content-area conversations are types of classroom talk that emphasize the use of academic language. When thoughtfully incorporated and appropriately scaffolded, classroom talk simultaneously fosters the active engagement of students, promotes language development, and facilitates the comprehension of content concepts.

The key to successful classroom talk is in the planning and the scaffolding. Teachers need to determine points in a lesson or unit of study that warrant the inclusion of focused student talk. Teachers also need to decide on the academic words and phrases that students should use to practice academic talk and how she/he will scaffold the conversation so that students are mandated to use those target words and phrases. The following scenario based on a sixth-grade mathematics lesson exemplifies each of these steps.

In a series of lessons focused on order of operations, the teacher has provided enough direct instruction and guided practice using the acronym PEMDAS (parentheses, exponents, multiply, divide, add, subtract) to help students remember the steps to following in solving multistep equations. The goal is to provide students an opportunity to engage in independent practice and to explain their application of PEMDAS. An instructional strategy that can be integrated to content conversations to achieve this goal is consensus boards (Fisher et al., 2008; Harste, Short & Burke, 1996). This strategy involves dividing students into groups of four and giving them a large piece of butcher paper to place on the table in front of them. Students divide the paper (i.e., their consensus board) into four sections with an additional section in the center. Each student claims one of the four sections. The teacher provides the prompt, in this case a math problem that includes several of the operations in PEMDAS. The teacher allows students several minutes to work on the problem in their portion of the consensus board. This is an individual's time to think and should be free of conversation. Students may use their notes or other aids to help them solve the problem, and can use words, symbols, or a list of steps to notate their process in their individual squares.

In order to scaffold the conversation to ensure that students are practicing and applying academic language, the teacher should have the target words and phrases easily visible in the front of the room or on papers for the group to consult as they converse. Target words for this example could include: parentheses, exponent, product, solution. Target phrases could be written as sentence stems such as, "The first step to solve this problem is to _____ because _____." As the students explain their individual processes, the teacher should be circulating and giving students feedback on their application of PEMDAS as well as their use of academic language. After all students have shared, the group's goal is to reach consensus regarding the prompt or, in this case, how to solve the problem.

This type of lesson brings language to the forefront of instruction by mandating and scaffolding the use of academic language by students. Not only does the inclusion of content-area conversations promote language acquisition, but these conversations provide a time for students to process and practice content-area concepts. Furthermore, the inclusion of listening and speaking standards for *all* students in the CCSS provides educators an opportunity to explore how classroom talk can benefit all students, not just their EALs.

However, just as extended classroom talk and discipline-specific discourse practices need to be scaffolded, so do reading and writing need to be extended beyond the single word/sentence response. For example, we advocate that secondary teachers provide students with a topic sentence for a paragraph in their subject, and have them rely on their notes or other resources to write four or five supporting detail sentences. For longer writing assignments, such as an essay or research report, rather than assuming that students already know how to structure such an assignment, we suggest that teachers make the content of each section (or even each paragraph) explicit for the students. This is essential because different disciplines organize and present information in different ways (Shanahan & Shanahan, 2008). For example, writing a lab report in biology has a distinctly different structure than a persuasive essay in history class. Being explicit about expectations regarding written assignments promotes student success—especially for those developing academic proficiencies in English—because it demystifies the process and provides a clear expectation of the product.

AN EIGHTH-GRADE SOCIAL STUDIES INSTRUCTIONAL SCENARIO

The scenario below exemplifies a mainstream content area classrooms instruction that scaffolds the language and literacy development that are particularly beneficial for EALs. We present readers a skeleton of four closely related lessons within a larger unit of study. This topic of the social studies unit is the American Revolution. The class is composed of 28 students, of whom nine are EALs. Five of the EALs are have been tested at the advanced English proficiency, and four tested at the low–intermediate proficiency level (their native languages are Spanish, Mandarin, and Arabic). All nine EALs receive specialized ESL (English as a second language) instruction for 2 hours a day, but are in mainstream content-area classes for the remainder of the day.

The four successive mini-lessons we present here focus on the theme of "Taxation without Representation" using four events: (1) the Stamp Act, (2) the Townshend Acts, (3) the Boston Massacre, and (4) the Boston Tea Party. Five key vocabulary terms that are part of each lesson: *patriot*, *resistance*, *protest*, *tax*, and *impose*. Through a series of instructional activities, including direct instruction, small-group work, and individual assessment, this scenario demonstrates how a social studies teacher can integrate language and literacy instruction and scaffold that integration for the various degrees of English proficiencies among the students. Note that each lesson contains both content and language objectives, describes the series of activities, provides examples of some of the materials and structures, and includes a discussion of the rationale for and intended goal of each activity.

Lesson 1: Direct Instruction

Content Objective

Students will be able to make connections among four historical events leading up to the American Revolution.

Language Objectives

Students will be able to:

- Complete Cloze (fill in the blanks) notes.
- Using at least two of the key vocabulary terms, describe two ways in which the historical events (from the content objective) are connected.

Activities

Asking students to share whether they, or their parents, have ever participated in a protest, or whether they remember any recent protests in the news is likely to generate some interest and establish broad background knowledge/experience on the topic. Students can be expected to take notes of a lecture-style lesson, with an accompanying PowerPoint presentation (which would incorporate key facts about each of the events, in addition to visuals and brief video clips). The five key vocabulary terms (*patriot*, *resistance*, *protest*, *tax*, and *impose*) are also defined in the presentation and integrated into it meaningfully and as often as they are applicable. For example, a slide titled "The Boston Massacre" contains the following facts:

- Occurred on March 5, 1770.
- A group of Boston **patriots** was **protesting** the Townshend Acts.
- British soldiers killed five colonial **protestors.**
- Resulted in the removal of troops from Boston.

Notice the use of bold to highlight key terms as well as the limited amount of information. The goal for the presentation is an initial familiarity with the key terms and events, not a comprehensive understanding of events and relationships. However, to supplement the basics, the slide could then be followed with a visual or a short video clip. Websites such as *www. history.com* and *www.pbs.com* are stable and provide images of primary source documents as well as a wide variety of video clips. These nonlinguistic inputs help students develop initial understandings of content-area concepts. The use of visuals and video is particularly beneficial on the first day of instruction.

Although there are several ways of taking notes, Cloze notes are helpful to EALs and easy for teachers to prepare from their digital presentation. For example, the above "Boston Massacre" slide could be copied and pasted into a Word document, and then the teacher can simply replace some of the key words with blank lines:

- Occurred on _____ 5, 1770.
- A group of Boston **patriots** was **protesting** the _____.
- British soldiers _____ five colonial **protestors.**
- Resulted in the _____ of troops from _____.

This form of notes allows EALs to pay attention to what the teacher is saying and still record accurate content information. It is often difficult for EALs to attend to a teacher's lecture and take notes simultaneously because of the high levels of language such an act entail. Reducing the linguistic demand while still providing access to academic language allows EALs to develop both content-area concepts and academic language.

Lesson 2: Expert Groups

Content Objective

Students will be able to describe in detail one event that led to the American Revolution.

Language Objectives

Students will be able to:

- Read a text to identify important causes and effects of their focal event.
- Add two key details to the previous day's notes.
- Create a simple visual of the event that also incorporates two key vocabulary words.

Activities

The "expert group" component of the jigsaw structure allows teachers to differentiate independent reading tasks. Therefore, prior to the lesson the teacher should select and/or adapt three brief texts related to each event. The published social studies textbook as well as websites like the two mentioned in the previous section are excellent sources for texts. Using different sources provides ready-made differentiation because they tend to include varying degrees of detail. For example, one source could provide a brief summary, whereas another would have an extended description. Because this reading task will primarily be an independent one, EALs with lower levels of English proficiency should be provided with a shorter, simpler text.

At the onset of instruction, the teacher places students into heterogeneous groups of three, mixing EALs among the mainstream students. Each group gets a set of readings related to one of the four events. In order to guide their reading, students receive the following prompt: "Determine the Who, Why, and So What of your focal event. Identify specific places in the text that support your answer." This prompt gives students a purpose for reading and expands on the basic information presented in the previous lesson. It also provides a way for the teacher to monitor student comprehension as they circulate while students are reading.

After individual group members finish reading their text, the group has a brief discussion of their individual readings focused on the Who, Why, and So What of the event. Then they determine the two best pieces of information to add to the previous days' presentation about their event. Their final step is to develop a simple visual that depicts their event and relates at least two key terms. Each group member makes his or her own version of the visual to help describe the event to a new group in the next lesson. Students may also write words or phrases on the back of the visual to help them remember what to say. This scaffold is particularly useful to EALs and other students who are uncomfortable sharing in group situations.

Lesson 3: Mixed Groups

Content Objective

Students will be able to make connections among four historical events leading up to the American Revolution.

Language Objectives

Students will be able to:

- Clearly describe their focal event including at least two key vocabulary terms.
- Complete a graphic organizer connecting the four key events.

Activities

The teacher places students into groups of four, with one representative from each event per group. Students are given about 5 minutes to present the information about their event using their visual to guide them. Listening students should add new information to their notes from the first day's lesson. While students are working, the teacher circulates to monitor use of academic language and ask questions of group members to check for comprehension.

When all members have presented, groups complete a graphic organizer to compare and contrast the four events; a modified Venn diagram or a semantic feature analysis chart would work well in this situation. After completing the organizer, groups need to write several sentences explaining the connections among the four focal events.

Although there is a lot of language use and production in this lesson, the group structure helps EALs of varying English proficiencies access the content. Students listen to the content, add a few pieces of information to their notes, and work collaboratively to compare/contrast the four events. The multiple modes of input and the group structure facilitate comprehension and participation among EALs.

Lesson 4: Assessment

Content Objective

Students will demonstrate their understanding of four events leading up to the American Revolution.

Language Objectives

Students will be able to:

- Construct a comparison/contrast paragraph of at least two focal events.
- Incorporate at least three vocabulary terms into their paragraph.

Activities

A brief assessment of students' understanding related to the four events leading up to the American Revolution is warranted after 3 days of instruction. Straightforward multiple-choice questions that are based on students' notes are appropriate for EALs of all proficiency levels. The main difference in assessment for EALs is the teacher's expectation regarding paragraph development. The content of paragraphs should be correct, but EALs might write less and have sentence construction errors. The goal is to assess their understanding of content and provide another opportunity for them to practice and apply the academic language embedded in the content area.

CONCLUSION

This chapter attempted to underscore that although secondary EALs are developing English language proficiency, they are likely to already be proficient in one or more languages or dialects. Also, after explaining the range of these students heterogeneity, the chapter outlined several instructional strategies and activities to help secondary teachers put language at the forefront of content instruction, to ensure the successful academic achievement of students for whom English is an additional language.

DISCUSSION AND ACTIVITIES

1. Who are the EAL students across your classes? What do you know about their prior formal education experience?

2. Which one of the strategies provided in this chapter could be implemented in your content area?

3. Review the texts (including, of course, visual texts) your students will be exposed to, and try to compose one or two language objectives to make the linguistic demands of the text explicit both to you and your students.

REFERENCES

August, D., & Shanahan, T. (2010). Response to a review and update on *Developing literacy in second-language learners: Report of the National Literacy Panel on Language Minority Children and Youth. Journal of Literacy Research, 42,* 341–348.

Fisher, D., & Frey, N. (2012). Close reading in elementary school. *The Reading Teacher, 66*(3), 179–188.

Fisher, D., Frey, N., & Rothenberg, C. (2008). *Content-area conversations.* Alexandria, VA: Association for Curriculum and Supervision Development.

Gándara, P. C., & Contreras, F. (2009). *The Latino education crisis: The consequences of failed social policies.* Cambridge, MA: Harvard University Press.

Grosjean, F. (2010). *Bilingual: Life and reality.* Cambridge, MA: Harvard University Press.

Guan Eng Ho, D. (2005). Why do teachers ask the questions they ask? *RELC Journal, 36,* 297–310.

Harste, J., Short, K., & Burke, C. (1996). *Classrooms for authors and inquirers.* Portsmouth, NH: Heinemann.

Lingard, B., Hayes, D., & Mills, M. (2003). Teachers and productive pedagogies: Contextualising, conceptualizing, utilizing. *Pedagogy, Culture and Society, 11,* 399–424.

Moschkovich, J. (2012, December). *Mathematics, the Common Core, and language: Recommendations for mathematics instruction for ELs aligned with the Common Core.* Paper presented at the meeting "Understanding Language Institute," Stanford University, Stanford, CA.

National Governors Association Center for Best Practices & Council of Chief State School Officers. (2010). *Common Core State Standards.* Washington, DC: Author.

Rubinstein-Ávila, E. (2003). Facing reality: English language learners in middle school. *English Education, 35*(2), 122–136.

Rubinstein-Ávila, E., & Johnson, J. (2008). Meaningful content for middle school students for whom English is an additional language. In K. A.

Hinchman & H. K. Sheridan-Thomas (Eds.), *Best practices in adolescent literacy instruction* (pp. 20–38). New York: Guilford Press.

Shanahan, T., & Shanahan, C. (2008). Teaching disciplinary literacy to adolescents: Rethinking content-area literacy. *Harvard Educational Review,* 78(1), 40–59.

Wong-Fillmore, L. W., & Fillmore, C. J. (2012, December). *What does text complexity mean for English language learners and language minority students?* Paper presented at the meeting "Understanding Language Institute," Stanford University, Stanford, CA.

CHAPTER 3

The Role of Motivation in Engaged Reading of Adolescents

David G. O'Brien
Deborah R. Dillon

This chapter:

- Discusses the role of motivation in engaged reading by exploring how general motivation constructs can inform better practices.

- Explores why motivation can play a particularly crucial role in adolescents' literacy learning and practices.

- Shows how specific motivation constructs can be used to guide "best practices" for all students, including those who struggle with literacy.

What is motivation? What are some common conceptions and misconceptions about the importance and role of motivation in adolescents' reading? Before we explore the complex topic of motivation and consider instructional possibilities for improving motivation related to adolescent reading, we examine some common misconceptions and oversimplifications of the term.

When we started to explore the construct of motivation in instructional settings about 15 years ago, we created an organizer to characterize the way educators talk about it. We believe that the following statements, gleaned from anecdotal records, classes, and professional development sessions, exemplify common but inaccurate perceptions about motivation.

After each statement, in italics, we explain how the characterization in the statement shapes misconceptions many educators have constructed about motivation.

- "I wish my students were more **motivated**." *This comment intimates that motivation is something people do or don't have. In fact, motivation is something individuals develop as a result of experiences with particular tasks, subjects, people, and at various moments in their lives.*
- "My students last year were more **self-motivated**." *This statement promotes the idea that motivation is connected to one's self-discipline, and that regardless of tasks and instructional factors, some individuals are just more determined and self-directed, which really is not accurate.*
- "I just don't know what I can do to **motivate** these students." *Here we see that motivation is perceived as some kind of immediate encouragement teachers can offer that suddenly sparks students' interest and activity.*
- "I think my class is losing some of its **motivation**." *Unfortunately, here we see that educators believe that motivation is a diminishing, nonrenewable resource. It appears like you can lose motivation with a group of kids during a given year, and that it might be gone for good.*

As we illustrate in this chapter, the definitions of motivation implicit in the statements above represent common but inaccurate conceptions of both the construct of motivation and the degree to which teachers can influence it in the arena of literacy practices and learning. In fact, the statements are antithetical to research on best practices for facilitating motivation and engaged reading because they construct motivation as something that is magically present or that mysteriously disappears in some students regardless of the instructional environment, quality of teaching, or specific strategies that good teachers employ. Some statements also portray motivation as something elusive—beyond teachers' control. However, these perceptions do not adequately capture what motivation is or how it is developed or sustained.

So how might we define motivation? In their edited *Handbook of Motivation at School*, Wentzel and Wigfield (2009) state that motivation is the energy that students bring to tasks and "the beliefs, values and goals that determine which tasks they pursue and their persistence in achieving them, and the standards they set to determine when a task has been accomplished" (p. 2). The research literature on motivation yields a range of perspectives and definitions and includes students' beliefs about their abilities (e.g., whether these are fixed or can change over time); their self-efficacy or expectations related to succeeding on future tasks (or not); what students attribute their success or failure on particular tasks to (e.g., their ability, effort, the difficulty of the task, or help/hindrance from others); and why students choose to pursue particular tasks (e.g., the value students place on assignments and the goals they set to achieve).

The concept of motivation has recently been expanded to focus on the characteristics of individual learners and how students' motivations are shaped by developmental, ecological, and socialization factors. What we do know is that a complex web of issues shapes students' motivations, including the contextual features that surround students in their home and school lives (see Guthrie &Wigfield, 2000; Taboada, Tonks, Wigfield, & Guthrie, 2013; Wentzel & Wigfield, 2009). Some of the common dimensions associated with motivation like *interest* and *attitude* are sometimes presented as similar to motivation in the literature, but we know that motivation is much more (e.g., Mazzoni & Gambrell, 1999). For example, *interest* might refer to preferences for certain topics, genres, or reading tasks. If readers are interested, they may be more *intrinsically* motivated— that is, they read because they want to and they find it enjoyable. If they choose reading over other activities, we could say that they have a positive *attitude* toward reading. As we get into some of the dimensions of motivation, the interrelation and interdependence of these dimensions is obvious. For example, persons who have generally positive perceptions about their abilities feel self-efficacious; that is, they believe that they have the ability and strategies to succeed at specific tasks they have yet to face. This is an incredibly important aspect of motivation. In addition, if students are working toward goals that they believe are important, they place high value on reading and related tasks and hold more steadily to performance goals (Guthrie & Coddington, 2009). Our goal is to promote the development of engaged reading. The best way to understand the research base for best practices in promoting motivation and engaged reading is to know about the various dimensions that make up the concept of motivation to understand how they intersect.

WHY MOTIVATION IS IMPORTANT FOR ADOLESCENTS

Developmental trends indicate that a marked change occurs in students' motivation as they progress through school. Research findings show us that the school learning climate becomes increasingly performance oriented (vs. mastery driven) as students move through the grades. A huge transition occurs in middle school as the emphasis on performance and grades increases, as social comparisons are made, and as ability tracking often occurs in subjects like math and reading (see Eccles et al., 1983). At the same time, young people are also highly aware of how they are perceived by their peers and express concerns over the performance of others in comparison with themselves.

Perceptions about one's competence affect the value and interest placed on particular subjects and tasks and, in the end, one's motivation. For example, global and national profiles of adolescent readers in general indicate a crucial need for a focus on motivation approaches that can increase adolescents' engagement in reading. For example, Guthrie (2008) noted that U.S. fourth graders are "astonishingly low" in intrinsic motivation compared with peers from other countries using an indicator of attitudes toward reading and reading by adolescents' own interests outside of school. What Guthrie and his colleagues call a "general disengagement" from reading among adolescents they attribute to a range of issues, from a lack of parental support, to media distraction away from print, to negative perceptions of reading in school.

Before we start the central discussion about motivation, adolescents, and the subject of reading, we acknowledge that the term *adolescence* has many definitions and that individual students' identities are much more complex and significant than membership in a community, developmental stage, or age group (see Dillon & Moje, 1998; Moje & Dillon, 2006). We touch on developmental issues aligned generally with chronological age in two groups of students: (1) typically progressing, competent readers; and (2) so-called "struggling" readers. For the first group, we look at learners who have traversed the excitement of the earliest stage of learning how to read, the engaging experience of accessing new worlds through texts, the identification with characters in stories who are like friends, and the association of reading with community and enjoyable time with peers and teachers.

Many youth in the age range of 10–11 years have learned to read narrative texts, take an interest in series books, and have favorite authors and genres. But many of these same students start to feel reservations about reading as a school subject or reading related to learning across the curriculum. They start to dislike reading textbooks in school subjects and form some soon-to-be deeply engrained notions of reading tasks related to schoolwork that may mitigate against their future motivation to read a range of texts for a variety of purposes.

The latter group, the struggling readers, by age 7 or 8 have started to see themselves as less competent than their peers. At this relatively early age they are becoming painfully aware of the difference between ability and effort. They are starting to disengage from reading and other literate practices to preserve self-esteem, realizing that getting better seems beyond their control. Overall, they read much less than more competent peers, they develop coping strategies to negotiate school tasks without reading, and they fall further and further behind. Next, we present frameworks for thinking about how to motivate and engage readers—with some distinctions between competent and struggling or disengaged readers.

MOTIVATION FRAMEWORKS
FOR GUIDING BEST PRACTICES

Why hasn't the topic of motivation found its way into discussions about reading and literacy learning and into teachers' practices? First, much of the current discussion about adolescent literacy concerns struggling readers, particularly how to bring these readers "up to grade level." The predominant model for "not leaving anyone behind" embraces the most technically efficient solution for equipping these youth with strategies and skills that will help them read more proficiently, that is, proficient reading as defined by performance on large-scale standardized assessments (see a critique of this idea and No Child Left Behind by Dillon, 2003). Using motivation to engage readers, although currently a popular topic, has been theoretically elusive, and the intersecting frameworks that define the field have been difficult to incorporate into either instructional frameworks or assessment plans. We propose a new way to think about these intersecting frameworks (see Figure 3.1, pp. 48–49). Specifically, we note that (1) a strategy must foster the deliberate cognitive processing that a reader uses in selecting and monitoring a plan to attain a goal and (2) the reader must be supported in assessing the goal as valuable, the latter being tied to motivation and engagement theory.

Nevertheless, for practitioners who want to delve into the rich theoretical traditions in achievement motivation, the inquiry will yield some strong, time-tested practices. For example, researchers have revisited the constructs of intrinsic and extrinsic motivation and unearthed some common misconceptions in relation to achievement. Several scholars (Sansone & Harackiewicz, 2000) have analyzed reward systems to determine which ones work and which do not in various instructional contexts. For example, a recent study found no statistically significant effects on standardized math or reading outcomes in Chicago, New York City, or Washington, D.C., to support the effect of financial incentives on student achievement (Fryer, 2011). Other scholars have reviewed 30 years of research and presented current work on achievement motivation, including how instructional practices can actually contribute to increased motivation (Wigfield & Eccles, 2001). In addition, several researchers have taken great pains to translate the knowledge base on achievement motivation into specific practices for teachers (e.g., Alderman, 2008). Guthrie and his colleagues have directed their attention to motivation in literacy, particularly in the area of reading. For example, Guthrie, Wigfield, and Perencevich (2004) examined elementary school classroom contexts that promote engaged reading, focusing specifically on Concept-Oriented Reading Instruction (CORI)—a relatively new framework with potential that has yet to be realized, especially with adolescent learners, through ongoing development.

One of the most significant early discussions of how motivation frameworks relate to specific practices in reading, particularly as reading actually occurs in classroom contexts, is Guthrie and Wigfield's (1997) *Reading Engagement: Motivating Readers through Integrated Instruction*. In this foundational text they present a framework in the form of a graphic that guides discussions, showing the intersection of factors that support individual engagement with those that contribute to coherent classroom contexts. *Motivation* and *engagement* are not sets of isolated cognitive constructs but the result of complex factors that play out in situated practices. Similarly, the North Central Regional Educational Laboratory (NCREL, 2005, p. 8) compiled findings on key elements required for adolescent student engagement. This resulted in a four-level pyramid model that seeks to promote student achievement. The levels, working from the bottom up, include teacher's care and encouragement; teacher's knowledge of effective research-based reading strategies; teacher's recognition of student interests, [leading to] high student confidence, meaningful choices of literacy activities, relevant and interesting texts; [leading to] student engagement in using literacy strategies and skills, [which ultimately leads to] achievement. We like this model because it shows the many facets of motivation that educators want to address to enhance motivation and achievement.

We are partial to Wigfield and Eccles's (2001) manner of organizing motivation frameworks. They propose three questions learners might ask: "Can I do this activity?", "Do I want to do this activity and why?", "What do I need to do to succeed?" We think this question framework is particularly effective because it allows practitioners to ponder how their students might answer each question and the reasons they may give for answering affirmatively or negatively (based in the frameworks), and then the specific ways teachers might shift students' answers from negative to positive responses. Wigfield and Eccles note that these complex intersecting frameworks deviate considerably from older models in which researchers focused on processes such as reinforcement or constructs such as internal drives, with a shift toward a focus on developing beliefs, values, and goals. They also emphasize the importance of looking at the developmental trajectory of motivation, not only in how children and youth change over time, but in how their *perceptions* of the constructs—at least at an intuitive or self-reflective level—change, and in turn change their beliefs, values, and goals. In Table 3.1, we use Wigfield and Eccles's three questions to organize, at a very general level, a way of thinking about key motivation constructs in terms of struggling and normally achieving adolescent readers.

INTEGRATING MOTIVATION INTO EXISTING INSTRUCTIONAL FRAMEWORKS

Teachers can make subtle but powerful changes to their practices that can improve students' motivation. We have developed sets of these possible practices, based on many motivation frameworks, including the ones

TABLE 3.1. The Relation of Three Key Motivation Questions to Adolescents' Literacy Learning and Instruction

The key motivation question (posed by Wigfield & Eccles, 2001)	Constructs the question taps	Implications for struggling adolescents' literacy practices and growth	Implications for normally achieving adolescents' literacy practices and growth
1. **"Can I do this activity?"** *Literacy examples:* • "Can I read as well as I can do math?" • "Can I read as well as Erin or Alex?"	*Self-competence*; *expectancy beliefs*—expectations of success across various academic areas, and in relation to others.	Struggling adolescents develop negative perceptions about ability by second grade; early in academic careers they start to disengage from reading and define themselves as incompetent; they read less, get less practice, and fall further behind peers. Individual tasks define various facets of incompetence; although they may have a generally negative set toward school reading, they may feel more positively toward reading related to enjoyment or to an after-school job.	Normally achieving adolescents believe that they are competent; they persist longer and work harder; when presented with difficult texts and tasks, they take on the challenge. Because they work hard and use effective strategies, they get feedback that their effort and strategies pay off, and they continue to achieve. Nevertheless, even for these youth, research shows that perceptions of academic competence decline the longer they are in school due to competition, norm-referenced grading and tests, and less individual attention (e.g., Covington & Dray, 2001; Schunk, Meese, & Pintrich, 2013).
• "Do I believe that I can read and understand this text?" • "Can I answer the questions at the end of a text at this level?"	*Self-efficacy*—belief about one's ability to learn or perform at certain levels in connection with specific tasks (Schunk & Pajares, 2009).		

(continued)

TABLE 3.1. (continued)

2. "Do I want to do this activity, and why?" *Literacy examples:* • "Which book would be easier to understand?" [Choice = possibility for success = easier text or a skill set I have.] • "How important is it to read the biology chapter and answer the questions at the end?" [Value = grades; looking competent to teacher; doing as well as peers. • "Will reading critically in this class result in anything important?" [What do I need to do to get a grade; to be perceived as competent by the teacher or a valued peer?]	*Expectancy–value model*—expectations for success and the value placed on success determine motivation to perform various tasks.	As in the first question, research shows that early in their academic careers, children distinguish competence across school subject domains. By mid-primary grades, they have sorted out what they choose to work on, based on expectations for success. Struggling readers, who start to have trouble in early grades, do not expect success and hence place little value on working at texts and tasks at which they expect to fail. However, particularly as adolescents, they may place value (subject task value judgments) on texts and task independent of their expectations for success—for example, things they like; desire to identify with social peers, etc. Girls have higher competency beliefs than boys for reading.	Similar to the response to the first question, even normally achieving students show declining expectations for success and diminished beliefs in their competency (e.g., Dweck & Elliot, 1983; Eccles et al. 1998). In this model, adolescents are particularly interesting because they are more capable than children of distinguishing between more finely tuned components of task values; they are also better at "reading" their environments, interpreting feedback, and looking at subject task values in relation to social environments. Adolescents could decide to work harder and more strategically at something, based on a carefully elaborated set of values.
3. "What do I need to do to succeed?" *Literacy examples:* • "How should I read this history unit to do well on the exam?"	*Self-regulation—of cognition, motivation, and affect when presented with various tasks and contexts* (Pintrich & Zushio, 2001).	It is well documented that struggling readers do not self-regulate as well as normally achieving readers (e.g., Pressley, 2006).	Normally achieving readers can self-regulate and employ strategies; however, they lack the opportunities in school to read critically, to get feedback

(continued)

TABLE 3.1. *(continued)*

The key motivation question (posed by Wigfield & Eccles, 2001)	Constructs the question taps	Implications for struggling adolescents' literacy practices and growth	Implications for normally achieving adolescents' literacy practices and growth
[What is particularly challenging about text structure and content? What are some strategies I can use to learn from this text?] • "How will I know if I am not understanding the text and not using effective strategies?" [Or the reverse: how will I know what is working well?] • "Based on the texts and the tasks I need to complete, and my knowledge of this subject and pertinent strategies, how can I do the best job on reading for the exam [or on reading to engage in a class discussion or to complete a project]?"	Planning and goal setting, along with activating perceptions of the task and context in relation to self. Monitoring various aspects of self, task, and context. Using a repertoire to regulate self, task, context.	They rely on ineffective strategies and are not adept at monitoring their understanding; they are not as facile at relating what they know to the topic at hand (they are likely to actually know less because they read less than normally achieving peers) and are not as likely as skilled readers to vary their strategies according to text types and difficulty or variations in task demands.	on the effectiveness of their strategies, and to develop personally relevant purposes and goals. In short, much or most of the reading they do does not require them to use and get feedback on the self-regulation of which they are capable. If they succeed in understanding difficult texts, they need feedback about which strategies work to meet specific goals and to feel confident that they can read difficult texts because of strategies within their control (e.g., the WestEd apprenticeship model).

highlighted in Table 3.1. Because the frameworks overlap, one set of practices based on a particular foundation might engender other sets of practices based on complementary research. For example, there are motivating ways of presenting books and other reading material to children and youth; there are motivating ways to engage adolescents who have become disengaged with reading in school; and there are motivating ways to design and present tasks related to reading that learners find more engaging than typical school tasks.

Also, when looking more at the panorama of a classroom rather than at a particular reader interacting with a text, it is apparent that there are motivating ways of engaging students in an academically and socioculturally important manner. There are also discourses that cause readers to feel more confident and competent as readers—ways of respecting individual meaning constructions and opinions, as well as discursive practices, including feedback, that encourage students to tackle difficult texts and to sort out strategies that they can continue to use effectively. Overall, in the best of all possible classroom scenarios, one might see practices that tap various intersecting frameworks in creating supportive classroom environments populated by engaged readers who are motivated to critically understand texts. These students persevere to meet goals and feel in control of a repertoire of strategies. In theory, this sounds great. But how might we set up our classrooms and design instruction for all adolescent readers—especially with the range of competence and perceptions of competence in a typical classroom?

We revisit the frameworks and implications outlined in Table 3.1 in the following sections of this chapter. We realize that the dichotomy presented in the table is somewhat contrived, and that the criteria for assigning persons to the respective groups are often ambiguous and range greatly from setting to setting. Nevertheless, we use the classifications as one way to make several generalizations that we believe are important in thinking about adolescents. Specifically, we examine why adolescents are much more than simply older readers, and why some adolescents did not develop the reading skills and strategies typically associated with a given developmental stage, grade level, or chronological age.

PRACTICES FOR NORMALLY ACHIEVING READERS

As is apparent from Table 3.1, many adolescents who *are* competent readers and *believe* they are competent readers are increasingly unlikely to want to read in school and less likely to choose reading for pleasure the longer they are in school. Reading, which had almost universal appeal when these youth were in preschool and primary grades, has been replaced with reading-as-subject. Reading, which used to be an adventure, an engaging and nurturing social experience, becomes a set of tedious tasks leading to the demonstration of narrowly defined competencies—grades on homework assignments, quizzes and tests, and meeting standards. The trust that toddlers and primary-age children gave freely to teachers who guided them to exciting encounters in stories has been replaced by a distrust of teachers who assign reading in textbooks students view as ill-structured exposition and as compendia of not-so-useful information. This disengagement and lack of motivation can be reversed, at least in some measure, by drawing from the frameworks in Table 3.1.

"Can I Do This Activity?"

Normally achieving adolescents would usually respond, "Yes, I believe I have the ability to read and complete most tasks related to what I read." They would qualify this confidence by subject areas, perceiving that they are more competent as readers in some subjects than others. But some practices may further motivate them to read—especially in school—because the longer they encounter reading in school, the less motivated they are. These practices include:

  • Providing more compelling reasons to read and to practice and build fluency with a range of texts accompanied by procedural feedback; this feedback includes information on what readers understand and how they understand it—not just competition and comparative performance or reading to cover the content, but a focus on reading to learn interesting things.

  • Providing more instruction in important strategies coupled with more demanding reading. For example, the reading apprenticeship framework (Schoenbach, Greenleaf, Cziko, & Hurwitz, 1999) includes a focus on academic apprenticeship and feedback that enables readers to attribute success to something at which they are getting better. Readers talk to one another about what they understand in reading challenging texts and which strategies they used to understand the text.

"Do I Want to Do This Activity, and Why?"

The implications column of Table 3.1 state that even confident adolescents' perceptions about their competence as readers declines somewhat as they move up through the grades. This decline is due to increased competition, a focus on grades, difficulty of texts, and reading and task demands related to wider ranges of text genres with less assistance from teachers. The following practices are supported by motivation constructs:

  • Providing more access to a range of engaging texts, particularly texts that are not like textbooks, including hybrid texts such as "pseudo-narratives" and graphic text forms such as graphic novels, manga, and Web pages.

  • Providing choice among texts and options on tasks related to reading. A typical activity such as reading to answer questions at the end of a section or chapter would compete with options such as reading to summarize thoughts in a blog; reading to augment a media presentation; and reading multiple texts on a topic to compare authors' perspectives and credibility (Shanahan, 2003; Shanahan, Holschuh, & Hubbard, 2004).

• Allowing students to construct purposes for reading that meet personally relevant goals or enable them to engage in useful or interesting activities (e.g., O'Brien, 2003), such as reading to find out how to organize a neighborhood project or reading to complete an inquiry project.

"What Do I Need to Do to Succeed?"

Ironically, many normally achieving adolescents feel successful in reading, but they have little idea about what makes them successful, and they don't know how they can get even better at reading. As already noted, because they often lack goals that require critically reading difficult texts, they receive little guided practice, independent practice, and feedback regarding their efforts to read effectively. Given the underlying foundation that motivated reading is reading in which readers feel self-efficacious because they have control of their reading, here are some practices teachers can employ that are supported by the research in motivation:

• Using explicit teaching of strategies appropriate for specific disciplines and in a range of texts in those disciplines; explicit instruction must then lead to guided practice, independent practice, and the successful daily use of strategies learned. We have modified the traditional notion of strategies instruction and strategic reading into strategic engagement (Figure 3.1), in which we ask teachers to systematically consider both strategies and motivation and engagement.

• Providing ample opportunities (built into explicit instruction to independent reading frameworks) for students to receive feedback on their reading from teachers and peers; the feedback focuses on identifying what they are doing that can be attributed to their own knowledge and control, their self-regulation, their strategies, and their effective monitoring. This feedback is the key to the development of intrinsic motivation and feeling self-efficacious.

• Reducing the focus on competition, assessment, and grades and increasing opportunities to read strategically to meet different purposes.

• Providing multiple experiences wherein teachers and peers discuss both the content and the process of reading a range of texts for a variety of purposes.

PRACTICES FOR STRUGGLING READERS

Struggling readers are typically characterized as older readers who lack the skills and strategies of their more competent peers. Although this characterization partly captures who these readers are, for many readers, it

Almasi and Fullerton (2012) define strategies as "The deliberate cognitive processing a person uses in selecting and monitoring a plan to attain a goal" (p. 3). In comparison, our strategic engagement model adapts their notions to focus systematically on twin strategies, with motivation and engagement at the core. We (Dillon & O'Brien) posit that both traditional strategies steps and specific plans to foster motivation and engagement must be made explicit, side by side. For example, to foster agency in meeting a goal, two things must happen: (1) a strategy must foster the deliberate cognitive processing that a reader uses in selecting and monitoring a plan to attain a goal and (2) the reader must be supported in assessing the goal as valuable, the latter being tied to motivation and engagement theory.

Current Positions on Strategic Reading (Almasi & Fullerton (2012)	"Strategic Engagement" Emphasis—Making the Engagement and Motivation Explicit
The reader should have a goal in mind.	1. Tying the goal to **value** and **expectation** for success: Part of the instruction should explicitly focus on **clearly defining** the goal—for example, Goal = . You will read to make three inferences about the passage. 2. Clearly defining the **value** of the goal—for example, if you can draw inferences, you can better understand the text and make connections to your experiences, which makes the reading more meaningful. 3. Discussing explicitly reasons that the goal is attainable and within the reader's scope of experience and ability (remember to define ability as open and within one's control).
The reader should plan actions to meet the goal.	**Presenting contingencies and choices:** 1. Teachers should discuss with readers how possible plans might be effective; readers should be allowed to choose actions they prefer to meet the goal, reassess, and try new plans. 2. You should focus, via interacting with student, on the autonomy and control associated with choosing from contingences. For example, students might read and jot down possible inferences as they go; they could wait until the end of a section of text and jot down a main inference; or they could read the whole text and then jot down three things that they know for sure (explicit information) and three things that they are pretty sure are inferences that could be drawn.
The reader is motivated to actually enact the strategic actions.	**Reviewing/reinforcing:** By this step, the reader is already moving toward motivation. But this is a good point for a reminder—that the goal is **clear** and **valuable**; the reader is reminded that she/he has formulated a plan and chosen strategies that are **expected to work and that readers have control over**.

FIGURE 3.1. (*continued*)

The reader has the ability to monitor the process to see whether he/she has attained the goal and to make adjustments as necessary (combined Almasi points 4 and 5).	**Explicitly tie monitoring to "online" agency and recursive agency:** Monitoring is attention to whether the chosen actions are working strategically **toward** meeting the goal and include a stance of control. As a reader, I have options if this is not working and it is my choice to pick action *B*. If at the end of the reading, I assess that I did not meet the goal, it is my choice to start over with a new plan.
Example: This could be applied to instructional routines leading to strategic reading—for example, one could modify list–group–label or SQ3R so that the specific strategic components are aligned with motivation and engagement components.	

FIGURE 3.1. Strategic engagement: Making explicit connections.

is an oversimplification that favors definitions of competence grounded in achievement performance and psychometrics over broader sociocultural issues (Murdock, 2009). Unfortunately, these same issues are based on a deficit ideology that has defined struggling adolescent readers in many major research and policy reports. The instructional complement to this insufficient deficit view is that educators simply need to provide struggling adolescents with the skills and strategies instruction that will move them up the developmental ladder—up to grade level and up to established state and district benchmark scores. The deficit perspective ignores or subordinates most of the "affective" and identity construction dimensions of reading, which, from a contemporary perspective, include a range of both sociocognitive and sociocultural aspects of motivation. With reference to more traditional theories of motivation, like self-efficacy theory (Bandura, 1977), expectancy value theory (Eccles et al., 1983), attribution theory (Weiner, 1986), and achievement goal theory (Ames & Archer, 1988), struggling readers are defined as having beliefs about the inadequacy of their abilities, not valuing perceived goals, or being unable to attribute success to factors within their control. What is noticeably absent, from a contemporary position, although unclear from research, is how racial and ethnic factors constructed from a sociocultural rather than sociocognitive orientation intersect with motivation. Instead of focusing on the individual and assessing motivation based on general perceptions about ability or goals assessment, sociocultural theorists posit that membership in cultural groups or social classes, through its contribution to identity construction and assignment of stereotypes, influences, for example, a reader's stance toward tasks. And this could happen primarily due to racial and class identification and class membership.

Murdock has synthesized some perspectives organized around the three questions posed by Wigfield and Eccles (2001) that we used to organize part of this chapter. In reality, struggling readers do lack requisite reading skills and strategies, but they also experience failure on a daily basis, develop negative self-perceptions, and position themselves as incompetent based on early self-appraisals, formal and informal appraisals from others, and cultural identity and its discursive formations and practices (Hall, 2009). In response to this failure, students develop accompanying intricate rationalizations and coping strategies that protect them from additional failure. These factors must be as systematically addressed as the teaching of skills and strategies—even more so with disengaged learners. Practices based on key motivation constructs can be used by educators to revive students' confidence and self-efficacy and convince struggling readers that they can use and develop skills and strategies that result in meeting goals that are attributable to factors within their control. Of course, there is some overlap in addressing the three questions above for normally achieving students, but in the case of struggling readers, the instruction may be more like a targeted intervention due to the severity of disengagement and the need to resurrect something positive within relatively few remaining years in school. The sociocultural factors do not as neatly map onto the three questions addressed below as more traditional motivation constructs because ongoing discursive identity construction based on cultural membership is more complex and continually sustained over time.

"Can I Do This Activity?"

The answer many struggling adolescent readers give to the question "Can I do this activity?" is "No" or "I'm not so sure." These readers have years of evidence that convinces them that they might not succeed, and they weigh this evidence against future effort. When young people say "I think that I lack the ability" or "I might not be successful," they often convince themselves not to try. They also believe that the factors that lead to their reading failure are beyond their control: They didn't get to pick the texts, tasks, and tests; they have relatively little power to change teachers' decisions regarding what to include in the curriculum; they have a limited repertoire of strategies to apply on various texts and tasks. From Murdock's (2009) synthesis of sociocultural dimensions, two intertwined factors mitigate against approaching tasks with confidence and self-efficacy: (1) persons whose identities are significantly grounded in race and class membership outside of the dominant achievement ideology of schooling are treated differently by others and (2) they subconsciously internalize the negative competence stereotype from experience as members of marginalized groups. In short, these students' academic positions are socially constructed. The following instructional practices, based on the frameworks introduced in Table 3.1, address the motivational challenges associated with struggling adolescent readers:

- Reversing disengagement with self-efficacy. Struggling readers have already disengaged, and educators who work with adolescents can't turn back the clock to intervene in early grades or easily change some students' generally negative self-perceptions about ability. However, teachers can try to build or *re*build self-efficacy, which depends on an individual's beliefs about his or her ability to perform a particular task. A practice that could yield results is to break larger tasks that seem formidable and difficult down into specific steps with very clear benchmarks for success and a focus on meeting goals one by one.

- Designing specific forms of feedback that show students that their progress can be attributed to actions and abilities within their control. If students successfully read longer and more difficult books, educators can build specific feedback into the task on how these readers are traversing the text features, structure, and vocabulary by using specific reading or study strategies. Educators can also share how students' use of particular reading processes and strategies contributes to specific outcomes, such as the ability to summarize, tell peers about a section of the text, or explain which strategies they have used to understand the text.

- Reducing the anxiety over reading as a performance or process, in and of itself, by focusing on reading as just one avenue toward activity or action. For example, reading may be one source of information students use to complete a multimedia project, or reading may be just a tool to learn about something you need to be able to do to demonstrate it for peers.

"Do I Want to Do This Activity, and Why?"

Table 3.1 explains that struggling adolescent readers are seldom enthused and often mildly to moderately disinterested in most reading tasks in school. They have the same negative, escalating feelings about reading in school that their more competent peers have: The longer they are in school, due to the factors noted, the less they like reading and the lower their perceptions about their ability. Struggling readers realize in about second grade that they are behind their peers, that effort did not yield results, and that they lacked strategies for reading to learn. These negative perceptions explain in large part why struggling readers don't want to participate in reading activities and related tasks. But again, we must draw an important distinction between task value related to engagement or avoidance based on typical sociocognitive dimensions versus sociocultural views.

We can use the traditional approach to goal orientation to clarify the differences. Traditionally, tasks might have value because completing them assures one that she or he has learned important concepts (mastery goals) or simply because one wants to feel competent in completing them (ego orientation) (Nicholls, 1989). In contrast, members of cultural groups may take stances toward tasks shared by group members that are based on values assigned by the group. Not only do persons from different broad cultural groups exhibit different performance-avoidance stances, groups may devalue academic achievement based on whether academic achievement yields jobs or other attainments of success for that group. One may simply take a stance that devalues academic achievement to preserve self-esteem against this historical backdrop of group members failing to capitalize on the value of something that others enjoy, like high-paying jobs following from college degrees. This contrast is not to devalue our instructional approaches tied to the category but to make you aware of the deeply ingrained complexity of placing values on academic tasks and goals and to alert you to our belief as to why this category is more difficult to tackle when dealing with sociocultural factors.

In addition, issues from the expectancy–value model cited in Table 3.1 influence adolescent readers' beliefs and actions. Struggling students do not expect to gain anything tangible from reading; they read to meet externally established and imposed goals (e.g., read to answer the questions and complete the unit quiz). Furthermore, based on past feedback, self-appraisals, and the way they have been positioned in the institution of school (e.g., labels, special programs), even if they did decide to meet externally imposed goals, they would not expect to be very successful. In the following section we provide several instructional practices that can begin to address this seemingly intractable problem, some of which are variations on the practices provided earlier for normally achieving readers:

• Focus on accessibility. Accessibility—dimensions of a text that make it available to a reader—is not synonymous with matching reading ability to text readability. It is more like leveling, based on a range of factors including text difficulty, but also considering how difficulty can be mediated by interest, stance toward a topic, and determination and perseverance to read something one has decided to read. If students read something they really want to read and are invested in, then they choose to read it, in spite of the perception that it is difficult. This is true as long as the text is not *too* difficult on the word recognition/decoding level. The point we wish to make is that text accessibility leads to more reading, and practice leads to more fluency and competence.

• Promoting reengagement in reading for enjoyment and excitement. This can be achieved by providing students with many choices of reading materials from among a wide range of trade books and genres. This range would include texts that are popular among adolescents, such as graphic novels, manga, and digital texts. Reading these engaging texts should also be part of instruction in various disciplines and should supplement or supplant textbooks when possible. Use of these texts should *not* lead to typical outcomes such as writing reports or answering questions. If exciting texts lead to disengaging typical tasks, it defeats the purpose of using them.

• Providing positive, specific feedback directed at facilitating self-efficacy, personal goals, and strategy use, with a focus on successes. If students choose—even with reservations—to engage in a reading task, they are more likely to want to engage in this task in the future if they have evidence that they were successful and accomplished something. Stiggins, Arter, Chappuis, and Chappuis's (2004) ideas that focus on formative assessment directed back to learners apply here. Good vehicles for providing this kind of feedback include teacher conferences or peer-to-peer conferences, wherein students share and discuss reading and strategies.

• Focusing on more appealing reading outcomes instead of requiring only typical outcomes such as answering questions, writing reports, and writing summaries (e.g., constructing a menu of variations). In previous sections of this chapter we noted several examples of outcomes that would be appealing to adolescent readers, such as writing a blog (or contributing to a wiki) or producing a multimedia project. In curriculum planning, it makes sense to list all of the typical tasks educators might assign to students in one column and then in another column list possible options that meet the same or similar instructional objectives. We have had success with media inquiry projects in which students self-selected project partners, outlined and storyboarded self-selected project ideas, and then worked from daily contracts in which they (and we) could track how they met their daily, weekly, and project goals (O'Brien, 2006). These projects required students to use a range of media, including print; they read to do research on the topic using both print and digital sources; and they synthesized their reading into multimodal texts.

• Eliciting self-selected purposes. This is a strategy already listed for normally achieving students. Rather than giving students topics and purposes for reading, educators can construct projects in which learners select topics and outcomes. Student choice and autonomy lead to motivation and engagement. The multimedia projects discussed above are a good example of this concept.

"What Do I Need to Do to Succeed?"

Struggling readers often draw a blank when this question is posed to them. As noted in Table 3.1, these adolescents lack a repertoire of strategies, have difficulty selecting appropriate strategies from ones they do know, or continue to use ineffective strategies. As in the case of normally achieving readers, although less often, some struggling readers think they are improving but aren't sure why and, across the curriculum, they receive too little instruction and practice in comprehending challenging texts. We reiterate the motivation construct stated for competent readers that underlies this question: Motivated reading is reading in which readers feel self-efficacious because they have control of their reading, and they can read with confidence and an expectation of understanding what they read. The following instructional practices tap into some of the ideas already discussed for normally achieving readers, but focus more on both the lack of typical skills and strategies among struggling readers and the effect of students' negative perceptions about their ability to succeed on various tasks during particular literacy performances:

• Providing explicit instruction leading to guided and independent practice. Most struggling readers need explicit instruction in literacy strategies appropriate for specific disciplines and in a range of texts in those disciplines, particularly in using strategies with the highest utility that meet both teachers' and students' goals. For example, summarizing, exploring question–answer relationships, inferring, and monitoring understanding are processes that should be supported with explicit strategies instruction. Some of the lowest-performing struggling readers need to work on word-level strategies and build fluency. We emphatically repeat, however, that *explicit instruction must lead to guided practice, independent practice, and the successful daily use of strategies.* For example, in reviewing 20 years of strategies instruction, researchers (Dole, 2003; Duffy, 2003) concluded that educators are very good at teaching instructional strategies but not as proficient at providing opportunities for learners to use them.

• Providing specific feedback. Struggling readers need more feedback about specific skills they are doing well and those on which they need additional work. Feedback helps readers know that what they are doing is both effective and attributable to something within their control. Understanding the implications of their actions will positively affect adolescent readers' perceptions about their ability and, more specifically, their self-efficacy. Written individual feedback, specific classroom feedback and praise, and feedback in teacher or peer conferences are all formats that could help struggling readers understand how well they are learning effective strategies and monitoring their understanding. Other helpful practices include reducing the focus on competition, assessment, and grades; increasing opportunities for students to read strategically to meet different purposes; and providing time for teachers and students, and students and their peers, to talk about both the content and the process of reading a range of texts for a variety of purposes.

CONCLUSION

As we have discussed in this chapter, motivation is not a fixed construct. Teachers can use their understanding of motivation and engagement to improve literacy practices, achievement, and students' perceptions of their abilities. Examining motivation constructs from the perspectives of learners and responding to the three questions in Table 3.1 provide tools educators can use to map significant research-based ideas and eloquent theoretical models onto day-to-day practices. Obviously, from both the initial discussion of the motivation frameworks and the instructional practices based on them, there is a lot of overlap and intersection of various constructs within the framework. But if educators employ most of the constructs to reframe or modify instruction, positive benefits will ensue.

DISCUSSION AND ACTIVITIES

In order to work to transform relatively complex theoretical frameworks and models of motivation into practices, we have read widely in the fields of motivation in general and achievement motivation in particular. We have also implemented many of the ideas we have gleaned in both middle and high school settings, studied what happened, and modified our approaches to reflect what we learned. The instructional practices section of the chapter, organized around several key questions, could lead to many specific activities. We want to recommend the following ideas:

1. Read the research base and work leading to key motivation constructs. An understanding of these constructs will help you comprehend why particular modifications of tasks and literacy contexts should make a difference in students' perceptions and achievement.

2. Systematically map out modifications that could be made to your current instructional plans. A planning activity that we have used successfully with our school-based colleagues is one in which they have listed current reading assignments and related activities in one column, and then have used a multiple-column bridging chart to explore alternatives. Part of this activity requires using some existing frameworks for systematically critiquing current practices with a goal of modifying as many as possible so that they are more motivating. For example, we use the "Six C's" (*choice, challenge, control, collaboration, constructing meaning*, and *consequences*), generated by Turner and Paris (1995), to provide a way to critique existing instructional frameworks. The purpose of the Six C's is to help teachers think of open-ended tasks rather than the more typical closed tasks. Table 3.2 defines each of the C's and shows possible transformations of closed tasks to open-ended tasks.

3. Videotape several classroom lessons (e.g., lessons you teach and lessons taught by peer educators). The taped lessons should include interactions between you and your students and segments where you provide feedback to students during reading instruction and related tasks. Using a framework for analyzing classroom interactions, critique your lesson interactions or a peer's interactions and list ways you or your colleagues could improve on how you motivate students via your comments, suggestions, and feedback.

TABLE 3.2. Transforming Literacy Tasks Using the Six C's

The Six C's (Turner & Paris, 1995)	Typical closed literacy tasks	Transformation to more open-ended, motivating literacy tasks
Choice: Provide students with authentic choices and purposes for literacy. Recast activities to emphasize the enjoyment and informational value of literacy; do not refer to daily tasks as work but instead rename them by their function (e.g., ask students to plan an event by writing. . . . and reading).	In an eighth-grade science class, students read an assigned portion of Chapter 3 and then work on the follow-up lab. Each lab group is responsible for writing up an oral report of their findings and the group leader, assigned by the teacher, presents it to the class.	Using the classroom library and a menu of web pages, students can choose any combination of books or other texts that they think will help them complete a lab. They collaborate on the lab and choose among several different products for presenting the results, including a presentation on a web page.
Challenge: Allow students to modify tasks so the difficulty and interest levels are challenging. Demonstrate the many ways one can complete a tasks; show concrete examples to students of successful but different approaches to tasks; teach students to assess whether tasks are too difficult or too easy for them and how to adjust goals or strategies for appropriate difficulty; point out how students have molded tasks to their interests; and assign tasks that can be modified in many ways.	In a high school reading lab designed for students who struggle the most in reading (defined as the lowest 2-3% in performance on comprehension and vocabulary subtests of the state achievement test), students can pick partners and choose among several topics focusing on the impact of violence in the media on adolescents. Each pair completes an inquiry project based on teacher guidelines.	The students in the reading lab are given the broad topic, "The impact of violence in the media on adolescents." Each pair is asked to submit a plan in which they decide on which medium (e.g., film, TV, video games) they want to use. In addition, they have to plan and storyboard the process they will use and then plan a possible outcome of their project based on their perception of the level of difficulty and challenge they think is appropriate for their abilities and time frame (e.g., design a web page or a multimedia project presentation on PowerPoint; make a mini-documentary).
Control: Show students how they can control their learning. Teach students how to evaluate what they know and how to evaluate and monitor their learning. Students are probed by teachers with such questions as: Are you focused?	In a middle school language arts class, students read portions of the book *Maniac McGee* for homework, in which they have discussions or answer questions about the portion of the book assigned for each day.	In a middle school reading "intervention" class for the lowest- level readers in the school, students read *Tears of a Tiger*. In between whole-class discussions, the students participate in peer groups focused on metacognitive conversations (Schoenbach et al., 1999).

(continued)

TABLE 3.2. (*continued*)

What's more important? Students are guided to use inner speech to self-monitor.	They often turn answers to the questions posed by the teacher for each portion of the book.	The students share their evolving understanding as well as the strategies they use to meet different goals in reading the text. Through sharing both their meaning-making and the ways they tackle the text, each learner feels more control and confidence.
Collaboration: Emphasize the positive aspects of giving and seeking help. Provide students with opportunities to work with many different peers; students are taught how to teach each other by emphasizing the giving of clues, not answers; many individual tasks are recast as paired or group tasks (e.g., paired reading vs. oral round-robin reading).	The teacher engages in recitation with students in a middle school health class. The topic is how to administer first aid to someone who has accidentally consumed poison. The teacher asks a series of questions, calling on one student after another. Students respond by rapidly reciting information from the text.	Students in a high school biology class, work in self-selected peer groups. The members of each group divide up tasks, with some members using resources to find answers to study guide questions, some introducing information they have done as homework, and some writing to synthesize information that the group will turn in as a shared product.
Constructing Meaning: Emphasize strategies and metacognition for constructing meaning. Provide students with a repertoire of strategies in order to respond flexibly in reading and writing situations; students need extensive applications of comprehension as well as encoding and decoding strategies to assist them in acquiring an understanding of what literacy is as well as how to use and understand it.	In a high school history class, the students read a chapter entitled, "Early Americans." They are assigned to read sections of the text each night for homework and to turn in questions after reading each section. When the students read, they usually read only to find answers to the questions; a typical strategy they use is skimming to find a statement in the section that relates to or includes information needed to answer each question.	In a high school history class studying the Civil War, the students are critically reading a portion of the text entitled "The Story Behind the Story of Pickett's Charge," using a variation of the three-level comprehension guide (Herber, 1970). In the first level students find information in the text that supports statements and explain if the information is directly stated or requires minor inferencing. In the second level they find multiple places in the text that support inferences. In the third level they reread sections to synthesize main themes that they use to construct applied-level comprehension statements.

(*continued*)

TABLE 3.2. (continued)

The Six C's (Turner & Paris, 1995)	Typical closed literacy tasks	Transformation to more open-ended, motivating literacy tasks
Consequences: Use the consequences of tasks to build responsibility, ownership, and self-regulation. Acknowledge that group evaluation is a regular part of literacy instruction; encourage students to share their successes and failures; help students see that errorless learning is not learning at all; rather, real learning comes through error, because errors provide information about needed improvement; emphasize the value of effort and honing strategies because these tools equip students to attempt more and more challenging tasks.	Middle school language arts students work on a collaborative inquiry project in which teacher-assigned groups study a "famous person." To pick the person, each member puts his or her preferred name on a piece of paper and one group member draws a name out of a can. The groups are given an outline to follow in constructing the project and a fixed number of points are assigned to each section of the outline.	Students in a high school literacy lab select an inquiry topic based on interest. Then they plan the project based on available resources, the amount of time needed, and the deadline for completion (e.g., a school open house when they will present their work to parents/caregivers). For each workday they write up task goals that are reviewed first by them and then by a teacher. Based on review/conferences, they revise goals when necessary.

To analyze classroom interactions to determine what motivates students and enhances literacy learning, we have used several frameworks, including one adapted from Alderman (2008), titled "Guidelines for Effective Praise" (p. 254). Alderman's table is based on the work of Jerry Brophy (1981) and juxtaposes effective versus ineffective praise offered by teachers to students. For each type of praise listed as ineffective, it is useful for educators to reflect on how to modify praise, monitor what it "looks like" via videotaped lessons, and then note the effect of the modification on student motivation. Videotaping lessons, analyzing interactions, and reflecting on the acts of teaching and learning are powerful ways to study motivation constructs and set goals to enhance adolescents' literacy learning.

REFERENCES

Alderman, M. K. (2008). *Motivation for achievement: Possibilities for teaching and learning.* New York: Routledge.

Almasi, J. F., & Fullerton, S. K. (2012). *Teaching strategic processes in reading* (2nd ed.). Guilford Press.

Ames, C., & Archer, J. (1988). Achievement goals in the classroom: Students' learning strategies and motivation processes. *Journal of Educational Psychology, 80*, 260–267.

Bandura, A. (1977). *Self-efficacy: The exercise of control*. New York: Freeman.

Brophy, J. E. (1981). Teacher praise: A functional analysis. *Review of Educational Research, 51*, 5–32.

Covington, M. V., & Dray, E. (2002). The developmental course of achievement motivation: A need-based approach. In A. Wigfield & J. S. Eccles (Eds.), *Development of achievement motivation* (pp. 33–56). San Diego: Academic Press.

Dillon, D. R. (2003). In leaving no child behind have we forsaken individual learners, teachers, schools, and communities? In C. Fairbanks, J. Worthy, B. Maloch, J. Hoffman, & D. Schallert (Eds.), *Fifty-second yearbook of the National Reading Conference* (pp. 1–31). Milwaukee, WI: National Reading Conference.

Dillon, D. R., & Moje, E. B. (1998). Listening to the talk of adolescent girls: Lessons about literacy, school, and life. In D. E. Alvermann, K. A. Hinchman, D. W. Moore, S. F. Phelps, & D. R. Waff (Eds.), *Reconceptualizing the literacies in adolescents' lives* (pp. 193–223). Mahwah, NJ: Erlbaum.

Dole, J. A. (2003). Professional development in reading comprehension instruction. In A. P. Sweet & C. E. Snow (Eds.), *Rethinking reading comprehension* (pp. 176–191). New York: Guilford Press.

Duffy, G. G.(2003). *Explaining reading: A resource for teaching concepts, skills, and strategies*. New York: Guilford Press.

Dweck, C. S., & Elliott, E. S. (1983). Achievement motivation. In P. H. Mussen (Ed.), *Handbook of child psychology* (3rd ed., pp. 643–691). New York: Wiley.

Eccles, J. S., Adler, T. F., Fetterman, R., Goff, S., Kaczala, C. M., & Meece, J. L. (1983). Expectations, values, and academic behaviors. In J. T. Spence (Ed.), *Perspectives on achievement and achievement motivation* (pp. 75–146). San Francisco: Freeman.

Eccles, J. S., Wigfield, A., & Schiefele, U. (1998). Motivation to succeed. In N. Eisenberg (Ed.), *Handbook of child psychology* (5th ed., Vol. 3, pp. 1017–1095). New York: Wiley.

Fryer, R. G. (2011). Financial incentives and student achievement: Evidence from randomized trials. *Quarterly Journal of Economics, 126*, 1755–1798. Advance access publication on November 2, 2011, Oxford University Press.

Guthrie, J. T. (2008). Reading motivation and engagement in middle and high school: Appraisal and intervention. In J. T. Guthrie (Ed.), *Engaging adolescents in reading* (pp. 1–16). Thousand Oaks, CA: Corwin Press.

Guthrie, J. T., & Coddington, C. S. (2009). Reading motivation. In K. R. Wentzel & A. Wigfield (Eds.), *Handbook of motivation at school* (pp. 503–525). New York: Routledge.

Guthrie, J. T., & Wigfield, A. (Eds.). (1997). *Reading engagement: Motivating readers through integrated instruction*. Newark, DE: International Reading Association.

Guthrie, J. T., & Wigfield, A. (2000). Engagement and motivation in reading.

In M. L. Kamil, P. Mosenthal, P. D. Pearson, & R. Barr (Eds.), *Handbook of reading research, Volume III* (pp. 403–422). Mahwah, NJ: Erlbaum.

Guthrie, J. T., Wigfield, A., & Perencevich, K. C. (2004). *Motivating reading comprehension: Concept-Oriented Reading Instruction.* Mahwah, NJ: Erlbaum.

Herber, H. L. (1970). *Teaching reading in content areas.* Englewood Cliffs, NJ: Prentice Hall.

Hall, L. A. (2009). Struggling reader, struggling teacher: An examination of student–teacher transactions with reading instruction and text in social studies. *Research in the Teaching of English, 43*(3), 286–309.

Mazzoni, S. A., & Gambrell, L. B. (1999). A cross-cultural perspective of early literacy motivation. *Reading Psychology, 20*(3), 237–253.

Moje, E. B., & Dillon, D. R. (2006). Adolescent identities as mediated by science classroom discourse communities. In D. E. Alvermann, K. A. Hinchman, D. W. Moore, S. F. Phelps, & D. R. Waff (Eds.), *Reconceptualizing the literacies in adolescents' lives* (2nd ed., pp. 85–106). Mahwah, NJ: Erlbaum.

Murdock, T. B. (2009). Achievement in racial and ethnic context. In K. Wentzel & A. Wigfield (Eds.), *Handbook of motivation at school* (pp. 433–461). New York: Routledge.

NCREL. (2005). *Using student engagement to improve adolescent literacy: An NCREL quick key 10 action guide.* Naperville, IL: Learning Point Associates, North Central Regional Educational Laboratory. Retrieved from *http://education.ucf.edu/mirc/Research/Using%20Student%20Engagement%20to%20Improve%20Adolescent%20Literacy.pdf.*

Nicholls, J. G. (1989). *The competitive ethos and democratic education.* Cambridge, MA: Harvard University Press.

O'Brien, D. G. (2003). Juxtaposing traditional and intermedial literacies to redefine the competence of struggling adolescents. *Reading Online, 6*(7). Retrieved from *www.readingonline.org/newliteracies/lit_index.asp?HREF=obrien2.*

O'Brien, D. G. (2006). "Struggling" adolescents' engagement in multimediating: Countering the institutional construction of incompetence. In D. E. Alvermann, K. A. Hinchman, D. W. Moore, S. F. Phelps, & D. R. Waff (Eds.), *Reconceptualizing the literacies in adolescents' lives* (pp. 29–46). Mahwah, NJ: Erlbaum.

Pintrich, P. R., & Zushio, A. (2001). The development of academic self-regulation: The role of cognitive and motivational factors. In A. Wigfield & J. S. Eccles (Eds.), *Development of achievement motivation* (pp. 249–284). San Diego, CA: Academic Press.

Pressley, M. (2006). *Reading instruction that works: The case for balanced teaching* (3rd ed.). New York: Guilford Press.

Sansone, C., & Harackiewicz, J. M. (Eds.). (2000). *Intrinsic and extrinsic motivation.* San Diego, CA: Academic Press.

Schoenbach, R., Greenleaf, C., Cziko, C., & Hurwitz, L. (1999). *Reading for understanding.* San Francisco: Jossey-Bass.

Schunk, D. H., Meece, J. L., & Pintrich, P. R. (2014). *Motivation in education: Theory, research, and applications* (4th ed.). Boston: Pearson.

Schunk, D. H., & Pajares, F. (2009). Self-efficacy theory. In K. R. Wentzel & A. Wigfield (Eds.), *Handbook of motivation at school* (pp. 35–53). New York: Routledge.

Shanahan, C. (2003). *Using multiple texts to teach content.* Naperville, IL: Learning Point Associates.

Shanahan, C., Holschuh, J. P., & Hubbard, B. (2004). Thinking like a historian: College students' reading of multiple historical documents. *Journal of Literacy Research, 36*(2), 141–176.

Stiggins, R. J., Arter, J. A., Chappuis, J., & Chappuis, S. (2004). *Classroom assessment for student learning: Doing it right—using it well.* Portland, OR: Assessment Training Institute.

Taboada, A., Tonks, S. M., Wigfield, A., & Guthrie, J. T. (2013). Effects of motivational and cognitive variables on reading comprehension. In D. E. Alvermann, N. J. Unrau, & R. B. Ruddell (Eds.), *Theoretical models and processes of reading* (6th ed., pp. 589–610). Newark, DE: International Reading Association.

Turner, J., & Paris, S. G. (1995). How literacy tasks influence children's motivation for literacy. *The Reading Teacher, 48,* 662–673.

Weiner, B. (1986). *An attributional theory of motivation and emotion.* New York: Springer-Verlag.

Wentzel, K., & Wigfield, A. (Eds.). (2009). *Handbook of motivation at school.* New York: Routledge.

Wigfield, A., & Eccles, J. S. (Eds.). (2001). *Development of achievement motivation.* San Diego: Academic Press.

CHAPTER 4

Using Discourse Study as an Instructional Practice with Adolescents to Develop 21st-Century Literacies of Critically Conscious Citizens

Margaret C. Hagood

This chapter examines the uses of Discourse study in order to develop the literacies of 21st-century critically conscious citizens. It covers the following:

- Situating contemporary literacies within a growing and diverse U.S. population.

- Defining Discourse and its importance for understanding literacies of self and other.

- Illustrating Discourse study instruction with adolescents.

- Discussing benefits of Discourse instruction for teaching literacies.

- Connecting Discourse instruction to the development of 21st-century literacies defined by principles of the Common Core State Standards, media literacy education, and participatory culture.

The United States is more diverse than ever before. Of its more than 315 million people, the 2010 U.S. Census shows a noteworthy breakdown (see Table 4.1). It is projected that by 2043, people who identify themselves

TABLE 4.1. 2010 U.S. Census

Demographics of the United States	Percentage of U.S. Population
Hispanic or Latino population	16
African American	12.9
Asian American	4.6
White/European American	64
Native American, Alaskan Native, other	2

as white will no longer make up the American majority (*www.census.gov/2010census*). Part of this shift is due to the fact that the fastest-growing demographic in the United States is the children of immigrants. This growth is so substantial that it's projected that by 2028, groups currently identified as racial and ethnic minorities will become a majority among adults ages 18–29. It seems that many Americans are also feeling less inclined to associate with a singular identity group. Unpublished U.S. Census data show that millions of people shunned singular race categories such as black or white, preferring to write in their own cultural or individually defined identities (Yen, 2012). Another important trend in the U.S. Census data reveals a blurring of racial identities. By 2060, people who identify themselves as multiracial are projected to more than triple, from 7.5 million to 26.7 million.

Diversity cuts across identity categories of race, class, gender, cognitive abilities, language, ethnicity, and the body itself. The diversity of the U.S. population also includes the diversity of their literacies and reflects various ways of being as seen in language use, beliefs and values, clothing, traditions, and even pop culture choices. Diversity of literacies includes reading and writing, listening and speaking, and viewing and designing of print, nonprint, and digital texts.

While the demographics of the U.S. population rapidly changes, the demographic of the teaching field in the United States remains constant. In 2010 the U.S. Department of Education (2010) reported that 83% of public school teachers were white, while only 7% were Hispanic or Latino, 7% African American, and fewer than 3% were Pacific Islander, American Indian, Alaskan Native, or other. It is more critical now than ever before to ensure that teachers not only understand the connections between diversity, identity, and literacies but also teach students about these connections.

In this chapter, I demonstrate how instruction built on analysis of adolescents' diverse literacies reflective of their identities goes a long way toward addressing the diversity of literacies in the U.S. population and in the development of 21st-century literacies necessary for success in adulthood. I discuss how teachers can use the concept of Discourse as an instructional strategy to analyze both the structures of literacies and the shifting relations of those structures to acknowledge and value adolescents' diverse literacies. I argue that instruction that explicitly examines adolescents' contemporary literacies is not only beneficial but also is critical for meeting the goal of adolescents' facilities with 21st-century literacies as responsible citizens.

DISCOURSE THEORY, IDENTITY, AND LITERACIES

Discourse can be examined in a lot of ways. Sometimes it is defined as language exchange. But for the purposes of this chapter, I draw on structural and poststructural theories to describe Discourse as a structure that frames a social or cultural group's habits of interpretation and their related literacies. Defined in this way, a Discourse organizes and constrains thoughts, words, and actions. Each Discourse has its own sets of rules and procedures to determine what counts as meaningful (or not). Discourses are also interwoven; sometimes they match, sometimes they clash. While Discourse as a structure might seem rigid and stable, another structure of another Discourse may work to destabilize it.

In *Social Linguistics and Literacies*, Gee (1990) outlined a theory of Discourse (with a capital *D* to differentiate from other kinds of discourse described above as language exchange), highlighting the comprehensive social and situated contextualized literacies connected to identity. Gee likened Discourse to a personal identity kit that people have at their disposal and includes language, behavior, and social expectations of self and others related to beliefs, values, and actions accepted within the Discourse.

People develop these identity kits—Discourses—in their home context first. A person's first learning of these literacies is referred to as a Primary Discourse (Gee, 1996). Primary Discourses inculcate people into community membership. For example, family members teach children their own beliefs and values about how to dress, act, behave, think, speak, listen, read, and write. These Discourses are acquired mostly through tacit inculcation, and they create and shape children's identities before they enter school.

People take their Primary Discourse identity kits into Secondary Discourses. That is, people take their acquired home language, beliefs and values, style in clothing, views of the world that make up their literacies with them into Discourses outside the home (Gee, 1996). School, for example, is considered a Secondary Discourse. Secondary Discourses have their own associated identity kits that include behaviors, beliefs, attitudes, values, and literacy practices about how to be a member in the group and to interact with others. As distinct from Primary Discourses, Secondary Discourses are learned (rather than acquired).

Primary and Secondary Discourses are also interwoven. Sometimes they match; sometimes they clash. When Primary and Secondary Discourses match, people move from one Discourse community to another without much thought about the associated identity kits. Related to literacies, the identity kits are the same across Discourses, or are similar enough that people don't consciously think about shifting or changing the literacies of their identities in the ways they read, write, speak, dress, or value certain ideas. Matches between Primary and Secondary Discourses reflect at least some portions of the identity kits acquired in Primary Discourses. So, for some people, the literacies taught in the Secondary Discourse of schooling reflect those implicitly taught in the Primary Discourse of home. The interwoven structures of the Discourses are seamless enough, and free movement from one Discourse to the other often means taken-for-granted, assumed literacies.

For some people, interwoven structures of Primary and Secondary Discourses don't match. When this happens, movement from one Discourse community to another requires explicit thought and attention to the differences in identity kits—and with the associated literacies—needed for success in the different communities. Secondary Discourses are learned, not acquired. For example, sometimes the literacies of an identity kit from a Primary Discourse aren't reflected in the literacies valued in the identity kits of the Secondary Discourse. Going back to schooling as a Secondary Discourse, such examples are apparent when students bring Primary Discourses of language, culture, values, and beliefs to school that differ from the Secondary Discourse identity kits valued and taught at school. If a person's home language and literacies per se differ from the language and literacies of the identity kit valued and taught in the Secondary Discourse of school (e.g., Spanish vs. English; slang vs. academic language), then a mismatch in the structures and in identities occurs. When the structures of Primary and Secondary Discourse identity kits aren't aligned, students perceive the shifts, either explicitly or tacitly.

In the case of mismatches of interwoven identity kits in Discourses, individuals have several options:(1) assume the identity kit of the Secondary Discourse, (2) reject the identity kit of the Secondary Discourse, (3) acquire enough information about an identity kit of the Secondary Discourse—its structure—to get by, or (4) assert Primary Discourse literacies such that the structure of the Secondary Discourse must acknowledge the working of the Primary Discourse, and in doing so make room for the diversity of individuals' literacies and identities, which ultimately causes shifts in the Secondary Discourse itself.

Indeed, each of these options related to mismatches in Discourse produces different outcomes. In the case of the first choice, sometimes people feel that when they learn a Secondary Discourse they must put aside their Primary Discourse identity kits and the related literacies. They learn a new identity and literacies in school and then resume their acquired identity and literacies when at home. In this case both Primary and Secondary Discourses remain intact, one not influencing the other.

In the second option, when the identity kit associated with a Secondary Discourse is wholly refuted, the person has difficulty succeeding in that Secondary Discourse because there is no acknowledgment of any shared structure. In this case, the person either chooses not to learn the Secondary Discourse or the person doesn't understand how to learn the Discourse because acquisition of the Discourse is not explicitly taught. As in the first option, nothing changes between the Primary and Secondary Discourses.

The third option refers to what Gee (1990) calls "mushfake." This approach to Discourse mismatch requires the partial acquisition through meta-knowledge and tactical uses of the Secondary Discourse—just enough of the associated literacies—to create an identity kit to make do within the Discourse. The person learns the structure of the Secondary Discourse to work within and to navigate it, but doesn't really buy into it. Such learning of Secondary Discourse is a means for getting by, not for making any changes to the structure of the Discourse itself. When this happens, folks are fine with getting along in that way.

The fourth choice, however, opens up possibilities for acknowledgement, growth, and change related to diversity of literacies found in Secondary Discourses. This choice recognizes the power of the person and the power of the Discourse, each to influence the other. Gee (1999) described this work as *borderland discourse*. A borderland discourse is a community discourse wherein members of different Secondary Discourses through mutual recognition identify the disparities between their Secondary Discourse and use meta-knowledge of both Discourse group's identity kits to influence the literacies of both Discourses. Of all the choices, this one allows for most movement and change within the structures of Discourses via attention to different and diverse literacies of the identity kits of the Discourses. Borderland discourses have the potential to transform both Discourses. Borderland discourses have been documented in the literacies of diverse ethnic groups of urban middle and high school students in a common outdoor space during break from school (Gee, 1999) and in Alsup's (2006) study of preservice teachers' identity formation. In both cases, the groups' cognitive dissonance of their understanding and uses of Secondary Discourses influenced the others' literacies. The Secondary Discourse structures of both groups shifted so as to open up new spaces for identities and related literacies.

Invariably, all people experience matches and mismatches between Discourses that affect their literacies and learning. Research over the past decade *about* Discourses of various groups has documented matches and mismatches between their literacies associated with their identities and has revealed outcomes reflected in the choices described above. (See, e.g.,

Rogers's [2002] Discourse analysis of family literacy, Sheehy's [2002] Discourse analysis of constructivism in a middle grades classroom, and Wohlwend's [2009] Discourse analysis of young girls' identities and Disney princesses, all of which demonstrate the workings of the structures of Discourse affected by pop culture, social norms, and contextual beliefs.)

But very few studies have applied Gee's concept of Discourse as an instructional strategy *with* students to deepen their literacies and their power and agency to shape the identity kits within both Primary and Secondary Discourses. The following examples illustrate how explicit instruction *with* adolescents about structures of Secondary Discourses and associated literacies serves as a useful framework for acknowledging diverse literacies—reflective of the shifting demographics in the United States—and for influencing shifts in the structures of the Discourses.

EXAMPLE OF INSTRUCTION
USING DISCOURSE IN AN IN-SCHOOL SETTING

In their work with 91 African American high school students, Fisher and Lapp (2013) employed Discourse instruction to teach students how to identify, deconstruct, and use language appropriate within different Secondary Discourses. Acknowledging students' Primary Discourses constructed from identity kits that used African American Vernacular English (AAVE), they incorporated contrastive analysis instruction to explicitly teach students the differences between different home (Primary) and school (Secondary) language patterns. As students learned to analyze differences, they developed metacognitive skills that allowed them the power to choose different literacy practices appropriate for different Discourses.

Instruction occurred for at least 15 minutes (and up to 85 minutes) 4 days a week during English class over 2 years to develop their language skills (for reading, writing, speaking, and listening) across Discourses at the word, phrase, and sentence level. Careful to acknowledge the validity of Primary and Secondary Discourses, Fisher and Lapp designed several activities. Students learned how to compare the identity kits of home/Primary and school/Secondary Discourse by identifying different audiences, the purpose of communication, and the best word use for sharing information with a specified recipient.

Beyond teacher modeling of academic English, contrastive analysis and situationally appropriate language instruction over the 2 years included the following:

1. Study of five different forms of language and students' self-reflection of their uses of these five forms.
2. Analysis of language patterns in a children's book that uses AAVE

and academic English, which revealed to students that different Discourses make for richer understandings of self and others.

3. Research project of students' analysis of YouTube videos to demonstrate different perspectives about using academic English, and student-created PhotoBooth presentations of their findings comparing AAVE to academic English.

4. Identification, transcription, and analysis of written and spoken language patterns of prominent African Americans (e.g., Barack Obama, Langston Hughes, Shukar, Zora Neale Hurston), and then student rewriting of the language, code switching from the author's presented language to either Academic English or AAVE.

5. Students' creation of a list of common Academic English language frames that they posted on their English classroom wall to use in their writing.

6. Dialogue writing in pairs using Academic English scaffolded by the students' generated list of language frames of Academic English that differed from their AAVE language patterns.

7. Production of videos and participation in debates in which students demonstrated their uses of both AAVE and Academic English and evaluation by peers and teachers.

Careful to respect students' Primary Discourses, Fisher and Lapp purposefully and systematically taught students about situationally appropriate language. As students developed their knowledge, skills, and uses of multiple language patterns, they became more aware of their agency and power to choose how they wanted to communicate within different Discourses. From their study, they realized that rejection of certain Secondary Discourses shut them out of conversations, while learning and using Secondary Discourses yielded more opportunities for mushfaking and borderland discourses. This intervention instruction, undertaken after none of the African American students passed the state standardized English test required for graduation, yielded a 78% and 97% passing rate in the 2 years of the intervention.

EXAMPLE OF INSTRUCTION
USING DISCOURSE IN AN AFTER-SCHOOL SETTING

Blackburn (2005) documented in a 3-year study the explicit exploration of Secondary Discourses of identity kits of LGBTQ adolescents who frequented an after-school hangout called The Attic. Blackburn worked with a group of mostly queer African American adolescents as an after-school facilitator. During her time with these adolescents, they created a dictionary of terms deemed Gaybonics, which they described as gay language that uses Ebonics. The adolescents discussed at length the relationship between their uses of Gaybonics as borderland discourses in response to Secondary Discourses of standard English and heterosexual associated identities of the youth who engage these Secondary Discourses.

As they worked on the dictionary at The Attic, Blackburn learned how the adolescents identified, defined, and performed the words. Through in-depth discussions about different language use in different secondary Discourses, she examined with participants how they acquired and learned Gaybonics vocabulary through both observation and overt teaching. She also helped participants make sense of the multiple meanings the words conveyed and the difference these meanings made to the identities these participants created for themselves both within and outside the Secondary Discourse of The Attic and in the larger Secondary Discourse of LGBTQ.

Adolescents spent considerable time explicitly discussing the relationship between Gaybonics and power for inclusion and exclusion within a Secondary Discourse community. This instruction and exploration at The Attic helped them to examine how they used language within discourses of race and gender to include and exclude different people. Gaybonics as a borderland discourse created intimacy among members in the Secondary Discourse of The Attic. In this space, the adolescents tried on language and identities that fit within Gaybonics as created by the group. Blackburn observed and examined with the adolescents how they practiced with language in playful and humorous ways. Their creation of a borderland discourse gave them agency to practice ways to subvert heterosexist, homophobic, and racist Secondary Discourses and identities.

Through their study of the Secondary Discourses the adolescents at The Attic learned how to use language to position themselves as agents with power in order to confront and talk back to other Secondary Discourse communities. Blackburn argued that participants developed a metacognitive awareness of language via their discussions and creation of the dictionary, which in turn helped them to make purposeful language choices about what they wanted to achieve. Adolescents recognized that their language use was often associated with pleasures of membership in the Secondary Discourses of The Attic and of a LGBTQ identity. Sometimes this pleasure was expressed by subversion of oppression and by the retaliation against the hatred they felt from others in Secondary Discourses whose identities and literacies disagreed with those who frequented The Attic. Attention to this awareness helped adolescents tap into their agency of then making conscious and purposeful choices about which discourse to use in a particular situation or setting to accomplish a particular goal.

Interestingly, the Gaybonics dictionary the adolescents wrote and published ultimately was used only within the Secondary Discourse of The Attic. Although some members of The Attic who had graduated and moved into other communities (e.g., work, college) approached Blackburn to publish the dictionary for wider audiences, the members of The Attic felt that it could be used against them. In this case, they chose to use the text only among frequenters of The Attic. In this study, adolescents' discussions led to cognitive dissonance and created contexts where the study of identities and literacies led to action and advocacy for diverse perspectives.

BENEFITS OF DISCOURSE INSTRUCTION
FOR TEACHING LITERACIES

These two studies exemplify how Discourse juxtaposition of contemporary print and nonprint texts across Discourses helps adolescents develop deeper knowledge and understandings of their own and others' literacies. Adolescents in these studies drew from the texts important to identity kits created from Primary and Secondary Discourses. These texts included oral language (slang and formal language), digital and pop culture texts (YouTube, Photobooth, movie creations), and print-based texts (language frames, dictionaries, children's picture books), to name a few.

Through explicit instruction about Secondary Discourses, of which the adolescents initially had tacit knowledge, the adolescents (and, I'd venture to say, the adults, too) developed a meta-awareness of the workings of literacies in different contexts. The adolescents' and adults' analyses of juxtaposed Discourses facilitated the growth of a meta-knowledge of the Discourses that enabled them to remove themselves enough from the Discourses so they could talk about them, describe them, and explain how they get used. In this way, they interrogated not only the Secondary Discourse of which they were a part (i.e., AAVE language use or LGBTQ) but they also examined the wider Secondary Discourses (i.e., schooling and homophobic contexts). This work required the ability to step outside the Discourse, albeit briefly, to see it deeply from another perspective, and then to analyze and synthesize various members' ideas.

The study of literacies and identities using cognitive dissonance deepened everyone's understandings and uses of competing Discourses and the associated literacies. With this recognition came a newfound understanding of agency and power that the adolescents and adults could use as they saw fit. Certainly, this awareness prompted independence, but even more, it allowed both adolescents and adults to decide how they wanted to engage with various Secondary Discourses. In this sense, they learned valuable lessons to mushfake in order to get by; but more important, their conscious efforts and ultimate meta-awareness of the uses of Discourses helped them to create borderland discourses such that the literacies of the identity kits of their Secondary Discourse could be more overtly woven into other Secondary Discourses. In this way, the structures of both Secondary Discourses could shift and open up as they became more accepting of the literacies—and ultimately the identities—of the other group. Such work supports the learning of the literacies of diverse groups, develops more conscientious citizenship, and holds potential to affect larger changes to society.

Using explicit instruction and a focus on literacies within Discourses, the teachers/facilitators in these studies also demonstrated respect for the Secondary Discourses important to the adolescents' identities. Utilizing culturally relevant pedagogies (Ladson-Billings, 1995) the adults struck a balance, acknowledging the adolescents' literacies of Secondary Discourses while also explicitly teaching them about other Secondary Discourses that provided the adolescents alternative perspectives about literacies for their consideration and ultimately helped them to navigate the literacies of Secondary Discourses with which they were unfamiliar. This mutual respect for the organization and structure of Secondary Discourses aided adolescents' learning of audience, purpose, task, and discipline within a specific context.

DISCOURSE STUDY EMBEDDED
INTO 21ST-CENTURY TEACHING AND LEARNING

Three central documents are shaping literacies instructional practices in the United States: the *Common Core State Standards* (CCSS; National Governors Association Center for Best Practices and Council of Chief State School Officers, 2010), *Core Principles of Media Literacy Education* (MLE; National Association for Media Literacy Education, 2007), and *Confronting the Challenges of Participatory Culture: Media Education for the 21st Century* (PC; Jenkins, Clinton, Purushotma, Robison, & Weigel, 2006). These documents take into account the teaching and learning of print, nonprint, digital, and media texts for the development of reading, writing, listening, speaking, viewing, and designing literacies. The foci of three areas of these documents overlap: the purposes for learning, qualities of learners who are 21st-century literate, and approaches of implementation (see Table 4.2). This is interesting, because although school systems across the United States are focused on the CCSS, the MLE, and the PC documents predate and, as will be shown later, are in some ways more comprehensive than the CCSS. Also, although not explicitly stated, attention to the literacies of various Discourses runs through all of these documents. In this section I examine and provide brief explanations of how Discourse study relates to the goals of literacy instruction in the United States as outlined in these documents.

First, all of the documents aspire to create 21st-century learners who positively contribute to society through their skills and knowledge. The CCSS state that students who progress through the standards will be

TABLE 4.2. Comparison of Literacy Initiatives in the United States

Common Core State Standards for English/language arts (2010)[a]	Core Principles of Media Literacy Education in the United States (2007)[b]	Confronting the Challenges of Participatory Culture (2006)[c]
	Purpose of Learning	
1. College and career readiness as a 21st-century literate person. 2. To be literate in the 21st century means to "reflexively demonstrate the cogent reasoning and use of evidence that is essential to both private deliberation and responsible citizenship in a democratic republic" (p. 3).	To develop "habits of inquiry and skills of expression that they need to be critical thinkers, effective communicators, and active citizens in today's world" (*http://namle.net*).	"To encourage youth to develop the skills, knowledge, ethical frameworks, and self-confidence needed to be full participants in contemporary culture" (p. 8).
	Qualities of learners who have attained the skills outlined	
Learners exhibit these qualities as college and career ready: 1. Independence. 2. Respond to varying demands of audience, task, purpose, and discipline (set purpose and appreciate nuance). 3. Comprehend and critique. 4. Value evidence. 5. Use digital media and technology strategically and capably. 6. Understand other perspectives and cultures (p. 7).	Learners exhibit these qualities through media literacy education: 1. Active inquiry and critical thinking about messages received and created (p. 3). 2. Expands concept of literacy from reading and writing to include all forms of media (p. 3). 3. Builds and reinforces skills. Skills require integrated, interactive, and repeated practice. • Co-learning pedagogies (p. 4). 4. Develops informed, reflective, engaged citizens who are skeptical, value diverse viewpoints, and explore (mis)representation (p. 4).	Learners exhibit these qualities in social skills and cultural competencies in core media literacy skills: 1. Play. 2. Performance. 3. Appropriation. 4. Multitasking. 5. Distributed cognition. 6. Collective intelligence. 7. Judgment. 8. Transmedia navigation. 9. Networking. 10. Negotiation—the ability to travel across diverse communities, discerning and respecting multiple perspectives, and grasping and following alternative norms" (p. 4).

(*continued*)

TABLE 4.2. (*continued*)

5. Recognizes media as
   part of culture and
   function as agents of
   socialization.
   • Presents diverse
     perspectives.
   • Examines alternative
     media.
   • Shares responsibility
     with media owners to
     facilitate discussion of
     media effects (p. 5).
6. Affirms individual
   skills, beliefs, and
   experiences to construct
   own messages.
   • Welcomes different
     interpretations.
   • Values group
     discussion and
     analyses (p. 5).

Approaches for implementation		
What to know, what to teach, but not how to teach.	"To know what to teach and how to teach it" (p. 2).	Know what to teach and gives examples of how to teach it.

[a]*www.corestandards.org/ELA-Literacy*

[b]*http://namle.net/publications/core-principles*

[c]*http://digitallearning.macfound.org/atf/cf/%7B7E45C7E0-A3E0-4B89-AC9C-E807E1B0AE4E%7D/JENKINS_WHITE_PAPER.PDF*

college and career ready. To that end, the CCSS intends to produce learners who "reflexively demonstrate the cogent reasoning and use of evidence that is essential to both private deliberation and responsible citizenship in a democratic republic" (p. 3). The other documents hold similar foci. The purpose for learning the MLE is to develop active citizens as effective communicators and critical thinkers. Similarly, the purpose of the work of the PC is to develop youths' abilities to be "full participants in contemporary culture" (p. 8). The purpose of all the documents is to use students' literacy learning to mold them into responsible and active citizens who participate fully as effective communicators and critical thinkers using reasoning and evidence. Because the United States continues to become more diverse, an active citizenry must be aware of the various literacies and related identity kits, which influence the structures of Primary and Secondary Discourses and literacies in people's lives.

The three documents also outline similar and overlapping descriptions of qualities that 21st-century literacy learners will acquire (see row 2 of Table 4.2). For example, the CCSS state that students who have learned the skills should be able to "respond to varying demands of audience, task, purpose, and discipline" (p. 7). The MLE includes a core principle to "develop informed, reflective, engaged citizens who are skeptical, value diverse viewpoints, and explore (mis)representations" (p. 4). And the PC describes this idea a bit differently, stating the value of negotiation: "the ability to travel across diverse communities, . . . grasping and following alternative norms" (p. 4). In order to be able to do this work of identifying, analyzing, and negotiating different viewpoints, learners must understand the perspectives and literacies from which they came. Through a study of Primary and Secondary Discourses, adolescents will have the language to use for deeper analyses.

Third, all three documents explicitly give a content focus on developing multiple perspectives and valuing of diversity. The CCSS states that students who are college and career ready "understand other perspectives and cultures" (p. 7). The MLE values qualities in the learner who knows how "to present diverse perspectives" and "welcomes different interpretations" (p. 4). And the PC likewise values students' learning to discern and respect multiple perspectives (p. 4). Clearly, these documents purport to understand the diversity among students and to value explicit goals that will address diversity of literacies.

The analysis of these documents is more illustrative than exhaustive in order to make the point that Discourse study is already embedded into the necessary knowledge and skills needed for developing 21st-century literacy skills. I now return to the examples of the two studies to demonstrate how the key components of Discourse study as an instructional strategy could be overlooked, thus derailing the potential benefits.

THE CRITICAL NEED FOR EXPLICIT FOCUS ON DISCOURSE STUDY AS AN INSTRUCTIONAL PRACTICE

Fisher and Lapp's (2013) and Blackburn's (2005) studies point to several benefits of using Discourse study as an instructional strategy to help students understand the relationship between structures that define literacies and their ability to influence those structures to affect change. Across both studies, the benefits as described earlier included the following:

- Values literacies within print and nonprint text.
- Employs explicit instruction to develop meta-awareness.
- Develops multiple perspectives.
- Analyzes agency and power.
- Creates conscientious citizenship.

Table 4.3 shows an analysis of the benefits of Discourse study relative to the purposes for learning, qualities of learners who are 21st-century literate, and approaches of implementation across the CCSS, MLE, and PC. The benefits of Discourse study as an instructional strategy maps clearly onto the core values and principles of three specific areas outlined in these documents: (1) valuing print and nonprint text, (2) developing multiple perspectives, and (3) creating conscientious citizenship.

TABLE 4.3. Analysis of Discourse Study in 21st-Century Literacy Education Documents

Discourse study as instructional strategy	Common Core State Standards for English Language Arts (2010)	Core Principles of Media Literacy Education in the United States (2007)	Confronting the Challenges of Participatory Culture (2006)
Values literacies within print and nonprint text.	Uses "extensive range of print and nonprint text in media forms old and new" (p. 4).	"Expands concept of literacy from reading and writing to all forms of media" (p. 3).	"Contemporary culture" (p. 8).
Employs explicit instruction to develop meta-awareness.			
Develops multiple perspectives.	Understands other perspectives and cultures.	"Presents diverse perspectives" (p. 3). "Welcomes different interpretations" (p. 4).	Develop "ethical framework"; "Respecting multiple perspectives, and grasping and following alternative norms" (p. 4).
Analyzes structures of Discourses to identify agency and power to effect change.		Citizens who are skeptical, value diverse viewpoints, and explore (mis) representation. Recognizes media as part of culture and functions as agents of socialization.	
Creates conscientious citizenship.	"Responsible citizenship in a democratic republic" (*www. corestandards.org/ ELA-Literacy,para6*).	"Informed, reflective, engaged citizens" (p. 2).	Development of "ethical frameworks" (p. 8).

However, two benefits specific to instructional practices of Discourse study found in the two studies analyzed don't clearly map onto the development of 21st-century literacy learners as described by these three documents. These include the following: (1) the use of explicit instruction to develop a meta-awareness of discourses, and (2) the analysis of structures to identify agency and power to effect change.

None of the documents state anything about the need for explicit instruction in order to develop a working meta-awareness of how language works across settings, contexts, or Discourses. And only the MLE addresses the larger issue of analysis of structures to identify agency and power to affect change. This document encourages instruction to create "citizens who are skeptical, value diverse viewpoints, and explore (mis) representation" and who "recognize media as part of culture and functions as agents of socialization" (p. 4).

Looking more closely at the CCSS and at the college and career anchor standards for language further exemplifies the point. College and Career Readiness Anchor Standards for Language of the Common Core State Standards of secondary students give two standards for teaching the conventions of standard English. Standards 1 and 2 address students' command of standard English (grammar, usage, capitalization, punctuation, and spelling) (p. 51). Standard 3 addresses the knowledge of language, stating that students will "apply knowledge of language to understand how language functions in different contexts, to make effective choices for meaning or style, and to comprehend more fully when reading or listening" (p. 51).

Although conventions of Discourse structures of standard English are addressed through knowledge and skills, these Standards do little to examine how Discourse study points to larger issues of power structures and students' agency for changing or influencing those structures. Furthermore, the anchor standards say nothing about the development of meta-awareness of when to use different language or about the abilities to analyze how agency and power play into the uses of literacies in Secondary Discourses. Without explicit instruction of Discourse study to the development of meta-awareness of power structures for acknowledging and building on agency, teachers and students might think they are doing the work of deep analysis to create critically conscious learners but instead are only reifying the structures of language already in place. The development of a critically conscious citizenry—of people who understand and value diverse literacies—the point of implementing these standards in the first place—isn't met.

The value of Discourse study as an instructional strategy with adolescents cannot be overstated. Although the three documents define what literacies should look like for adept 21st-century learners, they don't present instructional strategies for teaching. The CCSS, for example, explicitly states its purpose as an outline for what learners should know, what teachers should teach, but not how to teach it. The MLE similarly states the import of knowing "not only what to teach but also how we teach it" (p. 2), but doesn't give specific instructional strategies for the core principles outlined. And while the PC document provides detailed vignettes of users' facility with the core skills outlined and possible activities, it doesn't give instructional strategies for teaching the skills described.

Without specific pedagogy or curricula about how to teach these standards, teachers and curriculum developers must design pedagogy and instruction for implementation. On one hand, it is refreshing that authors of these documents value teachers' expertise and autonomy to create contextually meaningful instruction. But for some teachers, especially those who haven't explored the nuances of different kinds of literacies of diverse groups, this autonomy may be debilitating rather than freeing.

CONCLUSION

In the case of using Discourse study as an instructional strategy, teachers must understand how the strategy serves as means to examine not only the structure of the literacies within a Discourse, but also how that structure changes as literacies of different Discourses interact. In short, explicit Discourse study helps teachers and students learn the difference between assuming, rejecting, mushfaking, and creating borderland discourses. Discourse study as an instructional strategy must include analysis of others' work, but needs also to turn inward, so adolescents learn how to apply these concepts to their own work, and to their own literacies and identities. Through instructional practices that examine Discourses, literacies, power, and agency can we actually help to develop the literacies of adolescents prepared to live successfully as critically conscious citizens in a diverse society.

DISCUSSION AND ACTIVITIES

1. After teaching students about Primary and Secondary Discourses, have students create a chart reflecting these categories. Have them brainstorm a list of the literacies they use at home and ones they use at school. Then have them subgroup the lists according to various literacies: texts I read, texts I write, texts I listen to, texts I speak, texts I produce. Have them bring one example of text for each Primary and Secondary Discourse to school.

2. Create opportunities for cognitive dissonance: Have students share their text examples in small groups. Have other students guess whether the text is a Primary or Secondary Discourse text and state why. Then have students discuss the text lists in small groups. Have each person choose a text from those brought to class and have them analyze it and create a Primary or Secondary text from it, based upon their own experiences.

3. Have students analyze how they use Primary and Secondary Discourses to assume, reject, mushfake, and create borderland crossings in their lives.

4. Have students examine various published works (e.g., favorite blogs, movies, Facebook posts, or language used by characters in literature) to determine the Discourses used. Students can analyze the text by the language and images used and the identities presented.

5. Invite community members to the class to discuss the importance of understanding and using different Discourses in their work.

REFERENCES

Alsup, J. (2006). *Teacher identity discourses: Negotiating personal and professional spaces.* Mahwah, NJ: Erlbaum.

Blackburn, M. (2005). Agency in borderland discourses: Examining language use in a community center with black queer youth. *Teachers College Record, 107*(1), 89–113.

Fisher, D., & Lapp, D. (2013). Learning to talk like the test: Guiding speakers of African American Vernacular English. *Journal of Adolescent & Adult Literacy, 56*(8), 634–648.

Gee, J. P. (1990). *Social linguistics and literacies: Ideology in discourses.* London: Routledge.

Gee, J. P. (1996). *Social linguistics and literacies: Ideology in discourses* (2nd ed.). London: Routledge.

Gee, J. P. (1999). *An introduction to discourse analysis: Theory and method.* London: Routledge.

Jenkins, H., Clinton, K., Purushotma, R., Robison, A.J., & Weigel, M. (2006). *Confronting the challenges of participatory culture: Media education for the 21st century.* Chicago: MacArthur Foundation.

Ladson-Billings, G. (1995). Toward a theory of culturally relevant pedagogy. *American Educational Research Journal, 32*(3), 465–491.

National Association for Media Literacy Education. (2007, November). *Core principles of media literacy education in the United States.* Retrieved from *http://namle.net/wp-content/uploads/2013/01/CorePrinciples.pdf.*

National Governors Association Center for Best Practices and Council of Chief State School Officers. (2010). *Common Core State Standards: The standards for English language arts and literacy in history, social studies, science, and technical subjects.* Washington, DC: Author. Retrieved from *www.corestandards.org/the-standards.*

Rogers, R. (2002). Between contexts: A critical discourse analysis of family literacy, discursive practices, and literate subjectivities. *Reading Research Quarterly, 37*(3), 248–277.

Sheehy, M. (2002). Illuminating constructivism: Structure, discourse, and subjectivity in a middle school classroom. *Reading Research Quarterly, 37*(3), 278–308.

U.S. Department of Education, National Center for Education Statistics. (2010). *Teacher attrition and mobility: Results from the 2008–09 teacher follow-up survey* (NCES 2010-353). Retrieved February 15, 2013, from *http://nces.ed.gov/fastfacts/display.asp?id=28.*

Wohlwend, K. (2009). Damsels in discourse: Girls consuming and producing identity texts through Disney princess play. *Reading Research Quarterly, 44*(1), 57–83.

Yen, H. (2012, Dec. 13). In focus: The changing face of America. *The Portland Press.* Retrieved February 13, 2013, from *www.pressherald.com/news/nationworld/in-focus-majorities-and-minorities-_2012-12-13.html.*

CHAPTER 5

Teaching Literacy to Youth Who Struggle with Academic Literacies

Leigh A. Hall
Aubrey Comperatore

The purpose of this chapter is to consider how to understand and respond to youth who struggle with academic literacies. We consider how students' reading identities contribute to the development of their academic literacies. Specifically, this chapter:

- Defines the term academic literacies.

- Explains what reading identities are, how they are developed, and how they can be changed.

- Provides ways for responding to youth who struggle with academic literacies while taking their current reading identities into account.

BACKGROUND INFORMATION

And we need to listen to the youths. We need to see them as people who want desperately to succeed, as people who are demonstrating in numerous ways that they are capable and cognitively sophisticated beings.
—MORRELL (2010, p. 149)

What does it mean to teach literacy to youth who struggle with academic literacies? If we listen to reports of how our youth perform on a national level, we get the message that most of them have limited literacy skills and will have regular difficulties comprehending and learning from texts (National Assessment of Educational Progress, 2011). These messages may be further supported by looking at assessment data in our own school, which is likely to show many youth reading 1 or more years below grade level. Finally, many teachers of adolescents report that students with academic literacy difficulties appear disinterested in reading and learning.

Often, teachers ask what they can do to help these students improve. As Mr. Cook, a sixth-grade social studies teacher, once explained to Leigh Hall, "Most of my students who struggle with reading are often very intelligent and seem to have the potential to succeed. I can't figure out what the difficulty is." There are a number of explanations offered for why some students have continued, regular difficulties with academic literacies and why, as a result, they fail to learn content. Many of the reasons are placed squarely on the students, including a lack of motivation, little enjoyment of reading or learning, and a lack of necessary reading skills. The message often sent to teachers is that they need to do something *to* youth who struggle with academic literacies. For example, teachers need to find ways to motivate students. They need to provide better or more instruction focusing on the skills students lack and provide them with texts to read that are on an appropriate reading level. While such practices may help, they are no guarantee that students will apply the skills they have learned or engage with the texts they encounter.

In short, common understandings about youth who struggle with academic literacies has been framed in terms of their deficits and what they cannot do. Rarely are they seen as capable members who have something significant to contribute about the texts they read in school and who, as Morrell (2010) says, "want desperately to succeed." If we want to make a difference in the lives of youth who have academic literacy difficulties, we have to widen our scope and do more than focus on what skills to teach and what texts to give them, and we need to come up with ways to motivate them. We have to frame our instruction so that we work *with* them.

FOSTERING ACADEMIC LITERACIES

What are academic literacies? At their core, academic literacies are about helping students learn not just knowledge but how knowledge is created and communicated within each discipline (Moje, 2008). In addition, students should learn how to evaluate and critique the knowledge presented to them in school and should learn how to participate in the different academic communities.

How we approach working with our youth in relation to developing their academic literacies is changing. The implementation of the Common

Core State Standards (CCSS) has shifted greater attention to how students' academic literacies develop across all subject areas and grade levels. Developing academic literacies, for all students, has become the responsibility of every teacher. No longer can the argument be made that youth who have academic literacy difficulties are the primary responsibility of English teachers or special pull-out classes.

The CCSS provide each subject area with its own set of reading standards that are intended to support academic literacy development for each domain and grade. On the surface, the standards appear to be generic. For example, in social studies/history and science, students are expected to pay attention to how texts are structured and cite textual evidence in making claims. Although the standard is worded the same for both domains, how they are enacted and carried out will look unique to each area. Students will need to learn how texts are structured and how to use those texts to make arguments in ways that are specific to social studies/history and science. As a result, teachers in both disciplines will need to work with students to help them develop these abilities.

While the CCSS are a step in the right direction, they also carry the risk of promoting literacy only as a skills-based endeavor (Burns, 2012). Developing strong instruction that will support the needs of youth who struggle with academic literacies will require doing more than identifying and teaching skills in an isolated, autonomous manner. As Lea and Street (2010) explain, instruction that utilizes an academic literacies model will treat literacy instruction "as social practices that vary across context, culture, and genre" (p. 368). The reading and writing practices that students engage in will be viewed as situated and varied and will change across the different disciplines.

Working toward the standards set forth by the CCSS can be a challenge to even the most experienced teacher. The standards require us to rethink how we engage students with texts and what our instruction to support them in developing the literacies they need to read, write, view, and otherwise use texts looks like. However, the standards also require and create space for students to learn how to engage with a variety of texts in new ways, including critically reading and analyzing nontraditional texts, such as media, and creating multimodal texts (Dalton, 2012/2013). We see this as an exciting time to rethink how we approach developing academic literacies with our students.

Reconceptualizing Our Understandings

Before we can think about how to teach youth with academic literacy difficulties, we have to rethink how we understand them. Although they are often positioned as unmotivated and uninterested in reading and school in general, most of them are unhappy with their status and would like to make positive changes (Hall, Burns, & Edwards, 2011). When speaking to them, you are likely to find they often enjoy reading, want to learn, and wish to become better readers of academic texts. Even when they appear disengaged or resistant, they are often watching and listening in an attempt to learn something (Hall, 2010).

If youth with academic literacy difficulties are interested in changing their situation, what is causing the holdup? First consider that students' understandings of who they are as readers, or their *reading identities*, are formed early in their lives (Brown, 2011). According to Hall (2012a, p. 369):

> The term *reading identity* refers to how capable individuals believe they are in comprehending texts, the value they place on reading, and their understandings of what it means to be a particular type of reader within a given context (Hall, Johnson, Juzwik, Wortham, & Mosley, 2010; McRae & Guthrie, 2009).

Although students can assign themselves a reading identity, they are often assigned one by their teachers, peers, and family members (Gee, 2000/2001). In school, there exists a collective understanding about what it means to be identified as a particular type of reader. Students are typically presented with three possible reading identities: good, average, or poor reader. These identities are usually formed according to how successful students are at understanding and engaging with texts in the ways sanctioned by teachers, schools, and curriculum (Collins, 2013). While students may not always agree with the identities they are assigned, they often have little say about the reading identities placed on them in school.

Being assigned an identity comes with steep consequences, both positive and negative. Students who engage with texts and use reading instruction in ways that are sanctioned by teachers and schools are more likely to receive assistance from their teachers, be publicly praised as good readers, and given authority to determine what texts mean. Students who do not attempt to acquire the socially accepted identity of a good reader risk being marginalized by their teachers and peers and often have little agency in their classrooms.

Attempting to shed the *struggling reader* identity is not simply a matter of reading more or applying instruction differently. Attempting to change reading identities carries social risks. Youth with academic literacy difficulties are aware that they stand to increase their comprehension if they ask questions about texts, participate in discussions, and apply the skills and strategies taught to them. However, doing so often requires them to show their peers they are not strong readers—something they are often not willing to do. When faced with publicly revealing their perceived weaknesses or silently remaining a struggling reader, many students will often choose to remain struggling readers and limit their learning. Their decision to do so is an act of social preservation and should not be seen as a desire to maintain their current position as poor readers.

Why Should You Address Reading Identities?

By the time students enter middle school they have established identities and histories of themselves as readers based on their experiences with reading (Hall, 2012a). For example, Cheryl, a sixth-grader, told Leigh Hall she was a "bad" reader. When Leigh asked why she believed herself to be a bad reader, Cheryl explained that she learned she was a bad reader back in first grade, "Because ever since first grade people told me I couldn't read. I never got the right answer, and no one calls on me. I'm just not good at reading. It's always been like that."

Students' reading identities influence the decisions they make with texts. Students who self-identify as poor readers often limit their interactions with texts, ask fewer questions, and limit the amount of reading they do with academic texts. In addition, they may not apply reading instruction even if they understand what to do and know how it could benefit them. Their decisions are often attributed to the fact that they see themselves as poor readers who have little chance of improving. Their repeated negative experiences with reading have reinforced for them that they are unlikely to improve and there is nothing they can do to change their situation. Their apparent disengagement is not from a lack of interest, but from an understanding that they cannot succeed.

However, students who have a positive reading identity may also limit their interactions with texts. Although these students may be more likely to engage with texts in positive ways, they may do so only on a superficial level. For example, they may view the purpose of reading in school as finding the one "right" answer, and they may not know how to engage with texts in more complex ways. However, because they hold a positive reading identity they may believe they do not need to engage with texts any differently. For example, Jacob, an eighth-grader, explained:

> "Yeah, like I think I'm a pretty good reader. I read all the time and get good grades. So there's not really much more I need to learn, you know, about how to read. I already know how to read."

For some students, how they identify as readers does not always align with how they might be identified or positioned as a result of a reading comprehension assessment or what grade level teachers have been told they read on. This means that students who read below grade level, but self-identify as good readers, may interact with texts in ways you may not have thought they were capable of. Conversely, students who read above grade level, but self-identify as poor readers, may fall below your expectations in their engagements with texts.

Therefore, improving the academic literacies of youth is about more than selecting quality texts and teaching skills and strategies. While such things are important, the research done on reading identities reminds us that how students understand themselves as readers plays a significant role in their academic development. When students receive instruction that takes their reading identities into account, the potential exists to change how they interact with texts, improve their reading comprehension, and increase their understanding of academic subject matter.

BREAKING THE CYCLE: HOW CAN READING IDENTITIES BE CHANGED?

If we want to change how youth engage with texts and develop their academic literacies, we have to understand and respond to their reading identities. When we talk about how reading identities can be changed, we do not mean getting students to conform to our version of what it means to be a "good" reader. Instead, we mean helping students express their current understandings of who they are as readers and getting them to imagine how they would like those identities to shift over time. As a result, we ultimately leave it up to the students to decide what it means to be a reader, what they need to do to become the kind of reader they desire, and to communicate to us how we can support them.

In this section, we provide two approaches teachers can use to work toward changing students' reading identities. In the first approach, we focus on how teachers can understand students' reading identities and then help students take control of shaping their reading development. In the second approach, we share how teachers can make the struggles that any student has with reading become a normal process that we all experience and can learn from. Both approaches are suitable for teachers who work with adolescents of any grade and with any subject matter.

Taking Control of Your Reading Development

Empowering youth with reading difficulties requires them to take ownership of their reading development. However, the dominant approach to reading instruction has focused on the idea that by providing better or more reading instruction, teachers can transform students into stronger readers. School then becomes a place where students get little voice in what they read, have limited opportunities to read texts that are interesting and relevant to them, and receive instruction that does not map onto what they need or want to learn (Allington, 2011). As a result, most adolescents who have academic reading difficulties have been disempowered and have experienced reading instruction as something teachers do *to* them and not *with* them.

Doing something *to* students means making most, if not all, of the decisions for what skills and strategies they need to learn, how they need to learn and use them, and what texts they should read. By comparison, reading instruction that focuses on engaging *with* students allows them to provide input on how they would like to improve and is responsive to such input. Teachers first work to learn how students understand themselves as readers and how they would like to improve. They then make explicit the kinds of things students need to know and be able to do with texts that will allow them to develop as academic readers and make progress toward their own goals.

The first step is to learn how students identify as readers, how they would like to improve, and how they might like their existing identities to change. Teachers can ask students to provide short written responses that might address questions such as:

- "How would you describe yourself as a reader?"
- "Why do you think this description fits you?"
- "How would you like to improve your reading abilities this year?"
- "How might you achieve your reading goals?"
- "What is one thing I could do to help you achieve your reading goals?"

Students' responses provide information about the kinds of labels they place on themselves and what evidence they use to ground their responses.

To think about how such information could be used in practice, we take a look at how one eighth-grade English teacher, Ms. Winters, was observed by Leigh Hall as she used her students' responses to the above question.

In the fall, students in Ms. Winters's class described themselves as readers in a variety of ways, including a good reader, a bit of a slow reader, or not a great reader. Nearly all students wanted to improve in some way, with the most popular goals being to expand their vocabulary and learn skills and strategies that would help them comprehend difficult texts. For example, Tara wrote, "I would describe myself as an ok reader because some books are very hard for me, and I don't understand them." Tara noted that she would like to "learn some things about how to read hard books."

Asking students to identify one to three goals for improvement is a reasonable amount for them to focus on (Hall & Greene, 2011). It is also important to be supportive of the goals students set. Simply provide space for students to articulate how they want to improve, and respect their ideas. For example Nolan said, "I mostly want to improve my reading speed and understanding." Nolan's teacher, Ms. Winters, did not have any problems with his goals, but they were not the ones she would have identified for him. She wanted Nolan to work more on sharing his ideas about texts with the class. However, Ms. Winters did not suggest her ideas to Nolan. Instead she acknowledged his goals and noted to herself that she would find space to work on the goals they both had for him.

If a student gets stuck on setting a goal, it is fine to help him or her think it through. Our suggestion is to start by reviewing how the student identifies as a reader. For example, look at the student's response and say something like, "You say here that you are not a very good reader. How would you like to describe yourself at the end of this year?" After the student has provided a response, follow up by asking, "What do you think you might need to do to get where you want to be?" or provide suggestions if necessary.

Teachers can ask students to share how they describe themselves as readers and/or how they want to improve over the year. Such discussions can be especially important for youth who have experienced regular difficulties with reading academic texts, as they will have the opportunity to hear that everyone can improve as readers. Sharing can expose students to new ways of thinking about reading and help them see that they are not alone in their desire to improve. However, participation in such a discussion should be voluntary and should be limited to sharing only what each student is comfortable with. Not all students will feel safe in sharing their goals or descriptions of themselves as readers in front of their peers, and this decision needs to be respected.

The next step is to create instruction that addresses the goals students have for themselves and also the ones you have for them. First, review students' goals and look for commonalities such as improving vocabulary or learning how to respond to comprehension difficulties. During instruction, make connections between how you are helping students work toward achieving their goals while also providing them with new ways to think about how they engage with texts.

For example, Ms. Winters knew that most of her students were interested in improving their vocabulary and/or comprehending difficult books. One day, she assigned them O. Henry's *The Ransom of Red Chief*. She asked students to identify words they did not understand as they began their initial read of the story for discussion later. Ms. Winters explained to her students why she wanted them to pay attention to the vocabulary by saying:

> "Why am I asking you to pick out words you don't know? A lot of you have said that you want to improve your vocabulary. One way to do that is to pay attention to words that don't make sense and then discuss them and learn what they mean. But a lot of you also want to learn

how to read more challenging stories, and I think this story is pretty challenging. The character in the story likes to use all these big words but doesn't necessarily use them correctly. So paying attention to the words that get used, how they are used, and what they actually mean will help you get better at understanding stories that are a bit more complex."

In the above example, Ms. Winters bridged students' beliefs about what they needed to work on with what she wanted to teach. While she explained that she wanted to help expand students' vocabulary, she also explained that she wanted her students to read and discuss elements of a short story. Learning how short stories worked was never something her students expressed interest in. However, it was an important part of the English curriculum in eighth grade.

Students generally responded positively to the instruction they received. Sylvia explained, "Ms. Winters helps me get better at reading because she listens to what I ask for help on." Antony said, "I have a lot to learn, and I know some of what I need. But [Ms. Winters] knows a lot and what she says helps me. It helps me learn things I didn't know I needed to learn."

As a result, both Ms. Winters and the students were able to have collaborative discussions about reading development, what texts should be read, and the different ways one could engage with them. Ultimately, Ms. Winters saw benefits to the instruction as well, explaining:

> "The reading in this class just really took off, and it's carried over into other classes that you don't get to see. Like Mr. Sampson, the science teacher, told me that the kids are asking him for more time to read in his class and they want harder things to read! It's like they took this idea that they could have a say in their own development and really ran with it. It's been amazing."

Celebrating Struggles

Too often, struggling to understand texts or being labeled a struggling reader is viewed as something shameful. Students experience school as a place where finding the "right" answers in texts is celebrated and being confused, or wrong, or having a radically different interpretation is seen as a problem. While there are concrete, correct facts found within texts, many of the more complex ideas are often open to constant analysis and reinterpretation. When students are asked to answer questions and discuss texts, they are often expected to identify their teachers' interpretation of those texts (O'Flahavan & Wallis, 2005). When students repeatedly fail to identify their teachers' interpretations, they often get the message that they are not good readers and stop participating.

Although students may think some people always understand texts and others do not, this is far from the case. Everyone, regardless of their reading ability, experiences comprehension difficulties from time to time. Some students may find they are more successful at comprehending science texts due to their personal funds of knowledge but may have a more difficult time understanding a history text because they have less familiarity or interest with the subject matter. Within a given discipline, some texts are more or less difficult for any student.

Rather than try to avoid reading difficulties, or perceive them as something negative, we believe such struggles should be celebrated, tackled head-on, and viewed as normal in school, at home, and at any age/stage of life. Often, youth with reading difficulties believe they are alone and that no one understands their situation. However, when they realize that others share in their difficulties to comprehend, they start to see such struggles as normal and may begin to increase their participation with reading and discussing texts (Hall, 2012b).

There are several approaches teachers can take that will position students' struggles with texts as a normal, and even celebrated, part of classroom life. First, make discussions about struggles with texts a regular part of classroom discourse. Give students a piece of text to read. As they read to themselves, have them pay attention to places they do not understand or have questions. Students should mark these places in some manner either with a sticky note or by recording the page and paragraph where the disruption occurred on a separate paper.

Students can think about how they identify reading struggles and questions in a variety of ways. Examples include passages or words they did not know or understand fully, passages that made them ask questions, and passages they partially understood but wanted to know more about. It may be helpful to discuss with the class what struggles and questions look like and generate a list of possibilities before having students do it on their own.

After students have finished, ask them to share the places they marked in the text. A primary point of sharing is to help all students, but particularly youth with regular reading difficulties, see they are not alone in their difficulties and that we all have questions and confusions about what we read. A second point is to help students become comfortable openly sharing questions and difficulties.

In Mrs. Johnson's sixth-grade class, we observed as students were intentionally given a difficult article from a medical journal and asked to read it (Comperatore & Hall, 2013). After a few minutes of attempted reading, Mrs. Johnson noted that many students were losing interest quickly. "They looked at their shoes, they played with bracelets, they stared at the ceiling, they patiently waited for me to tell them they could stop reading and when they did there were several audible sighs of relief."

Mrs. Johnson next asked students to raise their hands if they had experienced difficulties while reading it. Sixteen of the 17 students in her class raised their hands, along with Mrs. Johnson. The students expressed surprise that Mrs. Johnson would have problems with the text. One exclaimed, "But you're the teacher!"

Mrs. Johnson then gave the class two more articles to read. One was about video gamesand the second was about a popular entertainer. The students agreed that both articles were easier to understand when compared to the medical article.

Following these experiences, the students brainstormed reasons people might have difficulties with understanding texts, including lack of background knowledge and reading about topics that they are disinterested in. Mrs. Johnson was then able to discuss with the class how everyone struggles with reading texts at some point, even the teacher. She also expressed how amazed she was at how willing the students were to share the struggles they experienced:

> "I think my students appreciated being able to see me struggle. I think they took away from the lesson that is it ok to not always know how to do something or how to read something. I hope that they will also remember the confidence they felt when they read the passages that featured a topic they were interested in and continue to look for books with similar topics."

Once students have gotten comfortable sharing and discussing their difficulties, the next step is to work toward solving them as they read. As students identify areas of confusion, they can document how they tried to address them. For example, did they reread the passage? Did they look up a word in the dictionary? Or was the section so difficult they just didn't know how to tackle it?

Students should also evaluate their level of understanding after attempting to address a difficulty or question. They can note what they learned when they responded to their struggles, or if nothing changed about what they knew. However, students should know it is also acceptable if they did not know how to approach a problem or were unable to resolve it, as this is also a normal part of reading.

Next, have students share how they worked toward solving their problems, what they learned, and where they would like more help when reading texts in the future. If they did not solve a problem, they can share what they did and other students can offer suggestions. The emphasis is placed on processes for resolving comprehension difficulties and learning new ways of perceiving them. As students present the questions and confusions they had, discussion can start about how others interpreted the same section and how they arrived at their conclusions. As a result, students stand to learn more about a text and will gain new ideas for solving future issues and questions.

When having students discuss their difficulties, we suggest asking them how they responded to their struggles and not how they attempted to fix them. This is a subtle, but we believe important, language shift. Asking students how they tried to "fix" their comprehension problems places the emphasis on finding a solution. We want students to focus being comfortable with having difficulties and open to multiple ways to approach them. Teachers can also emphasize that sometimes our attempts to understand do not end in success or result in finding a clear answer, and this is normal. Finally, teachers should be careful not to force participation, particularly in the beginning. Students who have a long history of reading difficulties may not feel comfortable openly discussing them. Over time, and as they see they are not alone in their struggles, their participation will likely increase.

Students can also discuss questions they have about texts and how they attempted to resolve their issues through small-group discussions. Small-group discussions have a benefit over whole-class discussions in that they can allow students to form bonds and begin to feel safe in sharing the struggles they have with reading. Such discussions can focus both on the content of what was read as well as the difficulties students encountered while reading.

A central aspect of small-group work is keeping the groups as constant as possible. For groups to form bonds, and for members to take risks, they need to meet on a regular basis (once or more each week) and retain membership. If possible, forms groups based on a shared interest or goal to create an initial basis for bonding.

In preparing students for small groups, it is helpful to suggest ways students might approach discussing their readings. For example, in reading a text, teachers can ask students to do the following:

1. "Identify areas where you have questions or simply want to talk more about the text."
2. "If you solved a comprehension difficulty while reading, be prepared to share what you did."
3. "Identify at least two passages in the text you found interesting and would like to talk more about."

The idea is to have students talking about content, places they were confused about, and ways they approached solving comprehension problems in a flowing manner as opposed to a disjointed discussion in which students first talk about problems, then content, and so on.

Students who have academic reading difficulties have expressed how helpful sharing their challenges in a small group can be (Hall, 2012b). For example, Mason explained, "I didn't even know other people had problems like me or that I could help them." Sophia said, "It was good being able to help someone learn something about what we read in here. It was like, yeah, I'm helping someone get better." Finally Nate said, "We get to talk about the stuff, which is fun because it helps me learn. Like when someone tells me what they thought about it I think, 'Oh! I never knew that,' and that is cool. Everyone helps each other."

What Happens When Students' Reading Identities Change?

Over time, students can shift from holding negative to positive reading identities, and youth who have positive reading identities can deepen their understandings about who they are as readers. However, such shifts require patience and time. We have found that changes to youths' reading identities often occur within 2 to 3 months of actively working with them. For example, in September Sylvia identified herself as "not a great reader" because when she read she noticed that "some of the words are big, and I don't know what they mean." However, in December she identified herself as "a good reader," because "I understand a lot more of the words in the books."

Despite the positive shift that students like Sylvia may experience in their reading identities, it can take 4 to 6 months from the start of doing such work before changes in their engagement with texts begin to surface (Hall & Greene, 2011). Hall's (2011) research on understanding how reading identities are constructed and enacted has shown that when students shift from a negative to a positive reading identity they will also experience the following changes in their interactions with texts:

- Increase the amount they talk about texts.
- Begin to talk about texts in more substantive ways.
- Demand more opportunities to read in school.

As students begin to shift from a negative to a positive reading identity, they begin to participate more in class when discussing texts. Over the course of an academic year, students can increase their talk about texts by as much as 50%. In addition, what students talk about also changes. Prior to identity shifts, students with negative reading identities often talk about texts in two ways: (1) answering questions asked by a teacher or student and (2) asking a teacher or student to clarify what they are supposed to do when reading a piece of text. However, after students have shifted to a more positive reading identity their talk about texts can became more substantive. Teachers may notice that students begin asking questions about the content of texts, volunteer their ideas about texts, and expand on ideas being discussed about a text.

Finally, teachers may notice that students began to demand they be given more opportunities to read in school. As students start to feel more in control of their reading development, they may ask for more time to read in school on a regular basis across subject matter. Students do not think that such time should always be for free reading. Instead, they often want regular, sustained silent reading time with texts relevant to their classes. Students may also appreciate teachers making recommendations for further reading related to the content being taught. Finally, students have said that teachers should allow them to suggest books for their classes and that teachers seriously consider including those books in their instruction.

However, there are also issues to be aware of as students undergo changes with their reading identities. As students who have struggled with academic literacies begin to speak up more, students who already held a positive reading identity and may have been in positions of power in their classrooms, may respond by engaging in what we call *disruptive talk*. We define disruptive talk as occurring when a student (1) attempts to silence another, (2) interrupts another, and/or (3) devalues the ideas of another when discussing texts.

It can often be difficult to know that disruptive talk is occurring or that one student is actively working to silence another. The disruptive talk we have observed is most common in small-group and one-on-one interactions and less common in whole-class discussions about texts. Given that it can be difficult to overhear, and even more difficult to see the pattern of the talk, we recommend that teachers assume such talk is happening as youth who struggle with academic literacies begin to develop positive reading identities and start to speak more.

In considering how to respond to disruptive talk, first know that it is likely a normal response for some students who are used to providing valued information about texts. Students may benefit from developing social skills that will allow them to be more inclusive of students who have often not been involved with classroom literacy practices for many years. Most likely, when students engage in disruptive talk they are not aware they are doing anything that could be considered hurtful.

Therefore, fostering a supportive classroom environment plays a critical role in helping youth who struggle with academic literacies find their voice. One way to do this is to co-create a framework with students to guide discussions and interactions (Brookfield & Preskill, 2005). Students can reflect on their experiences in discussions to consider what has and has not worked well or fostered a supportive environment for their participation. Such guidelines can and should be revisited and refined throughout the year and can serve to help students and teachers know how to identify and respond to disruptive talk.

CONCLUSION

A common perception of struggling readers portrays them as deficient in reading skills and strategies, having little motivation to engage in academic literacy practices, and disinterested in improving their academic literacy abilities (Hall, 2010). Such perceptions fail to capture the complexities that make up the reality of these students' lives and that influence their decisions with academic literacy practices. Once students are assigned and adopt the struggling reader identity, it shapes what they believe they can do with texts and mediates their participation in school. To change students' engagement with texts, then, requires more than simply teaching them skills and strategies or providing them with an appropriate text. It requires understanding how their reading identities influence what they do and finding ways to help them craft more positive ones.

An important step in disrupting the negative cycle students face is to empower them to take charge of their literacy development. Empowering students requires, in part, helping them unpack their current reading identities as well as crafting new ones for them to take up. It also involves changing the classroom culture around what it means to be a reader in school. Being explicit with students about the reading obstacles we all face disrupts fixed ideas about what it means to be a particular kind of reader and instead makes reading difficulties acceptable and normal for everyone.

Helping adolescents with academic literacy difficulties requires schools to relinquish some control over molding students into specific kinds of readers and instead allow students to play a major role in the development of their literate identities. Teachers, administrators, and district leaders need to encourage the formation of learning partnerships with their students and foster collaborative and supportive school and classroom climates that make it safe for students to take risks and to share their worries, ideas, and questions about literacy. By creating these shared spaces, educators can cultivate growth and success in literacy for all students.

DISCUSSION AND ACTIVITIES

1. Find a text that is written for a specialized audience (chemical engineers, botanists, discrete mathematicians, lawyers, etc.) that is outside of your expertise. Were there any passages in the text that were particularly difficult to comprehend? Did you use any strategies that helped you to better understand the text, and, if so, what did you learn about this process? Try sharing the results of this experience with your students and facilitate a discussion about their own encounters with reading obstacles.

2. Create a survey asking students how they perceive themselves as readers, their beliefs about reading and writing, and any literacy practices they

engage in both inside and outside of class. Schedule a time to meet with each student individually to discuss the survey and allow them to elaborate on their answers. Think about how their perceptions of themselves challenge your own and how you can use this information to help modify your instruction.

3. With your students, construct a list of possible reading and writing goals that would be realistic to achieve during the school year. Talk about your goals for them as their teacher and how they may be different, but no more important, than the goals they may have for themselves. Once students have identified two to three goals, help them develop a plan that will help them succeed in reaching the goals. Encourage students to discuss with their peers strategies they will need to complete their plan and to give advice on how to help one another achieve their goals throughout the school year.

4. Hold a class forum to elicit student feedback on the climate of your classroom. Do students feel safe to share their questions, opinions, and concerns with you and their classmates? Do all students seem to have a voice during class discussions? Is the environment conducive to working in partnerships and small groups, as well as a whole class? Use student input to develop a plan to create, foster, or improve the cooperative and supportive climate of your classroom so that all students feel secure in participating.

REFERENCES

Allington, R. L. (2011). Reading intervention in the middle grades. *Voices from the Middle, 19,* 10–16.

Brown, S. (2011). Becoming literate: Looking across curricular structures at situated identities. *Early Childhood Education Journal, 39,* 257–265.

Brookfield, S. D., & Preskill, S. (2005). *Discussion as a way of teaching: Tools and techniques for democratic classrooms* (2nd ed.). San Francisco: Jossey-Bass.

Burns, L. D. (2012). Standards, policy paradoxes, and the new literacy studies: A call to professional political action. *Journal of Adolescent and Adult Literacy, 56,* 93–97.

Collins, K. M. (2013). *Ability profiling and school failure: One child's struggle to be seen as competent* (2nd ed.). New York: Routledge.

Comperatore, A., & Hall, L. A. (2013, April). *Disrupting the common place.* Paper presented at the annual meeting of the International Reading Association, San Antonio, TX.

Dalton, B. (2012/2013). Multimodal composition and the common core state standards. *Reading Teacher, 66,* 333–339.

Gee, J. (2000/2001). Identity as an analytic lens for research in education. *Review of Research in Education, 25,* 99–125.

Hall, L. A. (2010). The negative consequences of becoming a good reader: Identity theory as a lens for understanding struggling readers, teachers, and reading instruction. *Teachers College Record, 112,* 1792–1829.

Hall, L. A. (2011, December). *Developing eighth-grade students' engagement and identity as readers.* Paper presented at the annual meeting of the Literacy Research Association, Jacksonville, FL.

Hall, L. A. (2012a). Rewriting identities: Creating spaces for students and teachers to challenge the norms of what it means to be a reader in school. *Journal of Adolescent and Adult Literacy, 55,* 368–373.

Hall, L. A. (2012b). The role of reading identities and reading abilities in students' discussions about texts and comprehension strategies. *Journal of Literacy Research, 44,* 239–272.

Hall, L. A., Burns, L. D., & Edwards, E. C. (2011). *Empowering struggling readers: Practices for the middle grades.* New York: Guilford Press.

Hall, L. A., & Greene, H. T. (2011, December). *The role of identity in reading comprehension development.* Paper presented at the annual meeting of the Literacy Research Association, Jacksonville, FL.

Hall, L. A., Johnson, A., Juzwik, M. M., Wortham, S., & Mosley, M. (2010). Teacher identity in the context of literacy teaching: Three explorations of classroom positioning and interaction in secondary schools. *Teaching and Teacher Education, 26,* 234–243.

Lea, M. R., & Street, B. V. (2010). The "Academic Literacies" model: Theory and applications. *Theory Into Practice, 45,* 368–377.

McRae, A., & Guthrie, J. T. (2009). Promoting reasons for reading: Teacher practices that impact motivation. In E. H. Hiebert (Ed.), *Reading more, reading better* (pp. 55–78). New York: Guilford Press.

Moje, E. B. (2008). Foregrounding the disciplines in secondary literacy teaching and learning: A call for change. *Journal of Adolescent and Adult Literacy, 52,* 96–107.

Morrell, E. (2010). Critical literacy, educational investment, and the blueprint reform: An analysis of the reauthorization of the elementary and secondary education act. *Journal of Adolescent and Adult Literacy, 54,* 146–149.

National Assessment of Educational Progress (2011). *2011 reading assessment results.* Retrieved from *http://nationsreportcard.gov/reading_2011.*

O'Flahavan, J., & Wallis, J. (2005). Rosenblatt in the classroom: Her texts, our readings, our classrooms. *Voices from the Middle, 12,* 32–33.

PART II

Developing Literacy Strategies

CHAPTER 6

Text Complexity and Deliberate Practice

Common Cores of Learning

Kristen A. Munger
Maria S. Murray

This chapter provides:

- Background on text complexity, including what it is, why it is important, and how it is measured.
- An overview of the principles of "deliberate practice."
- Justification for using a deliberate practice framework to advance students' abilities to read and understand complex texts.

The most recent results from *Reading Today's* annual "What's Hot, What's Not" literacy survey (Cassidy & Grote-Garcia, 2012) indicate that for 2013, adolescent literacy is considered an "extremely hot" topic, and both text complexity and the Common Core State Standards are rated in the "very hot" category. Because this chapter covers all three of these hot topics, it is especially relevant to educators seeking to integrate them into their teaching practices.

BACKGROUND INFORMATION

The *Common Core State Standards for English Language Arts & Literacy in History/Social Studies, Science, and Technical Subjects* (CCSS; National

Governors Association [NGA] & Council of Chief State School Officers [CCSSO], 2010a) is a nationwide initiative exerting influence on U.S. educational practices. Previous state standards have been replaced by new national standards that guide teaching and learning in the vast majority of public schools. Predictably, these changes are causing quite a commotion in educational circles. For example, in a recent article in *Education Week*, Ronald Wolk (2012) cautioned against the use of standards and testing as the principle means for improving student achievement:

> We know from experience that standards do not educate people. Without the organization, resources, and trained workforce necessary to meet them, standards are worth little, and people cannot be compelled to meet them. Keep in mind that the U.S. Congress mandated that every student would be proficient in reading and math by 2014. How's that working out? (para. 16)

And it is not just educators who are keeping an eye on "the Standards." Joel Stein, the *Time* magazine columnist, has forecasted the death of fictional texts in favor of informational texts (Stein, 2012), based on recommendations of the CCSS. His prophesy carries its own irony, given that his column is regularly assigned by English teachers as nonfiction reading.

Although the CCSS document still encourages the use of narrative fiction, it stipulates that educators must increase the use of informational texts as well:

> Most of the required reading in college and workforce training programs is informational in structure and challenging in content; postsecondary education programs typically provide students with both a higher volume of such reading than is generally required in K–12 schools and comparatively little scaffolding. The Standards are not alone in calling for a special emphasis on informational text. The 2009 reading framework of the National Assessment of Educational Progress (NAEP) requires a high and increasing proportion of informational text on its assessment as students advance through the grades. (NGA & CCSSO, 2010a, p. 4)

Many English and content-area teachers regularly incorporate informational texts into their classes, making the topic of text complexity span all disciplines, with special emphasis on informational text complexity. For example, consider the level of complexity of the *Declaration of Independence* (n.d.). Here is an excerpt:

> But when a long train of abuses and usurpations, pursuing invariably the same Object evinces a design to reduce them under absolute Despotism, it is their right, it is their duty, to throw off such Government, and to provide new Guards for their future security.

A reader can immediately recognize the high level of complexity of this text, but as a teacher, how do you know how complex it actually is? Who is likely to struggle with reading and understanding it, and what strategies can be used to enable the comprehension of such a complex text? The CCSS attempt to address these exact questions.

The CCSS's (2010b) Appendix A contains useful explanations regarding why text complexity matters, as well as how the standards specify using more complex texts to improve reading levels of students. One study completed by American College Testing (ACT, 2006) found meeting or exceeding the reading benchmark score on the ACT is predicted more by the questions students can answer about complex texts, rather than a general ability to think critically. The CCSS's (2010b) Appendix A also discusses the concern regarding the steady increase in the complexity of texts used in college and career settings over the last several decades, along with a corresponding decrease in the complexity of texts used in schools. Thus an important goal of the CCSS is to "move students into more complex texts earlier in their schooling to significantly improve the text levels they can read by the time they enter college or begin a career" (Goatley, 2012, p. 18). While the recommendations to increase students' exposure to complex texts hold true at middle and high school levels, they are unlikely to apply to texts read by very young students since it is difficult for texts which are at the "ground floor" of reading to actually decrease in complexity (Hiebert, personal communication, December 7, 2012).

THE CCSS MODEL OF TEXT COMPLEXITY

The CCSS feature three equally important components for measuring text complexity. These are quantitative measures, qualitative measures, and reader and task considerations. Figure 6.1 illustrates the CCSS model of text complexity, using a triangular framework. What follows are descriptions of each of these components, as well as examples of how teachers can integrate the components into their practice.

Quantitative Measures

Standard 10 of the CCSS specifies that students should read and understand texts that gradually increase in complexity from grade to grade in a "staircase" fashion (NGA & CCSSO, 2010c). But how can teachers determine the complexity of texts or whether a sequence of texts is actually advancing in complexity? One way is to use quantitative measurement tools. Quantitative tools gauge the readability of texts based on formulas including word repetition, word and sentence length, vocabulary, and syntax.

Although measuring text complexity is not new (see Mesmer,

FIGURE 6.1. CCSS model of text complexity. Copyright 2010. National Governors Association Center for Best Practices and Council of Chief State School Officers, Washington, DC. All rights reserved.

Cunningham, & Hiebert, 2012), advancements in the sophistication, variety, and availability of digital text leveling tools have led to a text readability renaissance. Digital measures are popular because they use a common scale to gauge the readability of texts, and some (e.g., Lexiles; MetaMetrics, 2013) can even gauge the reading levels of students. CCSS's Supplemental Information for Appendix A (NGA & CCSSO, 2010c) shows difficulty ranges for six popular quantitative text complexity measures, which are matched to CCSS grade bands and illustrate the staircase of increasing expectations across grade levels (see Figure 6.2). These tools make matching students with appropriately leveled texts relatively straightforward, at least in terms of quantitative levels.

According to Nelson, Perfetti, Liben, and Liben (2012), field testing of popular quantitative measures of text complexity showed no single measure to be superior. They found that all of the measures were "reliably, and often highly, correlated with grade level and student performance-based measures of text difficulty across a variety of text sets, and across a variety of reference measures" (p. 46). Second, the measures showed some of the same patterns in how they scaled texts. For example, metrics estimated the difficulty of informational texts more precisely than narrative texts and more precisely for texts used in lower grades than upper grades. Differences between the measures largely related to the sophistication of the formulas used for each measure. For example, measures based mostly on word difficulty and sentence length (e.g., Lexiles) were less precise than those including additional linguistic features (e.g., semantics). In spite of some of these technical differences, Nelson et al. (2012) concluded that each measure "can support the goal of the Common Core Standards to increase student achievement by closing the large gap that currently exists between typical high school level and college texts" (p. 4).

In order to close this large gap, quantitative measurement tools can

Common Core Band	ATOS	Degrees of Reading Power®	Flesch-Kincaid®	The Lexile Framework®	Reading Maturity	SourceRater
2nd–3rd	2.75–5.14	42–54	1.98–5.34	420–820	3.53–6.13	0.05–2.48
4th–5th	4.97–7.03	52–60	4.51–7.73	740–1010	5.42–7.92	0.84–5.75
6th–8th	7.00–9.98	57–67	6.51–10.34	925–1185	7.04–9.57	4.11–10.66
9th–10th	9.67–12.01	62–72	8.32–12.12	1050–1335	8.41–10.81	9.02–13.93
11th–CCR	11.20–14.10	67–74	10.34–14.2	1185–1385	9.57–12.00	12.30–14.50

FIGURE 6.2. CCSS grade-level bands associated with quantitative measures of text complexity. Copyright 2010. National Governors Association Center for Best Practices and Council of Chief State School Officers, Washington, DC. All rights reserved.

be used not only to select texts based on a reader's present level of ability but also to select texts that increase in complexity (see Table 6.1 for links to text complexity resources). Websites such as *The Lexile Framework for Reading* (MetaMetrics, 2013) provide tools to search for books at a student's estimated reading level, estimate a specific text's level of difficulty, and monitor a student's progress by recording each Lexile level of texts he/she reads.

Although quantitative measures are useful when evaluating the complexity of most texts, as mentioned previously, they have been criticized for their inaccurate leveling of complex narrative fiction (see NGA & CCSSO, 2010b). A good example of inaccurate leveling is featured in the CCSS's Appendix A. *The Grapes of Wrath*, by John Steinbeck (1939), is a popular book assigned in American high schools. Using only quantitative measures, the text appears appropriate for second- and third-grade students because of the relative simplicity of the words in the text's dialogue (the text's estimated Lexile level is 680). It is only when additional qualitative elements are considered, such as the maturity of the dialogue, that the text's true complexity is better understood. It is likely that teachers already know not to assign *The Grapes of Wrath* to second-grade students, but this example shows what can go wrong if only quantitative measures are used, especially for texts that are less well known. There is also the danger that because quantitative tools yield numbers, they may appear to have greater precision than they actually do (Nesi, 2012).

An additional concern is that certain texts may be offered or denied to students based on quantitative measures alone since they are both widely available and efficient to use. Directing a student away from a text because it appears to be at too high a level, in spite of a student's interest, extensive background knowledge, or high level of motivation to read it, is a potential misuse of quantitative measurement tools. A final concern relates to the idea of "leveling mania," a term used by Szymusiak and Sibberson (2001) to describe the extreme focus of some teachers on organizing, leveling, and attaching students to books, while paying little heed to other important characteristics of both readers and texts (e.g., cognitive skills, motivation, background knowledge, and life experiences; RAND Reading Study Group [RRSG], 2002).

Qualitative Measures

Limitations in quantitative measures require the use of other tools, such as qualitative measures, when making decisions about texts. The CCSS feature four domains involved in the qualitative evaluation of texts (see Table 6.2): levels of meaning, text structure, language conventionality/clarity, and knowledge demands. Table 6.1 provides links to CCSS rubrics used in the qualitative evaluation of both narrative and informational texts.

The CCSS's Appendix A (NGA & CCSSO, 2010b) features a clear example of how qualitative measures can be used to examine the complexity of *The Grapes of Wrath*. Recall that the text's Lexile level is quite low—around 680—which falls within the second- to third-grade band of

TABLE 6.1. Text Complexity Resources for Teachers

CCSS model	Text complexity resources for teachers
Quantitative measures	Lexile analyzer: *www.lexile.com/analyzer*
	ATOS analyzer: www.renlearn.com/ar/overview/atos
	Accelerated Reader BookFinder: *www.arbookfind.com*
	For more readability formula resources and digital tools, visit the Kansas State Department of Education website: *www. ksde.org*
Qualitative measures	CCSSO text complexity qualitative measures rubric for informational text: *http://programs.ccsso.org/ projects/common%20core%20resources/documents/ Informational%20Text%20Qualitative%20Rubric.pdf*
	CCSSO text complexity qualitative measures rubric for literary text: *http://programs.ccsso.org/projects/common%20 core%20resources/documents/Literary%20Text%20 Qualitative%20Rubric.pdf*
Reader and task considerations	Questions for professional reflection on reader and task considerations: *http://programs.ccsso.org/projects/ common%20core%20resources/documents/Reader%20 and%20Task%20Considerations.pdf*

TABLE 6.2. Qualitative Measures of Text Complexity

Domain	Lower complexity	Higher complexity
Levels of meaning	• Single level of meaning • Explicitly stated purpose	• Multiple levels of meaning • Implicit, hidden, or obscure purpose
Structure	• Simple and conventional structures • Events in chronological order • Conventions of genres and subgenres followed • Simple graphics that are unnecessary/supplemental	• Complex, implicit, unconventional structures • Flashbacks, flash-forwards, manipulations of time/sequence • Conventions of genres and subgenres not followed • Complex graphics that are essential to understanding text or provide an independent source of information
Language conventionality/clarity	• Language that is literal, clear, contemporary, conversational	• Language that is figurative, ironic, ambiguous, deliberately misleading, archaic, unfamiliar, and/or contains discipline-specific vocabulary
Knowledge demands	• Few assumptions made about cultural, literary, and content/discipline knowledge	• Many assumptions made about readers' life experiences and knowledge

complexity. When examining levels of meaning, text structure, language clarity, and knowledge demands (see Table 6.3), it becomes clear that the text is far more advanced than what quantitative measures approximate.

The contrasting simplicity of the sentence structure (see below), with the sophistication of the text's meaning and use of vernacular, show that qualitative measures trump quantitative measures in terms of their validity for judging the complexity of this piece of narrative fiction:

> "May soun' funny to be so tight," he apologized. "We got a thousan' miles to go, an' we don' know if we'll make it." He dug in the pouch with a forefinger, located a dime, and pinched in for it. (Steinbeck, 1939, p. 175)

Reader and Task Considerations

Quantitative text complexity formulas and qualitative rubrics featuring gradients of thematic complexity do not take into consideration the specific

TABLE 6.3. Levels of Meaning, Text Structure, Language Conventionality and Clarity, and Knowledge Demands Applied to *The Grapes of Wrath*

Levels of meaning

Although the plot relates to a family's journey across the Midwest, Steinbeck's copious use of metaphor and themes related to social justice may be missed by readers unfamiliar with recognizing and interpreting different levels of meaning.

Structure

The text is very simple in its structure, follows the conventional framework of most narrative fiction, and presents key events in chronological order.

Language conventionality and clarity

Although the language used is largely conventional, there are some higher demands related to vocabulary knowledge. In addition, the vernacular used by the characters complicates the seeming straightforwardness of the text.

Knowledge demands

A certain degree of knowledge is assumed on the part of the reader, for example, that there was a period in history called the "Great Depression."

characteristics of readers or the tasks in which they engage. Factors such as student motivation, stamina, verbal reasoning, general reading ability, English language proficiency, or prior knowledge require thinking deeply about readers when selecting and using complex texts. Determining the complexity of texts is important, but only to the extent that they are combined with effective instruction to support thinking and learning. Consider the particular tasks students will be asked to do in connection to texts they read. If students read *The Grapes of Wrath*, is the goal to improve their ability to understand complex themes or to read for enjoyment? Will students read the text with peers or independently at home? What tasks must students complete related to their reading?

According to Hiebert (2012), three dimensions of readers and tasks are important when planning and delivering instruction: social configuration (teacher-led, peer, independent), type of response (oral vs. written), and allocation of time (fixed immediate blocks of time such as assessments vs. open-ended assignments) (see Table 6.1 for a link to "Questions for Professional Reflection on Reader and Task Considerations"). Depending on various dimensions of the particular readers (e.g., their levels of background knowledge, general reading ability, stamina), teachers must continually gauge and adjust the amount of support provided to students in each of the dimensions. For example, if a new comprehension strategy is introduced, such as integrating prior knowledge while reading a text, and students need a lot of support, the social configuration will be teacher led and will include explicit modeling of the use of the strategy. At this point, student responses may be limited to oral comments and questions, which the teacher uses to monitor learning and adjust instruction. Once students develop an understanding of the strategy, the role of the teacher changes to include teacher-mediated discussions. The teacher facilitates peer interactions, creates peer-supported practice opportunities, and provides feedback to help students adjust their application of the strategy. Student responses may be discussion based and include oral and/or written responses drawn from group-supported applications of the strategy. Engaging with peers in organized, teacher-mediated discussions and activities enables students to respond to texts more interactively and spontaneously than when only written responses are required. There may be considerable time devoted to this phase of learning since successful application of the strategy is critical to future applications. If it is determined that the text or an associated task is too challenging, or the application of the strategy is not transferring or generalizing to new contexts, the teacher may step in once again to model and facilitate more guided practice opportunities. Eventually, students must learn to apply strategies independently, and at this point, may be required to generate an individually written response. Considerably less time may be devoted to this phase of learning, unless responses indicate a need for additional instruction and practice.

DELIBERATE PRACTICE

In their recent article "The Challenge of Challenging Texts," Shanahan, Fisher, and Frey (2012) feature an analogy comparing text complexity and weight lifting. Quite obviously, gradual increases in weight are required to build muscle, but perhaps less obviously, gradual increases in text complexity are required to strengthen reading skills. We would like to further develop this analogy using a "deliberate practice" framework (Ericsson, Krampe, & Tesch-Römer, 1993).

Pause and consider for a moment a skill that you acquired in sports, music, or some other area in which you think of yourself as either proficient, or perhaps expert. How did you learn to hit a baseball with accuracy or learn to speak a second language fluently? It was likely a mix of frequent practice sessions at an appropriate level of difficulty, with just the right progression of difficulty, immediate and frequent corrective feedback, and some level of determination on your part and that of your teacher/coach. These elements of deliberate practice can be traced back to the body of work by K. Anders Ericsson and colleagues (Ericsson, 2004; Ericsson et al., 1993; Ericsson, Nandagopal, & Roring, 2009), who have written extensively on how improvements in learning and expert performance develop.

MetaMetrics researchers Stenner, Koons, and Swartz (2009) explicitly situated the comprehension of complex texts within a deliberate practice framework. They made the point that students spend 13 years in class-rooms with daily practice reading texts. In spite of this, many students are still not prepared to read and understand the texts used in college and career settings. What could be missing? Using the CCSS and a deliberate practice framework, we will generate possible answers to this question.

The Influence of Practice

Ericsson et al. (1993) used the term "deliberate practice" to describe a framework in which teachers help learners progress on the novice-to-expert continuum, including the following: (1) knowledge of previously acquired abilities of the learner, (2) a steady progression of task difficulty designed to advance skills and prevent skill plateaus, and (3) immediate and valid feedback to the learner (see Figure 6.3). Plus, learners must exert and sustain effort during selected activities, making motivation an important component as well.

If our learning experiences lack one or more of these components, we are not likely to make progress, or we may make only very slow progress relative to others whose practice experiences are more complete. For example, when learning to play an instrument, if we only practice songs that are easy to play rather than taking on the challenge of incrementally more difficult pieces, we are unlikely to improve very much. Playing only easy music violates the deliberate practice framework because it does not involve a steady progression of more difficult tasks and completely disregards the previously acquired abilities of the learner.

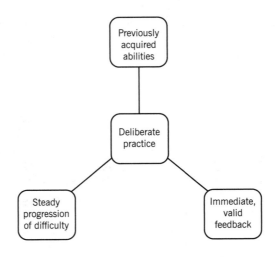

FIGURE 6.3. A framework of deliberate practice.

The deliberate practice framework corresponds with what Vygotsky (1978) termed the zone of proximal development. In this zone, tasks that are just beyond the learner's current knowledge or capability are presented, and teacher support is offered until the student can complete tasks with high rates of success. Support is withdrawn as the student becomes more proficient. Then tasks that are more difficult are introduced, along with temporary teacher support. This practice sequence is precisely what is recommended in the CCSS, where students benefit from initially scaffolded activities, but ultimately, "By the time they complete the core, students must be able to read and comprehend independently and proficiently the kinds of complex texts commonly found in college and careers" (NGA & CCSSO, 2010b, p. 2).

What Do Good Readers Do to Become Good Readers?

An important aspect in helping adolescent readers learn to comprehend increasingly complex texts is to think beyond "what good readers do" and consider the equally important but less prosaic question "What did good readers do to get to be good readers?" While this distinction might seem trivial, we will use an example from the book *Talent Is Overrated: What Really Separates World-Class Performers from Everybody Else*, by Geoff Colvin (2008), to illustrate why this distinction matters.

When *average* tennis players are served the ball, their eyes tend to fix on the ball. Conversely, when *expert* players are served the ball, their eyes fix on the body parts of their opponents (e.g., hips, arms, and shoulders). Expert players subconsciously use body cues from their opponent to foresee where the ball will be directed, and this awareness enables them to react swiftly and accurately to return it. But what happens when average tennis players are told to do what experts do and focus their attention on their opponent's body parts? *There is no improvement in their ability.* This is because experts developed the ability to automatically interpret what these cues mean only after hundreds of hours of training. Their training set up a feedback loop that helped them develop and hone strategies that resulted in the most success. An average tennis player has not acquired the many hours of deliberate practice needed to learn to read and use bodily cues, and thus telling average players to act like experts does little to improve their skills.

Similarly, advanced readers have engaged in hundreds, if not thousands, of hours of reading. What they attend to, and do, will be different, at least in part, from what they attended to and did when they were less experienced readers. In this respect, highly skilled readers have developed and adapted their expertise over countless text reading occasions, and encouraging nonproficient readers to mimic what expert readers do, outside of the deliberate practice framework, is risky. Less experienced readers have not had the opportunity to enable automaticity in certain skills required to use the highly sophisticated strategies that skilled readers regularly use. Just as the expert tennis player progresses from focusing on the ball to automatically focusing on body cues, less experienced readers require practice in a wider variety of skills before successfully integrating them to read and understand complex texts.

Whereas proficient readers have read more and have read often, advanced readers have not only read even more and more often, but they also have *deliberately engaged in reading texts that are challenging to them.* Expert readers do not merely assimilate ideas from various texts but integrate new and sophisticated ideas. Working toward this apex of inference is not only consistent with the spirit of the CCSS but is probably only achievable within a framework that includes reading increasingly complex texts.

COMBINING TEXT COMPLEXITY AND DELIBERATE PRACTICE

Steady Progression of Difficulty

Now that we have reviewed the CCSS model of text complexity and the framework of deliberate practice, we will discuss decisions teachers face when choosing texts. We know students need to engage in a great deal of reading in order to advance in skills, and purely enjoyable reading experiences using self-selected texts are necessary to maintain students' enthusiasm for reading (O'Brien & Dillon, 2008). But simply reading more, at the same level, is insufficient to promote reading that leads to the steady progression of skills specified by the CCSS. The following example from the *New York Times* article titled "A New Assignment: Pick Books You Like," by Motoko Rich (2009a), raises an important debate related to students' self-selection of texts. He wrote about Lorrie McNeill, a teacher who experimented with teaching literature by having students only read books that they selected. Getting her students excited about reading and having them genuinely interested in books were high priorities—as they should be.

Alternatively, when we situate Ms. McNeill's approach into the deliberate practice framework, it is clear that something is missing. In a follow-up article by Rich (2009b), appearing in the next day's *New York Times*, a reader commented:

> The student who loves reading "Captain Underpants" but who is never forced to move beyond that material has done nothing to prepare for a life of active, intelligent, inquisitive citizenship (which is something training in the humanities ought to prepare us for) and has been poorly served by her educators. It sounds as though teachers such as Ms. McNeill are presenting reading to students as a hobby, not an academic discipline. (para. 2–3)

This does not mean that *all* texts should be teacher assigned or even incrementally challenging. Clearly, a combination of reading experiences is needed to simultaneously promote students' engagement in purely enjoyable reading activities, along with reading experiences that promote the thinking skills required for texts encountered in college and career settings. A persistent challenge educators may face in trying to meet these goals is students' resistance to reading texts that seem less enjoyable and are more difficult to read. For this reason, it makes sense to share with students why they are being challenged. This can be done by using analogies, such as the one provided below, to show how learning can be weakened when challenges are avoided.

As illustrated by Colvin (2008), simply doing an activity over and over will not lead to any extraordinary improvement. For example, he points out that even if we have spent thousands of hours driving a car, driving experience does not automatically lead to our becoming expert drivers. In fact, our driving probably improved only toward the beginning, and additional hours of driving do not lead us anywhere beyond basic proficiency. Colvin describes the three stages that most drivers experience, and pins down when progress stops:

> The first stage demands a lot of attention as we try out the controls, learn the rules of driving, and so on. In the second stage we begin to coordinate our knowledge, linking movements together and more fluidly combining our actions with our knowledge of the car, the situation, and the rules. In the third stage we drive the car with barely a thought. It's automatic. And with that our improvement at driving slows dramatically, eventually stopping completely. (p. 82)

What this means is that once we develop automaticity at something, and no additional demands are made on us through deliberate practice (i.e., there are no gradual increases in difficulty) improvements largely cease. This is not to say that for some abilities, automaticity in one or more skills is not required to successfully develop more complex skills, such as becoming automatic with multiplication facts to solve complex math problems. But simply reading more at the same level of difficulty (i.e., the "Captain Underpants" effect) is no more likely to improve someone's reading ability than simply driving a car will improve someone's driving ability. The notion that skills do not improve much once they become automatic is one reason teachers who use repeated reading of texts to build reading fluency do not involve students in reading the same passage a dozen times. After a certain number of times reading an appropriately leveled text—usually around three—students generally develop sufficient fluency with the passage, and further practice is mostly a waste of time. What we can take from discussions based on learning theory is that challenging tasks are required to improve skills and that not all of these challenges will be enjoyable. People training to run a marathon do not run steeper and steeper hills because it feels particularly good; they do it because they want to reach a goal, and they know that making progress toward that goal requires a sustained effort.

On occasion, adolescents may prove to be unwilling to read much of anything without a great deal of prodding on the part of their teachers, causing some teachers to use what we recognize as extreme scaffolding to support or motivate their students. This is most likely to happen when levels of texts are far above students' reading abilities or when students' motivation is low. It is important to keep in mind that heavily scaffolding all tasks to motivate students will not necessarily result in the gains specified by the CCSS. Teachers who assign more difficult texts but then incorporate so many supports that the texts are no longer challenging is akin to carrying students up the text complexity staircase. Yes, students are exposed to more complex texts, but they are not doing much of the work, and ultimately they end up no better conditioned to climb the staircase independently.

In a book titled *Never Work Harder Than Your Students*, Robyn Jackson (2009) discusses her Herculean efforts to get students to learn, as she scrambled for countless hours to motivate and engage them. She finally realized that most of the time she was working much harder than they were, with little return on her investment. Teachers who work harder, while their students do less, are unlikely to see advancements in their students' abilities. Starting with easy or heavily scaffolded tasks might be a good initial strategy to promote engagement, but ultimately, high levels of learning require a deliberate and sustained effort on the part of students, not just teachers.

Just as marathon runners map out their practice activities related to their running goals, teachers and students can use measurement tools to map out practice activities related to reading goals. Engaging students in reading more challenging texts, while still allowing self-chosen reading so that students continue to read a lot, will lead to movement up the staircase of complexity and improve students' ability to read difficult texts independently. Using measurement tools can ensure that the complexity of a chosen text is consistent with the goals for reading it. For example, Stenner et al. (2009) specifically discuss using the Lexile framework to increase and design reading opportunities for students, in which readers' abilities and text difficulties can be considered on the same scale. To challenge readers, they recommend using texts with a Lexile level 100 or more points above students' reading level. To improve fluency, they recommend a Lexile level 250 points below students' reading level (although more research is needed investigate the use of quantitative measures in this way).

Teacher Knowledge of Previously Acquired Abilities of the Learner

It is important to take into consideration not only the staircase of text complexity but also what students bring to specific learning situations. Like a good coach, teachers recognize what students already know and can do—consistent with Vygotsky's zone of proximal development. When we think about Ms. McNeill's version of reading workshop, in which students selected all of the texts they read, text difficulty and any increases in difficulty were entirely determined by her students. Students who exclusively self-select texts may have difficulty taking into account their own previously acquired abilities to advance their reading skills. In an analogy related to math, Rich (2009b, para. 4) asks: "Would students ever learn difficult equations or formulas if they were allowed to choose what to study in these classes?" Some students will consistently make choices that do not challenge them, whereas others will make choices according to their interests but that may be far too difficult. Considering their previously acquired abilities can help students prepare for and face academic challenges as well as help them decide when to ask for support if overly complex texts lead to high levels of frustration.

Teachers using the deliberate practice framework will frequently ask themselves, "If I use this text, how will an individual student or group of students interact with it based on their unique abilities, backgrounds, and experiences?" This is going beyond the exclusive use of qualitative or quantitative measurement tools to combine the deliberate practice framework with reader and task considerations. Just because a text is theoretically at a student's reading level does not mean it will result in a successful reading encounter. For example, if students' stamina levels are low, have students read only some portion of the text or have sections read aloud. Break the text into smaller sections to be read over a longer period, or perhaps, select abridged texts. If a text requires students to have advanced levels of inferencing, such as *The Grapes of Wrath*, consider students' analytical reasoning skills, social maturity, and knowledge of history, in addition to other measures of text complexity. (A link to a more complete list of reader and task considerations is available in Table 6.1.) These practices will ensure that students will not only read texts but their efforts will result in an improved ability to comprehend future texts as well.

Immediate and Valid Feedback

The final element of the deliberate practice framework is providing immediate and valid feedback to learners. When learners are provided with appropriately leveled tasks and clear goals, feedback supports focused problem solving as well as self-exploration of methods to improve task performance (Ericsson et al., 2009). Feedback can be intrinsic to a task, such as successfully hitting a pitched baseball, or supplemental, such as feedback regarding students' use of evidence to support a conclusion based on reading informational texts.

Ericsson (2004) provides a clear example of the critical role of feedback related to physicians in training to read and interpret mammographic images. When they do not receive immediate and valid feedback regarding diagnoses they make and must instead wait for biopsy results, any improvements in their diagnostic skills occur very slowly, no matter how good their training is otherwise. Now consider when training includes examination of hundreds of mammographic images, along with immediate feedback, using previously confirmed diagnoses. Couple these with diagnostic images that increase incrementally in complexity, and the principal components of deliberate practice are present: steady progression of more difficult tasks and immediate and valid feedback. Skill levels increase markedly under these conditions.

Computer-assisted instruction is used in schools' literacy teaching practices in order to take advantage of the benefits of immediate and valid feedback (e.g., *MyReadingWeb*, in Stenner et al., 2009). Although the quality of these programs varies, high-quality computer-assisted instruction can maximize this feedback component and gradually increase levels of task difficulty. Where computer-assisted instruction is weaker, however, is in taking into account characteristics of learners (reader considerations), as well as bridging practice tasks to more authentic learning situations (learning transfer and task considerations).

Using computer-assisted instruction is not the only way that real-time feedback can be provided to students. Multiple strategies are needed to build comprehension of complex texts. For example, concept-oriented reading instruction (CORI) focuses on goals created for reading complex informational texts (Raphael, George, Weber, & Nies, 2009). Students are taught strategies to gain information from the texts, and through collaborative teacher and peer interactions (real-time feedback), students refine their insights and eventually present what they learn to an audience (summative feedback). Additional concrete examples of real-time feedback that can be used include giving feedback related to students' class discussion points, oral or written responses to questions, handwritten or online journal entries, or construction of concept maps. Peers can be taught to deliver feedback as well (e.g., peer-to-peer talk).

A Final, Cautionary Tale Related to Talent

Even teachers who are knowledgeable about the active ingredients of deliberate practice can neglect to use them with certain students. For example, when students are recognized as more "talented," teachers may provide more and better practice opportunities for them but not for students who appear "less talented." As illustrated in Malcolm Gladwell's book *Outliers* (2008), talent can be tricky to judge, and the effects of misjudgments can be harmful. Sometimes, individuals who appear more talented have simply had more practice opportunities.

In *Outliers,* Gladwell reviews research by Roger Barnsley, who discovered that expert Canadian hockey players are significantly more likely to be born in the first half of the year. Why? Because the cutoff date for hockey players to join junior teams is January 1. Children who are the most physically mature tend to be recruited most often to advanced teams, and of course, the most physically mature children also tend to be older. But the more mature children *do* have better skills compared to the less mature children, right? Wrong. Well, sort of. The older children are taller and stronger, so their skills are generally better at the time teams are picked, but when they were younger, shorter, and weaker, many will have had the same level of "talent" as children who happen to be younger at the time junior teams are formed. The age variable causes coaches to confuse talent with practice, and unaware teachers may be similarly tricked into believing certain students have talent rather than considering which students have had more practice. In hockey, when older children make the team, they get far more (and better) practice opportunities. They get the best ice time, are more challenged in more frequent practice sessions, and have more skilled coaches. All of this high-quality, deliberate practice eventually leads to their being disproportionately recruited to professional hockey teams, with many younger players, who had the same potential, left behind. Just as young hockey players with strong potential can be inadvertently denied opportunities to advance their skills, readers with strong potential may experience this same disadvantage in a system that recognizes and rewards high levels of ability but neglects the history of how this ability developed.

There is also the equally harmful assumption that talented students may require little or no practice because their innate abilities will automatically enable them to flourish. Remember that deliberate practice is required to advance skills, and while we want to celebrate the talent we see in our adolescents, there are many students who possess the same potential but have not had sufficient deliberate practice opportunities to improve. In other words, regardless of students' current levels of reading ability, an essential component to their becoming more advanced readers involves promoting and supporting the reading of texts that are the right level of challenge. Teachers who use knowledge of text complexity within the context of the deliberate practice framework are well positioned to maximize the growth of all of their students and less likely to mistake the results of successful practice as intrinsic talent.

CONCLUSION

In this chapter, we provided background regarding what text complexity is, why it is important, and how it is measured, based on the three components of the CCSS text complexity model. We also described a framework of deliberate practice to help guide teachers of adolescent learners to promote meaningful practice opportunities enabling students to independently read and understand increasingly complex texts. We believe both teachers and students must be involved in setting reading goals as well as practice activities purposefully designed to achieve them, since responsibility for improving reading must gradually shift to students as they transition from high school to college and career settings. In addition, although the chapter does not expressly focus on disciplinary literacy strategies, we would like to point out that teaching students to understand more complex texts is the purview of all teachers—not just English teachers—at all grade levels. Elementary school teachers, middle and high school content-area teachers, intervention specialists, and educational consultants must all understand how to provide high-quality deliberate practice opportunities for all students.

Text complexity is unquestionably a hot topic in education (Cassidy & Grote-Garcia, 2012). Because of its popularity, text complexity runs the risk of becoming a narrow focus of teachers (i.e., "leveling mania"), to the exclusion of other equally important but less "hot" topics, such as student motivation. The risk is similar to what we see when we watch a team of 6-year-olds play soccer; they know that the aim is to kick the ball into the goal of the opposing team, but they tend to remember and use only one strategy. When an especially energetic child kicks the ball, you can only sit back and watch as every child surrounds it, like a swarm of angry bees attacking an intruder. Eventually, when another child manages to kick the ball out of the scrum, the hive is on the move again. The goals of the CCSS will not be realized if text complexity becomes the next soccer ball we surround. Instead, text complexity must be placed within a complete strategic framework designed to enhance students' enjoyment and motivation of reading as well as advance their skills.

DISCUSSION AND ACTIVITIES

1. Using the links in Table 6.1, determine the quantitative and qualitative levels of two texts you might use in your classroom. Next, compose a list of reader and task considerations for these two texts. With whom would you use these texts? What supports would you provide? With whom would you not use these texts, and why?

2. Discuss with others a set of skills you have acquired in sports, music,

languages, or another area. Think back to what it took for you to achieve these skills. How did your coach or teacher consider your previously acquired abilities? How did he or she advance your skills by steadily making your lessons or practice sessions more difficult? How did your coach or teacher provide real-time, corrective feedback to you, so that you were able to efficiently advance your skills?

3. Now consider what it will take for your students to be able to become good readers and comprehenders of complex texts. In addition to "more reading time," discuss other strategies you can use to engage students in successfully reading and understanding challenging texts. Consider the three CCSS measures of text complexity, the three aspects of deliberate practice discussed in this chapter, and any other possible influences related to motivation or determination.

4. The adoption of the CCSS is being implemented quickly. What kind of supports and scaffolds do *you* need, not only to learn the standards but to prepare your students to successfully read and understand challenging texts? Use the deliberate practice framework to discuss practice opportunities you need to help you advance along the novice-to-expert continuum.

REFERENCES

American College Testing. (2006). *Reading between the lines: What the ACT reveals about college readiness in reading.* Iowa City, IA: Author.

Cassidy, J., & Grote-Garcia, S. (2012, August/September). Defining the literacy agenda: Results of the 2013 What's Hot, What's Not literacy survey. *Reading Today, 30,* 9–12.

Colvin, G. (2008). *Talent is overrated: What really separates world-class performers from everybody else.* New York: Penguin.

The Declaration of Independence (n.d.). Retrieved from *www.archives.gov/exhibits/-charters/declaration_transcript.html.*

Ericsson, K. A. (2004). Deliberate practice and the acquisition and maintenance of expert performance in medicine and related domains. *Academic Medicine, 79*(10), 70–81.

Ericsson, K. A., Krampe, R., & Tesch-Römer, C. (1993). The role of deliberate practice in the acquisition of expert performance. *Psychological Review, 100*(3), 363–406.

Ericsson, K. A., Nandagopal, K., & Roring, R. W. (2009). Toward a science of exceptional achievement: Attaining superior performance through deliberate practice. *Longevity, Regeneration, and Optimal Health, 1172,* 199–217.

Gladwell, M. (2008). *Outliers: The story of success.* New York: Little, Brown.

Goatley, V. (2012). Slicing and dicing the ELA Common Core Standards. *Principal, 92,* 16–21. Retrieved from *www.naesp.org/sites/default/files/Goatley_SO12.pdf.*

Hiebert, E. H. (2012). *The text complexity multi-index* (Text Matters series).

Santa Cruz, CA: TextProject. Retrieved from *http://textproject.org/teachers/text-matters/the-text-complexity-multi-index*.

Jackson, R. (2009). *Never work harder than your students*. Alexandria, VA: Association for Supervision and Curriculum Development.

Mesmer, H. A., Cunningham, J. W., & Hiebert, E. H. (2012). Toward a theoretical model of text complexity for the early grades: Learning from the past, anticipating the future. *Reading Research Quarterly, 47,* 235–258.

MetaMetrics. (2013). *What is a Lexile measure?* Retrieved from *http://lexile.com/about-lexile/lexile-overview*.

National Governors Association Center for Best Practices & Council of Chief State School Officers. (2010a). *Common Core State Standards for English Language Arts & Literacy in History/Social Studies, Science, and Technical Subjects*. Washington, DC: Author. Retrieved from *www. corestandards.org/assets/CCSSI_ELA%20Standards.pdf*.

National Governors Association Center for Best Practices & Council of Chief State School Officers. (2010b). Appendix A: Research supporting key elements of the standards; Glossary of key terms. In *Common Core State Standards for English Language Arts & Literacy in History/Social Studies, Science, and Technical Subjects*. Washington, DC: Author. Retrieved from *www. corestandards.org/assets/Appendix_A.pdf*.

National Governors Association Center for Best Practices & Council of Chief State School Officers. (2010c). Supplemental information for Appendix A. In *Common Core State Standards for English Language Arts & Literacy in History/Social Studies, Science, and Technical Subjects*. Washington, DC: Author. Retrieved from *www.corestandards.org/assets/E0813_Appendix_A_New_Research_on_Text_Complexity.pdf*.

Nelson, J., Perfetti, C., Liben, D., & Liben, M. (2012). *Measures of text difficulty: Testing their predictive value for grade levels and student performance*. Retrieved from *www.ccsso.org/Documents/2012/Measures%20ofText%20Difficulty_final.-2012.pdf*.

Nesi, O. (2012). *The question of text complexity: Reader and task trump traditional measures*. Retrieved from *www.slj.com/2012/10/opinion/on-common-core/the-question-of-text-complexity-reader-and-task-trump-traditional-measures-on-common-core*.

O'Brien, D. G., & Dillon, D. R. (2008). The role of motivation in engaged reading of adolescents. In K. A. Hinchman & H. K. Sheridan-Thomas (Eds.), *Best practices in adolescent literacy instruction* (pp. 78–96). New York: Guilford Press.

RAND Reading Study Group. (2002). *Reading for understanding: Toward an R & D program in reading comprehension*. Santa Monica, CA: RAND.

Raphael, T. E., George, M., Weber, C. M., & Nies, A. (2009). Approaches to teaching reading comprehension. In S. E. Israel & G. G. Duffy (Eds.), *Handbook of research on reading comprehension* (pp. 449–469). New York: Routledge.

Rich, M. (2009a). A new assignment: Pick books you like. Retrieved from *www.nytimes.com/2009/08/30/books/30reading.html?pagewanted=all&_r=0*.

Rich, M. (2009b). Where does a love of reading come from? Retrieved from *http://artsbeat.blogs.nytimes.com/2009/08/31/where-does-a-love-of-reading-come-from.*

Shanahan, T., Fisher, D., & Frey, N. (2012). The challenge of challenging text. *Educational Leadership.* 69(6), 58–62.

Stein, J. (2012, December 10). How I replaced Shakespeare. *Time.* Retrieved from *www.time.com/time/magazine/article/0,9171,2130408,00.html.*

Stenner, A. J., Koons, H. H., & Swartz, C. W. (2009). *Text complexity, the text complexity continuum, and developing expertise in reading.* Durham, NC: MetaMetrics.

Steinbeck, J. (1939). *The grapes of wrath.* New York: Viking.

Szymusiak, K., & Sibberson, F. (2001). *Beyond leveled texts.* Portland, ME: Stenhouse.

Wolk, R. (2012, December 14). Common Core vs. common sense. *Education Week.* Retrieved from *www.edweek.org/ew/articles/2012/12/05/13wolk_ep.h32.html.*

Vygotsky, L. S. (1978). *Mind in society: The development of higher psychological processes.* Cambridge, MA: Harvard University Press.

CHAPTER 7

Active Engagement with Words

Karen Bromley

> If you ask students what makes reading hard,
> they blame the words.
> —SHANAHAN, FISHER, AND FREY (2012, p. 59)

Of course, it is more than the words that make reading difficult for some students. A reader's ability to comprehend text is also related to the text's sentence structure, coherence, organization, and background knowledge (Shanahan et al., 2012). But the words an author uses can cause many middle school students to stumble as they read conceptually dense subject area material. This chapter discusses:

- The role of a large vocabulary.

- How words are learned.

- A rationale for active engagement.

- Strategies for word learning.

There are alarming numbers of secondary school students today who can't read well enough to be successful. They struggle with making sense out of print. They disrupt. They clown around. They withdraw. They fake it. They fail and drop out. There are also many resistant older readers who can read but choose not to engage with subject-area materials (Lenters, 2006). Both struggling and resistant readers often lack interest in topics and genres used in school. They reject school assignments that aren't meaningful or relevant to them. These students need choices, not only in topics, texts, and assignments, but also in how they learn new words. They need direct instruction and active involvement in strategies they can adopt and use independently. Middle school teachers need to be intentional about vocabulary instruction and use a variety of strategies in order to develop engaged and successful readers (Bromley, 2007).

THE ROLE OF A LARGE VOCABULARY

Words are essential building blocks of comprehension and cognition. Unlocking, understanding, and remembering difficult words are keys to learning subject-area concepts. So it is critical that subject-area teachers realize they are just as responsible for teaching vocabulary as are language arts teachers. Possessing large vocabularies:

- Boosts comprehension. Vocabulary knowledge influences comprehension and may comprise 70–80% of what students comprehend (Nagy & Scott, 2000; Pressley, 2002). For example, understanding animal migration is easier if students know that in this context a *pod* is "a group of whales" and not "the shell in which peas grow."
- Improves achievement. A large vocabulary means a fund of conceptual knowledge that makes learning easier. Students with large vocabularies score higher on achievement tests and classroom assessments than those with small vocabularies (National Center for Education Statistics, 2011; Stahl & Fairbanks, 1986).
- Enhances thinking and communication. Words are tools for analyzing, inferring, evaluating, and reasoning. Large vocabularies allow students to communicate verbally in precise, powerful, persuasive, and interesting ways (Cunningham, 2009). Large vocabularies also make students better writers (Cunningham & Cunningham, 2010).
- Promotes fluency. Vocabulary influences fluency and may comprise as much as 70% of fluency (Fuchs, Fuchs, Hosp, & Jenkins (2001). When students recognize and understand many words, they read more quickly and easily than if they know few words (Allington, 2006; Samuels, 2002). Thus they read more material and meet more words than students who read slowly.

Vocabulary is an important element of the *Common Core State Standards for English Language Arts and Literacy* (National Governors Association [NGA] Center for Best Practices & Council of Chief State School Officers [CCSSO], 2010) because words are basic to listening, speaking, reading, writing, and language use in general. The K–12 standards require students to be able to:

- Determine the meaning of unknown or multiple-meaning words (use context, analyze meaningful word parts, and use reference materials).
- Understand figurative language, word relationships, and nuances in word meanings.
- Acquire and use accurately a range of academic and domain-specific words and phrases.
- Demonstrate independence in gathering vocabulary knowledge when encountering an unknown term important to comprehension or expression.

Usually the most troublesome words for students are domain specific and central to building knowledge and conceptual understanding in science, history, and math. These domain-specific words are the most difficult of three following types of words (Beck, McKeown, & Kucan, 2008):

- Tier Three—rare, sophisticated, and specific to a subject area (*flavenoids, cholesterol, immunity*).
- Tier Two—important and appear frequently across subject areas (*contains, lower, protect*).
- Tier One—basic high-frequency, usually recognized on sight (*in, and, not, they*).

Of course, both Tier Two and Three words can be multisyllabic and cause problems for many adolescent readers. Tier One words are often one-syllable words and don't usually present adolescents with trouble.

HOW ARE WORDS LEARNED?

Many factors affect word learning, including schema, facility with the English language, availability of supportive models, mentors and coaches, socioeconomic status, wide reading, and the purpose and relevance of learning words (Bromley, 2012; see Figure 7.1). Some words are learned as a result of *vicarious experiences* when students encounter them in casual ways, such as in a conversation or during reading when a term like *soul patch* is used and students discover it is "a small tuft of hair growing below a man's lower lip." Some words are learned as a result of *direct experiences*, such as when students visit a *blog* online and discover it is a "web log or diary written by an individual" (omit the *w*, *e*, and space between *b* and *l*). Other words are learned as a result of *direct instruction* in the word's meaning and orthography. For example, when students are taught that *metamorphosis* is a noun that comes from two Greek roots, *meta* (new) and *morph* (to transform) they learn that the word describes what

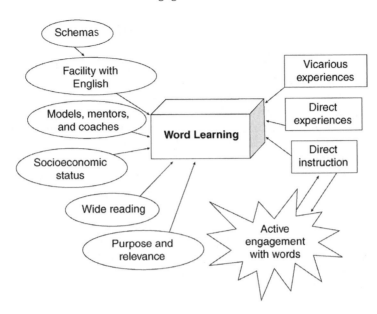

FIGURE 7.1. Factors in word learning.

occurs when a caterpillar hardens into a chrysalis and changes into a butterfly. As well, *metamorphosis* is related to other words like *meta-analysis* and *endomorph*.

While students may learn words as they listen, read, take part in class discussions, keep vocabulary notebooks, use word walls, and consult dictionaries and thesauruses, direct instruction is a key component for learning domain-specific Tier Two and Tier Three words. Both types of words are multisyllabic and need more direct, in-depth instruction in order for students to learn them than do Tier One words. Tier Three words are more difficult than Tier Two words because students often lack prior knowledge/schemas for them, and Tier Three words are also more conceptually dense than Tier Two words.

Teachers who provide direct instruction understand that learning a word occurs in both linguistic and nonlinguistic ways (Paivio, 1990). They teach the linguistic elements of a word (spelling, pronunciation, graphics, meaning, and grammatical function) and reinforce this with the nonlinguistic elements of a word (a visual, auditory, or other sensory image that connects to the word). Teachers who practice sound vocabulary instruction don't just assign, define, and test students on new words. They teach words in a meaningful context, associate new words with related words, repeat new words often, and offer opportunities for active engagement with words (Bromley, 2012; Stahl, 1986).

A RATIONALE FOR ACTIVE ENGAGEMENT

Active engagement in learning includes having students work together to teach each other and learn from each other. "Adolescents already exist in a social world, so it is easy for them to extend this natural talent to their own learning" (Santa, 2007, p. 473). Working together can help struggling and resistant learners connect with school and with other students. In fact, research indicates that when students participate in peer teaching, both observers and teachers experience learning gains (Harmon, 2002). In addition, as a result of peer teaching, the traditional classroom context changes to create a community of learners who share in the learning process (Greenwood, Delquadri, & Hall, 1989).

Active engagement with words involves interacting with others to learn new words, and it involves using metacognitive strategies to analyze and figure out unknown words. When teachers model the following metacognitive strategies with an unfamiliar word from a selection, students learn how to use the strategies on their own:

- Think what makes sense.
- Read the sentence again.
- Skip it and keep reading.
- Think about words that look like it.
- Find a small word or "chunk" you know.
- Sound it out using these words or "chunks."

Once students have seen you model these strategies a few times for them, it's time to ask students to talk about the strategies they use to analyze and learn a new word. Whether students work alone or with peers, giving them the option to share the metacognitive strategies they use can improve learning for everyone and be an effective way for others to learn these strategies. Analyzing new vocabulary, studying difficult words, and teaching these words to each other is an effective practice because students use their own words and they often listen better to each other than they do to their teachers.

STRATEGIES FOR WORD LEARNING

Here are five easy strategies for engaging adolescents actively in interactive work with their peers and/or independent work to learn new words. I have seen these ideas used successfully by middle school teachers with struggling and resistant readers who have trouble learning domain-specific vocabulary.

K-W-L

K-W-L (Know, Want to know, Learn) is a prereading strategy designed to tap students' prior knowledge and use it in preparation for reading new material (Ogle, 1986). But K-W-L is also a handy strategy for introducing new words (Bromley, 2012). When you use K-W-L to introduce vocabulary, you help students set their own purposes for reading. The strategy allows students to cooperatively unlock a new word as they take control of their own learning. For example, you can model K-W-L for students with the word *endangered* (See Figure 7.2).

First, have students brainstorm the "K," or what they think they know about the word. Have them look at the word and its parts or "chunks" and make guesses about how the new word connects to something they already know. Next, move to the "W" and have students think about what they want to know about the word. At this point, you can introduce the word by pronouncing it, giving its meaning, and praising any of the "K" or "W" statements that reveal part or all of the word's pronunciation or meaning. You can also wait until students have read the material that contains the word. Then students can contribute the "L," or what they learned about the word from their reading.

One advantage of K-W-L is that it helps students access information they already have, and it helps them use this prior knowledge as a bridge to learning something new. Second, K-W-L is an easy to remember acronym that students can adopt and then use independently. Third, K-W-L puts learning squarely in the hands of students; thus they have a purpose for figuring out meaning and pronunciation of new words.

Teach–Teach–Trade

Teach–Teach–Trade is a strategy I observed in a seventh-grade biology class where Katie, a special education teacher, was co-teaching with her

K—Think I **Know**	W—**Want** to Know	L—What I **Learned**
It's like dangerous.	Is it a science word?	
Danger means "stay away" or "be careful."	What animal will we read about?	
I've heard of "endangered species."		
Is it about Rodney Dangerfield?		

FIGURE 7.2. K-W-L chart for *endangered*.

content-area peer. The strategy involved students in writing, drawing, reading, talking, teaching, and learning new words to/with each other. Before using Teach–Teach–Trade, be sure to explain the purpose and procedure. Tell students why the strategy will help them learn difficult words and how it works. Katie suggests these directions for teachers who want to try Teach–Teach–Trade (my additional ideas are in italics):

- Identify important words from what students have just read. *(Be sure to find one word for each student.)*
- Write each word on a separate 5″ x 8″ card or half sheet of paper and have each student choose a card.
- On the front of the card, have students define the word and draw a picture to represent the word *(and write the word again)*. On the back of the card have them use the word in one or two sentences (see Figure 7.3). *(Encourage students to use references like their texts, the glossary, and/or notebooks.)*
- *(Check each card for accuracy and have students redo their work if the card includes inaccuracies.)*
- Partner students and have them teach each other their word *(by reading the word, definition, and sentence to the partner).*
- Have students trade cards, find a new partner, and teach the new word to another person *(or have students continue teaching the same word to others).*
- Continue Teach–Teach–Trade until each student has taught a new word to everyone in class *(or if time is an issue, stop part way through and have each student teach their word to the class).*

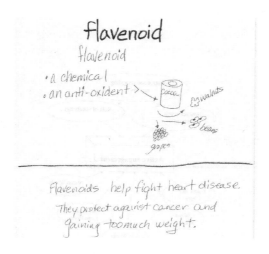

FIGURE 7.3. Example of a Teach–Teach–Trade card.

As I observed Teach–Teach–Trade, I saw students sharing some inaccurate information. Thus I added *"Encourage students to use references"* and *"Check each card for accuracy . . . "* I also saw some students showing the written work and drawing to each other without any oral exchange. Thus I added (. . . *by reading the word, definition, and sentence to the partner*). This reinforces the visual mode with the oral mode. To provide additional reinforcement, rather than having students trade cards, you can have them find a new partner and teach the same word to someone else. Then continue teaching the same word to several students. When each student has taught the word several times, there is a greater likelihood that s/he will make that word his/her own.

Another option includes having students select the words *they* believe are important enough to learn; this gives students choice and voice in the strategy. And to shorten the in-class preparation time, after each student has chosen a word to teach, you can assign completion of the word card as homework. This allows parents to connect with what students are studying in school and gives them an opportunity to be involved in their child's learning.

Teach–Teach–Trade requires students to search for clues to the meaning and pronunciation of new words. Challenge students to be detectives and use bits of text information and meaningful "chunks" of letters first to figure out the new words. The strategy also shows students that meanings for some words are not found in the text, so for these words they can consult the dictionary or glossary. The strategy allows students to work independently first and then together to share orally with each other the information they found. It gives a nonparticipating student a chance to shine, and students see how they can learn from each other.

Teach–Teach–Trade is a novel way to do an end-of-unit review when there are many concepts to relearn and/or review before a writing assignment or a test. The strategy gets students out of their seats and physically moving around the room, which is important. You can also have students keep a vocabulary notebook with the class's words, pictures, sentences, and definitions since writing involves a physical component that reinforces learning. Then students have something concrete to use as they review terms with a partner in school or at home with a family member.

A Word a Day

A Word a Day (AWAD; *www.wordsmith.org/words*) sends a daily e-mail to subscribers with a new word appropriate for middle school and high school students (Bromley, 2012). AWAD includes a vocabulary word, its definition, and pronunciation information including an audio clip, etymology, a usage example, an example of the word used in a sentence, and other interesting tidbits. Each week there is a different theme, and each daily word fits that theme.

Students can learn much about words independently when they subscribe to this website. Or you can subscribe and share a word a day on a bulletin board or a special AWAD chart. Recently, when the theme was *toponyms* and *eponyms*, I learned: "They are words derived from places or people, real and fictional, from history and mythology. They are known as *toponyms* and *eponyms,* from Greek *topo-* (place) + *-onym* (name), and *epi-* (upon) + *-onym* (name). This week we'll see five words coined after the names of people and places."

The first word posted on Monday as part of that theme was *serendipity*. It is a Tier Three word worth teaching to middle grade students. It is "a term used by scientists when they make an accidental discovery leading to something important." For example, in an explanation of serendipity on Wikipedia (*www.wikipedia.com*), the story of Newton's theory of gravity is attributed to the serendipitous event he witnessed as he sat under an apple tree and saw an apple fall straight to the ground.

You can use the information from AWAD to deepen students' understanding of these words. For example, you can tell students that *serendipity* is pronounced *ser-uhn-DIP-i-tee* and it means "The faculty of making fortunate discoveries by chance." AWAD reports that *serendipity* comes from the fairy tale "The Three Princes of Serendip," in which the princes supposedly made happy discoveries they were not looking for. The word's origin is from Persian *sarandip* (Sri Lanka) and from Arabic *sarandib,* and it was first used in 1754.

Within the AWAD website, students can also explore a word like *serendipity* by clicking on a visual thesaurus embedded there. This visual display of synonyms can make word meanings easier to remember than some of the etymology information. For example, students can see a "Think Map" or graphic there that shows *serendipity* related to "good luck," "fluke," and "good fortune." This visual display lets students explore the connections among words and their relationships to each other. Reproducing a concept map or visual web (see Figure 7.4) with synonyms and discussing the map with students is an excellent way to reinforce the word and its meanings visually and orally. You might also have several students research the word and share other examples of serendipitous findings in science.

Or you can combine AWAD with K-W-L to help students learn the word. For example, in a K column on the K-W-L chart, a student might notice that *seren-* looks like *serene* and identify it as meaning "calm" or "placid." Another student might note that the first part of the word is spelled almost like *siren*. While these connections may or may not be fruitful in learning the meaning of *serendipity*, they provide an opportunity for

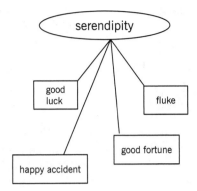

FIGURE 7.4. A Word a Day concept map for *serendipity*.

students to tap their prior knowledge, and these connections also give you a way to teach or reinforce some Tier Two words.

One advantage of having students subscribe individually to AWAD, or using it yourself as a teacher, is that students typically are introduced to multisyllabic words. Second, these are the words that are difficult for struggling and resistant readers because the words often include Greek or Latin roots. In fact, the vocabulary in science, social studies, and math in most middle school text books and other assigned reading often contains Greek or Latin roots. The many multisyllabic technical terms found in this reading makes content-area learning difficult.

All sorts of interesting word knowledge are available from AWAD (Bromley, 2012). Recently, when "text messaging" was a theme, I learned that this kind of language is not a new phenomenon. Hundreds of years ago, English poets such as Charles Bombaugh used numbers and the sounds of letters to represent words. In 1867, 130 years before mobile phone messaging, Bombaugh used the phrases in one of his poems, "I wrote 2 U B 4" and "He says he loves U 2 X S/U R virtuous and Y's." ("He says he loves you to excess. You are virtuous and wise.")

Root Words

We do not always do a good job of teaching middle school students about the roots of English. It may be that middle school teachers believe students learned about these roots in elementary school. Or some middle school teachers may teach vocabulary by giving students definitions, rather than attending to deep conceptual meanings, building students' independent word learning skills, and teaching them about roots. At any rate, "Middle school students have much yet to learn about the structure of words" (Ivey

& Broaddus, 2000, p. 74). And creating visual displays of related words with similar roots can help build students' vocabularies through associations.

Because a good portion of the English language has Greek and Latin origins, it is essential to familiarize struggling and resistant readers with the spelling and meanings of some of the most often appearing roots and affixes (Figure 7.5) (Bromley, 2012). In fact, students can infer meanings of 60% of the multisyllabic words they meet by analyzing word parts (Nagy & Anderson, 1984). So knowing the meaning of a prefix, suffix, or root makes it easier to figure out the meanings of other words that contain those roots. Here are some ideas for teaching Greek and Latin roots:

- On the Internet, find a dictionary of Greek and Latin roots that includes roots, meanings, and example words. Print copies for students or have them bookmark a site like *english.glendale.cc.ca.us* that is an easily accessible resource to refer to when meeting new words.
- Teach students to analyze morphemes and determine the meanings of roots and affixes because they give clues to the meanings of

Most Common Prefixes			
un- (not, opposite)	under- (too little)	pre- (before)	semi- (half)
re- (again)	in-, im- (in ,into)	inter- (between, among)	super- (above)
over- (too much)	mis- (wrongly)	anti- (against)	mid- (middle)
in-, im-, ir-, il- (not)	non- (not)	en-, em- (cause to)	trans- (across)
dis- (not, opposite)	sub- (under)	ex- (out)	de- (away, from)
com- (together, with)			

Most Common Suffixes			
-s (plural)	-ible, able (can be done)	-ity, y (state of)	-ness (state of)
-ed (past tense)	-al, -ial (having characteristics)	-less (without)	-er, -or (person)
-ing (present tense)	-y (characterized by)	-en (made of)	-ion, -tion (act)
-ly (characteristic)	-ful (full of)	-ment (action)	-est (most)

Common Latin and Greek Roots			
audi (hear)	spect (see)	bio (life)	photo (light)
dict (speak)	struct (build)	graph (written, drawn)	scope (see)
port (carry)	tract (pull, drag)	hydro (water)	tele (distant)
rupt (break)	vis (see)	meter (measure)	ology (study of)
auto (self)	bio (life)	scrib/script (write)	cred (believe)

FIGURE 7.5. Common roots and affixes in English.

words. For example, *audi-* means "hear," so students can infer the meanings for *audible, auditorium,* and *audience.*

- Give students a number of words with the same root (e.g., *-rupt*), and the meaning "to break." Then have them extend this knowledge and figure out the meanings of *disrupt* (to break apart), *interrupt* (to insert words between someone's words; *inter-* means "between or among"), *disruption* (a noun since *-ion* is added), *eruption* (to blow up).
- For Bell Work, which is a brief activity students engage in when the bell rings to begin class (Moore & Hinchman, 2006), put two or three multisyllabic words on the board. Words can be real (e.g., *photosynthesis* or *hypotenuse*), or nonsense words you and/or student(s) make up (e.g., *pyrgamy, contrapent, tetrathan*). Then have students form pairs to determine each word's meaning by analyzing its morphemes.
- Create a Word Wall in your classroom to reinforce learning roots and derivatives. List word parts alphabetically, or draw a graphic organizer like a Root Word Web using a root vegetable such as a carrot with leaves (see Figure 7.6). Then invite students to add other words that contain that root. When everyone contributes, students can see how many other related words they can now infer meanings for.

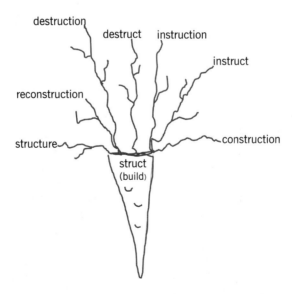

FIGURE 7.6. Example of a Root Word Web for *struct.*

- Have each student make a Portable Dictionary from a file folder by dividing the inside of the folder into boxes where students list words with the same word part in a square. Have students review the multisyllabic words or their file folder dictionary lists with partners during "Bell Work."

Teaching these Greek and Latin word parts, how to spell them, pronounce them, and what they mean can reap huge rewards in the number of Tier Two and Tier Three words struggling and resistant readers understand independently. Remember, the linguistic and nonlinguistic aspects of words including graphics and visual pictures often help cement these words and their roots in students' memories.

Digital Words

The CCSS (NGA & CCSSO, 2010) and the International Reading Association's (IRA) position statement *Integrating Literacy and Technology in the Curriculum* (IRA, 2012) suggest that full literacy in today's world includes proficiency in technology use. Technology and the digital world often appeal to unmotivated students who are disengaged from learning.

Making meaning by combining visual and verbal modes through technology is termed multimodality. In fact, we are told that "many literacy educators have tapped multimodality because it often recasts students who are labeled 'at risk . . . as students 'of promise' " (Siegel, 2012, p. 674). So there is a strong rationale for using multimodal practices in teaching. Some examples follow:

- Have students use PowerPoint to create slides that depict new words. Then they can teach classmates the meaning and pronunciation of a word like *economy* (see Figure 7.7). With PowerPoint, a seventh grader made the dollar sign pulsate, which gave the slide a 3-D quality.
- Let students visit Wordle (*www.wordle.net*), where they can cut and paste or type the text from their content reading to create a "splash" of words. The most often used words appear largest and may be the most important to learn. Students can change colors, fonts, styles, and languages as well as omit common Tier One words.
- Invite partners to collaborate as they use Inspiration (*www.inspiration.com*) to create an organizer that shows words that contain for example, the root -*tract* (see Figure 7.8). Students can use clip art and an online dictionary before printing their work and sharing it perhaps in a handout with classmates.
- Pair students to work together to explore multimedia authoring tools like Animoto (*www.animoto.com*) and Glogster (*www.*

"economy"—the study of money

Economists are scientists who watch and predict
how money affects people (and vice versa).

FIGURE 7.7. Example of a PowerPoint slide for *economy*.

glogster.com). These programs will inspire your students, who will enjoy using them to teach their peers what they have learned about difficult vocabulary. The websites reinforce vocabulary by creating visual representations of words that include graphics and illustrations.

Middle school students enjoy working together to explore digital creations that represent new and difficult Tier Three words multimodally. "By harnessing their fascination and familiarity with multimedia, educators are striving to re-engage students—many of whom are left cold by traditional text-based learning" (Adams, 2005). You can have students design

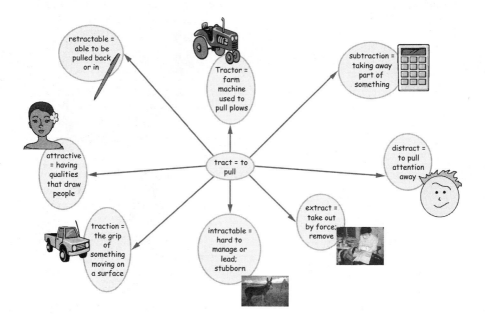

FIGURE 7.8. Example of an Inspiration organizer for *tract*.

multimedia presentations and digital video clips to represent new vocabulary and then teach the new words to classmates. The active engagement students experience when they work with peers to create Digital Words makes it challenging and fun for all students to learn new vocabulary and practice technology skills.

CONCLUSION

Knowing a word well means understanding the word's meaning, pronunciation, and spelling when it is heard and read, as well as using the word correctly in speaking and writing. Actively engaging students with new words and with each other as they learn vocabulary can promote learning words well. Peer interactions also build a positive classroom environment and establish a community of learners who support each other.

Direct instruction that includes active engagement is important when helping struggling and resistant middle school readers learn to meet the heavy vocabulary load in content-area materials. First, we need to teach students to search text and their prior knowledge for clues to a new word's meaning. Second, we need to teach students to identify known word parts that will help them unlock meaning and pronunciation. Judicious use of strategies like those provided in this chapter that deepen students' understanding of vocabulary is important for students to be able to read increasingly complex text independently, which is a goal of the CCSS.

DISCUSSION AND ACTIVITIES

1. For a strategy to be used successfully by all teachers and students across grade levels and curriculum areas, there often needs to be a schoolwide commitment. How would you establish a schoolwide initiative for improving students' vocabulary? How would you introduce it and what steps would you take to ensure its success?

2. What do you think the term *word consciousness* means? Why do you think it might be important for both teachers and students to possess word consciousness? As a teacher, how would you act if you were intent upon fostering word consciousness?

3. What does a best-practice vocabulary teacher look like? What are the characteristics that set this teacher apart from a teacher who is not committed to the notion that vocabulary and comprehension go hand in hand? List five characteristics and share your ideas with someone.

4. "The difference between a word and the right word is like the difference between a lightning bug and lightning" (Mark Twain, 1888). Is it important to teach this concept to middle school students? How would you teach it to

a seventh-grade writing class in a mini-lesson? How would you engage their prior knowledge? What examples might you use? How would you have students apply the idea?

REFERENCES

Adams, L. (2005). The digitization of learning. *T.H.E. Journal.* Retrieved from *www.thejournal.com/articles/17321.*

Allington, R. (2006). *What really matters for struggling readers: Designing research-based programs* (2nd ed.). Boston: Allyn & Bacon.

Animoto. Retrieved from *www.animoto.com.*

A Word a Day (AWAD). Retrieved from *www.wordsmith.org.*

Beck, I. L., McKeown, M. G., & Kucan, L. (2008). *Creating robust vocabulary: Frequently asked questions and extended examples.* New York: Guilford Press.

Bromley, K. (2007). Nine things every teacher should know about words and vocabulary instruction. *Journal of Adolescent and Adult Literacy, 50*(7), 528–539.

Bromley, K. (2012). *The next step in vocabulary instruction.* New York: Scholastic.

Cunningham, P. M. (2009). *What really matters in vocabulary: Research-based practices across the curriculum.* Boston: Allyn & Bacon.

Cunningham, P. M., & Cunningham, J. W. (2010). *What really matters in writing: Research-based practices across the elementary curriculum.* Boston: Allyn & Bacon.

Fuchs, L. S., Fuchs, D., Hosp, M. K., & Jenkins, J.R. (2001). Oral reading fluency as an indicator of reading competence: A theoretical, empirical, and historical analysis. *Scientific Studies of Reading, 5*(3), 239–256.

Glogster. Retrieved from *www.glogster.com.*

Greek and Latin roots. Retrieved from *http://english.glendale.cc.ca.us/roots. dict.html.*

Greenwood, C. R., Delquadri, J. C., & Hall, R. V. (1989). Longitudinal effects of classwide peer tutoring. *Journal of Educational Psychology, 81,* 371–383.

Harmon, J. M. (2002).Teaching independent word learning strategies to struggling readers in facilitated peer dialogues. *Journal of Adolescent and adult literacy, 45*(97), 606–616.

Inspiration. Retrieved from *www.inspiration.com.*

International Reading Association. (2012). *Integrating literacy and technology in the curriculum.* Position statement of the International Reading Association. Newark, DE: Author. Retrieved from *www.reading.org/downloads/positions/ps1048_technology.pdf.*

Ivey, G., & Broaddus, K. (2000). Tailoring the fit: Reading instruction and middle school readers. *Journal of Adolescent and Adult Literacy, 54*(1), 68–78.

Lenters, K. (2006). Resistance, struggle and the adolescent reader. *Journal of Adolescent and Adult Literacy, 52*(2), 136–146.

Moore, D. W., & Hinchman, K. A. (2006). *Teaching adolescents who struggle with reading: Practical strategies.* Boston: Allyn & Bacon-Pearson.

Nagy, W. E., & Anderson, R. C. (1984). How many words are there in printed school English? *Reading Research Quarterly, 19*(3), 304–330.

Nagy, W., & Scott, J. (2000). Vocabulary processes. In M. L. Kamil, P. B. Mosenthal, P. D. Pearson, & R. Barr (Eds.), *Handbook of reading research* (Vol. 3, pp. 269–284). Mahwah, NJ: Erlbaum.

National Center for Education Statistics. (2011). *National assessment of educational progress: The nation's report card.* Washington, DC: Institutes for Education Sciences. Retrieved from *http://nces.ed.gov/nationsreportcard.*

National Governors Association Center for Best Practices & Council of Chief State School Officers. (2010). *Common Core State Standards in English Language Arts and Literacy.* Washington, DC: Author. Retrieved from *www.corestandards.org.*

Ogle, D. (1986). K-W-L: A teaching model that develops active reading of expository text. *The Reading Teacher, 39,* 564–570.

Paivio, A. (1990). *Mental representations: A dual coding approach.* New York: Oxford University Press.

Pressley, M. (2002). Comprehension instruction: What makes sense now, what might make sense soon. *Reading online, 5*(2). Retrieved from *www.readingonline.org/articles/art_index.asp?HREF=/articles/handbook/pressley/index.html.*

Samuels, S. J. (2002). Reading fluency: Its development and assessment. In A. E. Farstrup & S. J. Samuels (Eds.), *What research has to say about reading instruction* (3rd ed., pp. 166–183). Newark, DE: International Reading Association.

Santa, C. M. (2007). A vision for adolescent literacy: Ours or theirs? *Journal of Adolescent and Adult Literacy, 49*(6), 466–478.

Shanahan, T., Fisher, D., & Frey, N. (2012). The challenge of challenging text. *Educational Leadership. 69*(6), 58–62.

Siegel, M. (2012). New times for multimodality? Confronting the accountability culture. *Journal of Adolescent and Adult Literacy, 55*(8), 671–744.

Stahl, S. (1986). Three principles of effective vocabulary instruction. *Journal of Reading, 29*(4), 662–668.

Stahl, S., & Fairbanks, M. M. (1986). The effects of vocabulary instruction: A model-based meta-analysis. *Review of Educational Research, 56*(1), 72–110.

Wikipedia. Retrieved from *www.wikipedia.com.*

Wordle. Retrieved from *www.wordle.net.*

CHAPTER 8

Comprehension in Secondary Schools

Douglas Fisher
Nancy Frey

This chapter:

- Explores the role of disciplinary content and students' reading of content-area texts.

- Identifies the various ways in which a text can be complex so that teachers can target their instruction on aspects of text complexity.

- Describes the role of vocabulary in comprehension and understanding of texts.

- Outlines aspects of instruction required for students to comprehend at high levels.

As noted on the Common Core State Standards (CCSS; National Governors Association Center for Best Practices & Council of Chief State School Officers, 2010), students who are college and career ready in reading, writing, speaking, listening, and language share several characteristics. Specifically, they:

- Demonstrate independence.
- Build strong content knowledge.
- Respond to the varying demands of audience, task, purpose, and discipline.
- Comprehend as well as critique.

- Value evidence.
- Use technology and digital media strategically and capably.
- Come to understand other perspectives and cultures. (p. 7)

Schooling prior to the middle grades focuses on developing students' literacy skills. In middle school students explore disciplinary content, and in high school students must demonstrate their competency in many different content areas. In high school, students collect grades, grade point averages, and credits necessary to graduate and to be admitted into college. They also hone the technical and interpersonal skills that are necessary for success in life. Furthermore, the high school years are a time when students want to explore their independence and begin to distance themselves from adults and focus increasingly on their peers.

Above all, the secondary school years are devoted to knowledge building. Students deepen and extend their understanding of concepts and topics that are specific to the various disciplines that they study, from algebra and biology to history and vocational classes. More to the point, secondary students engage in the cognitive and metacognitive processes that are unique to each discipline, such as the ability to factor sourcing information and corroborating evidence when analyzing a historical document (Wineburg, 1991), or using formal reasoning to query the results of a scientific article (Aufschnaiter, Erduran, Osborne, & Simon, 2008).

A significant portion of knowledge building is accomplished through interactions with texts, which means that deep comprehension is essential. Students face increasingly complex print and digital texts that may be dense, draw on substantial background knowledge, and offer multiple layers of meaning. Skimming the surface is inadequate, and yet many learners don't even realize when they need to mine the text for insights that are not readily apparent in a first reading. In this chapter, we address the demands that complex texts place on adolescents. This includes disciplinary and vocabulary knowledge that increases the need for students to read for deep meaning. We also review instructional practices that support deep comprehension, including close reading and annotation of texts.

CONTENT IS KEY

Secondary school students face a challenge the moment they walk into a typical school: their experiences are unnaturally segmented into silos of information. Without meaning to, school schedules unintentionally convey a falsehood, namely that learning is neatly divided into finite blocks of time. Therefore, many students have little experience with applying their knowledge of history, for instance, when reading a poem in English. The do not use their scientific knowledge while writing argumentatively.

Comprehension requires that students marshal what they know from a range of experiences and disciplines to fully understand texts.

And make no mistake: Text is central in the secondary school classroom. The CCSS have certainly located text at the center of the curriculum, but this refocusing has been gaining traction for a number of years. Advances in our understanding of disciplinary literacy (e.g., Shanahan & Shanahan, 2008), adolescent English learners (e.g., Short & Fitzsimmons, 2007), and college and career readiness (e.g., Achieve, 2012) have heralded a return to meaningful reading and discussion of text. Students in grades 6–12 utilize a balance of informational texts and narrative ones across the school day, and secondary school teachers are not in the business of teaching reading—they teach content. But in order to teach for understanding of the written content, educators must understand how their texts work and engage students with text-dependent questions that cause them to consider concepts they may have overlooked. Discussion is critical, as comprehension is strengthened in the company of the ideas of others. Therefore, it is essential to integrate academic language into all aspects of instruction. In the next section, we examine how each of these instructional factors—texts, questions, and discussion—propel comprehension.

The Nature of Texts

During the secondary school years, students are expected to significantly increase the amount of informational text they consume across the school day. This has implications for the English classroom, where the curriculum is primarily literary (stories, dramas, poems). While English educators should not eliminate literary works from the curriculum, there should be a purposeful attention to informational texts that develop students' essential cultural and historical knowledge of. Examples of such informational texts include comparative literature essays, memoirs, speeches by historical figures, and literary criticisms. Science, history, and technical subjects classes focus on expository texts, including primary and secondary source documents, as well as a wide range of text types that students will encounter in the world, such as news articles, memos, technical manuals, editorial cartoons, reports, public documents, and advertisements. That is not to say that a history teacher would not use a poem to facilitate students' understanding of the content or that a science teacher would not use an essay. For example, a U.S. history teacher may use the poem "In Flanders Field" (McCrae, 1915) to focus students on various aspects of World War I, and a science teacher may use an essay from Stephen Jay Gould to discuss natural selection.

It is important to note that secondary school students should be reading appropriately complex texts, as determined by quantitative and qualitative measures. The CCSS have positioned text complexity at the heart of curricular discussions. The 6–8 band is defined quantitatively as 925–1186 (Lexile range), the 9–10 band is defined as 1050–1335L, and the 11–12 band is 1185–1385L. These bands are notably higher than has been commonly expected among high school students and reinforce the need for consistent academic emphasis as students are regularly challenged to read, discuss, and analyze complex texts accompanied by meaningful teacher instruction. The texts selected for instruction should challenge students' thinking. As one consideration, teachers in grades 6–12 should consider the quantitative measure of the text. In addition, they should consider the qualitative factors that contribute to a given text's complexity, which can range from the structure of the text to the role of the narrator to the genre or even the graphic and visual information used by the author. Figure 8.1 contains a rubric for qualitatively assessing a piece of text across 13 factors that can contribute to a text's complexity. Those factors that weigh more heavily become the teaching points for lessons involving the selected reading.

For example, an analysis of Anna Quindlen's (2001) essay "A Quilt of a Country" suggests that several factors contribute to the complexity of the text: the levels of meaning, density, text structure, and background knowledge. These aspects of text complexity would then be appropriate teaching points for students in grade 10 as they read and discuss the essay. Finally, teachers should evaluate the tasks students will be asked to complete relative to the text in making their final selections.

Questioning to Deepen Comprehension

Simply surrounding students with complex texts and then expecting something to happen is magical thinking—if that was all that was necessary, we could merely send students to the school library and be done with it. But assigning students to independently read, think about, and then write about a complex text is no better. Quality questions are one way that teachers can check students' understanding of the text. Questions can also facilitate students' search for evidence and their need to return to the text to deepen their understanding. Teachers take an active role in developing and deepening students' comprehension by asking questions that cause them to consult the text again, resulting in multiple readings of the same text. In other words, these text-dependent questions provide students with a purpose for rereading, which is critical for understanding complex texts.

While the use of text-dependent questions may seem obvious, in fact too many questions are text independent and therefore take students too quickly away from the text. Asking students how they would vote if they were present for the Emancipation Proclamation in 1865 is premature when they know little about the document itself. On the other hand, students are able to offer a more measured and thoughtful response when

Score	3 pts (Stretch):	2 pts (Grade Level):	1 pt (Comfortable):
	Texts that would stretch a reader and/or require instruction	Texts that require grade-appropriate skills	Texts that are comfortable and/or build background, fluency, and skills
Levels of Meaning and Purpose			
Density and complexity	Significant density and complexity, with multiple levels of meaning; meanings may be more ambiguous	Single, but more complex or abstract level of meaning; some meanings are stated, while others are left to the reader to identify	Single and literal levels of meaning; meaning is explicitly stated
Figurative language	Figurative language plays a significant role in identifying the meaning of the text; more sophisticated figurative language is used (irony and satire, allusions, archaic or less familiar symbolism); the reader is left to interpret these meanings	Figurative language such as imagery, metaphors, symbolism, and personification are used to make connections within the text to more explicit information, and readers are supported in understanding these language devices through examples and explanations	Limited use of symbolism, metaphors, and poetic language that allude to other unstated concepts; language is explicit and relies on literal interpretations
Purpose	Purpose is deliberately withheld from the reader, who must use other interpretative skills to identify it	Purpose is implied but is easily identified based on title or context	Purpose or main idea is directly and explicitly stated at the beginning of the reading
Structure			
Genre	Genre is unfamiliar or bends and expands the rules for the genre	Genre is either unfamiliar but is a reasonable example of it *or* it is a familiar genre that bends and expands the rules for the genre	Genre is familiar and the text is consistent with the elements of that genre
Organization	Organization distorts time or sequence in a deliberate effort to delay the reader's full understanding of the plot, process, or set of concepts; may include significant flashbacks, foreshadowing, or shifting perspectives	Organization adheres to most conventions, but digresses on occasion to temporarily shift the reader's focus to another point of view, event, time, or place, before returning to the main idea or topic	Organization is conventional, sequential, or chronological, with clear signals and transitions to lead the reader through a story, process, or set of concepts

FIGURE 8.1. (*continued*)

FIGURE 8.1. (*continued*)

Score	3 pts (Stretch):	2 pts (Grade Level):	1 pt (Comfortable):
Narration	Unreliable narrator provides a distorted or limited view to the reader; the reader must use other clues to deduce the truth; multiple narrators provide conflicting information; shifting points of view keep the reader guessing	Third-person limited or first-person narration provides accurate, but limited perspectives or viewpoints	Third-person omniscient narration or an authoritative and credible voice provides an appropriate level of detail and keeps little hidden from the view of the reader
Text features and graphics	Limited use of text features to organize information and guide the reader; information in the graphics are not repeated in the main part of the text, but are essential for understanding the text	Wider array of text features includes margin notes, diagrams, graphs, font changes, and other devices that compete for the reader's attention; graphics and visuals are used to augment and illustrate information in the main part of the text	Text features (e.g., bold and italicized words, headings and subheadings) organize information explicitly and guide the reader; graphics or illustrations may be present but are not necessary to understand the main part of the text
Language Conventionality and Clarity			
Standard English and variations	The text includes significant and multiple styles of English and its variations, and these are unfamiliar to the reader	Some distance exists between the reader's linguistic base and the language conventions used in the text; the vernacular used is unfamiliar to the reader	Language closely adheres to the reader's linguistic base
Register	Archaic, formal, domain-specific, or scholarly register	Register is consultative or formal and may be academic but acknowledges the developmental level of the reader	Register is casual and familiar
Knowledge Demands			
Background knowledge	The text places demands on the reader that extend far beyond one's experiences and provides little in the way of explanation of these divergent experiences	There is distance between the reader's experiences and those in the text, but there is acknowledgement of these divergent experiences, and sufficient explanation to bridge these gaps	The text contains content that closely matches the reader's life experiences

Score	3 pts (Stretch):	2 pts (Grade Level):	1 pt (Comfortable):
Prior knowledge	Specialized or technical content knowledge is presumed, and little in the way of review or explanation of these concepts is present in the text	Subject-specific knowledge is required, but the text augments this with review or summary of this information	Prior knowledge needed to understand the text is familiar and draws on a solid foundation of practical, general and academic learning
Cultural knowledge	Text relies on extensive or unfamiliar intertextuality and uses artifacts and symbols that reference archaic or historical cultures	Text primarily references contemporary and popular culture to anchor explanations for new knowledge; intertextuality is used more extensively but is mostly familiar to the reader	The reader uses familiar cultural templates to understand the text; limited or familiar intertextuality
Vocabulary knowledge	Vocabulary demand is extensive, domain specific, and representative of complex ideas; the text offers little in the way of context clues to support the reader	Vocabulary draws on domain-specific, general academic, and multiple-meaning words, with text supports to guide the reader's correct interpretations of their meanings; the vocabulary used represents familiar concepts and ideas	Vocabulary is controlled and uses the most commonly held meanings; multiple meaning words are used in a limited fashion

FIGURE 8.1. Qualitative measures of text complexity. From Fisher, Frey, and Lapp (2012, pp. 47–48). Copyright 2012 by the International Reading Association. Reprinted by permission.

they are first deeply grounded in the text. Table 8.1 provides examples of text-dependent and text-independent questions for *A Quilt of a Country* by Anna Quindlen.

Text-based Discussions

Discussion drives learning in the high school classroom. Long gone are the days when teaching meant lectures, with little exchange between teacher and learner. The text-dependent questions developed by the teacher should not be viewed as homework assignments, but rather as a means to frame extended discussion in the classroom. Discussion about texts is valued by adolescents, who recognize it as a pathway to understanding text (Alvermann et al., 1996). Discussion can and should also occur among small groups of students, especially to increase participation and active learning.

TABLE 8.1. Examples of Text-Dependent and Text-Independent Questions for "A Quilt of a Country," by Anna Quindlen

Text-dependent questions	Text-independent questions
• "What is the main idea of the essay? What is the author's major idea?"	• "What surprised you in the essay?"
• "Where are three examples of freedom and oppression in the essay?"	• "What do you love about America?"
• "What other juxtapositions does our author use?"	• "What are some additional failures of America that the author could have included?"
• "What role does the word *conundrum* play in this essay?"	• "What are some addition successes of America that the author could have included?"
• "What is the structure of the essay? How does the author build her argument?"	• "What do you think would be a patriotic act?"
• "Look at the date of this essay, and then let's talk about why the author might have written it."	
• "Whose side of the story is not being told? How do you know?"	
• "What does the author believe about the benefits and limitations of tolerance?"	
• "To quote, the author says, 'These are the representatives of a mongrel nation that somehow, at times like this, has one spirit.' What does that mean and what evidence does she provide for this statement?"	
• "How does the author's perspective change from the time when she wrote 'The Melting Pot'?"	

Educators understand the need for collaboration and decision-making opportunities among students, who will soon be applying these skills in their careers or college classrooms. The text-based questions posed to groups can offer interesting tasks and challenge students to draw on their resources. More extended small-group discussion around a common piece of text requires members to arrive prepared. In addition, they must establish goals and deadlines for task completion, while applying the rules and procedures that govern work groups, such as reaching consensus, listening to opposing ideas, and moving the group forward when needed. Frequent use of extended small-group discussion further positions students to take ownership for building one another's understanding as they interpret a text.

These instructional factors—text selection, text-dependent questioning, and text-based discussion—frame lesson development. But it is language that undergirds these instructional factors. In the next section, we discuss why vocabulary is an essential component of comprehension.

VOCABULARY IS VITAL

When children are emergent readers in their first years of school, they learn how to break the code to unlock the printed word. They learn the 44 sounds of the English language, called phonemes, and the alphabetic principles that represent these sounds on paper, called phonics. In due time they string the sounds and letters together more fluidly and in a short time they learn to recognize the code automatically, freeing up attention to focus on meaning (LaBerge & Samuels, 1974). These early code-based processes are constrained, in the sense that there is an end point at which you are finished; in other words, once you know the phonemes and their representations, you're done. But comprehension and vocabulary are unconstrained; that is, we all continue to improve across a lifetime (Paris, 2005).

The evidence of the importance of vocabulary knowledge for comprehension is extensive. Vocabulary knowledge is a strong predictor of the reader's comprehension abilities (Baumann, Kame'enui, & Ash, 2003). As well, vocabulary use in text is a good indicator of how difficult a reading may be (Stahl, 2003). The link is an obvious one. When students understand the terminology of a discipline or topic, they are more likely to understand a reading containing that vocabulary.

The explosion of vocabulary words and phrases accelerates in secondary school, and it is essential that students be equipped with the tools they need to resolve unknown terms without teacher support. Readers frequently encounter unknown or partially understood vocabulary words and phrases when reading complex text. But the simplistic advice to skip the confusing portion and hope that the context will give you a clue is inadequate. After all, how many times can one skip forward before the text is rendered meaningless? High school students need a multipronged problem-solving process in order to determine the meaning of unknown words and phrases. We advocate teaching students how to look inside and outside of confusing words in the text (Fisher & Frey, 2008). This problem-solving process includes looking inside the word to perform a structural analysis, especially in noting how affixes, roots, and bases can reveal meaning. Readers and listeners also look outside the word to consider the contextual clues that might further corroborate meaning. The third method is to consult outside resources, especially dictionaries and glossaries, which also provide more information regarding etymology and usage:

- Teach students to look inside a word by analyzing its structure. Morphological and derivational clues can sometimes be located within an unfamiliar word. For instance, the meaning of the word *turbid* is more clear when *turb-* is understood to mean agitated or stirred up. Words such as *disturbance*, *perturbed*, and *turbulent* share this root.
- Not all words and phrases are made clear through structural analysis, so that is when context can be helpful. For example, idioms are rarely unlocked by examining the structure. A character with *egg on her face* isn't someone who is a messy eater. By examining the context in which the idiom was used, a student may determine that the character was embarrassed by a turn of events.
- Looking outside an unknown word or phrase at the context isn't foolproof, either. In these cases, we encourage students to look further outside toward resources such as glossaries, dictionaries, and even by asking others.

Vocabulary knowledge extends beyond local meaning of a sentence or paragraph; it provides insight into how the text works more broadly. The craft and structure of a text is understood in part by being mindful of the choices the writer makes in word selection. Students are challenged to view the text as a whole in order to understand the perspectives of the writer, as in a historical document, or the concepts related in a scientific article or technical reading. Writers establish mood and tone by artful selection of words and phrases and link them to rhetorical purposes, especially in history. For instance, consider the use of the word *their* in the first sentence of the Declaration of Independence: "We hold these truths to be self-evident, that all men are created equal, that they are endowed, by *their* Creator with certain inalienable Rights, that among these are Life, Liberty, and the pursuit of Happiness." *Their,* not *the.* One word subtly shifts the meaning to acknowledge the existence of more than one belief system. Seemingly small word choices can profoundly affect analysis and interpretation of a reading.

Vocabulary is treated differently in the science and technical subjects, especially as it relates to the use of symbols and the role of discipline-specific vocabulary and the way words and phrases influence how the information in a text is presented to the reader. The author's purpose is also addressed quite differently, given that most scientific texts are not constructed with controversy in mind. Instead, the emphasis is on the author's use of explication. As students progress through high school, they analyze vocabulary use in order to detect the gaps in knowledge that explanation cannot fully address.

KEY INSTRUCTIONAL PRACTICES

There are a number of instructional practices that have been useful in improving reading comprehension, chief among these a gradual release of responsibility (Pearson & Gallagher, 1983). As the content becomes increasingly sophisticated and complicated, students need to be guided to higher levels of understanding and performance by a skilled, expert teacher. Teachers in grades 6–12 should be familiar with focused instruction, guided instruction, collaborative learning, and independent learning as they design lessons. A few of the aspects of high–quality core instruction bear additional attention for students in middle and high school.

Purpose for Learning

Adolescents want to know why they have to learn specific things. They want to know whether the content of the class will help them out later in life, and whether they will ever use the information that is being presented to them. It's a fair question, and one that should be addressed in every lesson. Having a purpose for learning focuses student attention, alerts them to key ideas and details, and ensures that the content is relevant. It's this last point that is so important. A purposeful classroom has an objective (what we will learn today), as well as relevance (why we will learn this). Sometimes relevance is established because students will need to use the information outside the classroom, either in their daily life, at college, or at work. Other times, relevance is established because the content allows the student to learn about him- or herself, such as how to solve problems or compose effective arguments. And at still other times, relevance is established when students come to understand that learning contributes to one's confidence and competence. In other words, sometimes we learn things because it's fun and interesting. Establishing a purpose and building relevancy aids in comprehension by motivating students to attend to the text and providing them with a learning target for the lesson.

Modeling

In middle and high school, much of the content is very sophisticated and students need to apprentice into the thinking of an expert. Because thinking is invisible, students need to experience their teachers' thinking in other ways. Often this is accomplished as teachers model their thinking during reading. Essentially, the teacher explains his or her thinking using "I" statements rather than *you* directives. For example, rather than saying "First you have to figure out whether you can make the bases equal. If you can make them equal, then you know that the exponents can be made equal" a teacher modeling might say, "When I see two bases with exponents equal to each other, I first ask myself whether I can make the bases equal. I do this because I know that if the bases are equal, or can be made equal, then the exponents have to be equal." In addition, the teacher integrates metacognition into the modeling by providing the reasons, rationale, or explanation for the statements. In essence, the teacher attempts to open up his or her brain and describe the processes that are used to complete the task at hand, in this case comprehending a complex text. Most modeling events are brief glimpses into the thinking required to reach understanding. Modeling allows students to observe the problem-solving process of other human beings.

Close Reading

Close reading is a type of guided instruction in which students explore a complex and worthy text, mining it for all types of information. Close readings are done with short passages, either stand-alone texts or strategically selected sections of a longer text. Typically the students encounter the text first, with limited frontloading or pretaught vocabulary. That is not to say that the teacher does not scaffold instruction, but rather that students meet the text and attempt to make some meaning from it, knowing that they will return to the text several times. There are several keys to an effective close reading.

Repeated Reading

Students read the selected text several times, often with different purposes or to respond to different questions. In some cases, the teacher also reads the text aloud or students read sections to their peers. Repeated reading has been an effective way to improve comprehension and close readings are a way to ensure that students get instructional opportunities to reread for meaning. In their seminal text, *How to Read a Book*, Adler and Van Doren (1940/1972) built a case for engaging in repeated readings with accompanying annotation:

> Why is marking a book indispensable to reading it? First, it keeps you awake—merely conscious, but wide awake. Second, reading, if active, is thinking, and thinking tends to express itself in words, spoken or written. The person who says he knows what he thinks, but cannot express it, usually does not know what he thinks. Third, writing your reactions down helps you remember the thoughts of the author. (p. 49)

Annotation

Ideally, students write on the text, underlining key points and writing in the margins. Sometimes this is not practical and students write on bookmarks, self-sticking notes, or on paper as they read. Annotation helps students prepare for the discussions they have with their peers and to integrate evidence into their writing. Types of annotation include circling confusing words, underlining important statements, noting questions and connections, and enumerating arguments.

Text-Dependent Questions

As we have noted elsewhere in this chapter, text-dependent questions provide students an opportunity to cull the text for evidence that supports their responses. These questions should not be limited to recall questions, but rather should give the student an opportunity to consider the text from a number of angles and perspectives. For example, 11th-grade students might be asked about major themes or central ideas, the structure of specific parts of the text and how that contributes to the meaning, and how two different texts treat a theme or topic.

General Comprehension Strategies Instruction

As stated earlier in this chapter, learning in grades 6–12 is about knowledge, rather than process, and understanding, or comprehension, should be the outcome of instruction, rather than application of strategies. For example, an expectation is that students must learn to analyze explicitly what the text says. Students are not expected to be able to predict or visualize as an end goal, but rather to leverage these reading comprehension strategies as needed in order to analyze how an author's choices influenced the structure a text and the order of events within it. Comprehension strategies, then, should be used as tools to support students' understanding of the text rather than as performance expectations (e.g., Frey & Fisher, 2013). Students should be taught and expected to use the following comprehension strategies to access complex texts:

- *Self-questioning strategies* to predict and anticipate what might occur next in the text, to resolve problems, and clarify their understanding.
- *Summarizing strategies* to identify important information and provide an accurate recount.
- *Inferencing strategies* to "read between the lines" in order to identify clues in the text.
- *Self-monitoring strategies* to determine when readers understand what they have read and notice when they have not.
- *Connection strategies* to integrate what readers have experienced and have learned with the information being read.
- *Analysis strategies* to identify literary devices, determine author's purpose, and evaluate texts.

As students encounter complex texts, they are likely to need to deploy these comprehension strategies more often, especially if they have been accustomed to reading most texts only once and then answering surface-level comprehension questions.

NEEDED: AN INTEGRATED APPROACH
TO COMPREHENSION

In the same way that the high school curriculum should be integrated to support cross-disciplinary thinking, so should comprehension instruction. Reading comprehension isn't solely about reading; students regularly utilize speaking and listening, as well as viewing and writing in order to understand text. Consider the literacy demands embedded in these content standards from California:

- Discuss the human costs of the war [World War II], with particular attention to the civilian and military losses in Russia, Germany, Britain, the United States, China, and Japan (California Department of Education, 2010, History/Social Studies Standard 10.8.6).
- Students know how to analyze published geological hazard maps of California and how to use the map's information to identify evidence and geological events of the past and predict geologic changes in the future (California Department of Education, 1998, Earth Science standard 9.d).
- Plan, conduct, and evaluate social, recreational, and educational activities appropriate to the physical, psychological, cultural, and socioeconomic needs of individuals and families (California Department of Education, 2006, Career and Technical Education standard D12.3).

Competency in these standards requires that students mobilize their reading, writing, speaking, listening, and language skills. In effective high school classrooms, students use language in their learning. For example, for students to demonstrate their understanding of the history/social studies standard noted above, they would have to interact with their peers, having read and researched material under study, work with peers to set rules for collegial discussions and decision making, and respond thoughtfully to diverse perspectives and summarize points of agreement and disagreement. Students in an earth science class tasked with analyzing published geological hazard maps would need to acquire and use general academic and domain-specific words and phrases and develop claims and counterclaims fairly, supplying evidence for each while pointing out the strengths and limitations, and establish and maintain a formal style and objective tone while attending to the norms and conventions of the discipline in which they are writing.

Reading comprehension involves the integration of multiple modalities and sources of information. It is not a purely receptive act. The learner is acting on his or her understanding of the text. In other words, reading comprehension is not passive. It requires that students interact with one another, with the teacher, and with the text itself. This has implications for the teacher as well. Simply assigning complex texts without proper scaffolded support will prove frustrating for everyone. However, modeling one's thinking gives students insight into how an expert (the teacher) makes meaning. Thoughtfully crafted text-dependent questions offer students a progression as they move from literal understanding to implicit understanding. Importantly, the discussions students engage in with their teacher and peers can be structured such that readers return to the text to locate information and justify their claims. Their conversations set the stage for writing as they begin to produce original texts that extend beyond the readings.

CONCLUSION

Comprehension of complex texts is possible when teachers align their instruction with student needs. This requires an understanding of the factors that contribute to a text's complexity, an exploration of the vocabulary demands of a text, and high-quality instructional moves that apprentice students in learning to read for information and ideas. Together, these create the ideal conditions that prepare students for success in their future endeavors, whether that be higher education or a rewarding career, or both.

DISCUSSION AND ACTIVITIES

1. Take a look once more at the list of developmental characteristics we selected for the chapter opening. Are students in your school or district appropriately prepared for college and careers? What needs to change to ensure students are ready?

2. Obtain a copy of Anna Quindlen's essay described in this chapter. After reading the essay, compare your analysis of the text complexity factors with those presented in the chapter. Also consider the text-dependent questions and what is required of you as a reader to determine the answers to those questions.

3. Select a piece of text that students in your content area should read. Analyze the text for its complexity and determine your teaching points. With colleagues, develop text-dependent questions and try them out with your students.

REFERENCES

Achieve, Inc. (2012). *Closing the expectations gap 2012: An annual 50-state progress report on the alignment of high school policies with the demands of college and work.* Washington, DC: Author. Retrieved from *www. achieve.org/ClosingtheExpectationsGap2012.*

Adler, M. J., & Van Doren, C. (1972). *How to read a book.* New York: Touchstone.

Alvermann, D. E., Young, J., Weaver, D., Hinchman, K. A., Moore, D. W., Phelps, S. F., et al. (1996). Middle and high school students' perceptions of how they experience text-based discussions: A multicase study. *Reading Research Quarterly, 31,* 244–267.

Aufschnaiter, C., Erduran, S., Osborne, J., & Simon, S. (2008). Arguing to learn and learning to argue: Case studies of how students' argumentation relates to their scientific knowledge. *Journal Of Research in Science Teaching, 45*(1), 101–131.

Baumann, J. F., Kame'enui, E. J., & Ash, G. E. (2003). Research on vocabulary instruction: Voltaire redux. In J. Flood, D. Lapp, J. R. Squire, & J. M. Jensen (Eds.), *Handbook of research on teaching the English language arts* (2nd ed., pp. 752-785). Mahwah, NJ: Erlbaum.

California Department of Education. (1998). *Science content standards for California public schools.* Sacramento, CA: Author.

California Department of Education. (2006). *California Career and technical education model curriculum standards.* Sacramento, CA: Author.

California Department of Education. (2010). *History–social science content standards for California public schools.* Sacramento, CA: Author.

Fisher, D., & Frey, N. (2008). *Word wise and content rich: Five essential steps to teaching academic vocabulary.* Portsmouth, NH: Heinemann.

Fisher, D., Frey, N., & Lapp, D. (2012). *Text complexity: Raising rigor in reading* (pp. 47–48). Newark, DE: International Reading Association.

Frey, N., & Fisher, D. (2013). *Rigorous reading: Five access points for helping students comprehend complex texts, K–12.* Thousand Oaks, CA: Corwin.

LaBerge, D. I., & Samuels, S. J. (1974). Toward a theory of automaticity information processing in reading. *Cognitive Psychology, 6,* 293–323.

McCrae, J. (1919). *In Flanders Fields and other poems,* London: Arcturus Publishing.

National Governors Association Center for Best Practices & Council of Chief State School Officers. (2010). *Common Core State Standards for English Language Arts and Literacy in History/Social Studies, Science, and Technical Subjects.* Washington, DC: Author. Retrieved at *www.corestandards.org/the-standards.*

Paris, S. G. (2005). Reinterpreting the development of reading skills. *Reading Research Quarterly, 40*(2), 184–202.

Pearson, P. D., & Gallagher, M. C. (1983). The instruction of reading comprehension. *Contemporary Educational Psychology, 8,* 317–344.

Quindlen, A. (2001, September 26). A quilt of a country. *Newsweek.* Retrieved from *www.thedailybeast.com/newsweek/2001/09/27/a-quilt-of-a-country.html.*

Shanahan, T., & Shanahan, C. (2008). Teaching disciplinary literacy to adolescents: Rethinking content area literacy. *Harvard Educational Review, 78*(1), 40–59.

Short, D. J., & Fitzsimmons, S. (2007). *Double the work: Challenges and solutions to acquiring language and academic literacy for adolescent English language learners. A report to Carnegie Corporation of New York.* Washington, DC: Alliance for Excellent Education.

Stahl, S. A. (2003). Vocabulary and readability: How knowing word meanings affects comprehension. *Topics in Language Disorders*, *23*(3), 241–247.

Wineburg, S. S. (1991). On the reading of historical texts: Notes on the breach between school and academy. *American Educational Research Journal*, *28*, 495–519.

CHAPTER 9

Expanding Adolescent Writing

Building upon Youths' Practices, Purposes, Relationships, and Thoughtfulness

Randy Bomer
Michelle Fowler-Amato

This chapter:

- Outlines some core principles about what is most important in writing instruction.

- Describes ways to understand and build upon students' existing writing lives.

- Discusses two purposes for classroom writing: writing to think and writing for audiences.

- Introduces teaching structures that support student writers.

Obviously, writing is an important part of a literate education. However, writing has not always received the emphasis in literacy curricula that it seems to warrant. All literacy necessarily involves composing; there are no texts to read if no one makes them. But it is, nevertheless, quite common for students to have very few invitations to write whole texts in a given school year, in English or any other class (Applebee & Langer, 2009, 2011). Sometimes, teachers may think they are working on composing when they are really working on students' knowledge about grammar. Sometimes, the writing that does get assigned to students involves them only in a small bit of a writing process, for example, providing evidence for someone else's claims. And sometimes, students may be asked to write, but only about a text created by someone else—someone who is considered the *real writer* in this exchange. So like many writing scholars, we want to argue for the importance of writing, sometimes even its primacy. And we want to argue, too, that we should emphasize certain messages about writing over others.

DIRECTING TEACHER AND STUDENT ATTENTION TO WHAT REALLY MATTERS IN WRITING

When we literacy teachers create classrooms where students will grow as writers, our choices direct students' attention to particular dimensions of composing. We promote some aspects of writing and suppress others. When teachers compose curriculum in their classrooms—as when writers compose pieces of writing—we select themes to emphasize and themes to deemphasize or leave out all together. Those choices comprise the clearest message that students receive about writing. Because of this shaping influence, we should make sure we are focusing our attention—and, therefore, that of our students—on the most substantial, meaningful, and important dimensions of writing. Because this focus may not always match the teacher's own experiences in school, it may be necessary to pay special attention to our assumptions, so that we can make sure we are not inadvertently teaching things we do not mean.

Writers Attending to Their Own Thinking

Writing involves, first of all, paying attention to your own thoughts, remaining focused on them, and developing these invisible, fleeting notions into something purposeful. Generating written language requires a writer to attend to what is as-yet unsaid, to focus into silence and bring nascent ideas into words. To turn attention inward in this way means that we have to turn away, for the moment, from what others say or want from us. Although people do all kinds of *thinking* in varied situations, this is the contemplation we often associate with the word *thinking*, and it's the foundation of writing.

This thinking is not always supported in school, where, when students attend to their own thoughts, they are likely to be accused of daydreaming or inattention. Because this process of generating thought and catching it on the fly is at the core of writing, many writing teachers have found that it is best supported by making students responsible, as much as possible in any given situation, for initiating and developing their own topics and subject matter for writing (Atwell, 1986). Sometimes, encouraging this effort means making students *completely* responsible for developing content, for example, in units of study on writing memoirs or writing for political purposes. In other cases, such as when students are writing about shared content because the focus is an exploration of a text or topic, teachers may open up student topic choice as much as possible within a set of parameters. For example, rather than answering a teacher's questions about a shared text, students might write to think several times during the reading, then return to that writing to formulate an assertion they would like to make to an audience, building upon their own observations, insights, and trails of thought. The important point is that students can only learn to trust their own thinking and take on a process of developing content when they actually have a chance to do so.

Writers Reworking Large Chunks of Meaning

Another fundamental understanding about writing to which we need to direct students' sustained attention is that for most writers, most of the time, whole texts seldom come out right away the way they look when they are finished. Many good, successful writers produce first drafts that do not come close to satisfying their purposes (or even saying what they mean). Their writing gets stronger with successive rewrites in which they look at what they have said so far, compare that to the ideas that are still emerging in their mind, and make substantial changes. That doesn't mean just changing spelling, word choice, or even sentences, but rather serious rethinking, or new attempts to get at what they would like to accomplish in this text.

Again, for writers and their teachers, writing is a matter of controlling *attention*. A writer needs to attend to meanings, the development of the ideas, the substance underlying the sentences—and to be able to ignore strategically, temporarily, surface "correctness" and other such considerations. The surface features of language can be a distraction from this other, truly more essential, part of the composing process. Here we are talking about changes in the larger structures of meaning, and in order for students to learn to do these kinds of revisions, they need experience with looking for those structures. Because students typically think of revising as something they would do to correct mistakes or to fix poorly worded parts, they need guidance to attend to the parts of a draft that have potential that is not yet realized. They need experiences thinking of writing as having sections, figuring out which sections to expand and which to shrink or cut, and determining various possible arrangements of those sections. They need also to learn that writing can involve changing your mind entirely about what the text will say. This kind of revision often involves actually inventing new content on the second, third, and fourth pass through a piece of writing. The process of writing, in other words, teaches the writer what the text will be about. To learn to use writing this way, students need time to revisit what they have written and to *try* to rethink—rather than being asked to produce a final statement in a first draft. Teachers often do this simply by having a due date for a complete first draft and then scheduling ample time in class after that date for students to revisit their writing and ask new questions about it. The important thing, as often as possible, is for student writers to see writing as something that grows thought, rather than simply leaps from some genius's great first ideas.

Writers Designing for Particular Purposes and Audiences

Writers are engineers, or designers. They attempt to construct an experience for the users of their designs. To do that, they need to learn how to hold the user, the audience, in mind—the people for whom they are making this text. And they also need to hold in mind the purpose of the designed object—what they are trying to do to that audience. As we discuss below, that means writers need, much of the time, to have audiences beyond the teacher, so that the teacher can function as a coach, helping them to achieve their purposes with the audience *out there*.

Writers have to make the peculiarities of the content in their texts work to achieve their purpose. There are, of course, lots of tricks, strategies, and structures they might consider as they craft their content to achieve those purposes. However, prescriptive formulas that teachers often impose only serve in the end to distract writers from developing the structure that will work organically with their material to achieve their purpose. When they are given formulas—like, say, five-paragraph essay structures or prescriptions about the function of each sentence in a paragraph—the purpose they focus on is obedience to the authoritarian formula, rather than their actual, rhetorical purposes as a writer trying to reach an audience. The goal instead should be for writers to figure out the patterns, the design, that will work for future readers to have the right kind of experience when they are engaged with this text. Writers can learn to think about design from studying and discussing the ways other writers have constructed published texts that are considered high quality in this discipline or general form, then trying to apply some of the same structures they have discovered empirically from those texts. Once they have applied the design principles they have drawn from the study of text, they then need opportunities to test their own designs on readers to see whether the text is actually working on an audience as they had envisioned. As with the other shaping influences we named above, the teacher's designs for the classroom and curriculum contribute to shaping the design of a purposeful and effective text and an experience that will be educative, as well, for future writing experiences when the teacher is not around.

ADOLESCENTS' WRITING LIVES: RECEIVING WHAT STUDENTS ARE ALREADY DOING OUTSIDE SCHOOL

People learn by pulling themselves into new understandings using their existing knowledge. That means, to support learning, teachers need to find out about students' existing writing practices—the activities and places in their lives where engagement with composing is the strongest—and to design instruction on the basis of what students already understand. Recent research in adolescent literacy has revealed much more competence, artistry, and sophisticated knowledge in adolescents' unofficial, out-of-school writing lives than educators ever understood existed before (Christenbury, Bomer, & Smagorinsky, 2008). At times, students may have already set themselves on the road toward the academic goals we have in mind for them. The task is to recognize that knowledge, get it into the classroom, convince the students of its legitimacy, and then connect it to various important goals in school, including (but not limited to) official academic standards. Let's look at some examples.

Seventeen-year-old Shawna began writing poetry in fifth grade after receiving a compliment from a teacher for a poem she wrote in class. Although she usually begins a poem in a notebook or on her phone, in response to something she sees or hears, it lives there in the notebook only temporarily. Often, she posts stanzas of poems in process on her Facebook page so she can get feedback from friends, many of whom are also poets, as well as from others who represent her wider audience. When a piece is complete, she uploads it to her website and prepares to share her work at a local "open mic" night or a poetry slam. On nights when she performs, Shawna brings books of her poetry, which she has put together herself, and sells them to those who would like to return to the moment in which she shared her story in performance. All of this activity is independent of school.

Fifteen-year-old Ben says he's a "nerdfighter," which means he's an active participant and contributor on the social networking site *nerdfighters.ning.com*. (Don't worry; as you'll see if you look at the site, this is decidedly not a community of bullies who pick on kids they call nerds.) After reading John Green's *The Fault in Our Stars* as part of his school's summer reading program, Ben became one of the 966,000 subscribers to this Ning (a number that will no doubt have grown by the time you read this), which is run by author John Green and his brother, Hank. Like many other "nerdfighters," Ben contributes to the Ning through blogging, interacting with others in online discussions, and uploading videos and images that are likely to generate conversation among members of this community. Influenced by the work of author John Green, Ben and a few of his fellow "nerdfighters," who he met through his participation in this online space, decided to join a new online community, challenging themselves to participate in National Novel Writing Month (NaNoWriMo) by each committing to write 50,000 words over the month of November. Ben's teachers did not know about any of this.

Although these snapshots focus, specifically, on the writing students are doing outside the classroom, both of these young people were encouraged to write as a result of an experience they had in a school—Shawna's encouragement from a teacher, Ben's connection to a series of books via a summer reading program. It is always our hope as teachers that our students will draw on what they learn in our classrooms. But we can also learn from our students about the composing in their everyday lives and build our curriculum on what already exists.

Like the students we describe above, young people are writing more than they might even recognize, and more than youth ever have in history (Lenhart, Arafeh, Smith, & Macgill, 2008). Some keep journals, diaries, and sketchbooks to document and reflect on their experiences. They engage in writing to pursue artistic endeavors, creating scripts that become the text of plays or movies, and composing lyrics, which they often put to music. Sometimes, the writing that youth do is different than the writing that is traditionally valued in our schools. For example, some young people take up the practices of graffiti artists, "tagging" walls or other unofficial writing spaces. They might text their peers, participate in social networking sites, and create online identities in MMPORGs (massively multiplayer online role-playing games). Even though, if you ask them, they probably will not say these activities are "composing," they really are. In order to help students draw upon what they know about writer–reader relationships, writerly habits, and the varied environments in which writing gets done, many teachers find it helpful to create space in a writing classroom to inquire into these practices and to connect them to the kinds of literacy required in academic work—across the curriculum—and in careers (Bomer, 2011).

Teachers sometimes start by taking some time to think with students about what literacy really is, looking around at the spaces in which they write and their motives for taking literate action in them. Although students will be able to list a few of these contexts and practices pretty easily, these teachers also send them out in the world with their notebooks to jot down when they engage in these practices, how they do so, and what they hope to accomplish. Students then return to class to think with others, in small groups or with the entire class. The teacher documents what each writer says, filling the classroom's walls with lists of the motives and processes of writing, recognizing that these experiences can be built on in future conversations with individual writers as well as in the development of a writing curriculum. Figure 9.1 lists a variety of activities that have supported students' study of their existing literate lives. These and other approaches to bringing literate lives into the classroom are more thoroughly

- Student/student interviews.
- Public interviews in which everyone questions a particular writer.
- Keeping a journal in which we "spy" on ourselves as writers.
- Focused, ethnographic investigations of one another's homes, rooms, habits, and writing conditions.
- Metaphorical drawings about what writing is like for us.
- Acting out critical incidents in our writing lives.
- A letter-writing cycle about life as a writer initiated by the teacher writing about her or his own life as a writer, with students writing back in dialogue.
- A timeline of our experiences with writing that have led us to become the writers we are today.

FIGURE 9.1. Activities for investigating existing literacies.

described in Bomer's (2011) *Building Adolescent Literacy in Today's English Classroom.*

College and Career Readiness as Part of a Writing Life

One interesting irony about students' writing outside school is that it may do as much to prepare students for their future as the instruction they receive in the school curriculum. We all hope that our students will leave our classrooms prepared to engage in the wide variety of writing tasks they need to do in all of the different arenas of their lives, including the relatively few years that some of them will spend in college. As most American teachers know, the Common Core State Standards' (CCSS) College and Career Readiness Anchor Standards for Writing (CCRA; National Governors Association Center for Best Practices & Council of Chief State School Officers, 2010) express an opinion about what young people should be able to accomplish in writing for their future lives. These standards suggest that students need opportunities to write habitually, within short and extended time frames (CCRA.W.10). It is often students' writing lives outside school—journaling, spiritual practices, songwriting, and participation in digital culture—that see them composing most frequently and in varied timeframes. They suggest that students should have experiences writing in a variety of genres (CCRA.W.1, CCRA.W.2, CCRA.W.3), recognizing that the decisions writers make while composing are always influenced by the writer's purpose, the audience, and the choice of genre itself (CCRA.C.W.4, CCRA.W.10).

Apparently, variety is what the standards are seeking, and the widest range in young people's composing occurs in the context of their participation in the arts, in family life, in personal relationships, in religious life, and in sports and other activities. These are the locations of their real audiences, their collaborators, and their topical variation. The CCSS call for students to be given opportunities to draw on multiple sources, including digital texts, to support their thinking in the writing they do, assessing the validity of each of these resources (CCRA.W.8), as well as to make use of technology when composing, publishing, and collaborating with others throughout the writing process (CCRA.W.6).

Unfortunately, the goals in these standards are not necessarily supported by the kinds of school experiences that many middle school and high school students are having. Some research (Applebee & Langer, 2011) suggests (as does our experience as professionals) that students may experience few extended writing opportunities even in their language arts classes (as well as across the disciplines) and rarely share their writing with audiences beyond the classroom community. As we mentioned above, students are often taught formulaic structures with the goal of preparing them for standardized tests or for the completion of a writing task that requires a fixed response. Similarly, the use of technology in the writing classroom is limited, mostly serving teachers rather than students (Applebee & Langer, 2011). Because students may be learning the most from unofficial locations outside school, the practices and habits they take on in those settings might be especially valuable to bring into school, as a foundation for academic learning. Although academic literacies require different skills and forms of knowledge than those that young people often call upon when writing for their own purposes, the motives, processes, and forms of thinking are similar (Daniels, Zemelman, & Steinecke, 2007). So why not start there? Why not begin by seeking an understanding of what writing is to them, building on what they are already doing, in an effort to connect the curriculum to the lives of the students who are experiencing it?

WRITING TO THINK

Although it's important to build upon students' existing writing practices, secondary school literacy instruction ought to *expand* students' literate repertoires. In particular, most teachers of writing want to develop students' capacities in two main directions: using writing as a tool for thinking and communicating effectively through writing with real audiences.

Here, we want to consider the writing that students do for themselves— how people use language in talking to themselves to mediate their thinking. This type of writing provides students with the space to figure out how they feel and what they have to say. Teachers might plan for students to engage in this type of writing in order to speak back to the texts that they read as well as to the ideas about which they are working to make sense of in school. But many teachers believe that writing to think should serve an even broader purpose in a literacy curriculum. In addition to having opportunities to respond to conversation in the classroom, our students should experience what it is like to attend to their own thinking, becoming aware of the moments in which they have a thought, using writing as a tool to further develop the idea while, at the same time, preparing to participate in conversations that take place beyond the walls of the classroom.

Writers' Notebooks

When students write to think, they are typically talking to themselves about things that matter to them: their memories, their dreams, their interests, the people and places that are important to them, and the things they see and hear that call them to respond. Although this writing could live anywhere (writers jot down their thinking on napkins, old envelopes, and paper menus), many teachers find value in the use of a writer's notebook, a tool in which ideas take shape, ideas that a writer might eventually return to when addressing an audience (Bomer, 1995, 2011).

Like a journal, a notebook allows writers to return to and reflect on their thinking over time. But whereas a journal often consists of a collection of reflections that stand on their own, a writer's notebook is a compilation of entries, each with the potential to be part of a bigger conversation. When a writer composes a notebook entry, he does so with an understanding that he is likely to return to this piece of writing, building on his thinking in future entries and, later, in a piece of writing that speaks to a particular audience. Or he might find, through the process of writing and reflecting on his thinking within the notebook, that he is not interested or ready to take this topic further. In the meantime, this piece will remain inside the notebook, allowing the writer to return to his thinking in the future, if he is called to do so.

In addition to serving as a tool that allows writers to collect and document their thinking over time, it is our hope that keeping a notebook will encourage students to change the way they pay attention to the world. When a writer knows that he will be expected to write regularly in a notebook, he begins to notice what he sees, hears, feels, and wonders about, and each of these experiences becomes a possible topic to explore through writing.

Notebooks in the Classroom

In order to create a classroom space in which students are thinking like writers, arriving ready to put their thoughts down on paper, it is important that they are given time to write every day. A teacher must encourage each writer's independence, yet provide enough support to ensure that each writer grows as a result of engaging in the process of writing. This support might be provided through the implementation of mini-lessons as well as through the conferring that takes place while writers are at work. Early on, these mini-lessons and conferences are likely to focus on practices and habits of keeping a notebook, teaching students the purposes of this tool and thinking with them about how best to set up individual notebooks. It is important that each writer finds his own notebook to be user friendly, allowing him to return to previous entries, thereby building on past thinking. A teacher might also implement mini-lessons and facilitate conferences that explore how writers generate ideas and build stamina and concentration. Similarly, a teacher is likely to design mini-lessons and engage in conferences early in the school year, in an effort to encourage variety within student writing.

A notebook is a tool in which students experiment with language as well as with different ways of representing their ideas. In order to encourage variety in notebook entries, teachers create space for writers to share their work as well as their practices and processes, so students have the opportunity to learn from each other. In Figure 9.2, we include a list of some of the kinds of entries that we have seen writers try out in their own notebooks. We share these only to open students' and teachers' eyes to some of the possibilities that might exist within student notebooks, not as a set curriculum or a complete list. Because writers' notebooks serve as self-sponsored tools for thinking, teachers help students by introducing a variety of strategies that they might call upon, as needed, in an effort to get their material out of their mind and onto a page, to see what they have to say. That way, when they make a piece of writing for an audience, it's mainly a matter of design.

Writing for Audiences

To create opportunities for students to write for audiences teachers have to play the role of a social engineer. The job is to design a system that connects students with people waiting to hear what they have to say—possibly classmates, but when possible, it's even better for the class to be performing for a larger public outside the classroom. Some teachers accomplish this by arranging for their own different classes to be audiences for each other. Or an audience may comprise other students in the school, people in the larger community, organizations or students who are geographically distant, or an even larger audience made possible through the Internet. The point is to create an audience other than the teacher. That way, the teacher's role can become one of coach, preparing students to share their thinking with people out in the world who are waiting to hear what they have to say,

- Observations—things I notice in the world.
- Questions—things I wonder about.
- Thinking about what events might mean.
- Response to things I read, see, and hear.
- Drawings, sketches, diagrams.
- Clippings and photos and my thoughts about them.
- Kernels of blog posts or status updates.
- Memories.
- Stories my family tells.
- Plans and goals.
- Quotes and things people have said to me.
- Revisits to previous topics.

FIGURE 9.2. Examples of entries writers make in writers' notebooks.

rather than an authority figure demanding that students write "for me" in the required way so that their work may be judged.

With those social relations established, the writer's task is to design experiences for those readers—to define purposes and agendas toward those people and to devise a text strategically to achieve those purposes. Sometimes, the purpose is to share experiences, maybe to let the readers know what the writer's life is like and to try to make them care. At other times, the purpose is to change the reader's mind, perhaps about a matter of public policy, a topic of interest in their shared community, or a way of thinking about a text. In a context in which the writer knows what she is trying to do to a reader, some of those typical things people remember hearing about from traditional teachers of writing might become useful—ways of organizing texts, patterns of arrangement that some writers have called upon, even the way readers might expect sentences to be arranged. All of these formal considerations get their meanings from the real social interactions into which they fit. Too often, as we discussed above, the meanings are lost in all of the attention given to the forms themselves—uninspired formulas or grammatical prescriptions. Instead of focusing on fixed, ready-made recipes for writing, good writing teachers show students the processes writers use to make decisions about structure, about detail, about supporting claims, about language, and about other features of quality in a particular form of writing.

Structures for Teaching

By now, it is probably clear that, as with any craft, people get better at writing mainly from the experiences they have as writers. They pick up strategies from trying them out in practical situations, and every time they do this, they expand their repertoire of things they know to try in order to get a text to work for a reader. They pick up ideas from reading experiences, trying in their own writing the designs they notice in other writers' work. But they only do this because they have developed the eyes of a craftsperson from their own attempts as writers to make texts do what they want them to. There is really not much to say to writers before they start writing. They don't need lectures or prescriptions; they mainly need to get to work. So a writing classroom is a place where people work. That is not to say that there is no role for a teacher, for instruction. Once a writer is trying to make something she cares about, in order to have an impact on a particular audience, she will have all kinds of motivation to learn things that can help her accomplish her purpose. Here, we suggest a few teaching structures that provide opportunities for writers' own work time and also for teachers to influence the choices writers make within that time.

Writing Time in Class

In order for a teacher to have a chance to coach student writers, it is best for students to be writing during class time, in the classroom, where the teacher can see them and talk to them individually as they work. Most committed writing teachers think that it's important to value writing as an activity—to actually make time for literate activity in the school day and to demonstrate to students that it is important enough for the school to give time to it. With many students, this is the time when writing will actually happen. This is the most important structure in writing pedagogy, and all of the others depend on it.

Individual Writing Conferences

When students are writing in class, the teacher can get to work conferring with individuals. The purpose of a writing conference is to understand the writer's intentions and to teach a strategy that can help her pursue those intentions, not just for this particular writing experience, but so that she can use this same strategy in the future. In other words, we are teaching into the writer's decision making, not just fixing up the piece (Anderson, 2000; Murray, 1985). For most teachers who confer in this way, writing conferences range between a few seconds and a few minutes, and people try to have six or seven such conversations during a half hour or so of writing time. During a week, then, they get around to each student at least once. With this level of one-to-one attention, this structure helps to meet the goals of individualized, student-tailored teaching articulated in approaches such as response to intervention.

Whole-Class Mini-Lessons

When students are writing during class and the teacher is conferring with individuals, it becomes clear to the teacher what kinds of things everyone in the class could benefit from hearing. These become the topics of mini-lessons, which are very focused, short lessons for the whole class—maybe 5 to 10 minutes long. Because they are short, many teachers teach a string of mini-lessons about one idea across several days, perhaps introducing a strategy on one day, demonstrating the next, and then giving students a chance to try that same strategy on the third day. So if the purpose is to teach students to create a sense of place by detailed sensory information, the teacher introduces the idea and shows an example on the first day, demonstrates it by revising in front of students on the second day, and asks them to identify one place or setting in their own piece of writing and try building up the sensory information on a small sheet of paper on the third day.

Response, Collaboration, and Sharing

In a writer's life, fellow writers play an important role, and students in a writing classroom fill that role. Often, they are thinking partners for one another, and offer additional, generous thoughts about possible notebook entries, or the initial plan for a piece of writing. Even just keeping one another company during the writing process, offering encouragement and a sounding board, can be fortifying for writers. Other times, a writer might bring a draft to another student or writing group, explain what they are trying to do, and then think strategically together about how to accomplish what they have in mind for their readers. As part of a design process, as we described writing for audiences, user testing might be viewed as an expected part of engineering a text so that it works in practice the way the designer had in mind.

CONCLUSION

As everyone knows, we are living in a new era of literacy, one in which *participation* is the key word—participation in a digital culture, participation in a democracy, and participation in a global conversation. What this participation mostly entails is *writing*. It may have seemed acceptable in earlier eras to focus on reading alone—in times when workers simply needed to receive instructions and follow orders. But the emerging world involves speaking up with one's own voice, responding, telling what our lives are like, and how we see things. For our students to take their rightful place in this world, they need ample opportunities for flexible, thoughtful engagement with writing.

DISCUSSION AND ACTIVITIES

1. Make a timeline of your own life history as a writer. Label on it all of the writing experiences you remember, in and out of school. Be sure to count the holiday plays you made up with your cousins, the songs you wrote for girlfriends, the letters to and from your grandfather, the journals, blogs, and the video you made that one summer. Label these moments on your timeline: the most helpful thing that ever happened to you, the most hurtful thing that ever happened, the time in your life when you felt the most like a writer, and the time in your life when you felt least like a writer.

2. Interview adolescents about the range of composing activities they engage in throughout their lives. Remember that they may not count lots of things they do as writing. See if you can help them revalue the composing they already do as similar in some underlying ways to academic forms of writing.

3. Buy yourself a notebook that seems inviting to you, one that inspires you to write freely. Spend several weeks writing every day about a range of different things, varying topics as well as forms—just to think through them and try them out. Then read through your notebook and see what emerges as possible topics. What single entries draw you? What themes can you see across your writing? What kind of piece could you make from those entries?

4. Find a short story or essay that you think students could relate to. Identify five things you could teach from that story about good writing—not punctuation or grammar, but craft, style, invention, and deeper structures. How could you talk about those things in a way that might make sense to student writers, so that they could use those strategies in their own work?

REFERENCES

Anderson, C. (2000). *How's it going?: A practical guide to conferring with student writers*. Portsmouth, NH: Heinemann.

Applebee, A. N., & Langer, J. A. (2009). What is happening in the teaching of writing? *English Journal, 98*(5), 18–28.

Applebee, A. N., & Langer, J. A. (2011). A snapshot of writing instruction in middle schools and high schools. *English Journal, 100*(6), 14–27.

Atwell, N. (1986). *In the middle*. Portsmouth, NH: Heinemann.

Bomer, R. (1995). *Time for meaning: Crafting literate lives in middle and high school*. Portsmouth, NH: Heinemann.

Bomer, R. (2011). *Building adolescent literacy in today's English classrooms*. Portsmouth, NH: Heinemann.

Christenbury, L., Bomer, R., & Smagorinsky, P. (Eds.). (2008). *The handbook of adolescent literacy research*. New York: Guilford Press.

Daniels, H., Zemelman, S., & Steineke, N. (2007). *Content-area writing: Every teachers' guide*. Portsmouth, NH: Heinemann.

Lenhart, A., Arafeh, S., Smith, A., & Macgill, A. (2008). *Writing, technology, and teens.* Washington, DC: Pew Internet and American Life Project. Retrieved from *www.pewinternet.org/Reports/2008/Writing-Technology-and-Teens.aspx.*

Murray, D. M. (1985). *A writer teaches writing.* Boston: Houghton Mifflin.

National Governors Association Center for Best Practices & Council of Chief State School Officers. (2010). *The Common Core State Standards.* Washington, DC: Author. Retrieved from *www.corestandards.org/ELA-Literacy/CCRA/W.*

CHAPTER 10

Reading and Writing across Multiple Texts

Cynthia Shanahan

This chapter:

- Makes an argument for teaching students to understand, think about, and write multiple texts on the same topic.

- Discusses research and practice regarding multiple text reading and writing strategies.

- Provides activities that can be used with students in English, social science, science, and mathematics classes for reading and writing using multiple texts.

THE CASE FOR MULTIPLE TEXTS

We make decisions every day regarding the various aspects of our lives. Should we go on this diet or that one—or should we adopt more realistic body images? Is this candidate's plan for the budget realistic? What will the consequences of global warming be, and what should we be doing about it? These decisions are all quite difficult to make because we rely on information from multiple viewpoints, in multiple genres (letters, essays, reports, advertisements, lectures, etc.), and through various venues (newspapers, television, podcasts, websites, billboards, books, magazines, and so on), that is often contradictory. The information changes depending on who said it, when it was said, what evidence was used to support it, and on and on. There is no one definitive answer, yet there may be many messages claiming to be just that. Regardless of how confusing the messages are, however, we are compelled as citizens to vote for the person who has garnered our trust, and we either do something about global warming (like taking public transportation and buying better light bulbs) or do nothing, but either way, respond.

Our nation is based on an informed citizenry, and that means we have an obligation to learn about the issues that affect our nation and ourselves. If we don't inform ourselves about the issues related to global warming, for example, we end up making decisions on the basis of an 8-second sound bite or because a celebrity said so.

The necessary reliance on multiple messages that conflict or disagree and through which we find no right answer is also part of most disciplines. Think of the discipline of history, for example. Historians use evidence from multiple sources (film, newspapers, autobiographies, letters, firsthand accounts, and interviews) to *construct* plausible interpretations of historical events and make cause–effect claims or claims of significance about them. They construct those claims based not only on the evidence, but also on their particular viewpoints. For example, if a historian believes that history is a story of progress (things just keep getting better and better), she will be interpreting the evidence in a different way than a historian who believes that the past is glorious and that the future is getting worse. A grassroots historian will be looking for different kinds of evidence than a biographer of presidents, even though the two may focus on the same era and even the same events. In addition, historians often argue about the meaning of events as new evidence becomes available or because of a new outlook. Christopher Columbus, for instance, has been lauded as a great man who discovered the new world and initiated the Columbian exchange; scorned for how he took advantage of the Taino people and decimated their population; and defended as an individual acting within the constraints of his time, each view depending on when historians were doing the writing. Historians not only read multiple genres when creating accounts and interpretations, but they also write them. Academic prestige is achieved through writing scholarly books, but historians also write journal articles and books for the popular press, take elaborate notes, engage in conversations with other scholars, and so on.

Multiple texts are also the purview of science. Scientists reinvent the world. What we think of as scientific truth at one time is later discarded as new tools (like the telescope), new theories (like quantum physics), new procedures for analysis, and new experiments are created. Even though scientists' views of the world are constrained by scientific methods, and what counts as evidence is subject to the rigors of experimentation, scientists decide what is significant and what is accepted as scientific fact only after evaluating numerous experiments and after reading numerous documents—not all of which look at the subject matter in the same way. And if we consider phenomena that are difficult to measure, such as the phenomenon of global warming, then, scientists are often divided in their views. Too, when scientists write, they do not write in only one format for one purpose. They write multiple documents—scientific reports, proposals for funding, laboratory observation notes, explanations of science for popular consumption, and so on. Bazerman (1998) discusses how important it was to incandescent lighting that Edison could communicate in writing via the patent application, the newspaper, technical journals, legal briefs, and so on. The transformation of information from one domain to another is perhaps the hallmark of a skilled language user *and* a successful scientist.

Even in a highly constrained field such as mathematics, experts read and write multiple texts for a variety of purposes, especially when mathematical principles are applied to the real world. Mathematical principles, for example, are sometimes applied to political purposes in order to make particular claims (such as in claims that a state can afford a new health plan), and these claims can be refuted by a look at the same issues with different sets of figures. In summary, although the various disciplines are far from similar in the ways experts approach reading and writing and in the challenges they present to adolescent readers (see Shanahan, Shanahan & Misischia, 2011), discipline experts all read and write multiple texts.

In today's information-rich society, adolescents also are awash in multiple, conflicting messages. The world's teens are channel switchers; they are constantly searching the Web for information, blogging their views, and, sadly, becoming victims of misinformation, fraud, and exploitation. A series of studies (Leu, 2007) shows that, even with all of the practice adolescents seem to be getting at reading multiple documents, they are alarmingly unfamiliar with search strategies and are unaware of issues such as the credibility of information sources. Students do not know how to refine their search terms, choosing the first Google hit without examining its relevance. Once on a website, they do not know where to find, or they choose not to read, text that might tell them about the source of the information on the page and the particular biases of the site owner. A colleague of mine tells about a teenager who definitively announced to his teacher that the Holocaust was a hoax after having read the views of a professor at a university on a website he discovered. It seemed credible, considering the university affiliation; yet the student had not been taught that the tilde after the university URL indicated that the website he had accessed was not an official university site; and he had not noticed the professor's affiliation with the Ku Klux Klan.

In addition, despite the writing practice adolescents seem to be getting when they write to their peers using blogs, e-mail, and text messaging, adolescents also continue to have difficulty providing appropriate evidence for claims, engaging in more formal writing activities, and writing about the same topic from multiple viewpoints or for multiple purposes (American

College Testing, 2006). In other words, adolescents need instruction in reading and writing multiple texts, especially in academic and public environments.

Yet as important as reading and writing multiple texts are, much of our instructional effort in literacy has been focused on teaching the understanding and creation of single texts on any one topic. We have rarely taught students to read across various texts and to write about the same topic in multiple ways and for multiple purposes.

This lack of focus on instruction with multiple texts may be most evident in the performance of students in college. When I taught college reading classes, I sometimes took classes with students so that I could help them meet course demands. Without exception, these courses required students to read not only a textbook but primary documents in history; issues briefs in political science; lab books and science articles in science; and short stories, essays, and full-length books in English. Students were expected to integrate information from their course notes, the textbook, and their other course readings and assignments to prepare for tests; yet most students did not know how do this. They were often expected to show that integration in the way they answered questions and wrote papers, and they were expected to know how to write for the particular discipline-based audience, but those assignments proved difficult. For example, students often wrote essay test answers in history or science class as if they were writing a five-paragraph English essay, taking great care to engage the reader with a clever first paragraph, when the instructor just wanted them to answer the question. Most college students I talked to were overwhelmed by the reading and writing demands of many of their courses. It is no wonder that 4- and 6-year graduation rates of public institutions are abysmal (an average of 31% and 56%, respectively). Although there may be myriad reasons why graduation rates are low, the lack of focus on teaching students to read and write using multiple texts certainly hinders students' success in dealing with the kinds of reading and writing tasks prevalent in college-level coursework.

For those states following the Common Core State Standards (CCSS), however (National Governors Association Center for Best Practices & Council of Chief State School Officers, 2010), the practice of focusing solely on single texts is changing or about to change. In these standards, students are asked to make distinctions between two texts as early as kindergarten. Multiple texts are referenced in virtually every section: literature and nonfiction, speaking and listening, history/social studies, science and technical subjects, and writing. Students are expected to progress steadily from making general comparisons of more than one text (e.g. comparisons of genre or style) to making comparisons of structure (e.g. chronology, comparison, cause–effect, or problem–solution), to identifying and comparing specific arguments in texts (e.g. claims, counterclaims, and evidence), to evaluating credibility and usefulness. Thus for those using the CCSS, teaching will be focused on reading across multiple texts. For example, a 9-10 ELA "Integration of Knowledge and Ideas" standard states: Analyze seminal U.S. documents of historical and literary significance (e.g., Washington's farewell address, the Gettysburg Address, Roosevelt's "Four Freedoms" speech, King's "Letter from a Birmingham Jail"), including how they address related themes and concepts. A History/Social Studies Reading Standard for grades 11–12 says: Evaluate authors' differing points of view on the same historical event or issue by assessing the authors' claims, reasoning, and evidence.

The ability to understand and respond to multiple texts is also a focus of the assessments that are being developed by the Partnership for Assessment of Readiness for College and Career (PARCC) and Smarter Balance. For example, one PARCC exercise has students answering questions about one text, then adds another text and expects students to use information from the first text to interpret the second. If instruction does not include multiple text understanding, then states implementing the CCSS will undoubtedly fall short of helping their students to meet those standards, and students will be at a disadvantage on assessments of them.

Although we haven't previously done very much instructionally to ensure that students read and write multiple texts, there is a research base supporting such instruction. The research that has been done on multiple-text reading and writing is synthesized in the next section.

RESEARCH AND PRACTICE WITH MULTIPLE TEXT STRATEGIES

We know from studies of multiple text reading in history that students do not independently use effective strategies for reading several texts on the same topic. Wineburg (1991) had high school students and historians read several documents on a particular event in history. The students had already learned about the event in school, so had some background information. The event was not part of the expertise of the historians; thus they lacked background information. The historians, however, engaged in a highly sophisticated reading of the documents. In addition to learning the information in the texts, they engaged in three processes: sourcing, contextualization, and corroboration. When sourcing, they looked for information about the author, they checked the sources of information the author used, they looked at the kind of document it was, and so on. When contextualizing, they thought about the time in which the document was written in terms of the political or socioeconomic climate, for example, and they thought about the kind of history being portrayed, among other considerations. When corroborating, they looked for agreements and disagreements across the texts and with their own knowledge and experiences. In short, the historians were evaluating the documents for their credibility. They thought of the documents as arguments for particular interpretations of history, and they used the credible information to form their own interpretations. The high school students, on the other hand, treated each of the documents as a separate entity and engaged in fact collection. Wineburg's findings have been corroborated by a number of other studies (Britt, Rouet, & Perfetti, 1996; Perfetti, Britt, Rouet, Mason, & Georgia, 1993; Stahl, Hynd, Britton, McNish, & Bosquet, 1996; VanSledright & Kelly, 1998). In the Stahl et al. (1996) study, for example, students did seem to learn the information in common across the various texts, but there was no indication that the students were utilizing corroboration—just that they remembered the information that was repeated. They did not seem to notice when information in the various texts conflicted, and with few exceptions, they did not seem to engage in sourcing or contextualization. Researchers have also confirmed that *experts* in various subject areas, unlike students, do use information from many sources in learning, critiquing, and applying ideas in their respective fields (Bazermann, 1988; Shanahan et al., 2011).

Could students learn to engage in the processes the historians used? Several studies confirm that the answer to that question is yes. Hynd-Shanahan, Holschuh, and Hubbard (2004) found that college students not only engaged in sourcing, contextualization, and corroboration when reading multiple texts, but also changed the way they thought about history. In thinking about the texts as arguments for historical interpretation, they ended the study with more sophisticated strategies, more engagement in reading, and a more nuanced and critical view of what it meant to learn historical information. It is not only college students who can use those strategies. VanSledright (2002a, 2002b) taught fifth graders to use historical reasoning to read multiple texts, concluding that the students learned "how to make sense of historical documents as evidence, identify the nature of the documents as sources, judge the reliability and perspective of those documents, and corroborate details across accounts in order to construct evidence-based assumptions" (VanSledright, 2002b, p. 131). Wolfe and Goldman (2005) taught low-performing middle graders to think across two texts about the fall of the Roman Empire and found that even these struggling readers could make cross-textual connections, given easy texts. De La Paz (2005) found that instruction of middle school students in historical reasoning strategies using multiple texts helped them to write more accurate and persuasive historical essays than students who did not have such instruction. Monte-Sano (2011) studied an 11th-grade history class whose teacher taught them to annotate multiple primary sources, write about historical perspectives, and synthesize major issues, with an emphasis on using evidence. She found that students gained skill in historical reasoning and wrote better essays as a result. Later, Monte-Sano and De La Paz (2012) gave four document-based writing tasks to

10th- and 11th-grade students on the topic of the Cold War. They asked some to engage in sourcing, corroboration, and causal analysis before writing and others to imagine themselves as historical agents. The students who engaged in sourcing, corroboration, and causal analysis significantly improved their historical reasoning, whereas students who were asked to imagine themselves as historical agents, writing in first person, did not do as well. And Reisman (2012) provided 11th-grade history teachers a number of "document" lessons they integrated into their regular history curriculum. She found that students who experienced these multiple document lessons did significantly better than those who did not on measures of historical thinking, were able to tranfer historical thinking strategies to current issues, and did significantly better on tests of factual knowledge and general reading comprehension. So studies across grade levels provide evidence that students are capable of learning multiple texts strategies in history for both reading and writing.

In the sciences, Prain, Hand, and their colleagues engaged in a series of studies of models of writing in science, and found that students benefit from instruction that involves them writing for a variety of purposes to a variety of audiences, and in a variety of genres (Hand, 1999; Hand, Prain, & Wallace, 2002; Prain & Hand, 1999). They recommend that students be given writing assignments in science that include explanation, sets of instructions, letters, reports, diagrams, and so on for the purpose of clarifying, applying, or persuading peers, younger students, a government agency, and others. Elizabeth Moje and her team (Textual Tools Study Group, 2006) developed units to teach science by pairing a textbook passage with a popular science passage on the same topic, and they taught students to translate science information into different forms (e.g. from text to diagram, to data table) Students had to write explanations that their peers reviewed for quality. Students across all classrooms—regardless of entering skill level—demonstrated more developed and scientifically accurate and appropriate explanations when compared to their writing at the outset of the interventions, as well as significant gains in science concept knowledge (Textual Tools Study Group, 2006; Moje, 2007; Moje, Sutherland, Solomon, & Vanderkerkof, 2010).

Greenleaf and associates taught science teachers, through an apprenticeship, to develop science lessons focused on the use of multiple texts and multiple representations of data. The teachers taught students to engage in sense-making from these texts, to monitor their comprehension, and to solve problems in understanding as they arose. A randomized experiment of high school biology teaching and learning showed that the students improved their skills at integrating information across sources and representations. They also made significant achievement gains on their on state language arts, reading comprehension, and biology tests (Greenleaf et al., 2009).

In summary, in these two fields at least, there are numerous indications that reading across texts leads to a number of academic benefits.

ISSUES WITH MULTIPLE TEXTS

Teachers usually want to know several things before they teach students multiple text strategies. Some of these issues are addressed in this section.

Text Complexity

Adolescent readers often struggle with their content area texts for a variety of reasons. Perhaps they have general reading difficulties, such as word recognition and fluency problems that affect all of their reading. Maybe they lack adequate general vocabulary knowledge or struggle with the abstract, decontextualized nature of academic language. It could be that the text genre (e.g., a scientific journal article) or structure (e.g., a mixture of narrative and expository text) is unfamiliar. It could be that the student lacks appropriate background information or that the text itself is "inconsiderate" (e.g. Beck, McGowan, & Worthy, 1995)—that is, it fails to provide explanation of technical vocabulary, lacks appropriate explanations and examples, or uses arcane language. In addition, perhaps students do not approach reading within a particular disciplinary lens and therefore do not understand what to pay attention to or what questions to ask. Whatever the reason, these struggles are still evident when there is more than one text, and may be magnified if the texts represent different genres, were written in different contexts, or have contradictory purposes and messages. Thus the difficulty level of the texts students read is an issue, but the measurement of difficulty is complex. For a single text reading, any one of the conditions noted above could make the texts too difficult, and most often, more than one of the conditions interact. For example, Britton and Gulgoz (1991) found that students who lack background information are more troubled by inconsiderate texts than students who have high levels of background knowledge, especially when the text comprehension requires extensive inferential thinking. Multiple text reading compounds the complexity. Depending on what the problems are, different solutions are called for—and not all of them involve finding texts at lower readability levels.

An ACT study (American College Testing, 2006) found that students' preparation for college depended on the extent to which they could read complex texts. Too often, students do not get the practice reading these kinds of texts that they need, even though, with a high level of instructional support, students can often read text that is too difficult to read independently.

The CCSS make it even more imperative that we find ways to support students as they read complex texts. This set of standards expects students to read more difficult texts than they have read in the past. They define text complexity as the interaction of three factors: a qualitative evaluation of the text, a quantitative evaluation of the text, and an interaction of text and task that is matched to the characteristics of readers.

Different solutions are called for depending on the reasons students experience difficulty reading the texts, as represented in the following list. Teachers could:

- Encourage close reading of texts.
- Preteach potentially troublesome vocabulary.
- Have students read an easier text or otherwise provide information to build background knowledge (e.g., an anchor text or experience) before reading a more difficult text.
- Teach students to use strategies that will help them better interpret the texts.
- Teach students about various genres and structures used in particular texts and how texts within those genres signal important information.
- Teach students information about the discipline in which they are reading—about how experts in that discipline approach and use information in text to build on existing knowledge.
- Set up cooperative grouping structures that would allow students to support one another's interpretations.
- Use one of the online translation sites to translate text to a student's primary language.

Using more than one text about a particular topic may actually facilitate gains in text comprehension about a particular topic. The easier texts in the set could build background that makes the more difficult texts easier to understand. Also, multiple readings of information that are repeated across texts may increase the likelihood that students will gain a deeper understanding of the information.

I would like to say more about the first item: "Encourage close reading of texts." The term "close reading" is extremely popular in educational circles lately, yet there is a great deal of disagreement about what it means. Some think that close reading is a strategy or set of procedures; some think it is a lesson. I define close reading as the careful reading of texts to explore their meaning on various levels, actively negoiating with the texs to unearth and evaluate possible meanings. This kind of reading requires self-regulation to engage in problem solving and to overcome challenges to interpretation. If students are reading *multiple texts* closely, not only are they focusing on one text's interpretation, but they are also comparing that interpretation with others. Close reading in history might involve looking for the source of information and the perspective of the writer, and students might surmise the context in which the text is written so that differences in what various texts say might be attributed to these things. Close reading in science might entail looking at the data and reading the graphic information and the prose information recursively, inferring from this information what a text means and how trustworthy it is, then reading other texts in the same way to add to their understanding of the scientific information.

To get students engaged in this kind of close reading, teachers need to create a climate for reading that recognizes students' difficulties with text and honors their persistence in using problem-solving strategies to overcome those difficulties. That is, students must have permission to struggle, to reread, to discuss difficult words or passages with others, and to not be satisfied until they have deeply understood and thought about what they have read. Teachers need to help students feel competent enough to figure out what they find challenging (providing support but not answers).

How Many Texts?

I've found that teachers who introduce multiple text instruction sometimes make the mistake of assigning too many texts, too soon. The middle school and high school history teachers I work with have had success with this beginning to multiple text instruction: Have students read an easy background text (an "anchor" text) that sets the context and introduces key vocabulary. Then introduce a second text and study it. Then introduce a third text, studying it as well and comparing and contrasting it to the second text. With that introduction to multiple text study, it will be easier in the future to introduce a larger text set.

What Kind of Instruction?

Students need to learn how to think about more than one text about a topic. My research has convinced me that, without this instruction, just having students read more than one text will have minimal effect on comprehension or learning. But the answer to the question, "What kind of instruction?" depends somewhat on the discipline one is teaching, the kinds of texts that are being introduced, and the purpose for reading. For that reason, this section discusses the application of multiple texts strategies within disciplines and for specific purposes that are to some extent discipline specific.

History

As discussed earlier in this chapter, historians are always reading texts with a critical eye—that is, as arguments for particular interpretations of historical events. Thus, when reading multiple texts in history, the most authentic purpose for reading is to determine a credible interpretation of an event—what caused it, what effects it had, how significant it was. In reading any document in a set of documents, then, the reader must determine the credibility of the source, evaluate the context in which the message was written, weigh the evidence that is being offered for the interpretation, and evaluate how well that interpretation agrees or disagrees with others in order to decide what to believe.

In my teaching of multiple texts in history, I first ask students to what it is that historians do. My research (Hynd-Shanahan et al., 2004) suggests that students begin to answer that question in a way that assumes historians to be nothing more than than documenters. They believe historians write down exactly what happened. In the discussion, however, they soon come to realize that that is an inadequate description—because historians search for many different accounts of what happened, and they begin to view them as synthesizers. Some subsequently start to shift their opinions to note that historians need to judge the accuracy of accounts—thus they believe historians act as arbiters. If they keep on discussing the issue, some will even come to recognize that historians have their own viewpoints and biases that influence their final interpretation. These emerging notions of the historian's role in interpreting historical events are key. To read and write like historians, students need to understand that they are reading arguments rather than truth when they read historical text.

I teach students about the strategies that historians use when they read: sourcing, contextualization, and corroboration. That is, I explain what they are, I model how they are used by thinking out loud about them as I read a text excerpt, and I have the students practice using the strategies, both as a whole group and independently or in small groups. It is only after I know that students understand the task (to determine a credible interpretation of an event) and the strategies (sourcing, contextualization, and corroboration) that I introduce a text set. As noted earlier, three texts are an optimal beginning point. The first text sets up the context and provides background information. The second and third texts are read using the strategies.

Other teachers, however, have introduced the idea of history reading in a slightly different way, without teaching the strategies first. After asking students what historians did, one history teacher I work with at Project READI began a unit on the Columbian Exchange by having students read three texts: one was a document by a local priest castigating Columbus for decimating and torturing the peoples they conquered. The other two texts were written by historians who both used the first document as evidence. One author used it almost exclusively, taking the position that there was no Columbian exchange—rather, there was only exploitation. The other historian minimally used the first document and included evidence pointing to the ways both Europe and the "New World" benefitted—a true Columbian exchange. These three texts help students realize that historians had different perspecives, used evidence in different ways depending on the perspectives, and were, indeed, interpreters of history. While students were reading this text set, the teacher was introducing the concepts of sourcing, contextualization, and corroboration, making these strategies explicit during and after instruction.

To help students engage in the strategies, I ask them to create two comparison and contrast charts. On one chart, students take notes about the *source* of each text (the author, the kind of text, the publisher, where the information came from) and the *context* of each text (when it was written, for what audience, and in what political, social, economic climate). To find this information, a student might have to search a website or search the jacket of the book or read the preface and the table of contents. To find out the political, social, or economic climate, students may have to search outside sources; the teacher at this point might want to provide her expertise in helping students understand contextual issues or point them to key sources of information, such as the anchor text they read for background information.

The second chart I have students create is a comparison–contrast chart of the issues for the purposes of *corroboration*. For example, when we studied the Gulf of Tonkin incident of the Vietnam conflict, students knew from the background text that historians argued about three points: (1) what happened, (2) whether the United States instigated it, and (3) whether President Johnson pushed the Gulf of Tonkin resolution through Congress knowing that the justification he used was not entirely truthful. Students wrote these points in the form of questions that could be answered "yes" or "no" (or, in some cases, "maybe") across the top of their chart and wrote the text titles down the side of their chart. That is, they wrote these three questions: (1) Did North Vietnam attack the U.S.S. *Maddox*? (2) Did the United States intentionally provoke North Vietnam? (3) Did President Johnson manipulate Congress? When they came to evidence in their reading that spoke to one of the points, students answered the question, then paraphrased the evidence in the appropriate box and wrote down the page number where they found it. They could then compare the texts on those three issues.

Students need to discuss what they find using the charts with a more knowledgeable other, such as the teacher. This discussion is important because students do not have the expertise or the mature viewpoints of practicing historians. For example, my students thought that a book that was "self-published" was automatically just as credible as a book produced by a reputable publishing company, and that an article in a local newspaper carried the same evidentiary weight as an article published in a newspaper like the *Washington Post* or *New York Times*, papers which are (or which used to be) known for their dogged pursuit of reliable information. They also held a considerable bias for authors who "were there" over historians, believing, for example, that Dean Rusk was a more credible source of information than the historian who had written his dissertation on Vietnam and who had published a three-volume set of annotated primary documents. When I asked questions, however, that got them to examine these beliefs, they changed their thinking. For example, when I asked students what made them think that Dean Rusk was without bias, some students brought up the idea that he had his own reputation on the line and, in defending that reputation, might not be giving his audience the most unbiased presentation of the facts. I set up a scenario for them of an accident site and asked them who would have the more credible account—any one person who witnessed the accident or the reporter who interviewed all of the witnesses. But students were rightly quick to point out that the reporter, too, could have had biases. These discussions helped students form more nuanced interpretations of the event.

In their essays that were part of the exam about the Vietnam conflict, students were asked to take a stand on one of three questions and provide evidence for their viewpoint. Because they all had thought very deeply about their stand and the evidence to support it before taking the test, they could easily write coherent, well-supported essays.The first time I engaged students in a multiple text project I was surprised by the quality of their writing; as I continued to engage students in this kind of instruction, I came to expect it. However, I am still amazed at the transformation that takes place in students' understanding of what it means to read history and how much more students are engaged in learning history when they take responsibility for interpretation.

OTHER MULTIPLE TEXT STRATEGIES FOR HISTORY

Questioning the Author (QtA; Beck, McKeown, Hamilton, & Kucan, 1997) can be adapted for use with multiple texts. It is appropriate, because the purposes of the strategy are to help readers understand that each text has a human, fallible author and to read texts with a reviewer's eye. The idea is that students "question" the unseen author in order to determine the meaning he or she intended. The teacher initiates the discussion (What is the author trying to say?), helps students focus on the author's message (That's what the author says, but what does it mean?), links information, in this case, to the other texts they have read (How does this connect with what we already read?), identifies difficulties (Does that make sense?), and encourages a close reading of the text (Did the author tell us that? Where?). For multiple text lessons, these questions can be used with the texts as they are read to help students comprehend them and to ensure that students are able to make appropriate links to the other texts.

In addition, teachers can construct other guiding questions that students can use in collaborative work to help them think critically about the various texts they are reading. Steve Stahl and I (Stahl & Shanahan, 2004) called these "procedural facilitators," in that they facilitate the use of the same procedures historians use (see Table 10.1).

When historians are reading the text, they look for evidence of bias in the language authors use by asking themselves questions about the connotation of particular words, by evaluating what was *not* said about the topic, and so on. All of these questions, if students learn to ask them, help them to evaluate a particular text and compare it with the others they are reading. The final result should be that students are better able to decide what kind of cross-textual evidence is credible as they learn to make their own interpretations of historical events.

Science

As noted, scientists read multiple texts on any one topic and engage in writing across multiple contexts for multiple purposes. Teachers need to invite their students into the various discourses used in science. Scientists approach reading somewhat differently than do historians, however. Shanahan et al. (2011), found that the chemists they studied engaged in two

TABLE 10.1. Procedural Facilitators for Considering History Texts

Questions about sourcing

- Who wrote this?
- Who published it?
- What biases did the author have?
- How might those biases affect the content?

Questions about context

- When was this document written?
- To whom was it written?
- What was occurring at the same time?

Questions encouraging critical reading

- What kind of history is this [political, social, economic, and so on]?
- Whose voices are represented in the contents? Whose voices are left out?
- What is this author's view of the past? (Is the past glorified or considered a problem?)When did the author begin and end the story [of a person's life or of a particular event]? Could the story have begun or ended in a different place in a way that might have affected its meaning?

distinct kinds of reading, depending on the kind of text they read and their level of knowledge about the topic. Bazerman (1998) found that physicists engaged in those two processes as well. That is, when their topic knowledge was low, the scientists read uncritically, for the purpose of learning. When we asked the chemists about how students should read their textbooks, they emphasized this kind of learning-focused reading. If they knew a lot about the topic or if they were reading a journal article or piece in the popular press (e.g., a newspaper article), they would adopt a critical reading style, engaging in many of the same processes the historians used when reading (sourcing, contextualizing, and corroborating).

So how should multiple texts be used in science classes? Certainly, students should read the various discourses of science, classified by Wignell (1994) as (1) procedure (to provide instruction for experiments); (2) procedural recount (to record what has already been done in an experiment); (3) science report (to organize information by setting up taxonomies, parts, or steps, or by listing properties); and (4) science explanation (describing how and why phenomena occur). Note that (3) and (4) appear most often in science textbooks, and (1) and (2) appear most often in scientific journals. In addition to these, Prain and Hand (1999) note other genres that are appropriate for science writing such as field notes, a diagram, a brochure, or a letter. Considering Bazerman's (1998) reminder that scientists have to cross genres to gain funding, secure patents, and disseminate findings to a lay audience, asking students to read and write these different types of texts in science class makes sense. For writing assignments, Prain and Hand recommend that teachers vary these four elements on any given topic: (1) the genre, (2) the purpose, (3) the audience, and (4) the method of text production. If the topic were "the urban heat island," for example, students might be asked to write a scientific explanation in order to clarify ideas for another student, using pen and paper, or write a proposal to a government agency to alter the effects of the urban heat island for the benefit of the city's inhabitants (a persuasive argument that includes how the ideas are applied), using a computer. For our purposes, (teaching students to process multiple texts) students would be asked to engage in both types of writing. Because each of these genres uses distinct structures and rhetorical moves, these need to be taught.

Moje's (2007) idea of pairing a textbook-like scientific explanation with an article in a popular science magazine or other type of text showing an application of the scientific phenomenon makes sense as well. When reading the scientific explanation in the textbook, students would be in learning mode. They would engage in strategies to help them learn the information in the text, such as transforming text into diagrams (or vice versa), identifying and learning key vocabulary through activities such as concept cards, and so on. When reading the "popular science" application text, they would be engaged in sourcing, contextualization, and corroboration.

That is, they would be finding out who the author is and to what audience he or she is writing, what the context of the writing is about, and how well the text corresponds to the science.

Another pairing of articles to help students make sense of scientific study might be an experimental article on a particular topic paired with a newspaper or popular science article on the same topic. In such a pairing, students could evaluate the science (How well did the scientists follow the scientific method? Did their findings make sense?) and then see how those findings are translated to another audience. Alternately, an article on a particular topic written in the past paired with one on the same topic written more recently would help students to understand how scientific findings change with new methodology, new measurements, and so on.

I used two popular science texts on sea turtles to help students engage in critical thinking about science information. One text is dated, and some of the information is no longer thought to be true. If students don't pay attention to the date of the articles, they can become confused. That text is written to persuade the audience to back conservation efforts of a particular government agency. The other text is written to provide information about sea turtles to students. For science topics, I suggest focusing on learning the information first. Students read one of the texts, write down the information they learn, then group that information and label it. For the sea turtles topic, for example, students write down information and group it under such labels as (1) physical appearance, (2) reproduction, (3) habitat, and so on. They place this information on a chart, with the labels along one axis and the two texts along another, and the actual information (e.g., weight = 150 pounds; large flippers) in the boxes next to the first text. Then students read the second text. If the second text agrees with the first text, they place a check in the box next to the second text. If it is new information, they put a plus and add the new information, and if it disagrees with the first text, they put an x in the box and write down the disagreement. Students can complete this task in small groups or alone. When they are finished, the class discusses the similarities and differences between the texts. The differences provide the teacher with the opportunity to help students pay attention to the source of the information and the context in which it was written. The contextual analysis includes seeing *when* the text was written, to *what audience,* and for *what purpose.* Students see that one of the texts is dated and are then able to evaluate the credibility of the information. The final step is to have students write a synthesis of the two texts, using only the information that appears to be credible. The activity loosely mirrors the processes used by scientists when they read several texts on the same topic.

Science inquiry projects (such as those required in science fairs) all involve the synthesis and critical evaluation of multiple texts as well as the ability to use scientific method to answer a question. Yet students are expected to know how to think about the information in more than one text without being taught how to do so. That assumption may be unfair to students, as they will flounder in their attempts to engage in true scientific inquiry.

Mathematics

The Shanahan et al. (2011) study found that the mathematicians they studied did not view sourcing and contextualization as key elements in reading mathematics. One of the mathematicians explained to us that it just doesn't matter when a mathematics text was written. Years later, it could still be the object of intense study. In the same vein, it doesn't matter who did the writing, according to him. What matters is the text on the page. These mathematicians engaged in critical reading, but it appeared different than the critical reading done by the chemists and historians in our study. Mathematicians, they told us, look for a kind of precise sense-making. They want to make sure that the math is without error, and that every word and term is accurately used, that a logical progression of ideas unfolds. So reading and writing multiple texts in mathematics will look different than it does in science or history. In the application of math to everyday life, precision truly matters. For example, it is a matter of life and death that an engineer correctly calculates the weight that can be borne by a particular floor.

That a sloppy or inaccurate application can be quite important is an idea that is easier communicated to students through multiple texts. As in the science example above, a typical textbook explanation of a mathematics principle could be paired with an applied text, such as in a magazine or journal article. The textbook passage is read in a "learning" mode. That is, students learn key vocabulary and the processes that are described. They write explanations of the processes in their own words, solve problems using the process, and engage in other activities such as writing their own problems. When they are asked to read the applied text, they are to read critically. That is, they look for errors in the text—to see whether all vocabulary, formulae, explanations, and so on are accurate, that they are appropriately applied, that there is a logical progression of ideas, and that the unit of measurement makes sense. Corroboration, too, is an important process to be used in mathematics. Mathematics teachers commonly complain that students can do the problems assigned after reading the text, but have difficulty figuring out how to solve problems on a test, when they have to decide among several different processes for solving them. They say that students don't know how the problems on the test compare with the ones they learned to do in their assignments. Thus comparing the test problems with the textbook problems may help students come up with ways to categorize text problems. When writing, students could write multiple texts about the same process. One might be an explanation of the process and another might be an application of the principle.

CONCLUSION

This chapter has made a case for using more than one text when teaching content-area subjects. I used three discipline examples to discuss how this might be done—history, science, and mathematics. Even beyond these examples, however, more needs to be done to teach students how to take into account multiple messages when they read and write for different audiences. Students are already reading multiple texts in their daily lives and they are increasingly reading multiple texts in school, but they won't be able to process these texts critically unless they are provided some instruction in how to do it.

DISCUSSION AND ACTIVITIES

1. What difficulties do adolescents experience when they have more than one text to read about a particular topic? How can these difficulties be ameliorated?

2. Think of a topic you would teach in your subject area. What kinds of texts would be good choices for involving students in learning about that topic? Where would you find them?

3. How would you teach students to search for multiple texts they might find on the Internet regarding topics in your subject area? How would you help them to evaluate them for credibility?

4. How would you react to students who, after evaluating the credibility of the texts they are reading, decide to believe a harmful or untenable position (e.g., racist or in some other way biased or offensive)?

5. What writing genres are used in your subject area? How could you help students to write in these various genres?

ACKNOWLEDGMENT

Project READI is a multiinstitution collaboration to improve complex comprehension of multiple forms of text in literature, history, and science. It is supported by the Institute of Education Sciences, U.S. Department of Education, through Grant R305F100007 to the University of Illinois at Chicago. The opinions expressed are those of the authors and do not represent the views of the Institute or the U.S. Department of Education.

REFERENCES

American College Testing. (2006). *Reading between the lines: What the ACT reveals about college readiness for reading.* Retrieved from*http://act.org/ path/policy/reports/reading.html.*
Bazerman, C. (1998). *Shaping written knowledge: The genre and activity of*

the experimental article in science. Madison, WI: University of Wisconsin Press.

Beck, I., McKeown, M. G., & Worthy, J. (1995). Giving a text voice can improve students' understanding. *Reading Research Quarterly, 30,* 220–238.

Beck, I., McKeown, M. G., Hamilton, R. L., & Kucan, L. (1997). *Questioning the author: An approach for enhancing student engagement with text.* Newark, DE: International Reading Association.

Britt, M. A., Rouet, J. F., & Perfetti, C. A. (1996). Using hypertext to study and reason about historical evidence. In J. F. Rouet, J. T. Levonen, A. Dillon, & R. Spiro (Eds.), *Hypertext and cognition* (pp. 43–72). Mahwah, NJ: Erlbaum.

Britton, B., & Gulgoz, S. (1991). Using Kintsch's computational model to improve instructional text: Effects of repairing inference calls on recall and cognitive structures. *Journal of Educational Psychology, 83*(3), 329–345.

De La Paz, S. (2005). Effects of historical reasoning instruction and writing strategy mastery in culturally and academically diverse middle school classrooms. *Journal of Educational Psychology, 97*(2), 139–156.

Greenleaf, C., Hanson, T, Herman, J., Litman, C., Madden, Rosen, R., et al. (2009). *Integrating literacy and science instruction in high achool biology: Impact on teacher practice, student engagement, and student achievement* (Final report to National Science Foundation, Grant #0440379). Retrieved from *www.wested.org/sli/downloads/nsf-final-report.pdf.*

Hand, B. (1999). A writing-in-science framework designed to enhance science literacy. *International Journal of Science Education, 21*(10), 1021–1035.

Hand, B., Prain, V., & Wallace, C. (2002). Influences of writing tasks on students' answers to recall and higher-level test questions. *Research in Science Education, 32*(1), 19–34.

Hynd-Shanahan, C., Holschuh, J., & Hubbard, B. (2004). Thinking like a historian: College students' reading of multiple historical documents. *Journal of Literacy Research, 36,* 141–176.

Leu, D. (2007, May). *What happened when we weren't looking? How reading comprehension changed and what we need to do about it.* Paper presented at the annual meeting of the International Reading Association, Toronto, ON.

Moje, E. (2007, May). *Adolescent literacy: The crisis and the solutions.* Paper presented at "Reading and writing are more than elementary: A summit on adolescent literacy," Wisconsin Department of Education & Alliance for Excellent Education (with support from Carnegie Corporation of New York & Great Lakes West Comprehensive Center), Madison, WI.

Moje, E. B., Sutherland, L. M., Solomon, T. E., & Vanderkerkof, M. (2010). *Integrating literacy instruction into secondary school science inquiry: The challenges of disciplinary literacy teaching and professional development.* Retrieved from *www.personal.umich.edu/~moje/pdf/ MojeEtAlScienceLiteracyTeachingStrategies2010.pdf.*

Monte-Sano, C. (2011). Beyond reading comprehension and summary: Learning to read and write by focusing on evidence, perspective, and interpretation. *Curriculum Inquiry,41*(2), 212–249.

Monte-Sano, C., & De La Paz, S. (2012). Using writing tasks to elicit adolescents' historical reasoning. *Journal of Literacy Research, 44*(3), 273–299.

National Governors Association Center for Best Practices & Council of Chief State School Officers. (2010). *Common Core State Standards.* Washington, DC: Author.

Perfetti, C. A., Britt, M. A., Rouet, J. F., Mason, R. A., & Georgi, M. C. (1993, April). *How students use texts to learn and reason about historical uncertainty.* Paper presented at the annual meeting of the American Educational Research Association, Atlanta, GA.

Prain, V., & Hand, B. (1999). Students' perceptions of writing for learning in secondary school science. *Science Education 83*(2), 151–162.

Reisman, A. (2012). Reading like a historian: A document-based history curriculum intervention in urban high schools. *Cognition and Instruction, 30,* 86–112.

Shanahan, C., Shanahan, T., & Misischia, C. (2011). Analysis of expert readers in three disciplines: History, mathematics, and chemistry, *Journal of Literacy Research, 43,* 393–429.

Stahl, S., Hynd, C., Britton, B., McNish, M., & Bosquet, D. (1996). What happens when students read multiple source documents in history? *Reading Research Quarterly, 31,* 430–457.

Stahl, S., & Shanahan, C. (2004). Learning to think like a historian: Disciplinary knowledge through critical analysis of multiple documents. In T. Jetton & J. Dole (Eds.), *Adolescent literacy research and practice* (pp. 94–118). New York: Guildford Press.

Textual Tools Study Group. (2006). Developing scientific literacy through the use of literacy teaching strategies. In R. Douglas, M. Klentschy, K. Worth, & W. Binder (Eds.), *Linking science and literacy in the K–8 classroom* (pp. 261–285). Washington, DC: National Science Teachers Association.

VanSledright, B. (2002a). Confronting history's interpretive paradox while teaching fifth graders to investigate the past. *American Educational Research Journal, 39,* 1089–1115.

VanSledright, B. (2002b). *In search of America's past: Learning to read history in elementary school.* New York: Teachers College Press.

VanSledright, B., & Kelly, C. (1998). Reading American history: The influence of multiple sources on six fifth graders. *Elementary School Journal, 98*(3), 239–265.

Wignell, P. (1994). Genre across the curriculum. *Linguistics and Education, 6*(4), 355–372.

Wineburg, S. S. (1991). On the reading of historical texts: Notes on the breach between school and academy. *American Educational Research Journal, 28,* 495–519.

Wolfe, M. B., & Goldman, S. R. (2005). Relations between adolescents' text processing and reasoning, *Cognition and Instruction, 23*(4), 467–502.

PART III

Developing
Disciplinary Literacies

CHAPTER 11

Fostering Acquisition of Mathematics Language

Codruta Temple
Kathleen A. Hinchman

The purpose of this chapter is to illustrate several principles of best practices for fostering the development of mathematical language, as required by the Common Core State Standards for Mathematics. The chapter includes:

- A brief description of mathematics language.

- Principles of classroom practice illustrated with observation snippets from one teacher's classroom.

- Conclusions and instructional implications.

- Points for discussion and suggested activities.

The Common Core State Standards for Mathematics (CCSSM), like the Common Core State Standards for English Language Arts, have been adopted in most of the United States (National Governors Association [NGA] Center for Best Practices & Council of Chief State School Officers [CCSSO], 2010a, 2010b). The CCSSM emphasize the development of students' conceptual understandings, procedural skill and fluency, and flexible application in and outside the classroom. The CCSSM build on those expectations spelled out previously by the *Principles and Standards for School Mathematics* (National Council of Teachers of Mathematics, 2000) and *Curriculum Focal Points* (National Council of Teachers of Mathematics, 2006). However, the new standards require more complex approaches to mathematics content, demanding that students in all grades learn to complete newly complex, challenging tasks with appropriate mathematical thinking that they explain in viable arguments.

Thus, as Siebert and Draper (2012) explain, communication is central to successful engagement in mathematical processes. The CCSSM preface notes the role language plays in mathematics learning:

> Mathematically proficient students understand and use stated assumptions, definitions, and previously established results in constructing arguments. They make conjectures and build a logical progression of statements to explore the truth of their conjectures. . . . They justify their conclusions, communicate them to others, and respond to the arguments of others. . . . Students at all grades can listen or read the arguments of others, decide whether they make sense, and ask useful questions to clarify or improve the arguments. (NGA & CCSSO, 2010b, pp. 6–7)

In other words, part of engaging in the complex mathematical processes required by the CCSSM is learning to use mathematics language in ways that are specific to the discipline of mathematics. Determining ways to help all students learn this language, including those who are typically marginalized by mathematics instruction and assessment, will be central to the success of the new standards (Larson, 2012).

WHAT IS MATHEMATICS LANGUAGE?

The idea that learning mathematics means learning to use language in specific ways was first articulated by the linguist Halliday (1978) in his discussion of the "mathematical register," which he defined as "the meanings that belong to the language of mathematics . . . and that a language must express if it is used for mathematical purposes" (p. 195). Building on Halliday's and others' discussions of this definition, Schleppegrell (2007) pointed out that the mathematical register includes not only oral and written language, but also symbolic notation and visual representations (e.g., graphs); that the linguistic, symbolic, and visual systems work together to construct meaning; and that, therefore, students need to learn to interpret and use all three systems of representation in an integrated manner as they learn mathematics.

In addition, Fang (2012) elaborated on the linguistic challenges that mathematical texts pose for students, given their tripartite (linguistic, symbolic, and visual) structure. He explained that understanding and producing mathematics texts involves not only familiarity with technical vocabulary (usually words of Latin or Greek origin, such as *polynomial* or *diameter*), but also the ability to identify the technical meanings of everyday terms when used in mathematical contexts (e.g., *acute, power,* or *product*). Moreover, mathematics texts use "semitechnical terms" (Fang, 2012) created through nominalization (i.e., through converting verbs into nouns, such as *add—addition, equate—equation*), which refer to abstract concepts rather than to concrete operations, and which are critical to developing and communicating conceptual understanding.

Fang (2012), as well as Schleppegrell (2007), also pointed out that, besides acquiring discipline-specific vocabulary, learning mathematics language involves developing familiarity with the grammatical patterns (sentence structures) used to express mathematical meanings. The grammatical patterning of mathematics typically consists of technical or semitechnical vocabulary packed densely in noun phrases that are brought together in clauses with *being* and *having* verbs. For example, the sentence "The slope of a line is the tangent of the angle formed by the line with the x-axis in its positive direction" consists of two noun phrases ("the slope of a line" and "the tangent of the angle formed by the line with the x-axis in its positive direction") connected by the verb *is*.

Finally, scholars working in the field of genre pedagogy note that mathematics knowledge is communicated through discipline-specific genres, or text types, such as definitions, explanations, justifications, problems, and proofs (Marks & Mousley, 1990). Therefore, besides familiarity with the vocabulary and grammatical patterns of mathematics language, understanding and communicating mathematical ideas also requires the ability to comprehend and produce such texts.

Most of us learn the language we use to communicate each day through our attempts to use it, along with others' guidance of our efforts (Scribner & Cole, 1981). Even though mathematics language bears some resemblance to the language of everyday interactions, young people typically do not so easily acquire an understanding and ability to use its complex technical or semitechnical vocabulary, grammatical patterns, and multisemiotic texts. How to build on students' everyday language resources in a way that would support their acquisition of mathematics language has been a key question for educators over the past two decades. Scholars in the fields of both content-area literacy and mathematics education (e.g., Moschkovich, 2010; Schleppegrell, 2004, 2007) suggest that the answer includes (1) exposing students and drawing their attention to the ways in which linguistic, symbolic, and visual representations are used to express mathematical meanings, as well as (2) providing and mediating opportunities for students to use mathematics language orally and in writing to construct meaningful mathematics texts.

PRINCIPLES TO HELP STUDENTS LEARN MATHEMATICS LANGUAGE

Codruta Temple spent a year gathering data in a 10th-grade Romanian mathematics classroom with a teacher whose practices encouraged students' acquisition of mathematics language. We share this teacher's approach to teaching one mathematical concept (the slope of a line) in the following sections, segmenting one instructional unit to point out principles for teaching mathematics language that are illustrated by her classroom orchestrations.

1. Invite Students to Use Their Prior Mathematical and Linguistic Knowledge to Explore New Concepts

At the beginning of the first lesson in the unit, the students discussed the new concept, the slope of a line, starting from the word *slope*, which they said meant "inclination" or "steepness." Ariadna, the teacher, drew an oblique line on the board that intersected the *x*-axis of a system of Cartesian coordinates and asked the students to hypothesize how they might find the slope of the line. In the conversation that followed, a student suggested drawing a triangle and finding the tangent of the angle formed by the line and the *x*-axis. Starting from this suggestion, the class eventually produced a more precise definition of slope: "the tangent of the angle formed by a line and the *x*-axis, positive direction." Then they discussed the slopes of lines that were parallel or perpendicular on the *x*-axis.

In the episode transcribed in Figure 11.1, Ariadna wanted to take the students one step further and have them use the new concept to find, and then to define, the slope of a line determined by two points. She framed this as a problem for students to solve and then asked them to explain their solutions to the class (see Figure 11.1, lines 1–4). It is noteworthy that solving the problem required that the students construct a visual representation and use symbolic notation, while explaining the solutions required translating the visual and symbolic information into words.

Misha's explanation of his solution (see Figure 11.1) was less than clear, so Ariadna rephrased it before she evaluated it as a possible variant for solving the problem (lines 4–7). Raul volunteered a different solution and explained it clearly enough for Ariadna to be able to point out its fallacy, namely that it required information not given in the problem (lines 9–14). Iolanda proposed a third solution and, prompted by Ariadna's questions, she explained how she had reached it (lines 28–36).

Up to this point in the lesson, Ariadna encouraged the students to use their prior mathematical knowledge and linguistic resources to explore the problem, make conjectures, and explain them. Through her questions and feedback, she clarified students' contributions, pointed out fallacies in their solutions, and pushed them to elaborate on their explanations, thus helping them to express their reasoning in detail. What she did *not* do was ask them to use more precise language; the emphasis was on students' thinking and reasoning rather than on the precision with which they explained their solutions.

The principle here is that an important instructional move for helping

ARIADNA: . . . I have two points, A, of coordinates x_1 and y_1, and B, of coordinates x_2 and y_2. I would like you to determine the slope of line AB function of the coordinates of the points. . . . Please think and let's see what ideas you have for determining the slope.

Students start talking among themselves, some in pairs, and some in spontaneously formed small groups. They turn around to face the people sitting behind them. Some move their chairs to join a group at a different table. Some are writing in their notebooks, alone. Cristina is having a heated argument with Ovid. At one of the front tables, Dean and Raul are laughing heartily. June and Carmela are laughing, too, while drawing lines and angles in the air. There's much noise, but they are all working on the problem. I hear Chip say to Ada, "And there goes my axiom, right down the drain." Nobody volunteers for about 5 minutes. Ariadna waits in silence.

MISHA (*over the noise*): If we take . . . if we take the projection of B on the x-axis, and we take the projection of A on the i-axis, we get two small triangles, and the slope would be the tangent of the angle between the line and x.

ARIADNA: You want to construct a parallel to AB through this projection point. It's a variant. Yes, Raul, how did you do it?

RAUL: I prolonged the line to make it intersect x and . . . we need the coordinates of the point of intersection.

ARIADNA: But do you know . . . ? I don't know what coordinates the point of intersection has.

RAUL: And y . . . and then the tangent is $y_2 - y$ over $x_2 - x$.

ARIADNA: Well, yes, except you are introducing an x and a y in the formula that I don't need, because I want the slope to be only a function of the coordinates of A and B.

IOLANDA: If I write $y_B - y_A$ over $x_B - x_A$ . . .

ARIADNA: I know where you want to get but I'm asking you, how do you get there? You're perfectly right, Iolanda, but what did you do to get there?

IOLANDA: I drew a parallel to x through B, I got similar triangles, corresponding angles . . . and then the angle is the same and I can write the tangent.

ARIADNA: I got you. But I want to see what Laurel understood. He will dictate the solution and I will write it on the board.

LAUREL: We draw a parallel and we will have similar triangles.

ARIADNA: So, we construct a parallel to the x axis . . .

As Laurel begins his explanation, Ariadna starts drawing and writing on the board, converting his words into symbolic language. Several other students join in the explanation.

ARIADNA: This means that the slope of a line determined by the points of coordinates (x_1, y_1), (x_2, y_2) will be . . . ?

MARIA: The slope of a line determined by the points of coordinates (x_1, y_1), (x_2, y_2) will be $y_2 - y_1$ over $x_2 - x_1$.

Classroom transcript and field notes, March 2, 2006.

FIGURE 11.1. Genres: Definition and explanation.

these students to construct a new concept involved inviting them to explore it, to form conjectures, and to explain their thinking, drawing on their existing conceptual knowledge and linguistic resources, and with limited initial concern for the precision of their verbal expression.

2. Model Use of Mathematics Language for More Precise Concept Explanation

Once Iolanda shared her solution, the exploration of the problem ended, and the focus of the activity shifted to constructing a clearer explanation of the steps used in solving the problem and of the reasoning behind them (see Figure 11.1, lines 39–45). Ariadna asked Laurel to restate Iolanda's explanation, which he did with help from other classmates, while Ariadna assisted them in expressing their ideas by rephrasing and completing them (Laurel: "We draw a parallel and we will have similar triangles." Ariadna: "So, we construct a parallel to the x-axis . . . "), by providing sentence starters (Ariadna: "This means that the slope of a line determined by the points of coordinates (x_1, y_1), (x_2, y_2) will be . . . ?" Maria: "The slope of a line determined by the points of coordinates (x_1, y_1), (x_2, y_2) will be $y_2 - y_1$ over $x_2 - x_1$"), and by converting the verbal solution to the problem into symbols that she wrote on the board.

Through these instructional moves, Ariadna helped her students to recast the explanation of the new concept in more precise mathematical terms. She also helped them to construct both a verbal and a symbolic definition. She supplied technical vocabulary for everyday words (*construct* for *draw*), provided a sentence pattern that students could use to define the concept, and showed the students how the verbal definition could be represented symbolically.

The principle being enacted here is that a clear understanding of a mathematical concept involves being able to explain/define it using mathematics language. Once Ariadna's students had an initial grasp of the concept being studied, the teacher modeled the use of mathematics language to scaffold students' construction of suitable mathematical texts.

3. Invite Students to Connect the New Concept to Previously Learned Concepts Orally and in Writing

At the beginning of the next lesson, Ariadna had the class return to the definition of the slope of a line determined by two points and embed it in a written summary of what they had learned about the slope of a line. Besides allowing the teacher to gauge students' learning, this task also served the purpose of pushing students to extend and deepen their understanding of the new concept by connecting it to previously learned concepts. To scaffold the task, Ariadna asked the class to use a list of words, which she wrote on the board, to compose their summaries: *slope, number, x–y plane, value, two points, the difference of the ordinates, the difference of the abscissas, ratio, increasing oblique line, decreasing oblique line, horizontal line, and vertical line.*

Except for the new term/concept *slope*, all the other terms were part of students' mathematical vocabularies. However, the terms *ratio, the difference of the abscissas,* and *the difference of the ordinates* had not been used in defining the slope of the line determined by two points. Ariadna's including them on her list of terms to be used pushed the students to rephrase the definition they had constructed in the previous lesson ("The slope of a line determined by the points of coordinates (x_1, y_1), (x_2, y_2) will be $y_2 - y_1$ over $x_2 - x_1$") in more general terms.

When students had finished writing and had submitted their papers, Ariadna asked, "Who would like to try to formulate a text, remembering what they wrote in their paper, that includes all the words on the board?" Figure 11.2 is an excerpt of the dialogue that ensued.

Just like the written assignment, this sharing episode provided students with the opportunity to practice using the newly learned vocabulary, the sentence pattern, and the symbolic notation in conjunction with

---

RADA: I said that the slope of a line represented the tangent of the angle formed by a line and the abscissa of the system in which the line is situated .. . and that the line is in the *x–y* plane.

THEO: The slope is the angle made by the line and the *x*-axis, direction plus.

ARIADNA: The slope is the angle?

STUDENT: The tangent.

ARIADNA: The tangent of the angle, be careful! So, the slope is the tangent of the angle made by the line and the *x*-axis, positive direction.

DEAN: I said that the tangent was determined by the angle.

ARIADNA: It's okay if you said that it was determined by the angle and then said that it was the tangent of the angle. What else . . . ?

MISHA: The value of a slope . . . The value of the slope of a line in a *x–y* plane, which passes through two points equals the difference .. . the ratio between the difference of the abscissas and .. .

MARIA: The other way around! Of the ordinates.

ALEX: Of the ordinates and of the abscissas.

MISHA: Of the ordinates and of the abscissas.

ARIADNA: And then?

Classroom transcript and field notes, March 3, 2006.

FIGURE 11.2. Student oral explanation.

mathematics language that was already familiar to them. As Figure 11.2 demonstrates, using all of the mathematical terms in sentences was not an easy task for the students, so Ariadna provided assistance in the form of corrective feedback. For instance, she repeated students' statements as questions, expecting self-correction (lines 5–8); she rephrased parts of their sentences using mathematical terminology (when Theo used the phrase "direction plus," Ariadna recast it as "positive direction"); she allowed students to correct one another (lines 12–17); and she invited students to produce more language through questions that contained continuatives ("What else . . . ?" "And then . . . ?").

Four samples of student written summaries are included in Figure 11.3 to illustrate the students' range of success on the writing assignment. They were ranked by the teacher as low, medium, medium–high, and high according to the number of terms used correctly from a mathematical point of view.

Trying to use all the key words pushed the students to create explanations and definitions that not only had a higher degree of generality, but were also more syntactically elaborate. For example, compared to students' initial definition of the slope of a line determined by two points ("The slope of a line determined by the points of coordinates (x_1, y_1), (x_2, y_2) will be $y_2 - y_1$ over $x_2 - x_1$"), the definition in Sample 4 of Figure 11.3 ("The slope of a line that crosses two points on a x–y plane equals the value of the ratio between the difference of the ordinates and the difference of the abscissas of the two points") shows both a generalized understanding of the concept and better control of the grammatical patterning of mathematics language (the definition consists of two noun phrases, "the slope of a line that crosses two points on a x–y plane," and "the value of the ratio between the difference of the ordinates and the difference of the abscissas of the two points," connected by the verb *equals*).

Ariadna's asking the class to write, and then to share orally, summaries of what they had learned about the mathematical concept that the instructional unit was built around thus served to consolidate and extend students' mathematical understanding of the concept as well as to develop their ability to use language effectively and efficiently to express their understandings. The relatively reduced cognitive load of the task (which only required recalling and connecting familiar concepts, as opposed to constructing new concepts) was likely to allow students to pay attention to the language needed to complete the tasks, and thereby to support their use (and possibly retention) of the technical vocabulary and grammatical structures required by the task. Students need such opportunities for practice in which they focus on the precision of their expression in order to develop fluency in mathematics language (Temple & Doerr, 2012).

The twofold outcome of the writing/sharing assignment makes Ariadna's scaffolding of the task (her supplying the terms to be included in the

Sample 1. (low) Although I was absent from the last math class, I know that the title of the last lesson was the slope of the line. In an x–y plane the slope of the line is the angle formed by a line and an angle. The value that this slope takes is the ratio between the difference of the ordinates and the difference of the abscissas. To be able to realize the slope of the line, we need two points (the projections of the tips of the angle).

Sample 2. (medium) The slope is the steepness of the line that crosses an x–y plane. It has a value equal to the ratio between the difference of the ordinates and the difference of the abscissas of the two points that it crosses. If the line is an increasing oblique line, then the value of the slope is a positive number, if it is a decreasing oblique line, then the slope has a negative number as its value. If the line is vertical, then the value of the slope is 0. The value of the slope is calculated using the function of the tangent of the angle formed by the line with x, positive direction.

Sample 3. (medium–high) In our last lesson we studied the slope of a line. We represented two points on an x–y plane, thus determining a line. The slope of the respective line is the tangent of the angle formed by the line with the x-axis if the line intersects the x-axis. If it doesn't, we draw a horizontal line parallel to x through the first point and a vertical line parallel to y through the second point. If the line is an increasing oblique line, the angle will be acute, and if the line is a decreasing oblique line, the angle will be obtuse. To find the value of the slope, we tried to determine the tangent of the angle formed. This was equal to the ratio between the difference of the ordinates and the difference of the abscissas, and the result was a number that gave us the value of the slope.

Sample 4. (high) The slope of a line that crosses two points on an x–y plane equals the value of the ratio between the difference of the ordinates and the difference of the abscissas of the two points. If the line is horizontal (parallel to x), then the slope equals 0. If it is vertical, then the slope cannot be defined (as the angle between the line and x has 90 degrees). If the line is an increasing oblique line, then the value of the slope is a positive number, and if it is a decreasing oblique line, then the value of the slope is a negative number. By definition, the value of the slope is equal to the tangent of the angle between the line and the x-axis, positive direction.

Student artifacts, March 3, 2006.

FIGURE 11.3. Student written explanations.

summary) worth special attention. Contrary to the widespread belief that understanding mathematical concepts is manifested through knowledge of the technical terms that name the concepts, Ariadna's writing/sharing task seems to suggest that such understanding involves primarily the ability to connect technical terms into sentences and larger texts. The task did not require students to recall vocabulary items in isolation; instead, the key terms needed to explain the concept were provided, and the challenge was for students to relate them to one another in sentences constructed in accordance with the grammatical patterning of mathematics language.

A similar view of conceptual understanding and its expression in language was theorized by Lemke (1990). According to Lemke, just as a concept does not stand by itself but is always part of a conceptual system, the word that stands for the concept does not have meaning by itself; rather, it derives its meaning from how it is related to other words that stand for other concepts. Lemke calls such words "thematic items," and calls the pattern of connections among their meanings in a particular discipline a "thematic pattern." Furthermore, he argues that teaching disciplinary content is teaching students how to use language to construct thematic patterns (sentences and texts, that is) to express the conceptual system of the discipline.

The principle here is that a teacher can extend students' conceptual understanding by creating opportunities for them to connect new concepts to previously learned concepts and to express those connections in written and spoken mathematical texts; and that creating such opportunities has the additional benefit of developing students' fluency in mathematics language.

4. Provide Feedback to Develop Awareness of Features of Mathematics Language

In the feedback that she gave students on their written summaries, Ariadna first clarified some conceptual confusion that had surfaced in the papers (the fact that the slope of a line was not a line and not an angle). Then, after having the class briefly review and clarify the definition of the slope, she directed the students' attention to the precision of their written expression (see Figure 11.4).

ARIADNA: Another observation: when you write, "The slope is the ratio between the difference of the ordinates and the difference of the abscissas," from the point of view of a reader who knows mathematics, that means that the numerator is the difference of the ordinates and the denominator is the difference of the abscissas. That's what "the ratio between" means. If you write, "the slope is the ratio between the difference of the abscissas and the difference of the ordinates," then you are obviously saying quite the opposite. . . . "Positive angle," somebody said. "For any line, we take the positive angle." We talked about the angle between the line and the x-axis, positive direction. There are such things as positive angles, but we haven't studied them. They are oriented angles. So, if I go this way (draws an angle and an arrow on the board), it will be a positive angle, and if I go this way, it will be a negative angle.

Classroom transcript, March 9, 2006.

FIGURE 11.4. Feedback to writing (I).

Two phrases that some of the students had used inaccurately in their papers (*ratio between* and *positive angle*) gave Ariadna the opportunity to teach a mini-lesson in mathematical literacy. Besides clarifying the meaning of the phrases, she illustrated how the same technical terms had different meanings depending on how they were used in a sentence. Her reference to the "reader who knows mathematics" also suggested that mathematical texts are read somewhat differently from other texts, in that a reader's success in making sense of them depends critically on the writer's using technical terminology precisely and accurately.

Significantly, one of the inaccuracies that Ariadna pointed out was not due to students' not knowing the technical terms. Instead, it was caused by how the terms were related to one another in the sentence ("the ratio between the difference of the ordinates and the difference of the abscissas," as opposed to "the ratio between the difference of the abscissas and the difference of the ordinates"). This reinforces the point we made in the previous section, namely that conceptual understanding involves not only knowledge of words for concepts, but also (and primarily so) knowledge of the relationships among concepts and of the ways in which these relationships can be expressed in language.

Having discussed the need for precision in using technical terms, Ariadna went on to give students feedback on the structure of their texts (see Figure 11.5). This part of the feedback was meant to raise students' awareness of three features that a mathematical text should have. One feature is that it should include a clear definition of the concept being discussed. Another is that it should be complete, including all the information needed for the reader to fully understand it. The third is that it should be coherent, that is, organized in a way that shows logical connections between the concept being explained and other related concepts—mirroring the internal logic of the larger conceptual system.

The principle here is that a teacher should provide feedback to students to help them refine their conceptual understanding and the linguistic

---

ARIADNA: As for the construction. . . . Those of you who tried to include all the phrases that I gave you succeeded in constructing a fairly coherent text, in the sense that you started with a definition, (you said) that the slope was . . . , after which, since you had the phrase "the *x–y* plane" there, you tried to place the line on a plane. When you saw "value," "the difference of the ordinates," "the difference of the abscissas, "ratio," all of these made you think of the expression of the slope when we know two points that the line crosses, and then, of the slope of an increasing and decreasing oblique line, of a horizontal and vertical line.

Classroom transcript, March 9, 2006.

FIGURE 11.5. Feedback to writing (II).

expression of their understandings. She can give feedback in such forms as written notes, conferences, or class mini-lessons, helping them clarify the meaning and use of technical terms, and supporting them as they learn in more detail about expectations for the construction of mathematical texts. In doing so, she issues invitations to the greater mathematicians' discourse community with her requests for students to produce texts for "the reader who knows mathematics."

5. Invite Students to Create Mathematics Texts for an External Audience

At the beginning of the last lesson in the unit, the students had the opportunity to demonstrate their learning in another written assignment. This time their task was to define the concept of slope and to construct a problem based on their definition. Figure 11.6 includes four samples of student writing.

What is remarkable about the definitions that students produced for this assignment is that they are all accurate, even though, as the differences in wording and notation among them show, they had not been memorized word for word. The students' ability to use mathematics language flexibly to define the concept and to construct problems based on their definitions suggests that they had understood the concept, even though the difference in complexity among the problems in Samples 1–4 suggests that some students' understanding was more sophisticated than that of others.

Throughout this instructional unit, as they developed an understanding of the new concept, the students had learned ways to represent this concept visually and symbolically. They had also learned new vocabulary and new sentence patterns that allowed them to express the concept and its relationships to mathematical concepts. They had engaged in mathematical processes (forming conjectures, solving problems, and constructing mathematical explanations and definitions) that had allowed them to practice the newly learned language to construct oral and written mathematical texts.

If the first steps of this instructional sequence were meant to help students move from concrete visual representations toward increasingly elaborate generalizations of a new concept, the intent of the last step was to invite them to make the journey back, from the general concept to particular problem situations, thus closing the loop between the particular and the general and between the concrete and the abstract expressions of the key concept. Like many of the preceding tasks, this one also required that students use mathematics language (verbal and symbolic, with visual representations being required in order to solve the problems). The difference between this task and the preceding ones was that the problems that students were required to produce were potentially intended for an

---

Sample 1. The slope of a line is the tangent of the angle formed by the line and the x-axis, positive direction ($m = (y_2 - y_1) / (x_2 - x_1)$). Problem: Given the points $A(-4, 3)$ and $B(2, 4)$, calculate the slope of the line that crosses the two points.

Sample 2. The slope of a line situated on a plane that has a x–y system is equal to the tangent of the angle formed by the line and the x-axis in its positive direction. Problem: Points A and B belong to line d. Knowing that the coordinates of $A(1, 3)$ and $B(2, 4)$, find the slope of line d.

Sample 3. The slope of a line is the tangent of the angle formed by the line with the x-axis (positive direction). As a line is determined by two points, $P_1(x_1, y_1)$, $P_2(x_2, y_2)$, we can write the slope (m) as $(y_2 - y_1) / (x_2 - x_1)$, the difference of the ordinates / the difference of the abscissas. Problem: Find the slope of a line knowing that the points $A(2, 3)$ and $B(5, 9)$ belong to this line.

Sample 4. The slope of a line is equal to the value of the tangent of the angle formed by the respective line and the x-axis, positive direction. The formula of the slope: $m = (y_2 - y_1) / (x_2 - x_1)$. Problem: A line intersects the y-axis in point $A(0, 20)$. Find the area of the triangle formed by this line, the y-axis, and the line that forms an angle of 75 degrees with the x-axis. Find the slope of the line that divides the triangle into two similar triangles and intersects two of its sides in their middle.

Student artifacts, March 9, 2006.

FIGURE 11.6. Student definitions and problems.

audience other than themselves or their teacher (one may write a definition for oneself or for one's teacher, but only mathematicians write problems for others to solve). The task therefore positioned the students as mathematics experts, which meant that their texts had to meet the standards of expert writing.

The principle here is that a teacher can support students' concurrent conceptual and linguistic development to the point where they can assume expert identities and thus create mathematical texts typically produced by mathematicians.

CONCLUSION

To help students learn a new mathematical concept and the language needed to understand it and operate with it, Ariadna asked students to attend to the structure of language from a variety of stances. First, she invited students to explore the new concept and to use their prior mathematical knowledge and linguistic resources to describe it. Then she introduced new language (technical vocabulary and sentence patterns typical of mathematics language) to help students describe the concept with increased precision. Next she invited students to use the new vocabulary and sentence patterns in conjunction with previously learned technical vocabulary in writing, and then, orally, to explain and define the concept, providing feedback to illustrate the precision of mathematics language and to explain conventions of mathematical genres. Finally, she asked students to produce formal definitions and to draft problems of their own, applying knowledge of the new mathematical concept and of the language needed to express it in expert ways.

Ariadna's practice is an example of how a teacher can develop students' mathematical knowledge to include, beyond computational fluency, conceptual understanding and the ability to engage in mathematical processes. While the instructional unit included opportunities for students to develop computational fluency (mostly through homework problems), most of the instructional time was spent in activities that allowed students to broaden and deepen their understanding of the key concept as well as to develop their ability to use suitable mathematics language to talk and write about it.

If we view Ariadna's instruction as aimed at supporting students' mathematics language acquisition, we will notice that her instructional steps echo what we know about supporting language acquisition more generally (Cambourne, 1995). Cambourne emphasized that students' willingness to engage is key, and this brings us to another principle of Ariadna's teaching: Students are more likely to engage with learning subject-specific ways of using language when they feel safe about the risks they need to take. Ariadna respected students' contributions at all times. However, throughout the activities that she designed in order for her students to practice using language to operate with the new concept, she constantly provided feedback, modeling and explaining the conventions of mathematics language and genres along the way, thereby helping students to learn to communicate with the precision needed for "the reader who knows mathematics."

Research on subject-specific language acquisition suggests that best practice in mathematics literacy means finding ways to help students become members of the discourse community of mathematicians, that is, speakers/writers of mathematics language (e.g., Rittenhouse, 1998). In this view, simply asking students to read, write, speak, and listen as they engage in problem-based teaching, as is common in much current mathematics instruction, is not sufficient to develop mathematics language and in-depth conceptual understanding of mathematics. Similarly, content-area literacy strategies that help students build on prior knowledge, draw inferences, attend to text structure, learn technical vocabulary, or write to learn offer necessary but not sufficient exposure for students to gain entrée to this discourse community. A teacher must also understand, demonstrate, and explain the expectations of the mathematical discourse community, as well as encourage and provide responsive support to students' attempts to join this community, to which they can and should aspire.

DISCUSSION AND ACTIVITIES

1. Recognizing that the key principle involves providing students with supported entrée into the mathematics discourse community, consider alternatives to Ariadna's instructional cycle. For instance, how could students work together to analyze various written mathematical texts (e.g., explanations or definitions) to discern features of mathematics language descriptions of key concepts?

2. Work with other mathematics and literacy teachers to identify key concepts and the language needed to express them, and plan instructional sequences (including language development objectives) that echo Ariadna's efforts to teach students mathematics language so they will be able to describe key concepts for "the reader who knows mathematics." Such lessons could be observed and scripted for lesson study to ground discussion of how the lessons address this chapter's principles.

3. Consider features of the registers and genres typical of other disciplines and design instructional sequences that show students how to shape their language for use in these different discourse communities.

4. Invite local mathematicians, engineers, biologists, chemists, historians, or other professionals to share primary source documents from their respective disciplines with students. Invite students to compare and contrast features of the language used in such documents and to discuss connections between the language of the documents in each discipline and the language they are learning in their academic studies.

REFERENCES

Cambourne, B. (1995). Towards an educationally relevant theory of literacy learning: Twenty years of inquiry. *The Reading Teacher, 49*(3), 182–192.

Fang, Z. (2012). The challenges of reading disciplinary texts. In T. L. Jetton & C. Shanahan (Eds.), *Adolescent literacy in the academic disciplines: General principles and practical strategies* (pp. 34–68). New York: Guilford Press.

Halliday, M. A. K. (1978). *Language as social semiotic*. London: Edward Arnold.

Larson, M. R. (2012). Will the CCSSM matter in ten years?: Reflect and discuss. *Teaching Children Mathematics, 19*(2), 108–115.

Lemke, J. (1990). *Talking science: Language, learning, and values*. Norwood, NJ: Ablex.

Marks, G., & Mousley, J. (1990). Mathematics education and genre: Dare we make the process writing mistake again? *Language and Education* 4(2), 117–135.

Moschkovich, J. (Ed.) (2010). *Language and mathematics education: Multiple perspectives and directions for research.* Charlotte, NC: Information Age Processing.

National Council of Teachers of Mathematics. (2000). *Principles and standards for school mathematics.* Reston, VA: Author.

National Council of Teachers of Mathematics. (2006). *Curriculum focal points for kindergarten through grade 8 mathematics.* Reston, VA: Author.

National Governors Association Center for Best Practices & Council of Chief State School Officers. (2010a). *Common Core State Standards for English Language Arts.* Washington, DC: Author.

National Governors Association Center for Best Practices & Council of Chief State School Officers. (2010b). *Common Core State Standards for Mathematics.* Washington, DC: Author.

Rittenhouse, P. S. (1998). The teacher's role in mathematical conversation: Stepping in and stepping out. In M. Lampert & M. L. Blunk (Eds.), *Talking mathematics in school: Studies of teaching and learning* (pp. 163–189). Cambridge, UK: Cambridge University Press.

Schleppegrell, M. J. (2004). *The language of schooling: A functional linguistics perspective.* Mahwah, NJ: Erlbaum.

Schleppegrell, M. J. (2007). The linguistic challenges of mathematics teaching and learning: A research review. *Reading and Writing Quarterly, 23,* 139–159.

Scribner, S., & Cole, M. (1981). *The psychology of literacy.* Cambridge, MA: Harvard University Press.

Siebert, D., & Draper, R. J. (2012). Reconceptualizing literacy and instruction for mathematics classrooms. In T. L. Jetton & C. Shanahan (Eds.), *Adolescent literacy in the academic disciplines: General principles and practical strategies* (pp. 172–198). New York: Guilford Press.

Temple, C., & Doerr, H. (2012). Developing fluency in the mathematical register through conversation in a tenth-grade classroom. *Educational Studies in Mathematics 81*(3), 287–306.

CHAPTER 12

Reading Challenging Texts in High School

How Teachers Can Scaffold and Build Close Reading for Real Purposes in the Subject Areas

Elizabeth Birr Moje
Jennifer Speyer

In this chapter, we:

- Describe the complex connections between reader purpose, engagement, and knowledge; texts of the subject areas; and the social networks within which texts are embedded.

- Use short pieces of science and history texts to illustrate what youth need to know and be able to do to comprehend texts at the high school level.

- Summarize what teachers need to know and be able to do to mediate these challenges.

- Present content literacy teaching practices that can be adapted for particular youth, particular texts, and particular contexts of instruction.

- Link these teaching practices to the student outcomes called for in the Common Core State Standards and describe teaching needed to realize the goals of the Common Core.

WHAT'S THE BIG DEAL
WITH READING IN HIGH SCHOOL?

Imagine walking into your classroom, the teacher's lounge, or your office and being asked to read the following text:

Emergency Quota Act of 1921

AN ACT
To limit the immigration of aliens into the United States.

Be it enacted by the Senate and House of Representatives of the United States of America in Congress assembled . . .

Sec. 2. (a) That the number of aliens of any nationality who may be admitted under the immigration laws to the United States in any fiscal year shall be limited to 3 per centum of the number of foreign born persons of such nationality resident in the United States as determined by the United States census of 1910.

(Retrieved April 9, 2007, from *http://tucnak.fsv.cuni.cz/~calda/ Documents/1920s/QuotaAct1918.html*)

What is the first thing you would do upon being presented with this reading task? Can you identify the main idea of the passage? What kind of questions would you ask the person who demanded this reading act of you? What kinds of questions would you ask yourself? Perhaps most important, would you do it?

Many of you reading this chapter would probably ask, "Why? What do you want me to do with it?" if presented with this reading task. You might ask it simply because you are a good reader, and as such, you automatically seek to establish purpose for reading. Or you would ask these questions because you know that good readers attempt to establish a purpose for reading when presented with a text they have not chosen to read. When good readers have not chosen texts for themselves, they recognize that the purpose for reading is not up to them to decide. Finally, you might ask such questions because you know you have a choice and can refuse to read the text if the reason for reading is not to your liking.

This note about choice is an important one. Literacy theorists argue that choice in reading and writing tasks makes an enormous difference in one's motivation or engagement with a reading task (Guthrie & Wigfield, 2000). A number of studies have demonstrated that many young people do not read academic texts with proficiency or high interest (Moje, Overby, Tysvaer, & Morris, 2008; Perie, Grigg, & Donahue, 2005). The lack of proficiency has been variously attributed to low literacy skills, to motivation and engagement, and to text difficulty.

Studies have also indicated, however, that young people read many different kinds of texts—including challenging texts—outside of school, and they read them with fluency and comprehension (Alvermann, Young, Green, & Wisenbaker, 1999; Gee, 2003; Leander & Lovvorn, 2006; Moje, 2006). Many of these same scholars have suggested that motivation and engagement are at work in young people's abilities to read out-of-school texts. But research suggests that is it not just that youth *want* to read these texts. Motivation matters, but what may help youth persevere even in the face of challenging texts is that these texts are embedded in meaningful social networks of the young people's lives (Moje et al., 2008). As such, these social networks provide important background knowledge that helps youth establish a purpose, ask questions, monitor comprehension, and synthesize ideas for each new text they read.

By contrast, the texts of high school classrooms are not embedded in the social networks of most students' daily lives. They are embedded in the social networks represented by the disciplines, which means that they draw on different kinds of knowledge and skills. And yet, the Common Core State Standards (CCSS), which were released and adopted by the majority of U.S. states just a few years after we published the original version of this chapter, have set an expectation for all students to be deeply proficient at reading and writing a range of discipline-specific genres and media. Whether the standards speak to English language arts, history, or science and "the technical subjects," the expectations for developing readers and writers—and by extension, the teachers of those readers and writers—are vast. The CCSS initiative seeks to develop reading and writing skills that enable students to read and write to learn new ideas and information. Moreover, the authors of the CCSS have emphasized the need for teachers to focus students' attention to the words on the page, despite what literacy research demonstrates as the need to go beyond the page to enable deep comprehension and skilled composition.

In this chapter, we use one case of classroom practice both to complicate these demands of the CCSS and to demonstrate meaningful subject-area literacy instruction that meets those demands by drawing from what students know and can do and taking them, with scaffolding, to new skill levels and understandings of subject matter concepts. Specifically, we complicate the CCSS demands by highlighting the vast requirements of knowledge and skill required to read the texts of high school history and, by extension, other subject areas. Such knowledge and skills are often mentioned in discussing comprehension in general terms, but are rarely examined in terms of what it means to set a purpose for reading a historical document such as the Emergency Quota Act of 1921 (i.e., a primary [data] source in historical study). Likewise, producing a well-written argument in science or social studies depends on ability to set purposes for the writing. What follows is an analysis of some of the skills and knowledge that young people need in order to comprehend the texts of high school content areas. These skill and knowledge demands complicate secondary school reading and are unique to subject matter texts.

To frame the analysis, we draw from our experience co-teaching 11th-grade social studies students in a predominantly Latino/Latina neighborhood of a large Midwestern city. As hinted at by the Emergency Quota Act text excerpt with which we opened the chapter, we were studying a unit on U.S. immigration issues and history. We framed the problem under study in terms of contemporary questions around who should be allowed to immigrate into the United States, and whether and how immigration should be monitored. We started with a contemporary problem and then looked back in time to our nation's founding, moving forward until we returned to the present day. The analysis emphasizes the different types of knowledge necessary for purpose setting, comprehension monitoring, and sense making, with an examination of how knowledge and development intersect with engagement when it comes to reading. Our analysis of the text challenges students faced as they read primary sources throughout U.S. history is bolstered by findings from Moje's research with young people in and out of school.

Using this case, we demonstrate powerful subject-matter literacy instruction that can meet the CCSS demands by illustrating our teaching practices. We offer recommendations for teaching practices and specific strategies to help teachers mediate these challenges and support young people's reading comprehension and written production of the texts demanded for high school content-area learning. The suggested practices are not intended to supplant project-based practices described above, but to complement such teaching practices, in an attempt to support text reading, learning from text, and text production while conducting both natural and social science investigations, thus achieving the goals of the CCSS. Indeed, in our conclusion, we offer an analysis of how these teaching practices support the work of achieving the student outcomes called for in the CCSS. Our analysis focuses in large part on the question of *close reading*, a skill emphasized, but not well theorized, and thus largely undeveloped in the CCSS. The concept of close reading, in particular, is empty unless tied explicitly to the purposes for and nature of reading closely in a specific domain (whether disciplinary or otherwise). In addition, we take on the question of the role of knowledge in close reading and emphasize the point that proficient close reading attends to far more than the words on the page. Drawing from our analysis of the knowledge and skill needed to understand one brief text excerpt, we push for an understanding of close reading as being all about drawing from, connecting to, and expanding the "necessary knowledge" (Moje, 2010) readers bring to the act of reading.

TYPES OF KNOWLEDGE AND SKILL NECESSARY FOR PURPOSE SETTING AND COMPREHENSION

We feature the Emergency Quota Act of 1921 text because it was in the process of teaching that the complexity of knowledge and skill demands implicit in what is, at first glance, a seemingly straightforward piece of text, became obvious. Our analysis revealed at least six types of knowledge or skill necessary for purpose-setting and sense-making of this short passage: (1) semantic, (2) historical, (3) geographical, (4) mathematical, (5) discursive, and (6) pragmatic.

Semantic Knowledge and Skill

That semantic—or word—knowledge is needed to make sense of this passage may seem rather obvious and is often the first factor considered by content teachers, literacy coaches, and reading theorists. The technical words of the passage include *immigration, aliens, Senate, House of Representatives, Congress, assembled, fiscal year, per centum, nationality*, and *census*. The everyday terms that might give adolescent readers pause, particularly in terms of the syntax in this passage, include *enacted* and *resident*. Many of these terms are ones that most youth are likely to have heard before; however, the difference between their casual use and their meaning in this passage may be critical. Readers who do not know the technical or everyday meanings of these and other words in the passage could nevertheless work to comprehend the passage, provided they possess the semantic skill not only to locate words in dictionaries, but also to discern which meaning is more appropriate in the context of the passage. Such semantic skill, however, is complicated by the other knowledge demands embedded in the passage. As we used the Emergency Quota Act and other texts in the immigration unit we found ourselves repeatedly turning our students to the dictionary, asking students to read each of the definitions provided, and working with them to choose the best fit word for the context in which we were reading.

Mathematical Knowledge

As mentioned above, *per centum* is a key phrase in this text that needs to be understood in order to make sense of the text. However, the knowledge required is not merely definitional (i.e., it is not enough merely to know that the Latin phrase translates as "per one hundred," it is also essential that students understand what it means mathematically when a limit is set at 3 per 100). As obvious as this may seem to the adult reader, students in our classes answered the question, "If there were 100 people from Albania in the U.S. in 1910, then how many Albanians could immigrate to the U.S. in 1921?" with responses such as, "Five?" or "Twenty?" Students' responses indicated either a lack of skill in calculating percentages (or even a lack of conceptual knowledge of what a percentage represents), or a lack of interest in applying the mathematical concept to the historical information of the passage (in some cases, they seemed to simply call out a number without really stopping to think about the question). Both language and mini-math lessons were necessary, as we discussed both the meaning of *per centum*, using the Spanish for 100 as a way into the Latin word, and how to calculate three per centum of a given number of residents. Making sense of the numbers, however, raises questions about another kind of knowledge required for making sense of this passage: knowledge of history and geography.

Historical Knowledge

One of the most important types of knowledge for making sense of this particular historical document is knowledge of past events, data, people, and social and political issues and conflicts. Although a reader could comprehend the Emergency Quota Act's surface meaning to be that in 1921 U.S. immigration law set limits on immigration and that those limits were set to equal 3% of the people of a given nationality living in the United States in 1910, the significance of the text is only revealed when one either knows or examines the numbers of immigrants from different countries living in the United States in 1910. If readers know anything about U.S. immigration during the early 1900s, then they will know that the numbers of different nationalities living in the United States were vastly different. They might even know something about the nature of the differences (e.g., that the country was heavily populated by people of English and German descent and less heavily populated by people of Italian, Romanian, or Polish descent). If, for example, readers had knowledge of the information shown in Table 12.1, then they would be able to draw inferences about the intent of the act, and they might put a different spin on the word "emergency."

Armed with the knowledge that the number of British residents in 1910 was higher than the number of Romanian or Polish residents, the reader might infer that the law targeted 1910 as a way of limiting the numbers of Romanian and Polish residents and allowing British peoples to maintain dominance in the larger population (the same sort of argument could be made for German immigration in comparison to Italian immigration). However, to do so, readers would then have to employ their mathematical knowledge to determine that 3% of 65,923 (the number of Polish-born residents in 1910) is smaller than 3% of 1,221,283 (the number of British-born residents in 1910). But the need to make that mathematical calculation

TABLE 12.1. Foreign-Born Residents by Selected Country of Origin, 1890–1920

Country/region	1890	1910	1920
Great Britain	1,251,402	1,221,283	1,135,489
Ireland	1,871,509	1,352,251	1,037,234
Germany	2,784,894	2,311,237	1,686,108
Italy	1,887	1,343,125	1,610,113
Romania	NA	937,884	1,139,979
Poland	48,557	65,923	102,823

Note. (Based on information retrieved April 9, 2007, from *http://www.u-s-history.com/pages/ h1398.html*, April 9, 2007, and April 20, 2007, from *http://www.census.gov/population/www/ documentation/*, April 20, 2007).

depends on the knowledge that the groups differed in number. Without that knowledge, the words would be taken at face value and the law would appear to be equitable. With that knowledge, readers would have access to deeper and historically important interpretations of the text. Specifically, they would come to understand that the Emergency Quota Act of 1921, despite its seemingly equitable application of the same *percent* limit to all nationalities, was established to limit the immigration of certain groups (Eastern and Southern Europeans, in particular) into the United States. To draw that conclusion, however, one would also need to know that numbers of those groups immigrating were on the rise, as shown in Table 12.2.

It could be argued that the savvy reader would ask questions of that text that would demand the answers provided via these data. However, that savvy and the accompanying critical reading practice require additional

TABLE 12.2. Immigration Statistics, 1920–1926

Year	Total Entering U.S.	Great Britain	Eastern Europe	Italy
1920	430,001	38,471	3,913	95,145
1921	805,228	51,142	32,793	222,260
1922	309,556	25,153	12,244	40,319
1923	522,919	45,759	16,082	46,674
1924	706,896	59,490	13,173	56,246
1925	294,314	27,172	1,566	6,203
1926	304,488	25,528	1,596	8,253

Note. Based on information retrieved April 9, 2007, from *www.u-s-history.com/pages/h1398. html*, and April 20, 2007, from *www.census.gov/population/www/documentation*.

types of knowledge and skill, such as knowledge of geography and skill in making sense of geographic data.

Geographic Knowledge and Skill

A lengthy list of countries and population numbers included in the 1924 law requires either extensive knowledge of geography or well-developed geographic skill to find the countries and attempt to identify demographic characteristics of the populations of those countries (see Table 12.3). However, these knowledge and skill demands are even more complicated. To recognize the import of either the 1921 act or the 1924 law, one needs to recognize that the people of some countries were not as highly regarded as the people of other countries, at times on the basis of social class, at other times on the basis of race, ethnicity, or language. To know these differences requires deep geographic knowledge beyond simply knowing where a country is located on a map or globe.

Discursive Knowledge and Skill

One additional type is discursive knowledge, or the knowledge that the construction of texts is tied to the domain in which they are written and to the purposes for which they were originally written. Understanding the Emergency Quota Act of 1921 as more than a string of words demands that the reader possess and use discursive knowledge of how and why legal documents from a particular time period were written, to what audiences they were addressed, and to what issues they spoke. Discursive knowledge is even more useful in a later immigration law, the Immigration Act of 1924, wherein limits are reduced to two per centum of the foreign-born persons resident in the United States in 1890 (note both the reduction in percentage and the move by 20 years from 1910 to 1890), particularly in the final portion of the act, which reads:

> The immigration quotas assigned to the various countries and quota-areas should not be regarded as having any political significance whatever, or as involving recognition of new governments, or of new boundaries, or of transfers of territory except as the United States Government has already made such recognition in a formal and official manner.
>
> Retrieved April 9, 2007, from *www.u-s-history.com/pages/h1398.html.*

This attempt to disavow political intent in the law requires an understanding of the nature of political back-room negotiations, U.S. foreign policy, and of the likely targets of this law. A skilled reader should wonder about the politics at work in the time period upon reading these words. The skilled reader should question the intent behind the words. In the

TABLE 12.3. Country or Area of Birth Quota 1924–1925

- Afghanistan—100
- Albania—100
- Andorra—100
- Arabian peninsula—100
- Armenia—124
- Australia, including Papua, Tasmania, and all islands appertaining to Australia—121
- Austria—785
- Belgium—512
- Bhutan—100
- Bulgaria—100
- Cameroon (proposed British mandate)—100
- Cameroon (French mandate)—100
- China—100
- Czechoslovakia—3,073
- Danzig, Free City of—228
- Denmark—2,789
- Egypt—100
- Estonia—124
- Ethiopia (Abyssinia)—100
- Finland—170
- France—3,954
- Germany—51,227
- Great Britain and Northern Ireland—34,007
- Greece—100
- Hungary—473
- Iceland—100
- India—100

- Iraq (Mesopotamia)—100
- Irish Free State—28,567
- Italy, including Rhodes, Dodecanesia, and Castellorizzo—3,845
- Japan—100
- Latvia—142
- Liberia—100
- Liechtenstein—100
- Lithuania—344
- Luxemburg—100
- Monaco—100
- Morocco (French and Spanish Zones and Tangier)—100
- Muscat (Oman)—100
- Nauru (proposed British mandate)—100
- Nepal—100
- Netherlands—1648
- New Zealand (including appertaining islands—100
- Norway—6,453
- New Guinea, and other Pacific Islands under proposed Australian mandate—100
- Palestine (with Trans-Jordan, proposed British mandate)—100

- Persia—100
- Poland—5,982
- Portugal—503
- Ruanda and Urundi (Belgium mandate)—100
- Romania—603
- Russia, European and Asiatic—2,248
- Samoa, Western (proposed mandate of New Zealand)—100
- San Marino—100
- Siam—100
- South Africa, Union of—100
- South West Africa (proposed mandate of Union of South Africa)—100
- Spain—131
- Sweden—9,561
- Switzerland—2,081
- Syria and Lebanon (French mandate)—100
- Tanganyika (proposed British mandate)—100
- Togoland (proposed British mandate)—100
- Togoland (French mandate)—100
- Turkey—100
- Yap and other Pacific islands (under Japanese mandate)—100
- Yugoslavia—67

Note. Retrieved April 9, 2007, from *www.u-s-history.com/pages/h1398.html.*

absence of such knowledge, skill with navigating discourse communities can come into play and aid in comprehension. However, the discursive skill here involves imagining reactions from various countries around the world, as well as from various national groups within the United States at the time, and analyzing how the text was constructed in attempts to minimize those reactions. Thus the discursive skill requires knowledge of politics, rhetoric, history, and geography, a point that emphasizes the complicated, interrelated nature of bodies of knowledge and skill in making sense of texts at the high school level. No text is an island unto itself; an awareness of intertextuality—that is, the interconnectedness of multiple texts and ideas across texts—is especially important for both the high school reader and the teachers of high school readers.

Making sense of these texts also requires another kind of discursive knowledge or skill, one that is tied to the original question of purpose. The reader needs to recognize that one should get information, ideas, or perspectives from texts. The question, however, is which information, ideas, or perspectives are to be taken away from the text, and once one has them, what is to be done with them? Expert reader studies (Alexander, 2003; Alexander, Kulikowich, & Jetton, 1994; Pressley & Afflerbach, 1995; Wineburg, 1998) have demonstrated that expert readers ask for, articulate, or have in their minds an explicit purpose when approaching a text. To set such purposes requires discursive knowledge of historical reading practices and problem framing (Bain, 2006). For example, as we taught these texts, we provided an interpretive task for our 11th-grade students to complete after reading the Emergency Quota Act of 1921. The students were to draw a representation of what they read for placement on a timeline we were building as class. We saw this task as an excellent way to translate across communicative forms (from print to drawing), and the collection of drawings placed on the timeline helped to make the laws visual and to frame them chronologically. The timeline provided a stable referent as we worked through the unit.

The question remains, however, as to how clear we made *what* the students were supposed to take away and represent from the Emergency Quota Act text. It was in working with several small groups of students as they struggled through this text that we realized a weakness in our lesson design. Specifically, although our students could visually represent a surface-level meaning of the texts they read, they were not able to dig deeper into the texts to comprehend more nuanced meanings, and nothing in the task's purpose demanded in-depth reading. The task was a comprehension—or close reading—task, but comprehension/close reading to what end? This problem became especially clear with the Emergency Quota Act and the Immigration Law of 1924 because so much meaning lies beneath the surface of the words in those two laws. Thus the purpose we set of representing the laws visually provided one way into the laws, but it did not provide the students with the kind of purpose they really needed in order to develop a historical understanding of the importance of the laws.

In effect, high school readers and their teachers must juggle at all times different purposes for reading. As Wineburg (1991, 1998) demonstrated, historians read archival material with two purposes in mind. One is the purpose involved in doing history, that of constructing accounts from the range of sources they analyze. The other purpose for which they read is the purpose of the original writer, the context in which the text was written, and the probable effects of the text on other people or on historical events. Historians read with their working purposes in mind, and those purposes demand that they examine the author's purpose and context of text they study. Like historians, secondary school students must approach texts, then, with multiple purposes in mind: One purpose might be to complete the school task they have been assigned. But if we want students to learn the concepts of the discipline, then students in a history class must assess an original author's purpose; analyze the historical, geographic, political, and discursive contexts; corroborate evidence and information; and read between the lines of the texts (Wineburg, 1991; VanSledright & Kelly, 1998). In other words, they need to read as historians would, not so that they can become historians, but so that they can understand and question how historical claims are produced and can analyze the importance of the information for their lives as citizens (Wineburg & Martin, 2004).

Pragmatic Knowledge and Skill

One type of pragmatic knowledge is the recognition that texts can be questioned. The Emergency Quota Act (and its partner, the Immigration Act of 1924) provide excellent examples of texts that convey a simple piece of information and appear to lay down equitable laws but, in fact, are replete with hidden implications that depend on knowledge of history or, at least, of the knowledge that one should ask questions such as, "Why, in 1921, would the U.S. immigration law refer back to 1910 to calculate its immigration quotas?" And just who lived in the United States in 1910? Knowing that one can ask such questions of a text (and being motivated to do so) is something that may need to be taught. At one point in our unit, I said to one class, "So what do you think, is this Immigration Law [of 1924] equitable? It says that every resident ethnic/national group can have the same percentage of immigrants, right?" One young woman responded, "I would have thought so, until you showed us all of that [referring to the data tables presented previously]." In other words, this student may not have asked the question about the equity of the acts unless we had modeled how to ask and how to make sense of related information. On a related note, other students may not have recognized embedded inequities had we not probed this point through questioning and revisiting the ideas across multiple texts and sources of information.

The idea of making sense of related information links to two additional types of knowledge or skill required for reading the seven lines of the Emergency Quota Act of 1921: search skills/knowledge and analytical skills/knowledge. Even if one assumes that high school readers possess the different kinds of skills described above, they still need to build relevant historical knowledge or information (we can assume that they do not possess it in depth, or we would not be teaching them). Thus, they either need the information handed to them or they require knowledge of how to access relevant information and skill in doing so. Once they have access to the information, they must be able to make sense of relevant information.

Knowledge of and Skill in Retrieving Data or Information

This set of knowledge and skills may seem trivial and yet was central to us as teachers in preparing to teach this text. As adults with history degrees, we did not have the immigration statistics relevant to interpreting the text stored in memory; we had to search for them. In our current context, we relied heavily on the Internet, which meant that we not only needed digital search skills, but also needed critical digital search skills. We checked and double-checked sources, assessing the sites' provenance and checking the numbers across multiple sources. In this lesson, we supplied these materials for students, but our analysis of this text suggests that this data retrieval knowledge and skill would be an important comprehension skill to teach in future lessons.

Analytical Knowledge and Skill

Consider the data tables shown previously. Think of the many challenges in making sense of those tables, let alone in applying them to the print text they inform. First, one must know how tables work. This kind of knowledge is often assumed, but it is not clear when the reading of tables is taught. To read Table 12.1, for example, the reader must know that the items in the rows of the tables do not necessarily have a relationship to one another except insofar as each item in these particular tables represents a country of origin from which people have emigrated to the United States. The columns, however, do relate to one another because the columns represent trends in numbers of people from each of those countries over 10-year time periods. The time periods are written from least to most recent, and they represent the periods critical to the two pieces of immigration legislation under study.

Table 12.2, however, is arranged in exactly the opposite order, and includes a total immigration column. Both of these tables are types of primary historical texts that adolescents must be able to read and then apply to their reading of the immigration laws. The irony of the process of table reading in this case is that reading the tables depends at some level on knowing what one needs to learn from the tables. In other words, one must have a purpose for reading the tables as well, and that purpose derives from knowing what one needs to learn from the legislation under study. But reading the legislation requires knowing the importance of the numbers in the table. Again, these texts are interconnected and depend on relatively high levels of background knowledge and analytical skill. We can teach such knowledge and skill simultaneously. Thus, as we taught this unit, we found that we needed to guide our students in making sense of these tables and that we had to make direct links back and forth from legislation to tables. Our students could engage in analysis of the numbers and the words and ideas, but only with our support and direction.

THE ROLE OF MOTIVATION AND INTEREST IN BUILDING KNOWLEDGE AND COMPREHENDING TEXTS

Thus far, we have emphasized the role of knowledge and skill in making sense of high school content-area texts. However, understanding this text may depend most on readers' interest in the topic or motivation to make sense of the text for some purpose beyond being interested (e.g., to get a school task done, to use the text as evidence in a debate). That is, people need to want to know what texts mean in order to spend the time asking questions, searching for information, or questioning contexts.

There are many possibilities for building on students' motivation to and interest in reading various texts, particularly if teachers choose topics that appeal to youth interests. Many young people in this urban neighborhood read texts outside of school that address issues and topics commonly covered in social studies (Stockdill & Moje, 2013), which suggests that they should find school social studies to be a fascinating and useful subject; in other words, young people *are* motivated to learn social and natural science concepts. The same research, however, yielded data that report the opposite finding: These same students rated social studies among their least useful and enjoyable subjects, with science a close second. What explains this contradiction?

One challenge to interest and motivation may be that although adolescent students may be highly interested in a topic, they are often less engaged with academic texts about the topic because of the writing style of the text. Several researchers have found that the lack of voice of academic texts make them difficult for students to access (Paxton, 1999; Schleppegrell, 2004). Indeed, as we taught our unit on immigration, we noted that many of the youth appeared to be highly engaged in our K-W-L ("what I *know*, what I *want* to know, what I *learned*"; Ogle, 1986) brainstorming discussions about immigration, but groaned when we passed out written texts to read to help us learn what we wanted to know.

One notable exception was the reading of "The New Colossus" (Lazarus, 1883), a poem that we read together, engaging in a close reading and analysis of each stanza. Although neither of us would claim that the students were enthralled with this text, they did appear to be more engaged than when they were asked to read texts independently, even when the activities attached to the independent reading were ostensibly engaging (e.g., drawing a political cartoon to represent the texts of immigration laws). Their interest in "The New Colossus" may have something to do with its narrative form. However, we would also assert that working through the text with the students, focusing closely on connecting what the words and concepts meant in relation to concepts in their own lives or in other historical periods (e.g., to understand the "new" colossus one must know what the "old" colossus was) helped to maintain their engagement. In that sense, close reading demanded much more than merely reading the words on the page; close reading demanded that we engage the students in a conversation about (1) why Lazarus wrote the poem, (2) how her use of metaphor and analogy communicated her views, (3) the contradiction inherent in the fact that her poem was inscribed on the base of the Statue of Liberty at the very time when laws were being passed that prevented poor and diseased people from immigrating to the United States, and about (4) how Lazarus's words and the conflicts of that time period might mean something for their lives in 2007, among many other possible topics. Thus, we suggest spending a fair amount of time on whole-class think-alouds of readings, especially early in a unit, to model for students how to set a purpose, ask questions of the text, and troubleshoot when comprehension goes awry. Even reading small portions of challenging texts as a whole class (or in small groups) can make a difference. Navigating such points of confusion can make an important difference in students' motivation to keep reading.

Another important way to engage youth and maintain their engagement even as they encounter lengthy print texts, is to build units on the issues and concerns about which they care deeply. However, as we learned with the immigration unit, teachers need to be prepared to address students' well-developed beliefs about the concepts under study. Adolescent youth, more so than young children, also possess deeply entrenched views and opinions, as well as self-interested perspectives. These opinions and perspectives are useful for building interest and motivation to learn more, but they can also serve as a roadblock for learning information or ideas that may contradict the youths' deeply held beliefs or perspectives. Our students' views on immigration were shaped by important life experiences and thereby shaped what they were willing to hear, read, or discuss. Many were either immigrants themselves or knew people who had immigrated. Many of them knew stories of immigration challenges. At the same time, they appeared to lack extensive knowledge outside of their own experiences. This lack of knowledge outside themselves, coupled with their belief that they already knew what was important to know about immigration, made deep learning of new or different ideas challenging. Keeping the students focused on the texts we presented, while simultaneously drawing out the knowledge they brought to bear on these texts, allowed us to support a purposeful and meaningful close reading of the material in a way that fostered new learning without denying the value and power of their personal experiences and knowledge.

Students' beliefs also played a role in their interest in and willingness to read the texts of U.S. immigration history. Encouraging them to use the information they had learned throughout the unit—much of which actually bolstered their perspectives—was challenging because they said that their arguments were strong without the benefit of additional historical information. However, discussion of what these texts meant for their beliefs, and explicit attention to how the students might use the texts to support or challenge particular ideas, seemed to generate interest in the texts. For example, at the end of the unit, as we reviewed immigration laws throughout history, one student objected to the name of one law, *Operation Wetback* (Garcia, 1980), stating that the name of the law was racist. That statement inspired a different student to raise the question of when racial slurs are considered racist, and when they are not. The heated and difficult discussion that ensued was generated from word and text and pointed back to word and text, as well as to the central issue we were investigating, the role of race in immigration law. Ultimately, the texts we read and the discussion we had about racist language helped to frame an argument that many of them planned to make in their final essays. The opportunity to discuss their beliefs and values stemmed from and supported their readings of text. Although this discussion felt, in the moment, as if it veered too much from our careful reading of the texts and from the larger issues we were investigating with the students, we realized in our analysis of this conversation that to have shut it down because it did not hew closely to the text and activity goals would have been to close off a powerful learning space for the students. In other words, we could have forced the students back to the words of the Operation Wetback law, arguing that they had to attend to the words on the page if they were to improve their reading skills, but to do so would have constructed a reading act without a purpose, with no frame of reference, and with little reason to continue reading.

Another excellent motivational resource in working with the youth in our classrooms was the rich vocabulary and experience students possessed, usually from interactions with previous classes, families, peer groups, and popular cultural texts. Students were familiar, for example, with a number of terms relevant to immigration, such as *alien, quota, undocumented, bracero* (worker), *green card, visa, passport,* and many others. They also knew many technical terms from their previous history courses. They were less familiar, in this case, with nontechnical vocabulary such as *per centum* (see above), *teeming* or *colossus* (both from the Lazarus poem), or *pauper* and *moral turpitude* (used in an 1891 immigration law).

We spent a great deal of time defining such terms, but we were also able to make use of students' extensive knowledge of popular culture in interesting ways as we defined vocabulary or built background knowledge.

For example, when discussing the Chinese Exclusion Act of 1882, one student volunteered that he had played a computer game in which the goal was to protect Chinese workers who were building railroads in the United States during the 1800s. Other students drew on their knowledge of the African slave trade from past history courses to raise questions about whether and how African were counted in immigration quotas or about the history of world wars in developing hypotheses about which immigrant groups were most accepted during different time periods of U.S. history. In another instance, while engaging in a think-aloud of a journal entry written by a Mexican *bracero* (worker), my colleague commented that the worker's mention of being fed bread and bologna as "glory" indicated how hungry he must have been. Two students began to sing, "I'm from the ghetto homies, I grew up on bread and bologna," an excerpt of lyrics from a popular rap song, "Move Around" (B.G., feat. Mannie Fresh, 2006). The invoking of these lyrics led to a discussion of what bread and bologna signified in the *bracero*'s text. In each of these cases, and many others, our students exhibited a wealth of knowledge—albeit not always conventional, not always deep, and not always complete or fully accurate—that could be expanded to support their sense making of these historical texts.

DISCIPLINARY LITERACY TEACHING PRACTICES FOR MEANINGFUL CLOSE READING

Our analysis of these history texts demonstrates that the exhortation to read closely without teaching practices to support such reading will not address the greatest challenges presented by advanced content-area texts being read by a wide variety of youth (i.e., who may or may not be as interested in the content as those of us who chose to spend our lives teaching it). In what follows, we have chosen to highlight six overarching teaching practices high school content-area teachers can use to engage students in discipline-specific reading and writing: (1) problem framing and question asking, (2) whole-group knowledge elicitation and building, (3) scaffolded close reading, (4) questioning, (5) visualizing texts, and (6) summarizing and synthesizing ideas within and across texts. A variety of daily practices and content literacy strategies (see Buehl, 2002) can be embedded within these overarching practices, as described here.

Framing Problems, Setting Purpose

From our perspective, problem framing is the most critical practice in disciplinary literacy instruction. Indeed, we argue that instruction cannot be framed as "disciplinary" in orientation if it does not include problem framing because problem framing is at the core of disciplinary work. Members of the disciplines—whether basic or applied researchers—begin with problems to be solved or questions to be addressed. Thus, we suggest that at the beginning of a unit, teachers set a purpose for the entire unit by framing a problem for study. Project-based science curricula, for example, always begin by posing driving questions for students to investigate throughout the course of unit. Similarly, history and other social studies units could begin with the kind of problem framing we posed in our immigration unit, with a focus on a contemporary problem that requires knowledge of how the issue has evolved throughout history.

In our immigration unit, we set a purpose by asking students to free write to the problem of whether the United States should allow immigration by any person from any country at any time. We posed a new aspect of U.S. immigration issues each day for free writing. We cannot underscore enough the importance of this practice for setting a purpose for the reading and writing to be done and for building and maintaining student interest in a meaningful activity. This is perhaps one of the most troubling missing pieces of the CCSS: The standards call for practices and skills without a sense of why the practices and skills would be employed. The practices and skills are, in effect, generic, but an ample body of theory and research makes clear that literacy practice is never free of context or domain specificity. Some skills can certainly transfer across contexts, domains, or discourse communities, but how those skills transfer depends on the context. This is particularly true for disciplinary literacy practices (Lee & Spratley, 2010; Moje, 2007; Shanahan & Shanahan, 2008).

Following on the idea of problem framing, a disciplinary literacy approach would also preview texts and concepts before, during, and after a reading or writing task is given, using well-known literacy strategies such as K-W-L, anticipation guides, preview guides, and advanced organizers. When previewing, keep in mind the two levels of purpose—purpose of the reading task and purpose of the text in the discipline—discussed previously. Make explicit what you expect your students to do with the text (whether to ask questions, to use it in an essay, to link it to another text, and/or to critique or question its purpose in history). Second, discuss with students the purpose of the text for the context in which it was written. Who was its author? What did the author intend? To whom was the author writing? Although these are questions that historians routinely ask of texts in their work (Bain, 2006; Wineburg, 1991), they can be relevant for students reading texts in any content area, because no matter what the text is, they are reading it outside of the context in which it was written.

Whole-Group Knowledge Eliciting and Building

As illustrated in the prior analysis of the knowledge students needed to make sense of just five lines of historical primary source text, knowledge is a key ingredient in skillful reading (and writing). That means that teachers must be clear about the knowledge demanded by a given text (we call this *necessary* knowledge), have a general sense of the knowledge their students bring to the reading, and have a clear idea about what they want the students to learn from the text. With these three types of knowledge in mind, teachers can design instruction that builds the necessary knowledge for meaningful close reading. We suggest that although a teacher might occasionally lecture to students, the mainstay of one's teaching practice should be offering information and leading students in critical thinking and reasoning about the information, just as we did in our immigration unit when we presented students with primary sources, statistics, maps, and visual images. We also facilitated whole-group knowledge elicitation and building through the process of scaffolding close reading of various texts, as we discuss in the next section.

Scaffolded (Close) Reading

The CCSS famously call for close reading of texts, which we see as akin to what we referred to in our original chapter as *scaffolded* text reading. In fact, we argue here that the call for close reading in the CCSS is inadequate because it does not include attention to the kind of scaffolding that teachers can offer to support their students in drawing from and expanding their knowledge as they read the texts of the disciplines. We find this failure to attend to scaffolding ironic, given the concern that teachers and students remain focused on closely reading the texts, rather than drawing from past experience. The concern is that if one encourages students to connect texts to their experiences, then the conversation will quickly become only about students' experiences and will not help students learn new ideas and learn to read more and more complex texts. In what follows, we offer some suggestions for enacting close reading with the scaffolding students need but without descending into a discussion of students' experiences that fails to advance students' reading skill development and learning of new ideas.

Talk about the Texts

In addition to brief lectures or mini-lessons as knowledge-building activities, engage in text reading and discussion strategies such as close reading, dictionary searches, concept mapping of ideas in texts, and text–self–community–world connections. As you talk about texts, define words and interpret nuances in meaning. Model for students how to ask questions even at the word level. While defining the word *quota* with our group of 11th-grade students, for example, we read several different definitions and then talked about the definition that best fit our text and historical context.

Make Texts Visible

Project sections of text on overhead screen so that students can see and hear words read and so that you can point to words as you read. Look up important words together in the dictionary while also pointing to them on a common text. Look carefully at words, phrases, and syntax of sentences. Point out how headings signal what is coming up in the text. Refer readers to images that accompany the text.

Read Charts and Tables

Try not simply to refer readers to these images or to present charts and tables, but to work through them with students. Chart/table/graph reading is a skill that is often not explicitly taught. Reading images is an important skill and often dramatically supports the reading of print. As we worked through the charts we used in our immigration unit, we blocked out certain bits of information in the chart, in part to encourage students to focus on certain statistics before encountering other statistics, but in part to reveal a kind of logical progression in looking at the information. We walked the students through the chart, rather than simply offering it to them *in toto*. In this way, reading the chart was a kind of puzzle, as students tried to figure out how to interpret the numbers they saw. The important information was not contained in the numbers alone, but in what the trends or patterns in numbers over years and by immigrant groups meant for immigration history and law.

Questioning or Pressing for Understanding

One observation Moje made after a day in the classroom is that our students did not appear to have much experience answering *why* questions. For example, while brainstorming "Want to Know" items in our K-W-L activity, one young woman stated that she wanted to know why there were fences and guards at the United States' border with Mexico, but not at the United States' border with Canada. Elizabeth wrote her question on the board, and then said, "That's an interesting one. Anyone have any ideas why that might be?" Another student said, "Because they were ordered to go there." Not taking up the validity of that statement, Elizabeth simply asked, "Oh? Why would that be?"

"Because they were sent there," responded the student.

"OK, but why do you think guards were sent to the Mexican border and not the Canadian border?" asked Elizabeth.

The student appeared to be perplexed by the question, and none of the other students seemed able or inclined to help support or refute the claim. Eventually, the student said, "Because they think more Mexicans [than Canadians] want to come to the United States," but getting this idea out took approximately 5 minutes of probing around a single statement. We maintained this pattern of probing for reasons throughout the unit, and the students did shift to engaging the *why* questions, but it took some time and required us to make a trade-off between teaching youth how to ask questions of texts and themselves—even when their ideas may have been inaccurate or partial—and covering content. In related work in science classrooms, a number of researchers have found that teachers often resist what some researchers refer to as *pressing for understanding,* in part because they fear alienating or threatening students (Blumenfeld, Marx, & Harris, 2006; Blumenfeld, Kempler, & Krajcik, 2006). Although it is the case that rapid movement without much questioning pushes students through the curriculum and keeps students' attention focused on the points at hand, it does not engage students in the kind of questioning they need to develop for deep comprehension of advanced subject-matter texts or for taking inquiry to new levels.

Visualizing Texts

The students we taught needed help visualizing what these texts meant in terms of actual people. When we presented them with visual images of different groups represented by the numbers in the tables we presented, our students appeared to make connections to the implicit goals of the laws, underscoring the idea that literate practice, while focused on making sense of encoded symbols, is also about more than just print codes or other symbols (Moje, 2000). Images can help readers interpret texts (Eisner, 1994; Kress, 2003; Kress & van Leeuwen, 1996), and visual images can prove to be important tools in supporting students' comprehension.

That said, it is important to note that visual images should not *replace* print, especially for struggling readers. Some adolescent literacy researchers have noted a tendency to offer struggling adolescent readers ways to opt out of reading print in an effort to make content information accessible; these scholars have also noted that such options may make content accessible, but do not help adolescents improve their literacy skills (Dressman et al., 2005). Thus, the point of using visualization and images is that they should be used to support print reading and writing (and vice versa). One form of representation should not simply replace the other. Moreover, teachers can work with students to draw on past visual images to support their comprehension of print and other symbolic texts. New images do not need to be offered with each reading; rather, readers can be encouraged to visualize without the aid of actual images, but only if they are introduced to relevant images when they first encounter new material or concepts outside their experience.

Summarizing and Synthesizing within and across Texts

A final overarching practice is that of modeling for students how to summa- rize within a text and synthesize across texts. Central to this practice is the idea that teachers teach students *how* to summarize and synthesize, rather than summarizing or synthesizing key points or ideas for the students. This practice involves repeatedly coming back around to ideas covered in previous lessons and can be aided by literacy teaching strategies. For example, keeping a K-W-L chart visible in the classroom can allow a teacher to revisit ideas the students claimed to know at the outset of a unit, suggesting modifications, additions, or corrections to the original ideas. Having the chart as a visual prompt is an excellent management device for the teacher and students, as days or weeks into a unit, they may not recall the exact content of their ini- tial brainstorming. Similarly, the "Want to Know" items can be ticked off as they are covered and those that are never or partially addressed can be listed in a "Still Want to Learn" column at the end of the unit (Blachowicz & Ogle, 2001). For secondary school teachers who will be likely to have several different sections of students producing several different artifacts of student thinking, keeping a permanent record might seem to pose a problem. We found it useful to make notes on the students' ideas at the end of each class period and then to type and distribute them at the next class session for students to keep as references (for underresourced schools, teachers could make a single chart or overhead transparency for each class). Whatever the method, a permanent—but changeable—artifact facilitates the practice of coming back around and summarizing ideas throughout the unit.

Similarly, as our students in the social studies class prepared to write essays that expanded on their free writing from the first day of the unit, we reviewed with them the different laws they had learned (referring to our visual time line), the different texts they had read, and the different approaches they might take toward making an argument, incorporating an if–then writing strategy (see Buehl, 2002). In every case, our summariza- tion work always referred back to the texts that we had read in class. In many cases, we read excerpts of those texts again, both as a way of taking them back to the text and as a way of synthesizing ideas across texts. For example, when discussing a 1903 immigration statute, which prohibited *paupers* (among others) from entering the United States, we reread "The New Colossus" (after looking up the word *pauper* in the dictionary). In our read-aloud of "The New Colossus," we emphasized the line "Give me your tired, your poor, your huddled masses, yearning to breathe free," compar- ing it to the text of the statute, which reads:

> The following classes shall be excluded from admission to the United
> States. . . . All idiots, insane persons, epileptics, and persons who have

been insane within five years previously; paupers; persons likely to become a public charge; professional beggars; persons afflicted with a loathsome or with a dangerous contagious disease; persons who have been convicted of a felony or other crime or misdemeanor involving moral turpitude.

(32 Stat. 1214, sec. 2 of 1903 U.S. Statutes at Large)

We placed the texts side by side and asked the students to evaluate whether the law excluding paupers and sick people lived up to the sentiment expressed in Lazarus's poem. Through this process, we were teaching vocabulary; summarizing ideas within texts; synthesizing ideas across texts; modeling critical reading, questioning, and thinking; and, most important, teaching concepts, events, and actions central to the study of history and the social sciences. In short, we were engaging these youth in comprehension instruction in the service of social studies learning, not apart from it.

CONCLUSION: BUILDING DISCIPLINARY LITERACY BY TEACHING WITH TEXTS

Different subject-matter teachers can engage in similar kinds of teaching, setting up routines, habits, and practices that turn students to the texts of their content areas, whether textbooks, related real-world texts (e.g., newspaper articles), or primary sources. These turns to subject-matter texts can be engaging for young people if couched in meaningful purposes for reading the texts. Bringing text reading to the foreground and modeling for young people how texts of history and science can inform their everyday lives will not only improve their literacy skills, but also enhance their content learning and their possibilities for future participation as educated citizens.

DISCUSSION AND ACTIVITIES

1. Consider your own students. How could you connect from their interests to the central concepts of your subject matter? What might have you have to consider as you make those connections?

2. What are the major concepts of your subject area? How might you frame a problem for students to study or on which they could take a stand, using text resources from your area?

3. Considering those texts, what would your students need to know and be able to do to understand the big ideas and apply them to the problem or issue under study? Use the six types of knowledge/skill discussed in the chapter analyze the necessary language skills, content knowledge, and

discipline-based thinking skills needed to construct deep meaning from the text.

4. Once you've conducted the text analysis, construct a lesson or unit around the central problem or issue you've chosen, and then use the text or texts you analyzed. Try building in some of the teaching practices and strategies outlined in the chapter.

REFERENCES

Alexander, P. (2003). Profiling the adolescent reader: The interplay of knowledge, interest, and strategic processing. In C. Fairbanks, J. Worthy, B. Maloch, J. V. Hoffman, & D. Schallert (Eds.), *53rd yearbook of the national reading conference* (pp. 47–65). Milwaukee, WI: National Reading Conference.

Alexander, P. A., Kulikowich, J. M., & Jetton, T. L. (1994). The role of subject-matter knowledge and interest in the processing of linear and nonlinear texts. *Review of Educational Research, 64,* 201–252.

Alvermann, D. E., Young, J. P., Green, C., & Wisenbaker, J. M. (1999). Adolescents' perceptions and negotiations of literacy practices in after-school read and talk clubs. *American Educational Research Journal, 36,* 221–264.

Bain, R. (2006). Rounding up unusual suspects: Facing the authority hidden in the history classroom. *Teachers College Record, 108,* 2080–2114.

B. G., feat. Fresh, M. (Artist). (2006). *Move around: The heart of tha streetz: Vol. 2. i am what i am* [song].

Blachowicz, C., & Ogle, D. (2001). *Reading comprehension: Strategies for independent learners.* New York: Guilford Press.

Blumenfeld, P., Marx, R. W., & Harris, C. (2006). Learning environments. In I. Siegel & A. Renninger (Eds.), *Handbook of child psychology* (Vol. 4, pp. 297–342). Hoboken, NJ: Wiley.

Blumenfeld, P. C., Kempler, T. M., & Krajcik, J. S. (2006). Motivation and cognitive engagement in learning environments. In K. Sawyer (Ed.), *The Cambridge handbook of the learning sciences* (pp. 475–488). New York: Cambridge University Press.

Buehl, D. (2002). *Classroom strategies for interactive learning.* Newark, DE: International Reading Association.

Dressman, M., O'Brien, D. G., Rogers, T., Ivey, G., Wilder, P., Alvermann, D. E., et al. (2005). Problematizing adolescent literacies: Four instances, multiple perspectives. In J. V. Hoffman, D. L. Shallert, C. M. Fairbanks, J. Worthy, & B. Maloch (Eds.), *55th yearbook of the National Reading Conference* (pp. 141–154). Oak Creek, WI: National Reading Conference.

Eisner, E. W. (1994). *Cognition and curriculum reconsidered* (2nd ed.). New York: Teachers College Press.

Garcia, J. R. (1980). *Operation wetback: The mass deportation of Mexican undocumented workers in 1954.* Westport, CT: Greenwood Press.

Gee, J. P. (2003). *What video games have to teach us about learning and literacy.* New York: Palgrave Macmillan.

Guthrie, J. T., & Wigfield, A. (2000). Engagement and motivation in reading. In P. B. Mosenthal, M. L. Kamil, P. D. Pearson, & R. Barr (Ed.), *Handbook of reading research* (Vol. III, pp. 403–419). Mahwah, NJ: Erlbaum.

Kress, G. (2003). *Literacy in the new media age.* New York: Routledge.

Kress, G., & van Leeuwen, T. (1996). *Reading images: The grammar of visual design.* London: Routledge.

Lazarus, E. (1883). *The poems of Emma Lazarus* (Vol. 1). New York: Houghton Mifflin.

Lee, C. D., & Spratley, A. (2010). *Reading in the disciplines and the challenges of adolescent literacy.* New York: Carnegie Corporation of New York.

Leander, K. M., & Lovvorn, J. F. (2006). Literacy networks: Following the circulation of texts, bodies, and objects in the schooling and online gaming of one youth. *Cognition and Instruction, 24,* 291–340.

Moje, E. B. (2000). To be part of the story: The literacy practices of gangsta adolescents. *Teachers College Record, 102,* 652–690.

Moje, E. B. (2006). Motivating texts, motivating contexts, motivating adolescents: An examination of the role of motivation in adolescent literacy practices and development. *Perspectives, 32,* 10–14.

Moje, E. B. (2007). Developing socially just subject-matter instruction: A review of the literature on disciplinary literacy. In L. Parker (Ed.), *Review of research in education* (pp. 1–44). Washington, DC: American Educational Research Association.

Moje, E. B. (2010). Comprehending in the subject areas: The challenges of comprehension, grades 7–12, and what to do about them. In K. Ganske & D. Fisher (Eds.), *Comprehension across the curriculum: Perspectives and practices K–12* (pp. 46–72). New York: Guilford Press.

Moje, E. B., Overby, M., Tysvaer, N., & Morris, K. (2008). The complex world of adolescent literacy: Myths, motivations, and mysteries. *Harvard Educational Review, 78,* 107–154.

Ogle, D. M. (1986). K-W-L: A teaching model that develops active reading of expository text. *The Reading Teacher, 39,* 564–570.

Paxton, R. J. (1999). A deafening silence: History textbooks and the students who read them. *Review of Educational Research, 69,* 315–339.

Perie, M., Grigg, W. S., & Donahue, P. L. (2005). *The nation's report card: Reading 2005* (No. NCES 2006-451). Washington, DC: U.S. Government Printing Office.

Pressley, M., & Afflerbach, P. (1995). *Verbal protocols of reading: The nature of constructively responsive reading.* Mahwah, NJ: Erlbaum.

Schleppegrell, M. J. (2004). *The language of schooling: A functional linguistics perspective.* Mahwah, NJ: Erlbaum.

Shanahan, T., & Shanahan, C. (2008). Teaching disciplinary literacy to adolescents: Rethinking content-area literacy. *Harvard Educational Review, 78*(1), 40–61.

Stockdill, D., & Moje, E. B. (2013). Adolescents as readers of social studies: Examining the relationship between youth's everyday and social studies literacies and learning. *Berkeley Review of Education, 4,* 35-68.

VanSledright, B. A., & Kelly, C. (1998). Reading American history: The influence of multiple sources on six fifth graders. *The Elementary School Journal, 98,* 239–265.

Wineburg, S. S. (1991). On the reading of historical texts: Notes on the breach between school and the academy. *American Educational Research Journal, 28,* 495–519.

Wineburg, S. S. (1998). Reading Abraham Lincoln: An expert/expert study in the interpretation of historical texts. *Cognitive Science, 22,* 319–346.

Wineburg, S. S., & Martin, D. (2004). Reading and rewriting history. *Educational Leadership. 62,* 62.

CHAPTER 13

Teaching History and Literacy

Timothy Shanahan
Cynthia Shanahan

This chapter:

- Provides a rationale for history teachers to teach students the literacy of their discipline.
- Discusses what students need to know about history to read it well.
- Discusses research and practice regarding the teaching of disciplinary literacy during the study of history.
- Provides examples of instructional routines that will help students understand and think about history texts.

THE CASE FOR TEACHING LITERACY IN HISTORY CLASS

When we ask historians how much time they spend reading and writing, they say *all of the time*; and anyone who has studied history understands that making sense of the past requires intense reflection on the written word. Yet history teachers face a particularly knotty dilemma—they have students who, although they may know how to read, struggle with the history textbook and resist reading it ("Boring!"). The archaic language and unfamiliar text organization of historical documents may pose even greater challenges. Teachers may wonder, "Why haven't these students learned how to read in elementary school? And if they can't read, shouldn't the English teachers be teaching them?"

But reading literature isn't the same as reading history. Each discipline has its own way of communicating knowledge: a consequence of the unique kinds of knowledge they create and the different standards they have for determining what is worth studying. English teachers usually won't know enough about history to be able to teach students what to understand and think about history; nor do they typically engage in such reading themselves. In addition, as students move through the grades, the material they read becomes increasingly complex, abstract, and more specifically enmeshed within a disciplinary focus.

Students may start out in third or fourth grade reading science and social studies materials equally well. Subject-matter texts aren't that different initially, but by ninth grade, they are. By ninth grade the purposes, language, page formatting, organizational structures, relationships of prose to graphics, role of the author in interpretation, degrees of precision, nature of critical response, and so on, differ markedly. The problem is compounded by the fact that the texts for older students usually address content of which students have little prior knowledge. The reading taught in the English class likely won't support the reading of increasingly complex history texts. It is no wonder, then, that history teachers often eschew the textbook in favor of lectures or video, or having the better students read the text aloud with interspersed teacher explanations. The committed teacher is going to make sure students get the historical information, even if they can't or won't *read* history themselves.

The major job of the history teacher is not to tell students the information from the history books, but to enable them to make sense of this information in a sophisticated and appropriate manner. Such reading is essential for college, even in fields other than history (students are often required to learn the history of their major fields). Making decisions about who to vote for requires the kind of reading practiced by historians who consider evidence from multiple sources and opposing perspectives. Digging into the past helps one better understand and operate in the present. In the workplace, an individual who knows how the current situation came to be may have a better idea about how to change it. Yet digging into the past takes initiative and must be done without a teacher's support. Thus by the time students get through high school, they should be on their way to being *independent* and sophisticated readers of history.

The wide adoption of the Common Core State Standards (CCSS) for the English Language Arts (National Governors Association Center for Best Practices & Council of Chief State School Officers, 2010) emphasizes the notion that students in history classes should be *readers* of history. Perusing these standards, one realizes that there are not only literacy standards for English classes, but also reading and writing standards for history/social studies, science, and technical subjects. These standards indicate that students must learn to read history texts for understanding (e.g., "Determine the central ideas or information of a primary or secondary source"), how to analyze multiple texts, (e.g., "Integrate information from diverse sources, both primary and secondary, into a coherent understanding of an idea or event, noting discrepancies among sources"), and how to weigh the quality of historical evidence and use it to support their own arguments (e.g. "Integrate and evaluate multiple sources of information . . . to address a question or solve a problem").

To help students learn to read history, we call for an instructional focus on the discipline of history itself. We argue that, although most history teachers do not know how to teach reading, they do possess a great deal of knowledge as to what it takes to read history. History teachers can support students' reading not by teaching general reading comprehension strategies, but by imparting the kinds of thinking needed to interpret the past.

WHAT DO STUDENTS NEED TO KNOW ABOUT HISTORY TO READ IT WELL?

We thought deeply about what students needed to know about history to read history well during a Carnegie-funded study of expert readers in history, chemistry, and mathematics (Shanahan & Shanahan, 2008; Shanahan, Shanahan, & Misischia, 2011). We asked historians to think aloud about their reading processes as they read. To help interpret these responses, we drew on Wineburg's seminal study (1991) in which he compared the reading of historians and high school students, and we reviewed the work about history processes (e.g., Lee, 2005). As part of Project READI, an Institute of Education Sciences (IES)-funded Reading for Understanding grant, Cynthia Shanahan and her colleagues have further refined our understanding of what it means to understand history.

Wineburg found that historians engaged in processes that helped them think about the ideas, whereas high school students merely tried to remember facts. Historians used three processes not common among students: (1) they *sourced*—they thought about where information came from, who the author was, and when it written; (2) they *contextualized*—they looked at when the writing was produced and thought about the historical contexts under which it was written; and (3) they *corroborated*—they noted the agreements and disagreements across texts, ascribing confidence to corroborated information.

The historians in our study engaged in these processes too, but revealed additional ones. For example, a historian, while reading documents expressing different perspectives on the question "Was Lincoln the greatest president?" said:

"I don't know him very well, but [the author] is part of a right-wing group of Southern conservatives who is a secessionist. I'm not sure that the best model for thinking about Lincoln as a president is one that comes from a racist. So I have my critical eyes up a little bit, so it's a bit of a stretch to be friendly to, so I wanted to make sure to read it fairly."

The historian was sourcing, but also was evaluating his own potentially biased perspective.

Historians also try to determine what perspectives may have been left out. The historians we worked with strongly recommended that history teachers help their students think about whose voices are not being heard in the historical record. Are women's, Native Americans', or Vietnamese perspectives being omitted? Why?

Historians also evaluate a text's coherence. Are there gaps in the story or in the logic? Are events out of chronological order? What claims is the author making about the information, and what evidence does the author present to back up those claims? Are they coherent or contradictory? Often students are asked to read narrative history and they tend to view such text as a series of ill-connected stories. Historians relate such stories in a way that supports an argument, and showing students how to make connections among events can help them to uncover the argument.

Historians study change over time and use frameworks to guide that study. Perhaps they are interested in the political ramifications of an event, or its social, economic, artistic, religious, or technical causes and consequences, or maybe they are interested in the interplay of several of those frameworks. For example, consider historical accounts of the Little Rock Nine, the group of African American high school students who spent a year in what had been an all-white school in Arkansas, until Governor Faubus used a loophole in the state law to close the school. The integration of Central High School was affected by politics (e.g., Eisenhower used his presidential powers to send in federal troops; some say Faubus's resistance was to protect his own political power, and not because he was racist) and legality (e.g., *Brown v. Board of Education of Topeka, Kansas*, was the impetus for integration and Faubus used states' rights as a legal argument for resistance). However, these events were affected by social (e.g., Civil Rights Movement, KKK) and even technical (e.g., advent of televised reporting) influences, too. By thinking in terms of frameworks, historians can sharpen their analysis of change over time.

In addition to these frameworks, historians classify systems such as governments into categories like feudalism or monarchy; they think thematically (exploring "processes of migration," "expansion and retraction of rights," or "changes in economic systems,"), and they interpret the relationships among events. Just because a series of events is chronological doesn't mean the relationship is causative, or just because an author tells about events in a particular sequence does not mean that the events occurred in that order. Time sequences may reveal causation, but they also may be simply due to coincidence or chance.

Historians have varying theories of history. Some historians operate from the belief that history is a story of progress; others think that it is a documentation of social decline. Some believe history is a fueled by the great men (and women) that lead it; others believe it is fueled by the hopes and desires of the masses and that the so-called "great men" respond to the movements, like corks on the water. Note what one historian told us about the author's theoretical stance:

> "My response is, first of all, I'm always kind of very suspicious and weary of the kind of 'great man in history' approach, so I'm looking kind of carefully at how the author is embedding this argument. In other words, are they trying to undermine that great man in history, are they addressing the problem and dealing with the problem, or are they letting the problem just kind of fester without addressing it?"

All such considerations about history are based on a set of assumptions about historical accounts. The nature of historical inquiry leads historians to these beliefs. Unlike scientists, who rely on systematic descriptions of observed phenomena and experimental evidence, historians must rely on the study of primary (documents and artifacts) and secondary sources (e.g. the works of other historians) that already exist and must be found through inexact search processes. Whereas experiments may allow scientists to predict with a degree of certainty what will happen in the future, historians can make no such predictions. Scientists can determine probability; historians can only hope to determine *plausibility*, given evidence that is incomplete, often contradictory, possibly biased, and inconclusive. Because of that, historians are always aware that historical accounts consist of different interpretations or approximations of the past—not of the truth, and they know that one's interpretation of history is always contestable; much of history is argument. Events aren't significant unless they are claimed to be so, and this claim may be flawed or based on incomplete evidence. They understand that each interpreter of an event has a point of view and a historical context from which to study the past (e.g., during the first half of the 20th century, historians were particularly unkind to the "Radical Republicans" who worked to end slavery in the United States, but since the Civil Rights movement, they have been viewed more sympathetically). Given these limitations, historians recognize the need to be critical in determining the trustworthiness of any particular story of history.

The big idea here is historians see *everything* in history as argument—with a series of claims about the past and evidence for these claims—even if history is written as a story. Read, for example, the following excerpt from a history textbook:

> Their [bus boycotters] victory would inspire a new mass movement to ensure civil rights for African Americans. A series of local struggles to dismantle segregation—in the schools of Little Rock, in the department stores of Atlanta, in the lunch counters of Greensboro, in the streets of Birmingham—would coalesce into a broad-based national movement at the center of American politics. By 1963, the massive March on Washington would win the endorsement of President John F. Kennedy, and his successor, Lyndon B. Johnson, would push through the landmark Civil Rights Act and Voting Rights Act. (Farragher, Buhle, Czitrom, & Armitage, 2009, p. 1009)

This text follows a chronological account of the Montgomery Bus Boycott. That the historian chose this particularly well-known event as *the* event inspiring a new mass movement is his interpretation—a claim he makes presumably on the basis of evidence. Was it the very first nationally televised action by those seeking integration? Did he base the claim on the interpretations of other accounts? Historians would ask those questions rather than simply accept the claims.

The problem is that most historical accounts students read in class are from textbooks that tend to report history as a grand narrative. History in such books is told as an unfolding chronological story through which historians make implicit rather than explicit claims and bolster their claims with implicit rather than explicit evidence. To muddy the water, history texts report many widely accepted facts. World War II ended in 1945. Columbus sailed in 1492. To students, such historical accounts appear to be factual, cut-and-dried accounts of the past, and they don't think deeply about them. People's motivations, the relationship of one event to another, or whether the event was causative or coincidental are interpretations, hidden from students if they are not taught to pay attention to them.

Although students accept the truth of what is presented in a history class, historians use these insights about historical processes and the nature of evidence and argument to guide their reading. They approach a text seeking clues to the source and context even before beginning to read the text itself. When they do read the text, they seek clues that will help unmask an author's perspective or bias, the nature of the argument or claim, and the quality of the evidence. Historians continue to evaluate these things as they read, and based on their judgments of a text's trustworthiness, they determine their own stance toward the information. We argue that helping students to read like historians will lead to higher levels of engagement and, ultimately, a better understanding and use of history.

OTHER CONSIDERATIONS IN THE READING
AND WRITING OF HISTORY

Functional linguists have studied the differences among texts in different subject areas, including history (Fang & Schleppegrell, 2008). They find that sentences in history texts are unique because of their heavy emphasis on intention. History sentences are often about historical actors, their intentions, motivations, and goals, and the tactics they use to accomplish or attain these. Such sentences would be out of place in a science text, where the writing aims to suppress ideas of intention. Atoms do not choose to move; they are acted upon or implicated in scientific processes. In history, the sentences that describe the actors' goals and tactics also include information about time and place. Consider the following sentence: "One year after the Little Rock Nine integrated Central High School, Governor Faubus shut down further attempts to integrate by abruptly closing the Little Rock, Arkansas, public schools." In this sentence, time is construed as "one year after. . . . "; place is construed as "Little Rock, Arkansas"; and the actor is Governor Faubus. The goal that he acts toward is "to shut down further attempts to integrate," and the manner this is done is "by abruptly closing the Little Rock, Arkansas public schools."

Fang and Schleppegrell suggest that teaching students how to read history sentences can increase their basic understanding of history by keeping them focused on the historical purpose of such syntactic constructions. They also note that, whereas science text is filled with vocabulary that is technical in nature (e.g., *mitochondria, eutrophication, osmosis*), the challenge for history readers is not so much grasping the technical vocabulary, which is often borrowed from economics or other social sciences, but making sense of general academic vocabulary, which can be quite daunting. Note the following excerpt from a high school history textbook: "Dr. King's prophetic speech catapulted him into leadership of the Montgomery bus boycott—but he had not started the movement. When Rosa Parks was arrested, local activists with deep roots in the black protest tradition galvanized the community with the idea of a boycott" (Farragher, Buhle, Czitrom, & Armitage, 2009, p. 1008). Students may have difficulty with *prophetic, catapulted, activists*, and *galvanized*, none of which would be considered discipline specific or technical. In addition, given that history is an argument, vocabulary in historical accounts often carries ideological baggage (Shanahan & Shanahan, 2012)—it matters whether one writes of *affirmative action* or *reverse discrimination; protesters* or *agitators; the Civil War* or the *War Between the States*. Part of reading history is interpreting the perspectives evident in the choices of words, not just the word meanings.

We asked historians what difficulties they expected students to confront in reading history. They noted that reading historical documents could be challenging because language has changed over the years. If students are reading old documents, they will find that the vocabulary and writing style may be unfamiliar. Note the following excerpt from Ensign Jeremy Lister, a British Officer who writes an account of the night of Paul Revere's ride:

> I immediately offered myself a Volunteer in the room of Hamilton and was [ac]cepted of when I immediately returned to my lodgings to equip myself for a march, and met the Company on their way through the town in order to embark in boats to cross the bay above Charlestown, when we was just embarking, Lt. Col. Smith wish'd me to return to town again and not go into danger for others, particularly Hamilton whose illness was suppos'd by everybody to be feign'd which 'twas clearly proved to be the case afterwards, but wishing much to go, for the Honor of the Reg't thinking it would be rather a disgrace for the Company to March on an Expedition, more especially it being the first, without its compliment of Officers, therefore my offer was [ac]cepted. (Retrieved from *www.nps. gov/mima/forteachers/upload/Ensign%20Jeremy%20Lister.pdf*)

Even though the document is written in a rather informal style, familiar or modern conventions of spelling, sentence endings, and phrasing are missing.

Also, documents may be written in "legalese," or have some other arcane style. Note the language of the Thirteenth Amendment to the U.S. Constitution: "Neither slavery nor involuntary servitude, except as a punishment for crime whereof the party shall have been duly convicted, shall exist within the United States, or any place subject to their jurisdiction."

The meanings of vocabulary words can change, too, over time, or words may be dropped from common usage. Students may not know what the word "gilded" means since it is not used much anymore. They are often appalled when reading a document from the first half of the 1900s to read what is now considered a pejorative term, "Negro," and they make assumptions about the users of such terms. They lack what Lee (2005) refers to as "historical empathy," or the ability to interpret text in light of the time in which it was written (most likely because they lack background knowledge). This lack of empathy may appear in judgments about other social conventions, too. For example, students analyzed a photograph from the 1880s of a family. Because no one was smiling, students inferred that they were angry about the Native Americans nearby, not understanding that the lack of smiling was due to the long exposure times needed to make such photographs.

Such interpretive challenges can and should be the focus of instruction. It is incumbent upon those who teach history to read texts before having students read them, to note areas of potential difficulty, and to have ways ready to help students overcome these difficulties if they do, indeed, occur.

RESEARCH AND PRACTICE OF HISTORY LITERACY

Elsewhere in this volume, research regarding the teaching of reading and writing in history is explained as it relates to the reading of multiple texts. This research can be referred to in relation to both topics because, as the historians told us, reading more than one text and reading different genres is essential to history. With one text, there is no way to determine whether another perspective may have led to a different interpretation. Also, historians use primary source documents and artifacts to guide their interpretations, not relying merely on secondary texts written by other historians. The historians we studied were so adamant that more than one text be used that they suggested that, if nothing else were available, at least another textbook should be introduced for the purpose of comparison. Also, if students *never* encounter contradictory interpretations of an event, they will *never* understand what it is to be engaged in historical inquiry. At the heart of that inquiry is the idea that history is a complicated story, and that the "truth" about the past can never be fully known. The past can only be understood as an interpretation of the competing narratives of individuals who come from different perspectives.

To summarize the research on teaching history literacy, there is growing evidence that students as early as fourth grade and through college can be taught to read as historians do, and that such reading increases students' understanding of history and the depth of their engagements in reading, and leads to higher levels of reading comprehension and better writing of historical arguments (De La Paz & Felton, 2010; Hynd-Shanahan, Holschuh, & Hubbard, 2004; Monte-Sano, 2011; Monte-Sano & De La Paz, 2012; VanSledright, 2002a, 2002b; Wolfe & Goldman, 2005). For example, one study found that developmental community college students, when asked to engage in sourcing, contextualization, and corroboration while reading history, wrote significantly better essay test answers—more detail, better use of evidence, better organization—than students who were taught general reading strategies (Leahy, 2010). In one of the most recent studies, Reisman (2012) simply had teachers insert lessons on reading historical documents and writing about history into their existing units. Over the course of the study she found that teaching these led students to perform better on measures of historical thinking. Furthermore, these students transferred the thinking strategies they learned to the study of current issues, and they even did better on tests of factual knowledge and general reading comprehension.

The field of history teaching has gone further down the path of disciplinary literacy than other fields, perhaps because historians have been so articulate about what it means to read in their field. There are a number of resources available for teachers in this area. For example, the Reading Like a Historian website (*http://sheg.stanford.edu*) and the Teaching History website (*teachinghistory.org*) provide materials, primary source documents, instructional routines, and graphic organizers that students can use to read, write, and think critically about history, and The Teaching Channel (*teachingchannel.org*) has video clips of classrooms engaged in "reading like a historian."

In addition, major efforts are under way to study the teaching of historical thinking in relation to reading and writing. For example, an Institute of Education Sciences research project, Project READI, is studying the development of students' ability to understand and write arguments in history, science, and English literature in grades 6–12. This project starts from the premise that the nature of argumentation differs across these fields. In history, claims are often embedded in description and narration, although they may be more explicit in historical explanations. There are also different conventions for presenting evidence, and the warrants, or the linkages between the evidence and the claims, are often not explicitly stated and must be inferred. In reading history texts for implicit arguments, students cannot use the same strategies used in reading science. In Project READI, the history team is studying a middle grades and high school teacher as they infuse reading and writing instruction into their existing instructional practices. These teachers are teaching students to source, contextualize, and corroborate; to recognize claims and evidence in historical texts, looking for a source's interpretation of the relationship among events and their significance; and to use textual evidence in their own writing. They are also helping their students understand that reading historical texts closely in this new way—as historians do—requires a level of engagement and persistence they may not previously have applied to their reading of history, but that provides greater rewards. Both teachers have reported high levels of engagement with the reading and writing tasks.

HOW SHOULD WE TEACH THE LITERACY OF HISTORY?

Change Students' Ideas about What History Is

The biggest challenge in teaching students to read history is their abiding distaste for it. Students resist such reading because they find it boring or because the texts are challenging and don't seem worth the effort. Teachers need to disrupt these students' conceptions of history as being no more than a tedious compendium of past names, dates, and events. We need to change students' beliefs about what it means to read history, before trying to teach them the historians' reading and writing routines. Teachers can achieve this by providing students with contradictory texts, perhaps two texts showing differing perspectives (a British account of Paul Revere's ride and an American version) or differing uses of evidence (primary vs. secondary sources, one source vs. several). Focusing attention on such differences makes a point: accounts of the past are often based on incomplete and contradictory evidence. A teacher can help students *come to their own conclusions* that their history textbooks or the historical movies they watch or the stories they have grown up learning (e.g., stories about George Washington) are more uncomplicated and straightforward than history could possibly be.

There are other ways to begin the process of reading like a historian. In Project READI, one unit taught by history teachers started with photographs that students analyzed in relation to a question, "What caused the conflict between the Native Americans and the settlers in the Black Hills?" The photographs included some contextual information, such as their dates, so they could be placed in chronological order. Students made inferences that they would later confirm or disconfirm and asked questions that they would later answer through their reading. Reinforced in this lesson were several ideas about history reading: chronology is important, but it is not the same as causation; historians make hypotheses about the past based on the evidence they have; historians use artifacts such as photographs and texts to construct their interpretations; and understanding history is a process of inquiry into the past. We learned from that initial lesson, however, that even when using photographs, students lacked enough background knowledge to do much contextualization. In subsequent lessons we provided a short anchor text that set the stage for the question, and that seemed adequate to improve subsequent inferences. The big idea here is to help students see what history really is.

Teach Students the Processes Historians Use

As students dig into primary and secondary texts and artifacts, teach them to engage in the following strategies:

Sourcing

Have students find out about the author and think about what perspective that author may have. Include a discussion about whose perspectives are missing.

Contextualization

Support students' ability to contextualize by asking them to notice the date; if they don't know anything about that time period, help them find out about what was going on then. Guide them in making inferences about why an author wrote as he or she did. One strategy that combines sourcing and a kind of contextualization is called SOAPStone (Source, Occasion, Audience, Purpose, Subject, and Tone). In this activity, students have to think about the author's stance, but also about when it was written (the Occasion), whom it was written to (Audience), why it was written (Purpose), and what the writing was about (Subject). As students read, they confirm or disconfirm their hypotheses about an author's perspective based on what the author says and the way he or she says it (Tone).

Corroboration

Especially when using multiple texts, students should be engaged in comparison and contrast—looking for corroborated evidence and evidence that is unique or contradicted. Students can make comparison–contrast charts to keep track of this kind of information.

Historical Frameworks

Students can be tasked to look for political, economic, social, or legal tactics. Then they can be asked to reason about the interplay of these frameworks to answer questions such as: What tactics did Governor Faubus use to keep Central High School from being integrated? What tactics did civil rights activists use during the 1950s? How did these change in the 60s? One way to help students to reason using historical frameworks is a graphic organizer called a pattern organizer (See Figure 13.1). This organizer provides a visual way to display information using the frameworks.

Evaluations of Coherence

Help students notice when parts of a chronology are missing or out of order, or when the reasoning doesn't match the evidence. During a middle grades observation, a teacher was teaching students to engage in history discussions. He assigned roles so that one student looked into the source of the material; another considered the context, and so on. As they read texts about Custer's Last Stand from different perspectives, they noticed that the textbook version had presented the events out of chronological order, making it seem as if one event had led to another, when that could not have happened. The students were outraged and wrote the publisher about what they had discovered.

Argumentation

Expose students to claims and evidence in different genres. A teacher recently had students watch a PBS documentary on the Freedom Riders. They watched it for a short while and wrote down the claims and evidence they heard. Then they compared notes with a partner, watching a few minutes more. This exercise was more interesting than taking notes on names

Name _____

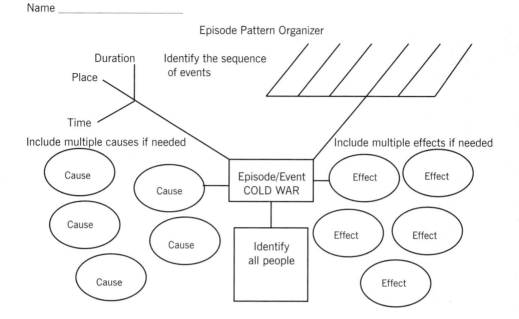

FIGURE 13.1. Pattern organizer.

and dates and provided insights about how documentaries pose arguments. Later, in discussions about the documentarian's decisions, the students exhibited sophisticated ways of thinking. Textbook narratives are usually full of claims without sufficient evidence, whereas popular history books usually cite sources of evidence in some way. Explorations of these traditions of interpretation can spark high-level conversation. Also, if students are reading to answer a historical question, having a multiple text comparison–contrast chart can provide fodder for writing their own essays. Ask students to put the guiding questions on top, and list the name of the different texts down the side. As students read the texts, they enter whatever evidence they found to answer the guiding question. When the students are done reading, they make their own claims based on their thinking about the trustworthiness of the source and its presentation of evidence. The chart, then, becomes a large part of the planning support for student essay writing.

Arcane Vocabulary and Structure

Teachers should create a climate for reading that honors struggle and problem solving. To read like historians, students must really dig into a text, understanding it at word and sentence level as well as more conceptually. In a sense, students are reading like detectives, looking for clues to an author's perspective, claims, evidence, and tone, and placing the text within a larger group of texts to get a more in-depth and complicated view of the past. Students must learn to do this independently, but initially they will need support. The challenge for teachers is to support them when they have difficulty *without telling them what the text means*. If students struggle with a key vocabulary term, lead them to try to get to the meaning themselves before telling them. Ask questions to lead students to higher levels of thinking. A high school history teacher admitted this was the hardest thing for her to do. Like most history teachers, she *loved* her subject matter, and got so excited about it that she wanted to tell them all about her insights before they had a chance to have any of their own.

Relationships among Events

As mentioned, events can be in chronological order without having a cause–effect relationship. Some events have multiple causes and some events have multiple effects. Some are simply coincidental. These relationships are the interpretations of historians, and students acting as historians can make inferences about them. Another graphic organizer we use with narrative history is our History Events Chart (see Figure 13.2), in which students summarize each of the historical events reported in the narrative and explain the connections between the events. Thus fifth graders, while reading a chapter on the American Revolution, had to summarize five sections of the chapter: the fall of Fort Ticonderoga; the Battle of Bunker Hill; the Second Continental Congress; Washington takes command; and the British leave Boston. As students examined the evidence, they started to discern an argument in the series of "stories." They decided the author was making an unstated claim about the importance of unification in a war (a sophisticated reading for a group of 11-year-olds).

CONCLUSION

The fundamental idea of disciplinary literacy is that texts are not read or written in the same ways, and that each discipline has its own rules of evidence and ways of using language. The only way students are likely to learn to be literate in these specialized disciplinary ways is through a kind of apprenticeship that brings them into participation in the discipline rather than as just an observer or a consumer. If students are to be sophisticated readers of history, they need to understand what historians are trying to do, and they need to be introduced to the nature of vocabulary in history or the ways sentences work or how narratives serve as implicit arguments or why we need to think about authors as we read. Research shows that engaging

Event	What happened?	Who?	When?	Where?	Why important?
Connection:					
Event	What happened?	Who?	When?	Where?	Why important?
Connection:					
Event	What happened?	Who?	When?	Where?	Why important?
Author's argument:					

FIGURE 13.2. History events chart.

students in reading history in the ways historians do is beneficial both for history learning and for civic engagement.

DISCUSSION AND ACTIVITIES

1. In what kind of a discussion of the processes of history would you engage students? What historical analysis processes would you involve them in, and then what questions would you ask to get them to think about the nature of history and historical writing?

2. Develop a text set for use in a history unit. Be sure to include both primary and secondary documents and documents that reveal different perspectives.

3. Try out the history events chart yourself. Identify a narrative history chapter, such as in your students' textbook, and then summarize each event and try to analyze the relations among these events to uncover the author's usually unstated arguments or claims. Pay attention to any insights that you develop about this process and how you would take advantage of those during lessons.

REFERENCES

De La Paz, S., & Felton, M. K. (2010). Reading and writing from multiple source documents in history: Effects of strategy instruction with low to average high school writers. *Contemporary Educational Psychology, 35,* 174–192.

Fang, Z., & Schleppegrell, M. J. (2008). *Reading in secondary content areas.* Ann Arbor: University of Michigan Press.

Farragher, J., Buhle, M. J., Czitrom, D. H., & Armitage, S. H. (2009). *Out of many: A history of the American people (Vol. 5).* New York: Pearson.

Hynd-Shanahan, C., Holschuh, J., & Hubbard, B. (2004). Thinking like a historian: College students' reading of multiple historical documents. *Journal of Literacy Research, 36,* 141–176.

Leahy, M. (2010). *Using disciplinary knowledge and intertextuality to improve college reading skills: A study of developmental community college students as they learn to read critically and think about historical documents.* Unpublished doctoral dissertation, Northern Illinois University.

Lee, P. J. (2005). Putting principles into practice: Understanding history. In S. Donovan & J. Bransford (Eds.), *How students learn: History, mathematics, and science in the classroom* (pp. 29–78). Washington, DC: National Academies Press.

Monte-Sano, C. (2011). Beyond reading comprehension and summary: Learning to read and write by focusing on evidence, perspective, and interpretation. *Curriculum Inquiry, 41,* 212–249.

Monte-Sano, C., & De La Paz, S. (2012). Using writing tasks to elicit adolescents' historical reasoning. *Journal of Literacy Research, 44,* 273–299.

National Governors Association Center for Best Practices & Council of Chief State School Officers. (2010). *Common Core State Standards for the English language arts and literacy in history/social studies, science, and technical subjects.* Washington, DC: Author.

Reisman, A. (2012). Reading like a historian: A document-based history curriculum intervention in urban high schools. *Cognition and Instruction, 30,* 86–112.

Shanahan, C., Shanahan, T., & Misichia, C. (2011). Analysis of expert readers in three disciplines: History, mathematics, and chemistry. *Journal of Literacy Research, 43,* 393–429.

Shanahan, T., & Shanahan, C. (2008). Teaching disciplinary literacy to adolescents: Rethinking content area literacy. *Harvard Educational Review, 78,* 40–59.

Shanahan, T., & Shanahan, C. (2012). What is disciplinary literacy and why does it matter? *Topics in Language Disorders, 32,* 7–18.

VanSledright, B. A. (2002a). Confronting history's interpretive paradox while teaching fifth graders to investigate the past. *American Educational Research Journal, 39,* 1089–1115.

VanSledright, B. A. (2002b). Fifth graders investigating history in the classroom: Results from a researcher-practitioner design experiment. *The Elementary School Journal, 103,* 131–160.

Wineburg, S. S. (1991). On the reading of historical texts: Notes on the breach between school and academy. *American Educational Research Journal, 28,* 495–519.

Wolfe, M. B. W., & Goldman, S. R. (2005). Relations between adolescents' text processing and reasoning. *Cognition and Instruction, 23,* 467–502.

CHAPTER 14

Literacy Support in English/ Language Arts Classrooms

Motivation, Dialogue, and Strategy Instruction

Leslie S. Rush
Todd F. Reynolds

The purpose of this chapter is to discuss instructional techniques that English/language arts teachers can use to support students' literacy development. It includes discussion and examples of instructional techniques related to:

- Supporting students' motivation to read.
- Engaging students and teacher in collaboration and dialogue.
- Teaching students reading strategies.

As suggested by Wilson (2011), the burden of teaching adolescents to read and write effectively tends to fall most heavily on English teachers, in spite of the growing movement to address disciplinary literacies in all content-area classrooms (Moje, 2008). As teachers whose focus is largely on reading and writing, it is reasonable to expect that English teachers would know most about teaching the skills of reading and writing. However, in our experience, many English teachers—although they love literature and find it important for developing lifelong learners—may not have a clear understanding of how to assist students who struggle with reading or who are not interested in reading. This chapter offers suggestions for English teachers who would like to foster the literacy development of their students.

We provide some important theoretical understandings as well as specific actions related to improving students' literacy skills.

What can we as English teachers do to help our students develop the kinds of reading skills that are essential for success, not only in English classes, but in life? In the first two sections of this chapter, we provide a discussion of instructional techniques that can encourage students' motivation to read and ways in which English/language arts teachers can incorporate dialogue in their classrooms. We also provide an instructional example, using a high school classroom's interaction with a scene from Shakespeare's *Hamlet*, that uses these techniques in pursuit of students' comprehension of this classic play. Both of these foci—motivation and dialogue—can play important roles in building students' desire and interest in reading, an important precursor for assisting students actively with strategy instruction. The third and final section of this chapter provides an instructional framework for teaching students the types of reading strategies that good readers use, a hallmark of reading and literacy instruction in English/language arts classrooms. For this chapter, we chose to use texts that we have either personally taught in the classroom or that we felt our readers would be familiar with. This does not mean, however, that we are prioritizing these classic texts. In fact, we believe strongly that teachers should choose texts that will engage the specific students they have in their classrooms. The concepts discussed here can work with any text the teacher chooses to meet the students' needs.

INSTRUCTIONAL TECHNIQUES THAT BUILD MOTIVATION TO READ

One important key for addressing the needs of struggling readers in English/language arts classrooms is recognizing the impact of motivation to read—or lack of motivation to read—on students. According to McRae and Guthrie (2009), students who avoid reading an assigned text usually have a reason for this avoidance. The reason may be one of skill; alternatively, it may be one of motivation. Research on motivation has shown us that internal or intrinsic motivations to read, such as seeking understanding, feeling successful, and finding enjoyment in reading, are connected with reading achievement. Likewise, external motivations—such as grades, requirements, and assignments—are not connected with reading achievement (Guthrie & Coddington, 2009).

McRae and Guthrie (2009) describe a set of classroom practices that are designed to help build students' motivation to read, including providing relevance, choice, opportunities for success, opportunities for collaboration, and opportunities for students' mastery of content knowledge. In this section of the chapter, we review those practices and provide examples that are specific to English/language arts classrooms.

Relevance

Teachers who are aware of their students' interests and cultural backgrounds can choose activities, experiences, and texts that students will be interested in and will enjoy. When students find that the reading they are engaged in touches on something they understand, on a theme that affects them, or on their own cultural backgrounds, they are more likely to persist with the class reading. As students experience repeated opportunities to read something that they find relevant, they will begin to see reading itself as enjoyable. In English classes, therefore, looking for relevance means choosing texts with which students are likely to connect. For example, teachers who provide their students with young adult novels such as Sharon Flake's *The Skin I'm In*, Sandra Cisneros's *The House on Mango Street*, or Lisa Klein's *Ophelia*, give students the opportunity to explore literature that is compelling, complex, and beautiful, but also relevant. The International Reading Association and the National Council of Teachers of English collaborate to provide resources for teachers at *ReadWriteThink.org*, where teachers unfamiliar with young adult literature can find book recommendations for adolescent readers, such as Jennifer Buehler's podcasts (*www. readwritethink.org/parent-afterschool-resources/podcast-series/text-messages-recommendations-adolescent-30214.html*). One English teacher of our acquaintance asks students to research local history and present their findings at a local museum, with the community invited to participate. Thrilled to engage in such relevant study, students peruse historical documents, interview senior citizens, and talk with their neighbors about issues and events that are truly relevant because they take personal ownership.

Choice

Teachers who provide students with meaningful, appropriate choices send the message to students that their opinions and preferences matter. What might students be given choice in? According to McRae and Guthrie (2009), teachers might offer choices on such decisions as the topic of study, what reading materials to use, how student work will be assessed, the order of activities, social arrangements, and procedural sequences, among others. When we think about giving students choices in English classes, the opportunities are endless. For example, on the larger end of the choice scale, a teacher might ask students to choose one of three to four novels to study in small groups, or students may choose the members of their small group or how the novel study will be evaluated. At the smaller end of the choice scale, a teacher might give students options for responding to texts (e.g., students can respond in a paragraph or in a bulleted list), or whether they wish to work alone or with a partner. In large or small ways, giving students the opportunity to make their own choices affirms that they matter as individuals, and these opportunities can help students to see the texts and tasks in English classes in a positive light.

Opportunities for Success

In order to improve motivation to read, students need to experience success with the reading tasks they are given, which does not mean that students should always be given easy tasks. Instead, teachers should assign reading tasks that will challenge students and provide sufficient support so that they will succeed. What might a challenging task look like? It might involve reading an unfamiliar genre of text. It might mean reading a text that contains challenging vocabulary, challenging concepts, unfamiliar dialect, or complex sentence structure. The nature of these challenges will vary widely among students; similarly, the types of support they need will vary. Teachers who want to provide support for their students to read challenging texts can model reading processes for their students. For example, if students are having difficulty with vocabulary in a particular text, a teacher might model how to use context to get clues about word meaning. Once a teacher has modeled this process, he or she might then ask a student to model the same behaviors, ask students to work with a partner to develop their skills on these behaviors, and then ask students to carry out those behaviors independently. Other ways to support students' interactions with challenging texts are provided in this chapter's section on strategy instruction. In whatever form the support comes, it should ensure that students do not fail continually, as this repeated failure undermines students' perceptions that they can be successful with reading challenging texts.

Opportunities for Collaboration

Another technique that English/language arts teachers can use to improve students' motivation—both overall and for reading—is to include discussion and collaboration with peers as a regular part of the classroom work. According to McRae and Guthrie (2009), creating opportunities for students to talk with each other and to collaborate around reading will improve students' embrace of reading as a personal goal. In English/language arts classrooms, students can work together around common texts in collaborative ways that involve talk among students. In order for such talk to be effective, of course, teachers need to model appropriate behaviors. For example, teachers need to help students learn to disagree with each other respectfully and to manage volume levels so that the classroom doesn't become chaotic. We provide more information on how to include peer classroom talk in English/language arts classes in the section on dialogue below.

Mastery of Content Knowledge

The final key to encouraging students' motivation to read in English/language arts classrooms is to support students' desire to become knowledgeable about content, what McRae and Guthrie (2009) call "mastery motivation" (p. 68). Here, teachers can introduce and then deepen students' knowledge about complex concepts to help students amass a complex web of knowledge and skills. This process involves helping students to see the connections among the tasks and processes that they carry out in an English class; in addition, it involves helping them see the overarching connections among texts. For example, in a high school course that includes British literature, a teacher might focus on the history of Great Britain and the impact of that history on the literature that students study. Of course, in the process, students may study classics such as *Beowulf, The Canterbury Tales*, and works by Shakespeare, as well as more modern texts that speak to the era of postcolonialism, such as Chinua Achebe's *Things Fall Apart* or Ngũgĩ wa Thiong'o's *The River Between*. The key to building mastery of content knowledge in this example is to present these important works as connected texts in the larger study of the history of Great Britain, rather than discrete works that are only important in isolation. This connection and focus on larger concepts may be strengthened by using wall charts or other highly visual realia to draw students' attention to the larger concept or learning goal, adding information to this visual as the course of study progresses.

USING DIALOGUE TO IMPROVE LITERACY IN ENGLISH/LANGUAGE ARTS CLASSROOMS

Another key to improving literacy in an English/language arts classroom is the use of authentic dialogue, which is characterized by a significant amount of time spent in discussion, using authentic or open-ended discussion questions, and characterized by uptake, or follow-up questions (Nystrand, 2006). Time spent discussing is a strong and important predictor of literacy achievement as indicated by assessment scores in the spring (Lawrence & Snow, 2011), yet less than 1 minute of classroom time is typically spent discussing (Nystrand, 2006). Instead, teachers focus on questions and answers under the guise of discussion. This format, commonly called initiation–response–evaluation (IRE), allows the teacher to ask a specific question to which he or she already knows the answer (Neal, 2008). When students respond, the teacher judges the student response as either correct or incorrect, and then moves on. Although this well-known cycle can ensure that classroom discussions are both manageable and content focused, the bulk of the work of critical thinking, analysis, and synthesis is always being undertaken by the teacher, not the students; the teacher also maintains complete academic and interpretive authority and keeps the dominant power structure in place (Neal, 2008). So how might teachers move away from this cycle of teacher-dominated discussion and incorporate authentic dialogue that will both engage students and encourage literacy development?

Lawrence and Snow (2011), in their review of research on discussion in the classroom, suggest four strategies that teachers can use to facilitate authentic discussion that will help students build stronger comprehension skills. First, teachers can create a situation in which students have more interpretive authority, establishing a classroom with a diversity of perspectives as students feel the ability to contribute to the interpretation of the text instead of having an interpretation given to them by the teacher. Second, the teacher can surrender control over who speaks and when they speak. This can be done by having students lead discussion, or by having an open format not based on raising hands. The teacher will need to create the expectations for this kind of discussion, but when students rely on the ebb and flow of the discussion instead of being called on by the teacher, the dialogue can be more fluid and genuine. Nystrand (2006) describes this dialogic classroom as containing more "conversational turns" instead of teacher questions, allowing all participants in the room to add ideas and thoughts to the discussion (pp. 399–400).

Third, teachers can control the guiding topic by focusing on a specific strategy or purposefully chosen questions that students can answer. This gives the discussion a focus, a purpose. Fourth, teachers should use open-ended and genuine questions, which Lawrence and Snow (2011) describe as "ones worthy of discussion and ones on which opinions can legitimately differ" (p. 331). The development of open-ended questions helps teachers move away from the IRE format because the questions do not have one specific answer that can be found in the text. Instead, these questions require interpretation and discussion and can have multiple answers that the students can argue with and discuss. For example, *why* questions typically require interpretations into character or author motives. The question strategy discussed later in this chapter can help guide teachers in authentic questioning.

Opening the classroom to discussion can lead to tension as students and teachers voice their possible disagreement over different interpretations of the text. Nystrand (2006) argues that teachers should embrace this disagreement, knowing that the discourse developed by competing perspectives contributes to sophisticated comprehension (p. 399). While dialogue with disagreement may be difficult to begin and maintain, it is crucial for students so they can make meaning and develop understanding through genuine responses, and not through predetermined questions with simple answers (Nystrand, 2006, p. 400). In their review of research on adolescents' views on the classroom, Intrator and Kunzman (2009) found that students preferred teachers who had a gift of guiding discussions and listening to students' voices, and that students actually longed for in-depth discussion on questions of purpose and meaning in their lives. Despite the possible tension, whole-class discussion remains one of the best ways to engage the students and helps them reach deeper levels of comprehension (Nystrand, 2006; Wilkinson & Son, 2011).

SUGGESTIONS FOR TEACHING *HAMLET* WITH MOTIVATION AND DIALOGUE

To describe the concepts we have introduced in a classroom context, we imagined an amalgamation of some of our own previous classroom settings. One such setting is a British literature class in high school; for this imagined setting, we are introducing students to Shakespeare's famous tragedy, *Hamlet*; however, the strategies discussed here would work with any drama, and with some slight modifications, with any text. In the bulleted paragraphs that follow, we provide some teaching suggestions, specific to *Hamlet*, that create opportunities for both motivation and dialogue. These suggestions are certainly not the *only* instruction that should take place around a complex and difficult text such as the one we are addressing; however, they provide an opportunity for an English/language arts teacher to develop instruction that will encourage students to participate in authentic dialogue—with the teacher and with each other—as well as to bolster students' motivation to engage with the text.

Offering Choice through Performance

At the beginning of the play, we will give the students a list of important passages and ask them to work with a small group to choose one passage to present to the class just before we read that passage as a class. They can present it in any way they choose, as long as they convey the characters present and the basic plot.

Developing Expertise through Research on Historical and Cultural Background

Students will be asked to work with a partner to do research on the Renaissance, the Globe Theater, the King's Men, the Bubonic Plague, and other topics related to Shakespeare's dramas. Throughout the reading and work on *Hamlet,* students will provide the information gained through their research and will be called upon as experts to relate the ongoing study of the play to this information.

Providing Authentic Dialogue through Small-Group and Whole-Class Discussions

Using film clips readily available on YouTube or other sources, we will ask students to watch particular scenes and provide them with questions to think about as they watch. After watching the film clips, students will discuss these questions in small groups, and then share out and discuss as a class.

Providing Opportunities for Success through Vocabulary and Concept Work

Students will periodically be placed into groups to read a short passage from the play, focusing on finding and deciphering unfamiliar words and concepts. After teacher modeling of this process, they will circle any words they don't know and, as a group, write what they think the word means, using the context and dictionaries to help them develop meaning.

Leveraging Relevance through Literary and Pop Culture Study

As we work through the texts, we will continually ask students to reflect on the scenes and actions of the characters, and make connections to their own lives. For example, we could ask what they have done when they thought someone did something wrong, but they didn't have proof, or how they could respond if their boyfriend or girlfriend starting acting toward them the way Hamlet acted toward Ophelia. We also want to find examples of *Hamlet* in popular or modern culture. We will make connections to *The Lion King* and show clips from *Hamlet 2000* with Ethan Hawke. We will ask students to think about the themes we discuss in class and have them find more examples in texts they are familiar with.

These instructional plans provide students with opportunities for meaningful and authentic dialogue with partners, with groups, and as an entire class. They can choose which scene they present, even though the choice is from a list that we provided; this gives them the opportunity to take ownership over what they are doing, especially since they choose how they present the scene. Students are given the opportunity to develop mastery knowledge of a concept and to provide this knowledge for their classmates. Finally, there is plenty of movement into groups and back to the whole class. By providing these kinds of activities, we can increase the likelihood that the students will be engaged and motivated.

STRATEGY INSTRUCTION
IN ENGLISH/LANGUAGE ARTS CLASSROOMS

Even with methods to both motivate students and give them a voice in the classroom, teachers still face the question of how to help students more directly to develop their comprehension abilities as they read the assigned literature for the class. Strategy instruction can be one of the answers teachers need in order to help their students. The goal of strategy instruction is to teach students the kinds of reading strategies that good readers of literary texts use naturally, with the idea that students' use of these strategies will eventually become automatic, and that students will be able to successfully transfer the use of the strategy to other texts and to other contexts. Research has demonstrated that strategy instruction has a positive impact on students' comprehension performance (Duke & Carlisle, 2011; Duke, Pearson, Strachan & Billman, 2011; Pressley, 2000; Wilkinson & Son, 2011). Wilkinson and Son (2011) show that *"when implemented well,* [strategy instruction] produces robust effects on measures of comprehension, including standardized tests" (p. 364, emphasis added). The key, according to the authors, is quality implementation.

Unfortunately, since the concept of strategy instruction has been implemented in different ways since the early 1970s (Pressley, 2000), school administrators and policy makers have tried to centralize the approach, leading to possible unintended consequences (Duke et al., 2011). Strategy instruction can become too mechanistic, with teachers and testing focusing on the strategy as the goal as opposed to the comprehension of the text; it can also become more difficult than the actual text, trapping students in "introspective nightmares" of metacognition (Wilkinson & Son, 2011, p. 360). Strategy instruction can become scripted, rigid, and inflexible (Duke et al., 2011), leaving students confused as to how to actually use the strategies independently. However, these are cautionary tales, and studies demonstrate that quality strategy instruction can work well (Pressley, 2000).

While the research is still unclear as to why strategy instruction helps students, Wilkinson and Son (2011) provide two possible explanations. Strategy instruction may succeed because of its commitment to active engagement with the text. It may also succeed because of its focus on dialogue about the text. Each of these reasons involves a layer of application to strategy instruction. By actively engaging students with the text through strategies, teachers ask students to think about what they read, to process it more than simply looking for facts to answer multiple-choice questions. By creating opportunities for genuine dialogue about the text, teachers give students voice, but they also require students to support and defend their interpretations, and to argue with others. These two methods are crucial when implementing strategy instruction.

Duke et al. (2011) give two more qualifications for quality strategy instruction. First, teachers should help students learn "when, why, and how to apply strategies" (p. 68). This is not a rigid and scripted instruction meant to apply universally, but a localized and specific instruction on how to use strategies with the text being read and discussed in the classroom. Second, teachers should demonstrate to students that using the right strategy at the right time can make the difference between understanding the text and not understanding the text. In other words, the use of the strategies depends on the needs of the individual student; using the wrong strategy, one that does not address the student's comprehension problem, will not help that student, but using the right strategy, one that does address the problem, will. A program or a script will not be able to determine which one is correct, but a student, well taught in a variety of strategies, will be able to apply the appropriate strategy.

Another area of difficulty in strategy instruction is the definition of *strategy*. Teachers are usually confronted with two terms when dealing with comprehension: skills and strategies. Sometimes they are used as synonyms, and sometimes they are used to describe very different things. Afflerbach, Pearson, and Paris (2008) work on both defining the terms and separating them so that teachers can focus specifically on the kind of instruction that students need. According to them, strategies are "deliberate, goal-directed attempts to control and modify the reader's efforts to decode text, understand words, and construct meanings of text" (p. 368). Skills, on the other hand, are defined as "automatic actions that result in decoding and comprehension with speed, efficiency, and fluency and usually occur without awareness of the components or control involved" (p. 368). The difference is between deliberate and automatic actions that readers use when attempting to comprehend a text. When a reader has difficulty with a text and chooses to apply the questioning technique, he is using a strategy, a conscious method used to try to find meaning in the text. However, the same reader may instantly visualize the scene being described, automatically using a skill to continue to process the text.

As readers gain competence with strategies, they may become more automatic; as readers encounter more difficult texts, what once was automatic may become more deliberate. Readers can move back and forth between strategy and skill, and, for the reader and the teacher, it is not necessarily important which one it is for that reader since the distinction between the two is fluid (Afflerbach et al., 2008). However, the goal is to constantly move students to more self-directed and automatic use of strategies, which will help them understand and comprehend more complex texts (Afflerbach et al., 2008; Duke & Carlisle, 2011).

Quality strategy instruction, then, focuses on the deliberate methods that readers use in order to process the text. Reviews of research conducted by Pressley (2000) and Duke et al. (2011) each describe some of the most successful strategies. While all the strategies mentioned can be quality tools for teachers, five strategies consistently appear in the research: questioning, summarizing, monitoring and clarifying, activating prior knowledge, and setting a purpose. To implement quality strategy instruction in the language arts classroom, teachers can begin with these strategies, discussing them with the students and having the students apply them to the texts.

Questioning

Questioning as a strategy should focus on moving beyond the literal level in the text. Pressley (2000) focuses on "why-questioning," with students pulling in prior knowledge to answer the questions and connect the meanings in the text to previous learning. He demonstrates a tactic of asking why a fact in a nonfiction text made sense (p. 553); however, the strategy of creating authentic questions can be used equally well for fiction and poetry texts. Why does a character choose to do or not do something? Why does the poet end the line with this word or choose this metaphor to represent something? As teachers, we use authentic questions to start discussions. Part of teaching this strategy is having students do it by themselves, asking these kinds of questions as they read, and as they come up with them. A second part of this strategy is working on answering the questions, something that can be done individually, in small-group discussions, in large-group discussions, or even in written assignments. The Common Core State Standards (CCSS) for Speaking and Listening ask students to "pose and respond to questions" (National Governors Association [NGA] Center for Best Practices & Council of Chief State School Officers [CCSSO], 2010, 6.1.c). By 12th grade, students should be able to question others' comments in order to "clarify, verify, or challenge" those viewpoints (NGA & CCSSO, 2010, 11–12.1.c). Valuing the questions as a way to understand the text, though, and not just as an exercise in class, requires engagement with the questions in some way. Asking students to develop their own questions about a text encourages ownership; engaging in discussion around students' own questions provides a means to move away from recitation-style talk into the kind of collaborative, authentic dialogue that promotes literacy skills.

Summarizing

Summarizing is mentioned specifically in the CCSS for reading, with students being required to "provide a summary of the text distinct from personal opinions or judgments" in sixth grade (NGA & CCSSO, 2010, 6.2), and to "provide an objective summary of the text" (NGA & CCSSO, 2010, 11–12.2) in 11th and 12th grades. Working with students on succinct summarizing will help them to grasp the content and understand the material. Frey, Fisher, and Hernandez (2003) explain the collaborative generating interaction between schemata and text (GIST) strategy, along with an example of how to scaffold the instruction. To use the GIST strategy, teachers break the text into small sections. At the end of each section, teacher modeling or group work lead to the crafting of a one-sentence summary. At the end of the text, the collection of one-sentence summaries serves as the beginning of the summary of the entire text. Beers (2003) introduces the "someone wanted but so" (SWBS) method of summarizing fiction. After a section of text, the writer chooses a character (someone); the sentence continues with what that character wants (wanted), a potential complication to what the character wants (but), and then the resolution to that complication (so). For example, from *The Scarlet Letter*, a SWBS statement could read: "Hester wants to remove the letter, but Pearl doesn't recognize her when Hester removes it, so Hester puts the letter back on." The process can be repeated for different characters, or for different "wants." These are only two possible strategies, but they can provide some guidance as teachers think about how to bring summarization into their classroom, and to their students' experiences as they read.

Monitoring for Understanding

Monitoring and clarifying requires students to think about their own thinking. This is the height of metacognition. As Duke et al. (2011) point out, "Good readers monitor their understanding of the text, making adjustments in their reading as necessary" (p. 56). Teachers should walk students through this process, showing them how to recognize that they don't know something. To effectively monitor understanding, students need to constantly be aware of whether they comprehend the material and what steps to take to solve any problems. Struggling readers do not pay attention to the words; they just gloss over the page, expecting not to understand, or remember, or make sense (Bomer, 2011). By creating purposeful reading tasks, teachers can help students monitor their understanding, and then start to find ways to fill in the gaps when needed (Bomer, 2011). While the CCSS for reading do not refer specifically to monitoring and clarifying, Anchor Standard 4 refers to making meaning in the text (NGA & CCSSO, 2010), and Anchor Standard 10 refers to students reading and comprehending texts independently (NGA & CCSSO, 2010). In each case, students need to be aware of their own difficulties in order to make adjustments as necessary; they need to use the monitoring and clarifying strategy in order to figure out what they know and what they don't know, which will, in turn, allow their understanding of the text to deepen.

Activating Prior Knowledge

Activating prior knowledge helps the reader connect to the text. However, it is important to note that good readers make connections when it will help them understand something, and refrain from making those connections when they become unnecessary (Pressley, 2000). Weak readers, on the other hand, make irrelevant connections that can actually disrupt their understanding of the text (Pressley, 2000). Part of this instruction is making sure that students start to make the distinction between relevant and irrelevant connections and connect to prior knowledge in useful and productive ways to help them understand the text. This is not to say that the teacher knows the only way to connect; a random thought a student has could shed light on the difficulty he experienced in the text. It is, though, important to examine whether those possibly random thoughts contribute to or harm the comprehension. By opening up a dialogue about prior knowledge, students and teachers can work together to find connections that make sense, and add to the understanding of the text.

Setting a Purpose for Reading

Finally, setting a purpose for reading gives the readers some clarity about why they are reading in the first place. Strong readers can read for pleasure, for learning, for scholarship, or for a variety of other reasons. As they do so, they constantly examine whether what they are reading meets those goals (Duke et al., 2011). Purposes can also be set in classrooms where reading is required. Purposeful reading can focus on graphic organizers on before, during, or after reading questions or strategies; on connections to a topic being discussed or studied; or on myriad other concepts or ideas. The point for the teacher, though, is to set a purpose for the reading before the students read, as opposed to just saying, "Read the chapter for tomorrow." When using the CCSS, or localized state standards, the purpose can place focus on a particular standard. For example, instead of just assigning a chapter from *Catcher in the Rye*, the teacher could ask the students to look at how Holden develops over the course of a particular chapter, having them look for character traits in the text that will help them determine Holden's change or lack thereof (NGA & CCSSO, 2010, R.9–10.3). Being this specific gives the students a reason to read the chapter and can help them understand more as they read.

A Model for Strategy Instruction in English/Language Arts Classrooms

As teachers move to incorporate strategies in their classrooms, researchers have documented the most successful methods for instruction (Duke et al., 2011; Pressley, 2000; Wilkinson & Son, 2011). Commonly referred to as explicit teaching, or gradual release of responsibility, this instructional model provides students with the guidance they need in order to fully grasp and apply the strategies that can help them comprehend difficult texts.

The first two steps, explain and model, typically go together since they are based on teacher talk. The teacher first explains what the strategy is, why it is used, and what it is for. Then the teacher demonstrates how the strategy is used in a selection of the text. The next step is to involve the students in collaborative and guided practice, encouraging them to use the strategy with another portion of the text and then discuss it with a group and with the class. During this time, the teacher is listening and interacting, providing feedback on how the students are using the strategy, and prompting them to continue or modify what they are doing.

At this point, it is important for teachers to remember to meet the needs of their students. If their students are familiar with the strategies already, then the explanation and modeling can be very quick, and the guided practice can be more advanced. However, if the strategies are new to the students, or if students are demonstrating difficulty in comprehension that the strategies can help, then the explanation and modeling can be longer and more detailed, and the guided practice can be very focused.

The final stage is independent application, having the students read on their own and apply the strategy. The goal in this independent application, though, is not the strategy, but comprehension of the text through strategy use. Teachers should set the purpose, including the strategy, but should always relate the use of the strategy back to the meaning of the text.

This is where the gradual release of responsibility is so important. Duke et al. (2011) found that teachers either moved very quickly from the modeling to independent practice, asking students to do more than they were prepared to do, or they spent too much time on the guided practice, not letting the students get to the independent practice that is crucial for students to learn how to self-regulate their use of the strategies. There is no universal way to determine how long to spend on modeling and guided practice or when to move into the independent practice stage. Instead, teachers need to listen to their students and see what they are producing and where they are having difficulty. Essentially, if students seem to have no problem, teachers can move more into the independent stage; if students seem to have difficulty, teachers should stay in the modeling/guided practice stage. Since strategy use is recursive and happens all year (Pressley, 2000), instruction on a strategy may move back and forth depending on the text. With one text, the class could demonstrate quality use of strategies to comprehend the text, but with a different text they could have problems applying the strategies to arrive at an understanding. The teacher needs to be attuned to the students and should be prepared to adjust as the year progresses.

An Example of Strategy Instruction with a Classic Text

When teaching a classic novel, such as *The Adventures of Huckleberry Finn*, a teacher could focus instruction on the strategy of monitoring for meaning and clarifying. In Chapter 8, Jim explains to Huck why he ran away. Jim does a lot of speaking, and since his speech is written in a heavy dialect, sometimes students have difficulty understanding what is happening. The teacher could begin by explaining the focus on monitoring for meaning and clarification:

> "Today, while we're reading this chapter, I want you to think about monitoring and clarifying, which is when you think about whether or not you understand the text, and then, if you aren't, doing something to try to understand it. In order to get the most out of this chapter, you need to be aware of whether you understand, and this strategy can help."

The next step is to move straight into modeling. The teacher could say:

> "For example, turn to page 33. When I read this page silently, as I like to do, I didn't understand any of it. I got to the bottom of the page and realized that I had no idea what Jim is saying. So I had to adjust. I decided to read this page out loud to see if that would work."

The teacher could then read a paragraph out loud, articulating afterward, "You know, that made a lot more sense. I can hear the text better, and I can understand Jim more." The teacher could then move the students into some guided practice:

> "What I want you to do now is get into your groups, and take turns reading paragraphs. Make sure everyone gets a chance to read some of Jim's speech. After each paragraph, take a minute to see if you all understood what was said. I want to you to read to the end of the chapter, and then we'll talk about it as a class."

As the class continued reading this novel, the strategy use would move more to the students' independent reading, with the teacher always checking to make sure that students understand. The goal, though, is to make sure that they understand the strategy, and that they are using the strategy to comprehend the text, not just as an exercise in class. With that goal in mind, and with the gradual release of responsibility, students can start to take more ownership of their metacognitive reading practices and become more self-regulated readers.

CONCLUSION

Teaching English/language arts in junior high school and high school settings is a complex and fascinating task; when we include the need to teach reading skills as part of teaching the literature of our discipline, the task becomes infinitely more complex. Our hope is that the suggestions in this chapter provide English/language arts teachers with a concrete place to begin intertwining instruction that will motivate, engage, and provide structure for students who have not been successful in becoming lifelong readers with the study of both classic and young adult literature.

DISCUSSION AND ACTIVITIES

1. The next time you lead a classroom discussion, ask a colleague to assist in videotaping or perhaps observing the interaction among you and your students. Does the discussion follow the IRE pattern described in this chapter? If so, how might you develop discussion questions and techniques that will improve the flow of your discussion?

2. Examine one of the texts that students in your classes read. How might you integrate the suggestions for dialogue, motivation, and strategy instruction with your instruction on this text?

3. Reflect on how strategy instruction has been presented in your school, through professional development or policies. What have you read in this chapter or in other resources that could influence your use of strategy instruction?

REFERENCES

Afflerbach, P., Pearson, P. D., & Paris, S. G. (2008). Clarifying differences between reading skills and reading strategies. *The Reading Teacher, 61*(5), 364–373.

Beers, K. (2003). *When kids can't read, what teachers can do: A guide for teachers 6–12*. Portsmouth, NH: Heinemann.

Bomer, R. (2011). *Building adolescent literacy in today's English classrooms.* Portsmouth, NH: Heinemann.

Duke, N. K., & Carlisle, J. (2011). The development of comprehension. In M. L. Kamil, P. D. Pearson, E. B. Moje, & P. P. Afflerbach (Eds.), *Handbook of reading research* (Vol. IV, pp. 199–228). New York: Routledge.

Duke, N. K., Pearson, P. D., Strachan, S. L., & Billman, A. L. (2011). Essential elements of fostering and teaching reading comprehension. In S. J. Samuels & A. E. Farstrup (Eds.), *What research has to say about reading instruction* (4th ed., pp. 51–93). Newark, DE: International Reading Association.

Frey, N., Fisher, D., & Hernandez, T. (2003). "What's the gist?": Summary writing for struggling adolescent writers. *Voices from the Middle, 11*(2), 43–49.

Guthrie, J. T., & Coddington, C. S. (2009). Reading motivation. In K. Wentzel & A. Wigfield (Eds.), *Handbook of motivation at school* (pp. 503–525). New York: Routledge.

Intrator, S. M. & Kunzman, R. (2009). Who are adolescents today?: Youth voices and what they tell us. In L. Christenbury, R. Bomer, & P. Smagorinsky (Eds.), *Handbook of adolescent literacy research* (pp. 29–45). New York: Guilford Press.

Lawrence, J. F., & Snow, C. E. (2011). Oral discourse and reading. In M. L. Kamil, P. D. Pearson, E. B. Moje, & P. P. Afflerbach (Eds.), *Handbook of reading research* (Vol. IV, pp. 320–337). New York: Routledge.

McRae, A., & Guthrie, J. T. (2009). Promoting reasons for reading: Teacher practices that impact motivation. In E. H. Hiebert, & R. L. Arlington (Eds.), *Reading more, reading better* (pp. 55–76). New York: Guilford Press.

Moje, E. B. (2008). Foregrounding the disciplines in secondary literacy teaching and learning: A call for change. *Journal of Adolescent and Adult Literacy, 52*(2), 96–107.

National Governors Association Center for Best Practices & Council of Chief State School Officers. (2010). *Common Core State Standards for English Language Arts*. Washington, DC: Author.

Neal, M. (2008). Look who's talking: Discourse analysis, discussion, and initiation–response–evaluation patterns in the college classroom. *Teaching English in the Two Year College, 35*(3), 272–281.

Nystrand, M. (2006). Research on the role of classroom discourse as it affects reading comprehension. *Research in the Teaching of English, 40*(4), 392–412.

Pressley, M. (2000). What should comprehension instruction be the instruction of? In M. L. Kamil, P. B. Mosenthal, P. D. Pearson, & R. Barr (Eds.), *Handbook of reading research* (Vol. III, pp. 545–561). Mahwah, NJ: Erlbaum.

Wilkinson, I. A. G., & Son, E. H. (2011). A dialogic turn in research on learning and teaching to comprehend. In M. L. Kamil, P. D. Pearson, E. B. Moje, & P. P. Afflerbach (Eds.), *Handbook of reading research* (Vol. IV, pp. 359–387). New York: Routledge.

Wilson, A. A. (2011). A social semiotics framework for conceptualizing content area literacies. *Journal of Adolescent and Adult Literacy, 54*, 435–444.

CHAPTER 15

Assisting Struggling Readers with Textbook Comprehension

Heather K. Sheridan-Thomas

The purpose of this chapter is to suggest ways that middle and high school teachers can assist struggling readers to read and comprehend textbooks. Specifically, this chapter:

- Explains the importance of textbook comprehension for adolescents.

- Defines what I mean by *struggling readers*, including possible attributes of struggling readers that need to be considered when teachers plan textbook reading instruction.

- Provides guidance for choosing considerate content-area texts.

- Provides ideas for engaging students in textbook reading and discussion.

- Suggests principles for organizing and delivering effective textbook reading instruction, including strategy instruction that is embedded and explicit.

- Provides examples of instructional methods teachers can use to deliver textbook reading instruction.

WHY TEACH TEXTBOOK COMPREHENSION?

The advent of the Common Core State Standards (CCSS) places new demands on adolescent literacy research and instruction. While interest in adolescent multiple literacies remains strong (Hagood, Alvermann &

Heron-Hruby, 2010; Lankshear & Knobel, 2011; Moje, Overby, Tysvaer, & Morris, 2008), the adoption of the CCSS by 45 states and the District of Columbia and the heavy emphasis on college and career readiness has resulted in an enhanced focus on ensuring that students can comprehend complex nonfiction texts (National Governors Association [NGA] Center for Best Practices & Council of Chief State School Officers [CCSSO], 2010). CCSS for Literacy in History/Social Studies, Science, and Technical Subjects, for the first time, clearly specify the role content-area teachers play in developing the literacies critical to adolescents' success in high school, as well as beyond, in college or careers.

But what is the place of textbook reading in this focus on improving students' content-area literacy abilities? Literacy educators and researchers recommend that content-area teachers use multiple text sources, either to replace or at least supplement textbook readings (Allington, 2002; Hinchman, Alvermann, Boyd, Brozo, & Vacca, 2003/2004). Textbooks can be dense, dry, and difficult to comprehend. Calkins, Ehrenworth, and Lehman (2012) note that "what's so ominous about some of these textbooks is that they are in difficult in part because they are also poorly written. They summarize, they organize, but they do not engage students in complex reasoning" (p. 90). Adolescents themselves describe textbook reading as "just hard and really boring" (Sheridan-Thomas, Ro, & Bromley, 2004, p. 14).

Nonetheless, textbooks and textbook reading remain central to many content-area classes. Textbooks are a bastion of secondary subject-area instruction and are unlikely to disappear in the foreseeable future. Content-area teachers use textbooks to convey an overview and summary of course information as well as to provide an easy reference for students working on classroom tasks and homework assignments. Textbooks are an efficient source of information and a readily available place to start in communicating main points related to a topic. They are also carefully sequenced so that each chapter provides information needed to understand the next one. These features make teacher planning easier, especially as current textbooks are often correlated with national and even state standards, curriculum, and assessments. Textbooks can clearly be useful to teachers, but they are only useful to students if the students are able to read and understand them (Allington, 2002).

Students who struggle with extracting important information and making meaning from textbook reading do not have the same access to course material as competent textbook readers. Helping all students comprehend textbook reading is an equity issue. For courses in which textbooks are used, whether as a main source of information or as a secondary reference, all students need to be able to use the textbook with as much competence and independence as possible. It is therefore the responsibility of content-area teachers to provide explicit strategy instruction, including modeling, to teach students how to read and comprehend textbooks. This approach is particularly important for students who struggle with textbook reading and other academic literacy tasks, but even otherwise competent readers often benefit from additional support with textbook reading, especially in middle school.

Furthermore the CCSS require that students develop the ability to read increasingly complex and sophisticated texts independently with reference to a staircase of increasing text complexity (NGA & CCSSO, 2010). The goal is to better prepare students for the reading demands of college, given that nationally, more than 50% of students entering 2-year colleges and 20% of students entering 4-year colleges currently require remediation before moving on to college-level coursework (Complete College America, 2012, p. 1). Students who choose to enter the work world directly out of high school nonetheless require the ability to read technical texts in most well-paying professions (Harvard Graduate School of Education, 2011) and the ending levels of CCSS text complexity are also keyed to workforce training materials. Carefully scaffolded instruction in textbook comprehension can assist students to be independent, college- and career-ready readers.

Despite the fact that textbooks are unlikely to be considered the kind of reading material that anyone would choose from the library shelf for pleasure reading, many are, in fact, carefully constructed to provide easy access to large amounts of information on a specific topic. Features such as headings that signal text organization, clear contextual definitions of technical vocabulary backed up with a glossary, abundant visuals, and chapter summaries that highlight the most important information assist readers in understanding main ideas or locating specific information quickly.

WHO ARE THE READERS WHO STRUGGLE WITH TEXTBOOKS?

This chapter focuses on assisting readers who struggle with academic literacy generally and reading textbooks in particular. The phrase *struggling readers* has replaced terms such as "at-risk" or "below-level" students as a more respectful way of describing the situated nature of the challenging interaction between reader and text. The struggles that these readers encounter in school can be seen as socially constructed—by how schools are organized and scheduled, by assumptions that are made about home life and school abilities, by a curriculum that is often devoid of connections to students' lives, and by texts that may be too difficult for students to read (Triplett, 2007).

We all struggle with some types of reading (Alvermann, Phelps, & Ridgeway, 2007), so it is important to note that adolescents who have difficulty comprehending textbooks are often proficient with other literacies. Some are competent users of technology (O'Brien, 2001), and others avidly consume high-interest literacy materials such as topical magazines (Sheridan-Thomas et al., 2004), graphic novels (Frey & Fisher, 2004), and manga comic books (Schwartz & Rubinstein-Ávila, 2006). Some boys may eschew reading as unmanly (Smith & Wilhelm, 2002), yet still engage in purposeful reading of auto repair manuals and sports-related websites. The term *struggling reader* is used in this chapter as an efficient shorthand, but with full awareness that it describes a relationship between a student and a text that is situated, variable, and unique to each student. I am clear that this label should not at any time be taken to represent the sum total of the literacy competencies of the students it designates.

When it comes to academic literacy, and reading textbooks in particular, students' difficulties can stem from a combination of factors. Some students may struggle because of cognitive processing, hearing, or vision problems. However, many more adolescent readers struggle because they are not motivated by textbook reading and do not know effective strategies for gleaning meaning from dense expository text. For many students, the only purpose for reading academic texts is the weak purpose of getting assignments done and getting a good grade. Strategies associated with these extrinsic goals, such as hunting for answers without actually reading the material, predominate. Adolescents who cannot see any meaningful purpose for reading textbooks become disengaged readers, passing their eyes over textbook pages without even the intention of gaining meaning. Assisting struggling readers to comprehend textbooks must begin, therefore, with attention to motivation. However, it cannot end there.

Once they are motivated to read textbooks, struggling readers need explicit instruction in how to make the most effective use of textbook features, and they need lots of guided practice embedded in lessons focused on understanding meaningful content-area concepts. All of this will be most effective if teachers begin by selecting "considerate" textbooks (Armbruster & Anderson, 1988; Hiebert & Mesmer, 2013)—texts that are coherent, well structured, appropriate for students' age and grade, and designed to include a variety of text features that assist readers in comprehending and retaining text content.

HOW CAN CONTENT-AREA TEACHERS IMPROVE TEXTBOOK COMPREHENSION?

Principles for textbook comprehension instruction that is effective and engaging to struggling students, as well as congruent with current recommendations for teaching content-area literacy, are listed in Figure 15.1 and explained in more detail throughout this chapter. Instructional strategies that exemplify these principles are included within the explanation of each principle.

- Select a considerate textbook.
- Engage students through purpose-setting, communicating relevance, and/or making connections to popular or multimedia texts.
- Embed literacy strategy instruction in the context of meaningful content and concepts.
- Provide explicit literacy strategy instruction, including modeling.
- Design guides and classroom opportunities for guided practice of literacy strategies.
- Build in a progression toward gradual release of responsibility.
- Reinforce strategies consistently across content areas and grade levels, as well as across classroom and special support settings.

FIGURE 15.1. Principles for textbook comprehension instruction.

Selecting Considerate Textbooks

It is helpful for teachers to review textbooks prior to purchase for considerate text features; however, in many cases teachers may have a textbook already in use rather than being in the position of choosing a textbook. Figure 15.2 suggests questions that can assist in reviewing a textbook, whether before purchasing it or as a way of determining how much additional guidance students may need in using it.

Engaging Readers

Because struggling readers are often disengaged readers, and textbooks are rarely inherently engaging, involving students in *prereading activities* is a crucial first step to improving comprehension. Initial interpretations of the CCSS suggested that in order to increase independent reading of texts, teacher guided prereading activities should be eliminated altogether (Shanahan, 2012/2013, p. 12). The revised Publishers Criteria clarified this stance, noting that "Care should be taken that initial questions are not so overly broad and general that they pull students away from an in-depth encounter with the specific text or texts; rather, strong questions will return students to the text to receive greater insight and understandings. The best questions will motivate students to dig in and explore further—just as texts should be worth reading, so questions should be worth answering" (Coleman & Pimentel, 2012, p .8).

Engagement has been shown to be enhanced by helping students understand the relevance of texts; by providing some degree of choice (in texts, tasks or both); and by increasing students' sense of self-efficacy (Guthrie, Klaudia, & Ho, 2013). There are a number of prereading strategies that engage readers by increasing the relevance of the text, at the same time as they motivate readers to look for supporting evidence in the

Text Feature	Textbook Selection/Review Question
Bold, italicized, or colored print	How is technical, discipline-specific vocabulary signaled?
Contextual definitions	What assistance is provided to help students understand new vocabulary? Possibilities include parenthetic definitions, and helpful contextual information.
Sidebars	What assistance is provided to help students understand new vocabulary? Possibilities include sidebars. Are sidebars focused on important vocabulary or other important information, or are they additional "nice to know" information?
Glossary	Is there a glossary to which students can refer?
Content	Is content accurate? Current? Matched to curriculum standards? Does content reflect bias related to race, gender, religion, sexual orientation either directly or by omission? Is chapter content organized logically in a way that improves comprehension?
Overviews/ summaries	Does the textbook include an outline or graphic organizer at the beginning of each chapter to signal text organization? Does the textbook include section or chapter summaries in written or graphic form?
Headings	Are there section headings? Do the section headings provide adequate information to assist students in predicting content, predicting text organization, and/or locating content?
Pictures/visuals, captions	Do visuals provide information that assists in comprehending the text information? Are they appealing to students without creating a "busy" layout that may distract students? Is any direct guidance provided for students in how to interpret the visuals?
Questions	Are questions provided for each section rather than only at the end? Do questions require students to go beyond the literal level to make inferences, evaluate text information, and apply text information to new problems or situations?
Redundancy	Are the most critical chapter concepts and supporting details provided in multiple ways (text, visuals, sidebars)?
Table of contents and index	Does the textbook have a well-organized table of contents that includes section titles as well as chapter titles? Is there an easy-to-use topic index?

FIGURE 15.2. Questions for selecting a considerate text.

text. One commonly recommended prereading activity is an "anticipation guide" (Kozen, Murray, & Windell, 2006; Lent, 2012). Students react to teacher-constructed statements about ideas that are covered by the text. This step allows students to start thinking about the content of the textbook selection and begin making connections to related prior knowledge before they start reading. Having taken a stand on such issues, they are motivated to read the textbook and see whether their position is supported. Another engaging prereading strategy is problem posing or "establishing problematic perspectives" (Vacca & Vacca, 2008, p. 191). The content-area teacher creates a problem scenario designed to pique students' curiosity and interest. Students discuss the problem before they read, brainstorming solutions or voicing their reactions. As students read the textbook passage, they have the immediate purpose of using the information to solve the given problem. A "comprehension canopy" (Vaughn et al., 2013) can also create relevance for readers by providing a multilayered overarching unit question that focuses students and provides a purpose for reading. This unit question is revisited after each new reading to reflect on new information gained and on how students' responses to the questions may have changed.

Students' sense of text relevance can also be enhanced by making connections to themes or media types that readers are familiar with and enjoy. Because adolescents who struggle with academic reading may be avid consumers of one or more forms of popular culture texts (Alvermann, Moon, & Hagood, 1999; Moje et al., 2008), one way to motivate struggling students to read textbooks is to provide a *popular culture bridge*. Teachers can create a "text twin" set (Camp, 2000) of a popular culture and a textbook reading on a topic. Students can be introduced to the topic through engaging with familiar media forms and popular culture materials such as songs, magazine or newspaper articles, videos/DVDs, trading cards, or video games. They can then be guided to read the textbook selection, looking for content similarities and differences between the popular culture source and the textbook. For example, Xu (2005) suggested using *Yu-Gi-Oh!* trading cards to focus on Egyptian deities and related symbols. Later students read about Egyptian religion and the origin of the symbols, completing a comparison chart with what they knew from the trading cards.

Going beyond text twins to create full "text sets" (Lent, 2012) builds in choice as well as relevance. A text set is "a collection of materials, usually created by a teacher (or media specialist), composed of diverse resources on a specific subject, genre, or theme" (Lent, 2012, p. 148). Text sets designed to motivate adolescent readers can include information from high-interest periodicals as well as digital sources. Engagement is maximized when visual and even auditory texts are included along with print texts. Providing texts at varied reading levels provides access to the full range of adolescent readers, and even students reading at higher levels may enjoy the visuals and themes of well-chosen topical picture books. Students can become part of the creation of a text set when they are asked to preview a textbook chapter and think about what texts might be included (what types and subjects or specific texts they might contribute) (Lent, 2012, p. 155). This activity provides an engaging reason to preview the chapter. When a course textbook becomes part of a text set, students are provided with opportunities to compare information and presentation styles across texts.

Use of texts sets can also provide practice in the critical CCSS reading skill of gathering evidence from multiple text sources.

An often overlooked source of motivation for reading textbooks is *critical literacy* (Luke, 2000). Focusing on critical literacy can raise the relevance level while also addressing the CCSS focus on cognitive engagement and higher-order reading/thinking skills such as synthesizing, analyzing, and evaluating text information (Calkins et al., 2012; Conley, 2011). Teachers know that nearly all textbooks include some erroneous information (Gould, 1991) and that no textbook reflects all of the possible views and opinions on a topic (Loewen, 1996). Textbook authors write from viewpoints that privilege some voices and silence others. Rather than trying to hide this reality, it can be used to motivate adolescents, who are at a prime age for questioning authority, to read their textbooks with a critical eye. For example, students can be encouraged to look at whose point of view is represented in a history textbook and whose voices are silenced (Wolk, 2003).

Embedded Comprehension Instruction

Although numerous strategies can be taught to support struggling readers, the best textbook comprehension lessons remain focused on the content of the reading and on making the content interesting and understandable (Hinchman et al., 2003/2004). Because lack of student engagement is one barrier to textbook comprehension, shifting instructional focus heavily toward learning textbook reading skills—not a particularly engaging endeavor—is unlikely to be a good solution. Research on engagement suggests that "classroom goals that emphasize students' understanding of meaningful materials are essential to motivation and cognitive strategy learning" (Guthrie & Davis, 2003, p. 72). Textbook reading strategy instruction is, therefore, best embedded in lessons designed to teach the content and concepts found in the textbook material.

Embedded strategy instruction can focus on the disciplinary literacy skills required to read a particular textbook in a specific content area. Scientific reading can be quite different from the reading of historical text, and math textbooks have their own unique format and text features (Shanahan & Shanahan, 2008). It is not the job of content-area teachers to be "teachers of reading" so much as to teach the kinds of texts and reading strategies most likely to be found in their subject area. Embedding textbook strategy lessons in conceptually focused units of instruction allows teachers to develop and support content-specific literacy skills.

Embedded strategy instruction also addresses the concerns of teachers who feel that there is too much content in their subject area to take time to focus on literacy strategies. Engaging and interactive lessons that teach literacy strategies while remaining focused on content serve to deepen student understanding of content. Although it is clearly not possible to teach literacy strategies in every lesson, it works well to integrate strategy instruction into lessons with the highest priority course content.

For example, a sixth-grade math teacher may provide embedded instruction on focusing on question words during a unit on exponential notation (Kenney, Hancewicz, Heuer, Metsisto & Tuttle, 2005). As students work on answering the directive "Write $7 \times 7 \times 7 \times 8 \times 9 \times 9$ in exponential notation," the teacher suggests they look at the words in the question carefully for clues as to what kind of answer might be expected. Students who focus on the words *write*, *exponential*, and *notation* realize that the problem involves translation, rather than calculation, and are able to come up with a correct answer. Literacy strategy instruction may also be embedded in other content areas, such as science. An example of embedded strategy instruction in a biology class, focused on using graphic organizers, is provided below, in the section on explicit strategy instruction.

In order for students to become independent users of textbook reading strategies, as well as to achieve independence in their ability to read increasingly complex texts, they must know when to apply strategies and which ones to select. Embedded strategy instruction promotes independence by giving students specific models of the appropriate use of particular strategies on particular types of subject-area textbook reading. To develop struggling readers' full independence, however, teachers need to plan a sequence of explicit introduction and ongoing practice for high-utility textbook reading strategies.

Explicit Strategy Instruction

Struggling readers often rely on a small number of strategies, which they use in all situations. Successful readers not only apply a larger number of strategies flexibly, but they can also articulate which strategies are best suited for specific texts and tasks (Paris & Myers, 1981). Explicit instruction in strategies can help bridge the gap between successful and struggling readers by helping struggling readers develop the metacognitive awareness necessary for independent reading (Gersten, Fuchs, Williams, & Baker, 2001). Evidence suggests that providing explicit vocabulary and comprehension strategy instruction improves students' reading comprehension achievement (Edmonds et al., 2009). Steps in effective strategy instruction include naming the strategy and explaining why and when it is useful; explaining the steps in the strategy; thinking aloud while demonstrating the strategy; providing opportunities for guided practice, especially within cooperative groups; and providing independent application opportunities (Vacca & Vacca, 2008). Strategy instruction has the greatest impact on discipline-specific literacy if strategies are taught in the context of, and with a focus on, understanding subject-area content (Conley 2008; Lenski, 2011/2012). Conley (2008) provides an example of how one 10th-grade science teacher, Mrs. Gunning, uses explicit strategy instruction to teach her students how to create and use graphic organizers at the same time as she is using the graphic organizer to help students organize new information about pollution. While teaching critical science content, this teacher also develops "graphic organizers as a component of students' cognitive tool kit" (p. 91). Mrs. Gunning starts by naming the strategy—graphic organizer—and then explains the strategy as a way for students to picture what they know, including what they already know and new information they learn. She then models how to create a graphic organizer, thinking aloud as she creates the overall structure and adds known and new information about pollution. Students are given the opportunity to create their own graphic organizers with their known information about pollution. They then apply this strategy by adding to their graphic organizers as they learn new information throughout the unit on pollution.

It may appear contradictory to suggest that strategy instruction should be both embedded and explicit. It is true that one teacher will need to introduce a strategy initially, providing direct explanation of what the strategy is, when it can best be used, and the steps for using it. Once that has been accomplished, however, content-area teachers can carry out the remaining steps in explicit instruction in short mini-lessons embedded in their content lessons. These mini-lessons focus on the tasks and texts central to the current topic of the class. One crucial literacy strategy for assisting students in comprehending textbooks is the use of text features designed to focus students on the most important text information.

In order to easily access textbook information and make the best use of the considerate features of well-designed textbooks, struggling readers need explicit instruction in how to utilize text features. These features can help readers identify the vocabulary and comprehension demands of reading assignments and can also guide students in finding definitions or specific information.

Early in the school year, teachers can introduce students to the overall organization of their particular textbook. Middle school students may enjoy engaging in a "scavenger hunt" for various parts of the textbook, such as table of contents, chapter overviews and summaries, glossaries, and index. Older students might be asked to work with a partner to review their textbook features using questions similar to those in Figure 15.2, focused on considerate text features and their usefulness. Once students are familiar with the overall organization and features of their textbook, they can be shown how these features can help them with high-utility textbook reading strategies. Strategies such as understanding subject-specific vocabulary, determining importance, noting text organization, and making inferences are at the heart of comprehending texts. Figure 15.3 provides an

Text Feature	Connection to Reading Strategies
Understanding of Discipline-Specific Vocabulary	
Bold, italicized, or colored print	Different typefaces alert students that a word is important.
Contextual definitions	Contextual definitions for highlighted words provided in nearby text assist students in making predictions about meanings of disciplinary vocabulary.
Sidebars	Definitions of important terms in a sidebar help students confirm and expand their understanding of disciplinary vocabulary.
Glossary	An alphabetized list of words allows students to easily check definitions arrived at through use of context clues.
Comprehension of Disciplinary Concepts and Supporting Evidence	
Content	Students can more easily learn curriculum content if textbook content is well matched. Biased content can distract students in addition to providing misinformation. A well-organized text can guide students through comprehension of a logical progression of concepts.
Overviews/ summaries	Chapter overviews or outlines that highlight important points at the beginning of the chapter help students set purposes for reading and assist students in determining importance. Chapter overviews can also signal text organization, especially when provided in graphic form. Summaries can assist students in determining important text content.
Headings	Text headings may signal the organizational structure of the text. Headings may include structure words such as *causes* or *effects* or signal a pattern such as compare–contrast through the use of several parallel headings (e.g., Life in Cities, Life in Small Towns, Life on Farms). Text headings call attention to important information throughout the chapter.
Pictures/ visuals, captions	Pictures or other visuals that restate and provide examples related to important information can assist students in determining importance and comprehending text concepts. Well-crafted captions and/or related questions can assist students in interpreting visuals and connecting information to text concepts.
Questions	Well-written text questions can assist comprehension by focusing students on major text concepts and making connections to supporting evidence/ details. Poorly written text questions may mislead students to focus exclusively on literal details.
Sidebars	Important details restated in sidebars assist students with determining importance.
Redundancy	Information that appears in two or more places assists students in determining importance.
Use of Textbook as Reference for Specific Information/Evidence	
Table of contents and index	When the textbook is used as a reference source in a multiple-text lesson or unit, a well-organized table of contents and index can help students easily locate specific information as needed.

FIGURE 15.3. Use of considerate text features to support reading strategies.

explanation of how textbook features can help struggling students engage in reading strategies.

Often content-area teachers introduce students to the textbook early in the school year but do not consistently refer them to text features throughout the year. Students who struggle with academic reading need consistent reminders and practice to get to the point where they become independent users of such features. This ongoing review and practice can be provided through teacher-guided textbook comprehension activities.

Teacher-Guided Comprehension

Once students have been introduced to a strategy through explicit instruction, multiple opportunities to practice the strategy can be provided through teacher-created guides. The major focus of reading guides in a content-area class remains on the content—on helping students comprehend the most important concepts and related details in a textbook section. At the same time, students using the guides are practicing textbook reading strategies. Effective textbook reading guides model the way a good reader would use the strategy and also provide explicit reminders of strategy steps. Because struggling readers are often disengaged readers, textbook guides need to be constructed to promote engagement. Interactive reading guides (IRGs) (Buehl, 2009) involve students in responding to questions or statements about the content of the text, using textbook organization to extract important information, making connections between textbook information and prior knowledge, and reflecting on deeper meanings. Teachers design IRGs to focus on a particular text section, guiding students to use and practice effective literacy strategies as well as focusing them on the most important content.

These guides are interactive in two ways: they encourage individual students to interact thoughtfully with the text, and they can also guide cooperative group sharing and discussion around a piece of text. The best reading guides resist student attempts to use "search and destroy" tactics for finding answers without reading or thinking about the text. IRGs can be designed to focus on one or several text reading strategies. An example of an IRG focused on comprehension at and beyond the literal level is discussed below.

Two crucial skills for comprehending textbooks are determining importance and making inferences. Harvey and Goudvis (2007) define determining importance as the ability to identify essential ideas and differentiate between these key ideas and less important ideas when reading. Inference can be defined as using text information plus prior knowledge to draw conclusions, make judgments, and form interpretations (Keene & Zimmermann, 1997). One instructional method that lends itself to helping students do both of these is question–answer relationships, or QARs (Raphael, 1986; Raphael & Au, 2005).

QARs focus students on different levels of questions and where answers can be found. Categorizing answers as those that can be found "in the text" and "in my head" helps students understand that, whereas some questions can be answered directly from the text, others require the reader to combine previously learned information and text information. The QAR terms for question–answer relationships are clear and direct students where to look for answers to different kinds of questions. "In the Text" QARs include "Right There" and "Think and Search," while "In My Head" relationships include "Author and You" and "On My Own" (Raphael & Au, 2005). Students who understand QARs can be guided to ask themselves questions beyond the Right There level as they read, leading to deeper comprehension of textbook material.

Once students have received explicit instruction in QARs, IRGs that use QAR language to help students with the toughest aspects of textbook comprehension can be created. QARs are particularly helpful for assisting students to make inferences from text, because they guide students to synthesize text information (think and search) and analyze it in light of their own prior knowledge (author and you). A sample IRG, provided in Figure 15.4, shows how such guides can direct student attention to specific features of a textbook section, help them comprehend the content of the section, and also teach a transferable reading strategy, such as QAR.

Another example of an IRG is the visually appealing Reading Road Map, specifically created to help students connect textbook information to digital source information, while reading both texts strategically (Wood, 2011). The Reading Road Map consists of a step-by-step map designed to guide students on a "trip" through a content-area topic, with missions (activities to guide the use of strategies on textbook reading), road signs (to cue changes in reading rate), and location signs (to direct students to specific textbook paragraphs or external sources such as websites). Additional engagement is created by students' collaborative completion of the Reading Road Map.

Gradual Release of Responsibility

Content teachers who consistently provide their students with reading guides may become disheartened when they ask students to read independently and comprehend a textbook chapter. It is clear that the CCSS require students to move toward independent reading of increasingly complex texts. Because students cannot rely on teacher guidance in college or later life, they must develop independence with text, and that can only happen through multiple opportunities for guided practice. Elementary teachers are likely to have a clearer sense of the importance of multiple opportunities for guided practice and peer modeling in order for students to gain independence and control in relation to a reading strategy. Once a strategy

A Call for Freedom Guide PLUS Textbook Reading Review
The American Journey, Glencoe/McGraw Hill, 2003, p. 473–477

Using Text Evidence to Support Inferences

Good readers look for important details (**Right There**), such as people, events and dates. Good readers also need to be able to make and support inferences. There are different kinds of inferences. Some inferences can be supported with information that is all in the text, but may be in more than one place (**Think and Search**). Other inferences must be supported with text information AND information you already know (**Author and You**).

- One common kind of **Think and Search** inference authors may expect you to make is to compare and contrast two events, people or ideas. Question 4 on p. 477 is a **Think and Search** question (How did Lincoln's personal stand on slavery differ from his political stand?").
- The answer to this question is in the reading but it is not all in one sentence AND you cannot find it by looking for exact matches to the words in the question.
- Here are some steps you can take to answer a question like this.

1. Decide if you are being asked to COMPARE, CONTRAST or BOTH. This question uses the word "Differ," so you are being asked to _____. When you answer this question you will only discuss how Lincoln's two stands were _____, not how they were alike.
2. Look for the section(s) of text that discuss the question topic. In this case there is no topic heading on "slavery" that can direct you to the answer. If you skim the first few paragraphs of this section, you see that Lincoln and his views on slavery are mentioned frequently on pp. 473–474.
3. Make a chart in your notes of the two ideas you are being asked to contrast. In this case it is Lincoln's _____ stand on slavery and his _____ stand, so your chart can look like this:
   _____ stand _____stand
4. Look for words that have similar meanings to question words and find answers nearby, either before or after these words. Remember that the information you need to answer the question may be in more than one place and even on different pages.
   a. The words "political stand" are not used in the text on pp. 473–474. But on p. 474 the words "official position" have a similar meaning. Where on that page do you find Lincoln's "official position." In your chart under "political stand" write what you think his official position was.
   b. Find words in a nearby sentence that you think mean the same as "personal stand." What words are used to mean personal stand? Look near these words to see what Lincoln's personal stand was and write it in your chart.
5. Now write two or three sentences that answer the question. In this case, tell how the two stands differ. It's a good idea to start your first sentence with words from the question. One possible frame for the answer to this question is provided below, but you can write the answer in different words if you wish.

President Lincoln's personal stand on slavery differed from his political stand during the Civil War. Personally, Lincoln believed that _____ but in the beginning of the Civil War, he had a different political stand. Lincoln's political stand on slavery was that _____.

FIGURE 15.4. Example guide using QARs to focus on inferences and text structure.

has been introduced in a large-group shared reading setting, students can practice it in small guided reading-group discussions and while discussing reading "knee to knee" with peer partners (Cole, 2003).

Modifications of these techniques can be used to good advantage in secondary content classes. IRGs, discussed above, can be used to promote not only student interaction with the textbook but with each other as well. Guides can be completed and discussed in small groups, or students can complete the guides at home and meet in small groups to discuss their answers.

Beyond discussing their responses to teacher-created reading guides, small groups and partner sharing can provide opportunities for students to move toward independent use of reading strategies. Students in cooperative groups can be asked to share strategies they used to comprehend a textbook section. Struggling readers who have been learning textbook strategies in support classes can take an active role in these discussions, especially if they have prepared by reading and discussing the specific text section with a reading, special education, or English as a second language (ESL) teacher ahead of time.

Students can also be asked to "think aloud" with a partner about their strategy use. For example, students might be asked to list the five most important points in a textbook section and to defend their choices to a classmate. The discussions should focus on the use of text headings; text features such as chapter overviews, summaries, and sidebars; and the over-all impact of redundancy in determining importance. Students might also be asked to think aloud about the questions they ask themselves to facilitate their own understanding of the text as they read (Davey, 1983). Opportunities to think aloud help students move beyond teacher-guided rehearsal of strategies to a cognitive integration of when and how to use each strategy (Conley 2008).

Consistent Strategy Reinforcement

It is difficult for any one content-area teacher to provide enough practice opportunities for each reading strategy to allow struggling readers to become independent strategy users. However, if teachers across content areas (horizontal reinforcement) or in departments across grade levels (vertical reinforcement) can agree to use a small set of target strategies, students can get enough cumulative practice to make the strategies "stick." Strategies that are generic enough to travel well across subject areas (e.g., using QAR as a guide to asking and answering questions) can be targeted for horizontal reinforcement across content-area classes in a grade-level team. Discipline-specific strategies (e.g., use of structure–function charts in science or charts focused on relationships between events in history;

Shanahan & Shanahan, 2008) can be targeted for vertical reinforcement as students progress through courses in a department.

A second advantage to agreeing to a set of target strategies across a grade level or department team is that it allows a different teacher to introduce each strategy through explicit strategy instruction, whereas the other teachers need only commit to reinforcing the strategies through teacher-created guides, classroom tasks, and homework assignments. To best assist struggling readers who receive additional support from academic intervention services (AIS), special education, or English for speakers of other languages (ESOL) teachers, it is crucial to also engage these support specialists in reinforcing target strategies. The increasing levels of support recommended by current response to intervention (RTI) approaches will only succeed in increasing students' academic success in content area classes if support is aligned with prioritized course content and skills. (Lenski, 2011/2012). Support specialists can provide a second dose of explicit instruction and can help students focus on target strategies as they assist in assignment completion. The fictional vignette below provides a glimpse into a middle school where teachers have agreed to work together to support students' reading of content-area textbooks.

It is 15 minutes into third period and Ms. V's eighth-grade science class is studying weather. Jake has already stepped outside to record the temperature, barometric pressure, and wind direction for the day and reported back to the class. Students have recorded all of this information in their daily weather journals along with their initial impressions of the day's weather as they came to school. Now students are working in small groups to discuss and complete an IRG related to the sun's energy and wind.

In one group, Brenda is explaining how "prevailing westerlies affect the United States" to her classmates. Although her English is accented, and she occasionally searches for exactly the right word, her explanations are clear: She knows what westerlies are and how they can affect weather. Her group mates accept her answer to question 9 of the guide, with appreciation and a few small additions, and they go on talk about why these winds are called "westerlies."

Another group is talking about how they can use a visual aid to show the slant of the sun's rays to figure out where the rays will be perpendicular to the Earth's surface. Jake points out that *perpendicular* means that there will be a right angle, and he suggests that they read the title of the figure to see if it will help them figure out the location of the 90-degree angle.

Yesterday in Ms. H's ESL class Brenda reviewed the content-related vocabulary for the section they would study today. Ms. H showed them how they could get definitions from the textbook—using context clues, sidebars, and/or the glossary. The students also previewed the reading, with particular attention to the figures/graphics that are a major focus of the IRG for this textbook chapter.

Ms. H reminded her ESL students that the figures in a textbook are a great way to get information visually with less reliance on their developing knowledge of the English language. Students in Ms. C's AIS class and Ms. G's special education resource room (including Jake) received a similar kind of advance instruction, focusing on both the science content and the literacy strategies addressed by the IRG. Ms. C and Ms. G reviewed the figures in the reading and talked with their students about how to interpret the graphs, pictures, and visual organizers in the chapter. Ms. G reviewed angles with her students, so that they could interpret the figure related to the angle at which the sun's rays hit the Earth. In addition, Ms. G co-teaches one section of eighth-grade science, which contains several of her learning-disabled students.

As students work in small groups on the IRG in their eighth-grade science classroom, Ms. V and co-teacher Ms. G check in with each group. They are pleased to see that their collaborative work, both in and out of the class, has helped the special education, ESL, and AIS students become active participants in group discussion focused on using text features to gain content understandings about the sun and wind.

CONCLUSION

Because textbooks remain a mainstay of secondary content-area instruction, content-area teachers need to know how to assist their struggling readers with textbook comprehension. Inadequate access to and understanding of textbook content will only exacerbate achievement gaps. Choosing a considerate content-area text is an important first step, but it is not sufficient. Teachers need ideas for how to motivate students to engage with textbooks and how to suggest ways in which students can motivate themselves. Embedding textbook reading strategies in lessons focused on high-priority, meaningful subject-area content enhances students' motivation and engagement, and also helps teachers deal with the "content crunch" often associated with standards-driven curriculum and high-stakes assessment.

Teachers also need to know how to use explicit instruction to help struggling readers understand when, why, and how to use textbook reading strategies. Explicit instruction, including teacher and peer think-aloud modeling, helps struggling readers develop metacognitive strategy awareness and the independent control exhibited by competent readers. However, numerous opportunities for practice are required before students truly gain independence in the use of textbook reading strategies. These opportunities can be provided by using teacher-designed IRGs, which engage students in

using textbook reading strategies as they learn content. Consistent reinforcement of textbook reading strategies across subject areas and between
regular education and support specialists' classrooms takes planning, but
pays off in terms of students' growing ease with use and transfer of strategies.

One possible future vision suggests that textbooks may become digital
resources or "flexbooks," with links to a variety of open-source Web content and customized teacher guidance designed to match prioritized standards, focus on areas of problem-based units, or on student interests and
abilities (Hill, 2010). Adolescents will be able to bring their out-of-school
knowledge of skills for interacting with digital texts to bear on these textbooks. Even under these conditions, however, some students will need assistance to read closely and use text evidence to comprehend course content.

Thoughtful, well-planned instruction in textbook comprehension
strategies can give struggling readers the kind of access to textbook information and resources taken for granted by students who are more comfortable with academic literacies. This access to textbook content is a critical piece of the puzzle of reducing academic achievement gaps, improving
adolescents' content-area literacy skills, and preparing adolescents to be
independent consumers of college-level textbooks.

DISCUSSION AND ACTIVITIES

1. Review a textbook that is currently used in your content area. Use the questions in Figure 15.2 to determine how considerate the text is. Decide how
   desirable this text is for use in your classroom. What weaknesses would you
   have to overcome through targeted lessons?

2. Design an activity that would motivate students to read a section of a textbook in your content area. You can design an anticipation guide or create
   a problem that can be solved using text information. You may also create a
   matched text set with one or more pieces of popular culture or real-world
   text (widely defined to include music, film, TV, video games, websites, as
   well as print text) to motivate students and help them connect to related
   prior knowledge.

3. Choose a section of text from a textbook in your content area. Make a list
   of the important content points you want students to get from their reading
   of the text section. Think about which reading strategies students need to
   effectively learn those main points. Also notice the text features that might
   help students choose and comprehend important text ideas. Now create an
   IRG that will help students use the strategies and text features to understand
   the most important information in the chosen textbook section.

4. Different schools have developed different ways to organize instruction in
   textbook and other content-area literacy strategies so that students receive

both the explicit introduction and the amount of ongoing guided practice they need. Think about how teachers are organized in your school (or make up a fictitious school and organization)—whether it is into grade-level teams or cross-grade departments. What kinds of conversations would need to occur for content-area teachers in your school to agree to a plan for introducing and reinforcing textbook reading strategies? What might such a plan look like?

REFERENCES

Allington, R. L. (2002). You can't learn much from books you can't read. *Educational Leadership, 60,* 16–20.

Alvermann, D. E., Moon, J. S., & Hagood, M. C. (1999). *Popular culture in the classroom: Teaching and researching critical media.* Newark, DE: International Reading Association.

Alvermann, D. E., Phelps, S. F., & Ridgeway, V. (2007). *Content area reading and literacy: Succeeding in today's diverse classroom.* New York: Allyn & Bacon.

Armbruster, B., & Anderson, T. (1988). On selecting "considerate" content area textbooks. *Remedial and Special Education, 9,* 47–52.

Armbruster, B., Anderson, T. H., & Ostertag, J. (1987). Does text structure/summarization instruction facilitate learning from expository text? *Reading Research Quarterly, 23,* 331–346.

Buehl, D. (2009). *Classroom strategies for interactive learning.* Newark, DE: International Reading Association.

Calkins, L., Ehrenworth, M., & Lehman, C. (2012). *Pathways to the common core: Accelerating achievement.* Portsmouth, N.H.

Camp, D. (2000). It takes two: Teaching twin texts of fact and fiction. *The Reading Teacher, 53,* 400–408.

Cole, A. D. (2003). *Knee to knee, eye to eye: Circling in on comprehension.* Portsmouth, NH: Heinemann.

Coleman, D. & Pimental, S. (2012). *Revised publishers' criteria for the Common Core Standards in English Language Arts and Literacy: Grades 3–12.* Retrieved from the Common Core State Standards Initiative at *www.corestandards.org/assets/Publishers_Criteria_for_3-12.pdf.*

Complete College America. (2012). Remediation: Higher education's bridge to nowhere. Retrieved from http://www.completecollege.org/docs/CCA-Remediation-final.pdf

Conley, D. (2011) Building on the Common Core. *Educational Leadership, 68,* 16–20.

Conley, M. (2008). Cognitive strategy instruction for adolescents: What we know about the promise: What we don't know about the potential. *Harvard Educational Review, 78,* 84–106.

Davey, B. (1983). Think-aloud: Modeling the cognitive processes of reading comprehension. *Journal of Reading, 27,* 44–47.

Edmonds, M. S., Vaughn, S., Wexler, J., Reutebuch, C., Cable, A., Tacket, K. K., et al. (2009). Synthesis of reading interventions and effects on reading comprehension outcomes for older struggling readers. *Review of Educational Research, 79*, 262–300.

Frey, N., & Fisher, D. (2004). Using graphic novels, anime, and the Internet in an urban high school. *English Journal, 93*, 19–25.

Gersten, R., Fuchs, L., Williams, J., & Baker, S. (2001). Teaching reading comprehension strategies to students with learning disabilities: A review of the research. *Review of Educational Research, 71*, 279–320.

Gould, S. J. (1991) The case of the creeping fox terrier clone. In *Bully for brontosaurus: Reflections on natural history* (pp. 155–167). New York: Norton.

Guthrie, J. T., & Davis, M. H. (2003). Motivating struggling readers in middle school through an engagement model of classroom practice. *Reading and Writing Quarterly, 19*, 59–85.

Guthrie, J. T., Klauda, S. L., & Ho, A. N. (2013). Modeling relationships among reading instruction, motivation, engagement, and achievement for adolescents. *Reading Research Quarterly, 48*, 9–26.

Hagood, M. C., Alvermann, D. E., & Heron-Hruby, A. (2010). *Bring it to class: Unpacking pop culture in literacy learning.* New York: Teachers College Press.

Harvard Graduate School of Education. (2011). *Pathways to prosperity: Meeting the challenge of preparing young Americans for the 21st century.* Pearson Foundation.

Harvey, S., & Goudvis, A. (2007). *Strategies that work: Teaching comprehension to enhance understanding.* York, ME: Stenhouse.

Hiebert, E. H., & Mesmer, H. A. E (2013). Upping the ante of text complexity in the Common Core State Standards: Examining its potential impact on young readers. *Educational Researcher, 42*(1), 44–51.

Hill, R. (2011). Turning the page: Forget about those bulky backbreakers, digital textbooks are the future. *School Library Journal, 56*, 24–27.

Hinchman, K. A., Alvermann, D. E., Boyd, F., Brozo, W., & Vacca, R. (2003/2004). Supporting older students' in- and out-of-school literacies. *Journal of Adolescent and Adult Literacy, 47*, 304–310.

Keene, E. K., & Zimmerman, S. (1997). *Mosaic of thought: Teaching comprehension in a reading workshop.* Portsmouth, NH: Heinemann.

Kenney, J. M., Hancewicz, E., Heuer, L., Metsisto, D., & Tuttle, C. L. (2005). *Literacy strategies for improving mathematics instruction.* Alexandria, VA: ASCD.

Kozen, A. A., Murray, R. K., & Windell, I. (2006). Increasing all students' chance to achieve: Using and adapting anticipation guides with middle school learners. *Intervention in School and Clinic, 41*, 195–200.

Lankshear, C., & Knobel, M. (2011). *New literacies: Everyday practices and social learning* (3rd ed.). London: Open University Press.

Lenski, S. (2011/2012) What RTI means for content area teachers. *Journal of Adolescent and Adult Literacy, 55*, 276–282.

Lent, R. C. (2012). *Overcoming textbook fatigue: 21st-century tools to revitalize teaching and learning.* Alexandria, VA: ASCD.

Loewen, J. W. (1996). *Lies my teacher told me: Everything your American history textbook got wrong.* New York: Touchstone.

Luke, A. (2000). Critical literacy in Australia. *Journal of Adult and Adolescent Literacy, 43,* 448–461.

Moje, E., Overby, M., Tysvaer, N., & Morris, K. (2008). The complex world of adolescent literacy: Myths, motivations, and mysteries. *Harvard Educational Review, 78,* 107–154.

National Governors Association Center for Best Practices & Council of Chief State School Officers. (2010). Common Core State Standards for English language arts and literacy in history/social studies, science, and technical subjects. Washington, DC:. Author. Retrieved from *www.corestandards.org/assets/CCSSI_ELA%20Standards.pdf.*

O'Brien, D. (2001). "At-risk" adolescents: Redefining competence through the multiliteracies of intermediality, visual arts, and representation. *Reading Online, 4*(11). Retrieved from *www.readingonline.org/newliteracies/lit_index. asp?HREF=/newliteracies/obrien/index.html.*

Paris, S., & Myers, M. (1981). Comprehension monitoring, memory, and study strategies of good and poor readers. *Journal of Reading Behavior, 13,* 5–22.

Raphael, T. (1986). Teaching question–answer relationships, revisited. *The Reading Teacher, 39,* 516–522.

Raphael, T. E., & Au, K. H. (2005). QAR: Enhancing comprehension and test taking across grade levels and contents. *The Reading Teacher, 59,* 206–221.

Schwartz, A., & Rubinstein-Ávila, E. (2006). Understanding the manga hype: Uncovering the multimodality of comic book literacies. *Journal of Adolescent and Adult Literacy, 50,* 40–49.

Shanahan, T. (2012/2013) The Common Core ate my baby and other urban legends. *Educational Leadership. 70,* 11–16.

Shanahan, T. & Shanahan, C. (2008). Teaching disciplinary literacy to adolescents: Rethinking content area literacy. *Harvard Educational Review, 78,* 40–59.

Sheridan-Thomas, H. K., Ro, J. M., & Bromley, K. (2004, November). *Educating ourselves: Teacher educators and graduate students explore the in and out of school literacies of local adolescents.* Paper presented at the annual meeting of the National Reading Conference, Scottsdale, AZ.

Smith, M. W., & Wilhelm, J. D. (2002). *"Reading don't fix no Chevys": Literacy in the lives of young men.* Portsmouth, NH: Heinemann.

Triplett, C. F. (2007). The social construction of "struggle": Influences of school literacy contexts, curriculum, and relationships. *Journal of Literacy Research, 39,* 96–126.

Vacca, R. T., & Vacca, J. L. (2008). *Content area reading: Literacy and learning across the curriculum.* New York: Allyn & Bacon.

Vaughn, S., Swanson, E. A., Roberts, G., Wanzek, J., Stillman-Spisak, S., Solis, M., et al. (2103). Improving comprehension and social studies knowledge in middle school. *Reading Research Quarterly, 48,* 77.

Wolk, S. (2003). Teaching for critical literacy in social studies. *Social Studies,* *94,* 101–107.

Wood, K. (2011). Real-time teaching: Bridging print literacies and digital literacies using strategy guides. *Journal of Adolescent and Adult Literacy,* *55,* 3.

Xu, S. H. (2005). *Trading cards to comic strips: Popular culture texts and literacy learning in grades K–8.* Newark, DE: International Reading Association.

PART IV

Addressing Program and Policy Issues

CHAPTER 16

Multimodality and Literacy Learning

Integrating the Common Core State Standards for English Language Arts

Fenice B. Boyd
Andrea L. Tochelli

In this chapter, we:

- Narrate a portrait of the classroom context where one teacher incorporated a variety of multimodal and multiple text types to help students analyze the diverse perspectives toward Melba Patillo Beals's experience as a member of the Little Rock Nine.

- Discuss how multimodal and multiple text types were used to enhance students' conceptual understanding about the Civil Rights movement in general, and specifically the integration of Little Rock's Central High School.

- Convey how the teacher designed a multimodal approach to teach students about multiple perspectives.

- Demonstrate how students used multimodality to represent their conceptual understanding about past and present issues.

- Share students' multimodal connections to convey how their lifeworlds were invited into the classroom.

We live in an era in which educational reform is exerting a sweeping influence on teachers and students. When we consider the national adoption of new learning (and teaching) standards across the curriculum; how classrooms are becoming increasingly diverse with varied student populations, languages, and academic abilities; and what multimodality adds to teaching and learning, students' educational experiences are becoming progressively richer. The *Common Core State Standards for English Language Arts & Literacy in History/Social Studies, Science, and Technical Subjects* (CCSS; National Governors Association [NGA] Center for Best Practices & Council of the Chief State School Officers [CCSSO], 2010) for example, present learning goals that are aligned from kindergarten through 12th grade. These goals center on students' reading, writing, language, speaking, and listening skills to position students to be prepared for college and careers. In addition, text complexity and close reading while using evidence to support reasoning is one prevailing tenet of the CCSS. As noted in the document:

> The Reading standards place equal emphasis on the sophistication of what students read and the skill with which they read. Whatever they are reading, students must also show a steadily growing ability to discern more from and make fuller use of text, including making an increasing number of connections among ideas and between texts, considering a wider range of textual evidence, and becoming more sensitive to inconsistencies, ambiguities, and poor reasoning in texts. (NGA & CCSSO, 2010, p. 8)

The CCSS's position on text complexity and close reading is applicable to photographs, film, and digital texts, as well as print.

For today's students—those who have never known a world without multiple modes for meaning making—multimodality is central to their everyday lives. They have access to information and entertainment at the click of a mouse, the touch of an iPad screen, and, when they choose to put their earphones on, the sounds from an iPod. And increasingly, diverse populations generate a prominent and valued advantage in classrooms, with opulent heritages and experiences, multiple languages, multiliteracies, cultural traditions, and ways to discern the world. With a focus on diversity, a multiliteracies and multimodal teaching perspective is a necessary and valuable part of a teacher's pedagogical repertoire and students' learning experiences.

As teachers provide students with varied ways to "read" text—whether it is a book, photograph, or song lyrics—these critical pedagogical resources permit students to think about topics from multiple vantage points. We ascribe to Jewitt and Kress's (2003) theory on multimodality and literacy learning: "A multimodal approach to learning requires us to take seriously and attend to the whole range of modes involved in representation and communication" (p. 1). Multiple text types, various resources, or *modes* assist in meaning making, and different modes have their own potential (Moss, 2003). For instance, gesture, gaze, image, movement, music, speech, and sound effects are all modes that propose opportunities to interpret and construct meanings (Jewitt & Kress, 2003). Whether we are admiring vibrant colors of leaves during fall, smelling the fragrance of spring flowers, or analyzing the emotions evoked from the sound effects of a movie, multimodality plays a role in the sense we make of these modes and in how we rely on them as ways of being and knowing. Based on these ideas, meaning making in schools should not rely solely on writing and reading print-based texts but be expanded to include reading multiple text forms as well as composing various text types (e.g., Boyd & Howe, 2006; Jewitt, 2008; Shanahan, 2013a, 2013b).

However, at the same time that multimodality is taking center stage for 21st-century teaching and learning, teachers, teacher educators, and students are faced with an unprecedented national education policy that at first glance assumes to privilege print-based texts. Responding to the current national focus on college and career readiness, in 2010, 45 states and the District of Columbia adopted the CCSS. Full implementation of the standards is under way, and teachers and students all across the United States anxiously await the release of assessments that will be produced by two consortia—Smarter Balanced and PARCC (see *www.smarterbalanced.org* and *www.parcconline.org*)—and aligned with the standards.

Yet before the CCSS were ever adopted, many teachers employed rigorous teaching standards and expectations for themselves and their students. In this chapter we narrate the story of Deborah and her seventh-grade students to portray a multimodal approach to literacy teaching and learning. Our portrayal demonstrates how—7 years before the standards were released and adopted—Deborah taught her students in a way that addressed many of the precise outcomes required by the CCSS through the integration of multimodal texts. That is, through one curriculum unit, we demonstrate when and how seventh-grade English language arts (ELA) standards were integrated into Deborah's instructional practice.

CLASSROOM PORTRAIT

Deborah begins class by directing students to the chapters read for homework.

> DEBORAH: Last night you read three chapters [from *Warriors Don't Cry,* by Melba Pattillo Beals, 1994] because I wanted you to get that whole first day and night in Melba's life where they try to go to school and were kept out by the soldiers. We're going to be looking first at a photograph and then at real film of this event

happening [to look at multiple perspectives]. And we're going to be learning how to look carefully at those photos and film and how to interpret what's really going on in those pictures and what's really going on in this film [CCSS RI.7.3 and RI.7.7]. And so it will be taking a closer look at stuff you've already read about. The purpose of doing the reading first is it makes you a bit of an expert, and how to come to the photo and come to the film with some knowledge. The photo we're going to study today is one you've already seen because it's in your *Warriors* book, but it is considered a very famous photo because it was a symbol of the racial hatred in our country at the time. It made the national newspapers and the international press [see Figure 16.1]. It was shown all over the world. . . . Photos are really important in terms of how people remember history. This is a small. . . . I don't know how big this event will seem to us 50 years from now, but when we were in the middle of the Iraq war, what video image or photo do you think most likely would be the one people are going to remember? Alexis?

ALEXIS: Um, like how those people were tearing down the statue of Saddam Hussein, um, when we took over Baghdad, or when we were fighting for Baghdad.

TYRONE: Like the emotional things, like maybe people dying.

DEBORAH: OK. We certainly have pictures . . . we've seen pictures of wounded people and they stick in our minds because it's graphic. But that video of the statue toppling to symbolize the downfall of that government is a picture that people will associate with that time in history.

This vignette conveys how Deborah layered multiple texts for meaning making with her students. What we find particularly poignant in this example is how Deborah also connected a historical event to a then-current event in her students' lives. By doing so, Deborah helped her students to think about the ways in which events are documented affect how we understand and think about them in a modern context, how to consider the importance of events in the time period in which they occurred, and what documented images might mean 50 years in the future.

Multimodality is central to this narrative because it highlights how multiple pieces of history come together with different types of text to enhance students' conceptual understanding. Moss (2003) argued that multimodality offers the potential to exploit our understandings in different ways based on the affordances and resistances that any mode offers and the use that is made of multimodal resources in any given case. Furthermore, the learning

FIGURE 16.1. Hazel Bryan, Elizabeth Eckford, and adult protestors. Reprinted with permission from the *Arkansas Democrat Gazette.*

potentials of the materials as well as the interactions of the teacher and students affect the learning environment (Jewitt, 2008). In this case, Deborah first called students' attention to chapters read from Beals's memoir the previous evening, a photograph, and then a video image from a television news report. Jointly, these multiple text types allowed the teacher and students to think closely about different texts to engage in "reading" and interpretations. These modes (i.e., print, still, and moving images) afforded the seventh graders a chance to engage in an analytic endeavor of meaning making. What is more, looking back, Deborah's pedagogical move is applicable to our present ELA CCSS era. Deborah's teaching foreshadows the CCSS focus on critical thinking and deeper understanding of texts. Consider CCSS RI.7.3—Analyze the interactions between individuals, events, and ideas in a text (e.g., how ideas influence individuals or events, or how individuals influence ideas or events)—and CCSS SL.7.c—Pose questions that elicit elaboration and respond to others' questions and comments with relevant observations and ideas that bring the discussion back on topic as needed. Both standards were inherent in Deborah's interaction with her students. Throughout this chapter, we highlight instances where Deborah's teaching exemplified the CCSS. We make the case that teaching standards are slightly different from "teaching to the standards," as principled teaching means having high expectations for one's pedagogical practices as well as students' literacy learning and practices. It means that a teacher has a repertoire of strategies and exercises her right to appraise critique, choose, discern, and assess curriculum for students.

CONCEPTUAL UNDERSTANDING
AND MULTIMODAL TEXTS

We now turn to discuss how multimodality, as a pedagogical tool, enhances conceptual understanding inside the classroom. Teaching for conceptual understanding is emphasized in inquiry-based learning in which students begin with a question, theme, or issue designed to focus attention on the context within which a concept is situated. In Deborah's classroom, the seventh graders had a range of reading abilities, but no student read below grade level. Most of their school reading experiences in the past had centered on more traditional texts such as novels, short stories, and textbooks. The challenge for Deborah was to teach students how to understand the Little Rock Nine event conceptually. The process of layered meaning making is central to Deborah's themed unit because students today are expected to read many different types of text that are complicated and that have a wide variety of content and information (e.g., video games, hypertext, film, and Internet content) (Jewitt, 2008). Teaching for conceptual understanding requires that students enact various strategies to help them make connections through a wide variety of multimodal texts.

It is important to look at Deborah's pedagogical moves through the lens of a *new literacies stance*. Bailey (2012) discusses a new literacies stance as one in which a teacher attempts to integrate new literacies in her curriculum, which is built on a solid foundation of theories as related to multimodality (e.g., Jewitt, 2008; Kress, 2003; Shanahan 2013a, 2013b), multiliteracies (e.g., New London Group [NLG], 1996), and an extensive knowledge of teaching and learning principles associated with sociocultural and constructivist approaches that are "active and critical" (Gee, 2003, p. 4). Therefore, Bailey (2012) conceptualized a new literacies pedagogical stance as one that is grounded in dialogic and collaborative learning, guided participation, and focus on consuming and producing various multimodal texts.

In schools we tend to focus on using conventional print materials (Bailey, 2012; Jewitt, 2008; Shanahan, 2013a, 2013b). Electronic and media texts introduce complexity that promotes conceptual understanding because they require skills and abilities beyond those required for comprehension of conventional print materials. When adolescents are engaged in conversations about popular electronic media, their readings of such texts often involve sophisticated interpretive and analytical skills. In viewing a movie for interpretative as well as entertainment purposes, the viewer must be able to understand movement, lighting, and camera angles to make reasonable interpretations about scenes, situations and the director's message. In print text, authors use metaphors, imagery, and other symbolic meanings in language to challenge readers to delve into thoughtful and extensive understandings. Thus Deborah infused a new literacies stance when she taught her students that "reading" is a complex interactive process that requires readers to perform multiple tasks simultaneously. Reading any type of text entails much more than decoding words; critically understanding multiple text types requires teachers to instruct students that while reading widely, they also must read interactively and critically.

MULTIMODALITY: DIVERSE PERSPECTIVES WITH MULTIPLE TEXT TYPES

Multimodality refers to the modes of representation beyond print, including such things as the visual, auditory, gestural, and kinesthetic. Kress and Van Leeuwen (2001) developed a multimodal theory of communication that focuses on practices and resources in relation to meaning. In doing so, they looked at multiple semiotic meanings derived from signs, varied levels, and modes within a culture rather than holding to a traditional view that meaning is made once (Love, 2005). In using multimodal and multiple text types, Deborah encouraged the students to consider how different modes within a text represent the Little Rock Nine in vastly different ways, thus making meaning through multiple expressions. In their theory of multimodality, Kress and Van Leeuwen discuss four domains of practice in which meanings are made: discourse, design, production, and distribution. Although each domain is arranged in a particular order, it is not viewed within any hierarchy, where one domain exists above another. In this next section we examine the concept of design and how it relates to the idea of multimodality and multiple text types for layered meaning making.

In framing key theoretical concepts from the work of Kress and Van Leeuwen, we draw on the earlier work of the NLG (1996) and their concept of design as it relates to multimodal texts and conceptual understanding. The NLG broadened the view of literacy to account for a multiplicity of discourses. In this view learning occurs in a social context. The NLG framed a multiliteracies pedagogy in which design is integral, and emphasized meaning making as an active and dynamic process, and not something governed by static rules. In discussing design, the NLG highlighted multimodality as it relates to all the other modes and accounts for the layered complexity that fosters active design. For example, we began our chapter with a classroom portrait where Deborah asked the students to connect the famous picture of Elizabeth Eckford and Hazel Bryan to their own lives. In this picture, Bryan heckles Eckford as she walks to Central High during the height of the school integration movement. Deborah juxtaposed two mediums—a photograph and a moving image—to invite students to think about the impact of the Eckford and Bryan photograph over 50 years later, and what they recalled of a current event for them, Saddam Hussein's statue toppling down in Baghdad.

DESIGN AND MULTIMODALITY

Design is multifaceted and includes a conceptual and an expressive side. Love (2005) writes, "Design is a way to understand discourses within a communication situation and involves deliberate choice of mode (form) for representation and how the presentation will be framed" (p. 304). To illustrate this point, we turn to another classroom portrait where Deborah placed multiple texts side by side to showcase how the modes have the potential to change the meaning in significant ways. Three texts were used for analytical purposes, chosen to assist students' thinking about how an event is portrayed and how the modes influence the representation and meaning. Each text portrayed this key event differently.

The scene at Central High was Minnijean Brown dumping hot chili on one of the white students who had been harassing her for extended periods of time. Deborah used each text to discuss with the students why this event might be portrayed so differently across modes, and the reasons the authors of each text might have for doing so. Deborah noted that in *Warriors Don't Cry* Minnijean's experience is told through Melba's voice: "We never get to hear from Minnijean. I don't have any interviews with her," notes Deborah, but "if I sat behind you in class and just kept doing this [harassing], eventually you will throw your book at me, right? I mean eventually you are going to lose it." In the memoir, Beals does not communicate the extent of Minnijean's frustration and harassment. This text minimizes Minnijean's experience because it was told in Melba's voice and conveys the overall experiences of the Little Rock Nine in general, and Melba's specifically.

After Deborah showed a short clip from *Eyes on the Prize, Part II*, a discussion ensued about how the documentary represented the chili incident compared with the memoir. Deborah pointed out that Minnijean does not speak for herself in the video *Eyes on the Prize* (Hampton, 1986) either, but the Little Rock Nine students Ernest Green and Melba Pattillo Beals report that Minnijean was constantly harassed. Again Minnijean's experience is highlighted; while not in her voice per se, it nevertheless shows the significance of this event as remembered by her peers.

The goal in showing one event across multiple texts is to show how the mode of the narrative distinguishes different points in the story. As told in Melba's memoir, the event is powerful. But when juxtaposed with the documentary, Melba's written description of Minnijean's harassment feels static in comparison to Ernest and Melba's verbal description of the chili incident, which, as members of the Little Rock Nine, they witnessed firsthand. In the documentary we see, hear, and feel the emotion in their voices and see their gestures as they describe how Minnijean and the cafeteria staff, who were primarily African American, reacted to her throwing chili on one white student, and the consequences Minnijean faced on her impending expulsion from Central High School. These layered modes in the documentary changed the way Deborah's students thought about the incident with the chili and its historical significance.

The third text, a docudrama titled *Crisis at Central High* (Johnson, 1980) is based on the journal of Mrs. Huckaby, an English teacher and the Dean of Girls at Central High School in 1957. This low-budget HBO docudrama depicts yet another perspective of the historical event and the only one in which the Little Rock Nine are portrayed in the third person. Each text shows a different perspective of Miniijean's experience. While none of the texts are in her voice, the memoir highlights how this event affected all of the Little Rock Nine. The documentary *Eyes on the Prize* emphasizes the event through two interviews and provides an additional context to the many reactions to the chili incident. The docudrama in comparison overly simplifies the event and shows how a telling from a particular perspective can mask the importance of real-life situations. Furthermore, Deborah called the student's attention to the fact that docudramas have actors, directors, producers, and editors who decide how and what is portrayed in film, and can silence some voices and perspectives—and highlight others—in the process. Although *Crisis at Central High* is based on a diary kept by Mrs. Huckaby, the film was edited. This became a central part of the discussion as students became aware that what is left out of an account is often just as important as what is told. How emotions get portrayed influences how events are perceived, remembered, and internalized.

These examples validate the significance of questioning, posing dilemmas, and wondering what is and is not represented in a text. It is important to teach students that asking questions about a text is not an admission of not knowing, but rather a powerful way of "reading" across multiple text types multimodally. When students read texts without posing questions, they may not be reading critically and thinking about what the design of modes affords them in meaning making. In addition, these examples illustrate how CCSS RI.7.1—Cite several pieces of textual evidence to support analysis of what the text says explicitly as well as inferences drawn from the text—was inherent in Deborah's instructional approach. A memoir, a documentary, and a docudrama (i.e., several pieces of textual evidence) were all included in the lesson to support the microanalysis of a particular incident (i.e., Minnijean and the chili incident) within a specific historical event (i.e., the integration of Central High School).

In the next section, we turn to examine students' multimodal connections across texts to explore how, when invited, they brought to the classroom texts from their own lives to exhibit their conceptual understanding of critical historical events. Deborah designed a culminating activity that required the students to make multimodal textual connections to the experiences of the Little Rock Nine by sharing different types of texts that would support multiple perspectives of an event or issue. Students selected movie clips, hip-hop, a canonical text, a different school integration story, the Iraq War, and personal struggles with peers in instances of teasing to make connections to issues they studied in *Warriors Don't Cry*. Their final presentations and papers conveyed critical perspectives about obstacles faced when attempting to think analytically about events from multiple perspectives.

STUDENTS' MULTIMODAL CONNECTIONS

Perhaps what was most striking in this classroom were the seventh graders' personal responses to Melba and her experience. Students conveyed that Melba was one of the bravest people they ever read about. Being bullied and teased is not something they have to imagine; many middle school students have experienced such harassment, albeit not to the degree of the Little Rock Nine. But navigating obstacles in order to acquire an education is not within their experiences. When they hear about daily, aggressive harassment and physical abuse going unchecked in school, and when they can visualize aspects of this type of harassment from a docudrama and documentary, they empathize with Melba and other members of the Little Rock Nine, about how difficult it would be to take the daily unrelenting abuse without retaliating. In students' final inquiry projects, there was greater depth to their conceptual understanding of the historical event because they were allowed to layer texts multimodally from their own lives. To examine the students' writing about their multimodal artifacts, we have divided their responses into three sections: personal connections, current events, and popular culture.

Personal Connections

Lindsay's personal connection to the experiences of the Little Rock Nine was focused on teasing in middle school. She wrote, "My experience was tough but Melba's put her life in grave danger. She had to walk her halls watching her back in fear of getting jumped, hurt, or killed. Even though my middle school experience had strong effects on me, it was just boys being stupid little boys. In Melba's case she was being teased and harassed by people who could seriously hurt her." In her essay, Lindsay specifically acknowledged the difference between what she endured versus Melba by speaking of danger and "boys being stupid little boys."

Like Lindsay, Tyrone also made a connection to the discriminatory perceptions people hold, but discussed Melba's experience as one removed from his own. "At CHS [Central High School] she [Melba] had her humanity taken away from her and treated as the Other by the white people, meaning they didn't consider her another human being like themselves.

If you treat someone as the Other you don't have to treat them with basic decency. Nothing in my life connects because that has never happened to me." Tyrone critically noted how people from diverse backgrounds are often "othered" as he capitalized Other in his discussion. Although not able to sympathize with Melba, Tyrone showed understanding and the ultimate consequence for looking at the color of one's skin rather than attempting to know the individual. These two examples are inclusive of CCSS Writing 7.2—Write informative/explanatory texts to examine a topic and convey ideas, concepts, and information through the selection, organization, and analysis of relevant content. Although Lindsay and Tyrone could never imagine any schooling experiences such as those of the Little Rock Nine, they wrote a personal narrative to convey past experiences with peers, in which they articulated similarities and differences to empathize with the experiences of Melba and her peers.

Popular Culture

Jamal selected an appropriate song from the hip-hop genre to bridge music from his lifeworld to that of the Little Rock Nine. He wrote, "2Pac also says in the beginning of his song 'I see no changes.' When Melba attended Central High she saw no changes in how integration was getting better; if anything it was getting worse and harder for her to survive in Central High. Melba wants integration to work out for the sake of all the black people in her city. She's trying so hard to hold on and stay in central high but she sees no changes in how kids are treating her, which she doesn't want. She wants them to get to know her and get to be good friends with her, which I think is reasonable and if I were in her position that's what I would do." Grace (2004) defines "culturally conscious hip-hop as oral text with lyrics and messages that enlighten with social consciousness, engage with politicized messages, and empower by instilling cultural and self-awareness" (p. 484), and notes that some hip-hop genres are not suitable for the classroom and may present risks for teachers and students. Deborah was not familiar with rap or hip-hop, but discussed with students the appropriateness of lyrics.

Mo chose to make connections to movies from which he had learned about race-related issues.

> "In the movie remember the titans they tried to integrate a football team. This started because of a new coach that was black in a white school. The white players would not play for the team because they did not want to play with the black players. They finally joined together. . . . This is the same as Melba because of the white people of Central are mad that these nine kids are coming into this all white school and starting integration. Another connection is that Melba gets hurt just

like some of the players in remember the titans. Melba gets hurt in the bathrooms, hallways, and in the classroom."

Here, Jamal and Mo illustrate a personal preference for self-selected text to make connections to the experiences of Melba. The New York State Education Department (NYSED) took advantage of the ability to add up to 15% new content to the CCSS by adding a Literature Anchor Standard that strengthens the focus on responding to literature through making connections. Jamal and Mo's self-selected texts are examples of student work that illustrates CCSS RL.7.11a—Recognize, interpret, and make connections in narratives, poetry, and drama, ethically and artistically to other texts, ideas, cultural perspectives, eras, personal events, and situations; a. Self-select text based on personal preferences.

Current Events

Still a different kind of connection made to Melba and the Little Rock Nine was a connection to a current event. At the time Deborah implemented this unit, the United States had just invaded Iraq. Earlier in this chapter, we portrayed Deborah's reference to the toppling down of Saddam Hussein's statue, and what that would mean 50 years in the future. Alexis extended the event Deborah opened to all students and called attention to the discrimination Muslims today might face in the United States. Alexis said, "This connection is similar to Melba's experience because the Muslims in America today are treated exactly how the blacks were treated by the whites in 1957. They are very much stereotyped because of what they look like and what they believe in. Also the Muslims in the United States today are the minority, just like the blacks were, so it is easier to pick on them." In Table 16.1 we present the students' multiple text types. Table 16.2 exhibits all multimodal texts Deborah used to teach students while studying *Warriors Don't Cry*.

CONCLUSION

What do multimodal texts contribute to students' critical understandings about a political and social event such as the integration of Little Rock's Central High School that a print-only text cannot? For a print text, finding the point of view can seem abstract, and given that Deborah's students were far removed from the era of school desegregation, the events were difficult to imagine. Deborah argued that even though *Warriors Don't Cry* is well written, students were always left with so many questions. Because students were always so bewildered about the adults' actions in the story—that the

TABLE 16.1. Students' Multimodal Connections

Students	Text Type	Themes
Mo	Movies • *Remember the Titans* • *Jackie Robinson*	• Integrating a high school football team • Integrating major-league baseball
Jamal	Hip-hop • "Changes" by Tupac (1998)	• Reality of being black and male in the United States
Tyrone	Book • *The Catcher in the Rye* (Salinger, 1951)	• Holden (the main character) was isolated as alienated and suffered emotionally • "Othering" of people who come from diverse backgrounds
Lindsay	Personal story • Teasing in middle school	• Exclusion from the "cool girls club"
Alexis	U.S. and international news events • September 11, 2001	• Discrimination against Muslims in United States

white segregationists' abuse was of no consequence—Deborah believed that if she had not used additional text types, the students might not have believed what they read.

When a photograph is used to teach adolescents to analyze an issue conceptually, they can literally place a finger on each individual face and shift the point of view while critiquing the picture and take a stance from which they can understand that person's motivation. The photograph does not reveal how the people in it really feel about the situation, but from "reading" body language (e.g., angry-looking faces), students can make reasonable interpretations and bring to bear layered meaning making about the context at hand. Watching a documentary, students can "read" voice, gestures, and so forth, compare and contrast the memories, and add yet another layer to their meaning making. A docudrama, inspired by true events, is additional fodder for critique and lends itself to discussions about behind the scenes voices (e.g., producers, directors, editors), and about whose voice contributed to or was deleted from the story. Engaging with multimodal texts allows students to develop sophisticated, complex, and yet quite concrete understandings of concepts and events that might otherwise have remained only vague, abstract references. Teaching using multimodal texts also provides opportunities to introduce and practice critical analytic tools that will serve students well as they "read" today's multimodal world.

TABLE 16.2. Deborah's Curriculum Materials

Text type	Title	Synopsis	Purpose
Main Book	*Warriors Don't Cry* (Beals, 1994)	A memoir written from the perspective of Melba Pattillo Beals—one of the Little Rock Nine—centered on the integration of Central High School.	Used as an instructional tool to show hostile and violent incidents in the hallways and classrooms that went virtually unreported by local and national media. Also the memoir shows the complex roles that all of the people involved play in integrating the school.
Supplementary books	*Leon's Story* (Tillage, 1997)	Told in regional dialect, the book is an oral history of a sharecropping family living in the Jim Crow South.	Used to convey Tillage's views on the horror of Jim Crow laws and answer questions of why it was hard to fight them.
	Gandhi (Demi, 2001)	A biography and picture book written to portray Gandhi's life.	Used to introduce Gandhi's life and the philosophy and practice of nonviolent resistance.
	The Century for Young People (Jennings, Brewster, & Armstrong, 1999)	A children's version of the popular book of photographs.	Contains interviews of some people involved in resistance to Central High School's integration.
	A Life Is More Than a Moment (Counts, 1999)	Interviews and photographs of Central High in 1957 and 1997 taken by a white student who attended Central High School.	Offers varying points of view at the time and shows how views have changed (or not) over time.
Documentary	*Eyes on The Prize, Part II* (Hampton, 1986)	An award-winning documentary series of the Civil Rights Movement from the 1950s–1960s.	Used to show real-time footage of the mob and to hear the Little Rock protagonists telling stories.

TABLE 16.2. (*continued*)

Docudrama	*Crisis at Central High* (Johnson, 1980)	A movie based on the journal of the assistant principal and English teacher.	Told from the perspective of a white adult in the school, the movie makes students aware that perceptions can differ. The docudrama shows actual footage shot at Central High School so that students understand the size and scope of the building.
Photographs	Water fountains in the 1950s	A visual demonstration of how separate is not equal.	Still photographs "freezes" a historical moment so it can be closely examined and critiqued.
	Beals's family and friends	A visual representation of a middle-class African American family with friends.	
	Elizabeth Eckford, Hazel Bryan	A visual of Elizabeth Eckford walking stalwartly toward school followed by Hazel Bryan and a mob of angry white adults.	
Encyclopedia articles	*Plessy v. Ferguson*	An article describing Plessy's arrest and the court case.	
	Makes clear how Plessy and others deliberately planned for his arrest so that he would have the opportunity to question the law's constitutionality.		
	Brown v. Board of Education	An article describing Linda Brown's school and the U.S. Supreme Court case.	Helps students see that when people challenge a law they benefit many people more so than they benefit themselves.

DISCUSSION AND ACTIVITIES

1. In what ways does using a multimodal approach allow students to bring their perspectives and identities into the classroom? How does "reading" across text types help students think about events and ideas differently? How might multimodal texts be used inside the classroom to promote critical literacy skills? How is conceptual understanding strengthened by the use of multiple text types? (These questions connect to CCSS RI.7.1, 7.7, and 7.9.)

2. Brainstorm with students several critical events that have occurred within their lifetime. Talk about how these events are retold, portrayed, and narrated across several kinds of texts (modes). Discuss how they may want to remember this event, and how they would place themselves in the telling. (These ideas connect to CCSS RI.7.3).

3. As a research project, form groups based on an event students want to research and have them find several kinds of texts that give one perspective of the event while leaving out another perspective. Have each group present their findings through the texts they find to lead the class in a critical conversation about how the event is captured through various types of texts. (These ideas connect to CCSS RI.7.7).

4. Have students consider how they might retell an event to connect it to their own lives and then create their own multimodal texts such as an original rap song, iMovie, poem, or PowerPoint in the process. This activity would open the classroom to critical inquiry and multimodal learning, allowing students the creative freedom to design their own texts about an event that is significant to their lives. (These ideas connect to CCSS W.7.2 and 7.3.)

REFERENCES

Bailey, N. M. (2012). The importance of a new literacies stance in teaching English language arts. In S. M. Miller & M. B. McVee (Eds.), *Multimodal composing in classrooms: Learning and teaching for the digital world* (pp. 44–62). New York: Routledge.

Beals, M. P. (1994). *Warriors don't cry*. New York: Washington Square.

Boyd, F. B., & Howe, D. R. (2006). Teaching *Warriors Don't Cry* with other text types to enhance comprehension. *English Journal, 95*, 61–68.

Counts, W. (1999). *A life is more than a moment: The desegregation of Little Rock's central high*. Bloomington, IN: University Press.

Demi (2001). *Gandhi*. New York: Simon & Schuster.

Gee, J. P. (2003). *What video games have to teach us about learning and literacy*. New York: Palgrave.

Grace, C. M. (2004). Exploring the African American oral tradition: Instructional implications for literacy learning. *Language Arts, 81*(6), 481–490.

Hampton, H. (Director). (1986). *Eyes on the prize*. Washington, DC: PBS Home Video.

Jennings, P., & Brewster, T. (1999). *The century for young people*. New York: Doubleday.

Jewitt, C. (2008). Multimodality and literacy in school classrooms. *Review of Research in Education, 32*, 241–267.

Jewitt, C., & Kress, G. (Eds.) (2003). *Multimodal literacy*. New York: Peter Lang.

Johnson, L. (Director). (1980). *Crisis at Central High*. Los Angeles: HBO.

Kress, G. (2003). *Literacy in the new media age*. New York: Routledge.

Kress, G., & Van Leeuwen, T. (2001). *Multimodal discourse: The modes and media of contemporary communication*. London and New York: Arnold/ Oxford University Press.

Love, M. S. (2005). Multimodality of learning through anchored instruction. *Journal of Adolescent and Adult Literacy, 48*(4), 300–311.

Moss, G. (2003). Putting the text back into practice: Junior-age non-fiction as objects of design. In C. Jewitt & G. Kress (Eds.), *Multimodal literacy* (pp. 73–87). New York: Peter Lang.

National Governors Association Center for Best Practices & Council of the Chief State School Officers. (2010). *Common Core State Standards for the English language arts and literacy in history/social studies, science, and technical subjects*. Washington, DC: Author.

New London Group. (1996). A pedagogy of multiliteracies: Designing social futures. *Harvard Educational Journal, 66*(1), 60–92.

Salinger, J. D. (1951). *The catcher in the rye*. New York: Little, Brown, and Company.

Shakur, T. (1998). *Changes*. Greatest Hits [CD]. Santa Monica, CA: Interscope, Amaru, Death Row.

Shanahan, L. E. (2013a). Multimodal representations: A fifth-grade teacher influences students' design and production. *Pedagogies: An International Journal, 8*(2), 85–102.

Shanahan, L. E. (2013b). Composing "kid friendly" multimodal text: When conventions, instruction, and signs come together. *Written Communications, 30*(2), 194–227.

Tillage, L. W. (1997). *Leon's story*. New York: Farrar, Straus and Giroux.

CHAPTER 17

Traveling Together over Difficult Ground

Negotiating Success with a Profoundly Inexperienced Reader in an Introduction to Chemistry Class

Cindy Litman
Cynthia Greenleaf

In this chapter, we:

- Introduce Eduardo, an 11th-grade student, as he presented himself in the class in the beginning of the year.

- Describe the literacy learning routines that his teacher, Will Brown, established to support his students' learning of chemistry.

- Show how Will sequenced instruction to build academic dispositions and skills for his Introduction to Chemistry students.

- Follow Eduardo's progress from the beginning to the end of the year.

Eduardo is an 11th-grade student enrolled in Will Brown's Introduction to Chemistry class at Skyline High School in Oakland, California. His journey as a reader and a student in Introduction to Chemistry was gleaned from a multifaceted study of high school students who were profoundly inexperienced in academic literacy and were enrolled in content-area classrooms where teachers required and supported high levels of disciplinary reading (Greenleaf, Brown, & Litman, 2004; Greenleaf & Litman, 2011; Schoenbach, Braunger, Greenleaf, & Litman, 2003).

We retrace Eduardo and Will's steps on this journey to demonstrate that profoundly inexperienced and academically unprepared students can make considerable progress as readers and learners—even late in their academic careers—when classroom teachers provide routines and support for their learning. Our description of negotiating success moves the discussion of adolescent literacy development beyond the implementation of structures and instructional strategies to consider the importance of the classroom climate fostered by a teacher's stance toward students and their learning. We describe the classroom support that was provided so that disinvested or struggling students can develop new dispositions and identities as readers and students. Furthermore, we hope to provide educators committed to the equitable participation of all students in the academic enterprise with a concrete example of classroom practice that serves that goal.

BACKGROUND INFORMATION

The recent education policy and reform focus on adolescent literacy and college and career readiness makes the work we report here timely (ACT, 2005, 2006; Carnegie Council on Advancing Adolescent Literacy [CCAAL], 2010; Lee & Spratley, 2010). Indeed, instruction that engages students in close reading and sense-making with complex academic texts across the subject areas is called for by the new Common Core State Standards (CCSS) in Literacy (National Governors Association [NGA] Center for Best Practices & Council of Chief State School Officers [CCSSO], 2010). The introduction to the CCSS describes the dispositions and skills envisioned for college- and career-ready students:

> Students who meet the Standards readily undertake the close, attentive reading that is at the heart of understanding and enjoying complex works of literature. They habitually perform the critical reading necessary to pick carefully through the staggering amount of information available today in print and digitally. They actively seek the wide, deep, and thoughtful engagement with high-quality literary and informational texts that builds knowledge, enlarges experience, and broadens worldviews. They reflexively demonstrate the cogent reasoning and use of evidence that is essential to both private deliberation and responsible citizenship in a democratic republic. In short, students who meet the Standards develop the skills in reading, writing, speaking, and listening that are the foundation for any creative and purposeful expression in language. (p. 3)

While this description of high-level literacy ends up highlighting the skills students need to develop, of equal importance (perhaps more importance), it describes a set of dispositions and relationships to reading and learning that students need to acquire to become the deeply literate beings envisioned. The sort of instruction that would prepare students to be such literate individuals remains quite rare in our nation's secondary schools, particularly in content areas such as science (Duschl, Schweingruber, & Shouse, 2006; Weiss, Pasley, Smith, Banilower, & Heck, 2003).

Paralleling the CCSS, the new framework for science education (National Research Council [NRC], 2012) underscores the importance of science reading. Unlike previous reforms that viewed reading as marginally relevant or even antithetical to science inquiry (National Committee on Science Education Standards and Assessment/National Research Council [NCSESA/NRC], 1996; see, e.g., Osborne, 2002; Pearson, Moje, & Greenleaf, 2010), the new science framework recognizes that "reading, interpreting, and producing text are fundamental practices of science in particular, and they constitute at least half of engineers' and scientists' total working time" (p. 74). The framework encourages learning through the range of inquiry practices engaged in by scientists, including close reading and hands-on experimentation to develop, refine, and critique models of the designed and natural worlds. These visions compel a renewed focus on high-level, academic, discipline-specific literacies.

The study in which Eduardo came to our attention focused on how a diverse group of middle and high school teachers involved in an ongoing professional learning community integrated an instructional model, Reading Apprenticeship, into their ongoing subject-area teaching. As part of this study, we observed and recorded Will's class at least once a week, took field notes, collected lesson materials and student work, administered reading assessments, conducted teacher and student interviews, and identified a few focal students for closer study to represent a range of the students in this class. Our intent was to document literacy learning opportunities in Will's Introduction to Chemistry class, the least demanding science class that could be taken toward admission to a community or state college. It covered about half the content of Will's college prep chemistry. Nearly 40% of the students in this class had scored below the 10th percentile on standardized reading tests, and only two scored above the 25th percentile.

A detailed analysis of classroom events and interactions using grounded theory methods (Corbin & Strauss, 1990) alerted us to how interactions fostered engagement and development of academic identity in Will's class. As Eduardo entered the unfamiliar landscape of rigorous academic work, we watched Will skillfully maneuver Eduardo from a resistant stance toward a more powerful academic identity. Will's teaching illuminated a pathway toward academic engagement that we have come to regard as key to student literacy learning, an instructional stance we term "negotiating success."

MEET EDUARDO

When we first met Eduardo, he was an uncooperative and unmotivated student in Will Brown's Introduction to Chemistry class. Eduardo's participation during the first weeks of class took the form of passive resistance and frequent interruptions and disruptions. He was slow in responding to directions or chose not to follow them at all. When Will asked students to add to their notes what they had learned from their classmates, Eduardo sat with his binder closed. During one lesson, Eduardo kept up a steady stream of negative patter, replying to Will's reminder to work quietly with, "We don't have to." He shunned collaboration, telling Will, "I like being alone." In a whole-class conversation about how to succeed in the class, Eduardo insisted that it didn't matter to him if he failed. Even we wrote Eduardo off: he was not initially selected as a focal student in our study because of his frequent absences.

There was little to suggest that things would change. As an 11th grader, time was not on Eduardo's side. A native Spanish speaker—he had been in English Language Development classes through ninth grade—Eduardo described his experience of reading in class as "frustrating" and claimed he "couldn't read, you know, that well." He was not a student who seemed likely to beat the odds. He seemed at first to have none of the personal qualities associated with resiliency—cooperativeness, a positive sense of self, a sense of self-efficacy, positive peer and adult interactions, social responsiveness and sensitivity, empathy, a sense of humor, low degrees of defensiveness, and critical problem-solving skills (Garmezy, 1983). He appeared to be a not very likeable student who seemed destined to contribute to the alarming dropout rate at Skyline High School. Even the most committed educator would be tempted to dismiss Eduardo as an unfortunate—albeit complicit—casualty of our educational system.

But Eduardo did beat the odds. After earning poor marks in the first grading period, largely due to incomplete assignments, Eduardo went on to earn an A in the second semester. Furthermore, Eduardo developed a preference for reading science texts and expressed the desire to become an engineer. While Eduardo's turnaround coincided with exposure to specific reading and science strategies and routines, our data suggest that the change was a result of his broader apprenticeship in the discipline-based literacies in Will's classroom, coupled with Will's constant promotion of the expectation that academic achievement was malleable, and that Eduardo could succeed through effort (Molden & Dweck, 2006). Frequent in-class metacognitive conversations throughout the fall semester, conversations that were wide ranging but focused on reading and science thinking processes and academic mindsets, supported Eduardo in rethinking his identity. He came to see himself as having the capability to succeed in class and consequently experienced the "joy of figuring things out through science inquiry and through reading science" that Will described as the goal for his students.

Eduardo's surprising turnaround was largely the result of a process that we describe as "negotiating success." Much of this negotiation between Will and Eduardo took place in the context of ongoing classroom discussions that gave Will a nuanced understanding of Eduardo's identity as a student, reader, and learner, as well as ongoing opportunities to engage and mentor Eduardo and his classmates in the thinking, language, and literacy practices of science. Will's interactions with Eduardo occurred during content-area instruction that benefited Eduardo and his classmates. Indeed, in this classroom where students had ongoing opportunities for teacher- and peer-supported science literacy learning, we witnessed many shifts in many students' conceptions of reading and reading practices and in their identities as readers and students (Greenleaf et al., 2004). In order to situate Eduardo's story in its educational context, we now turn to a description of Will Brown's Introduction to Chemistry class.

READING APPRENTICESHIP
IN INTRODUCTION TO CHEMISTRY

Eduardo's teacher, Willard Brown, was a member of an ongoing professional learning community of teachers in the Bay Area of California working to apprentice urban students to academic literacy practices by integrating Reading Apprenticeship into subject-area teaching (Schoenbach, Greenleaf, & Murphy, 2012). Reading Apprenticeship is an instructional framework for adolescent literacy development based on an understanding of literacy as a social, cultural, and cognitive activity, mediated by settings, tasks, purposes, and other social and linguistic factors (e.g. Newell, Beach, Smith, & VanDerHeide, 2011; Scribner & Cole, 1981; Smagorinsky, 2009; Street, 1995). According to this approach, if students are to become skilled readers of academic texts, the invisible processes involved in comprehending a text must be made visible and accessible to them as they engage in meaningful literacy activities (CCAAL, 2010; Delpit, 1995; Freedman, Flower, Hull, & Hayes, 1995; Gee, 1996; Lemke, 2006; Moje, 2008; Shanahan & Shanahan, 2008). Beyond these cognitive skills, to become the skillful and thoughtful readers envisioned in the CCSS, students need to acquire learner dispositions such as stamina for lengthy engagement with text, tolerance for the inevitable confusion that will accompany complex reading, and perseverance (Dweck, Walton, & Cohen, 2011; Farrington et al., 2012; Schoenbach & Greenleaf, 2009; Yeager & Walton, 2011).

In Reading Apprenticeship classrooms teachers reframe teaching as an apprenticeship into discipline-based ways of thinking, talking, reading, and writing. Instruction includes explicit attention to how we read and why we read in the ways we do, as well as what we read in content-area texts. Furthermore, Reading Apprenticeship focuses instructional attention on building students' dispositions to struggle with complexity and ambiguity by publicly acknowledging, sharing, and working through the inevitable challenges to meaning making that academic texts present to readers. By starting with what students don't understand or find confusing in texts in order to collaboratively resolve challenges to comprehension, Reading Apprenticeship instructional routines *normalize struggle* (Walsh, 2002), shifting the definition of success from performance to effort, and demystifying the often hidden work of disentangling complex ideas and representations for students who may be profoundly inexperienced doing such intellectual work with text.

The Instructional Landscape

The Reading Apprenticeship Framework was reflected in key features of the learning environment in Will's class, such as the frequency and nature of reading opportunities, explicit strategies instruction, collaboration and metacognitive support, and science inquiry. These activities made visible the ordinarily invisible processes of students' conceptual change. Through ongoing reflection and collaborative inquiry, students shared their ideas, texts, data, and inferences with one another, and apprehended others' ways of thinking about the subject of inquiry or the inquiry process itself. These inquiry conversations also allowed Will the opportunity to coach students through the otherwise invisible thinking processes of science. Just as Will engaged students in ongoing metacognitive conversations about how, as well as what, they read, science investigations provided rich opportunities to engage students in ongoing conversations about science processes—how we do science—as well as science content.

Yearlong Literacy Routines

The rigorous academic landscape of Will's classroom was alien to the majority of his students, who were accustomed to rote learning assignments that required little thought. As a Reading Apprenticeship teacher, Will focused explicitly on academic literacy throughout the year, emphasizing ways of reading, thinking, and talking that are particular to science. Rather than presenting a smorgasbord of activities, Will concentrated on a handful of reading and discourse routines that he used over and over again in different ways. Metacognitive literacy routines and tools such as Talking to the Text (TttT), in which students annotated the text as they read with their reading and thinking processes, and double-entry I Saw/I Thought journals, supported students in reading and discussing everything from laboratory equipment like well-plates to lab procedures to Lewis Dot Structures to numeric equations, and increased opportunities for science and literacy learning from these texts. Table 17.1 describes these reading and discourse routines.

Metacognitive Conversation

Among the routines that supported students' growth as science readers and learners were the many opportunities Will offered his students to discuss the ideas and texts of chemistry. In Will's classroom, conversational routines included the preambles, expert groups and Team Reads described in Table 17.1. These conversational routines generally began with individual reflection, then proceeded to small-group and whole-class discussion before returning to the individual, providing opportunities for students to revisit, revise, and deepen comprehension and content knowledge as well as to practice and refine discipline-based thinking and reading processes. Topics of these conversations were wide ranging—students might grapple with a difficult concept or operation, connect new ideas to prior knowledge, or discuss real-life applications of chemistry in a preamble; synthesize and consolidate information and ideas from multiple sources in an expert group; or tackle a particularly challenging section of text in a Team Read—but they nearly always involved reading and text of some kind.

EDUARDO'S JOURNEY

Will designed his classroom routines and structures to guide students toward more powerful academic identities, even though students were sometimes reluctant traveling companions. During their first weeks together, Will guided an unwilling Eduardo to find his footing in an unfamiliar and forbidding landscape. As they traveled together over this difficult ground, with Will's support Eduardo gained traction and enthusiasm and, eventually, the knowledge, skill, and will to move forward more confidently toward a new identity.

Fall: Finding Common Ground

Eduardo's turnaround began with Will's observation that, despite Eduardo's refusal to participate in most classroom activities, he seemed to enjoy being part of class discussions. At first, Eduardo's participation in classroom discussions was largely tangential—telling a classmate that he couldn't hear what she said, for example, or piggy-backing on another's idea with an offhanded "Sounds good." However, Will consistently demonstrated that he valued students' participation, including Eduardo's, however negligible his contributions may have appeared to outside observers. During a preamble

TABLE 17.1. Reading and Discourse Routines in Introduction to Chemistry

Preambles

Each day began with a "preamble," a daily warm-up that brought students' individual reading and thinking into the wider classroom community. Preambles were also the primary venue for reading instruction.

K-W-L

Students used the K-W-L strategy to monitor what they knew, wanted to know and what they learned about a topic (Ogle, 1986). K-W-L supported both reading and doing science. Each lab was accompanied by a K-W-L, and K-W-L was also embedded in every reading log.

Expert groups

Some preambles and assignments were done in "expert groups," in which each team responded to a different prompt about a topic-related problem. These problems often involved synthesizing information from multiple sources. After working on the problem as a team, groups presented their solution to the class and solicited their peers' feedback and assistance.

Reading logs

The primary tool to support students' reading of the textbook was a two-column I Saw/I Thought reading log. In one column, students recorded what they "saw" in the text; in the other, they recorded their thoughts—patterns they saw, questions they had, connections they made to prior knowledge. The focus of the reading log changed depending on the content, the demands of the text, and students' increasing academic literacy skills. In addition to supporting textbook reading, students also used the double-entry I Saw/I Thought format to record and interpret observations during labs.

Bringing reading into the classroom

Reading happened in the classroom. Because the students were not yet independent readers of the complex science texts of chemistry, Will explained: "We have to bring the reading into class, as well as the comprehension." When reading and conversations about reading materials took place in class, students' comprehension problems and their thinking were in evidence, and the class could work collaboratively to both build dispositions for problem solving and solve comprehension problems with the text.

Explicit strategies instruction

Reading comprehension strategies emerged in the context of in-class supported reading as students grappled with in-the-moment comprehension problems. Students often generated and shared their own authentic and resourceful strategies for solving comprehension problems. Will played a critical role by modeling his own strategy use, by creating ongoing opportunities for students to share reading difficulties and solutions, and by elaborating on student-generated strategies.

Team Reads

Team Reads were a modified version of Reciprocal Teaching (Palincsar & Brown, 1984) in which students alternately read a small section of text individually and
(continued)

TABLE 17.1. (*continued*)

discussed the section with three teammates. In both the individual reading and small-group conversations, students monitored their reading and thinking processes and practiced three cognitive strategies: clarifying, questioning, and summarizing. Through this cycle of reading and talk, students practiced discipline-based reading skills and gained stamina for challenging reading as well as knowledge of the chemistry content.

Cooperative labs

Lab roles (facilitator, reader, editor, and resource person) involved facilitating, rather than doing, each task. The "reader," for example, coached teammates' close reading of procedural and informational texts associated with the lab investigation and facilitated discussion—but team members shared responsibility for reading and making sense of the material.

Inquiry

To apprentice students to the inquiry thinking and reasoning at the heart of science, Will started the year focused on developing habits of observing and questioning. He helped students acquire a language for identifying common types of science questions (attention focusing, measuring and counting, comparing, action prompting, problem posing, values reasoning) and coached his students to see the connection between these question types and the types of inquiry that would be needed to answer them (Raphael & McKinney, 1983). The spirit of inquiry was a common thread binding literacy and science in the classroom.

discussion of summaries, for example, when Eduardo declined to share, saying his idea was similar to what a classmate had already said, Will asked him to share anyway, explaining, "It's important to hear different voices." By mid-October, with Will's mentoring, Eduardo was making more substantive contributions to discussions, even volunteering to be the spokesperson for his team's expert group report.

During group work, Will was careful to focus on Eduardo's potential contribution to his team rather than on any misconduct. Will coupled his expectations for Eduardo's participation with the support necessary to ensure Eduardo's success as a group member. During an expert group activity in mid-October, Will asked an idle Eduardo, "How are you contributing to the group?" When Eduardo explained that he didn't have a book because of a library fine, Will talked with him about coming in at lunch until he could get a book of his own. Will's focus on solving the problem that impeded Eduardo's participation rather than laying blame softened Eduardo's resistance. The following day, Eduardo came to class on time, took his assigned seat and announced to Will that he took off his hat—signaling a new willingness to participate. When his team made their expert group report to the class, Eduardo assumed the role of spokesperson.

In the ensuing weeks, frequent metacognitive conversations provided ongoing opportunities for the class to explore social, personal, and cognitive aspects of reading and doing science. During these conversations, Eduardo expressed concern that the material was too hard, and Will expressed confidence in Eduardo's capabilities. Will shared strategies he used to make science reading more interesting and comprehensible and had students discuss what was easy, hard, interesting, and confusing for them. The realization that reading science requires more effort from everyone, including expert readers like Will, along with metacognitive reading routines, helped Eduardo identify and address his confusions and increase his confidence.

Metacognitive conversations surfaced Eduardo's conceptions of schooling and what it meant to be a good student—conceptions that worked against his success—and put them on the table for negotiation. At the beginning of the year, when Eduardo learned that students could use their reading logs during tests, he snapped, "That's cheating." Metacognitive conversations challenged Eduardo's conception of reading proficiency as a fixed trait and helped him see that even good readers improve with practice and collaboration. Gradually, Eduardo came to see reading as a tool for learning, rather than as an exam for separating good students from bad. He came to value collaboration, both benefiting from and contributing to his classmates' learning.

Eduardo became increasingly willing to take risks as a reader and learner. In late October, despite complaining that an upcoming lab was "too hard," Eduardo participated and found the lab doable, as Will had predicted. When Eduardo completed his lab report early, Will, leveraging Eduardo's increasing confidence, gave him a related reading assignment from the textbook, modeling how to use the "I Saw/I Thought" metacognitive reading log. Although the double entry reading log was a well-established classroom routine, Eduardo had neglected his log assignments and was not yet proficient in its use. Eduardo read his textbook for the duration of the class, making notes in his log. The following week, during expert group reports on the lab, Eduardo was conspicuously engaged, serving as spokesperson for his group. He expressed interest in others' reports, asking one group a sophisticated question about measurement. When Will polled the class about who had their reading logs to use for a class discussion, only Eduardo had his. As he was leaving class, Eduardo asked Will for permission to take home his reading log, despite the fact that there was no assigned reading. He insisted, "I want to read tonight."

Will's grading policy, which awarded up to 80% credit for late assignments, was also instrumental in Eduardo's transformation. By allowing students to make up late work, the policy held students to high standards but did not undermine the motivation of students, like Eduardo, who got off to a bad start.

Winter: Gaining Momentum

Seeing his efforts pay off was a crucial factor in Eduardo's turnaround. In late November, this young man, who claimed a few months earlier not to care whether he failed, sang aloud after getting back a corrected test: "I got a B, and I'm so happy!" The following week, when Will consulted his grade book about Eduardo's grade, Will told Eduardo, "You're right on the border." In fact, despite making considerable progress, Eduardo ended up with a D during the first marking period due to missing assignments.

Despite his low grade, Eduardo's new identity as a student had taken root. During the first semester, Eduardo's progress appeared primarily in the form of increased engagement— a willingness to participate in classroom routines—with little corresponding progress in completing assignments. He showed signs of a new resolve, but this resolve was fragile and erratic. Eduardo continued to complain that the material was too difficult throughout the first semester. However, following the winter break, Eduardo emerged as an agent of his own learning with his focus clearly on chemistry. He was frequently the first student in the room and was often finished with his preamble before his classmates settled down. In January, when Eduardo was confused about what happened in a lab, rather than dismissing the lab as "too hard," he concluded that he needed to learn more about acids. With the introduction of Team Reads in January, Eduardo was able to work through an article on acids and bases, puzzling out the meaning of such technical words as *calorimetric* by examining its component parts.

With Will's guidance and encouragement, Eduardo practiced a variety of cognitive strategies, from questioning to clarifying. Reading in the article that "any acid will react with any base," he wondered, "Is that true?" He accurately explained the concept "driving force," to Will's apparent surprise. Although Eduardo and his teammates sometimes failed to notice what they didn't understand, and their summaries tended to identify the topic rather than capture the gist of the passage, Team Reads helped Eduardo gain access to text that would have prompted passive resistance—or outright defiance—just months before.

As Eduardo gained confidence and expertise as a reader, Will also encouraged him to use disciplinary language to describe his own thinking more precisely. During a lesson on summarizing, Will asked the class, "What is the important idea that keeps coming up [in this passage]?" When Eduardo responded, "The things about acids and bases," Will prompted, "[Can you use] another word?" Eduardo amended his response: "Properties." The following day, Will highlighted the importance of Eduardo's contribution of "finding the word *properties*" during a recap of the previous day's lesson. Eduardo also showed increasing interest in chemistry for its own sake. He chatted informally with Will, asking questions about chemistry—even when they weren't on the exam—and did extra reading for homework.

Spring: Traveling Companions

Will continued to mentor Eduardo in negotiating the demands of school. When Eduardo confided one day that he was tired, Will advised him, "Just work slow and steady when you're tired." Later in the period, Eduardo expressed surprise when he solved a problem about molecules and smells correctly. Will responded confidently, "Of course!"

Will also increasingly challenged Eduardo to think in discipline-based ways. During a preamble about smells, Will probed for the rationale behind Eduardo's prediction that two molecules with similar molecular formulas would smell similar, and encouraged Eduardo to evaluate differences between the molecules systematically. Will invited a teammate, Samuel, into the discussion and noted, "We have two different ideas that are both good ones."

Overcoming his initial resistance to working with others, Eduardo's collaboration with his teammate, Samuel, deepened over the year. While Samuel served as Eduardo's tutor initially, coaching him on how to study for quizzes and do his reading log, by the end of the year, Eduardo and Samuel interacted as equals. In May, during an exploration of the relationship between molecular characteristics and smell, Will, pausing in his rounds as itinerant mentor, pointed out to Eduardo's group, "These molecules have almost the same formula so that doesn't help. So there's something about the structure." Samuel suggested, "Hexagons." Will pointed to something that violated Samuel's theory that the hexagonal shape of the molecules accounted for their smell, "These are hexagons too, but they have what?" Eduardo noted, "Carbons on the inside." Will affirmed, "Carbons on the inside!" According to the teacher's guide, students rarely observed this relationship on their own. Eduardo was the first student in Will's class to draw this inference.

Eduardo also emerged as a leader among his peers. Eduardo admonished others for their tardiness, was intolerant of frivolity (except when he himself enjoyed an occasional lapse), and encouraged classmates' participation in class discussion. In assuming this role, Eduardo frequently appropriated Will's supportive language, showing a special affection for Will's characterization of the class as "bright young students." During a preamble discussion on Lewis dot structure, for example, Eduardo took a lead role, volunteering his solution and encouraging a classmate—whom he inveigled as a "bright young thing"—to do the same. In addition to getting his own problem right, Eduardo suggested corrections to his classmate's solution.

In April, as students worked on incomplete assignments, Will asked

Eduardo to tutor Seth, who had been absent. He explained to Eduardo, "You'll become a super expert." Indeed, in the course of tutoring Seth, Eduardo used the periodic table, his reading log, and other handouts and papers to explain how to figure out the number of bonds. Eduardo's efforts were successful. At end of the period, Eduardo told Will proudly, "Seth's got it," and Seth told another classmate, "I thought that was hard [before Eduardo taught him how]." Eduardo suggested to Seth that he ask Will for a periodic table so that he could finish the assignment at home, offering, "Come tomorrow and I'll help you."

Eduardo Looks Back

Will's actions and, through Will's influence, the actions of classmates carried individual students through the many challenges of negotiating the unfamiliar language and literacy practices of science. In an end-of-year interview, Eduardo articulated how Will's ongoing support and the collaborative learning environment he created turned him around academically.

> "I went to Dr. Brown, you know, and I seen that he cared for my grades and helping me out. When he told me I can get my grades up, I tried it and I seen it go up, so then I thought, from there on I said, you know, 'If I can do that, I might as well try harder.' And I started trying harder in school, in all my classes. . . . He just told me, 'Come, second lunch,' you know, 'and we'll talk it out.' Then we did labs I missed and it got my grade up. Dr. Brown made me realize you can [catch up]. So I thank him a lot.
>
> "Then Samuel [a teammate] helped me. I seen him, you know, working on this in class, on the labs. And since he was my partner for the whole year, he helped me out. We had some quiz, and the day before, he gave me a little sheet and he told me, you know, 'Just study this and you should get a good grade, just study.' And I started doing the preambles and he helped me out when I didn't understand it. . . . When I got my quiz back, I seen I got an A, I thanked him, and from there on, just started working hard."

When asked if there had been particular things Dr. Brown had done that year to support his reading of chemistry, Eduardo responded:

> "When I had my first [reading log] and I tried it, you know, I did it with [my teammate] Samuel in class, you know. And he helped me realize it wasn't hard, you know. And one day, I came during lunch and Dr. Brown helped me with what you're supposed to do, so from there, from both of their help, you know, I tried it at home and it came out. I got an A on it, you know."

Eduardo also expressed his preference for reading science: "You know, I rather read this than the English book. See, science seems interesting to me, so, you know, so I like to read."

Afterward: Traveling Solo

Eduardo repeated the first semester of Introduction to Chemistry as a senior to make up for the D he had received then in Will's class and continued to make progress begun that spring. His new chemistry teacher had him tutor classmates. Eduardo graduated on schedule and planned to attend community college en route toward his goal of becoming an engineer.

NEGOTIATING SUCCESS

The Reading Apprenticeship framework provided a starting point for our investigation into how teachers like Will Brown supported underprepared and underachieving students to see themselves as readers, thinkers, and students. Negotiating success emerged from our inductive analysis as a construct with the potential to explain the growth we witnessed in some classrooms in students' identities as readers and learners.

Will was fiercely committed to educational equity and worked with administrators and colleagues to implement structural and curricular reforms that promoted this goal. Yet we found that it was classroom pedagogy that determined whether such structural and curricular reforms were successful. Will explicitly encouraged students to make up missing assignments and implemented policies that rewarded students for doing so. Indeed, it was never too late to complete assignments in Will's class, and one student, who had virtually dropped out of school, continued to attend Introduction to Chemistry, working hard through the very last day of class to complete missing assignments and pass the course.

Policies and practices that valued learning over accountability were a salient feature of Will's classroom, where seemingly intransigent students made unexpected progress. By focusing a spotlight on student effort and improvement, encouraging students to remain engaged in the face of challenges, and ensuring that effort paid off, Will's classroom practices demonstrated a malleable theory of achievement, in which academic performance is believed to develop and change through a person's efforts (Molden & Dweck, 2006). Research has linked this explanation to a wide range of positive academic behaviors and mindsets. Table 17.2 summarizes key features of "negotiating success" with underprepared students.

Key elements of the Reading Apprenticeship framework—ongoing literacy learning opportunities, explicit strategies instruction, collaborative learning structures, and metacognitive inquiry into reading and

TABLE 17.2. Key Features of Classroom Practices That Negotiate Success with Adolescents

- *Classroom policies, norms, and assessments value learning rather than accountability.* The heart of negotiating success is ongoing formative assessment as embodied by the Latin *ad sedere*, meaning "to sit down beside." As its etymology implies, assessment is primarily used as a tool for providing guidance and feedback to students and to inform instructional decision making. For teachers who engage students in negotiating success, instructional decision making is guided by the question: "Will this encourage or discourage this student from investing him- or herself in the learning process?"

- *Teachers interpret student behavior generously, assuming all students want to learn.* Teachers assume that all students can and want to achieve to high standards and seize on any glimmer of student interest or disciplinary thinking—no matter how small or awkwardly expressed—as an opportunity to increase engagement and learning. This approach to elaborating on students' nascent instructionally focused thinking is akin to the powerful language facilitation strategy of responding to the intent rather than the form of children's speech with slightly more information or in a more sophisticated way (e.g., Whitehurst et al., 1988).

- *Teachers establish positive relationships with students strategically, to leverage learning.* Caring teacher–student relationships are used as a lever for raising student achievement. Although teachers often make themselves available to students at lunch and after school, positive teacher–student relationships develop in the context of the classroom, rather than through extracurricular contact, and are inclusive of all students in the class. Knowledge of individual student interests and acknowledgement of individual student contributions is used to foster academic engagement.

- *Teachers establish metacognitive conversation to bring students' resources, knowledge, and even misconceptions into the classroom.* Classroom discourse routines and structures provide opportunities for students to bring conceptions of reading, learning, and school that do and do not serve them well into the classroom where they can be acknowledged and influenced by the teacher and classmates. Ongoing conversations about problem-solving processes allow teachers to access, mentor, and guide student thinking and reading processes.

- *Teachers provide frequent opportunities and support for in-class reading, writing, and talk.* The *success* in negotiating success is measured by students taking on more powerful identities as readers and students and, ultimately, achieving to high levels of academic literacy. Frequent opportunities for in-class, teacher-, and peer-supported reading, writing, and talk help students to negotiate academic language and texts. Literacy routines engage students in complex discipline-based literacy and support them in gaining proficiency and capacity in academic reading and discourse.

- *Intelligence and performance are seen as malleable factors.* Instruction spotlights student effort and improvement, encourages students to remain engaged in the face of challenges, and ensures that effort pays off. Classroom policies, norms, and assessments demonstrate a malleable theory of intelligence and achievement in which academic performance is seen to develop and change through a person's efforts (Molden & Dweck, 2006).

learning—set the stage for instruction to foster academic achievement. Yet without classroom interactions that foreground student capabilities and reward effort toward learning, students may make little progress over the difficult terrain of high academic challenge. In order to benefit from high-quality curriculum and instruction, students must avail themselves of these learning opportunities. Will supported students' investment in the rich literacy and science learning opportunities in Introduction to Chemistry by filtering his interactions, classroom policies, instructional moves and decisions though a single criterion: "Will this encourage or discourage this student from investing him- or herself in the learning process?"

Negotiating success thus encompasses a broad range of classroom practices that position the teacher as a partner in a negotiation on behalf of students who may neither appreciate nor desire such advocacy. In negotiating success, teachers must navigate a course between support and challenge, and making headway requires insight, patience, flexibility, and generosity.

LEARNER DISPOSITIONS

Until recently, learner dispositions, such as tolerating ambiguity and demonstrating determination to succeed in the face of difficulty, were seen as fixed attributes of character (Dweck, 2008; Dweck et al., 2011). Consequently, in many content-area classrooms, typical instructional strategies for struggling readers involved simplifying, slowing the pace, and abandoning more rigorous coursework with the tacit understanding that the students were not capable of performing at grade-appropriate levels of rigor. Students held beliefs about their own efficacy and the degree to which they could control their educational outcomes, and these beliefs and dispositions affected the effort they would expend on learning tasks (Farrington et al., 2012). In the past few years, however, the role of learners' dispositions in mediating student engagement and achievement has become increasingly understood to be malleable to instruction (Yeager & Walton, 2011). Students can gain self-efficacy and determination, learn to tolerate ambiguity, increase their stamina and stick-to-itiveness, and increase their valuing and enjoyment of academic work (Dweck, 2008; Moje, 2008; Schoenbach & Greenleaf, 2009). Achieving the high-level literacy envisioned in the CCSS may depend on identifying instructional approaches that foster such academic mindsets (Farrington et al., 2012). Engaging students in learning the practices of science as described in the new NRC standards (2012) means fostering new dispositions toward science knowledge as a product of intellectual and collaborative inquiry and argumentation.

In this reform context, it is important to note that many students who have reached middle school or high school with little experience of academic success have established identities as nonstudents or nonreaders.

These negative reader identities coexist with multiple other identities in both students' in-school and out-of-school lives. Most adolescents need support to develop key dispositions for approaching and engaging themselves in challenging academic tasks. These include general dispositions to be interested and critical learners—such as curiosity, tolerance for ambiguity, and the habit of mind to construct understanding—or the expectation that one should be constructing understanding of a topic—rather than passively carrying out the prescribed procedures (Bloome, Puro, & Theodorou, 1989; Gutiérrez, Baquedana-López, & Asato, 2000; Hall, 2010; Jiménez-Aleixandre, Rodríguez, & Duschl, 2000; Rex, 2001; Rymes & Pash, 2001; Schoenbach & Greenleaf, 2009; Yore, 2004). Such dispositions also include the ways students can maintain confidence in the value of persistence and in their own abilities, even while struggling through challenging academic texts and tasks (Farrington et al., 2012).

A critical and often unacknowledged part of supporting adolescents' literacy development involves helping them transform identities of nonreader and nonlearner, formed in response to negative experiences in school (Gee, 1996; Mahiri & Godley, 1998). As adolescents explore possible selves, teachers can encourage them to try on new reader identities, to explore and expand their visions of who they are and can become (Davidson & Koppenhaver, 1993; Kanno & Norton, 2003). This is critical if students are to embrace literacy, re-engage as readers, and improve their academic performance. Feldman (2004) reminds us that "learning not only changes what we know and do, but it changes who we are" (p. 144). When we ask students to learn something new, we are asking them to become someone new. When teachers provide consistent support for students to try on new ways of acting, thinking, and interacting, we see significant shifts in academic identity over an academic year.

CONCLUSION

In this chapter, we described how one teacher's willingness and ability to provide learning opportunities that illuminated students' conceptions of reading, reading practices, and identities as reader and student, to investigate and interpret students' thinking processes and learning experiences, and to design and modify instruction and support based on this assessment of student need—a stance that we have labeled "negotiating success"—was a key factor in supporting one underprepared student to shift his identity as a reader and student. We believe the practices Will demonstrated in negotiating success for and with Eduardo offer a set of instructional approaches that foster learner dispositions students will need to tackle higher-level literacy with complex text, particularly when they are inexperienced with such tasks as is the case with so many students in our secondary schools. By offering the construct of "negotiating success," we hope to contribute to efforts to better understand how teachers might translate their commitment to equity into classroom practices that help all students achieve high levels of academic literacy. Moreover, we hope to move the discussion of adolescent literacy development beyond a focus on school structures and instructional strategies toward the quality of interactions in classrooms that support and foster new and more resilient learner identities.

DISCUSSION AND ACTIVITIES

1. Observe in a secondary classroom. Analyze teacher–student interactions using the key features of classroom practices that negotiate success with adolescents. Identify opportunities—both taken and missed—for the teacher to negotiate success with students. For each missed opportunity, generate an alternative response that sets the stage for negotiating success.

2. Interview a teacher about classroom policies, norms, and assessments. What are the underlying assumptions about students behind these policies, norms, and assessments? Analyze ways these policies support or undermine opportunities to negotiate success with adolescents.

3. Develop a grading policy that rewards learning rather than compliance. Consider what such a grading policy will demand of the classroom teacher.

4. Look back through Eduardo's development as a reader and learner in this class. What do the metacognitive conversations documented through field notes reveal about his capacities and resources? Consider how to structure ongoing classroom conversation to create ongoing opportunities for assessment of student motivations, interests, stamina, *and* knowledge and skill. Create a set of sentence stems for a teacher to use to support a stance of inquiry and negotiate success with learners in the classroom.

5. Interview one or more adolescents about their conceptions of reading, learning, and school (if possible, choose students who are not faring well in class). (1) Probe students' early reading experiences and current in- and outside of school reading habits and preferences, (2) ask students for their self-assessment and goals as a reader, and (3) solicit students' advice about what teachers could do to make reading assignments better for students and help students become better readers. Analyze responses to identify students' conceptions of reading, learning, and school and of themselves as readers and students, including students' beliefs about the malleability or stability of reading ability and achievement.

6. Negotiating success has profound implications for teacher–student interactions. What implications does negotiating success have for curriculum and instruction (e.g., pacing, participation structures, teacher's role)?

REFERENCES

ACT. (2005). *On course for success: A close look at selected high school courses that prepare all students for college.* Iowa City, IA: Author.

ACT. (2006). *Reading between the lines.* Iowa City, IA: Author.

Bloome, D., Puro, P., & Theodorou, E. (1989). Procedural display and classroom lessons. *Curriculum Inquiry, 19*(3), 265–291.

Carnegie Council on Advancing Adolescent Literacy. (2010). *Time to act: An agenda for advancing adolescent literacy for college and career success.* New York: Carnegie Corporation of New York.

Corbin, J., & Strauss, A. (1990). Grounded theory research: Procedures, canons and evaluative criteria. *Zeitschrift fur Soziologie, 19*(6), 418–427.

Davidson, J., & Koppenhaver, D. (1993). *Adolescent literacy: What works and why* (2nd ed.). New York: Garland.

Delpit, L. D. (1995). *Other people's children: Cultural conflict in the classroom.* New York: New Press.

Duschl, R. A., Schweingruber, H. A., & Shouse, A. W. (Eds.). (2006). *Taking science to school: Learning and teaching science in grades K–8.* Washington, DC: The National Academies Press.

Dweck, C. (2008). Can personality be changed? The role of beliefs in personality and change. *Current Directions in Psychological Science, 17*(6), 391–394.

Dweck, C., Walton, G. M., & Cohen, G. L. (2011). *Academic tenacity: Mindsets and skills that promote long-term learning* (White paper prepared for the Gates Foundation). Seattle, WA.

Farrington, C. A., Roderick, M., Allensworth, E., Nagaoka, J., Keyes, T.S., Johnson, D. W., et al. (2012). *Teaching adolescents to become learners. The role of noncognitive factors in shaping school performance: A critical literature review.* Chicago: University of Chicago Consortium on Chicago School Research.

Feldman, A. (2004). Knowing and being in science: Expanding the possibilities. In E. W. Saul (Ed.), *Crossing borders in literacy and science instruction: Perspectives on theory and practice.* Newark, DE: International Reading Association.

Freedman, S. W., Flower, L., Hull, G., & Hayes, J. R. (1995). *Ten years of research: Achievements of the National Center for the Study of Writing and Literacy. Technical report No. 1-C.* Berkeley, CA: National Center for the Study of Writing.

Garmezy, N. (1983). Stressors of childhood. In N. Garmezy & M. Rutter (Eds.), *Stress, coping, and development in children* (pp. 43-84). New York: McGraw-Hill.

Gee, J. (1996). *Social linguistics and literacies: Ideology in discourses* (2nd ed.). London: Falmer Press.

Greenleaf, C., Brown, W., & Litman, C. (2004). Apprenticing urban youth to science literacy. In D. Strickland & D. Alvermann (Eds.), *Bridging the gap: Improving literacy learning for preadolescent and adolescent learners in grades 4–12* (pp. 200–226). Newark, DE: International Reading Association.

Greenleaf, C., & Litman, C. (2011, November). *Negotiating identity and achievement in the eleventh hour: Designing inclusive spaces for literacy growth in secondary classrooms.* Paper presented at the annual meeting of the Literacy Research Association, Jacksonville, FL.

Gutiérrez, K. D., Baquedano-López, P., & Asato, J. (2000). "English for the children": The new literacy of the old world order, language policy and educational reform. *Bilingual Research Journal, 24*(1–2), 87–112.

Hall, L. A. (2010). The negative consequences of becoming a good reader: Identity theory as a lens for understanding struggling readers, teachers and reading instruction. *Teachers College Record, 112*(7), 1792–1829.

Jiménez-Aleixandre, M. P., Rodríguez, A. B., & Duschl, R. A. (2000). "Doing the lesson" or "doing science": Argument in high school genetics. *Science Education, 84*(6), 757–792.

Kanno, Y., & Norton, B. (2003). Imagined communities and educational possibilities: Introduction. *Journal of Language, Identity, and Education, 2*(4), 241–249.

Lee, C. D., & Spratley, A. (2010). *Reading in the disciplines: The challenges of adolescent literacy.* New York: Carnegie Corporation of New York.

Lemke, J. L. (2006). Towards critical multimedia literacy: Technology, research, and politics. In M. G. McKenna, L. D. Labbo, R. D. Keiffer, & D. Reinking (Eds.), International handbook of literacy and technology (Vol. II, pp. 3–14). Hillsdale, NJ: Erlbaum.

Mahiri, J., & Godley, A. (1998). Rewriting identity: Social meanings of literacy and "re-visions" of self. *Reading Research Quarterly, 33*(4), 416–433.

Moje, E. B. (2008). Foregrounding the disciplines in secondary literacy teaching and learning: A call for change. *Journal of Adolescent and Adult Literacy, 52*(2), 96–107.

Molden, D. C., & Dweck, C. S. (2006). Finding "meaning" in psychology: A lay theories approach to self-regulation, social perception, and social development. *American Psychologist, 61*, 192–203.

National Committee on Science Education Standards and Assessment/ National Research Council. (1996). *National Science Education Standards.* Retrieved from *www.nap.edu/catalog/4962.html.*

National Governors Association Center for Best Practices & National Council of Chief State School Officers. (2010). *Common Core Standards for English Language Arts and Literacy in History/Social Studies and Science.* Washington, DC: Author. Retrieved from *www.corestandards.org/ Standards/K12.*

National Research Council. (2012). *A framework for K–12 science education: Practices, crosscutting concepts, and core ideas.* Washington, DC: The National Academies Press.

Newell, G. E., Beach, R., Smith, J., & VanDerHeide, J. (2011). Teaching and learning argumentative reading and writing: A review of research. *Reading Research Quarterly, 46*(3), 273–304.

Ogle, D. M. (1986). KWL: A teaching model that develops active reading of expository text. *The Reading Teacher, 39*(6), 564-570.

Osborne, J. F. (2002). Science without literacy: A ship without a sail? *Cambridge Journal of Education, 32*(2), 203–215.

Palinscar, A. S., & Brown, A. L. (1984). Reciprocal teaching of comprehension-fostering and comprehension-monitoring activities. *Cognition and instruction, 1*(2), 117-175.

Pearson, P. D., Moje, E., & Greenleaf, C. (2010). Literacy and science: Each in the service of the other. *Science, 328*, 459–463.

Raphael, T. E., & McKinney, J. (1983). An examination of fifth-and eighth-grade children's question-answering behavior: An instructional study in metacognition. *Journal of Literacy Research, 15*(3), 67-86.

Rex, L. (2001). Remaking of a high school reader. *Reading Research Quarterly, 36*(3), 288–313.

Rymes, B., & Pash, D. (2001). Questioning identity: The case of one second-language learner. *Anthropology and Education Quarterly, 32*(3), 276–300.

Schoenbach, R., Braunger, J., Greenleaf, C., & Litman, C. (2003). Apprenticing adolescents to reading in subject-area classrooms. *Phi Delta Kappan, 85*(2), 133–138.

Schoenbach, R., & Greenleaf, C. (2009). Fostering adolescents' engaged academic literacy. In L. Christenbury, R. Bomer, & P. Smagorinsky (Eds.), *Handbook of adolescent literacy research* (pp. 98–112). New York: Guilford Press.

Schoenbach, R., Greenleaf, C., & Murphy, L. (2012). *Reading for understanding: How reading apprenticeship improves disciplinary learning in secondary and college classrooms* (2nd ed.). San Francisco: Jossey-Bass.

Scribner, S., & Cole, M. (1981). *The psychology of literacy.* Cambridge, MA: Harvard University Press.

Shanahan, T., & Shanahan, C. (2008). Teaching disciplinary literacy to adolescents: Rethinking content-area literacy. *Harvard Educational Review, 78*(1), 40–59.

Smagorinsky, P. (2009). The cultural practice of reading and the standardized assessment of reading instruction: When incommensurate worlds collide, *Educational Researcher, 38*(7), 522–527.

Street, B. (1995). *Social literacies: Critical approaches to literacy in development, ethnography and education.* London: Longman.

Walsh, F. (2002). A family resilience framework: Innovative practice applications. *Family Relations, 51*, 130–137.

Weiss, I.R., Pasley, J.D., Smith, S., Banilower, E.R., & Heck, D.J. (May 2003). *Looking inside the classroom: A study of K–12 mathematics and science education in the United States.* Retrieved from *www.horizon-research.com.*

Whitehurst, G. J., Falco, F. L., Lonigan, C. J., Fischel, J. E., DeBaryshe, B. D., Valdez-Menchaca, M. C., et al. (1988). Accelerating language development through picture book reading. *Developmental Psychology*, *24*(4), 552.

Yeager, D. S., & Walton, G. M. (2011). Social-psychological interventions in education: They're not magic. *Review of Educational Research*, *81*(2), 267–301.

Yore, L. D. (2004). Why do future scientists need to study the language arts? In E.W. Saul (Ed.), *Crossing borders in literacy and science instruction: Perspectives on theory and practice* (pp. 71–94). Newark, DE: International Reading Association.

CHAPTER 18

Differentiating Literacy Instruction for Adolescents

Zaline Roy-Campbell
Kelly Chandler-Olcott

In this chapter, we:

- Define differentiated literacy instruction.

- Consider the affordances and challenges of the Common Core State Standards for differentiated literacy instruction.

- Describe three models for conceptualizing differentiated literacy instruction.

- Describe a classroom where the teacher enacts the vision of the Common Core State Standards through differentiated literacy instruction.

Adolescent students in the United States represent a spectrum of cultural, socioeconomic, ethnic, and linguistic backgrounds and possess varied strengths, what Moll and Greenberg (1990) call funds of knowledge, derived from their out-of-school experiences. These differences influence how they process and communicate information, as well as interact with others. For educators who acknowledge that one size does not fit all, the challenge is to design literacy instruction to expand students' funds of knowledge while addressing diverse learning needs.

This chapter elaborates on what we mean by differentiated literacy instruction and offers three lenses for conceptualizing it: multiple intelligences, universal design for learning, and the sheltered instruction observation protocol. We then consider the affordances and challenges of the Common Core State Standards (CCSS) for differentiating literacy instruction. To illustrate what such instruction might look like, we describe a secondary English classroom where the teacher has committed to enacting the vision of the CCSS while honoring and addressing her students' diverse learning needs.

DEFINING DIFFERENTIATED INSTRUCTION

In this chapter, we define *differentiated literacy instruction* as the pedagogical responses teachers make to learner differences that they "encounter day by day and moment by moment" (Roe, 2010, p. 141), for the purpose of supporting all learners in the mastery of common literacy standards. We use "instruction" to describe a number of related constructs, including curriculum development, lesson planning, instructional delivery, and assessment. As Table 18.1 reveals, we see differentiated literacy instruction as a perspective, not a set of approaches to be adopted. Teachers working from such a perspective adjust for learner differences on numerous levels:

- For different sections of the same class (e.g., building in more time for partner talk prior to whole-class discussion in Period 2, which includes a higher percentage of English language learners [ELLs], than in Period 9).
- For groups of learners with similar needs (e.g., preteaching key vocabulary to several struggling readers before viewing a documentary while the rest of the class completes the previous task).
- For individual learners (e.g., offering a student with fine-motor difficulties access to a computer for word processing).

In our view, differentiating literacy instruction does not simply mean using a variety of teaching strategies over time, just for variety's sake. Our conception, like Nunley's (2006), is standards driven: We believe that differentiated literacy instruction should offer "a variety of instructional strategies for the same specific objective" (p. 11), enabling all students to meet that objective.

Tomlinson (1999) has articulated a framework for differentiation that encompasses four areas of modification: content (what students learn), process (how they learn), product (how learning will be demonstrated), and assessment (how learning will be evaluated). In addition, she argues that teachers should differentiate to address students' (1) readiness, (2) interests, and (3) learning styles. As she points out, differentiated instruction requires both careful planning and a clear sense of learning goals: "We have to know where we want to end up before we start out and plan to get there" (p. 12). One way of viewing differentiation is to consider a group of

TABLE 18.1. Differentiation Comparisons

Differentiation is . . .	Differentiation is not . .
• The how: pedagogical format	• The what: The content of instruction
• Different routes to the same objectives	• Different content according to students' abilities
• Different means of accessing the same content	• A strategy to be implemented
• Way of thinking about instruction	• What a teacher does when she/he has time
• Providing choices based on interests	• Individualized learning plans for students
• Providing lessons that cater to multiple learning styles	• An afterthought

students headed to the same event. The athletically inclined may choose to run; others may ride a bicycle. Those with access to a car may drive; others may ride the bus. Some may walk. Those who are mobility impaired may need assistance from others. They should all reach that same destination, although clearly not at the same time or via the same means.

DIFFERENTIATED INSTRUCTION IN THE AGE OF CCSS

To extend the journey metaphor further, the CCSS can be seen as the destination. The teacher's challenge is to help all students become college and career ready by the end of high school. Currently adopted by 45 states and the District of Columbia, the CCSS are divided into four strands—reading, writing, listening and speaking, and language skills—each of which outlines a cumulative learning progression, K–12. Although the purpose of these standards and the process used to devise them are open to critique (Calkins, Lehrenworth, & Lehman, 2012), they do provide a national framework for developing school literacy skills. In past years, when each state had its own standards, some students completed school (or worse, dropped out) with less developed literacies than others, with often-predictable inequities linked to social class, race, language, and ability. What we like most is that the CCSS enjoin teachers to have high expectations for all students and to assume that they can all reach the same destination. The document states that while it is "beyond the scope of the Standards to define the full range of supports appropriate for English language learners and for students with special needs," nonetheless "all students must have the opportunity to learn and meet the same high standards if they are to access the knowledge and skills necessary in their post–high school lives" (National Governors Association Center for Best Practices & Council of Chief State School Officers, 2010, p. 6).

If one accepts the CCSS as a desirable destination, one must also acknowledge that these standards cannot be attained without differentiated literacy instruction. We contend that teachers *must* differentiate to ensure that all students can meet these standards. Without a conceptual framework for such accommodations, as well as a repertoire of approaches for doing so, it is difficult to blame teachers who see the goal of college and career readiness for heterogeneous populations as a daunting, even impossible, task. It seems likely that some practitioners may resort to the view that the CCSS may be fine for some students but not all, a perspective with the potential to exacerbate educational inequities.

MODELS FOR DIFFERENTIATING LITERACY INSTRUCTION

Fortunately, teachers can draw on a variety of conceptual frameworks to help them differentiate literacy instruction and achieve the CCSS promise. In this section we discuss three: multiple intelligences (MI), universal design for learning (UDL), and the sheltered instruction observation protocol (SIOP). Although none of these three approaches has been studied extensively with research designs that meet What Works Clearinghouse (WWC) evidence standards, they have been implemented widely and shown to be useful through investigations using other designs. In selecting these frameworks, we considered one that recognizes differences that all students bring to the learning environment (MI), another typically associated with inclusion of students with disabilities in the general education classroom (UDL), and a third that was developed to address the needs of ELLs in the content areas (SIOP). In the next section, we describe how each framework can enrich all students' learning in classrooms organized around the CCSS.

Multiple Intelligences

One means of differentiating classroom instruction is to identify students' strengths and the ways they learn best, then to provide instructional activities that incorporate them. While some students can more readily access knowledge from reading or listening, others need visuals or hands-on experiences. The theory of multiple intelligences (Gardner, 1999) couples perceptual learning styles—visual, auditory, and kinesthetic—with various ways that students process information. It synthesizes contributions from brain research and studies of literacy acquisition (Sousa, 2001). It supplants the idea of a unitary, measurable intelligence with the proposition of nine complementary spheres in which students can manifest intelligence: verbal–linguistic, bodily–kinesthetic, visual–spatial, musical, logical–mathematical, intrapersonal, interpersonal, naturalistic, and existential (Gardner,

1999). This framework caters to the diverse body of students, including those identified with disabilities and as ELLs.

Although literacy has traditionally drawn upon verbal–linguistic intelligence, Armstrong (2003) describes how multiple intelligences are implicated in reading and writing processes:

> As [a child] reads meaningful information, she may visualize what she reads (*spatial intelligence*), experience herself actively engaged in a physical way in the text (*bodily–kinesthetic intelligence*), have emotional reactions to the material (*intrapersonal intelligence*), attempt to guess what the author or characters intend or believe (*interpersonal intelligence*), and think critically and logically about what she is reading (*logical–mathematical intelligence*). . . . In each of these cases our reader is bringing to bear different intelligences upon the multilayered processes of reading and writing. (pp. 19–20)

Highlighting language processing challenges, he notes:

> Some students have particular problems with the visual configuration of letters . . . , while others encounter difficulties primarily with the sounds of the language. . . . Other students can decode individual words but encounter obstacles in comprehending whole text. Some individuals have problems primarily with the underlying grammatical–logical structures of sentences. Others have difficulties visualizing what they have read, or understanding what the author's intent may be. (p. 20)

Armstrong poses a central question: "whether we as educators are going to teach literacy skills in such a way that the words lie dead there on the page for so many students" or "whether we're going to take positive steps towards the ultimate goal of *making the words come alive for all students*" (p. 21, emphasis original).

To address Armstrong's challenge, teachers need to tap different intelligences when delivering instruction and provide choices for students to demonstrate learning. After reading a text, students can role play, create a visual image, discuss how they think the characters feel about what transpires in the text, or represent their understanding through music. Recognizing that some students prefer working independently while others learn best through peer interaction, teachers can provide opportunities for flexible grouping as well as individualized work.

Universal Design for Learning

UDL, also grounded in brain research as well as in theories of individual differences (Center for Applied Special Technology [CAST], 2011), is an educational approach for teaching all students. Originally developed for students with physical and cognitive disabilities, it has morphed into a framework enabling teachers to create instructional goals, methods, materials, and assessments promoting high expectations for all learners. It draws on three primary brain networks—recognition (what), strategic (how), and affective (why)—by utilizing three key principles: (1) multiple means of representation, (2) multiple means of action and expression, and (3) multiple means of engagement (Rose & Meyer, 2002).

A key focus of UDL is to integrate technology and media with sound instructional strategies and curricula in order to create customizable learning experiences (Hall, Meyer, & Rose, 2012). Students listen to texts via audiobooks, read-alouds, or the text-to-speech function on digital devices, and they write, keyboard, or audio-record expressions of learning. They work with visual representations to promote understanding and help them connect their cultural backgrounds to new learning (Proctor, Dalton, & Grisham, 2007).

Although the idea of "universal" implies that one size fits all, UDL is premised on the view that designing instruction for diverse learning needs creates better outcomes for all students. For example, in teaching a short story, teachers may begin by activating students' background and cultural knowledge through questions and visuals related to the story's context. They may then conduct a read-aloud of part of the story, highlighting key vocabulary and utilizing interactive visuals (including sign language and/or bilingual texts or glossaries). The students may then be directed to finish the story by reading alone, following along with an audio recording, using a Braille version or a screen reader, or reading the story aloud with a partner. They may respond to questions individually by handwriting or using word processing, speech-to-text, or another form of audio recording, or by including visuals. Alternatively, they may choose to work in pairs or in cooperative groups.

Sheltered Instructional Observation Protocol

The SIOP is a research-based model for teaching academic content to ELLs while they develop English proficiency (Echevarría, Vogt, & Short, 2013). It utilizes theories of second language acquisition to help teachers adjust their instruction to accommodate the language proficiency of the students. Although the SIOP model was developed to provide sheltered instruction for ELL students in general education classrooms, research has shown that this model can be helpful to native English speakers as well (Short, Echevarría, & Richards-Tutor, 2011). It requires teachers to be explicit in their instruction and to provide scaffolding at different levels to promote understanding.

The SIOP model comprises 30 features grouped under eight components: (1) lesson preparation, (2) building background, (3) comprehensible input, (4) strategies, (5) interaction, (6) practice/application, (7) lesson delivery, and (8) review and assessment. To fully implement the model, it is recommended that "teachers participate in professional development for at least one year" (Echevarría et al., 2013, p. 281). However, aspects of this model can be incorporated into differentiated instruction by all teachers, even with less formalized training.

For example, the lesson preparation component recommends setting both content and language objectives for every lesson. This practice enables teachers to identify specific language needs required to meet the content objectives. Teachers can then note students with an insufficient grasp of those skills and make an explicit plan to address these gaps.

Another key aspect of SIOP is supporting students' use of background knowledge to provide a bridge between their prior knowledge and experiences and the content of the literacy lesson. Research (Echevarría, Short, & Powers, 2006) has shown that developing background knowledge prior to reading a text increases comprehension. The SIOP model identifies three features of background knowledge: building new knowledge, activating prior knowledge, and developing academic vocabulary. Whereas building new knowledge is particularly important for ELLs, who may have little or no exposure to some curricular topics, students with disabilities or other struggling learners may also require this preparation. Similarly, academic vocabulary development is important for all students (Zwiers, 2007), although some may have more vocabulary knowledge than others.

The comprehensible input component is particularly important when teaching ELLs, as it enjoins teachers to use a variety of presentation techniques in the lesson, bearing in mind students' language needs. An important feature of the interaction component of SIOP is flexible grouping to support the content and language objectives of the lesson. Each group can focus on a different pathway toward the objectives. The SIOP model suggests using at least two different grouping structures in each lesson.

Instruction that incorporates SIOP features begins with a clear delineation of the content teachers expect students to construct as well as the language skills they should develop to understand that content and manifest learning. Teachers would need to determine the essential knowledge for students and consider multiple ways of activating or providing that knowledge.

All three models—MI, UDL, and the SIOP—are distinct in their own right, offering useful ways of thinking and approaches to teachers seeking to differentiate literacy instruction. At the same time, they have areas of overlap and compatibility that allow for flexible incorporation of aspects of each model into a teacher's practice. We turn to such practice in the next section.

DIFFERENTIATED LITERACY INSTRUCTION IN CONTEXT: A PEDAGOGICAL SCENARIO

To help illustrate how these conceptions of differentiated literacy instruction can support students in meeting learning objectives linked to the CCSS, we created a classroom scenario to conclude this chapter. We envision the teaching being done by the fictional Ms. Taylor, an 8-year veteran exemplifying characteristics of teachers with whom we typically work in master's classes or in-service workshops: dedicated to her students, willing to do some reading to supplement professional development, and inclined to differentiate instruction, despite having little formal training in serving diverse student needs.

Ms. Taylor's 10th-grade English class has 26 students—slightly larger than the average in New York. A heterogeneous group has been assigned to Period 3. Fourteen are boys, and 12 are girls. Eighteen are classified by the school as African American, including 11 native-born students and 7 whose families immigrated recently from countries such as Somalia and Sudan; 5 as white, including 1 student originally from Bosnia; 2 as Asian, both from Burma; and 1 Latino, born in the United States. Sixteen are native speakers of English, while 10 are ELLs. On the New York State English Language Assessment Test (NYSELAT), 6 ELLs have tested at the intermediate level and 3 at the advanced level of English proficiency. One ELL has tested at the proficient level, although she still struggles with English language skills. Five students receive special education services for learning disabilities, attention-deficit/hyperactivity disorder, and autism. According to a district reading test, 5 students read above grade level, 7 at grade level or one grade below, and 14 below grade level, some significantly. The first quarter reveals that students are similarly diverse in their motivation and engagement: about a third complete little homework, and many complain that school is boring. Ms. Taylor clearly has some work in front of her to help them meet 10th-grade standards by the end of the year.

To keep current with state expectations, Ms. Taylor is a frequent visitor to EngageNY (*www.engageny.org*), a website maintained by the New York State Department of Education with a plethora of CCSS-related resources. She recently discovered grade-by-grade curriculum exemplars posted there, including a 10th-grade unit on making evidence-based claims that uses two Nobel Prize acceptance speeches, one by Reverend Martin Luther King Jr., the other by U.S. President Barack Obama, as core texts (Odell Education, 2013). The exemplar catches her attention because she knows that a focus on complex informational texts, attention to close reading, and textual evidence are all hallmarks of the CCSS. The exemplar unit is organized into five parts, each recommended to unfold over 2 to 3 days of instruction but with flexibility built in so that teachers can slow or accelerate the pace depending on students' response. Its primary alignment is with CCSS

RI.9–10.1—Cite strong and thorough textual evidence to support analysis of what the text says explicitly as well as inferences drawn from the text.

As Ms. Taylor reads through the lesson plans and supporting materials, she identifies numerous aspects of the instruction that she feels will suit her students' varying needs. She is impressed by how well sequenced the activities are, how they link informational reading with speaking and listening (SL.9–10.1) and writing (W.9–10.4), and how they break the skill of making an evidence-based claim into manageable parts. Still, she is concerned about the unit's reliance on linguistic representation, its exclusive use of complex texts for a class including many reading below grade level, and its lack of choice. She resolves to develop a unit that starts with the state exemplar but incorporates differentiated supports to address her students' learning needs at this time. Her adapted unit (see Table 18.2) has a number of features consistent with the frameworks for differentiating instruction outlined above, discussed next.

Unpack the Standard and Consider How Students Will Meet It

Once Ms. Taylor decides that she, like the state exemplar, is going to focus on CCSS 9–10.1, she unpacks the standard, tracing how it evolves across the grade levels by copying and pasting the language from each grade into a single document. This allows her to consider what additional support students who have not yet mastered the 10th-grade version might need.

Next, she notes what it will look and sound like in her classroom if students can meet that 10th-grade standard. With this in mind, she designs a culminating assessment through which students can demonstrate their ability to make claims based on textual evidence. In keeping with the multiple representations principle from UDL, she considers various ways students could complete this task utilizing different media. She ultimately decides to expand the options from the short written essay suggested by the state exemplar to include three options: the essay, a podcast, and an oral presentation using Prezi software to supplement it.

Finally, she begins to design daily plans to address these overarching learning standards. For this part of the process, she draws on advice from SIOP-trained teachers in her building to specify learning objectives focused on both content and language. For example, for one lesson she specifies a content objective that students will identify claims and find supporting evidence in the speech they are reading and a language objective that they will identify signal words an author uses to link one argument to another. (The latter is the kind of understanding that many struggling students fail to pick up on their own without explicit instruction.) Both kinds of objectives are posted publicly in Ms. Taylor's classroom, and she makes sure to call students' attention to them daily, frequently using them as the focus for

TABLE 18.2. Overview of Evidence-Based Claims Unit

Part	Focus	Activities
1	Introducing evidence-based claims	• Students are introduced to the lesson focus. • The teacher models making evidence-based claims with a text from a previous unit. • Students apply skills to an ad and a movie trailer.
2	Making evidence-based claims	• Students read a speech by Elie Wiesel, first independently, then with the support of the teacher and a short video clip. Between readings, the teacher elicits Holocaust background knowledge. • In pairs, students look for evidence to support a claim about the text made by the teacher. • The class discusses evidence found by pairs. • In pairs, students make and present a claim.
3	Organizing evidence-based claims	• The teacher shares images from the Civil Rights movement and asks students to discuss what they notice and what they know about the period. • The teacher reads a speech by Martin Luther King, Jr., and then plays an audio clip of King delivering the next portion, while students follow along. • The teacher uses a think-aloud to model organizing evidence to develop and explain claims. • Students read the next third of the text using a variety of means (e.g., independent reading of print text, shared reading with audiotape, paired reading) • Pairs develop a claim and organize evidence. • The class discusses the evidence-based claims developed by student pairs, using hand signals to signal the strength of the evidence.
4	Writing evidence-based claims	• The teacher models writing claims with the last third of the King text. • In pairs, students write additional claims, while the teacher circulates to provide assistance. • Pairs share their claims and receive feedback. • Students write an additional claim independently about either the Wiesel or King text or both.
5	Developing evidence-based claims	• Students choose a new text from a teacher-made list of options to read using a variety of means. • The teacher organizes a writer's workshop for students to compose an evidence-based essay, podcast, or Prezi in response to their chosen speech. • Students share their products in small groups.

Note. Based on Odell Education (2013).

students' tickets-out-the-door. She reviews this informal writing along with other artifacts generated during the class to see how individual students are progressing toward meeting the standard.

Link Text Selection to Students' Interests and Needs

As she plans, Ms. Taylor thinks carefully about text selection. Both the King and the Obama speeches featured in the state exemplar offer opportunities for students to make evidence-based claims, but she is concerned about the length of the Obama text (14 pages vs. 5 for King), given difficulties she anticipates learners will have with its vocabulary, sentence structure, and geopolitical content. She is supportive of the CCSS emphasis on persevering with complex text, but she is also pragmatic about how long some students can sustain focus while struggling to make meaning at this point in the year. Moreover, Ms. Taylor would like to offer students more diversity in authorship; while the King and Obama texts were written 45 years apart, both are male, African American, Christian, and native English speakers. Consequently, she decides to replace the Obama speech with a shorter one by Holocaust survivor Elie Wiesel, another male Nobel Peace Prize winner, but one who is Jewish, Romanian-born, and multilingual.

To further diversify the unit, Ms. Taylor decides to give students some choice about the text for the culminating assessment. Her list includes the Obama speech, toward which she intends to steer some of her strongest readers, but also features texts authored by Nobel-winning women, such as Jody Williams, an American anti-landmine activist, and Wangari Maathai, a Kenyan environmentalist. Ms. Taylor believes that the more global perspectives offered by her text selections will position members who emigrated from other countries to share relevant experiences to enrich everyone's reading. She also predicts that selecting by interest will increase students' motivation, allowing them to focus on claim-making longer than they might otherwise.

Employ Multiple Modes of Communication

In addition to diversifying the textual choices recommended by the state exemplar, Ms. Taylor resolves to employ multiple modes and media in her version of the unit, a decision in keeping with both MI and UDL. To this end, she searches for video and audio clips of Nobel Prize winners. Midway through Part 2, the state exemplar recommends viewing the King speech to help students grasp King's use of a rhetorical device called anaphora, repetition intended to create impact. Ms. Taylor resolves to show a clip of King's delivery even earlier in the lesson sequence, during Part 1.

Although she is unable to find a recording of Wiesel delivering his Nobel lecture, she finds a number of video clips for talks he has given on similar topics. She resolves to show one of these in between students' first and second readings of the short text, both to remind students that Wiesel's activism is grounded in personal experience and to provide a powerful model for all students of English proficiency achieved by someone who is not a native English speaker.

Also in keeping with UDL's emphasis on multiple representations and media, Ms. Taylor plans to employ technology to assist some students. The state exemplar provides graphic organizers to help students make and support their claims, with instructions suggesting that the curriculum developers expected students to fill in responses by hand. Ms. Taylor knows that some students, particularly those with laborious handwriting or more limited English, may spend too much time recording answers and too little thinking about the content of their claims. For this reason, she recreates several organizers in digital form, loading them on laptop computers she reserves for several classes. After she assigns the computers to several students whom she thinks will benefit from them the most, she invites others to sign up to use them on a rotating basis, a practice to which students are accustomed. For three students, one identified with learning disabilities in reading and written expression and two with insufficient English proficiency, she creates a simplified version of the organizing claims graphic organizer that requires fewer pieces of evidence and offers more room for students to develop and explain their selections.

Ms. Taylor also resolves to offer her students some choice around how they represent their learning related to evidence-based claims. The state exemplar recommends that students write a claim related to one or both of the King and Obama texts. Ms. Taylor wants everyone to practice making an evidence-based claim but not necessarily in an essay format. Influenced by both MI theory and UDL, she decides to offer three choices: (1) the essay as the exemplar presents it, (2) a podcast, and (3) an oral presentation supported by Prezi. In each case, students will use the same graphic organizers to represent their claims and evidence, but some will produce extended written text while others will use more oral and visual language.

Assess and Activate Prior Knowledge

One of Ms. Taylor's concerns about the state exemplar is its stance toward teachers' assessing and activating prior knowledge. The unit authors argue that all students should "independently engage in productive struggle with complex texts" (Odell Education, 2013, p. 5), and "be allowed to approach the text freshly" to "make their own inferences based on textual content" (p. 3). Ms. Taylor understands that students need some practice of this sort (there will certainly be times when they need to make meaning from a text with no teacher scaffolding). At the same time, she is aware that approaching the text "freshly" can mean different things for students whose experiences and reading levels vary widely and that frustration with texts that are too difficult or inaccessible can lead students to give up on reading altogether. She is aware that frameworks like SIOP call for teachers to tap into and build students' background knowledge, while some CCSS advocates de-emphasize the practice (Gewertz, 2012).

Given these debates, Ms. Taylor adopts a middle position. She decides to invite students to complete their first reading of the Wiesel text independently because it is short and will allow many students to draw on knowledge from their global studies class. She is confident she can convince them to persevere with the first reading and then provide some support with background knowledge if needed before the second read. She is less sanguine about students successfully navigating a cold reading of the King text so she decides to share images about the Civil Rights movement as well as engage students in a discussion of what they know about King and the period to help students link what they already know to new knowledge they will gain from reading.

Vary Groupings Deliberately

Ms. Taylor appreciates that the state exemplar suggests various grouping configurations over the unit, including teacher-led discussion, pair work, and independent reading. Both her experience and her introduction to SIOP suggest that the repeated opportunities for pair work over Parts 2–5 will offer ELLs a lower-risk context to produce academic language. Mixed formats for social interaction will build on strengths for students who identify as interpersonal learners in the parlance of MI theory, and they will offer more practice in this area for those who need it. The exemplar notes that use of these structures will address a secondary standard: CCSS SL.9–10.1—Participate effectively in a range of collaborative discussions, building on others' ideas and expressing their own clearly and persuasively. Ms. Taylor likes this integrated approach.

At the same time, she notices that the exemplar offers little guidance about how to organize the pairs beyond the following from the Part 2 instructional notes: "Pass out the worksheets and have students work in pairs to find evidence to support the claims" (n.p.). Ms. Taylor knows that she will need to be deliberate about her grouping strategies to ensure success for all pairs in her heterogeneous class. Because she groups and regroups students frequently, sometimes even within the same class, she has a stack of index cards with students' names on them to facilitate the process quickly, based on her instructional goals.

For the first paired task, requiring students to identify evidence from the Wiesel speech to support teacher-made claims, she pairs students according to whether she thinks they can work well together socially, and not according to predicted facility with the new skill or general levels of success in the class. She expects the task to be a challenge for most students, even the handful of students who read above grade level according to the district assessment, so it seems like a good time to go with groupings that maximize heterogeneity. She is mindful of the SIOP protocol's caution against isolating ELLs in the classroom community by grouping them repeatedly with one another, and this seems like a good time to mix them with native speakers of English, as well as to mix students with disabilities with those who lack such labels.

Later, during Part 4, when students are asked to write evidence-based claims with a longer and more difficult text (the King speech), she intends to create more homogeneous pairings, using data from student work and her prior observations to indicate who is struggling to make claims and who is grasping the concept quickly. As she circulates the room during the pair work, such groupings will allow her to provide extra challenge for those who are ready, by encouraging them to write a more sophisticated claim that includes counterclaims. Similarly, she can offer additional support to pairs who continue to struggle with this task, either by re-explaining the task in new ways or by offering them the simpler graphic organizer she has loaded onto the laptops. At this point in the instructional sequence, she seeks to avoid a pairing where one partner's skill might obscure another's need for additional instruction.

Draw on Others' Expertise and Support

Although the state exemplar explicitly states that it "is designed to support real exposure and interaction with complex texts for *all* students," it also acknowledges that students identified with disabilities "should be further supported by the local professionals who are familiar with their individual learning profiles." At different points in Ms. Taylor's career, she has had a partner certified in special education or ESL co-teaching in her classroom to help support students identified with those needs. This year, however, she is teaching her Period 3 section alone. Fortunately, she has learned to draw on her specialist colleagues' expertise even when they are not assigned to her class. For example, she e-mails a link to the state exemplar during her pre-unit planning, sharing her initial thoughts and inviting the ESL and special education teachers for her grade level to read it and provide feedback. Ms. Taylor and Ms. Hardy, the ESL teacher, have a shared free period during the day, so they meet in person. Drawing on two aspects of the SIOP, one associated with comprehensible input and the other with varied methods for assessing lesson objectives, Ms. Hardy suggests that Ms. Taylor devise some visuals and some hand motions to associate with the relative strength of the textual evidence for a given claim. She suggests that students' use of the hand motions will help reinforce the concepts for ELLs, as well as provide visual data for Ms. Taylor to gauge understanding on the fly for students who don't volunteer much information orally in class.

Ms. Taylor isn't so lucky around schedule matching with Ms. Cheever, the special educator, but Ms. Cheever e-mails ideas about making the instructions for the three choices in the culminating assessment more explicit, to ensure that all students understand what to do. She also suggests modeling the claim-making process explicitly with a teacher think-aloud, an approach particularly useful for inexperienced or struggling writers (Gallagher, 2006). Ms. Taylor makes those changes to her plans and materials.

Midway through the unit, Ms. Taylor texts Ms. Cheever to ask for advice about how to support Jason, a student diagnosed with ADHD who is struggling to stay on task during whole-class discussions and, to a lesser degree, while working with a partner. Ms. Cheever reminds Ms. Taylor that it is helpful for Jason and other kinesthetic learners to move as part of instruction, something that the state exemplar, which relies on discussion, reading, and writing (all associated with MI theory's linguistic intelligence), doesn't address. Ms. Cheever recommends the use of a fidget kit, a collection of sensory items to help calm and focus Jason. Ms. Cheever also advises Ms. Taylor to incorporate physical movement such as getting up and moving chairs into the transitions between whole-class, partner, and individual work outlined in the exemplar, to break up literacy activities that learners would typically pursue while seated.

Expand Available Learning Time

Ms. Taylor's vertical reading of the key standards addressed by the state exemplar helps her to identify gaps in students' knowledge and skills from earlier grades—for instance, the ability to distinguish between claims that are supported by reasons from those that are not, slated for consideration in Grade 6, and the ability to evaluate the strength of textual evidence, from Grade 8. Some issues can be addressed by differentiated approaches during Ms. Taylor's regular class time, but there are limits to what she can accomplish in 42 daily minutes, particularly for students with significant gaps. For this reason, she plans opportunities for additional support and time on task for students whom she identifies as missing foundational content or skills needed for the unit.

Ms. Taylor uses various approaches to expand learning time for individuals. If Period 3 students are in study hall during another period when she is teaching English 10, she writes them a pass to her room, figuring they will benefit from additional practice with making claims. She sponsors extra-help sessions on strategies for reading multisyllabic words during lunch and after school, extending invitations on sticky notes to students who need that support. To incentivize these sessions, she extends the penalty-free deadline for the culminating assessment up to a week for students who attend at least twice. She also uploads resources to her website such as completed graphic organizers on evidence-based claims for to a text from a previous unit; such samples will supplement her in-class modeling and think-alouds of the claim-making process.

In addition, Ms. Taylor takes care to link individual students with additional support within the larger school community. She makes sure that the school librarian and teachers staffing the resource room have copies of anchor texts, graphic organizers, and the culminating assignment, so they can better support students who seek help. She recommends several students to the guidance counselor to be matched with retired teachers serving as volunteer tutors during the day and on two Saturdays a month. And she explains the unit expectations carefully to college students observing in her classroom, directing them to sit with students who will benefit from adult interaction and offering tips to support students' meaning making without fostering dependence. She makes these moves not to deflect from her own responsibility in supporting students' literacy development but rather to marshal all resources on their behalf. She realizes that differentiating literacy instruction is a big job, too big for a single person to accomplish.

CONCLUSION

In this chapter we present differentiated literacy instruction as a standards-driven perspective catering to a wide range of learner differences typical in secondary classrooms. The three models we profile have clear overlaps, enabling teachers to combine them flexibly as they accommodate their students' diverse needs. They offer ways of thinking about diversity at large when planning classroom instruction while not confining teachers to a specific approach. Collectively, the three models provide a range of approaches teachers can use to address students' learning styles and intelligences, to provide multiple modalities for students to access and demonstrate learning, and to accommodate students' linguistic and cultural needs.

We focused on the CCSS because they are the new bar that teachers and students must reach together or risk being labeled as failing. One of their most challenging features is their focus on complex texts. Many teachers are unsure about how to help learners with varying backgrounds and skill levels negotiate these texts. In our chapter we illustrate how teachers can build differentiation into instruction by focusing on a unit tied to the CCSS (Odell Education, 2013) that has been offered as a model to educators in our home state of New York (our browsing of other states' Web-based CCSS resources revealed that it is a typical exemplar). Although the exemplar's authors claim to have grounded it in UDL, we found it did not adequately differentiate for the diverse learners in our scenario. In describing Ms Taylor's thought processes related to varying needs in her 10th-grade English classroom, we hope to offer a framework teachers can use to maximize the potential of the CCSS while addressing their challenges.

DISCUSSION AND ACTIVITIES

1. Identify the different forms of diversity in your classroom, and classify students with respect to those differences. Think about why you classified them in that way. Focus on one lesson and consider how you could diversify instruction so that all students can meet the same objective while representing their learning in different ways.

2. Consider the students in one class and think about which intelligences you may associate with each of them. Focus on one of your lessons and design at least three ways students can meet your lesson objective by utilizing a different intelligence for each. You may want to review the Armstrong (2003) book or other resources on multiple intelligences for ideas.

3. Use the text exemplars for your grade level in Appendix B of the CCSS document to guide your selection of a complex text to anchor a lesson or unit you're planning. Make a list of texts, both print and multimedia, catering to your students' readiness and interests that could be combined with the anchor text, preferably allowing for some student choice.

REFERENCES

Armstrong, T. (2003). *The multiple intelligences of reading and writing: Making the words come alive.* Alexandria, VA: Association for Supervision and Curriculum Development.

Calkins, L., Ehrenworth, M., & Lehman, C. (2012). *Pathways to the Common Core: Accelerating achievement.* Portsmouth, NH: Heinemann.

Center for Applied Special Technology. (2011). *Universal Design for Learning guidelines, version 2.0.* Wakefield, MA: Author.

Echevarría, J., Short, D., & Powers, K. (2006). School reform and standards-based education: An instructional model for English language learners. *Journal of Educational Research, 99*(4), 195–211.

Echevarría, J., Vogt, M. E., & Short, D. (2013). *Making content comprehensible for English learners: The SIOP model* (4th ed.) Upper Saddle River, NJ: Pearson.

Gallagher, K. (2006). *Teaching adolescent writers.* Portland, ME: Stenhouse.

Gardner, H. (1999). *Intelligence reframed: Multiple intelligences for the 21st century.* New York: Basic Books.

Gewertz, C. (2012, April 24). Common standards ignite debate over prereading. *Education Week.* Retrieved September 20, 2012, from www.edweek.org/ew/articles/2012/04/25/29prereading_ep.h31.html.

Hall, T. E., Meyer, A., & Rose, D. H. (Eds.). (2012). *Universal design for learning in the classroom: Practical applications.* New York: Guilford Press.

Moll, L., & Greenberg, J. (1990) Creating zones of possibilities: Combining social contexts for instruction. In L. Moll (Ed.), *Vygotsky in the classroom: Instructional implications and applications of sociohistorical psychology* (pp. 319–348). New York: Cambridge.

National Governors Association Center for Best Practices & Council of Chief State School Officers. (2010). *Common Core State Standards for the English language arts and literacy in history/social studies, science, and technical subjects.* Washington, DC: Author.

Nunley, K. (2006). *Differentiating in the high school classroom.* Thousand Oaks, CA: Sage.

Odell Education. (2013). *Making evidence-based claims: Common core state standards English language arts/literacy lesson, grade 10.* Retrieved February 13, 2013, from *www.engageny.org/resource/making-evidence-based-claims-unit-ccss-ela-literacy-grade-10.*

Proctor, C. P., Dalton, B., & Grisham, D. L. (2007). Scaffolding English language learners and struggling readers in a universal literacy environment with embedded strategy instruction and vocabulary support. *Journal of Literacy Research, 39,* 71–94.

Roe, M. F. (2010). The way teachers do the things they do: Differentiation in middle level literacy classes. *Middle Grades Research Journal, 5*(3), 139–152.

Rose, D., & Meyer, A. (2002). *Teaching every student in the digital age: Universal design for learning.* Alexandria, VA: ASCD.

Short, D., Echevarría, J., & Richards-Tutor, C. (2011). Research on academic literacy development in sheltered instruction classrooms. *Language Teaching Research, 15*(3), 363–380.

Sousa, D. (2001). *How the brain learns.* Thousand Oaks, CA: Corwin Press.

Tomlinson, C. (1999). *The differentiated classroom: Responding to the needs of all learners.* Alexandria, VA: ASCD.

Zwiers, J. (2007). *Building academic language: Essential practices for content classrooms, grades 5–12.* San Francisco: Jossey-Bass.

CHAPTER 19

Assessment for Literacy Growth and Content Learning in Secondary Schools

William G. Brozo

In this chapter:

- The concept of assessment for literacy and learning is explained and supported.

- The unique nature of literacy and learning assessment in the secondary school is explored.

- Evidence-based literacy and learning assessment practices are described and exemplified.

More than 30 years of theory development and research has characterized literacy as an interactive, context-bound, purposeful process of meaning construction (Ruddell & Unrau, 2004). During the same time, we have progressed in our understanding of what literacy behaviors should be assessed and how that assessment should be represented (Johnston & Costello, 2005). At the secondary school level, these changes have translated into an emphasis on teachers' defining what it means to be literate and knowledgeable in their classrooms and designing a variety of performance-based activities and authentic opportunities to assess their students as they interact with content-area information and concepts (Clark & Clark, 2000).

In this chapter, issues and strategies of assessment are presented relative to one basic assumption: The goal of secondary literacy assessment is to provide teachers with knowledge about how best to improve and support learning for students and self-knowledge for students that will allow them to become more reflective, active, and purposeful readers and learners.

By the time students reach secondary school, they are fully aware of the importance of tests and their results. They know that completing a course, entering a specific academic program, graduating from secondary school, and gaining admission to college and university are all largely dependent on how they perform on tests. It is important for teachers to realize, however, that these summative assessments of students are a representation of the teaching that preceded them. That is, test scores tend to get better when teachers have an ongoing and developmental assessment focus, which guides them in the here and now of their daily teaching (Brozo & Afflerbach, 2011).

Effective teachers meet students at their current levels of ability and then scaffold attention and learning so students can move to the next levels of achievement. Working in these zones of proximal development (Vygotsky, 1978), secondary teachers can build on adolescents' competencies by presenting them with challenges that foster reading and learning growth. Critical to presenting students with appropriate reading and learning challenges is detailed and "fresh" assessment information that helps teachers direct the instructional focus. William (2000) asserts that "If schools used assessment during teaching, to find out what students have learned, and what they need to do next, on a daily basis" (p. 106), student achievement would rise.

Teachers of science, mathematics, history, languages, and other subjects of instruction in secondary schools must have a good deal of knowledge of their individual student readers in order to customize learning experiences for them. When contextually valid and ongoing assessment information is available, secondary teachers are in the best position to provide their adolescent students with responsive instruction that leads to successful reading experiences with a textbook chapter, a newspaper or magazine article, a graphic novel, or any other print or electronic text source (Afflerbach, 2004).

THE UNIQUE NATURE OF SECONDARY LITERACY AND ASSESSMENT

Mention secondary literacy today to nearly anyone but an insider to the field, and thoughts of failing and disinterested readers and learners are invoked. To be sure, there are plenty of indicators that U.S. middle and high school students are in need of special literacy supports (Brozo, 2011). Secondary literacy, however, encompasses much more than concerns about and practices for struggling adolescent readers and writers. Missing from this one-dimensional perspective is the fact that our secondary students are continually growing as readers and writers. In fact, most of us never stop learning to read better. Literal readers must become inferential readers, and all readers must become proficient at critically appraising the accuracy of textual information and the validity of authors' ideas and at judging the value and trustworthiness of the things they read (Afflerbach, 2007).

Moreover, each of the academic disciplines youth encounter daily in secondary schools around the United States demands particular reading mind-sets, strategies, and prior knowledge. Teaching students to use specialized literacy strategies to expand learning in the disciplines has been advocated for nearly a hundred years (Gray, 1919); however, only recently has this approach taken on new urgency with the influence of the Common Core State Standards (CCSS) movement. The literacy strand of the CCSS emphasizes the importance of reading and writing in the English language arts classroom as well as in the sciences, social studies, and technical areas. The goal is for students to grow increasingly more sophisticated and independent in their use of literacy processes while expanding their knowledge about content-area topics.

Also, within the past two decades researchers have been emphasizing the role of multimodal forms of representation and meaning making in the lives of young people. Those on the vanguard of multiliteracies argue that teachers "must now account for the burgeoning variety of text forms associated with information and multimedia technologies" (New London Group, 1996, p. 60). Many (cf., Kajder, 2010; Kress & Van Leeuwen, 2001) urge secondary schools to make room in language and disciplinary curricula for students' different experiences and outside-of-school discourses that are expressed through a variety of media.

These new perspectives and conditions impinge on our assessment of students' literacy and learning in secondary schools, and on our assessment of struggling adolescent readers and learners. Struggling readers represent the diversity of the adolescent population itself. This means youth from every socioeconomic group, ethnicity, culture, and gender may be in need of extra literacy supports. We also know, however, that certain groups of students are privileged in academic settings because the discourse at home and at school are congruent, while other students who bring different discourse traditions and patterns to secondary classrooms are more likely to encounter difficulties meeting literacy and learning expectations. The clash of school and home discourses and values seems to place a particularly heavy burden on youth who are recent immigrants and those who may be in poverty. For example, a disproportionate number of adolescent youth from poor households and those who are African American and Hispanic American find themselves near the bottom on our National Assessment of Educational Progress (NAEP, 2011) and global literacy assessments (Organization for Economic Cooperation and Development, 2010).

One national approach to addressing problems of struggling readers has been response to intervention (RTI). Although the specific features of RTI systems vary across states, districts, and schools, common components and processes are shared by all who employ the approach. These include some form of universal screening or testing all students for possible learning concerns; progress monitoring, the goal of which is to document growth; and tiered interventions for whole groups, small groups, and individuals.

The degree to which assessments for universal screening and progress monitoring are contextually sensitive and responsive to students' authentic literacy and learning processes will determine whether interventions in this approach are effective (Brozo, 2011). For example, 1-minute timed readings to gauge oral reading fluency is often used for progress monitoring, because, according to its advocates (cf., Shinn, 2007), it can serve as a proxy for overall reading ability, including comprehension. Yet this approach has been challenged on the grounds that it is not a viable way to assess adolescents' reading progress, given the complexities of texts and learning expectations at the secondary level (Brozo, 2011). Furthermore, when assessment approaches are reduced to standardized testing for universal screening and measures of the most basic elements of reading, such as speed or oral reading, teachers may gain little more information than what they already know or can be used to make an informed guess about struggling secondary students.

At the same time, reconciling school reading and assessments with real-life reading and uses can be challenging for any youth and lead to problems with academic texts and tasks. Adolescents who struggle with school-related reading tasks may participate extensively in out-of-school literate activities for personally meaningful, identity-affirming, and socially functional purposes (Alvermann & Wilson, 2007). They might read the sports page of the newspaper to find out more about a favorite player, find rap lyrics on a website as a guide for writing their own, or text with friends to plan a movie for the evening. Youths' competence with these real-life literacy practices may not be valued in or connected to academic settings, resulting in frustration, disengagement, and depressed performance (Dredger, Woods, Beach, & Sagstetter, 2010; O'Brien, 2006).

In the next section, the literacy assessments described and exemplified demonstrate authentic and viable practices in secondary classrooms. Because these assessment practices reveal rich and directly useable information about students' literacy competencies, they can inform responsive instruction for all students, especially diverse learners.

THE CONTENT-AREA READING INVENTORY: ASSESSING HOW STUDENTS READ CONTENT TEXT

A content-area reading inventory (CARI) is a tool that assesses students' reading, thinking, and study processes with content texts that the teacher plans to use and from which students are expected to learn (Readence, Bean, & Baldwin, 2004). The results can be turned into instructional practices to address reading and learning needs of a whole class, small groups, or individuals.

The CARI is a highly flexible, teacher-made inventory designed to detect (1) aspects of the text that may present potential problems for students, and (2) important skills and strategies students may lack for effective reading of particular texts.

Teachers can design their own CARI to assess whatever reading skills and strategies they believe their students need to possess. The process of constructing a CARI involves the following steps:

- Identify the reading, writing, and thinking skills essential to using the primary text effectively. This crucial first step requires consideration of the literacy skills needed to demonstrate competence with content text, so teachers should reflect carefully on the processes and outcomes of reading, writing, and thinking in their content area.
- Select a typical excerpt or excerpts from the text. The selections need not include an entire chapter or story but should be complete within itself and not dependent on other sections. In most cases a few pages will provide a sufficient excerpt from the text.
- Design questions and prompts for students that will provide an adequate reflection of how they navigate through, read, and study from a text. To increase the accuracy of the CARI each section should include three to five questions/prompts.

Below are typical sections of a CARI along with sample questions. Keep in mind that teachers determine sections to include in a CARI depending on aspects of content literacy they wish to emphasize in this form of assessment.

Using Book Parts

In this section, students are prompted to demonstrate the ability to use the table of contents, glossaries, indexes, headings and subheadings, highlighted terms, and so on.

Sample Questions for a World History Textbook

1. On what pages can you find information on the Silk Road?
2. In what part of the book can you find the meaning of Shari'a?

Understanding Visual Information

In this section, students are prompted to demonstrate the ability to read, understand, and gather information from graphs, charts, diagrams, illustrations, photos, and so on.

Sample Questions for a Health Textbook

1. According to the chart on page 61, what is the second largest cause of death among children?
2. What does the graph on page 334 imply about the relationship between cancer and cigarette smoking?
3. What does the cartoon on page 101 suggest about ways obesity influences national health policy?

Understanding Content Vocabulary

In this section, students are prompted to demonstrate their prior knowledge of key concepts and terms as well as their ability to use context to determine word meanings.

Sample Questions for a Science Textbook

Suppose you could send a robot to another planet. What kinds of (1) conduct, trials, experiments would you (2) list, program, code the robot to carry out? Before you programmed the robot, you would need to figure out what (3) information, order, rank you wanted it to (4) arrange, gather, group. Scientists are currently (5) emerging, mounting, developing robots that they plan to send to Mars. These robots are being (6) designed, deliberate, planned to examine the (7) atmosphere, ambiance, population, rocks, gravity, and magnetic (8) meadows, fields, turfs of the planet.

Determining and Summarizing Key Ideas

In this section, students are prompted to demonstrate their ability to identify and summarize important ideas, points, and arguments in content text.

Sample Prompts for a Mathematics Textbook

1. Write a one-page summary for the section entitled "What is a hyperbola?" on page 55. Be sure to include in your summary the key ideas and any other pertinent information. Use your own words as you write your summary.
2. In your own words, state the key idea of the paragraph on the Pythagorean Theorem on page 262, second paragraph from the top.

Creating Study Reading Aids

In this section, students are prompted to demonstrate their ability to create a record of their reading for ongoing study and review.

Sample Prompts for a History Textbook

1. Imagine that you will have a multiple-choice and short-answer test on the section in Chapter 18 entitled "Dangers of Fascism." Organize the material in that section by taking notes about it in a way that would help you prepare for the test.
2. If you prefer another study aid, create that one over the section in Chapter 18.

Using the Results from the CARI

Once students have completed a CARI, teachers can analyze the results and organize them into a whole-class profile, small-group profiles, or individual profiles that depict areas of strength and need. Check marks are placed under the number of the question that was missed and alongside the name of the student who missed it. Thecheck marks can be tallied to derive an overall score or for determining patterns of errors to guide instructional emphasis.

After filling out the CARI classroom analysis sheet for students in a class, teachers can determine individual student's strengths and needs. The form in Figure 19.1 can be useful for relating strengths and needs to appropriate instructional strategies to expand content literacy skills and abilities.

The following two scenarios will help you better appreciate the value of assessment *for* literacy and learning at the secondary level using a CARI-type approach. Read this Scenario 1 carefully. After reading it, try filling out the Assessment Reflection Sheet (Figure 19.2) for one of Marcus's students.

SCENARIO 1

Marcus is a history teacher in a secondary school. His school principal decided that all students should be tested at the beginning of the school year, so teachers would know how well they read. For the first week of school, students were required to complete a standardized reading test.

Student's Name	Strengths	Needs	Instructional Strategies
1.			
2.			

FIGURE 19.1. Determining individual students' strengths, needs, and strategies.

Student:
Assessment Tool:
Student Work: Areas of Strength
Student Work: Areas of Weakness
Teacher Practice: What instructional approaches should be used?
Teacher Practice: What interventions or unit modifications should be made?
Unanswered Questions:

FIGURE 19.2. Assessment reflection sheet.

The test consisted of questions about general vocabulary in the first section and short reading selections followed by comprehension questions in the second section. Neither the vocabulary nor comprehension sections had words or passages related to the history content in his textbook. Once the results of the test were processed for each student, teachers received a spreadsheet (see Figure 19.3).

Now read Scenario 2 just as carefully. After reading it, fill out the Assessment Reflection Sheet (Figure 19.2) for Maria's student, Christina. Compare and contrast your responses to the first and second scenarios. (If you are reading this chapter as part of a course or with colleagues as part of professional development, discuss the cases and your responses.) Also, compare your responses to the Assessment Reflection Sheet for Christina in Figure 19.4.

Student	Vocabulary (total correct/total possible)	Comprehension (total correct/total possible)
DeAngelo	40/50	37/50
Beatriz	35/50	32/50
Salim	29/50	27/50
Ana	47/50	44/50

FIGURE 19.3. Standardized reading test results.

SCENARIO 2

Maria is an eighth-grade science teacher. After attending a professional development workshop on content area assessment procedures, she became interested in discovering more about her students' ability to comprehend textbook information. She realized she needed alternative assessments to the tests at the end of the chapters in her science book. Maria was relying more and more on these tests for grading purposes and less on other assessments of her students as readers and learners. Moreover, she was not using the chapter test results to adjust the way she taught the textbook content.

The professional developer emphasized the need to tie content material to the processes for learning it effectively. The professional developer made suggestions for ways teachers could teach and assess at the same time. Maria decided to use this information to develop her own assessment tool using the class textbook. For an upcoming unit on geology, she designed an assessment that was consisting of several short sections with a few questions in each section. The textbook assessment with sample questions can be found in Figure 19.5.

Student Profile: *Christina*

Section I: Reading Engagement and Interest
Very little interest in the topic of geology

Section II: Prior Knowledge
Limited background knowledge on geology, including rock types, volcanoes, and earthquakes

Section III: Vocabulary
Supplied 1 out of 6 correct words in the blank spaces and may have guessed

Section IV: Comprehension
Answered 2 out of the 4 questions correctly

Section V: Reading Strategies
Her notes were disorganized and were taken verbatim from the paragraphs.
She underlined nearly the entire text, making it difficult to distinguish between important and less important information and ideas.
Her summary was too long and was not in her own words.

FIGURE 19.4. Assessment reflection sheet for Christina.

VOCABULARY SELF-AWARENESS: ASSESSING WORD KNOWLEDGE IN THE SECONDARY CLASSROOM

Because students bring a range of word understandings to the reading of content area texts, it is important to assess their vocabulary knowledge before reading (Fisher, Brozo, Frey, & Ivey, 2010). This awareness is valuable for secondary teachers as well as for students because it provides a reflection of the critical academic language they know, as well as what they still need to learn in order to fully comprehend the reading (Goodman, 2001).

The process involves providing students a vocabulary self-awareness chart before they begin reading new material. The chart should list key terms from the passage students should be expected to know and learn. Students are asked to rate each vocabulary word according to their level of familiarity and understanding. A plus sign (+) indicates a high degree of comfort and knowledge, a check mark (√) indicates uncertainty, and a minus sign (–) indicates unfamiliarity. Also students should to try to supply a definition and example for each word. For words with check marks or minus signs, students may have to make guesses about definitions and examples. Students should not be given definitions or examples at this stage.

Over the course of the readings and exposure to other information sources throughout the unit, students should be told to return often to the chart so they can revise original entries and add new information about each vocabulary word. The goal is for students to replace all the check marks and minus signs with plus signs by the end of the reading or unit. Because students continually revisit their vocabulary charts to revise their entries, they have multiple opportunities to practice and extend their understanding of important content terminology.

This vocabulary self-awareness activity provides another formative assessment of students' content-area vocabulary knowledge and learning. Information about students from this assessment can be added to the other assessment information gathered from the CARI to guide instruction in content area vocabulary building and reading. The vocabulary self-awareness activity, like the CARI, is evaluated informally.

Using Vocabulary Self-Awareness Results

Students can use vocabulary self-awareness to determine the extent of their prior knowledge for key content-area vocabulary and monitor their growth in word learning. By observing students' responses to the key terms on the vocabulary self-awareness chart, teachers can identify students who need vocabulary instruction before, during, and after reading.

Name:

Unit: Geology

Section I: Reading Engagement and Interest

1. It is hard to pay attention to what I'm reading in the science textbook.
Not at all like me!   Not much like me   Can't decide   Kind of like me   A lot like me!

2. I get nervous when I read on a new topic like geology.
Not at all like me!   Not much like me   Can't decide   Kind of like me   A lot like me!

3. I like to read about rocks, volcanoes, and earthquakes.
Not at all like me!   Not much like me   Can't decide   Kind of like me   A lot like me!

4. Reading will be easier for me because I like rocks, volcanoes, and earthquakes.
Not at all like me!   Not much like me   Can't decide   Kind of like me   A lot like me!

Section II: Prior Knowledge

1. **I know a lot about rocks, volcanoes, and earthquakes.**
Not at all like me!   Not much like me   Can't decide   Kind of like me   A lot like me!

2. I have read other books and magazines about geology.
Not at all like me!   Not much like me   Can't decide   Kind of like me   A lot like me!

3. I have a rock collection and know the names of several rocks.
Not at all like me!   Not much like me   Can't decide   Kind of like me   A lot like me!

Section III: Vocabulary

1. _____ rocks form from **2.** _____. **3.** _____ is made up of pieces of rock, shell, sand, mud, or organic matter that have been transported from one place to another by a force such as wind, water, ice, or simply gravity. When the movement stops, these particles settle layer upon layer forming. When these layers **5.** _____, **6.** _____ rock forms.

igneous, metamorphic, sedimentary, magma, lifthify, sediment

Section IV: Comprehension

1. According to the paragraphs you have just read, what are the three main types of rocks?
2. Name one characteristic of each type of rock.
3. How are these rocks different?
4. What words or phrases did the author use to cue you that the rocks were different in some ways?

Section V: Reading Strategies

1. Using the information from the paragraphs just read, construct a set of organized notes for studying
2. Underline the key ideas in the paragraphs just read.
3. Write a summary of the paragraphs just read.

FIGURE 19.5. CARI example from geology.

A teacher's analysis of student Nathan's performance with this vocabulary self-awareness activity (see Figures 19.6 and 19.7) could read:

- "His prior knowledge of key vocabulary was sufficient to aid in comprehending the passages, and he enriched his understanding of key terminology through reading."
- "Nathan does not appear to need any additional vocabulary instruction of these key terms."

A teacher's analysis of student Jodi's performance with this vocabulary self-awareness activity (see Figures 19.8 and 19.9) could read:

- "Jodi's low-level of familiarity with key vocabulary from the passages before reading and her difficulty acquiring new vocabulary knowledge through reading appeared to contribute to her overall problems with comprehension."
- "Jodi will require additional instruction related to these and other key science terms before reading: preteach key vocabulary and use vocabulary cards; during reading: use concept of definition and student friendly definition approaches; after reading: word study guides."

ASSESSING COMPETENCIES WITH ACADEMIC CONCEPTS THROUGH YOUTH MEDIA

By eliminating barriers between students' competencies with outside-of-school texts and classroom practices it is possible to increase engagement in learning and expand literacy abilities for adolescent readers (Sturtevant, Boyd, Brozo, Hinchman, Alvermann, & Moore, 2006).

Word	+	√	–	Definition	Example
artifacts		X		Unsure, maybe like facts from art	
archaeology			X	I'm not sure what this means	
specialized		X		I think it's anything that's real special to you	Like, someone who's real special to you
anthropology			X	It's some kind of scientist, but I'm not sure	

FIGURE 19.6. Nathan's vocabulary self-awareness responses *before* reading about early civilization.

Word	+	√	−	Definition	Example
artifacts	X			Something made or given shape by man, such as a tool or a work of art	A gold chain from ancient Egypt
archaeology	X			Study of human activity in the past by analysis of the physical culture	Learning about ancient Egyptian culture by analyzing the pyramids and tombs
specialized			X	I think it's having a special skill or being able to make something that does one thing	Ancient Egyptians had a special tool for making jewelry
anthropology	X			Study of humans in the past and today	Margaret Mead was an anthropologist who studied Samoans

FIGURE 19.7. Nathan's vocabulary self-awareness responses *after* reading about early civilization.

Teachers can take advantage of students' relative strengths with language and literacy outside of school, such as playing computer and video games, reading comic books and graphic novels, participating in fan fiction and various hobbies (e.g., skateboarding, collecting, sports), listening to music, and writing songs and lyrics [Hinchman, Alvermann, Boyd, Brozo, & Vacca, 2003/04]). It's possible to embed these youth literacies into assessment plans to gather robust emblems of what students have learned in secondary classrooms and how students apply their learning to new and novel contexts.

To illustrate what this approach to assessment might look like,

Word	+	√	−	Definition	Example
subdividing		X		To divide something	
application		X		Apply to a job	Like at McDonald's
interdependent			X	I don't know	
antibiotics		X		It's some kind of medicine	

FIGURE 19.8. Jodi's vocabulary self-awareness responses *before* reading *An Introduction to Science.*

Word	+	√	–	Definition	Example
subdividing		X		Something to do with categories	Animals
application		X		Using something	Using science
interdependent		X		Living together	Like birds and bees
antibiotics		X		Some kind of medicine	For the flu

FIGURE 19.9. Jodi's vocabulary self-awareness responses *after* reading *An Introduction to Science.*

consider how a high school English teacher struggles to make the literary device of allusion clear to his literature students. Allusions are difficult for even the most "with-it" students to appreciate, because they are often indirect or brief references in a literary work to a person, character, place, or thing in history or another work of literature. If readers don't know the events and characters to which an author alludes, then the allusion loses its impact.

To help sensitize his students to this literary device and thereby appreciate its significance, the teacher gives the class its initial exposure to allusion through a YouTube video clip of *Shrek 2*, a popular animated film for youth. The 3-minute clip includes several visual allusions to other films and film characters, both real and animated, with which the students are already familiar. As the clip plays, the teacher asks students to note any images that reference other movies or movie characters, and then holds a discussion afterward. This visual approach, using media from his students' everyday lives, proves quite successful, as they are able to identify several allusions in the video.

Next, the teacher guides his students through a class blog he has established. He indicates where they are to make entries and respond to their classmates. In his homework assignment he asks students to find examples of allusion in their own media—books, films, games, music—and post each example on the blog with an explanation of the allusion. Each student is required to post two examples on the blog and write two entries in response to their classmates.

The English teacher uses these entries as assessment data to determine the extent to which his students understand the concept of allusion and whether additional instruction around the concept is warranted for the class, small groups, or individuals. The teacher meets with students, goes over a scoring rubric like the one in Figure 19.10, and provides needed clarifications and additional practice. The approach produces many interesting

5 Points (A). The example of the allusion is unique and shows depth. Description is thoughtful and accurate and connects directly to the allusion.

4 Points (A). The example reveals an understanding of allusion. Description is accurate.

3 Points (B). Selection of the allusion is acceptable but doesn't stand out. Some connection to the allusion in the description.

2 Points (C). Selection of the allusion shows general understanding but description lacks direct connection to the allusion. Will need additional guided practice.

1 Point (D). A weak example of an allusion with limited and inaccurate description. Will need additional instruction and guided practice.

0 Points (F). No allusion example provided.

FIGURE 19.10. Assessment rubric for allusion assignment.

and accurate allusions from most students in his class, like the two examples below.

Student 1

"My allusion is from the anime *Lucky Star* (which no one has probably heard of, but is the only one I can think of at the moment). In one of the episodes, the main character, Konata, cosplays (dresses up) as a character from another anime, Haruhi from *The Melancholy of Haruhi Suzumiya*, at a cosplay café. The function of this allusion, in a way, is self-promotion because the writers of *Lucky Star* also wrote *The Melancholy of Haruhi Suzumiya*."

Student 2

"In a *Jimmy Neutron—Boy Genius* episode, Jimmy goes to find out why the Bermuda Triangle has so many problems. On his way into the ocean to search for an underwater entrance, we see a small pineapple. As all Nickelodeon viewers know, SpongeBob Squarepants lives in that pineapple. This was the producers' allusion to SpongeBob and their way of saying 'Hi' to the cast of SpongeBob."

From here, the English teacher transitions his class from exploring their media for allusions to searching out and uncovering allusions in traditional print texts, such as poems and plays in the class literature anthology. In using this assignment and its assessment, the teacher is able to take advantage of his adolescent students' competencies with literacies and interests outside of school to achieve his goal of motivating them to read and respond on a more thoughtful level to required texts in his classroom.

DISCUSSION AND ACTIVITIES

Assessment of literacy and content learning at the secondary level is a process of improving instruction for teachers and increasing self-knowledge for students. Text-specific and assignment-based assessment strategies can guide teachers to craft more responsive instruction that helps meet the literacy and learning needs of all students. To ensure assessment practices inform instruction and raise student awareness, teachers should seek answers to the following questions:

1. What literacy and learning skills do my students need to possess in order to be successful in my classroom?

2. What outside-of-school literate practices do my students engage in that can be used to assess them over required reading and learning?

3. How can I design assessments with the materials of instruction that inform and guide my literacy and content practices?

REFERENCES

Afflerbach, P. (2004). Assessing adolescent reading. In T. L. Jetton & J. A. Dole (Eds.), *Adolescent literacy research and practice* (pp. 369–390). New York: Guilford Press.

Afflerbach, P. (2007). *Understanding and using reading assessment, K–12.* Newark, DE International Reading Association.

Alvermann, D. E., & Wilson, A. A. (2007). Redefining adolescent literacy instruction. In B. J. Guzzetti (Ed.), *Literacy for the new millennium* (Vol. 3, pp. 3–20). Westport, CT: Praeger.

Brozo, W. G. (2011). *RTI and the adolescent reader: Responsive literacy instruction in secondary schools.* New York: Teachers College Press.

Brozo, W. G., & Afflerbach, P. (2011). *Adolescent literacy inventory: Grades 6–12.* New York: Pearson.

Clark, D., & Clark, S. (2000). Appropriate assessment strategies for young adolescents in an era of standards-based reform. *The Clearing House,* 73(4), 201–204.

Dredger, K., Woods, D., Beach, C., & Sagstetter, V. (2010). Engage me: Using new literacies to create third space classrooms that engage student writers. *Journal of Media Literacy Education,* 2(2), 85–101.

Fisher, D., Brozo, W. G., Frey, N., & Ivey, G. (2010). *50 instructional routines to develop content literacy.* New York: Pearson.

Goodman, L. (2001). A tool for learning: Vocabulary self-awareness. In C. Blanchfield (Ed.), *Creative vocabulary: Strategies for teaching vocabulary in grades K–12.* Fresno, CA: San Joaquin Writing Project.

Gray, W. S. (1919). The relation between studying and reading. (*Proceedings of the 57th annual meeting of the National Education Association*, pp. 580–586). Washington, DC: National Education Association.

Hinchman, K., Alvermann, D., Boyd, F., Brozo, W. G., & Vacca, R. (2003/04). Supporting older students' in- and out-of-school literacies. *Journal of Adolescent & Adult Literacy, 47*(4), 304–310.

Johnston, P., & Costello, P. (2005). Principles for literacy assessment. *Reading Research Quarterly, 40*(2), 256–267.

Kajder, S. (2010). *Adolescents and digital literacies: Learning alongside our students.* Urbana, IL: National Council of Teachers of English.

Kress, G., & Van Leeuwen, T. (2001). *Multimodal discourse: The modes and media of contemporary communication.* New York: Oxford University Press.

National Assessment of Educational Progress. (2011). *The nation's report card: Reading 2011.* Retrieved December 15, 2012, from *http://nces.ed.gov/nationsreportcard/pubs/main2011/2012457.asp.*

New London Group. (1996). A pedagogy of multiliteracies: Designing social futures. *Harvard Educational Review, 66*(1), 60–92.

O'Brien, D. G. (2006). "Struggling" adolescents' engagement in multimediating: Countering the institutional construction of incompetence. In D. E. Alvermann, K. A. Hinchman, D. W. Moore, S. F. Phelps, & D. R. Waff (Eds.), *Reconceptualizing the literacies in adolescents' lives* (pp. 29–45). Mahwah, NJ: Erlbaum.

Organization for Economic Cooperation and Development. (2010). *PISA 2009 results: Learning trends. Changes in student performance since 2000* (Vol.V). Paris: Author.

Readence, J., Bean, T., & Baldwin, R.S. (2004). *Content area literacy: An integrated approach.* Dubuque, IA: Kendall/Hunt.

Ruddell, R., & Unrau, N. (2004). *Theoretical models and processes of reading* (5th ed.). Newark, DE: International Reading Association.

Shinn, M. (2007). Identifying students at risk: Monitoring performance and determining eligibility within response to intervention: Research on educational need and benefit from academic intervention. *School Psychology Review, 36*(4), 638–646.

Sturtevant, E., Boyd, F., Brozo, W., Hinchman, K., Alvermann, D., & Moore, D. (2006). *Principled practices for adolescent literacy: A framework for instruction and policy.* Mahwah, NJ: Erlbaum.

Vygotsky, L. S. (1978). *Mind in society: The development of higher psychological processes* (M. Cole, V. John-Steiner, S. Scribner, & E. Souberman Trans.). Cambridge, MA: Harvard University Press.

William, D. (2000). Education: The meanings and consequences of educational assessments. *The Critical Quarterly, 42*, 105–127.

CHAPTER 20

Coaching and Growing Literacy Communities of Practice

Josephine Peyton Marsh
David R. Krauter
Lettice Pelotte

In our chapter, we:

- Review the literature on peer coaching and communities of practice.

- Describe the infrastructure and leadership that encouraged the communities of practice to develop and flourish at an urban charter school.

- Describe a community of practice created by adolescent peer-writing coaches.

- Offer a set of tools and practices that we found important in growing communities of practice and encouraging peer coaching.

"I have just witnessed too many examples of schools waiting for the communities of practice to develop organically only to find that it takes a lot of behind-the-scenes work to really make it happen and seem organic. It is like gardening—you can grow organic vegetables and fruits, but it takes a lot of work to create the right compost and know how to use to amend the soil, a lot of knowledge from the gardener to know how to pair plants for maximum benefit and what birds and insects are necessary so you do not have to use pesticides, and what climate, water, and light conditions create the best yield. If you do not know how to attend to all these issues, you can get lucky with one crop, but it will not be sustained without the requisite knowledge and attention."

As schools work to improve literacy instruction, they employ a wide range of professional development initiatives and strategies in order to help teachers improve instruction and boost academic outcomes. Some schools rely on top-down or stand-and-deliver models of professional development. Others employ literacy coaches or purchase books and other professional development materials to help teachers learn new ways of teaching. ASU Preparatory Academy (ASU Prep), a Title I urban public charter school sponsored by Arizona State University in partnership with a local K–8 school district, invests time and effort into developing communities of practice and the peer coaching that often takes place. This sort of collaborative professional development uses the broad base of experience held by our administrators and teachers. This chapter is dedicated to sharing the authors' experiences as coaches, participants, and observers in these communities of practice. Understanding that communities of practice can be intentionally framed and developed like an organic garden, as Deborah Gonzalez, Chief Academic Officer of ASU Prep, implied in the quote above, we describe the practices we believe nurtured these communities and helped them to grow.

Communities of practice—learning communities in which participants share and make use of their accumulated experiences and knowledge—have become part of the culture at ASU Prep. These communities of practice provide spaces for educators in our school to have professional conversations; share and create knowledge about teaching, learning, and students; and work collaboratively. We believe these interactions have contributed to the improved schoolwide reading scores and increased literacy integration across the academic disciplines. During the 2 years since the seeds were planted and communities of practice began to grow, we observed increased literacy integration in the content areas and witnessed the development of instructional practices that encouraged deeper readings of texts and the use of evidence-based writing. Schoolwide reading achievement scores improved 25 percentage points over these first 2 years. In spring 2013, 90% of our 10th graders passed the high school reading exit exam on their first attempt and 79% of them passed the writing exit exam. While we do not assume a direct correlation between academic literacy performance and the development of communities of practice, we posit that these communities contributed to this sustained growth. Like an organic garden, we found that effective communities of practice require continued thoughtful planning, requisite knowledge, and plenty of attention to grow.

COMMUNITIES OF PRACTICE AND PEER COACHING

Wenger (2006) defines communities of practice as clusters or groups of people who formally and informally learn together and develop a collection of shared knowledge, practices, resources, and ways of doing. Communities of practice cultivate a sense of belonging among individuals as they discuss common passions or concerns (Wenger & Snyder, 2000). They constitute social spaces in which members are given opportunities to learn from one another. They are similar in many ways to the peer-coaching partnerships described by Jewett and Macphee (2012) and Marchese (2012).

Like peer coaching models, participants within communities of practice engage with their peers in meaningful problem-solving tasks, rely on one another's expertise, and become collaborative colearners (Jewett & Macphee, 2012; Marchese, 2012). Communities of practice include both experienced and nonexperienced individuals who take part in shared, dynamic learning experiences (Lave & Wenger, 1991). The participants grow to respect and value each other's expertise as they interact regularly. In this sense, communities of practice encourage peer coaching among the participants.

The administrators at ASU Prep knew and understood that successful communities of practice allowed people to participate in a variety of ways. Lave (1991) terms these possible roles as: old-timers/newcomers, masters/apprentices, and full participants/peripheral participants. The more formal communities of practice, known as clusters at ASU Prep (e.g., high school cluster, middle school cluster, humanities cluster, STEM cluster), in which peer coaching occurs, are the focus of this chapter.

Our teachers, teacher leaders, and administrators each participated in these communities of practice differently, coaching one another as they learned new ways of teaching and as they collaborated to create new methods for teaching. While their levels of experience and expertise varied, the participants worked together as colearners and collaborators within their clusters. They met during common planning times, before or after school, and informally between classes or at lunch. Their meetings often focused on ways to support students' literacy instructional needs, aiming to help students meet and exceed the expectations of the Common-Core State Standards (CCSS; National Governors Association [NGA] Center for Best Practices & Council of the Chief State School Officers [CCSSO], 2010) and Cambridge International Examinations (Cambridge) used at ASU Prep. (For information about Cambridge see *www.cie.org.uk*.) While developing effective communities of practice takes work and effort, we have seen the benefit of creating and sustaining these communities and deem the effort worthwhile and valuable. As one teacher reflected in a schoolwide survey, "I like the collaborative atmosphere at ASU Prep . . . teamwork is encouraged among teachers. I believe that this collaboration helps us provide great educational opportunities for all students." This collaboration is nourished within the communities of practice. Communities of practice are not always easy to grow and sustain, as the opening quote implies. Planning and cultivation are needed for them to flourish within schools. The role of the gardener, in this case, the administrators and teacher leaders, should not be underemphasized.

A Snapshot: Peer Coaching in Action

The peer coaching that occurs in communities of practice is fluid and flexible. It follows lines of focus determined through collaborations among teachers, teacher leaders, and administrators. Though each participant in a community of practice plays a role in the creation and sharing of knowledge, the leadership team (the school administrators and teacher leaders) initiates conversations and guides discussions. In order to illustrate the role of leadership in fostering peer coaching at the school, we begin this part of the chapter with a snapshot of a community of practice in action. In this excerpt from a humanities cluster meeting, reading, English, and social studies teachers discussed problems students were having writing summaries. All student and teacher names used in the chapter are pseudonyms.

> ALICE: [We] have done it [summarizing] informally, we go over it, we are historians, we care about facts not opinions. In my class I have problems with getting to the heart, getting to the meaning of the text.
>
> JOSE: No problem inserting personal experience, they do summarize notes. They do have a little trouble paraphrasing.
>
> KRISTY: Alice?
>
> ALICE: Yeah, I notice same the thing. They use headings or phrases instead of writing it in their own words.
>
> RANDY: We have to scaffold writing the summarizing together. They can put together a sentence and it sort of makes sense, it is OK. So I am trying to just get them to get the main idea and find significant details.
>
> BETTY: I use "Somebody wanted but _____ so _____." One–sentence summary—helps them get to the theme.
>
> BETTY: What is the paragraph mostly about—what do the title and headings tell you about the main idea? That helps them find two details that support main idea.
>
> KRISTY: Is there transfer to social studies?

JOSE: No, it seems like they are having hard time summarizing in my class.

KRISTY: I am not trying to make anyone feel funny, I am trying to figure out what we all have in common to find a common strategy.

JOSE: Information text-wise—pulling out information from informational text. The more advanced students pull out information from [a text about] an immigrant from Romania writing about immigrating to the U.S. They have trouble pulling our information that is more about inference. More straightforward OK, but getting deeper into it is harder.

BETTY: I can go over some strategies with them. So . . .

KRISTY: Sounds like the kids get it in some classrooms and not in others. So in the next couple of weeks, let's teach central theme and details and then share what you did and how the students did. Bring in the best, average and worst.

As the conversation continued the participants shared different strategies, describing them in more detail and giving examples about how they could be used to teach summarizing and finding main idea and details.

In this snapshot, the teachers coached one another, sharing and developing strategies for teaching literacy in the content areas. The discussion that took place in the meeting was purposeful and relevant. During the meeting, the teacher leader, Kristy, initiated and facilitated the discussion, inviting participants to talk. She also periodically summarized what had been said. Although seemingly spontaneous, the discussion was set up by the leadership team and facilitated by the teacher leader in such a way that it led to collaborative peer coaching and shared knowledge building. In the following sections, the roles of the leadership team and the teacher leaders are described in order to make clear the parts that they had to play in setting up and maintaining communities of practice in which productive peer coaching could take place.

ADMINISTRATORS: PLANTING AND TENDING THE GARDEN

"We develop professional behaviors through collaboration with our peers and guided reflection."

Administrators, like the one quoted above, are the constant gardeners of communities of practice in schools. At ASU Prep, the leadership team included the building- and district-level curriculum and administrative leaders, a dean, and a professor in residence acting as a literacy coach. The leadership team created the infrastructure that supported communities of practice and peer coaching. In order to be effective, participants needed time to meet and to collaborate. In an effort to provide sufficient time for communities of practice to develop and flourish, the administrators designed the school day so that grade-level or content-area teachers had common planning times. This required a solid commitment to and a belief in the importance of professional collaboration. Some creative scheduling was also necessary. For instance, in order for all humanities teachers to meet, administrators scheduled weekly morning meetings like the one in the snapshot above. Having an established day and time for regular meetings is important. It provides a consistency that allows participants to get to know each other, share more freely, and build on each other's expertise.

Throughout the school year, administrators attended as many cluster meetings as possible. They participated in a variety of ways—sometimes facilitating, sometimes colearning, and sometimes observing. Their presence signified the importance of developing and nurturing communities of practice and the administration's belief in them. By devoting time to the cluster meetings, the administrators demonstrated that they were committed to peer coaching and supportive of the burgeoning communities of practice.

The administration plays a vital role in making sure that meetings are purposeful and relevant to the instructional needs of students and teachers. Prior to cluster meetings, administrators meet with teacher leaders to coconstruct an agenda. The agenda includes a discussion of assessment data and classroom observations. Using these data and their collective knowledge and experiences, the administrators and teacher leaders develop goals and objectives for upcoming cluster meetings. During the cluster meetings, the administrators and teacher leaders participate in and observe conversations among participants. They, in turn, bring their observations as well as any subsequent data from classroom observations and teacher feedback back to the leadership team meetings. This "circular process," as one participant described the sequence, allows them to revisit and revise the goals that had been determined during the first set of leadership team meetings.

The goal of administrative support was not to be a directive but to be supportive. For instance, prior to the cluster meeting presented in the snapshot above, administrators reviewed benchmark-testing data and observed that students were having difficulty answering questions that asked them to support main ideas with evidence or to summarize. They collectively decided to focus walk-throughs (unscheduled, short observations) on opportunities for students to learn strategies for summarizing and finding supporting evidence in fiction and informational texts. They reported their findings at the next leadership meeting. After gathering these observational data and discussing what they observed, the administrators decided to bring this issue to the attention of the teacher leaders. So during the next leadership meeting with teacher leaders, administrators brought up their observations and the benchmark testing results. Instead of imposing a desired outcome on them, the administrators presented the data and the observations and said, "Here is the issue; what do we do?" The teacher leaders then discussed the issue and decided to take it to the cluster meeting. After the cluster meeting, the next leadership meeting with teacher leaders served as a debriefing session, a place to make refinements and to coach each other on best ways to facilitate and interact within the clusters.

It is important to note that while in the example above the administrators initiated the focus on summarizing, often it is the teacher leaders who bring a concern to the attention of the leadership team. The circular process we described can begin at any point in the process. As one administrator said, "It can be in the classroom, in what we do in cluster, it can be in the leadership team meeting, or the leadership meeting with teacher leaders." For example, at one cluster meeting, social studies teachers said that they needed help teaching the students to interpret historical events from multiple perspectives. The teacher leaders took this to the leadership team, and the cycle began anew.

In addition to helping to determine the foci of cluster meetings, administrators coached the teacher leaders about how best to facilitate professional conversations and how to work with the different personalities present in the clusters. In one leadership meeting with teacher leaders, for instance, the team had an extended conversation about how to navigate interactions with a couple of the teachers who were reluctant to infuse literacy strategies designed to trigger divergent thinking into their instruction. The administrators engaged teacher leaders in brainstorming sessions that began with a teacher leader saying, "We could tell them to do it, be more directive. . . . " The administer then commented, "This is tough, accountability without looking like oversight." The conversation continued as they worked out how best to present the concern to the cluster in such a way that the issue and possible solutions to it would become self-evident to the teachers, and not be perceived as a mandate. Conversations such as these prepared the teacher leaders to facilitate cluster meetings, like in the snapshot above, and foster peer coaching within the clusters. The conversations also contributed to the development of shared knowledge within the community of practice and to the creation of teaching practices better suited to meet the needs of the students. The knowledge produced in these sessions and the practices that the leadership team implemented became a part of the school's culture as indicated in Figure 20.1.

What We've Learned from the Administrative Team	Tips for Administrators
• Participants need time to meet and to collaborate in communities of practice. • Administrators are a part of communities of practice in their schools. • The process used to develop and maintain communities of practice conducive to peer coaching is circular.	• Establish regular meeting times. • Schedule optimal common planning times. • Attend meetings, contribute, and listen. • Conduct classroom walkthroughs before and after meetings. • Collect observational and quantitative data on student growth. • Present the issues and ask teachers and teacher leaders to brainstorm with you about what to do about it.

FIGURE 20.1. Lessons learned from and tips for administrators.

TEACHER LEADERS: TENDING THE GARDEN

"It's all about relationships."

In the quote above, one teacher leader sees her role as a peer coach as being derived from professional interactions. Recent literature supports peer coaching as an effective strategy for meeting teachers' growing professional development needs (Jewett & MacPhee, 2012; Vogt & Shearer, 2011). The CCSS (NGA & CCSSO, 2010) and Cambridge demand a high level of academic literacy across all grade levels and content areas. A collaborative peer-coaching model affords teachers opportunities to learn from one another as knowledgeable equals in order to help students achieve higher standards and meet benchmarks. According to Marchese (2012) collaborative peer coaching helps foster an "authentic community of learners" who "engage in ongoing dialogue" and "support one another's professional growth" (p. 47). At ASU Prep, embedding peer coaching into communities of practice seemed like a natural pairing. Tending these communities often involved the consistent interaction of teacher leaders.

Teacher leaders at ASU Prep, sometimes referred to as mentor teachers, department heads, lead teachers, literacy coaches, and peer coaches coordinate and moderate the regularly scheduled cluster meetings, observe in classrooms, conduct formal and informal evaluations, and confer with individual teachers. They provide professional development in a variety of formats, adjusting to meet the needs of the teachers and students. At times, they meet in formal, structured settings like the clusters we described earlier. At other times, they meet with teachers informally and in less structured environments. They provide tailored professional development, sometimes coaching teachers directly and at other times setting up conditions under which peers coached one another.

Every week, as described in the previous section, teacher leaders at ASU Prep met with administrators and their grade-level or content-area clusters to identify common goals and/or to discuss methods and strategies to meet these goals. The focus and consistency of the meetings allowed participants in communities of practice to, as one teacher leader said, "feel really comfortable talking together, sharing ideas, and working together." Paramount in these meetings was a respect for the collaborative process and an awareness of the value of teacher input, as the teacher leader quotation at the beginning of this section indicates. While coconstructing knowledge along with the teachers, teacher leaders at the school created a safe place within the garden walls for new ideas to develop and grow.

In addition to creating positive learning environments, teacher leaders at the school developed ways of working with teachers that were supportive and collaborative rather than exclusively directive. They worked with an understanding that effective teacher leaders do not necessarily tell teachers what they need to know, what they ought to be doing in the classroom, or how they should work with other teachers. As one of our teacher leaders pointed out, "[Effective leadership is] looking for organic fits, and not saying, 'You will try this right now.'" Teacher leaders at ASU Prep listened to the needs of teachers, helped teachers to solve problems and make adjustments in instruction, and helped them to find the resources that they needed in order to improve student achievement. They asked, "What does my team need at the moment?" and looked for resources within the team to meet those diverse needs. This involved helping teachers see how to apply strategies across multiple disciplines, asking prompting questions to help teachers collaborate more effectively, and occasionally simply sitting back, listening, and taking notes. In one cluster meeting, for instance, the teacher leader introduced a topic of conversation and then sat quietly as the teachers talked. Two of the teachers in the meeting spent a considerable amount of time coaching a third teacher in managing small-group literacy instruction. Following the meeting, the teacher leader looked for resources that would help these teachers to effectively apply the strategies and solutions discussed.

Developing a sense of mutual respect and collegiality also allowed teacher leaders to create environments in which they can facilitate productive informal meetings alongside the more formal meetings. As one of the teacher leaders at the school said in an interview, "We have such a good staff in my department that I don't feel like I need to manage in any way; it's just facilitating the conversations. And then on an individual level you just sort of tailor to what the individual teachers need."

While formal cluster meetings provided teachers at ASU Prep with structured venues in which to conduct collaborations and develop relationships conducive to peer coaching, teachers also interacted informally in a wide variety of contexts. Many interactions occurred over coffee, during lunch, and while supervising students on the playground. Teachers and teacher leaders had e-mail conversations about academic goals and discussed teaching strategies as students changed classes. Calling these types of meetings "one-legged meetings" because they are short and to the point—you can't stand on one leg too long—one teacher leader posited that informal meetings and casual interactions among teachers and mentors eliminate the need for more frequent and formal meetings. Teachers at the school also noted the value of these types of interactions. In an e-mail to a teacher leader, one of the high school teachers wrote:

> "Hi, Thanks for a chat in the hall! I just remembered that there was something else I wanted to run by you. For the second quarter, I want to do some sort of project based learning with my ninth-grade English class that involved poetry/literature/art from around the world, technology, and public speaking. Do you have any good books for project based learning or any other ideas?"

The teacher leader, in response to this e-mail, provided feedback and suggested resources that could be used to develop her project.

As teachers and teacher leaders participated in these sorts of informal, collaborative interactions during the school day, they discussed student progress, shared observations about the teaching strategies that they had been using in the classroom, and compared notes about their successes and failures. They also devised new ways of working and coached one another as they came upon problems that required creative solutions. They drew on resources available to them through their peers.

At ASU Prep, teacher leaders, along with administrators, conducted formal and informal evaluations of teachers. Viewed as more than simply instruments used to administer performance payouts or to make personnel decisions, teacher evaluations were considered opportunities for reflection and colearning. Teacher evaluations, including the postobservation meetings, were often the topic of the leadership meetings. These conversations prepared and supported teacher leaders in this aspect of the circular process described above. Postobservation meetings were typically set up after the formal evaluation observations, although some were held after informal classroom walkthroughs. One teacher, for instance, made a point of grabbing some coffee from a teacher leader's room after a walkthrough observation to share with a teacher leader. While drinking their coffee, the teacher asked for feedback on the observations and discussed with the teacher leader the decisions he had made during instruction.

Meetings after formal evaluations typically followed a predictable pattern. Beginning with a period of reflection, teacher leaders asked teachers to comment on the parts of the lesson they thought were success-ful and parts of the lesson they would have changed. Next, the teacher leaders shared observational data and evaluation scores with the teachers. The teacher leaders identified areas of strength and weaknesses as deter-mined by the evaluation protocol and rubric. This portion of the meet-ings generally led to conversations about teaching strategies, resources for improving instruction, and ideas about how lessons might be taught in the future. Teachers generally valued this time to talk about their prac-tice. As one teacher wrote in a follow-up e-mail to the teacher leader who had evaluated her, "I wanted to tell you how much I valued our conversa-tion yesterday morning. I feel so lucky to work at a school where I can have fellow teachers observe my practice. Our meaningful conversation gives me concrete ways to improve and helps me to feel confident in my strengths."

Meetings such as this one helped grow communities of practice and the collaborative culture at ASU Prep. This result was particularly evident during one postobservation conference. A teacher in the middle school used a postevaluation meeting as a time to talk about ways to improve students' questions and engagement in discussions about texts. Stating that the students in her class were becoming less motivated as the school year progressed, the teacher asked for help to put some fire back into classroom discussions. The teacher leader was able to help the teacher reflect on her own practice. She guided the teacher to make a connection between the help she requested and what had been observed during the evaluation observation. Using the observation as the foci, they reflected together about how engaged the students were when they had an oppor-tunity to respond directly to each other and co-created an activity that they both thought would motivate students to participate in discussions about text.

Evaluations, in addition to providing opportunities for peer coaching and collaboration within communities of practice, are useful in determin-ing foci for future conversations in cluster meetings. They are a part of the circular design process mentioned in the section above. Teacher leaders and administrators evaluated teachers at the school, observational data were discussed in leadership meetings, and administrators and teacher leaders used the data to design and facilitate cluster meetings. Recognizing the importance of this process, one of the teacher leaders said, "I sort of see myself as a liaison between the administration and . . . the whole high school."

The mentor teachers in each of these settings acted as facilitators, determining the structure of meetings and creating environments in which teachers could work together to reach common goals. They participated in communities of practice in a variety of ways, coaching teachers and helping teachers to coach one another. Whether in formal or informal meetings, teacher leaders at ASU Prep created conditions conducive to communities of practice and aided in the development of peer coaching at the school. Figure 20.2 provides tips for creating these conditions.

ADOLESCENT PEER COACHES: HARVESTING YOUNG GARDENERS

"I feel that we're all alike. We're all like a family. We all work at helping get a better education. So I feel that I'm just another family member that we all look up to and that we all talk to whenever we need help. So we all contribute to each other's education."

The peer-coaching and community of practice model is part of the culture at ASU Prep not just with the administrators and teachers, but also among the students. We present one example of how the students and their writing teachers created a community of practice to support and build knowledge surrounding academic writing and peer-writing coaching. Like the communities of practice described previously, it is

What We've Learned from the Teacher Leaders	Tips for Teacher Leaders
• By creating a positive, comfortable, and collegial environment in formal meetings, teacher leaders help teachers to become productive peer coaches during scheduled meetings and in informal interactions. • One-legged meetings, short and informal interactions among teachers and teacher leaders, are just as important as formal meetings. • Effective teacher leaders are supportive rather than exclusively directive. They help teachers to solve problems, make adjustments to instruction, and find the resources. • Formal and informal evaluations can lead to conversations about teaching strategies, collaborations with teachers, and opportunities for peer coaching.	• Develop a sense of collegiality and collaboration among teachers. • Help teachers to feel comfortable and safe in sharing what they know and what they want to know. • Make time for the teachers with whom you work. Remember that people participate in communities of practice and engage in peer coaching in many different ways. • As you consider the needs of teachers and students, look for resources within your team and work with teachers to find creative solutions for problems. • When conducting observations and postobservation evaluations, be respectful and state your observations based on the approved evaluation protocol or rubric.

FIGURE 20.2. Lessons learned from and tips for teacher leaders.

important to note that the transformation of a group of peer-writing coaches into a community of practice was carefully cultivated and took time and patience.

Peer coaching is one model that has been effective in positively affecting both the coach and the peers with whom they collaborate (Dale, 1994; Downing, Brewer, Reid, & Rhine, 2003; Yong, 2010). As Yarrow and Topping (2001) point out, collaborative peer coaching can lead to metacognitive gains as well as skill gains for all students involved in the coaching process. Peers receiving coaching from trained peer tutors benefit from the immediate one-on-one practice, while the coaches learn through teaching and explaining. As well as increasing the writing skills of coaches and their peers, adolescents who participate in peer-writing groups can build collaborative coaching communities (Yarrow & Topping, 2001). Accordingly, they develop a sense of identity, learn collaborative social interactions, and share their expertise (Yong, 2010).

If one were to walk into Room 262 at ASU Prep on a Tuesday or Thursday afternoon, one would often see a cohort of three or four peer writers working with their 9th- and 10th-grade peers. The snapshot below represents the kinds of conversations that commonly take place between the writers and the coaches during a typical 45-minute session. During their writing class earlier that week, the students had been introduced to literary analysis by using a fairytale to model and to practice writing one. In this peer-writing session Darlene, a 10th-grade peer-writing coach worked with another 10th grader, Anna, through this process.

DARLENE: Hi, how's it going today? I see you're working on your literary analysis paper. Let's begin by reading it out loud to see what we want to focus on. Would you like me to read it or would you like to read it?

ANNA: You can read it.

DARLENE: (*Reads the paper out loud*) OK, so what do you think the strengths of your paper are?

ANNA: I think I have topic sentences and I have my context . . . and I've said Cinderella is obedient.

DARLENE: When we read it I noticed that not all of your paragraphs included quotes. How do you think you might be able to include some quotes in your paragraphs?

ANNA: I think I could . . . oh, OK, I think I know . . . (*Begins to make margin notes on her own paper.*) When the narrator says that "the poor girl suffered it all patiently . . . " I could use that.

DARLENE: Good. OK. Let's look at the next part. (*Reads out loud.*)

"The Character of Cinderella is betrayed as obedient. The reason being is because in the beginning of the story the narrator states that Cinderella was obedient her stepsisters and her stepmother . . . " Let's look at that. I wonder if *betrayed* is the right word there. What do you think?

ANNA: Um . . . I'm not sure. I wanted to say that is the way the author writes the character. Like that is the way we see her when we read the story. The narrator says she "was obedient to her stepsisters" . . . oh, I think there needs to be a *to* there.

DARLENE: OK. Add it in. (*Anna does.*) What else? So, that's how she's portrayed? Is that the word you mean?

ANNA: Yes, *portrayed*, not *betrayed* . . . (*Edits her paper.*)

The session continued along similar lines, with the Darlene and Anna working through the writing process engaged in conversation and reflection. Through prompting, questioning, and guidance, Darlene helped Anna to analyze, edit, and revise her own writing. If Darlene had needed guidance as a coach or had been unsure as to what kinds of questions could best help Anna, Darlene may have consulted the other peer-writing tutors who were in the room with her at the time or she may have asked Lettice Pelotte (the third author of this chapter), who acts as the facilitating teacher during peer tutoring sessions. Most of the time, however, Darlene expertly handled the situation on her own, as did the other trained peer-writing tutors. In an interview Darlene discussed her process when engaged in a peer-coaching session:

"First, when I ask them a question I try restating the question. And then I try having them read over their work to me and see if they catch their error. So, first I have them try to catch it, then I ask the question and I'll rephrase it. I know what I'm doing is working by just the way they look me in the eye. The way they just start fixing things on their paper. I know when they're struggling or they don't understand what I'm trying to say. I know that if I were to get somebody that doesn't really understand, then I will go to another peer writer and say, 'Hey, you know, I'm having some trouble.' "

The peer-writer coaching project began in the summer of 2011 as collaboration between Josephine Peyton Marsh (first author of this chapter), and the writing center staff at Arizona State University. A core group of peer-writing coaches was invited to participate in a training camp at the end of their eighth-grade year. Teachers recommended students who were either good writers, potential leaders, or both to be in the first group of 12 peer-writing coaches in the new ninth-grade. During training camp, students participated in writing and tutoring activities to help them develop as both writers and peer coaches. The camp taught strategies for working with peers, suggested ideas for assisting other students during different stages of writing, engaged students in role-playing demonstrations of peer-writing coaching, and provided opportunities to participate in get-to-know you activities and writing activities. The training ended with a practicum in which the newly trained peer-writing coaches tutored elementary students and reflected on their experiences.

The original idea for the peer-writing coaches was to have a few peer coaches in each English class assist their peers in becoming more proficient academic writers. This idea took off in many directions. Over the next 2 years of the project, the initial core group remained relatively stable, and, with the guidance of teachers, mentored about 20 additional peer-writing coaches, now known as peer-writers, into the community of practice. These coaches began tutoring elementary students during lunch; they conducted peer-writing coaching during the final period of the day; and, finally, they developed an entirely student-run writing center offering reading and math tutoring to elementary students and peer coaching to other high school students as portrayed in the above snapshot.

The quote at the beginning of this section, taken from an interview with Darlene, describes how the peer-writing coaching community felt like family to her. It is clear that she saw the group as a community of people working together to improve their own writing and help others improve theirs. She further stated that the group is "linked through writing" and noted that "writing has a deeper meaning than just the words on the page." Similar to the communities of practice described in the previous sections of the chapter, the peer-writing coaches were "bound by shared expertise and passion for a joint enterprise" (Wenger & Snyder, 2000, p. 139), and they were goal oriented and focused on helping each other and other students think deeply about their writing. Peer-writing coaches work collaboratively and take a leadership role in the school.

Peer writers continue to participate in ongoing training delivered by their English teachers and the staff of the nearby university writing center. During this time, they share successes and difficulties encountered in their sessions and learn strategies for continued improvement. Each of the peer writers was given a coaching notebook in which they are encouraged to write and reflect after each session. Figure 20.3 contains more lessons learned. After one session, Darlene reflected:

> "I feel like we all take leadership in the group. And we all just enter ideas. I don't think that there's a single person that's the leader. We all contribute to the understanding of how to be a peer writer."

What We've Learned from the Peer-Writing Coaches	Tips for Peer Coaches and Their Teachers
• Adolescents can benefit from the collaborative learning structure of communities of practice. • Peer coaching helps develop the skills and metacognitive processes of both the coach and the recipient of coaching. • Collaborative peer coaching helps adolescents develop not only their literacy skills, but also their leadership skills.	• Make time for training to build tutoring strategies and confidence in the peer coaches and find time for ongoing training to address ongoing needs. • Help develop a sense of shared purpose among the peer coaches and the students they work with. This sense of community will help drive the project forward. • Remind coaches that they are not expected to know everything. Make sure they know they can rely on the other coaches and teachers for support.

FIGURE 20.3. Lessons learned from and tips for peer coaches and their teachers.

CONCLUSION

Darlene's statement that she feels like a member of a learning family reflects our deepest belief that real learning and knowing happens when people come together for a common goal and engage in intrinsically meaningful activities that result in the betterment of the group as a whole. Sociocultural learning theory asserts that learning takes places within social interactions (Vygotsky, 1978). Communities of practice provide a space for learning to take place socially—whether it is among peers or among peers and mentors.

Collaborative peer coaching in communities of practice is not an accidental happening, but a way of life at ASU Prep. Intentionally cultivated through administrative leadership, tended to by teachers and their leaders, and harvested by our students, communities of practice are continually growing, expanding, and changing in order to meet the needs of our school.

DISCUSSION AND ACTIVITIES

1. What is a community of practice? Describe the benefits and the problems that might be associated with developing communities of practice in the workplace.

2. Think about how you might initiate a community of practice that would encourage professional discussions about literacy instruction and learning among your peers. How would you do it? What conditions would need to be present in order for it to become a community?

3. Peer coaching can be beneficial for students and teachers. Imagine you were a teacher leader to an experienced teacher on your staff. How would you facilitate and build a peer coaching collaboration?

4. You agree that peer-writing coaches would assist your students in becoming better writers. You have tried peer editing before, and it was a total flop. After reading about the success of the peer-writing coaching community of practice you would like to try it again. Develop a plan including goals and outcomes.

REFERENCES

Dale, H. (1994). Collaborative writing interactions in one ninth-grade classroom. *Journal of Educational Research, 87*(6), 334–344.

Downing, J. A., Brewer, R. D., Reid, M. S., & Rhine, B. G. (2003). Peer coaching: Students teaching to learn. *Intervention in School and Clinic, 39*(2), 113–126.

Cambridge International Examinations. (2013. Cambridge, UK: University of Cambridge

Jewett, P., & Macphee, D. (2012) Adding collaborative peer coaching to our teaching identities. *The Reading Teacher, 66*(2), 105–110.

Lave, J. (1991). Situating learning in communities of practice. In L. Resnick, S. Levine, & L. Teasley (Eds.), *Perspectives on socially shared cognition* (pp. 63–82). Washington, DC: American Psychological Association.

Lave, J., & Wenger, E. (1991). *Situated learning: Legitimate peripheral participation.* Cambridge, UK: Cambridge University Press.

Marchese, J. (2012). Leading from the middle: Enhancing professional practice through peer coaching. *Independent School, 71*(4), 40–47.

National Governors Association Center for Best Practices & Council of Chief State School Officers. (2010). *Common Core State Standards for the English language arts and literacy in history/social studies, science, and technical subjects.* Washington, DC: Author.

Vogt, M., & Shearer, B. (2011). *Reading specialists and literacy coaches in the real world.* Boston: Pearson.

Vygotsky, L. S. (1978). *Mind in society: The development of higher psychological processes* (M. Cole, V. John-Steiner, S. Scribner, & E. Souberman, Eds.). Cambridge, MA: Harvard University Press.

Wenger, E. C. (2006). *Communities of practice: A brief introduction.* Retrieved from *www.ewenger.com/theory.*

Wenger, E. C., & Snyder, W. M. (2000). Communities of practice: The organizational frontier. *Harvard Business Review,* January-February, 139145.

Yarrow, F., & Topping, K. J. (2001). Collaborative writing: The effects of metacognitive prompting and structured peer interaction. *British Journal of Educational Psychology, 71,* 261–282.

Yong, Y. M. (2010). Collaborative writing features. *RELC Journal, 41*(1), 18–30.

Index

Page numbers followed by *f* or *t* indicate figures or tables.

ASIAN AMERICANS:
PERSONALITY PATTERNS, IDENTITY,
AND MENTAL HEALTH

ASIAN AMERICANS
Personality Patterns, Identity, and Mental Health

LAURA UBA

The Guilford Press
New York   London

Printed in the United States of America

This book is printed on acid-free paper.

Last digit is print number: 9 8 7 6 5 4 3 2

Library of Congress Cataloging-in-Publication Data

Uba, Laura
    Asian Americans: personality patterns, identity, and mental health   /
by Laura Uba
        p.   cm.
    Includes bibliographical references and index.
    ISBN 0-89862-372-3
    1. Asian Americans—Mental health.   2. Asian Americans—Mental
health services.   I. Title.
    [DNLM: 1. Mental Health.   2. Mental Disorders—ethnology.
3. Asian Americans—psychology.   WM 31 U12a 1994]
RC451.5.A75U23   1994
362.2′08995073—dc20
DNLM/DLC
for Library of Congress   93-41723
                                                                              CIP

Foreword

In 1982, Jim Morishima and I wrote *The Mental Health of Asian Americans*, the first textbook to deal with the mental health of Asian Americans. The book was widely used in Asian American and psychology courses at universities throughout the nation. Since the writing of that book, much has occurred in terms of the population growth of Asian Americans, newly emerging mental health issues, ethnic and race relations, and research findings and theories pertinent to Asian Americans. There is a critical need to address these contemporary events in an updated textbook.

This volume, *Asian Americans: Personality Patterns, Identity, and Mental Health*, is a scholarly contribution that clearly addresses major, contemporary issues facing Asian Americans with respect to personality and mental health, including family, socialization and personality, stress, immigration, mental disorders, assessment, and mental health treatment. In her presentation of these topics, Dr. Uba relies on the very latest research findings; her grasp of the available literature is, indeed, impressive. The references that she cites and lists should enable readers to appreciate the voluminous amount of research now being conducted on Asian Americans.

Two features of this book are noteworthy. First, there is coverage of Asian Americans in terms of the different and distinct Asian American groups. For years, researchers have had to conduct research primarily on Asian Americans as an aggregate, because it has been difficult to find sufficient numbers of members of individual groups (e.g., Chinese, Japanese, Koreans, Filipinos, and Vietnamese). Yet, we have become increasingly aware of the cultural, historical, and experiential differences among these distinct groups. Dr. Uba focuses not only on Eastern versus Western differences but also on differences within Asian groups. In the process, she demonstrates an in-depth understanding of the variability among Asian Americans.

Second, Asian Americans are an *ethnic minority* group. As implied in the phrase, the experiences of Asian Americans are a function of ethnicity (and cultural differences) as well as minority group status (i.e., being treated as a minority group). Uba clearly examines the influences of culture and the effects of acculturation. She also pays considerable attention to stereotypes and forms of prejudice and discrimination directed toward Asian Americans. The effects of these two variables—ethnicity and minority group status—are discussed throughout the book. They are indeed powerful influences, affecting personality development, mental health, and utilization of mental health services.

Having coauthored a similar book on Asian Americans, I can well appreciate the hard work and complexity of tasks that go into the writing of a successful book. Laura Uba has taken on those tasks and has written a highly important book in the field of Asian American psychology.

Department of Psychology   STANLEY SUE
University of California at Los Angeles
June 1993

Preface

In Asian epistemology, there is the idea that one cannot appreciate a flowing river by scooping up some of the water in one's hands and examining what one has collected (Watts, 1951). Outside of its context, the water cannot be truly apprehended for what it is. Analogously, to understand the psychological functioning of Asian Americans one cannot just study Asian Americans outside their psychosocial context. In this book, the personality patterns, ethnic identity, and mental heath of Asian Americans are examined in the context of cultural values and perspectives, experiences with racism, and, in the case of some Asian Americans, immigrant or refugee experiences.

Watching a river flow by, one notices the confluence of different tributaries flowing into the river, with some parts hitting rocks or taking wider turns, and others taking different paths. Similarly, there is diversity among Asian Americans, who come from different places, have different experiences, and encounter different obstacles, though appearing on the surface to have a common identity. Just as collecting handfuls of the river's water will not suffice to discover the river's true nature, so likewise by perusing this book and scooping up information on a particular Asian American group, you will not end up with a complete picture of that group, much less of a particular Asian American individual. You can, however, look for patterns in the flow. This book presents patterns of empirical research on Asian Americans.

This volume is a review of psychological research on Asian Americans. Studies of Asians residing in Asia are not included—for example, even though there has been psychological research on Chinese in Taiwan, such research is not included in this book unless it has also dealt with Chinese in America. The reason for excluding the Chinese in Taiwan is that they are living in a different cultural, social, economic, and racial milieu than Chinese in America. The focus of this book is on Asian Americans, not Asians in general.

This book is divided into three sections. The first section, comprising Chapters 1 through 5, looks at Asian American personality patterns and their antecedents. More specifically, the first chapter presents a demographic and historical profile of Asian American populations. The second chapter discusses Asian American cultural values and the presence of racism against Asian Americans as a conceptual framework for understanding Asian American personality patterns. Chapter 3 examines general characteristics of many Asian American families. Research on Asian American families is reviewed because family structure helps to explain personality tendencies, values, identity, sources of stress, and patterns of utilization of mental health services. Chapter 4 presents research findings on personality differences between Asian Americans and Euro-Americans. The fifth chapter looks at ethnic-identity issues.

The second section of the book, comprising Chapters 6 and 7, reviews the sources of stress for Asian Americans.

The third section, Chapters 8 through 10, focuses on the mental health needs of Asian Americans. Chapter 8 reviews empirical studies of rates of mental disorder among Asian Americans, predictors of mental disorders, and common manifestations of mental disorders among Asian Americans. In Chapter 9, the reasons why Asian Americans seem to underutilize available mental health services are discussed. Chapter 10 looks at Asian Americans in psychotherapy. The final chapter provides a brief concluding note.

Acknowledgments

I would like to thank Dr. Stephen Fugita, Dr. Karen Huang, Ms. Kitty Moore, and Dr. Elizabeth Shon for their valuable feedback on rough drafts of this book. I would also like to thank Dr. Stanley Sue for his valuable insight into the book publication process. Thanks to the anonymous students who let me quote them and to the students who provided useful feedback on a rough draft of this book. Thanks also to Dr. Kenyon Chan and the Asian American Studies Department at California State University Northridge for providing institutional support. Finally, thanks to my family for all their support and encouragement, including my dad for his support and confidence-building before I started this book.

Contents

1

A Diverse Population

ASIAN AMERICAN POPULATION

The terms "Asian American"[1] and "Asian/Pacific Islander American" apply to members of over 25 groups that have been classified as a single group because of their common ethnic origins in Asia and the Pacific Islands, similar physical appearance, and similar cultural values. The Asian Americans studied by psychologists have been confined primarily to those of Cambodian, Chinese, Filipino, Hmong, Japanese, Korean, Lao, Mien, or Vietnamese ancestry. Other Asian American groups—such as Asian Indians, Guamanians, Indonesians, Samoans, and Thais—rarely have been studied by psychologists.[2]

---

[1]The term "Asian American" has been in common use since the late 1960s. It arose in the context of the civil rights movement. Just as African Americans generally discarded the term "Negro" because it carried so many disparaging stereotypes, most Asian Americans discarded the term "Oriental." In the 1960s, most people of Asian ancestry in the United States were American born. But since the 1965 Immigration Act, there has been a large influx of Asian immigrants, not all of whom have become citizens of the United States. Although those who have not become U.S. citizens are technically not Americans, researchers in psychology generally have subsumed them under the preexisting term, "Asian American." Researchers usually combine citizens and noncitizens in their statistical analyses because of limited sample sizes. Therefore, in this book the term "Asian American" will include both Asian American citizens and Asian foreigners living in the United States.

[2]Most of the research on mental health among Asian Americans has focused on Chinese Americans, Japanese Americans, and, more recently, Southeast Asian refugees. When other groups are included in samples, they are regarded generally as Asian Americans, and separate analyses of different Asian American groups usually are not performed. Moreover, much of the research on Southeast Asians has treated them as a homogeneous entity, in part because small sample sizes mitigate against analyses of the

1

Psychological research on Asian Americans generally started in the 1960s. The Asian American population has changed quite a bit since then. In 1960, with a population of fewer than 1 million constituting 0.5% of the U.S. population, most Asian Americans were descendants of earlier Japanese and Chinese immigrants.[3] By 1990, the number of Asian Americans had increased to 2.9% of the U.S. population, or 7,272,662. Now most Asian Americans are foreign born, and the proportions of the different ethnic groups constituting the Asian American population have been altered radically. Census estimates appear in Table 1.1.

The classification of a multitude of groups under the single rubric Asian Americans carries some potential dangers. For example, important differences among groups can be overlooked. In fact, Asian Americans are culturally and experientially quite diverse: they differ in degrees of acculturation, migration experiences, occupational skills (Shu & Satele, 1977), cultural values and beliefs, religion, primary language, personality syndromes (D. W. Sue & Frank, 1973), income, education, average age (Jiobu, 1988), ethnic identity (D. W. Sue & Kirk, 1973), and so forth.

Subsuming disparate groups under the single category of Asian Americans also can blind the unwary to individual differences and can lead to the formation of stereotypes. In addition to interethnic differences (i.e., variations among Asian American groups), there are intraethnic differences (i.e., variations within each Asian American group) in gender, generation, attitudes, degree of assimilation, traumatic experiences, socioeconomic status, identity, and so forth, which affect personality patterns, sources of stress, identity conflicts, attitudes toward mental health services, and the need for mental health services.

Historical Background

To help you understand some of the bases for these interethnic and intraethnic differences, consider the immigration history of the various Asian American groups that usually are the subjects of psychological research on Asian Americans.

---

various Southeast Asian subgroups. While there are similarities in history and culture among the Southeast Asian countries, there are also differences. In this book, when researchers have focused on one Southeast Asian group, I note which Southeast Asian group was studied; and when researchers have included a variety of Southeast Asian groups in their samples, I refer to the samples as "Southeast Asians."

[3]At that time, about 52% of Asian Americans were Japanese Americans, 27% were Chinese Americans, 20% were Filipino Americans, and 1% were Korean Americans.

TABLE 1.1 Asian American/Pacific Islander Population Based on 1990 Census Estimates

Ethnic group	Population in U.S.	Percentage of Asian American population	Percentage of population foreign born
Chinese	1,645,472	22.6%	56%
Filipino	1,406,770	19.3%	64%
Japanese	847,562	11.7%	33%
Asian Indian	815,447	11.2%	57%
Korean	798,849	11.0%	71%
Vietnamese	614,547	8.5%	92%
Cambodian	417,411	5.8%	80%
Hawaiian	211,014	2.9%	n/a
Lao	149,014	2.1%	n/a
Thai	91,275	1.3%	n/a
Hmong	90,082	1.2%	n/a
Samoan	62,964	.9%	n/a
Guamanian	49,345	.7%	n/a

Note. Data from U.S. Bureau of Census. Calculation of the percentage of the population that is foreign born is based on the sample of residents who filled out the long form of the census. Basing the percentage of foreign-born Chinese on persons born in Taiwan, The People's Republic of China, and Hong Kong may underestimate the percentage of foreign-born Chinese because many ethnic Chinese were born in Vietnam. The percentage of foreign-born Lao and Hmong cannot be shown because the different ethnic groups both come primarily from one country, Laos: Therefore, a comparison of the number of foreign-born Laotians to the total number of different Laotian ethnic groups would not reveal the percentage of foreign-born Lao or the percentage of foreign-born Hmong.

Chinese Americans

The Chinese were the first Asians to immigrate to the United States in large numbers; they started coming to the United States around the middle of the nineteenth century. But Chinese immigration was severely restricted by the 1882 Exclusion Act and was completely forbidden by the 1924 Immigration Act. The 1882 Exclusion Act and subsequent extensions of the Exclusion Act, antimiscegenation laws, special taxes directed against the Chinese, and discrimination in housing and employment limited the size of the Chinese population, limited the number of Chinese women in the United States, and forced the Chinese into Chinatown ghettos. Because there were few Chinese women in the United States until the second half of the twentieth century, most of the Chinese men in this first wave of emigration from China, numbering over 300,000 (the majority of whom eventually returned to China), did not father children in the United States. There are now some third-, fourth-, fifth-, and sixth-generation Chinese Americans who are descendants of that first wave of Chinese immigrants who had children. However, since most Chinese men of that first wave of immigration did not have children in the United States, third-, fourth-, fifth-, and sixth-generation Chinese Americans constitute a relatively small proportion of the total Chinese American population.

A second wave of a few thousand Chinese came to the United States after World War II. During the war, the United States, fearing that China might join forces with Japan, sought friendly relations with China and repealed the Exclusion Act, conceding to the Chinese a small immigration quota. After the war, when the communists took control of China, the United States government encouraged Chinese scientists and professionals and their families to immigrate to the United States. Therefore, in addition to the descendants of the first wave of emigration from China, there are now in the United States those Chinese Americans composing the second wave of Chinese immigrants and the children and grandchildren of those immigrants.

A third wave of Chinese immigrated to the United States after the 1965 Immigration Act (and the 1990 extension of that act), which gives priority to immigrants who have special skills (needed in the United States) or who are joining their families already in the United States. Under the current quota, having relatives who are citizens or residents of the United States improves an individual's chances to immigrate. Thus, with the third wave of Chinese immigration, either entire families have immigrated at once or one family member has immigrated, has established himself or herself as a permanent U.S. resident or citizen, and then has sponsored other family members. The 1965 Immigration Act marked a radical change in U.S. immigration policy: Quotas were no longer based on race. Tens of thousands of Chinese have come to the United States every year since the 1965 Immigration Act became law. The fact that Taiwan, the People's Republic of China, and Hong Kong each have separate quotas has further increased the number of Chinese who can immigrate to the United States under the 1965 Immigration Act and its extension.

In recent decades, Chinese have come to the United States to seek better standards of living and higher education for their children, and, in the case of the Taiwanese, to help sons avoid the draft. These Chinese have primarily emigrated from Taiwan, Hong Kong, the

People's Republic of China, and (because Chinese immigrated to Southeast Asia centuries ago) Vietnam. Owing to the size of this third wave, most Chinese in the United States are foreign born.

Because some Chinese families have been in the United States for five or six generations (descendants of the first wave) and others have arrived in the United States as recently as last week (members of the third wave), there is a great diversity in the Chinese community. Consequently, some Chinese are very Americanized while others are much less familiar with American life; some speak only English or Chinese while others are bilingual or trilingual (speaking Chinese, Vietnamese, and English); some grew up in the staid American middle class while others experienced horrendous psychological and physical traumas before fleeing Southeast Asia.

Japanese Americans

Japanese immigrants started coming to Hawaii in large numbers in the 1880s and to the U.S. mainland in the 1890s to avoid the military draft in Japan and to work on plantations in Hawaii and farms on the mainland of the United States. Because of its fear of the military might that Japan had demonstrated in China and Russia at the turn of the century, the U.S. government did not immediately totally exclude the Japanese from immigration. However, the 1906 Executive Order #589 and the 1907 Gentlemen's Agreement, restricting but not excluding the immigration of Japanese to the United States, signaled to the Japanese immigrants that a total ban on Japanese immigration could happen quickly. Thus, many Japanese immigrants in the United States either sent to Japan for a "picture-bride" wife or went to Japan, found a wife, and returned to the United States. As a result of these marriages, the Japanese tended to establish families quickly. There were between 130,000 and 150,000 people of Japanese ancestry in the United States when the Immigration Act of 1924 prohibited further Japanese immigration.

Owing to these various immigration restrictions, relatively distinct generational cohorts of Japanese in the United States were established. The members of the first generation (called the *Issei*) were born in Japan and generally married between 1907 (the year of the Gentlemen's Agreement) and 1924 (when Japanese could no longer come to the United States); those belonging to the second generation (called the *Nisei*) were generally born in the United States between 1910 and 1940; Japanese Americans of the third generation (called the *Sansei*) were by and large born between 1940 and 1965; and the members of the fourth generation (called the *Yonsei*) have generally been born since 1965. Although there were Japanese war brides and occupation brides after World War II and a small number of Japanese immigrants after passage of the 1965 Immigrant Act, most Japanese Americans are American-born, second-, third-, or fourth-generation descendants of those who came to the U.S. mainland or to Hawaii before 1924. As a group, Japanese Americans are the most acculturated of the Asian American groups. Not only have Japanese Americans been in the United States the longest as families, but evidence suggests that the experiences of Japanese Americans during World War II pushed the Japanese American community toward assimilation and away from the retention of much of Japanese culture (Nagata, 1991).

Korean Americans

Most of the first wave of Korean immigrants came to the United States between 1903 and 1905, although a few hundred students/political refugees continued coming to the United States until the 1924 Immigration Act ended all Korean immigration. There were fewer than 10,000 Koreans in this first wave of immigration. Many of them stayed in the United States because they did not want to return to Korea while it was under Japan's harsh and exploitative rule. The vast majority of these Korean immigrants were males who were subject to the same antimiscegenation laws that applied to the Chinese and Japanese. Thus, very few Korean Americans today are the descendants of those first few thousand Koreans.

Another small wave of Koreans came to the United States after World War II, when Japan lost control of Korea. The Korean War was fought—Korea being divided into North and South Korea—and a small immigration quota for Koreans was established. Only a few hundred Koreans, primarily war brides and orphans, annually immigrated to the United States during the post-World War II period. Thus, there is now in the United States a small number of second-wave Korean immigrants and the children and grandchildren of those immigrants.

Since the 1965 Immigration Act, there has been a large influx of Korean immigrants seeking better standards of living and college educations for their children. About 30,000 Koreans have come to the United States every year since the 1965 Immigration Act. As with the post-1965 Chinese immigrants, most of the Koreans who immigrated to the United States after 1965 came over in one of two ways: An entire family immigrated or one member of a family immigrated and later sponsored the admission of the other members of the family. Most contemporary Korean Americans were not living in the United States prior to 1965. Therefore, most Korean Americans are immigrants, though there is quite a difference between Koreans who immigrated twenty years ago and those who have come more recently.

Filipino Americans

Filipinos[4] started to immigrate to Hawaii in large numbers around 1909 and to the U.S. mainland around 1920. The first wave of Filipino immigrants was primarily composed of male agricultural laborers. Over 100,000 Filipinos came to the United States in the first wave, yet there are few descendants because most of those laborers never married or had children. The first wave ended in the 1930s, when Congress essentially excluded Filipinos by establishing a quota of 50 Filipino immigrants per year. After World War II, the quota was raised to 100 per year; and this quota, plus the War Brides Act, resulted in a small second wave of Filipino immigrants.

It was not until the 1965 Immigration Act that large numbers of Filipinos immigrated to the United States. Like other Asians who immigrated to the United States, these Filipinos sought better employment opportunities and a better future for their children. Tens of thousands of Filipinos have immigrated to the United States every year since the 1965 Immigration Act. Most of the Filipinos in the United States today are immigrants or second-generation Filipino Americans. Because of American colonialism in the Philippines from the Spanish–American War to the end of World War II and the U.S. military presence in the Philippines until 1992, Filipino immigrants are much more familiar with American culture than most immigrants.

Southeast Asians

With the end of the Vietnam War, Southeast Asian refugees started coming to the United States in large numbers in 1975, when roughly

---

[4]There are differing opinions concerning the use of the terms "Filipino" or "Pilipino." Since the *f* sound is not used in native Filipino dialects, some think that the term Filipino is a symbol of the subjugation of the Philippines by colonial powers. For that reason, these Filipinos prefer to be called Pilipino Americans. Others think that using the term "Pilipino Americans" might be confusing or imply that they cannot pronounce the *f* sound. Because more Filipino Americans seem to use the term "Filipino" instead of "Pilipino" when talking with non-Filipinos, the term "Filipino" is used in this book.

130,000 Southeast Asian refugees came to the United States. Those who came were mostly Vietnamese, urban, relatively well-educated, and more proficient in English than subsequent refugees have been. Since 1978, a second wave of Southeast Asian refugees has come to the United States to escape persecution. This wave has included Vietnamese, Chinese-Vietnamese, Cambodians, Lao, Hmong, and Mien. In recent years, Thais have come to the United States in small numbers, but they have come as sojourners or immigrants rather than refugees.

In summary, Chinese Americans have basically come to the United States in three waves over 150 years. A sixth-generation Chinese American, being very acculturated and comparatively removed from China, will be very different from a first-generation Chinese person who arrived in the United States this year from Vietnam. Most Japanese Americans today are the descendants of Japanese who immigrated to Hawaii or the U.S. mainland before 1924. Because of their shared acculturation and experiences with racism, a fourth-generation Chinese American and a third-generation Japanese American might have more in common with each other (in terms of attitudes, behavioral styles, acculturation level, and socioeconomic status) than a fourth-generation Chinese American would have with a first-generation Chinese immigrant. Almost all Filipino and Korean Americans came to the United States in their third waves, yet the similarities between Filipino Americans and Korean Americans are limited. Since the Philippines was an American colony, in general the third-wave Filipinos are much more Americanized than third-wave Koreans or Chinese. But there are large differences among third-wave Filipinos. For example, some Filipino immigrants were financially well-to-do in the Philippines, while many were extremely poor; and there are cultural differences among these immigrants not only because they have come from different social strata but also because they have come from different areas of the country. Southeast Asian refugees are quite different from other Asian Americans, in their experiences and in their reasons for coming to the United States. There are also differences within each Southeast Asian group. For instance, the Vietnamese who came to the United States in 1975 were quite different from the second wave of Vietnamese (e.g., in education, social class, and familiarity with American culture). Thus, there is a wide array of interethnic and intraethnic differences among Asian Americans.

Readers interested in more information on the history of Asian Americans may find it helpful to refer to Sucheng Chan's *Asian Americans: An Interpretive History* (1991), Ronald Takaki's *Strangers From A Different Shore* (1989), and Roger Daniels' *Asian American: Chinese and Japanese in the United States Since 1850* (1988).

EXAMINING ASIAN AMERICAN PERSONALITY AND MENTAL HEALTH

Some Asian Americans ask, "Why are you focusing on Asian Americans as a different group? We're just human beings like everyone else." There are ways in which Asian Americans are just like all other people but there are ways in which Asian Americans are unique: beyond the universal or core similarities shared by all humans, there are also cultural differences among groups of people. Unfortunately for those interested in examining the core similarities between Asian Americans and other people, much of the research in Asian American psychology has focused on ways in which Asian Americans are different from other Americans. If a researcher studies different groups, including Asian Americans, and finds no differences among the groups (in effect, finding some support for universal similarities), the editors of psychology journals will usually reject such a study: It will not be published precisely because statistically significant differences were not found—and, therefore, the study will be judged to be insignificant. Therefore, our understanding of Asian American psychology is based largely on studies showing how Asian Americans differ from other Americans.[5]

However, this is not an altogether negative state of affairs. These studies add to a multicultural perspective that enhances not only one's understanding of Asian Americans but also one's appreciation of and respect for the differences that exist among people. These studies also clarify the universality and cultural limits of assumptions about psychological functioning (Ibrahim, 1984; S. Sue & Morishima, 1982) and the research results based primarily on non-Asian Americans.

The focus of this book is on Asian American personality patterns, ethnic identity of Asian Americans, sources of psychological stress for Asian Americans, manifestations of mental disorders among Asian Americans, and the use of mental health services by Asian Americans. There are differences between Asian Americans and other Americans in these areas. Two important elements contributing to differences between Asian Americans and other Americans in these areas are cultural values and experiences with racism. These elements will be discussed in the next chapter.

---

[5]In psychological research, Asian Americans are usually compared to Euro-Americans. When Asian Americans, Euro-Americans, and non-Asian American minorities are included in studies, the size of either the Asian American sample or the non-Asian American minority sample is usually too small to be a basis for generalizations. For that reason, most of the discussion in this book compares Asian Americans to Euro-Americans.

2

Culture and Race

The cultural and racial environments in which Asian Americans have been raised and in which they find themselves today affect their personalities and mental health needs. Asian Americans are not simply darker versions of Euro-Americans. When trying to understand why people behave the way they do, it does not make sense to ignore their racial and cultural background any more than it makes sense to ignore their gender and age. Certainly, an individual's gender, age, and ethnicity are largely irrelevant to some behaviors but not to the full range of behaviors.

Cultural and racial context cannot always explain an Asian American's behavior. Sometimes the experiences one has had as a member of a racial minority and the cultural values that one has been taught are irrelevant to a particular behavior or personality pattern. But the recognition of irrelevance can only come in the context of knowledge: It is important to have an understanding of the cultural and racial contexts in which Asian Americans live in order to recognize whether and to what degree cultural and racial experiences pertain to one's personality, experiences, and problems.

Assessing whether a behavior is psychopathological depends in large part on the context in which that behavior takes place. A person who believes that a given behavior is either normal/psychologically healthy or abnormal/psychologically unhealthy, without reference to social context, would probably be hard-pressed in trying to justify to a Kalahari bushman why American men wear neckties or American women wear uncomfortable, spiked, high-heeled shoes.

"Normal" psychological functioning is usually defined as the behavior that is most common. But that definition has a bias. Insofar as most Americans are Euro-Americans and most of the institutional power in the United States is in the hands of Euro-Americans, Euro-American behavior patterns would be considered normal for Americans. Cultural characteristics of Asian Americans that differ from those of Euro-Americans would be classified as abnormal (D. W. Sue & D. Sue, 1990; D. W. Sue & S. Sue, 1972b).[1] Often, what is considered to be normal or mentally healthy is that which fits within the boundaries of social norms. But social norms vary. For example, what is considered mentally healthy varies with culture, education, age, and sometimes gender.

Does a female college student have a psychological problem if she refuses to hold hands with her boyfriend when they are at her parents' house? Should her boyfriend infer that she is frigid? What if she drapes herself all over her boyfriend at school but keeps him at arm's length at her parents' house? Is the problem that she is fickle, or that she has multiple personalities, or that she is ashamed of him, or that he sometimes has body odor? You might judge her behavior differently if you heard that she was a Euro-American, or a fifth-generation Chinese American, or a Korean American immigrant from a very traditional Korean family.

Suppose a 17-year-old female has an elder brother who gruffly orders her to vacuum his room and wash his car. If she says, "Yes, older brother," and does the work without complaint, does it mean that she is a passive, spineless doormat or that she is a good girl? You need to know the cultural context to judge her behavior. If she is a Korean immigrant, her behavior would be in keeping with traditional Korean family norms; and, therefore, acquiescing to her brother's demand may not indicate poor self-esteem or pathological passivity. If she is an African American or a fourth-generation Japanese American, you may interpret her behavior as a symptom of poor self-esteem. If she responds, "In your dreams!" when her elder brother gruffly orders her to vacuum his room and wash his car, is she a disobedient, immature, uncultured girl or is she an independent person with

---

[1]If one permitted the definition of "normal" to be dictated by the dominant social norms in the United States, one would be saying, in effect, that "white is right." Such a Eurocentric perspective would show little appreciation for cultural diversity. This perspective would imply that mental health is defined by the social norms of the dominant group: Whatever the majority or the dominant group does is mentally healthy, and whatever anyone else does, which does not mirror the behavior of the majority or dominant group, is mentally unhealthy. If one allowed that definition of "normal" to be determined by the social norms of traditional Asian cultures, one would, in effect, be overlooking the relevancy of one's residence in the United States. A culturally sensitive definition of "normal" must be relativistic to some extent.

self-esteem (who will not kowtow to his demands)? Again, your interpretation or her interpretation of whether such a response indicates a psychological problem depends on the cultural context of her behavior.

Culture refers to the beliefs, attitudes, values, behavior patterns, and modes of communicating that are shared by a group. Insofar as culture affects what people perceive and how they understand and respond to their environment, Asian American cultures can be expected to affect family dynamics; personality; the meanings attributed to behaviors; the perception of what constitutes a psychological problem; the manifestation, appraisal, and treatment of psychological problems; and the perception of behavioral alternatives. To understand some of the behaviors of Asian Americans—and to understand whether the behavior of a particular Asian American is abnormal—one has to be familiar with Asian American cultural values and perspectives. The following discussion of cultural values and experiences with racism will be the basis for a subsequent examination of traditional Asian American family structure, Asian American personalities, and Asian American attitudes toward mental health services.

CULTURAL VALUES AND PERSPECTIVES

The term "Asian culture" is technically a misnomer. Although Confucianism, Taoism, and Buddhism underlie many Asian cultural values—and although the tenets of these belief systems are shared by many Asian cultures—there also are significant differences among Asian cultures. Similarly, to speak of "Asian American culture" as a singular entity is misleading. Insofar as different Asian Americans reconcile Asian cultural traditions and American culture in different ways, there is no single Asian American culture. Different Asian American groups are not even reconciling the same Asian cultural traditions (because they have come from different countries and at different times in history) to the same experiences in America. Therefore, the terms "Asian culture" and "Asian values" are used for heuristic purposes only.[2]

In psychological research, it is commonly assumed that traditional Asian American values are based at least in part on traditional Asian

---

[2]While some cultural values also derive from socioeconomic status (Slaughter-Defoe, Nakagawa, Takanishi, & Johnson, 1990), psychological research on Asian Americans has tended not to focus on socioeconomic status as a variable affecting cultural values so this aspect of cultural values will not be emphasized.

values but two things are never discussed: (1) the time frame used to define traditional values and (2) the differences between Asian American and Asian values. These have never been systematically analyzed or empirically examined. For present purposes, Asian American cultural values will refer to those values, beliefs, and attitudes that have been reported in psychological research as being traditionally promoted—or dominant—in Asian American communities.

Asian American cultural values are discussed in order to provide some understanding of the difference between Asian American values and (Euro-) American values and the implications of these differences for the behavior of Asian Americans. These values are also presented in order to provide a framework within which to understand the research findings.

There are differences among Asian Americans just as there are among members of other groups. For example, among Asian Americans there are significant differences in values. Asian Americans hold traditional Asian values to varying degrees. The traditional Asian values presented here represent a historical context for understanding values among Asian Americans. It may be that very few Asian Americans adhere to all of these traditional values. Moreover, the values of some Asian Americans might be relatively traditional whereas the values of other Asian Americans might be so typically "American" that it would be difficult to distinguish their values from that of the so-called average American. In between these poles would be innumerable variations.[3]

It is not even completely accurate to define the extremes of the values continuum as traditional Asian values versus American values. It is misleading to label one extreme as "traditional Asian values" when even the most traditional Asian Americans might hold Asian values that are not traditional. Asian values and cultures evolve just as other value systems and cultures do. The Asian values and cultures of today are not the same as traditional Asian values and cultures of

---

[3]Acculturation refers to cultural assimilation (i.e., the adoption of American cultural patterns). In practice, researchers have defined acculturation unidimensionally—that is, based on responses to questionnaires, individuals are placed on a continuum from Asian to American (S. Sue & Morishima, 1982). In subsequent chapters, I use the terms "unacculturated Asian Americans" and "traditional Asian Americans" to denote Asian Americans who tend to adhere to traditional Asian values; I use the term "acculturated Asian Americans" to refer to those who are relatively Americanized. These terms are intended only as hypothetical constructs for the sake of brevity and not because such a simple dichotomy exists.

centuries ago. At the other end of the continuum, it also is misleading to talk about "American values" as if they were homogeneous, clearly defined, static, and synonymous with middle-class, Euro-American attitudes and beliefs. Besides individual differences, there are numerous social-class, gender, and regional differences in American values. In addition, American values are not necessarily the opposite of Asian values; therefore, it is misleading to put these sets of American and Asian values at opposite ends of a continuum.

Moreover, an additive model would not accurately reflect how Asian Americans synthesize Asian and American values and perspectives. Individuals do not simply combine traditional Asian values and dominant American values as one would collect rocks: add a few here, throw out a few there. Rather, the very combining and balancing of values within different personal and social contexts is a dynamic, integrated process. Asian American individuals will vary in their syntheses of personal experiences, Asian culture, and American culture as a function of their intelligence, education, gender, exposure to Asian culture (which would depend on place of birth—whether abroad or in the United States—and on age at the time of immigration, if foreign born), and so on. Nevertheless, a benefit can be derived from reviewing traditional Asian values inasmuch as these values constitute some type of context for Asian American values.[4]

Asian American values are very rarely studied empirically. The following depiction of values is based primarily on clinical observations and historical analyses.[5] Intended as a starting point or a frame of reference for the uninitiated, this discussion may provide a basis for understanding the behaviors of some Asian Americans.

Traditional Asian values are largely grounded in Confucianism and Buddhism.[6] Among the traditional Asian values thought to

---

[4]Clearly, a full appreciation of Asian American cultural values requires a more thorough review of Asian histories, Asian American history, and Asian American cultures than can be provided here. Such an appreciation also requires experience in Asian American communities, which is beyond the purview of this book. Still, some accounting of values is necessary.

[5]"Clinical observations" refers to patterns that psychotherapists have seen. "Empirical studies" refers to studies using scientific methods.

[6]Around 500 B.C., Confucius introduced into religion (which up to then had focused on gaining luck and the propitious intervention of spirits) an emphasis on moral behavior. He thought that the solution to the political and social disorder plaguing China lay in adherence to the moral principles that he set forth. Among the values promoted by Confucius and neo-Confucianists were interpersonal harmony, knowledge and acceptance of one's place in society and the family (with males and elders assuming ascendant positions), obedience, and orientation toward the group.

characterize most Asian American groups is an emphasis on maintaining harmony in relationships (Abbott, 1976; Caplan, Whitmore, & Choy, 1989; JWK International, 1978; Union of Pan Asian Communities, 1978). Some other values are promoted, in part, because they help to maintain interpersonal harmony. These other values include the precedence of group interests over individual interests (Abbott, 1976; Goldstein, 1988; JWK International, 1978; Kitano & Kikumura, 1976; Shon & Ja, 1982; S. Sue & D. W. Sue, 1973; Timberlake & Cook, 1984), the precedence of duties over rights (Moore, 1967), and the importance of fulfilling obligations (Asian American Community Mental Health Training Center, 1976; JWK International, 1978), particularly obligations to family (Caplan et al., 1989; Chew & Ogi, 1987; Fong, 1973; Payton, 1985; Pedersen, 1991; D. W. Sue, 1989a; Takamura, 1991; Union of Pan Asian Communities, 1978). Some research has confirmed that family needs often take precedence over individual desires in both immigrant Chinese and American-born Chinese families (Young, 1972a, 1972b). The importance of reciprocating for the kindness of others is also emphasized (Lott, 1976; Union of Pan Asian Communities, 1978).

Individuals will adhere to many of these values, even when they are not directly aware that the values serve interpersonal harmony. If you ask them why they behave the way they do, they might say, "Because that's what is expected of me," rather than, "For the sake of interpersonal harmony."

Putting the group ahead of the individual may have been manifested in the instance that follows. Years ago, there was a Japanese American female who was an A student in high school. Her father, anticipating that she would be offered scholarships, told her not to apply for any scholarships because he could afford to send her to college; he told her to leave those scholarships for people who otherwise could not afford to go to college. When the school counselor told her to apply for scholarships and the student relayed what her father had said, the counselor informed the student that there were a number of scholarships that were not based on financial need. The counselor encouraged the student to apply for these scholarships because the student's chances of being awarded one were good. The student asked her father about the scholarships that were not based on financial need. He said that she should also leave those scholarships for people who could not afford college. One way to explain the father's behavior is that he was a generous man who believed that all people should have a chance for education and that America was better off with more educated people. While he was not foregoing the scholarships in order to maintain interpersonal harmony, by his generosity the father was putting the interests of the many ahead of his own personal, financial interest.[7]

The following behaviors are valued by traditional Asian culture in part because they promote interpersonal harmony: being patient (Caplan et al., 1989; Fong, 1973; Union of Pan Asian Communities, 1978), gentle (Fong, 1973), well mannered (Kalish & Moriwaki, 1973), and cooperative (Goldstein, 1988; Union of Pan Asian Communities, 1978); being accommodating, conciliatory, and receptive rather than confrontational (Tung, 1985); blending in with the group rather than distinguishing oneself through either good or bad behavior (Morrow, 1987); not being bumptious by talking about one's accomplishments or expressing one's opinions (Brower, 1989); and being humble and modest[8] (Chew & Ogi, 1987; Fong, 1973; Kobata, 1979; Union of Pan Asian Communities, 1978). For example, a Chinese American business-man might have an enormously successful company, but when his friends ask how his business is doing, he may say, "Oh, I'm scraping by." By responding this way, the businessman might avoid making his friends feel inferior and, thus, disrupting interpersonal harmony.

Other behaviors that historically have been valued, in part because they promote interpersonal harmony, include withholding the free expression of feelings (Chew & Ogi, 1987; Fong, 1973; Kalish & Mo-riwaki, 1973; Kobata, 1979; Payton, 1985; D. W. Sue & S. Sue, 1972a; Tashima & Ito, 1982; Timberlake & Cook, 1984; Union of Pan Asian Communities, 1978), suppression of conflict (Fugita, Ito, Abe, & Takeu-chi, 1991), "avoid[ing] potentially divisive arguments and debates, . . . talk[ing] about only safe subjects, . . . keep[ing] discussions on a superficial, nonthreatening level" (Watanabe, 1973, p. 394), communi-cating indirectly (Nagata, 1989a), and refraining from openly challeng-ing other's perspectives (Ho, 1976; L. N. Huang & Ying, 1989). A reliance on nonverbal communication (JWK International, 1978) also promotes harmonious relationships because disapproval can be com-municated in a way not as socially disruptive as verbal challenges.

There is also an emphasis on conformity to conventional behavior (Union of Pan Asian Communities, 1978). For example, a Japanese

---

[7]Throughout this book, explanations are posited for behaviors illustrated in anecdotes and reported in empirical studies. Recognizing that there can be a multitude of explanations and motivations for a given behavior—depending on such factors as psychological, social, and (in the case of psychological studies) methodological context—it is not assumed that the explanations suggested are the only ones possible.

[8]Asian Americans who value modesty may do so because of their exposure to Asian or American cultural values. It is possible that their modesty can be traced back to a confluence of these two cultural forces. In many cases, Asian Americans will not know which parts of their behavior can be traced to Asian, as opposed to Western, roots.

American college student, who normally did not participate much in class, one day participated more than usual. After class, the instructor asked the student what caused the change in his behavior. The student responded that he had been willing to talk because a certain Japanese American female was not in class that day. Although the student did not know her personally, he did not want to participate in class when she was present. When the instructor asked him what difference her presence made, the student said that he would sometimes see her in the cafeteria with her Japanese American friends, and while the student did not know any of her friends, he was afraid that if he said anything in class in her presence, she would tell them that he was a "banana" (the Asian equivalent of "oreo") and they would ostracize him. One way, therefore, to interpret the student's behavior would be to infer that he was worried about not conforming to the expectations of people he did not even know.

Social sensitivity is also emphasized in Asian American cultures (Fong, 1973; Kalish & Reynolds, 1976). To preserve interpersonal harmony and avoid embarrassment, Asian Americans are generally taught to be adept at noticing subtle verbal and nonverbal cues. For instance, Asian American parents are often very skilled at giving their children subtle looks that signal disapproval. Those looks do not have to be accompanied by frowns, furrowed foreheads, pulsating blood vessels in the neck, or thinned lips. They can be looks that just last a little longer than expected. But the children learn to recognize that look.

This social sensitivity may render some Asian Americans susceptible to being easily hurt (Kalish & Reynolds, 1976) because they may notice subtle behaviors, assume that these behaviors are intended as cues, and feel that someone is disapproving, when, in fact, that is not the case. Moreover, individuals who are socially sensitive may hide their pain in order to protect the feelings of the person who hurt them. For instance, two Asian American high-school girls were discussing a problem that one of them had. A third Asian American girl, a friend of the two, was sensitive enough to subtle body language to know that they were discussing something personal. Therefore, she quietly walked by, trying not to disturb them. One of the girls who was talking, however, assumed that the girl walked by without saying anything because she was mad at her. She was hurt and sad but she did not express her feelings to the friend because she feared hearing confirmation that she was disliked.

There is a syndrome among Asian Americans that involves a particular type of reserve, reticence, deference, and humility. Known by various names in different Asian American groups, in the Japanese American community the phenomenon is referred to as the *enryo* syndrome. This syndrome may be manifested in a number of ways, as in a hesitancy to speak up in class or to openly contradict a person in a position of authority. *Enryo*-ing may be manifested in the value that is placed on not dominating other people in social situations (Brower, 1989; Kikumura & Kitano, 1976): Japanese Americans are typically taught not to be loud or assertive (Kikumura & Kitano, 1976). Another part of the *enryo* syndrome is a modest devaluation of oneself (Union of Pan Asian Communities, 1978) and one's possessions (Kobata, 1979) so that others will not feel inadequate. *Enryo*-ing individuals might also gently disparage themselves or their children to others. Family honor is maintained because the listener is not expected actually to believe all of these negative things that individuals are saying: The listener is expected to assume that the persons making these disparaging statements are being modest and are *enryo*-ing. This *enryo*-ing behavior may not just reflect cultural values. It may also be seen as serving a protective function in a racist society: Being modest might cut down on the jealousy that others may feel toward Asian Americans—and could thus make Asian Americans seem less threatening.

Traditionally, Asian American values also emphasize respect for people of status. Related to that display of respect are values emphasizing obedience to authority figures such as parents (Anderson, 1983; Asian American Community Mental Health Training Center, 1976; Payton, 1985; S. Sue & D. W. Sue, 1973) and respect for the elderly (Anderson, 1983; JWK International, 1978).

Among Asian Americans, academic (S. Sue & D. W. Sue, 1973) and occupational achievement (JWK International, 1978; Kalish & Moriwaki, 1973; Payton, 1985) are valued in part because these achievements elevate the status of the person and the family and partially fulfill obligations to the family. By the same token, failure by an individual is believed to shame the entire family (L. N. Huang, 1989; S. Sue & D. W. Sue, 1973).

The emphasis on interpersonal harmony and achievement are supported by the presence of other values, including self-control (Kalish & Moriwaki, 1973; Kobata, 1979; Timberlake & Cook, 1984; Union of Pan Asian Communities, 1978), self-discipline (Caplan et al., 1989; Union of Pan Asian Communities, 1978), education, hard work (Caplan et al., 1989; JWK International, 1978; Kalish & Moriwaki, 1973; Mass, 1976; Young, 1972a, 1972b), delayed gratification (Caplan et al., 1989; Young, 1972a, 1972b), suppression of both positive and negative emotions—but particularly the latter (L. N. Huang & Ying, 1989; Kobata, 1979), and silent forbearance and perseverance when in unpleasant situations (Morrow, 1987; Tashima & Ito, 1982).

Traditionally Asians use shame and guilt to control behavior

(Chew & Ogi, 1987; Payton, 1985; D. W. Sue, 1989a; Union of Pan Asian Communities, 1978). For example, a 19-year-old Chinese American college student wanted to move out of his parents' home and into an apartment. The student's mother, a traditional Chinese parent, tried to make him feel guilty for abandoning his family. Whenever the student broached the subject of moving, his mother would talk about all of the things that she had done for him since he was a little boy. When he reached the point where he could listen to his mother's speeches about all she had done for him and still express a desire to move out, his mother pulled out the family album. Recognizing that she was really going to lay on the guilt, he knew that he was not moving out any time soon.

Exaggerated, Manichean distinctions between Asian American and non-Asian American values should not be made. Many of the values ascribed to traditional Asian Americans appear to overlap considerably with those of non-Asian Americans. Indeed, other Americans espouse values such as education, respect for parents, hard work, and politeness. Yet there are subtle differences in the degree, intensity, and expression of these values. For example, Euro-Americans and Asian Americans both value filial piety but frequently differ in the priority that they give to caring for parents as opposed to being independent. Euro-American parents, in general, expect their children to move out on their own at an earlier age than Asian American parents do. As groups, Euro-Americans and Asian Americans differ in their attitudes about when to hold back in order to be polite as opposed to when to express individuality. These differences do not represent some type of cultural deficit that Asian Americans must learn to overcome (S. Sue, & Morishima, 1982).

Most discussions regarding values among Asian Americans have focused on Chinese Americans and Japanese Americans. Although there is considerable overlap in traditional values among different Asian groups, the values are not identical. For instance, Filipinos are most often Catholic, while Koreans are most often Protestants; and a large percentage of Southeast Asians are Buddhist.

In addition to interethnic differences there are intraethnic differences. Not all Asian Americans hold traditional values. For instance, compared to other Asian American groups, proportionately fewer Japanese Americans probably hold traditional values because Japanese Americans have been in the United States for so long. Not even all Asian American immigrants or refugees adhere to traditional values as much as they might have in their country of origin. After moving to the United States, Vietnamese and Lao refugees have been found to undergo a number of changes in their values in areas such as male domination and unquestioning obedience to parents (Nguyen & Henkin, 1983). (Sampling shortcomings in that study, however, dictate the need to replicate these results.) Some Korean immigrants adhere less strongly to Korean values in the United States than they did in Korea; other Korean immigrants adhere to traditional Korean values more strongly than their former compatriots do in Korea.

Although different Asian Americans adhere to these values in varying degrees, many would not be able to articulate the values underlying their behaviors. For example, Asian Americans might be asked, "Why don't you say exactly what is on your mind as much as non-Asian Americans do?" Rather than say that they have been taught Confucian values concerning the importance of maintaining harmony, Asian Americans will often reply, "I don't want to hurt anyone's feelings," "It's better to get along with people," "I wouldn't feel right about doing that," or "Why should I (say what is exactly on my mind)?" Asian Americans often do not know that there are Asian roots to some of the values that they hold—just as many other Americans do not recognize the roots of American values in Puritanism, Calvinism, and the Enlightenment. Some Asian Americans think that they are "bananas," until they hear that some of the values that they have been taught might stem from Asian (or Asian American) cultural values— and are not just the idiosyncrasies of their family.

RACISM

At the beginning of this chapter, two reasons were given for differences in the behavior of Euro-Americans (the group on which most psychological research is based) and Asian Americans. The first reason was cultural. The second reason involves experiences with racism.

Racism refers to the denigration or subordination of a group because of racial or cultural characteristics that supposedly make the denigrated group inferior. A racist perspective has allowed many members of the dominant group to feel that the disproportionate amount of power and wealth that they have is justified and has led to efforts by the dominant group to impose on the subordinated groups such a pervasive sense of powerlessness that the latter will not try to disrupt the status quo (K. Chan, in press).

In the past, racism was often blatant. It was clearly racism when European immigrants sought the genocidal destruction of the Indigenous American population. Slavery and its ideological underpinnings were patently racist. Laws prohibiting Asians from immigrating to the United States or from becoming naturalized citizens were clearly racist.

But racism today usually takes a more subtle form. K. Chan (in press) noted that rather than claim that subordinated groups are biologically inferior, racists today often claim that members of other races lack character, American cultural values, or competence in American culture (such as English proficiency). Some racists use such arguments to try to justify the disparity in power and wealth among different racial groups. Such racists claim that America is color-blind, and that if minorities do not succeed, it is their own fault. Maintaining such a perspective allows racists to dismiss as mere whining the subordinated groups' protestations of unfairness.

These racists think that the lack of respect shown to subordinated groups is, therefore, justified. Sometimes the lack of respect becomes so automatic that racists do not even see whether an individual in the subordinated group lacks character, American values, or proficiency in American culture. For example, a 30-year-old Asian American woman and her father were sitting on lawn chairs next to a swimming pool. A Euro-American male in his 50s, in the swimming pool, told the woman to, "Come here," making no effort to move to a point in the pool that was closer to her. When she did not respond he asked, "Do you speak English?", to which she responded, "Yes." He said again, more loudly, "Come here. I want to talk to you." It is unlikely that this man gave her that order because of any age difference between them, because a woman in her 30s is old enough not to be treated like a child. Whether it was because he saw her as a female or as a member of a minority, he seemed to assume that it was his right to order this person to get up and go over to him. (Incidentally, when the woman replied, "If you want to talk to me, you come here," he looked surprised.)

Sometimes the subordinated groups are feared, not because of their purported lack of character, but because of their success. Asian Americans in math classes have often heard others, moaning at the sight of many Asian Americans in the class, lament over what will happen to the grading curve.

The desire to justify the disparity in wealth and power is also one of the reasons for attacks on multicultural curricula. These curricula undermine the assumption that the disparity in power and wealth is due to lack of character or deficient cultural values—and, thus, threaten the assumptions about the superiority of one race or culture.

To some, the notion that Asian Americans are victims of racism will come as a surprise. Even some Asian Americans think that they are not the victims of racism. As a defense mechanism, many Asian Americans deny the existence of racism against Asian Americans (Matsunaga-Nishi, 1980). That is, such Asian Americans do not recognize the racism because recognizing it would make them feel insecure and anxious. Consequently, they unconsciously defend themselves against the anxiety by not seeing the racism.

For instance, one day at a self-serve gas station, a Euro-American man, in pulling up to the pump, hit the car of an Asian American woman in front of him. He got out of his car and walked over to the cashier to pay in advance for his gas, completely ignoring the woman whose car he had bumped. A likely explanation is that he was arrogantly disregarding her because of a racist assumption that Asian Americans can be taken advantage of and will not even complain (or because of a sexist assumption that females can be similarly abused). Recognizing the reason for this man's behavior could be anxiety-provoking for an Asian American in this situation. She might unconsciously feel that if she recognized his racism, she would feel vulnerable or angry—and she does not want to feel that way. As a result, she may unconsciously make the decision not to see the racism. Instead, she may tell herself that maybe he did not hit her car—maybe it was a little earthquake that shook her car. Or she might tell herself that he is so stupid that he did not realize that he hit her car (even though he clearly hit the car hard enough to know what he had done). Neither of these alternative explanations makes her feel vulnerable or angry. At the same time, though, she fails to see his racist (and sexist) behavior for what it is.

Alternatively, often Asian Americans do not know that they have been victims of racism because the racism is subtle. For example, in a City University of New York study (cited by Matsunaga-Nishi, 1980) similar resumés were sent to potential employers. Some of the individuals sending resumés were identified as Euro-Americans and some were identified as Filipino Americans. When the individuals were identified as Euro-Americans, they were five times more likely than Filipino Americans to be invited for interviews. Since people submitting a resumé often do not know why they have been rejected, Asian Americans may be the victims of racism and not know it.

The notion that Asian Americans are victims of racism also might come as a surprise to other Americans. After all, the prevailing image of Asian Americans is that they are the model minority. Supporters of this image point to the purportedly low rates of mental disorders, high occupational status, and high average family incomes of Asian Americans. In looking at the incidence of mental disorders, one discovers that a low rate of usage of mental health facilities does not necessarily indicate a low need for mental health services. Instead, low usage rates reflect factors other than need, such as the stigma attached to psychological problems, the tendency to manifest psychological problems as physical maladies, and the lack of culturally relevant mental health services.

Asian Americans have also been cast as the model minority because of their high occupational status and higher-than-average family incomes. This is also misleading. While many Asian Americans have been able to convert their educational achievement into occupational success, many face the "glass ceiling" (i.e., Asian Americans can see and aspire to higher statuses, but most large businesses will not promote Asian Americans above a certain level in the corporation). The incomes of both immigrant and American-born Asian Americans are generally not commensurate with their levels of education (Barringer, Takeuchi, & Xenos, 1990).

Comparing the average family income of Asian Americans to those of Euro-Americans can be misleading on a number of counts. In general, Asian American families have higher family incomes because, on average, more people in Asian American families work than in Euro-American families. Additionally, Asian Americans tend to live in expensive urban areas (such as Honolulu, San Francisco, Los Angeles, and New York). The average resident in these areas makes more money than the average American in areas of the country with a lower cost of living. When the incomes of Asian Americans in these areas are compared to those of Euro-American residents in the same areas, rather than in the United States as a whole, the average incomes of Asian Americans are usually lower (Moritsugu & S. Sue, 1983).

Furthermore, a basic premise of the model minority thesis is incorrect: Underlying the notion that Asian Americans are *a* model minority is the assumption of homogeneity among Asian American communities. In fact, as mentioned in the first chapter, there are many differences among Asian American groups. For example, whereas some Asian American groups have slightly higher average family incomes than those of Euro-Americans, other Asian American groups have not only lower average family incomes than Euro-Americans but also higher rates of poverty. In addition, there are still many negative stereotypes of Asian Americans such as that they are incompetent drivers.

A nationwide increase in the number of hate crimes committed against Asian Americans demonstrates that individual racism (the racism of an individual *qua* an individual) is becoming more common—or at least more commonly reported. While Asians constituted less than 10% of Los Angeles County's population between 1986 and 1989, the Los Angeles County Commission on Human Relations reported that Asians constituted 15.2% of the hate crime victims in that period (U.S. Commission on Civil Rights, 1992), and while Asians constituted less than 4% of Philadelphia's population, the 1988 Philadelphia Human Relations Commission revealed that they were the victims of 20% of the hate crimes there (U.S. Commission on Civil Rights, 1992). Asian American students at the California State Universities have reported that they "often do not feel safe or welcome on campus," have "reported more personal experiences [with] racism than any other group," and were more likely than other groups to see racial harassment as a problem on campus (The Asian Pacific American Education Advisory Committee, 1990, p. 13).

Institutional racism (i.e., the use of an institution to treat racial groups differently and unfairly) also may explain the controversial admittance procedures of some of the more prestigious universities in the United States. Many of these universities have been accused of having a ceiling on the number of Asian Americans that are admitted (the law school of at least one university has put Asian Americans on a different waiting list than other Americans). For example, between 1982 and 1985, the admission rate for Asian Americans at Stanford University was between 65% and 70% of that for Euro-Americans (Bunzel & Au, 1987). Even when Asian Americans and Euro-Americans had the same academic standings, Asian Americans were admitted at lower rates (Bunzel & Au, 1987). Similarly, in 1982 the admission rate for Asian Americans at Harvard was 74% of that for Euro-Americans. Evidence does not suggest that Asian Americans are admitted at lower rates than Euro-Americans are because of a lack of character, less participation in sports and artistic endeavors, or lower SAT scores (Bunzel & Au, 1987).

Asians also are still subject to cultural racism (i.e., the presumption that aspects of their culture are inferior to another culture). For example, there are birthday cards that have offensive caricatures of Buddha, Confucius, or some other "Oriental sage" making silly statements. Yet there are few cards that display caricatures of Jesus saying something silly followed by a birthday greeting because *that* would be considered disrespectful.

CONCLUSION

There are some assumptions made when Asian American values are discussed in psychological research. Most characterizations of Asian American values have been based on clinical observations. It is assumed that these observations are accurate, but there is very little empirical research on Asian American values. It is assumed that some of these values are the motivating forces behind some behaviors, but there is little empirical research substantiating this. Furthermore, there is a broad assumption that traditional Asian values are traditional Asian American values, but this has not been explored empirically. It is possible, for instance, that some Japanese American values taught to *Yonsei* are not traditional Japanese values but are the embodiment of the experiences and values developed by preceding Japanese American generations during their lifetimes in the United States. But this supposition has not been studied to determine whether it is true, or to what extent it may be true. Finally, the foregoing discussion of values might give the impression that the values of Asian Americans are homogeneous. But probably many of the Asian Americans who read that exposition on values would identify with some values ("Whoa, someone has been interviewing my family!") but not with others ("I'm not like that, but I can see that some other Asian Americans are"). Most likely, variables such as gender, level of education, and degree of acculturation are responsible for the differences among Asian Americans in values held. Why are some Asian values transmitted in a family while others are not? Are there gender differences in the values adopted? Is there a relationship between values held by an Asian American and his or her social class, education, and acculturation levels? If so, how much variance is accounted for by these factors? These are among the research questions that have yet to be addressed.

3

Families

Cultures determine the skills that parents think their children need in order to be successful (O'Reilly, Tokuno, & Ebata, 1986); the criteria that parents use in order to assess the success and ability of their children (Gibbs & Huang, 1989); the values and child-rearing practices that parents consider to be effective, appropriate, and acceptable (Chiu, 1987); and the responses that parents think their children should have to various social stimuli (Kriger & Kroes, 1972). Insofar as Asian American cultures are different from the cultures of other Americans, there should, theoretically, be differences in the family practices of Asian Americans and other Americans. Indeed, there is empirical evidence of differences in such practices between Asian American and non-Asian American families.

An examination of Asian American families is called for because family dynamics and child-rearing practices affect values, attitudes, personality development, styles of interacting, and a host of other interpersonal factors (Chiu, 1987). Such an examination lays the groundwork for understanding Asian American personality patterns, communication styles, sources of psychological stress, manifestations of mental disorders, and attitudes toward mental health services.

This chapter is not designed to provide a comprehensive overview of different types of Asian American families but rather to provide a comprehensive summary of empirical research on Asian American families. Collectively, the research on Asian American families is too much of a hodgepodge to provide a comprehensive portrayal.

Chapter 3 is divided into four sections. The first is a discussion of the limitations of the generalizability of the research on Asian American families. The second section is a brief discussion of traditional Asian family structure. The third section is a review of the family dimensions that have empirically been found to characterize Asian American families in at least two Asian American ethnic groups. The fourth section is a review of empirical studies of particular Asian American ethnic groups for which there is no corroborative evidence in other Asian American groups.

LIMITATIONS OF FAMILY RESEARCH

It is necessary first to consider some of the limitations of the family research that has been done on the Asian American population so that there is a basis for interpreting the results presented in this chapter: the use of standard research procedures in these empirical studies, on the one hand, can be weighed against the limitations of these studies, on the other.

First, research on Asian American families has never captured the *zeitgeist* of psychological research on Asian Americans: There has never been a time when many researchers systematically examined the structure, function, and variety of Asian American families. Consequently, the empirically based picture of Asian American families is fragmented and incomplete. What research exists has been descriptive rather than explanatory—which is understandable inasmuch as descriptive data are needed before sophisticated theoretical studies can be conducted. But a lack of theoretical research undermines efforts to obtain a comprehensive understanding of the dynamics of Asian American families. One is left to guess what influence the characteristics of Asian American families have on the personalities of family members, the types of stressors they encounter, and their ability to cope. The psychological costs and benefits of Asian American family characteristics across contexts have not been analyzed empirically and systematically.

Second, most of the empirical studies of Asian American families have sampled only Chinese Americans and Japanese Americans (there seem to be no empirical studies of Filipino Americans or any of the Southeast Asian groups or Pacific Islander groups). In addition, sample sizes often are less than ideal, and no studies have been replicated. Therefore, it is not clear how reliable or generalizable the results are.

Third, scant attention has been given to between-group and within-group differences among Asian Americans. Instead, most of the studies either have had no comparison group or have compared Asian American families to non-Asian American (usually Euro-American) families. Furthermore, although many studies have found some characteristics to be more common in Asian American families than in non-Asian American families, most of the studies have not established whether these characteristics are common in either type of family. Additionally, a significant portion of this research was conducted decades ago. Since there are intergenerational differences in family orientation (Connor, 1974b), such as how much bringing honor to the family name is stressed in Japanese American families, some of these old results might not hold to form now. On the other hand, interesting parallels could be revealed through replications of this research on Asian Americans who have immigrated to the United States since the 1965 Immigration Act.

As a result of these limitations in research on Asian American families, one should not expect to obtain a complete picture of Asian American families because the data and theoretical models do not yet exist to establish such a picture. Instead, this chapter offers a nonempirical portrayal of traditional Asian American families and a review of existing research on Asian American families. Such a discussion can render more sophisticated schemata[1] or concepts of Asian American families and, in so doing, increase awareness of different aspects of Asian American families.

TRADITIONAL ASIAN FAMILY STRUCTURE

To provide a conceptual framework for understanding the research on Asian American families, it is helpful to discuss informal and clinical observations of traditional Asian family structure. To discuss these observations does not suggest that all Asian American families have a traditional structure or even that traditional Asian American families are the modal average; nor does it suggest that this is a model of how Asian American families should be structured. Rather, such a discussion is provided as a point of reference from which readers can understand how some Asian American families, because of culture, differ from other types of American families.

Members of traditional Asian American families are expected to adhere to their relatively clearly defined, specific position in the family hierarchy, based on age and gender (C. Ho, 1990; Strom, Park, &

---

[1] A schema (plural schemata) refers to information and concepts that an individual possesses and that influence the way in which that individual interprets information and goes about searching for additional information. In this way, a schema is analogous to a computer format, except that new information can bring about changes in old schemata.

Daniels, 1987). The old have higher status than the young; males have a superior position to females. This is based on Confucian thought and Chinese cosmology: The latter maintains that life involves the balance of yin (including that which is feminine, negative, inferior, and weak) and yang (including that which is masculine, positive, superior, and strong). If this supposedly natural balance is upset (e.g., if a wife domineers over her husband), the equilibrium within the family would be disrupted (Yang, 1991).

The traditional Asian American family structure is patriarchal, with the father maintaining an irreproachably authoritative, strict, dignified, and aloof relationship to the family (J. Lee & Cynn, 1990; D. W. Sue, 1989a, 1989b; S. Sue & Morishima, 1982). Indeed, the father might be uncomfortable about appearing uncertain in front of his children (Strom et al., 1987) or revealing his feelings to his children; thus, a distance is created between father and children (S. Sue & Morishima, 1982). Responsible for providing for the economic well-being of his family, the father is the leader and the principle disciplinarian in the family (Shon & Ja, 1982). "Because of this, he is frequently seen as somewhat stern, distant, and less approachable than the mother" (Shon & Ja, 1982, p. 212).

The maternal role is to monitor the emotional well-being of the family (J. Lee & Cynn, 1991). The mother is the parent most involved in nurturing the children, listening when the children have problems, and communicating the children's needs, concerns, and desires to the father (Shon & Ja, 1982). The children feel emotionally closer to their mother than to their father (Shon & Ja, 1982). The mother's most important bond is likely to be with her children (especially with the eldest son) rather than with her husband; her husband's strongest bond is likely to be with his mother (E. Lee, 1982). Traditionally, wives are publicly subordinate to their husbands but privately are not so demure (S. Kim, 1991).

Older members of the family, even siblings who are only slightly older, command respect in traditional Asian American families (L. J. Huang, 1981). For example, younger siblings show respect for elder siblings by addressing elder siblings with such (translated) titles as "older brother" or "second older sister" rather than by the sibling's name (L. J. Huang, 1981; Strom et al., 1987). Elder siblings are expected to be role models for younger siblings (L. J. Huang, 1981).

Traditionally, sons are valued more than daughters (Morrow, 1989; D. W. Sue, 1989b) because sons are the ones who symbolically carry on the family line and are the ones who are responsible for caring for the parents when they become old (Yang, 1991). The eldest son is considered to be the most important child. He commonly receives better treatment than his siblings (Shon & Ja, 1982). For example, when some traditional Asian American families have dinner, the eldest son will get the food that remains after each member has had a serving, if the father does not want it; other family members can only eat more if the elder brother does not want more food. The eldest son is also the recipient of more respect than is given to the other siblings (Shon & Ja, 1982). The other siblings are supposed to obey the eldest brother and follow his guidance throughout their lives (Shon & Ja, 1982).

Daughters have a devalued status because traditional Asian American families think of daughters as people who are raised to join another family when they marry (J. Lee & Cynn, 1991). As a Chinese-Vietnamese college student recounted:

> In the Chinese culture, boys are more valued than the girls. The sons are the ones who will carry on the family name and the ones that will be responsible for the parents in their old age. Girls are considered as water being thrown out of the house, it will never come back. Raising girls is like raising children for another family. The girls are not given as much freedom as the boys are.
>
> My brother, the only son in the family, had all the attention from my grandmother when we were young. Whenever we visited my grandmother, he was always the one with the most gifts and the one who got the best of everything. When she passed away a few years ago, on her death bed, she took out the most valuable thing she owned and asked for it to be sent to America for my brother. Even now, my parents tend to think of contributing some of their savings to help him buy a house. So in the future, they would have a place to live and someone to take care of them in their old age. (Student term paper, 1992)

There is often a large communication gap between the father and the youngest child in the traditional family (E. Lee, 1982). The youngest daughter is frequently the most acculturated if her family immigrated to the United States, and her primary sources of emotional support are usually her eldest brother, grandparents, and friends (E. Lee, 1982).

Traditionally, the family exerts a great deal of control over its members (S. Sue & D. W. Sue, 1973) and individuals are expected to be devoted to and rely on their family (Chew & Ogi, 1987; Fong, 1973; Lyman, 1974). Parents stress to their children that the children have obligations to the family (D. W. Sue, 1989a).

It is incumbent on each member of the family to minimize conflicts and problems and to maintain familial harmony and order (C. Ho, 1990). The good of the family and the interests of the family take precedence over the desires of individual family members (Abbott, 1976; Union of Pan Asian Communities, 1978). "Each member of the [traditional Asian] family is expected to [maintain familial] harmony and comply with familial and social authority to the point of sacrificing his/her own desires and ambitions" (C. Ho, 1990, pp. 133–134). For example, it is not unusual to hear about immigrant Asian Americans whose major in college was decided upon by their parents. Oftentimes among Asian Americans, what superficially appear to be parental suggestions or expectations are understood by both the child and the parent to be veiled demands. Independent behavior or expressions of emotions that might disrupt familial harmony are discouraged (D. W. Sue, 1989). Being loyal to and making sacrifices for parents and showing respect for elders are behaviors that are valued (Chiu, 1987; M-K. Ho, 1976). Parents expect to be obeyed without question (Morrow, 1989); even adult sons are expected to obey their fathers (Fong, 1973).

There is an emphasis on maintaining familial honor (Mass, 1976; Morrow, 1987; S. Sue & D. W. Sue, 1973; Union of Pan Asian Communities, 1978; Welty, 1985). The behavior of individual members of a family is believed to reflect on the family as a whole (Morrow, 1987). In fact, one study (Young, 1972a) of immigrant and American-born Chinese found that there were few reports of any emphasis on gaining personal recognition, although this paucity may have reflected a reticence to admit such motivation.

Communication within the traditional family is unidirectional, flowing from parent to child (J. Lee & Cynn, 1991; Morrow, 1989; D. W. Sue, 1989). Traditional and rigid family roles may promote stability and security, but they may also perpetuate emotional distance between father and children (S. Sue & Morishima, 1982) and may restrict the avenues by which family members can express or resolve their problems (Shon & Ja, 1982).

INTRAETHNIC DIFFERENCES AMONG ASIAN AMERICAN FAMILIES

Not all Asian American families are traditional. At least some intraethnic differences among Asian American families are due to differences in acculturation. It seems that as succeeding generations of Asian Americans become more acculturated, their child-rearing practices become more like those of most American families. For example, "The discrepancies between the sexes in duties and privileges, though still there, are not so glaring" (L. N. Huang & Ying, 1989, p. 36). Although fathers in Korea are not traditionally active in child care, most Korean American fathers make significant contributions to child care (Yu & Kim, 1983). Rather than expect their children to fulfill their filial responsibilities in the customary tradition, acculturated Asian Americans often rely on health and social service providers to fulfill many of these needs (Chen, 1982).

In acculturated Asian American families, the husband may be head of the family in public, but the wife may have a lot of decision-making power behind the scenes (L. N. Huang & Ying, 1989). For instance, while an Asian American couple was visiting friends, the wife thought it was time to leave, but did not want her husband to appear henpecked. Therefore, instead of saying to her husband that it was time to leave, she waited for a lull in the conversation and made momentary eye contact with him. The husband took the silent cue and announced, "Well, we had better get going." With a sigh the wife replied, "Oh, do we have to?" "Yes," the husband responded in an authoritative tone—and the couple departed.

EMPIRICAL STUDIES OF ASIAN AMERICAN FAMILIES

The following section summarizes empirical studies of Asian American families in general. In this section, various studies of specific Asian American groups are collated and generalizations are made based on these studies. For example, studies of Japanese Americans and studies of Chinese Americans have shown that families in these groups tend to encourage conformity more than Euro-American families do. Although there is no empirical evidence of this emphasis on conformity in other Asian American groups, such an emphasis probably exists in most of these groups. Consequently, the tentative generalization is drawn that Asian American families tend to encourage conformity. This generalization is only drawn when an emphasis on conformity has been found in more than one Asian American group.

The following section, then, deals with common dimensions found across different Asian American groups. The following areas are reviewed: communication styles, independence/supervision, cohesion, conformity, achievement orientation, and methods of social control. Table 3.1 presents these dimensions, as well as notes indicating to which groups these dimensions have empirically been found to apply. Blank spaces indicate that research has not been done on a dimension for a particular Asian American group.

Euro-American families have been used for comparison in these studies, not because Euro-American families are what constitute "normal," nor because they are the model to which Asian American

Table 3.1. Summary of Familial Dimensions and Groups Demonstrating the Characteristic More Than Euro-Americans

Familial dimension	CA[a]	FA[b]	JA[c]	KA[d]	SA[e]	SEA[f]	AA Mix[g]
Restrained and indirect communication style	x		x				
Indirect expression of emotion	x		x				
Conformity	x		x				
Supervision	x						x
Cohesion	x	x	x		x		x
Achievement	x		x	x			x
Social control:							
guilt/shame	x	x	x			x	
physical punishment		x				x	
social isolation			x			x	

Note. Scoring in this table is based on empirical research and represent comparisons with Euro-American families. The social control dimensions are an exception and are not based on empirical research.
[a]Chinese Americans.
[b]Filipino Americans.
[c]Japanese Americans.
[d]Korean Americans.
[e]Samoan Americans.
[f]Southeast Asians.
[g]Sample made up of a mixture of Asian American groups.

families aspire, nor because other types of American families are unimportant or irrelevant, but, rather, because they are more numerous than other types of families in the United States, and therefore it is easier to recruit members of Euro-American families as research subjects than it is to recruit members of other types of families.

In reading this section as well as the succeeding chapters, remember that scientific understanding is gained through a *process* in which studies build on previous research. It is not the case that a researcher does one study and discovers the "truth" about Asian American families or even families from particular Asian American groups. The expectation is that collectively studies can help people to understand the parameters of whatever it is they are studying. You are undoubtedly familiar with the tale of the blind men who felt different parts of an elephant and described the elephant in quite disparate ways, depending on what part of the elephant they were touching. Just as one blind person holding the elephant's tail described the elephant quite differently from another blind person who was feeling the elephant's torso, sometimes different studies reveal different aspects of a phenomenon, resulting in superficially discrepant findings. More research is needed to understand how these results fit together. In science, researchers try to understand what they are examining by comparing the findings of various studies, looking in the findings for limitations or biases that are due to methodological factors, hypothesizing explanations in order to account for these various findings, and then testing their hypotheses in subsequent studies. In the case of research on Asian American families (and in subsequent chapters), various studies are reviewed, some methodological factors are discussed when there is reason to suspect that these studies may have distorted findings, and hypotheses to explain these findings are presented.

Communication Style

Restrained, Indirect

Various studies have found that, compared to Euro-American families, verbal communication in Asian American families tends to be relatively restrained. These studies have derived their data from interview-administered questionnaires, from home observations, or from videotaped interactions. One interview-based study (Nihira, Mink, & Shapiro, 1991) found that Chinese American and Japanese American parents talked less than Euro-American parents did. A combined questionnaire and videotape study (Hsu, Tseng, Ashton, McDermott, & Char, 1985) reported that Japanese American spouses were more reticent about expressing their thoughts and feelings, were less comfortable discussing personal problems, and were more vague when expressing thoughts and feelings than their Euro-American counterparts were. Japanese American spouses also were judged to be more restrained, less warm, less empathic, and less affectionate than Euro-American spouses were (Hsu et al., 1985).

A number of factors could explain these findings. First, Asian Americans may be more inhibited than Euro-Americans when they are being observed, especially when the observers use videotapes. Compared to Euro-Americans, Asian Americans may be more self-conscious of the observations, more inhibited about revealing family conflicts to strangers, and more on their we-have-guests behavior than their natural at-home behavior. As a result, members of Asian American families may inhibit their communication more than their Euro-American counterparts do in such situations. When the interactions of Asian American couples and Euro-American couples are videotaped while they are doing assigned tasks or discussing assigned topics (e.g., in the Hsu et al., 1985 study), Asian Americans may be more concerned than Euro-Americans about meeting the needs and expectations of the experimenters; consequently, Asian Americans, feeling more uncertain, may talk less than Euro-Americans in an experimental situation.

Second, the Asian American spouses may have been just as warm and communicative as their Euro-American counterparts, but they may not have expressed their thoughts and feelings as overtly as or in the same way that Euro-American spouses did. For example, insofar as Japanese American culture teaches social sensitivity to subtle cues, Japanese Americans may not need to be as obvious in transmitting the same intensity of feeling as non-Japanese Americans would. It is possible that the Japanese Americans anticipated and met each other's needs in ways that were too subtle and nonverbal for the raters to detect (Hsu et al., 1985). Asian American values emphasize anticipating the needs of others so that those people do not have to verbally express what they need, and can thereby avoid seeming demanding or selfish. Asian American children learn to be ashamed of themselves when they are not insightful (Toupin, 1980).[2] Supporting the hypothesis that social sensitivity to the needs and feelings of others may account for these differences between Asian American and Euro-American communication styles, other researchers (Caudill & Frost, 1974) have found that Euro-American mothers try to stimulate their infants to vocalize so that the infants can communicate their needs, whereas Japanese American mothers try harder to anticipate the needs of their infants. Members of Asian American families may verbally communicate less than members of other families because the former are more adept at perceiving the needs of others.

Japanese American families value and rely on indirect and nonverbal communication more than Euro-Americans do (Hsu et al., 1985) and frequently communicate through gestures, facial expressions, intonations, and speech volume rather than through direct statements (Johnson, Marsella, & Johnson, 1974). Asian American parents might communicate with silent looks unnoticed by observers. For example, many Asian American parents will express their disapproval with a look that may appear to the outside observer as a glance but that may convey a great deal (e.g., anger, disappointment, pride) to the children. In keeping with this hypothesis about nonverbal communication, a study of Korean Americans (Yu & Kim, 1983) found

---

[2] What is emphasized here is having insight into the needs of others rather than having insight into one's own psychological functioning.

relatively little verbal communication between mothers and their children but a great deal of nonverbal, implicit communication.

When observational studies use raters to assess characteristics of Asian American families, results are skewed if raters are not accustomed to, geared toward, or adept at judging Asian American communication patterns. Raters might use measures that look for Euro-American patterns or manifestations of some dependent variable and then conclude that Asian American families lack that conceptually underlying characteristic to the same degree as Euro-American families, but, in fact, the Asian American families might just manifest that characteristic differently. For instance, Hsu et al. (1989), finding that both the Japanese American and the Euro-American families whom they studied were reasonably healthy, interpreted their data as indicating that Euro-American families were psychologically healthier than Japanese American families. It is quite likely that this judgment was based on Eurocentric standards. Those same researchers claimed that Japanese American spouses conversed in a way that was more vague than the way in which Euro-American spouses communicated. It is possible that the Japanese American spouses were just as clear but not as explicit.

Third, there might be less communication in Asian American families than in non-Asian American families because traditional Asian American values emphasize being deferential rather than assertive or individualistic. Chinese American, Filipino American, and Japanese American families emphasize deference to authority more than other non-Asian American families do (Tsui & Schultz, 1988). Perhaps there is less conversing in Asian American families than in other families because Asian Americans on the average, do not spend as much time asserting their rights, desires, and opinions or arguing with authority figures.

Fourth, limited communication could reflect family structure. Because members of Chinese American, Filipino American, and Japanese American families tend to have well-defined expectations of social behavior and social roles (Tsui & Schultz, 1988), there could be less need for direct verbal communication in such families than in other American families.

Fifth, indirect and limited verbal communication in Asian American families might reflect the fact that the dominant American society has rewarded minorities for being silent and inconspicuous and has punished them for being outspoken (D. W. Sue, 1989a).

Finally, as they become older, some Asian American children of immigrant parents use less of their parents' Asian language and more English. As a result, a language gap between parents and children can develop. For example, there was a Chinese American college student who lived in an apartment and visited his parents once a week. Six days out of the week he did not use Chinese at all. He soon found that when he went to his parents' home he could not remember many simple Chinese words when he talked with his parents. A language gap can lessen the amount of communication and create emotional distance between the generations (Yu & Kim, 1983).

The picture that emerges from research on communication styles is that Asian Americans parents, as a whole, talk less to each other than do Euro-American parents. The communication styles of Asian American parents are apparently more subtle than those of Euro-American parents and may be more circumscribed by the situation in which Asian Americans find themselves. Substantiating the reasons for these differences awaits further research.

Keeping in mind that not all Asian Americans are raised in families with limited, restrained, or indirect communication, consider some of the potential consequences for those who are raised in such families. One consequence is that Asian American children raised in such families may be less verbally expressive than they might otherwise be (Yu & Kim, 1983), which in turn, could affect their careers (Yu & Kim, 1983) and social relationships. Another consequence of limited or indirect verbal communication is that people may become so guarded about communicating their feelings that they do not develop an awareness of them (Kalish & Reynolds, 1976). Such a reticent conversational style also might interfere with the development or expression of intimacy within the family (Kalish & Reynolds, 1976) and result in confusion, misinterpretation, and misunderstanding (Kitano & Kikumura, 1980). Furthermore, a talkative Asian American child may be labeled a problem child in a traditional Asian American home (Fort, Watts, & Lesser, 1969).

Display of Emotions

Parents in Asian American families tend to teach their children to control the expression of emotions more than parents in other American families do. For example, whereas Euro-Americans tend to believe that family members should openly and directly express affection for each other (McDermott, Char, Robillard, Hsu, Tseng, & Ashton, 1984), Japanese Americans are often taught to limit their emotional expressiveness (Hsu et al., 1985; McDermott et al., 1984; Morris, 1990).

Such results probably reflect cultural values—emphasizing self-control and interpersonal harmony—and cultural differences in the way emotions are expressed. For instance, Asian American parents are more likely to demonstrate love and affection for their children indirectly (e.g., by fulfilling obligations to the family and by sacrificing for the children) than to demonstrate affection for their children through words, hugs, or kisses (JWK International, 1978; Nihira et al., 1991; Shon & Ja, 1982). Traditionally, in Chinese families, affection is not expressed openly. Traditional Chinese accept public demonstrations of affection by non-Chinese but consider such behavior by Chinese to be childish or in bad taste (L. J. Huang, 1981).

Many Asian Americans have never seen their parents hug or kiss each other (L. J. Huang, 1981), and they can not remember the last time that one of their parents hugged or kissed their children. One Chinese American college student said he had never seen his parents hug or kiss each other or their friends and relatives—much less say, "I love you." He remembered that, when he was about 10 years old, he saw his father hold his mother's hand at a fair. The student said that he was shocked. Then he started laughing at the unfamiliar sight. Later that day, his father told him that he only held his wife's hand so that she would not become separated from the family in the crowd. Since then, the student has never seen his parents hold hands, hug, or kiss.

Independence Versus Supervision

A number of studies have shown that Asian American mothers tend to be more restrictive about the independence of their children than non-Asian American mothers are. Both immigrant Chinese American mothers and fathers tend to exert more parental control over their children than Euro-American mothers and fathers do (C-Y. Lin & Fu, 1990). For instance, Chinese American mothers tend to supervise their children more and be more protective, restrictive, authoritarian, and nurturant than non-Chinese mothers (Chiu, 1987; Kriger & Kroes, 1972; Sollenberger, 1968).[3] Consistent with these findings, another study (Chiu, 1987) found that Chinese American mothers often select their children's playmates. The parents of Asian American children (from a variety of Asian American groups) in grades 5 through 11 have

---

[3]Consistent with these findings is evidence that Chinese American and Filipino American children are highly protected, quickly attended to, and indulged until about age 5 or 6 when parents rather suddenly impose discipline (Anderson, 1983; Chiu, 1987). Also consistent with the protectiveness found among other Asian American parents is the finding that Japanese American parents are less likely than Euro-Americans to think that children under 7 years of age should be allowed to know about unpleasant events in the family (McDermott et al., 1984).

reported having more influence than the children's peers over the selection of their children's clothing, extracurricular activities, and courses of study (Yao, 1985). For example, whereas 86% of the Euro-American parents said that their children's peers had more influence over what clothing their children wore than the parents did, only 50% of the Asian American parents said the same thing (Yao, 1985).

Chinese-American mothers also generally think that their children should become independent at a later age than Euro-American mothers do. According to one study (D. Sue, D. W. Sue, & D. Sue, 1983), both immigrant and American-born Chinese adults believe that the age at which children are competent to do such things as find their own way around the neighborhood, visit or stay overnight with playmates, and resolve problems with other children without adult intervention is greater than the age at which Euro-American parents sense such competency.

The strictness and restrictions imposed by Chinese American parents are intended to protect more than they are intended to inhibit the child (Chiu, 1987). A rather extreme example of this extensive supervision can be seen in the case of 16-year-old, Chinese American, high-school student.

> She was going out on her first date, dinner and a movie. When she and her date were eating dinner, she saw, sitting three booths away from the couple, her father unobtrusively drinking coffee and watching them. When the couple went to the movies, she looked around the theater. There he was, a few rows behind her. She told her date what was happening and told him to rush her home after the movie so they would arrive home before her father and she could ask him where he was. But just as they arrived at her home, she saw the automatic garage door closing.

The findings of one study apparently conflict with much of this research on independence, but the contrasting results may be illuminating. C-Y. Lin and Fu (1990) found that Chinese American parents of 7-year-old children claimed that they encouraged independence in their children more than Euro-American parents did. The researchers posited that a certain amount of independence is encouraged because it is necessary for achievement. In fact, they did find significant correlations between parental encouragement of independence, on the one hand, and achievement, on the other. Traditional Chinese values emphasize interdependence with the family but do not necessarily discourage individual independence in other ways (C-Y. Lin & Fu, 1990). Taken together, these studies suggest that Chinese

American parents may be more restrictive of the independence of their children than other American parents are, particularly in social activities and, perhaps, occupational choices (Yao, 1985), but they may encourage independence in areas that facilitate academic achievement.

One reason that Asian American parents supervise their children more closely than other American parents may be that many Asian American parents are not comfortable about physically or verbally expressing their love for their children. Hugs, kisses, and declarations of "I love you" fly in the face of traditional Asian American values that emphasize restraint of emotion. But Asian American parents do love their children and want to express their love. A culturally acceptable way to express that love is to be strict. Since other avenues of expressing love may seem closed to them, traditional Asian American parents may exaggerate one avenue they see for expressing love by being very strict. Unfortunately, the children may interpret their parents' strictness as rejection and hostility (J. Lee & Cynn, 1991; Rohner & Pettengill, 1985; Sung, 1985).

Another more general way to look at this research showing Asian Americans parents to be more restrictive than Euro-American parents is to hypothesize that parental restrictiveness is negatively related to the degree of the mother's (the parent most often studied) acculturation to American life. Supporting the hypothesis of a negative relationship between restrictiveness in child-rearing and acculturation, research has indicated that (1) acculturated Chinese American and Japanese American mothers were more likely than nonacculturated Chinese American and Japanese American mothers to allow their children to be independent and venturesome (Kurokawa, 1969; S. Sue & Chin, 1983); (2) the *Issei* were more restrictive than were subsequent Japanese American generations (Connor, 1974); and (3) Chinese American mothers apparently are becoming more acculturated, allowing increased independence for their children and becoming less restrictive about their children's aggression and sexual interest (Chiu, 1987). A comparison of Chinese in the United States with Chinese in Taiwan (who would presumably be more traditional) also supports the hypothesis that parental restrictiveness is negatively related to the degree of the mother's acculturation to American life (Chiu, 1987). That study revealed that although Chinese American mothers were more like Taiwanese mothers and less like Euro-American mothers in the degree to which they interceded in their children's lives, Taiwanese mothers were more restrictive and less democratic than their Chinese American counterparts. There is also evidence that American-born Chinese advocate independent behaviors for their children at an earlier age than immigrant Chinese do (D. Sue et al., 1983). For instance,

American-born Chinese mothers allow their children to stay with someone whom the children know well when parents are away for a few days, visit and stay overnight with a friend, and resolve problems with other children without adult intervention at an earlier age than immigrant Chinese mothers do.

In contrast to these studies, one study of Japanese American mothers found that they were more restrictive than immigrant Japanese mothers or mothers in Japan (Higa, 1974). If acculturation were the determining factor, the *Nisei* would be more permissive than immigrant Japanese and Japanese nationals. Higa's study has apparently been the only one that addresses independence and supervision among Japanese Americans. Additional research is needed in order to examine the reasons why Japanese American mothers tend to be comparatively restrictive. It has been hypothesized (Nagata, 1989b) that the *Nisei* were particularly restrictive with their adolescent offspring because they went through their own adolescence either right before or during World War II, when many were in concentration camps (where their freedom was severely restricted). Therefore, their standards were distorted by memories of their own restricted adolescence; or deep fear of censure affected their child-rearing practices.

Research is needed to confirm the validity of these studies on restrictiveness. Response biases could compromise the validity of many of these studies: The respondents could have answered the questionnaires in ways that made their families seem socially desirable rather than in ways that reflected the characteristics of the family. In addition, studies that rely on one parent's or one adolescent offspring's characterizations of the family may be relying on the perspective of an individual who is not very perceptive about the functioning of the family. There is usually no corroborating evidence to validate the perceptions of the one respondent in the family.

Cohesion

Research generally indicates that Asian American families are more cohesive than Euro-American families. A number of researchers have noted that Chinese Americans, Filipino Americans, and Japanese Americans tend to have strong commitments to family (Connor, 1974b; Morris, 1990; Tsui & Schultz, 1988). Cohesion has been measured in many different ways.

One approach to measuring cohesion is to examine the relationship between Asian American adults and their aging parents. Research has found that, compared with Euro-Americans, Japanese Americans tended to live closer to their parents, feel more obligated to their parents, provide more financial aid to their parents, and interact more frequently with their parents (Osako, 1976). Research has also found that young Japanese American adults were expected to live with their families until they married, elderly parents tended to live with family members rather than in nursing homes, and all age levels within the family were integrated into family activities (Johnson, 1977). It should be noted that most of this research was done almost twenty years ago. More recent research (e.g., Leonetti, 1983) has confirmed some consistency in these behaviors, but there are also differences (e.g., retired *Nisei* generally do not want to live with their grown children).

The way in which child care is handled also suggests high levels of cohesion in Asian American families. Comparisons of *Sansei* and Euro-American mothers have found that *Sansei* mothers diapered, touched, carried, lulled, coddled, and played with their babies more than Euro-American mothers did (Caudill & Frost, 1974; Connor, 1977).

Assessing the amount of familial cohesion by measuring attitudes toward intrafamilial sharing of thoughts and feelings, other researchers (McDermott et al., 1984) reported that Japanese American parents thought that family members should share their deepest thoughts more than did Euro-American parents who gave more emphasis to individual family members' right to privacy. Japanese American parents also thought that family members should discuss important family decisions more than Euro-American parents did (McDermott et al., 1984).

Cohesion can be assessed by looking at the amount of support that individuals receive from their families. A study of Asian American students at a middle school revealed that they received more praise and support from their parents under a variety of circumstances than Euro-American students did (Pang, 1991). Perhaps reflecting a reciprocal sense of cohesion, these Asian American students also wanted to please their parents more than the Euro-American students did.

There is evidence of cohesiveness in the extended Asian American family: Nuclear and extended Samoan American family members tend to see each other often (i.e., at least once a week) , and Samoan American adult children may live with parents or siblings even after marriage (Ablon, 1976). A study of Asian American families with a developmentally disabled child found that these families receive more child-care support from relatives than their Euro-American counterparts do (Nihira et al., 1991). This study also found that Chinese American and Japanese American parents did not see their children or share in their activities as much as Euro-American parents did—and in this way, therefore, Chinese American and Japanese American nuclear families were less cohesive. But using the amount of time that parents saw their children or shared in their children's activities as a measure of cohesiveness may produce misleading results. Since Asian American families are more likely to have both the husband and wife working than Euro-American families are, Asian American parents and Euro-American parents may not start with the same amount of available time. Moreover, if these Asian American families could not depend on their extended families for help as much as they do (i.e., if the extended families were not so cohesive), then more responsibility would fall on the nuclear families, and the cohesion of these nuclear families—looked at as the amount of time that parents spend with their children—would probably increase. In effect, compared to Euro-Americans, Asian Americans may appear to be less cohesive in nuclear families because they are more cohesive as members of extended families. Therefore, one can conclude that studies using various measures of cohesion point to Asian American families generally being more cohesive than Euro-American families.

The cohesion generally found in Asian American families could have roots in traditional Asian American values that emphasize family solidarity. Familial solidarity has been supported by the interdependence of family members, hierarchical relationships in the family, an orientation to the family as a whole rather than to the individuals within the family, the belief that one's behavior reflects on oneself and on the nuclear and extended family over generations, and Confucian ethics emphasizing filial piety (C. Ho, 1990).

Cohesion also may reflect a familial response to exogenous pressures on the family. For example, an immigrant family coping with adaptation to American culture—or a family coping with racism—can find solace, strength, succor, and identity by affiliating closely with the family. The emphasis on cohesion also could reflect the historical need for all members of Asian American families to work together and cooperate in order to contribute to the financial support and functioning of the family.

Conformity

Reportedly, Asian American values traditionally emphasize conformity to normative behavior (Hsu et al., 1985). For example, Japanese Americans are traditionally taught that "being yourself" and behaving in accordance with the way one feels are secondary to "behaving well" and complying with social expectations based on one's social role (O'Reilly et al., 1986; S. Sue & Morishima, 1982). Indeed, researchers have found that Euro-Americans value "being yourself" more than Japanese Americans do and that Japanese Americans value "behaving well" more than Euro-Americans do (O'Reilly et al., 1986). Consistent with these findings, another researcher has found that Chinese Americans mothers demand conformity more than non-Chinese American mothers do (Sollenberger, 1968).[4]

For instance, suppose Asian Americans are interacting with non-Asian Americans. Since non-Asian Americans customarily maintain more eye contact than Asian Americans do, Asian Americans are likely to increase their eye contact when interacting with non-Asian Americans. However, when Asian Americans are interacting with other Asian Americans, they may unconsciously decrease eye contact to conform to the amount of eye contact the others are making.

This emphasis on conformity could derive from traditional Asian values that promote conformity as a way of maintaining social harmony. Alternatively, the emphasis on conformity might be based on experiences with racism that have encouraged Asian Americans to blend in as much as possible. In fact, such emphasis could be rooted in experiences with racism generations ago. Even if members of the current generations of Asian Americans have not experienced blatant racism, they may have been taught the coping and behavior patterns adopted by earlier generations in response to racism (see the discussion of conformity in the next chapter).

Achievement Orientation

There is evidence that Asian American parents stress achievement in their children more than Euro-American parents do. Chinese American parents and immigrant Korean American parents often expect and demand high educational and occupational achievement from their children (Chia, 1989; B-L. Kim, 1980; Lin & Fu, 1990; Sollenberger, 1968; Young, 1972a); Chinese American mothers anticipate high educational achievement in their children more than non-Chinese American

---

[4]Although research has most often compared one Asian American group to Euro-Americans, occasionally researchers have identified the comparison group only as "Americans." I assume that in such cases the researchers have not given Asian Americans equal status with other Americans and have excluded other Asian American groups from the control group labeled "Americans." In such cases, I refer to the comparison group as non-Asian American or the like.

mothers do (Sollenberger, 1968). Japanese American—and, even more so, Chinese American—families with developmentally disabled children emphasize achievement more than Euro-American families with developmentally disabled children (Nihira et al., 1991). In a study of Chinese-, Filipino-, Korean-, Vietnamese-, East Indian-, and Euro-American parents of fifth through eleventh graders it was demonstrated that Asian American parents expected their children to obtain higher grades than Euro-American parents did and were less satisfied with their children's grades than Euro-American parents were (Yao, 1985).

In Asian American communities, the emphasis on scholarship could reflect a Confucian regard for scholarship. Or, more probably, the emphasis indicates that many Asian Americans believe that education will give their children an improved quality of life. Among Asian Americans, the emphasis on achievement could also reflect a belief that the effects of racism against Asian Americans might be mitigated if one becomes educated and economically successful. For instance, some Southeast Asians believe that, because many Southeast Asians are thought to be on welfare, they can avoid the animosity directed at welfare recipients by becoming educated and successful and moving higher up the economic ladder.

Even though (or perhaps because) Asian American parents frequently expect high academic achievement from their children, many Asian American parents are not effusive in their encouragement or reinforcement of academic excellence. For instance, "Japanese Americans tend not to give overt praise or verbal feedback to their children" (Nagata, 1989b, p. 102). Consequently, the children sometimes feel that their efforts are not sufficiently acknowledged. Consider the following example.

An Asian American student received all A's except for one B on her report card. Her parents said nothing about her A's but asked her why she received a B and told her she could receive all A's if she put more effort into studying. The student felt angry and confused because she knew the parents of her non-Asian American peers would be very pleased with such a report card. Subsequently, she received all A's and found that her parents were not generous with their praise because they expected her to receive all A's. In a sense, she was left feeling that receiving all A's was just meeting the baseline expectations of her parents.

While under this pressure to succeed academically, Asian American children may not be receiving the help they need. Chinese

American mothers reportedly focus more on motivating their children than on actually providing academic instruction (K. Chan, Takanishi, & Kitano, 1975 cited in Yu & Kim, 1983).[5] When Chinese American mothers do provide instruction, it more often is in the form of statements and feedback rather than in the posing of questions (Steward & Steward, 1973). As a consequence, Chinese American mothers may be of limited help in teaching their children to think.

If Chinese American children do succeed, they often do not receive personal credit for their success. Table 3.2 presents the reasons that Chinese American and Euro-American mothers gave for their children's success and failure, according to a study by Hess, Chang, and McDevitt (1987). Notice the pressure that the mothers' reasoning appears to impose on Chinese American children: If the children fail, it is because they are not trying hard enough, and the parents feel some responsibility for that failure (i.e., failure to force the child to work harder). But if the children succeed, the mothers tend not to attribute this success to hard work nor do they reward their children accordingly. Instead, the mothers think that their children's success is due to parental pressure or that success just came naturally to their children.[6] The picture that emerges is that, at least in the case of Chinese Americans, high grades are expected and demanded by parents, but the children might not receive much pedagogical help from their parents, might not receive a lot of praise for high grades, and might not receive much personal credit for their academic success.

Methods of Social Control

In Asian American families, it is common to find relatively strict discipline of children (JWK International, 1978). This discipline is maintained in a variety of ways.

---

[5]In contrast, Japanese American parents tend to give their children instructions that are more prescriptive than motivational (Morris, 1990).

[6]A study compared the reasons given by Japanese American and Euro-American university students for their own academic successes and failures (Powers, Choroszy, & Douglas, 1987). At this point it is difficult to draw conclusions based on both this study and the Hess et al. (1987) study because too many important factors were varied—such as ethnicity, whether the reasons given concerned one's children's or one's own success and failure, and the age of the student. Suffice it to say for the present that the responses of the Euro-Americans in both studies were similar and that the reasons given for failure were similar for the Chinese American mothers and the Japanese American students.

TABLE 3.2. Differences between Chinese American and Euro-American Mothers in What They Attribute to Be the Causes of Their Children's Academic Success and Failure (in Order of Highest Mean)

How Chinese American mothers account for children's success	How Euro-American mothers account for children's success
Home training	School training
Ability	Effort
Effort/school training	Ability
Luck	Home training
	Luck

How Chinese American mothers account for children's failure	How Euro-American mothers account for children's failure
Lack of effort	Lack of effort
Poor home training/lack of ability	Lack of ability
Poor school training	Poor school training
Bad luck	Poor home training
	Bad luck

Note. Adapted from Hess, Chang, and McDevitt (1987). Copyright 1987 American Psychological Association. Adapted by permission.

Internal Versus External Control

Asian American families often emphasize self-discipline rather than external controls (S. Sue & Morishima, 1982). That is, children are not only motivated to behave well because they fear external sanctions (such as punishment if they behave poorly) , but are also motivated to behave well because they have an internalized sense of morality and will feel bad if they misbehave. Many Asian American children are reminded of their obligations to others and of the negative effects of their unacceptable behavior on other people (Morrow, 1989). Not surprisingly, then, guilt (Morrow, 1987; Slote, 1972) and shame (Anderson, 1983; Morrow, 1987) are methods of social control that are reportedly pervasive among Chinese Americans (JWK International, 1978; D. W. Sue & Kirk, 1972) , Filipino Americans (Anderson, 1983) , Japanese Americans (JWK International, 1978) , and Southeast Asians (Morrow, 1987). (This reliance on guilt is more characteristic of the middle class than the working class in the United States.) When individuals fail to meet familial expectations (e.g., expectations of high achievement) or violate internalized familial rules of conduct, they often feel guilty, ashamed, alienated, and critical of themselves (S. Sue & Morishima, 1982). This guilt and shame can become so developed that they may be dissatisfied with their behavior or performance even when they are relatively successful.

Punishment

Interestingly, there is apparently a dichotomy among Asian American parents: Some have never physically punished their children, while others commonly beat their children. Many Japanese Americans use the threat of temporary isolation from the family as punishment (Kitano & Kikumura, 1980). For example, the errant child may be banished outside the house, to a basement, or to his or her room. In parallel fashion, punishment in Southeast Asian families may involve threatening to isolate, or socially or physically isolating the child temporarily from the family (e.g., by locking the adolescent out of the home) (Morrow, 1987).

Primary means of discipline among Filipinos include spanking, hitting, scolding, name-calling, and teasing for being crude or for shaming the family (Santos, 1983). Some Filipino Americans emphasize negative sanctions, such as teasing and frightening, more than rewards as means of social control (Anderson, 1983). Increasingly, however, Filipino American families indirectly discipline by providing positive reinforcement for approved behaviors (Santos, 1983).

Many Chinese American children are beaten by their parents. Southeast Asians commonly use physical discipline on their children, such as hitting their children with feathersticks (C. Ho, 1990). Cambodians and Laotians frequently use such sticks, hitting their children on their legs, arms, and buttocks while avoiding their heads, backs, or ribs; Vietnamese parents more often hit their children with their hands rather than with sticks (C. Ho, 1990).[7]

Reward

Many Asian American parents reward their children for their good behavior by simply not punishing them. Southeast Asian parents often do not think that rewards should be given for expected behaviors (Morrow, 1989); therefore, the reinforcement that their children receive for being responsible and succeeding academically is muted and indirect (Morrow, 1989): for instance, a parent might acknowledge good behavior by encouraging the child to do even better (Morrow, 1989).

---

[7]Embarrassing Vietnamese children in front of their peers usually does not occur; and when the child becomes an adult, parents pretend not to notice misbehavior (Slote, 1972).

Meanwhile, if persons outside the family compliment a child, Southeast Asians, in an effort to be modest, will often dismiss or negate these compliments with statements that deprecate the child (Morrow, 1989).

FAMILIES FROM SPECIFIC ASIAN AMERICAN GROUPS

At this point in the discussion of the traditional Asian American family structure and the empirical evidence for differences between Asian American families and Euro-American families, it would be helpful to be able to examine the empirical evidence for interethnic and intraethnic differences among Asian Americans. Unfortunately, research has not focused on these matters: There are interethnic and intraethnic differences among Asian American families, but direct comparisons among Asian American families have rarely been made by researchers.

This section, therefore, will cover research on the differences between Euro-American families and families from specific Asian American groups. Although the family characteristics discussed may be shared by different Asian American groups, researchers have linked these characteristics only to the particular Asian American ethnic group discussed—and, thus, these characteristics cannot be generalized to other Asian American groups.

Most of the research that has been discussed so far has focused on Chinese Americans and Japanese Americans. In addition to Japanese Americans, consider now some of the research on less-studied Asian American groups. There are no empirical studies of Filipino American families in published psychological research. Very few studies have been published on Korean American and Southeast Asian families. Nevertheless, that limited research base contains valuable information. Table 3.3 summarizes family studies of specific Asian American groups. Some degree of caution should be exercised when interpreting the information in this table: Some of the characterizations in this table are based on empirical data (including the studies cited in the previous section), some are based on informal observations by researchers, and some are characterizations based on research conducted over 25 years ago (before many of the foreign-born Asian Americans had arrived in the United States) and on a generation different from the one in more contemporary studies.

Chinese Americans

Most Chinese American families have maintained some aspects of Chinese culture, including values, cuisine, celebrations, and language

TABLE 3.3. Characterizations of Specific Asian American Groups

Chinese Americans
Think rearing children is mother's responsibility
Are less likely to allow married women to continue their education
Think communication style and emotional expression should be restrained and indirect
Emphasize conformity
Closely supervise children
Emphasize family cohesion
Emphasize achievement
Maintain social control through guilt and shame

Filipino Americans
Emphasize etiquette, getting along with others, and appropriate social behavior
Emphasize family cohesion
Maintain social control through guilt, shame, and physical punishment

Japanese Americans
Do more lulling, carrying, and playing with babies
More unilateral decisions made by couples
Do not present as strong a parental coalition
Restrained, indirect communication style (including indirect expression of emotion)
Emphasize conformity
Emphasize family cohesion
Maintain social control through guilt, shame, and isolation

Korean Americans
Think it is unnatural to put babies in a separate room
Tend not to think an individual needs privacy for personal development
Think parents' playing with children can undermine children's respect for parents
Tend not to think play is an important part of child's life
Tend not to think it is good for children to play for a long time
Tend not to tolerate children's having secrets
Tend to be unwilling to listen to children's expressions of fears and anxiety
Language gap between parents and children
Strict parental control may be seen by children as hostility and rejection
Emphasize achievement

Samoan Americans
Emphasize family cohesion

Southeast Asians
Have experienced disruption of some established patterns due to acculturation difficulties
Children are subject to increased discipline with age
Discipline children for disobedience, failure to fulfill responsibilities, and aggression (particularly toward siblings)

TABLE 3.3. (*cont.*)

Southeast Asians (cont.)

Give daughters less freedom than sons

Women are openly dominated by husbands more in Vietnamese than in other
    Southeast Asian families: Spousal abuse common among Vietnamese,
    Cambodians, and Laotians

Usually avoid frank, verbal communication between parent and child

Maintain social control through guilt, shame, physical punishment, and
    isolation

Note. Results are based on empirical research and represent comparisons with
Euro-American families.

(S. Sue & Chin, 1983). Chinese Americans reportedly are more likely
than Euro-Americans to think that raising children is primarily the
wife's responsibility (Chia, 1989). In addition, despite the value
traditional Chinese culture places on education, Chinese Americans are
less likely than Euro-Americans to think that a woman is entitled to
continue her education after she is married (Chia, 1989).

Filipino Americans

Because there are no empirical studies of Filipino American family
dynamics, published reports of the characteristics of Filipino American
families have apparently been based on informal observations, and it is
these observations that are the basis for the following discussion.

Filipino American children generally are taught that it is
important to get along with others (Union of Pan Asian Communities,
1978): Toward that end, Filipino Americans emphasize teaching
children to be socially sensitive and considerate; to anticipate the needs
of others; to reciprocate when receiving a favor; to use pleasant, correct,
and euphemistic language; and to avoid aggression, confrontation,
discourtesy, shame, criticism, and embarrassment (Anderson, 1983).
Underlying such values is the belief that etiquette and appropriate
social behavior protect the individual from exploitation, harm, and
shame (Anderson, 1983).

Japanese Americans

Japanese American parents do not appear to present as strong a
coalition as Euro-Americans do (Hsu et al., 1985). This may be because

Japanese American couples make more unilateral decisions than Euro-American couples do (Hsu et al., 1985). In turn, the former may make more unilateral decisions than the latter make because Japanese Americans tend to have clearer roles or because Japanese American couples, sharing a somewhat common background, do not have to confer constantly with each other in order to have a consensus.

Korean Americans

Very little psychological research has been published on Korean American families. Only a few studies were found. This review will focus on the results of only one of these studies, as the other studies have been discussed earlier in this chapter.

Many Korean American parents, particularly fathers, do not think it is good for children to play for a long time and do not think that play ought to be an important part of a child's life (Strom et al., 1987). Because Korean cultural tradition holds that there should be distance between children and adults—and that intimacy (such as playing with children) can undermine the children's respect for their parents (Strom et al., 1987) —parent–child play is often limited. In addition, Korean American parents often find "it difficult to sustain interest in pretending and [are] uncomfortable using play as a medium for teaching" (Strom et al., 1987, p. 99). But the longer that Koreans have lived in America the more likely they have been to acknowledge the need for parents to play with their children and for children to play with their peers (Strom et al., 1987).

Compounding this communication gap, some 1.5 Koreans (i.e., Koreans who, as children, immigrated with their parents) are not fluent in either Korean or English—and the lack of fluency in Korean makes establishing and maintaining communication with Korean-speaking parents difficult (J. Lee & Cynn, 1991); other 1.5 Koreans are fluent only in English, while their parents are fluent only in Korean.

Southeast Asians

Existing information on the family dynamics of Southeast Asian families has been based largely on clinical observations rather than empirical studies. What little information could be found in the psychological research has described Southeast Asian families in general or Vietnamese families in particular. Too little is known about variations in families among and within different Southeast Asian groups.

Southeast Asian families have undergone changes in the United States. Often Vietnamese parents have lost their former social and economic status, and there has been a role reversal in the family. Many Vietnamese fathers have lost their ability to be the sole support of their families, as they were in Vietnam, and may now be dependent on their children—who interpret for them, help them cope with American ways, and so on (D. Le, 1983). This can result in the disruption of family relations, as well as confusion and insecurity for the children and despondency for the parents (D. Le, 1983). Moreover, Southeast Asian children frequently are aware of the despondency of their parents and feel very obligated to improve their parents' situation and compensate for their difficulties (Nidorf, 1985). These changes in family situations and dynamics necessarily limit any generalization about Southeast Asian families in the United States that might be based on their experiences in Southeast Asia.

There have been only a few studies on Vietnamese families. Child-rearing practices among Vietnamese, Cambodians, Hmong, and Lao are reportedly similar in many ways (Morrow, 1989), but researchers have not explicated the ways in which they are similar. During the preschool years (ages 3 to 5), Southeast Asian parents expect increasing self-sufficiency in their children. Preschoolers are expected to dress and groom themselves (Morrow, 1989). With age, the children are subject to increased discipline (Morrow, 1989) : Among the behaviors for which Southeast Asian children are disciplined are disobedience, failure to fulfill responsibilities, and aggression (particularly toward siblings).

Southeast Asian girls are raised more strictly and given less freedom in activities than boys are (C. Ho, 1990). Some Laotian mothers think they should be more strict with their daughters than with their sons: one reason is that "girls need to suffer in order to survive in their society. This would also prepare girls to become obedient and subservient wives" (C. Ho, 1990, p. 141).

Southeast Asian children are generally taught that their relationship to the family is very important and carries obligations (Morrow, 1989). In Vietnam elder siblings assume much responsibility for the care and behavior of younger siblings (Slote, 1972). If a younger sibling misbehaves, the elder sibling, who may not even have been present at the time of the younger sibling's misbehavior, may be blamed: This situation can be exploited by younger siblings and can create resentment in the elder sibling (Slote, 1972).

However, Southeast Asian children are customarily taught to suppress aggressive behavior, strong feelings, and personal grievances (Morrow, 1989). Hostility toward peers and siblings is frowned upon in

Vietnamese families, and hostility toward parents is usually prohibited (Slote, 1972). Nevertheless, there is some evidence of increasing intergenerational conflict based on cultural conflicts in Vietnamese and Chinese-Vietnamese families in the West (Woon, 1986).

Candid verbal communications between parent and child are usually avoided in Southeast Asian families, and the verbal communication that does take place is usually unidirectional— that is, from parent to child (Morrow, 1989). In general, mothers talk with their children more than fathers do (Morrow, 1989).

As for spousal relations, a focus-group study of Southeast Asians in Seattle found that the domination of women in the family was more openly accepted by Vietnamese than by other Southeast Asian groups (C. Ho, 1990). Vietnamese women felt that they could not reject the sexual advances of their husbands without a good excuse and that they had to accept their husbands' extramarital affairs. Similarly, Cambodian and Laotian women felt they could not reject their husband's sexual advances.

CONCLUSION

As shown in this review, the empirical picture of Asian American families is very fragmented. Much more research on them is needed, particularly to study how Asian Americans differ from—and are similar to—not only Euro-American families but also other Asian American families and the families of other minorities. The variety among Asian American families needs to be explored: Not all Asian American families are traditional or even normative. Some Asian American families are intact, while others are not—because the parents are divorced; or because someone (e.g., the father) lives part of the time in Asia, where his business is located, and part of the time in the United States, where the family resides; or because someone in the family did not immigrate to the United States. Single mothers have reportedly been head of over 10% of Chinese American, Japanese American, Korean American, Filipino American, and Vietnamese families in the United States (Slaughter-Defoe et al., 1990). Asian American stepfamilies have apparently never been studied. Some Asian American families live with extended families, and some live as nuclear units. Research has not yet shown how these different structural arrangements affect the amount and type of stress encountered, the conflicts experienced, and the support network available. In the general field of psychology, there is a great deal of research on the relation between ordinal position (i.e., order of birth in a family), on the one hand, and personality, on the other; but this relation has not been empirically examined in Asian American families.

The Asian American cultural values and historical experiences briefly examined in the previous chapters and the family milieu that have been discussed in the present chapter affect personality patterns among Asian Americans. It is to these personality patterns that attention turns in the next chapter.

4

Personality Patterns

This chapter focuses on personality patterns among Asian Americans, but, in a sense, the discussion of personality is already under way because values make up part of a person's personality, and family experiences contribute to personality development.

There are different approaches to the study of personality. Four of the most common are the psychodynamic, learning, biogenetic, and trait approaches. Psychodynamic theories emphasize the working of the unconscious and the effects of past experiences on the personality. The behavioral/learning approach accounts for personality characteristics by examining which behaviors have been reinforced, which have been punished, and which have been observed. The biogenetic approach to personality focuses on genetic predispositions. In the field of psychology these three theories of personality are cornerstones in understanding human behavior. Yet these approaches to personality have rarely been applied to Asian Americans by those doing empirical research.[1]

Instead, the empirical research on personality among Asian Americans has, for the most part, adopted the trait approach, which focuses on describing what are believed to be relatively stable behavioral characteristics. This approach has limited the attention that researchers have given to the study of behavioral change across situations. In addition, the trait approach in general is atheoretical; and, therefore, it does not offer explanations for behaviors. Rather, the trait

---

[1]A notable exception is the study by Zane et al. (1991), which takes a social-learning approach.

approach simply provides descriptions of how people differ from each other. If the research on Asian Americans had a broader theoretical basis, such research would lend itself to both uncovering the ways in which Asian Americans are like other Americans and the ways in which culture affects personality.

You will notice that most of the research on Asian American personality was published 20 or more years ago. Perhaps this area of research has generally been abandoned because researchers fear lending credence to stereotypes. Another possible reason personality research has been abandoned is that there are other, more attractive areas of psychological research on Asian Americans (such as psychopathology, which differs from personality research in that it seeks to define deviational rather than typical characteristics) that can have more immediate implications for psychotherapy or public policy and for which there is more research funding available.

LIMITATIONS OF PERSONALITY RESEARCH

In order to better understand the research on the personality traits of Asian Americans, it is helpful to consider some of the conceptual and methodological criticism that has been leveled at this research. Its limitations are similar to the limitations of the research on Asian American families.

First, most of the studies of Asian American personality have been correlational. As a means of explaining personality characteristics, they have given insufficient attention to testing theories of Asian American personality (S. Sue & Morishima, 1982), showing causal relationships between personality characteristics and predetermining factors, or demonstrating the role these personality characteristics play in the adjustment of Asian Americans (Nicassio, 1985). For example, there is a lack of research that examines how experiences with racism affect the personalities of Asian Americans and there are no longitudinal studies of personality development among Asian Americans. Moreover, the studies that do exist have focused on individual personality traits rather than personality syndromes, thereby limiting their explanatory power.

Second, the studies suffer from sampling limitations. Typically, the research samples have included only Chinese Americans and Japanese Americans, and the studies were conducted before large numbers of post-1965 immigrants came to the United States. Thus, foreign-born Asian Americans and non-Chinese and non-Japanese Asian Americans have not been included in most of these samples even though they now constitute a large portion of the Asian American population.

In addition, the samples have generally been composed of college students (who are often atypical of the whole Asian American population, as far as age, marital status, education level, and so forth are concerned). College students are often used in psychological studies because they are an easy-to-access source of subjects for university researchers, who are able to administer questionnaires to and run experiments with a broad sample of freshmen and other students taking Introductory Psychology classes.

Furthermore, the subject pools generally are restricted to those who read English well enough to answer questionnaires written in English. Researchers usually hesitate to provide questionnaires written in different languages because of the expense involved in translating and printing questionnaires in foreign languages. Expense is an issue because federal funding for research on Asian Americans is often very limited: Social-science research is generally underfunded, and little money is spent on studying minorities—especially the so-called model minority—that constitute a small percentage of the American population.

Third, studies of Asian American personality typically compare Asian Americans with Euro-Americans. There have not been many studies that have compared personality patterns across Asian American ethnic groups or that have examined individual differences in personality among Asian Americans. Failing to look at individual differences is conducive to the development of stereotypes.

In addition, consistently using Euro-Americans as the control group can have the unfortunate effect of unconsciously establishing Euro-Americans as the standard (Olmedo, 1979), thereby unintentionally implying that personality differences between Asian Americans and Euro-Americans indicate that Asian American personality patterns are negative, abnormal, or in need of rectification (D. Sue & S. Sue, 1987). The following is an example of how an Asian American personality pattern might be seen as an indication of poor adjustment when viewed from the perspective of a Euro-American standard. Suppose Asian Americans generally indicated on personality questionnaires that they uncomplainingly obey their parents even when they disagree with them. Interpreting these responses from a Eurocentric perspective might lead to the conclusion that Asian Americans tend to be introverted and lacking in self-confidence, but interpreting the same responses from a multicultural perspective might lead to the conclusion that Asian Americans demonstrate filial piety and modesty (D. Sue & S. Sue, 1987).

Fourth, the meaning of the statement, "Asian Americans tend to have personality trait X more than Euro-Americans do," can be ambiguous. The research strategy most commonly employed—that is, comparing average Asian American and Euro-American group differences—can mislead people into thinking that some traits are common among Asian Americans when in fact they are just more common in Asian Americans than in the other group studied (S. Sue & Kitano, 1973). The traits could be rare in both groups. For example, Chinese Americans may conform more than Euro-Americans do, but perhaps neither group conforms very much (S. Sue & Kitano, 1973). Such a research strategy does not disclose whether an attribute is more often present than absent in Asian Americans (S. Sue & Morishima, 1982).

Fifth, studies of Asian American personality patterns have generally involved the administration of personality questionnaires; but there are a number of problems inherent in standard personality questionnaires. Such paper-and-pencil tests (i.e., measures that involve filling out questionnaires) tend to focus on a restricted range of behaviors, overlook others (Tong, 1971), and fail to reveal how individuals will behave in particular situations.

Suppose there is a personality questionnaire that purportedly measures passivity. The questionnaire might contain a number of questions about the respondents' behaviors in interpersonal situations. Such a measure might indicate that the immigrant Asian Americans being tested are rather passive. But if the questionnaire took into account the immigrant Asians' initiative in moving their family to a new country, learning English, and establishing a business, the Asian Americans would not appear to be so passive (S. Sue & Morishima, 1982).

Personality tests often ask respondents to characterize their behavior in general. But some evidence suggests that Asian Americans are more likely than other Americans to vary their behavior depending on the person with whom they are interacting. For example, a personality questionnaire item could be "I am outgoing," and the respondent must indicate the degree to which that statement is true or not true. Many Asian Americans are extremely outgoing with their friends but very withdrawn in the classroom. The respondents, therefore, do not know whether they should arbitrarily pick one situation as more representative of their behavior than another. Some respondents might arbitrarily choose a situation and base their response on that situation, but other respondents might choose to average their two extreme behaviors. This ambiguity can result in unreliable and invalid findings.

Personality questionnaires typically include questions about private feelings, behavior in public, and behavior with friends. Discrepancies in these areas typically are not examined. Instead,

psychometricians (i.e., people who design psychological tests) generally seem to have assumed that there is a great deal of similarity in
how people respond in different situations and a great deal of
congruence in how people feel and how they behave. But these
assumptions could be even less valid for Asian Americans than they
are for other Americans. Because of cultural roles and expectations,
there may be larger discrepancies in the behaviors and feelings of
Asian Americans in different settings than there are for other
Americans. For example, foreign-born Asian Americans may be more
likely than other Americans to suppress anger that they feel toward
their parents. Because of acculturative difficulties constraining their
perceived behavior options, many immigrant Asian Americans might
not behave in a way congruent with their feelings or with their
underlying personality predispositions. For instance, Asian Americans
who are not fluent in English might not voice disagreement with
people who are fluent in English because the former might think that
they are unable to explain their feelings in English. If personality is
defined as underlying behavioral preferences and actual behaviors in
different contexts, it would be helpful to analyze both components
separately and examine the differences between behavior preferences
and actual behaviors in various contexts. However, such analyses are
not done by researchers, and this calls into question the validity of
some assessments of personality, particularly the personality of those
Asian Americans who behave very differently in various settings and
also of those who, more than other Americans, behave in ways that are
congruent with the expectations of others rather than in ways that are
congruent with their own feelings. Indeed, there is often no evidence
that these personality questionnaires are valid for Asian American
samples (D. Sue & S. Sue, 1987). Given these limitations, there are
questions about how generalizable some of this research is.

Despite these limitations, a review of the existing research on
Asian American personality is warranted as a means of showing what
the initial forays into this area have produced. The discussion that
follows has three purposes. First, a review of the research on Asian
American personality as well as an analysis of the relation between
these personality characteristics on the one hand, and cultural
background and minority experiences on the other, may help to
explain why some Asian Americans have certain personality characteristics and may also help to explain why there are *group* differences
between Asian Americans and other *groups* of Americans. (It is very
important to remember that the research deals with group differences,
not individual differences; therefore, this research does not indicate
why individual Asian Americans behave as they do.) Second, people

from different racial or cultural backgrounds presumably have the same potential range of personalities, but different cultures reinforce different personality traits (Abbott, 1976). Consequently, an examination of personality characteristics among Asian Americans may highlight what personality characteristics Asian American cultures reinforce. Third, a review of the personality research provides a context for understanding attitudes and behaviors that bear on mental health needs and services, including what is perceived as stressful and what individuals do to cope with that stress. In this way, a review of personality research on Asian Americans will be one of the bases for discussions in subsequent chapters.

PERSONALITY TRAITS

The research on Asian American personality has focused on descriptions of singular personality traits rather than personality syndromes; therefore, in order to reflect the research that has been done, this review will present research findings on separate personality traits. The traits discussed reveal the principle dimensions on which the personality research has focused.

Studies with samples comprising several Asian American groups and samples comprising only one or two Asian American groups are summarized for what these studies show about Asian American personality characteristics in general. One will notice, for example, that only studies of Chinese Americans and Japanese Americans have dealt with conformity. Based on anecdotal evidence, conformity is probably just as applicable to such groups as Cambodians, Thais, and Filipino Americans; but there is no research on these groups. Therefore, they are not mentioned in the section discussing comparisons in conformity between Asian Americans and Euro-Americans because there is a lack of substantiating evidence, not because there are no differences in conformity between these groups and Euro-Americans. A synopsis of which Asian American groups showed more or less evidence of certain personality characteristics, compared with Euro-American groups, is shown in Table 4.1. Blank spaces indicate that research on a dimension has not been done for a group.

The analysis of personality differences between Asian Americans and other Americans that are a result of both cultural values and the status of Asian Americans as racial minorities should not be interpreted as a value judgment on the personality characteristics analyzed. Cultural values and minority status are posited as possible explanations for these findings, but there is no empirical evidence

TABLE 4.1. Summary of Personality Research

Personality Dimension	CA[a]	FA[b]	JA[c]	KA[d]	Mix[e]
More abasement	+		+		
More affiliation					
in self-reports		+	+		
behavior measures	–				–
More anxiety	+		+		+
Less assertiveness in self-reports	+		+		+
Situationally determined assertiveness	+		+		
Less autonomy	+	+	+		
More conformity	+		+		
Less expressiveness	+		+	–	+
Less extroversion	+		+		
More formality	+		+		
External locus of control	+		+		
Negative self-concept about physical appearance	+		+		
More femininity	+		+		
More masculinity	+/–		+/–		

Note. Comparisons are to Euro-Americans. Regarding the formality dimension for Chinese Americans, there were no direct studies, only findings consistent with their being more formal. Regarding the masculinity dimension for Chinese Americans and Japanese Americans, there were contradictory findings.
[a]Chinese Americans.
[b]Filipino Americans.
[c]Japanese Americans.
[d]Korean Americans.
[e]Sample was a mix of Asian American groups.

directly supporting these hypotheses. Indeed, Asian cultural values in some cases might be of negligible relevance to the American-born Asian Americans who were the subjects of most of these studies. An equal emphasis is not placed on immigrant status to account for these findings since most of this research was done at a time when the vast majority of the samples were American-born Asian Americans.

Abasement

Abasement refers to accepting responsibility for things when they do not go well, preferring to give in and avoid confrontation more than preferring to have one's own way, feeling depressed when not handling situations well, feeling timid around others who are considered superior, and feeling inferior to others in many ways (Connor, 1974c).[2] Research has found that Chinese Americans and Japanese Americans are more prone to feeling abased than Euro-Americans are (Connor, 1974a, 1974c, 1975; Fenz & Arkoff, 1962).

These results were derived from studies using the Edwards Personal Preference Schedule. This test consists of a series of statement couplets and it requires that respondents choose which statement most applies to them. But many of the forced choices (e.g., "I like to criticize people who are in a position of authority" versus "I feel timid in the presence of other people I regard as superiors" or "I like to use words which other people often do not know the meaning of" versus "I feel that I am inferior to others in most respects") have what could be culturally biased content, which can undermine the validity of these studies. In the first couplet, for example, criticizing others might seem like trying to dominate them, and, as mentioned in Chapter 2, dominating others is frowned upon by many Asian Americans. But that does not mean that Asian Americans regard others as their superiors or that they feel timid in the presence of those supposed superiors. Given the choice between two false statements, respondents are instructed to choose the less false, but that does not mean that the statement is true. Much more research using culturally appropriate measures is needed before conclusions can be drawn concerning whether Asian Americans today tend to be more inclined to feeling abased than other Americans.

Cultural Basis

A lack of follow-up studies has meant that the degree to which the EPPS distorted findings is not known. However, it may be that Asian Americans are more inclined to feeling abased than other Americans are. If so, it may be in part because some of their cultural values reinforce self-abasement, such as the emphasis they place on modesty, harmony in relationships, and deference to authority (Union of Pan Asian Communities, 1978). Indeed, Chinese Americans, Filipino Americans, and Japanese Americans have been found to be more deferential than Euro-Americans (Fenz & Arkoff, 1962). Having a

---

[2]There is reason to doubt that conceptually all of these various purported aspects of abasement truly reflect a single, underlying construct. Even when a factor analysis subsumes these characteristics under one dimension, that is no guarantee that the characteristics reflect one conceptual construct because researchers could be choosing inappropriate conceptual and numerical criteria for inclusion in a factor.

yielding manner is consistent with modesty and deference to authority and can help promote interpersonal harmony. Behaving in deferential way can be viewed simply as a way of getting along with others and avoiding unnecessary confrontation. Traditional Asian American family structure may reinforce this characteristic. For instance, feeling inferior and timid around "superiors" might reflect the traditional family's emphasis on a hierarchy within the family.

Suppose an Asian American woman has been taught to respect elders because they are purportedly superior. She is treated as an inferior person by her elders and, from the perspective of social-learning theory, is reinforced for behaving as though she is inferior. The script (i.e., the style of relating to other people) that she is learning is to behave as though she were inferior to her elders. To avert cognitive dissonance, her behavior can promote the feeling that she is inferior to elders or others. This feeling may become generalized so that she is behaving in an abased way toward other people.

Minority Basis

Some Asian Americans may develop feelings of inferiority because of personal experiences with racism or because of media images of Asians and Asian Americans. These experiences and perceptions could contribute to feelings of abasement.

In addition, generations of Chinese Americans, Filipino Americans, and Japanese Americans may have learned that behaving in an abased manner can lessen racial antagonism directed against them. Earlier generations may have passed this behavior pattern along in an effort to protect their children (by teaching them a way to defend themselves) or simply to have their children adopt the values that the parents had learned as "right." Moreover, it would not be surprising if research found that recent immigrants behave in a self-abased manner because of their uncertainty about behavior patterns in the United States. However, such research has not yet been conducted.

Affiliation

Affiliation refers to association with friends: doing things with and for friends, sharing with friends, and forming strong social attachments. In a comparison of Chinese Americans, Filipino Americans, Hawaiian Americans, Japanese Americans, and Euro-Americans in Hawaii, all but the Chinese Americans were more affiliative than Euro-Americans, with Filipino Americans being the most affiliative (Fenz & Arkoff, 1962). Other research has confirmed that *Sansei* are more affiliative than Euro-Americans (Connor, 1974c, 1975, 1977) and, consistent with these findings, that *Sansei* had more desire for succor (i.e., more desire to receive help, encouragement, and understanding from others) than Euro-Americans did.

However, one study found that Asian American children in grades 5 through 11 communicated and associated less with their peers (as measured by frequency of phone calls from peers and frequency of visits from peers) than Euro-American children did (Yao, 1985). Similarly, another study (Bourne, 1975) found that Chinese American male college students had relatively few friends, dated little, and did not spend much time in recreational or social activities.

On the surface, these findings seem to conflict with studies that show Asian Americans to be more affiliative than Euro-Americans. One important difference between the two sets of studies is that those studies showing Asian Americans to be more affiliative were based on the Edwards Personal Preference Schedule while those showing Asian Americans to be less affiliative were based on reports of actual behavior. A second difference between the sets of studies is found in the samples. The Connor subjects were Japanese Americans in California. The chances are that most of them were not immigrants. In contrast, the subjects in the Yao study included a number of Asian American groups in Texas (but not any Japanese Americans). Half of Yao's subjects were foreign born. Differences in the subject pools in combination with Connor's finding that *Nisei* were not more affiliative than Euro-Americans suggests that there may be an as-yet-unstudied relationship between affiliation and acculturation. It is possible that as people become more comfortable and familiar with their surroundings, they become more affiliative. The study in Hawaii may have found that Asian Americans were generally more affiliative than Euro-Americans because the large Asian American population in Hawaii makes Asian Americans more comfortable with their surroundings than Euro-Americans are. Foreign-born children between the fifth through the eleventh grades (the grades studied by Yao) probably will not be as familiar with American styles of social interaction as American-born children are. Thus, the former might be less affiliative because they feel less comfortable socially interacting with their American peers. Alternatively, the former may be less affiliative because they have less time to spend on friends: Their immigrant parents might be putting in long hours at work so their children have to take on more family responsibilities than their American-born peers do. Note also that affiliation refers only to association with friends, not sociability in general. It could be that immigrant Asian American children spend more time socializing with their family than with their friends.

The tentative picture that emerges is that 20 years ago acculturated Asian Americans may have been more affiliative than Euro-Americans, but it is not known whether this is still the case. It also appears that foreign-born Asian Americans may engage in less social activity with friends than Euro-Americans. Additional research is needed to clarify these findings.

Cultural Basis

Among the traditional Asian values that could account for greater desire for affiliation among Asian Americans than among Euro-Americans is the former's greater orientation toward the group than toward individualism. But this orientation is not a likely basis for the research discussed. If Asian cultural values were the determining factor in affiliative tendencies, foreign-born Asian Americans, expected to have more Asian values, would be more affiliative than American-born Asian Americans.

Minority Basis

It is possible that because some Asian Americans have felt excluded from the mainstream, they have sought out friends in order to gain a sense of belonging, bolster their sense of self-worth, or protect themselves from racism. This feeling of exclusion, rather than the affiliation–acculturation hypothesis, might be the reason that *Sansei* in California are more affiliative than Euro-Americans.[3]

Anxiety

Researchers have found that Asian Americans tend to be more anxious than Euro-Americans across a variety of situations (Meredith & Meredith, 1966; D. Sue et al., 1983; D. W. Sue & Kirk, 1973; Zane et al., 1991). For example, *Sansei* high-school students have been found to be

---

[3]Some of these explanations for findings are somewhat simplistic because of two constraints: (1) the dearth of research on the relation between Asian American experiences with racism, on the one hand, and the various personality dimensions discussed in this chapter, on the other; and (2) the effort to stay roughly within the confines of the available research.

more anxious and worried than their Euro-American counterparts (Onoda, 1977), and Chinese American and Japanese American male college students and Chinese American female college students have been found to be more anxious than other students (D. W. Sue & Kirk, 1973).[4] Consistent with these findings, Abbott (1976) reported that Chinese Americans tend to have low personality-test scores for poise and self-assurance. Asian American middle-school students have been found to have more test anxiety than Euro-Americans do (Pang, 1991).

Few studies have compared Asian Americans to groups other than Euro-Americans. An exception is a study that found no difference in anxiety between Korean American and African American children (Chang, 1975).

Cultural Basis

Asian Americans may be more anxious than Euro-Americans because Asian Americans experience more ambiguity in nonfamilial social relationships than Euro-Americans do. This ambiguity could arise from differences between Asian Americans and Euro-Americans in communication styles: Insofar as Asian Americans customarily accommodate themselves to Euro-Americans in social situations, the former may be on less familiar ground than the latter and, therefore, may feel more anxiety. Contributing to the increased anxiety for Asian Americans could be the differences between Euro-Americans and foreign-born Asian Americans in their facility with English or in their familiarity with unspoken behavioral norms; another contributing factor could be the differences between Asian Americans and Euro-Americans in the amount of cultural conflict that they experience because of their behavior. Insofar as Asian American cultures traditionally emphasize noticing subtle social cues, some Asian Americans may feel generally more anxious than other Americans because of the former's concern about missing social cues and, therefore, not behaving appropriately. It is also possible that Asian Americans who feel relatively uncomfortable in new situations come from conservative, traditional Asian American families that emphasize fixed traditions and ways of behaving (D. W. Sue & Kirk, 1972).

In addition, some Asian Americans feel more pressure to maintain interpersonal harmony (e.g., to conform, to avoid offending others, to recognize when someone has done a favor so that they can reciprocate)

---

[4]Incidentally, Asian American females reportedly are more likely than males to exhibit anxiety (Meredith, 1969).

than most Euro-Americans do. Because of this pressure, Asian Americans may feel more anxious than Euro-Americans in situations that are not harmonious.

Finally, the subjects of these studies were students. It is possible that Asian American students are more anxious than their non-Asian American peers because the former are under more pressure from their parents to do well in school. Some research bears out this possibility (Aldwin & Greenberger, 1987; Yao, 1985).

Minority Basis

The tendency for Asian Americans to be more anxious than Euro-Americans could reflect minority-group status. Some Asian Americans may have been stigmatized as intruders, enduring stinging jokes about their ethnicity, or feeling misunderstood by those who stereotype them. Such Asian Americans may sometimes feel anxious when they enter new relationships because they feel they do not fit in or are apprehensive about the possibility of racist rejection.

A distinction needs to be drawn between intergroup and social anxiety because Asian Americans could be demonstrating intergroup anxiety rather than social anxiety—and, when this is done, it may be seen that the former is not a reflection of the latter (Stephan & Stephan, 1985). It could be that some Asian Americans are anxious about interacting with non-Asian Americans rather than that they are socially anxious. Intergroup anxiety could elevate the anxiety scores of Asian Americans more than those of Euro-Americans because most Asian Americans have more intergroup contact than Euro-Americans do.

Assertiveness

The majority of studies, relying on self-reports of assertiveness, have found that Chinese Americans, Filipino Americans, and Japanese Americans are less assertive (Fukuyama & Greenfield, 1983; Minatoya & Sedlacek, 1979, cited in D. Sue et al., 1983) and more deferential (Arkoff, 1964; Connor, 1975; Fenz & Arkoff, 1962; Meredith, 1966) than Euro-Americans.[5] Asian Americans tend to be less assertive than Euro-Americans in that they are more hesitant about expressing their feelings, disagreeing with their parents, or complaining (Fukuyama & Greenfield, 1983). Consistent with this research is the finding that

---

[5]In psychological terminology, "assertiveness" does not carry the implication of violence that "aggression" does.

Chinese Americans tend to have high personality-test scores for self-control and tolerance (Abbott, 1976).

But these studies do not tell the whole story because self-report measures often do not closely reflect actual behaviors (Zane et al., 1991). Indeed, although Chinese Americans have reported being less assertive than Euro-Americans have, a role-playing experiment (D. Sue et al., 1983) showed that Chinese Americans behave as assertively as Euro-Americans.

Other research, using behavioral measures of assertiveness, has indicated that Asian Americans have the ability to be assertive and know how to be assertive but that they inhibit that assertiveness (Ayabe, 1971; D. Sue et al., 1983; D. Sue, D. M. Sue, & Ino, 1990). This research suggests, therefore, that verbal inhibition and deference among Asian Americans may reflect situational factors rather than global personality characteristics (D. Sue et al., 1983). For instance, a study found that the amount of deference exhibited by Japanese Americans varied with the situation (Ayabe, 1971). In that study, Japanese American and Euro-American females were instructed to speak in a loud voice in the presence of a fellow student and in the presence of a professor. When the subjects were instructed to speak loudly in the presence of a fellow student, there was no difference in the loudness of the Japanese American and Euro-American subjects. However, when the subjects were instructed to speak loudly in the presence of the professor (regardless of the authority figure's ethnicity), the Japanese Americans did not talk as loudly as the Euro-Americans. Apparently, the assertiveness of Asian Americans was more situation-specific than that of Euro-Americans (Yi, Zane, & S. Sue, 1986).

In school, if Asian Americans need to form or participate in discussion groups with non-Asian American peers whom they do not know, they will often let the non-Asian Americans dominate the conversation. Frequently (but not always, because there *are* quiet non-Asian Americans and loquacious Asian Americans) the non-Asian Americans will talk louder and longer than the Asian Americans. When the non-Asian Americans find that the Asian Americans are not talking much, they often assume a leadership role and direct questions to the Asian Americans—in effect, inviting the Asian Americans to talk. It might be helpful to remember the discussion of the *enryo* syndrome in order to understand the cultural basis for this hesitancy to speak up. Many traditional-minded Asian Americans hesitate to speak up in meetings, and they hesitate even more when non-Asian Americans are present. Yet these same Asian Americans will be very talkative in other situations.

In another approach used for the purpose of seeing how assertive

Asian Americans are in natural situations (Zane et al., 1991), researchers presented Chinese American, Japanese American, and Euro-American college students with descriptions of naturalistic social situations and gave them a forced-choice list of alternative responses. The researchers found that the Asian American students did not differ from Euro-American students in the assertiveness of their responses when dealing with acquaintances or those with whom they had intimate relationships. However, the Asian Americans gave less assertive responses when presented with situations involving strangers. The Asian Americans were less likely than the Euro-Americans to expect that assertiveness with strangers would be effective. The researchers suggested that this expectation may, in part, account for Asian Americans being less assertive than Euro-Americans when associating with strangers.

As a whole, these studies point to noticeable situational variability in the assertiveness of Asian Americans. These studies also show that different measures of assertiveness can produce quite different assessments of assertiveness among Asian Americans.

Cultural Basis

Many Asian cultural values and norms (rooted in Confucianism, Buddhism, and Taoism) deter assertiveness—including the emphasis on respect for others, conformity, emotional detachment, modesty, interpersonal harmony, concern for proper form and etiquette, deference to those of higher status, restraint of hostile and aggressive emotions, and acceptance of those aspects of life that cannot be changed. From a traditionally Asian perspective, inhibition usually is regarded positively as a manifestation of self-control, whereas spontaneity is frequently considered to be an indication of bad manners (D. W. Sue & Kirk, 1972). Assertive behaviors could cause anxiety in some Asian Americans because such behaviors run counter to Asian American cultural values; but the situational specificity of assertive behavior in Asian Americans suggests that Asian Americans are not less assertive than Euro-Americans simply because of anxiety or guilt about disrupting interpersonal harmony.

Traditional Asian American family structure can also indirectly deter assertiveness in a number of ways. Some Asian American males inhabit revered positions in the family and discover that they can remain passive because others will be responsive to their needs; they do not have to be assertive to affect events (Bourne, 1975). From the perspective of social-learning theory, assertiveness by family members who are lower in the family hierarchy may be met with punishment or admonitions to respect people higher in the hierarchy. People lower in the family hierarchy may feel that the family has ignored their assertive statements and that their assertive statements had no effect on events. Unreinforced assertiveness can lead to extinction of that behavior. In traditional Chinese American and Southeast Asian families, older members make decisions. That children are not accustomed to making decisions not only tends to prolong dependency in the Chinese American family (D. W. Sue & Kirk, 1972) but can also encourage passivity. If a child's self-image is that of a person who obeys rather than as a person who chooses how to behave, this could inhibit the child's assertiveness (Watanabe, 1973). Dependence on the family can make interactions with nonfamily members feel awkward (Abbott, 1976). Furthermore, reserve might be a result of the restrictive child-rearing attitudes of some Asian American mothers (Higa, 1974).

In addition, Japanese Americans are frequently taught to be sensitive to the feelings and responses of others. As such, they are taught not to be domineering, boastful, or preoccupied with their own activities or interests (Kikumura & Kitano, 1976). Therefore, their threshold for what constitutes too much assertiveness may be lower than that of other Americans: Asian Americans and Euro-Americans could have different criteria for labeling behavior "somewhat" or "very" assertive on Likert-scale questionnaires. Moreover, nonassertiveness may be more socially desirable for Asian Americans than for Euro-Americans, and, therefore, Asian Americans and Euro-Americans could have different response biases.

Consideration must be given to the possibility that Asian Americans are as assertive as other Americans but that they manifest that assertiveness in different ways not tapped by most measures. An Asian American may be assertive about doing research for a term paper but not about glad-handing at a party. Indirect communication patterns could cause Asian Americans to appear less assertive than Euro-Americans, even though the former may be equally assertive (Zane et al., 1991). The choice of alternative forms of assertiveness may be culturally circumscribed. In turn, differences in the situations in which assertive behavior is manifested and differences in how assertiveness is manifested can affect Asian Americans' self-reports of assertive behavior, particularly if the questionnaires ask about Eurocentric styles of exhibiting assertiveness.

Minority Basis

The fact that Asian Americans are minorities also could contribute to their more deferential behavior. Deference could be a way of surviving in a racist society (S. Sue & Morishima, 1982) or a way of eliciting sympathy and attention (D. Sue & S. Sue, 1987). Assertiveness and expressiveness by minorities are frequently punished by the larger society (Watanabe, 1973), which sees such behavior as disruptive or extremist; whereas obedience, conformity, and respect for authority are often reinforced by the larger society (Suzuki, 1977) in order to ensure that the power structure in America will not be challenged.

The deferential behavior of some Asian Americans may reflect a learned helplessness developed from their experiences as minorities (S. Sue, 1980). Consistent with this hypothesis is the previously mentioned study that found Asian Americans to be less likely than other Americans to believe in the efficacy of their assertiveness (Zane et al., 1991). Although stereotypes about the passivity and deference of Asian Americans can be dignified by pointing to purported cultural roots, the behavior, in fact, can reflect an inability to stop racism (Tong, 1971). In any case, measures of assertiveness do not elucidate the reasons for passivity.

Asian Americans might also choose to exercise different forms of assertiveness because of their minority status. Minorities sometimes strive for achievement so that they will be judged for their performance rather than for their minority status (E. Smith, 1985).

Autonomy

Research has indicated that Chinese Americans, Filipino Americans, and Japanese Americans tend to be less autonomous, less independent, more inhibited, and more obedient to authority figures (including parents) than Euro-Americans are (Connor, 1975; Fenz & Arkoff, 1962; Meredith, 1966; D. W. Sue, 1989a; D. W. Sue & Kirk, 1972, 1973). *Sansei* also reportedly have less desire for autonomy and dominance than Euro-Americans (Connor, 1974c).

The claim that Asian Americans have less desire or need for autonomy may be a methodological artifact. The Edwards Personal Preference Schedule (the measure that was used in these studies) purports to reveal needs and desires. In this inventory, one of the measures of the desire for autonomy is the statement, "I like to be able to come and go as I want to," coupled with various other statements. The respondents have to choose which statement is more applicable to them. But the research on Asian American families has shown that Asian American parents in general are more restrictive with their children than non-Asian American parents are. Consequently, in reading the sentence "I like to be able to come and go as I want to," Asian Americans may be more likely than Euro-Americans to think that they do not have enough experience coming and going as they please. Therefore, although the stimulus sentence would not have the same meaning for the different populations, the responses of Asian Americans would be compared to—or evaluated by—Euro-American norms. Skewed results can follow from that. It is an open question whether these findings can be replicated now with other measures.

Cultural Basis

Insofar as Asian Americans do demonstrate less desire for autonomy, it could conceivably stem from the Confucian emphasis placed on strong family ties rather than independence and individual autonomy (Shon & Ja, 1982) and the emphasis placed on interdependence over independence (Union of Pan Asian Communities, 1978). It could be that Asian American families in general emphasize values such as sensitivity to the desires of others (Endo, 1980), conformity, respect for authority, and the submergence of the individual to the group—all of which may lead to less autonomous behavior and less desire for autonomy (D. W. Sue & Kirk, 1972). For instance, Chinese American college freshmen are apparently more influenced by and dependent upon their families than other college freshmen are (D. W. Sue & Kirk, 1972). With its emphasis on preestablished roles that family members are expected to fulfill, the structure of traditional Asian American families seems to discourage autonomy, or, at least, not to provide an environment that nurtures certain types of autonomous action.

Recall that in the preceding chapter it was noted that Chinese American parents often restrict their children's independence. A history of strict supervision may squelch the development of autonomy. By restricting the independence of children, parents do not teach their children how to handle freedom and decision-making (Carlin & Sokoloff, 1985): To the extent that this is true, such culturally based child-rearing patterns can discourage autonomy.

Minority Basis

It is possible that another reason for less autonomy among Asian Americans as opposed to Euro-Americans is that the former somewhat inhibit expressing their autonomy for fear that they may arouse racist responses. Nevertheless, in general, cultural values may more strongly influence this pattern of behavior than minority status does.

Conformity

Chinese American and Japanese American students have been found to be more likely to behave in a conformist manner than Euro-American students (Meredith, 1966; D. W. Sue & Kirk, 1972).

Cultural Basis

In the interest of maintaining harmony and placing the interests of the group ahead of those of the individual, traditional Asian values have emphasized conformity. For example, Chinese American children are taught to be sensitive to cues in social situations so that they can adapt their behavior to that of the group (Chun-Hoon, 1973). Japanese values also stress conformity, conventional behavior, and obedience to rules (Union of Pan Asian Communities, 1978).

From a social-learning perspective, Asian American children in general probably tend to be reinforced for conforming, obeying, and putting the desires of the group before their individual desires, and they are punished for contrary behavior. Both children and adults in some ethnic communities are also subject to gossip for failing to conform.

Minority Basis

Minority groups frequently try to be invisible—for example, by dressing like the dominant group, belittling their own accomplishments, and remaining quiet at meetings in order to minimize vulnerability (E. Smith, 1985). It is possible that this desire to be invisible and to minimize vulnerability to racism contributes to the tendency of Asian Americans to conform. This conformist behavior pattern may be generalized to situations in which Asian Americans would not be subjected to racism.

Another possibility is that when some people experience racism they develop a more acute desire to be accepted, and they see conformity as a way to gain acceptance. For example, if some people were to reject an Asian American because of his or her ethnicity, that Asian American may try to move them to look beyond his or her physical characteristics, and show, by conforming, that he or she is not that different from them.

Expressiveness

A great deal of research, mostly using paper-and-pencil measures, has found that Asian Americans are less verbally and emotionally expressive than Euro-Americans (see, e.g., Fukuyama & Greenfield, 1983; Johnson & Marsella, 1978). This pattern was found even in Chinese Americans and Japanese Americans during the early 1970s (D. W. Sue, 1973; D. W. Sue & Kirk, 1973) when there were still relatively few foreign-born Asian Americans in experimental samples. The tendency to be verbally inhibited and cautious about directly expressing feelings has been confirmed in clinical assessments (Bourne, 1975) and in self-descriptions by Asian Americans (Li-Repac, 1980). An exception to the use of paper-and-pencil tests is an observational study of groups of Japanese American and Euro-American college students at the University of Hawaii (Ogawa & Walden, 1972). That study indicated that Japanese American groups provided less verbal feedback to others than Euro-American groups did.

In contrast, some researchers, using a single-question measure of the tendency to express anxiety or frustration about problems, have found that Korean American college students were more likely to express anxiety or frustration than their Euro-American counterparts (Aldwin & Greenberger, 1987). (However, expressing emotions was positively associated with depression among these Korean American students, perhaps indicating that this sample was not typical of Korean American college students.) A problem with this study is its use of a single question to measure the tendency to express emotions. The use of one question to measure a construct might not provide valid results, and its meaning is very difficult to interpret accurately (Uba, 1981). Consequently, this contrasting finding does not seriously undermine the weight of the other studies demonstrating that Asian Americans tend to be less expressive than Euro-Americans.

However, since most of these studies involved paper-and-pencil tests, there is a potential methodological problem with their findings. When questionnaires seek to measure expressiveness by asking respondents what they say or do in various situations, researchers may implicitly—and perhaps unintentionally—be looking for Euro-American ways of expressing. Since Asian Americans tend to rely on nonverbal cues more than non-Asian Americans do, the former may not need to *say* as much to convey their thoughts and feelings or do anything as overt as the actions posed by questionnaires.

For example, coming from families in which a great deal of thought and feeling can be communicated subtly and indirectly, many Asian Americans may transfer a subtle style of communicating to nonfamilial situations. In class discussions it is sometimes possible, by noticing their subtle body language, to know when Asian American students know an answer and are willing to participate. Rather than raise a hand in class, some Asian American students will express their desire or willingness to participate by sitting a little straighter in their chairs or making a little more eye contact with the teacher than they usually do. Personality tests which ask the respondents how much they "express" themselves can provide misleading results. Asian Americans may be expressing themselves by sending cues, but others may not be noticing, or, if they are noticing, they are failing to interpret the cues correctly. A teacher who does not notice changes in posture may not call on these students; consequently, they will not contribute to class discussion. In response to personality questionnaires, Asian Americans may assume that these tests equate expressiveness with verbal communication; therefore, they will report that they do not express themselves much.

Despite these reservations, in the absence of strong data to the contrary, research currently suggests that Asian Americans are less emotionally and verbally expressive than Euro-Americans.

Cultural Basis

Limited verbal expressiveness could reflect cultural values that are placed on reserve, restraint of strong feelings, obedience, conformity with the group, respect, and social sensitivity. Indeed, being talkative can be interpreted by some Asian Americans as attempting to dominate social interactions. To the extent that this is true, talkative Asian Americans would not receive much reinforcement for their expressiveness. Moreover, their parents are probably not expressive role models.

In addition, Asian Americans might be less expressive in experimental and clinical settings than in other settings—and less expressive than Euro-Americans in experimental and clinical settings because of the value placed on deference to authority. As the well-known Milgram studies have demonstrated, subjects tend to perceive experimenters, or anyone else with the title "doctor," as authority figures. In such situations, Asian Americans might be inhibiting their expressiveness in an effort to be polite and deferential to the experimenters or clinical psychologists. But this does not mean that they are consistently nonexpressive.

Since communication in traditional Asian American families is customarily unidirectional from parent to child, some Asian American children receive little reinforcement for discussing matters, and, thus, these children's language skills may not develop as quickly as in Euro-American families (Endo, 1980). Children's verbal ability depends in part on their experience in dominating interactions and their feeling that what they say can influence their parents (Plummer, 1971). If children raised in traditional Asian American families receive little reinforcement for discussing matters with their parents—and, thereby, influencing their parents—the children's verbal ability could be stunted. Moreover, insofar as Asian American children are not encouraged to engage in protracted family discussions in which both parents and children exchange ideas, they might not be accustomed to thinking about their opinions. Thus, some Asian American students who do not participate much in class discussions claim that they do not feel they are holding back from class discussions. They say that they do not have anything to add to discussions and that they are surprised at how much their non-Asian American peers have to say.

Difficulties in developing English-language skills are exacerbated when English is not spoken at home (Endo, 1980). Verbal inhibition among foreign-born Asian Americans can reflect an actual or a perceived inability to communicate clearly in English (Endo, 1980; D. W. Sue & Kirk, 1972). Some foreign-born Asian Americans fear that their lack of fluency in English will lead to embarrassing situations (such as people shouting at them as though they were hard of hearing or making them repeat what they said because others cannot decipher their accents). Rather than deal with these situations, such Asian Americans may avoid expressing themselves.

Minority Basis

Verbal inhibition could also be based on experiences with racism. Cultural values emphasizing inhibition of expressiveness may be reinforced by racist efforts to keep minorities silent and inconspicuous (Endo, 1980). Similarly, Asian cultural values stressing obedience to authority figures may be reinforced by racist individuals and institutions that have sought to make minorities subordinate.

Stereotypes of Asian Americans as quiet people may cause others to assume that individual Asian Americans are quiet. Those who expect Asian Americans to be quiet may not address them or may be slow to recognize when they do want to express themselves—or they may just ignore Asian Americans. Feeling so excluded can inhibit the expressiveness of some Asian Americans.

Foreign-born Asian Americans can find that racism inhibits their expressiveness in another way. Foreign-born Asian Americans who are not fluent in English or have accents may not express themselves much to other Americans because they fear that their lack of fluency could arouse racist and xenophobic hostility in others (with comments such as, "Why don't you learn English?" and "Why don't you go back where you came from?"). Rather than face such potential confrontations, foreign-born Asian Americans may not express themselves.

In the case of most studies, it is not clear whether the experimenter who interacts with the subject was of the same ethnic group or same level of acculturation as the subject. If the experimenter and subject were of different races, ethnic groups, or levels of acculturation, subjects may have inhibited their expressiveness because of intergroup anxiety or their fear of creating an embarrassing situation (Stephan & Stephan, 1985). As a result, Asian Americans could appear to be less expressive in experiments than they are in everyday life.

Extroversion

Research primarily with Chinese Americans and Japanese Americans has found that (with the exception of Japanese American females) these Asian Americans are generally less extroverted than Euro-Americans (Meredith, 1966; Meredith & Meredith, 1966; D. W. Sue & Kirk, 1972 & 1973). Perhaps reflecting these differences in extroversion, Japanese Americans differ from Euro-Americans in the degree to which the former ask other people specific questions about their attitudes, values, personality, background, and feelings (Gudykunst, Sodetani, & Sonoda, 1987). Also consistent with being less extroverted, Asian Americans report more social anxiety in general than Euro-Americans do (Leong, 1985; Newton, Buck, Kunimura, Colfer, & Scholsberg, 1988).[6]

But many Asian Americans who appear socially withdrawn at work are very extroverted when with friends in social situations; many Asian Americans may initially be more socially withdrawn at work than non-Asian Americans but eventually these differences disappear as they get to know their coworkers. It may turn out that future research will show that extroversion is as situation-specific as recent research suggests assertiveness is. In interpreting these findings, consideration also must be given to the fact that the studies focusing on extroversion (rather than on social anxiety or the tendency to ask other people questions) were done over 20 years ago. Behavior patterns among Asian Americans may have changed since then, but follow-up research has not been done.

Cultural Basis

One reason that some Asian Americans may be less extroverted than their Euro-American peers is that these Asian Americans do not feel

---

[6]Social anxiety and social inhibition may also account for evidence that Asian Americans feel more isolated and lonely than Euro-Americans (Bourne, 1975; D. W. Sue & Kirk, 1973). Additionally, social anxiety and inhibition could contribute to the tendency of Asian Americans to choose occupations that do not require a lot of social contact (D. W. Sue, 1975).

sufficiently sure of themselves. Traditional Asian American parents assume their children know they love them but infrequently tell their children so. Sometimes the children will report, "I know they love me, but sometimes I kind of feel like they don't." These nagging doubts could undermine some of the children's self-confidence, thus making them feel less sure of themselves—and, therefore, less extroverted.

In addition, Asian Americans may be more socially anxious—and, therefore, less extroverted—than Euro-Americans because American cultural patterns call for less formality in social relations than many Asian Americans are accustomed to (D. W. Sue & Kirk, 1973). Furthermore, social anxiety among foreign-born Asian Americans could arise from a lack of fluency in English.

Minority Basis

Reportedly, Asian Americans generally feel less comfortable with Euro-Americans than with members of their own ethnic group (Patterson & Sedlacek, 1979, cited in D. Sue et al., 1983). According to one study, Asian Americans have more anxiety about interacting with Euro-Americans, feel more negatively toward Euro-Americans, and have fewer positive contacts with Euro-Americans than Latino Americans do (Newton et al., 1988). Since Euro-Americans outnumber Asian Americans, there is a greater likelihood that the latter will interact with more non-Asian Americans than vice versa. Therefore, Asian Americans might more often encounter situations that generate intergroup anxiety than Euro-Americans, and this could account for their decreased extroversion.

Finally, experiences with racism can leave some Asian Americans feeling vulnerable. Consequently, they may not be sufficiently sure of themselves to be extroverted. Instead, they may defend themselves by trying to become invisible.

Formality

Almost 30 years ago, research showed that Japanese American men were more reserved, regulated, and socially precise than their Euro-American counterparts (Meredith, 1966). As with assertiveness, formality is very dependent on the situation.

In the following anecdote, Japanese American college students were preparing to interview *Issei* as part of an oral-history project. The students shared observations of the ways in which they should regulate their own behavior during the interviews. They reminded each other that they needed to avoid prolonged eye contact with the interviewee, decline the first offer by the interviewee to provide refreshments, bring a small gift for the interviewee, and attend to body cues indicating that the interviewee had begun to feel tired (even though the latter would not mention it). The students all recognized the need to observe these behaviors with the *Issei*, who required such consideration in order to feel comfortable. But this did not mean that they observed such formalities in a different situation: When they met with other members of the research project, they were not concerned about avoiding prolonged eye contact; when one of the students had a couple of pizzas delivered to the group meeting and the professor suggested starting in on the pizzas, no one had to nudge the students (or the professor) twice before they devoured the pizzas. What is striking is the easy flexibility in behavioral styles that the students could invoke depending on the situation. Neither style seemed uncomfortably foreign to them.

Cultural Basis

Some Asian Americans might take a more formal and reserved approach to social relations because of Asian cultural values emphasizing formality, self-discipline, self-control, social sensitivity, politeness, the maintenance of interpersonal harmony, and sensitivity to the relative status of others so that one can behave accordingly. Lending some credence to the notion that cultural values could underlie this formality was evidence that Chinese American males and *Sansei* wanted order more than their Euro-American counterparts (Connor, 1974a, 1974c, 1975; Fenz & Arkoff, 1962). Also contributing to the development of a formal manner in Chinese Americans is the value adults place on the conformity of children to strict social conventions (Chun-Hoon, 1973).

Furthermore, family relationships have a tremendous effect on the scripts that individuals take to other relationships. Insofar as Asian American families have encouraged formal styles of interacting based on each member's role in the family, Asian Americans from such families may tend to be more formal with others than people are who have not come from such families—that is, they may carry that script to new relationships.

Minority Basis

Generations of Asian Americans may have been taught (perhaps unconsciously) that behaving in a formal manner can decrease the chances of offending others or arousing racist hostility. For those racists who think that Euro-Americans are superior to people of color, informality and familiarity by a person of color has historically implied the equality of the people participating in the social exchange. In such cases, informality aroused racist responses. Some Asian Americans, therefore, may adopt a formal manner to protect themselves from racists, or they may have learned such a manner from their parents who experienced racism.

Locus of Control

Rotter (1966) distinguished between an internal and an external locus of control: Those who have a high internal locus of control think that they have control over their environment and explain events in terms of the skills that individuals bring to a situation; those who have a high external locus of control think that they have little or no control over their environment and explain the occurrence of events in terms of chance, fate, luck, and other external forces. A number of studies have reported that Chinese Americans and Japanese Americans tend to have more of an external locus of control than Euro-Americans do (Chiu, 1988; Cook & Chi, 1984; Hsieh, Shybut, & Lotsof, 1969; Padilla, Wagatsuma, & Lindholm, 1985).

Locus of control is an important aspect of personality and mental health because, in general, Americans with an external locus of control are more likely than those with an internal locus of control to develop a mental disorder (E. Smith, 1985); both Asian Americans and non-Asian Americans with an internal locus of control tend to be more satisfied with their lives than people with an external locus of control (Seipel, 1988). Chinese Americans with an external locus of control exhibit more psychological distress than Chinese Americans with an internal locus of control (Kuo, Gary, & Lin, 1975). (However, even if this is a causal relationship, the direction of that causation has not been established.)

Cultural Basis

It has been suggested that American cultural values and beliefs, with their emphasis on self-reliance, cultivate a belief in an internal locus of control to explain success, but that Asian cultural values and beliefs, with their emphasis on the interdependence of people and the primacy of the group's efforts over the individual's efforts, cultivate a more external locus of control as an explanation for success (Chiu, 1988; Shon

& Ja, 1982; E. Smith, 1985). For example, many Buddhist and Taoist ideas stress the inevitability of trouble in life and the individual's limited ability to counteract these troubles.

If the hypothesis is correct that an Asian cultural background accounts, in part, for the tendency to develop an external locus of control, one would expect that those who have more of an Asian cultural orientation would have a more external locus of control than those with less of an Asian cultural orientation. In support of this hypothesis, Chinese in Hong Kong tend to have a more external locus of control than American-born Chinese, who tend to have a more external locus of control than Euro-Americans do (Hsieh et al., 1969; Padilla et al., 1985).

Alternatively, the development of an internal or external locus of control may reflect acculturative stress. For example, *Issei*, who were less acculturated than subsequent generations of Japanese Americans, experienced acculturative stress and tended to have a more external locus of control than did subsequent generations of Japanese Americans (Padilla et al., 1985). One type of acculturative stress comes from the need to learn English and the difficulty some immigrants have learning English. Confidence in one's English proficiency has been found to be positively related to perceived control over one's life (as well as self-esteem and satisfaction with life) for Chinese in Canada (Pak, Dion, & Dion, 1985). These findings suggest that one reason less acculturated Asian Americans tend to have a more external locus of control than Euro-Americans is that the former encounter cultural difficulties. Less acculturated Asian Americans could have a more external locus of control than more acculturated Asian Americans and Euro-Americans because, in fact, less acculturated Asian Americans have less control over their lives than Euro-Americans do. The less acculturated Asian Americans are more likely to be immigrants or refugees who are adjusting to a foreign culture, and who have fewer economic resources and less mobility than the Euro-Americans. A study comparing foreign-born, non-English-speaking Asian immigrants and foreign-born, non-English-speaking non-Asian immigrants would be enlightening, but such research has not been done yet.

Finally, the measure of locus of control may not be a reflection of exactly the same construct for Asian Americans as it is for other Americans because of the way the Locus of Control Scale is worded. There is a difference between familial and individual efficacy (Caplan, Choy, & Whitmore, 1992). It could be that Asian Americans feel that the family has a lot of control but that individuals do not. However, the Rotter Locus of Control Scale only asks about individual control.

Minority Basis

Members of racial minorities may find that they have little control over many of the events in their lives because of their race (E. Smith, 1985). When experiences with racism undermine the efficacy of individual efforts, learned helplessness (Seligman, 1975; E. Smith, 1985), pessimism, passivity, hopelessness, depression, alienation, loss of self-esteem, anxiety, hostility (S. Sue, 1980; Uomoto, 1986), and external locus of control may result. Developing an external locus of control can not only reflect the reality of the lives of minority members, but can also protect them from blaming themselves for those difficulties, limited successes, and failures that are actually due to racism (E. Smith, 1985).

Because Asian Americans have had some control in some areas, pervasive learned helplessness can be mitigated (S. Sue, 1980). Yet the lack of full participation by Asian Americans in America's social, economic, and political life can increase Asian Americans' sense of helplessness (S. Sue, 1980).

Self-Concept

There is evidence that Asian Americans have lower self-concepts than Euro-Americans do when it comes to physical appearance. Studies a generation apart have found that Japanese Americans were more dissatisfied with some of their physical characteristics (e.g., height) than Euro-Americans were (Arkoff & Weaver, 1966; Pang, 1981); Korean American grammar-school children are reportedly less happy with their physical appearance than African American children are and become more dissatisfied as they grew older (Chang, 1975). Similar reports of negative self-concepts have been found among Chinese American graduate students and professionals (White & Can, 1983). Thus, reports of negative self-concepts have been found among Asian American children (Pang, 1981), college students (Arkoff & Weaver, 1966), and adults (White & Can, 1983).

Other researchers have found no differences between the overall self-concepts of Japanese Americans and Euro-Americans; therefore, this phenomenon of lower self-concept may be limited to physical appearance (Pang, Mizokawa, Morishima, & Olstad, 1985).[7] In

---

[7]It could be argued that research showing Japanese Americans to be more susceptible than Euro-Americans to the Barnum Effect (i.e., Japanese Americans are more likely than Euro-Americans to accept the veracity of vague and bogus personality profiles of themselves) indicates that there is a sense in which the former's self-concept

keeping with this hypothesis regarding self-concept and physical appearance, African American children had more positive self-concepts regarding their physical appearance and popularity than Korean American children did; but Korean American children had more positive self-concepts regarding their behavior, intellectual status, and happiness—as well as more positive overall self-concept—than African American children did (Chang, 1975). A study of Asian American and Euro-American middle school students in a high-track math class found no difference in self-concept between these two groups of students (Pang, 1991). Therefore, it appears that lower self-concepts among Asian Americans tend to be restricted to physical appearance.

Cultural Basis

There are no traditional Asian cultural values that would underpin a lower self-concept for Asian Americans than for Euro-Americans. One might conjecture that the emphasis on the importance of the group over the individual may result in a lower self-concept, but quite an intellectual stretch would be required to show how this subordination of the individual to the group could account for more negative body images among Asian Americans. Rather than use cultural values to explain reports of poor body images among Asian Americans, it may be more enlightening to cite cultural values to explain the responses— that is, the reports of dissatisfaction with their body images could, in part, reflect the cultural value placed on modesty.

Minority Basis

Some Asian Americans may have a diminished esteem for their physical appearance because the media provide often demeaning stereotypes of the physical characteristics of Asian Americans. For instance, non-Asian Americans commonly accept that Euro-American actors look Asian simply when they are wearing strange eye makeup. When a model is said to have "all-American good looks," that model is never an Asian American.

---

is less developed (Diamond & Bond, 1974). It is more likely, however, that these results reflect not only a reticence to disagree with the authority represented by the test but also by the tendency of Asian Americans to agree with statements in questionnaires more than Euro-Americans do.

Sex Roles

At times Chinese American females and males have scored higher on femininity and masculinity scales, respectively, than other Americans have (D. W. Sue & Kirk, 1973). At other times Chinese American and Japanese American females have ranked higher in femininity than their Euro-American counterparts, but Euro-American males have ranked higher in masculinity than Chinese American or Japanese American males (Meredith, 1969). The discrepancy in masculinity scores for Chinese American males aside, even the apparent consistency in the femininity scores of Asian American females could be a methodological artifact since Chinese American and Japanese American females have been found to have more feminine personalities than did their Euro-American counterparts on some scales, such as the Gough Femininity Scale, but not on other scales, such as the Franck Drawing Completion Test (Blane & Yamamoto, 1970; Meredith, 1969).[8]

Other research (Meredith, 1969) has found that Japanese American females generally have adopted more egalitarian orientations toward marital roles than Japanese American males have. Unfortunately, there have been no replications of this study; and, therefore, it is not clear whether these findings would hold up today.

The picture that emerges from these studies on femininity and masculinity is very murky. Conclusions drawn from these studies would be extremely tenuous.

Cultural Basis

Because these results are inconsistent, explanations of these results in the context of cultural values must be tentative. If Asian Americans fit into more well-defined sex roles than Euro-Americans, this could be explained by the influences of Asian cultures, which define and differentiate sex roles more clearly than is typically done in Western society (Miller, Reynolds, Cambra, 1987). Asian American cultural values and interpersonal styles may be more consonant with traditional femininity than the dominant American values and styles are. Roles in traditional Asian American families are based not only on age

---

[8]Asian American women who have responded to a sex-role test in a masculine or androgynous pattern have been found to have higher occupational statuses and more self-esteem than other Asian American women do (Chow, 1987). Moreover, the higher their occupational status, the more self-esteem and work satisfaction these Asian American women reported.

but also on gender. A traditional Asian American family structure, therefore, may reinforce the development of sex-typed behavior.

Minority Basis

Any basis for these patterns of behavior in minority status would probably be very indirect. It is possible that minority status does not enter into sex-role development. More research is needed before it will be possible to resolve the various conflicting results and to see what role, if any, racism plays in the development of sex roles in Asian Americans.

INTRAETHNIC VARIATION IN PERSONALITY

The cultural influences on the personality characteristics of Asian Americans include Asian cultural values, American values, and the interaction of values with the experiences of Asian Americans (Ford, 1987; S. Sue & Morishima, 1982). As such, in addition to intraethnic personality differences that derive from intelligence, education, genes, and so forth, there are individual and group differences in Asian American personality characteristics that have to do with level of acculturation, ethnicity, and experiences (S. Sue & Morishima, 1982).

Although there are a variety of bases for intraethnic differences, research has tended to focus on how personality characteristics vary as a function of acculturation level. For example, Japanese Americans have personality scores more like those of Euro-Americans than Chinese Americans do (D. W. Sue & Kirk, 1973). Japanese Americans have been found to be more autonomous and less bound to traditional authority than Chinese Americans are (D. W. Sue & Frank, 1973). This difference can be understood in the context of acculturation or the interfacing of values and experiences in America. In general, Japanese Americans are more acculturated than Chinese Americans not only because most of the former are not immigrants but also because they have felt more pressure to acculturate because of their experiences during World War II (Nagata, 1991).

There is an abundance of other studies that have found differences in personality as a function of level of acculturation. A study of Chinese immigrants and American-born Chinese revealed that the former were more anxious, more isolated, more lonely, less happy, less autonomous, less socially extroverted, and burdened with more socioemotional problems than the latter were (S. Sue & Zane, 1985). (Chinese immigrants who had been in the United States for at least six years had a pattern very similar to that of American-born Chinese.) Similarly, foreign-born Asian Americans have been found to be less extroverted than American-born Asian Americans, who, themselves have been found to be less extroverted than Euro-Americans (Abe & Zane, 1990). In addition, Chinese students in the United States on student visas have been found to be less self-confident, less accepting, and less tolerant of others than naturalized Chinese Americans were (Fong & Peskin, 1973). Yet another study found that the more Chinese American children became acculturated, the more they valued self-realization and personal growth (Leong & Tata, 1990).

Generational differences in personality characteristics also suggest that assimilation and acculturation can account for some of the differences in personality characteristics among Asian Americans. As mentioned earlier, *Issei* tended to have lower self-esteem and a more external locus of control than subsequent generations of Japanese Americans did (Padilla et al., 1985). *Issei* were also less likely to be concerned with their rights and more likely to obey authority figures than were *Nisei*, who, in turn, were more authoritarian than *Sansei* (Connor, 1977). Lending support to this pattern is research that found Japanese American daughters to be less deferential, less nurturing, and less orderly than their mothers, while Japanese American sons were found to be less deferential than their fathers (Berrien et al., 1967). Additionally, in regard to some personality dimensions, Japanese Americans in 1952 differed from Japanese Americans in 1974 (Connor, 1974a). These personality variations probably reflect both generational and acculturational differences.

Generational changes in personality and behavior are found among both Asian Americans and Euro-Americans: Both Japanese Americans and Euro-Americans are not as deferential, orderly, authoritarian, and subject to abasement as they were in earlier generations (Berrien et al., 1967; Connor, 1974c, 1977). Intraethnic generational differences in personality are often larger than differences between Asian Americans and Euro-Americans. For example, responses of *Sansei* to a personality measure were more similar to those of Euro-Americans in their age group than to those of their *Nisei* parents (Connor, 1974a, 1974b, 1977).

CONCLUSION

The finding of personality differences between Asian Americans and Euro-Americans is consistent with the idea that Asian American cultures reinforce some personality characteristics. However, at this point, one can only speculate whether cultural values and minority status are the reasons for the reinforcement of particular personality characteristics within Asian American cultures. Research is needed to clarify what roles cultural values and minority status play in the development of particular personality characteristics. Future research needs to take other perspectives in addition to the traditional trait approach to the study of Asian American personality. More emphasis on the situational specificity of some characteristics would probably be fruitful.

Some of the personality characteristics discussed in this chapter could exacerbate existing environmental stressors. For example, insofar as Asian Americans tend to be more abasing than Euro-Americans, the former may unduly blame themselves for events beyond their control. Being more inclined to feelings of abasement and less autonomous than Euro-Americans might conflict with internalized American standards of behavior, thus setting the stage for cultural conflicts. Before discussing stressors facing Asian Americans, it is necessary to examine one other area of personality, namely, ethnic identity.

5

Ethnic Identity

Personality encompasses behavior, attitudes, and self-concept. Ethnicity is an underlying factor in personality, for ethnicity refers to more than race (Westermeyer, 1984) and shared ancestry (Eisenbruch, 1984). It also refers to beliefs (De Vos, 1976; Eisenbruch, 1984; Westermeyer, 1984), ways of communicating (De Vos, 1976; Eisenbruch, 1984; Phinney, 1990; Westermeyer, 1984), attitudes (Westermeyer, 1984), values (Eisenbruch, 1984; Phinney, 1990; Westermeyer, 1984), and behavior norms (Eisenbruch, 1984; Phinney, 1990) shared by a group in a culture. Inasmuch as ethnicity affects a person's cultural environment and culture affects personality development, ethnicity contributes to personality.

Broadly speaking, ethnic identity refers to a person's sense of belonging with other members of the ethnic group, based on shared ethnic characteristics (Phinney, 1990; Shibutani & Kwan, 1965). It is a part of self-concept based on how a person defines himself or herself vis-à-vis his or her ethnic group (Phinney, 1990) and how a person is categorized by others (Ryan & Smith, 1989; H. Wong, 1985a). But ethnic identity is even more than that. It constitutes a schema that (1) engenders the general knowledge, beliefs, and expectations that a person has about his or her ethnic group (Phinney, 1990), (2) functions as a cognitive, information-processing framework or filter within which a person perceives and interprets objects, situations, events, and other people, and (3) serves as a basis for a person's behavior.

Ethnic identity can affect goals set (E. Smith, 1989), regulate behavior (E. Smith, 1989), serve as a reference point for evaluating oneself (E. Smith, 1989; K. Smith, 1983), validate values and behaviors (Palinkas, 1982), and help to establish self-understanding (E. Smith,

1989). In the case of Asian Americans, a search for, sense of, and commitment to ethnic identity has been found to be positively related to self-esteem (Masuda, Matsumoto, & Meredith, 1970; Phinney, 1990; Tomine, 1985).

There is preliminary evidence that ethnic identity is particularly salient for Asian Americans (J. Chin, 1983).[1] Such evidence is not surprising given the heightened awareness of ethnic identity that may arise from the minority status of Asian Americans, or the emphasis in American culture on racial and cultural differences (J. Chin, 1983)—or, in the case of immigrants, the sense of identification that these immigrants have with the country of their birth. For example, most Asian Americans have probably been asked their ethnicity more often than most Euro-Americans have. Such frequent inquiries or differential treatment could make ethnic identity comparatively salient for Asian Americans.

MINORITY/ETHNIC IDENTITY

Some time ago, four forms of ethnic identity among Asian Americans were distinguished (S. Sue & D. W. Sue, 1971). According to this classification, some Asian Americans were labeled "traditionalists": This term referred to those who adhere to traditional Asian values and who identify with an Asian culture to the exclusion of the dominant society (Nicassio, 1985; Phinney, 1990; S. Sue & D. W. Sue, 1971). Put another way, traditionalists strongly identify with the ethnic group but are not very assimilated. Traditionalists include many of the more recent immigrants. "Assimilationists" are those who adopt Euro-American values and behavioral norms (Nicassio, 1985) and who identify themselves as Americans to the exclusion of their Asian background (Phinney, 1990; Yu & Kim, 1983). They are highly

---

[1]Chin asked Asian Americans and Euro-Americans to answer the question "Who am I?" by listing adjectives in rank order of importance. The results showed that Asian Americans always listed ethnic-group identity as either the first or second adjective, whereas their Euro-American counterparts frequently did not mention their ethnic group among the top five adjectives that they used for describing themselves. But there are methodological questions. It is not clear, for example, how Chin recruited her sample of Asian Americans. If she advertised for Asian Americans or tested large groups of Asian Americans at once, this method of recruitment or testing could have influenced the cognitive availability of that identity: That is, if the Asian Americans knew that they were sought as subjects because of their ethnicity or if they noticed that an unusually large number of their fellow subjects were also Asian Americans, this knowledge could have activated their schema for ethnicity, thus making this schema more cognitively available than it would otherwise have been.

assimilated but have little ethnic identity. Their friends are mostly from the dominant culture and their adherence to the ethnic culture takes largely superficial forms such as eating ethnic food, occasionally participating in celebrations of ethnic holidays, and so forth (Kitano & Daniels, 1988). "Bicultural" Asian Americans maintain both Asian and American cultural values and try to participate in the American mainstream (Chen & Yang, 1986; Nicassio, 1985; Phinney, 1990; S. Sue & D. W. Sue, 1971; Yu & Kim, 1983). Bicultural Asian Americans tend to identify strongly with their ethnic group—and, simultaneously, tend to be very assimilated to the dominant, American culture (Kitano & Daniels, 1988). They are comfortable with both Asian Americans and members of the dominant culture. Asian Americans who are labeled "marginal" reject both American and Asian cultures and feel alienated (Nicassio, 1985; Phinney, 1990). Similar classifications of Asian Americans have been proposed by a number of researchers (e.g., Yu & Kim, 1983).

These forms of ethnic identity were originally intended to be heuristic devices rather than descriptions of individuals (S. Sue & Morishima, 1982). But quite a controversy arose as a result of this initial attempt to formulate a conceptual classification of Asian Americans. Charges were leveled that this attempt at classification was imprecise, simplistic, and stereotypical. Nowadays when researchers refer to this classification, it is generally only to provide historical perspective. The classification has rarely been used as an independent variable in empirical studies of Asian American identity, personality, or mental health—and, therefore, its empirical usefulness has never been established. Its conceptual usefulness has been largely supplanted by more sophisticated classifications such as the Minority Identity Development model, which provides a more developmental, process-oriented perspective (Atkinson, Morten, & Sue, 1989; D. W. Sue, 1989b).

The Minority Identity Development model has been applied to Asian Americans. Asian Americans are minorities not just in the simple numerical sense. More importantly, they also meet the criteria of minorities because they receive differential and unequal treatment and are excluded from aspects of American life owing to their physical and cultural traits (Solomon, 1985; Westermeyer, 1984).

As a perspective on the development of identity among members of minorities, the Minority Identity Development model roughly parallels Phinney's (1990) three-stage model of identity formation that portrays an initial stage of unexamined ethnic identity, a second stage of ethnic exploration, and a final stage of achieved or committed identity. The Minority Identity Development model depicts a process through which members of minorities try to understand themselves, their minority culture, the dominant culture, and the relationship between the minority and dominant cultures. Although five stages are distinguished in this model, it is assumed that the boundaries between the stages are fluid; one does not always proceed through all the stages; after reaching "higher" levels, one may revert to "lower" stages; and functioning at higher levels does not presuppose that one has gone through lower levels (Atkinson et al., 1989).

According to the Minority Identity Development model, Asian Americans at the first stage, the Conformity Stage, completely prefer—and, to a great extent, want—to adopt the cultural values and lifestyles of Euro-Americans and, at the same time, consciously and unconsciously denigrate the physical and cultural characteristics of their minority group (perhaps for the purpose, as Phinney [1990] suggested, of trying to elevate their status by identifying with members of the dominant group). Those at the first stage believe it is more desirable to be Euro-American than Asian American, and members of other minority groups who resemble Euro-Americans physically and culturally are viewed more favorably than members of minority groups who are dissimilar to Euro-Americans.

At the second stage, the Dissonance Stage, Asian Americans have ambivalent feelings about both the dominant group and their minority group because they have encountered "information and experiences that are inconsistent with previously accepted values and beliefs . . . [causing them] to question some of the previous attitudes and beliefs held in the conformity stage" (D. W. Sue, 1989b, p. 83). They have ambivalent attitudes toward Euro-Americans, toward other Asian Americans, and toward other minority groups. They may possibly begin to feel a connection with other oppressed groups.

Asian Americans at the third stage, the Resistance and Immersion Stage, totally reject the dominant group and completely embrace their minority culture. They unquestioningly accept their Asian cultural values and begin to question why they have felt ashamed of who they are. They develop a great deal of identification with and commitment to other Asian Americans as well as an interest in exploring their cultures and histories. An increased understanding of the effects of societal forces on minorities is accompanied by a growing but tentative alignment with other minority groups who have been similarly oppressed. However, the alliance can be fragile and may disappear when Asian Americans come into conflict with other minorities (D. W. Sue, 1989b).

Asian Americans at the fourth stage, the Introspection Stage, feel sufficiently secure about their identity to begin to question their previously held, dogmatic beliefs. They question not only blind allegiance to the minority group at the cost of personal identity and but also blanket disparagement of the dominant group: They seek individuality as members of minorities but also recognize some positive elements in the dominant culture.

At the fifth stage, the Synergetic Articulation and Awareness Stage, Asian Americans accept or reject the cultural values of the dominant and minority groups on an objective basis (i.e., regardless of the cultural roots of those values) and have a sense of self-worth and individuality. At this stage there is a recognition that accepting and valuing one's own ethnic group does not mean that other groups do not also have positive attributes.

This model was proposed as a schema for therapists rather than as a personality theory (Atkinson et al., 1989). The empirical validity of this model has not been assessed: The forms of minority identity in this model have apparently not been used as independent variables in empirical studies of Asian Americans.

There are aspects of the model that research might be able to clarify. For example, in the first stage would Asian Americans raised in predominantly African American neighborhoods and schools identify with this predominant minority or still identify with Euro-Americans who predominate in the United States as a whole? Might they adopt some of the styles of the predominant minority while still believing that it is more desirable to be Euro-American rather than African American or Asian American? If there is a large, though not predominant, population of Asian Americans in the neighborhood, does that make a difference in the stages people go through? And if the other Asian Americans are primarily immigrants, will that cause American-born Asian Americans to identify with non-Asian Americans? There is a question whether this model assumes more capacity for abstract rationality than children have. A lot of Asian American children may simply think it is better to be Asian American than a member of another group because they like rice more than they like potatoes or other foods associated with non-Asian Americans. Many children may also think that because their parents are Asian American it is best to be Asian American.

It is not clear whether Asian Americans at the third stage would identify with Asian Americans in general or just with Asian Americans from their particular ethnic group. A question also arises whether Asian Americans at this stage must totally reject the dominant group and completely embrace their minority culture. Given the existence of individual differences in the way people cognitively differentiate and integrate information—some people being more Manichean and others being more relativistic (Harvey, Hunt, & Schroder, 1961; Uba, 1981)— some people would never take such a dogmatic position.

The Minority Identity Development model does not—and, apparently, did not intend to—account for the development of identity among biracial Asian Americans. Biracial adolescents have an "ambiguous ethnicity and . . . need to define their identities in a society where race has always been a significant dimension" (Gibbs & Huang, 1989, p. 322). Being prodded by society to define and identify themselves as members of one group or another, many biracial Asian Americans feel alienated: They feel that they do not fit into either group. Yet research has found that biracial Asian Americans do not differ from monoracial Asian Americans in amount of psychological distress, sense of competence, sense of self-esteem, or degree of psychological adjustment (Cauce et al., 1992; Mass, 1992).

A model of biracial identity development needs to take into consideration factors beyond those in the Minority Identity Development Model. For example, if young friends do not include biracial individuals in their ethnic group, how do biracial children reconcile this lack of social validation of their identity with their perceptions of themselves? Do some go through periods rejecting one of their ethnic groups—and, if so, is there a corresponding conflict with the parent of that ethnic group? What distinguishes those who go through such periods from those who do not? Research in this growing field will shed light on the identity development of biracial individuals and of minorities in general.

BASIS FOR DIFFERENCES IN ETHNIC IDENTITY

As a way of conceptually organizing research on ethnic identity, consider another approach to understanding the variations in ethnic identity among Asian Americans. Think of different aspects of ethnic identity as well as the factors that may lead to variations in aspects of this identity.

Three Aspects of Ethnic Identity

The broad definition of ethnic identity that appeared in the beginning of this chapter is based on what is generally meant by the term "ethnic identity." But actually, three aspects of Asian American ethnic identity can be distinguished: (1) consciousness of ethnicity, (2) adoption of an ethnic identity, and (3) adhibition of that ethnic identity. (In contrast to inhibition, adhibition refers to putting into use or applying.)

Consciousness of Ethnicity

Ethnic consciousness is a knowledge of the cultural characteristics of one's own ethnic group. It includes both "ideological ethnicity," referring to knowledge of the group's customs and beliefs, and "behavioral ethnicity," referring to behavioral norms upon which a person bases his or her deportment in interpersonal interactions (Eisenbruch, 1984).

To have a consciousness of ethnicity, a person need not have the ability to articulate what it is that he or she knows. Some Asian Americans may expect certain behaviors from another Asian American (and, on that level, be conscious of ethnic behavior patterns) but may not be able to explain to someone else what they know or may not be able to recognize the ethnic roots of that behavior. For example, some Asian Americans, claiming that they are "white bread," will enroll in an Asian American Studies class. Oftentimes, they have misinterpreted Asian American values and behavior patterns, which they have learned to recognize at home as reflecting the idiosyncrasies of their particular family. They are shocked to find that what their parents taught them were not just familial idiosyncrasies but Asian American cultural patterns.

Adoption of Ethnic Identity

Consciousness of ethnicity is distinct from adoption of an ethnic identity. Whereas consciousness of ethnicity refers to an awareness of ethnic patterns of behaving, ethnic-group history, ethnic customs, and values and beliefs commonly found in an ethnic group, adoption of an ethnic identity entails the incorporation of ethnic behavior patterns, values, and beliefs into the personality and a feeling that a person has of being connected in some way to other members of the ethnic group.

Once there is consciousness of ethnicity (whether or not a person is aware that what he or she knows is based on ethnic culture), a person may adopt ethnic behavior patterns and an ethnic identity. In this way of looking at identity, adopting an ethnic identity means that a person develops a relatively constant sense of ethnic identity. This constant, underlying sense of ethnic identity, which is integrated into the personality, could be called a person's "latent ethnic identity."

Adopting an ethnic identity is not an all-or-nothing phenomenon: There are large individual differences in the degree to which ethnic identity is adopted. On the one hand, some Asian Americans will strongly identify with many aspects of Asian American ethnicity while, on the other hand, some will only acknowledge that they belong racially to an Asian American ethnic group, at the same time denying that they have anything in common with members of their ethnic group.

Some Asian American individuals might adopt certain customs and perform particular rituals and ceremonies; others might not adopt those customs but may develop friendship patterns or styles of communicating that reflect ethnic identification. Some may identify with their ethnic group to the extent of knowing the history of the ethnic group and yet see the ethnic group as irrelevant today; others may identify socially with the ethnic group but have no knowledge of its history. Some will manifest their ethnic identity by focusing on learning Asian arts; others will focus on becoming politically active in the Asian American community. Individual differences in ethnic identity may be associated with differences in historical and personal experiences (Phinney, 1990). Which aspects of ethnic identity are adopted depends, in part, on the individual's values, consciousness of ethnic identity, and the ideological and behavioral aspects of ethnicity to which the individual has been exposed. Unfortunately, studies and measures of Asian American ethnic identity generally do not distinguish between ethnic consciousness, on the one hand, and the adoption of ethnic identity, on the other; therefore, it is empirically unclear which factors determine Asian American ethnic consciousness and which affect the adoption of an ethnic identity.

Adhibition of Ethnic Identity

Consciousness of ethnicity or adoption of an ethnic identity does not necessarily mean that a person will find his or her ethnic identity relevant to a given situation and will automatically adhibit that identity. That is, a person does not automatically invoke and apply his or her ethnic identity. Ethnic identity is dynamic rather than static: Ethnicity can be viewed as a relatively fluid characteristic (Jeffres, 1983) that "can be called upon, hidden, or imbued with ultimate importance in line with the needs of specific social situations" (Hayano, 1981, p. 158).

Asian American ethnic identity can be thought of as a schema that may or may not be invoked, depending on the circumstances. Like other schemata, sometimes ethnic identity is invoked and sometimes it is left dormant. Since there are many identities, at times other, nonethnic identities will be invoked.

A person is not only a member of an ethnic group but also a member of a sex, an age cohort, a nation, and a group with particular mental or physical abilities and interests. Indeed, in contrast to the study finding ethnic identity to be the first or second identity noted by Asian Americans (J. Chin, 1983), another study found occupational and sex-role identity to be more important than ethnic identity among Asian Americans (Phinney & Alipuria, 1990). It can be argued that individuals who identify *only* with their ethnic identity have a dysfunctional identity (Palinkas, 1982).

When an ethnic-identity schema is adhibited in a particular situation, it could be called the "manifested ethnic identity." Manifested ethnic identity refers to the temporary, though perhaps recurring, implementation of an ethnic-identity schema in a given situation. Inasmuch as ethnic identity is integrated into personality, this implementation of the ethnic-identity schema in a given situation is usually not based on a conscious decision. Nevertheless, the manifested ethnic identity may be thought of as the ethnic identity in use as a schema. Some ethnically reinforced traits might be adhibited in one situation but not in another: The tendency to avoid being loud could be an aspect of ethnicity that is adhibited at school; with friends, this aspect of ethnicity might not be applied. In this case, the latent ethnic identity could remain constant across both situations; nevertheless, the ethnic identity is manifested in the first instance but not in the second. A person may have a relatively constant, latent ethnic identity; but whether that identity is invoked at a particular time would depend on the context. The frequency with which a person may find himself or herself in contexts calling for the demonstration of ethnic values and customs, as well as which contexts elicit an ethnic-identity schema, and for whom the schema is elicited, are bases for individual differences in the adhibition of ethnic identity.

Factors Affecting the Three Aspects of Ethnic Identity

A number of factors can account for individual differences in the consciousness, adoption, and adhibition of ethnic identity. Consider a few of them.

Developmental Differences in Cognition

One basis for individual differences in the consciousness, adoption, and adhibition of ethnic identity is the presence of age-related differences in cognitive functioning. Very young children do not have ethnic-identity constancy: That is, just as they think they can change their gender, if they so wish, when they become older, they believe that their ethnicity is mutable. Young children might say they are Filipino American one day, and the following week they might decide that they no longer want to be Filipino—and might pick another ethnic identity. Ethnic-identity constancy, which requires concrete operational thinking, generally does not occur until about the age of 8 (Aboud, 1984). Preschool and early elementary-school-age children are, in some ways, cognitively and emotionally too immature to understand the meaning of their ethnicity (Gay, 1985); they are often able to identify who is a member of their ethnic group, but they might deny that they belong to that ethnic group (Gay, 1985).

Also affecting ethnic identity are developmental differences in cognition that are not age bound. A person is not automatically conscious of his or her own ethnic identity at birth, nor does ethnic identity develop automatically when a person reaches a particular age. A person must have certain cognitive abilities associated with age in order to develop a basic consciousness of ethnicity but beyond that, some individuals develop a more complex sense of ethnic identity than others. In this sense, developmental differences have to do with growing sophistication in a person's thinking processes rather than with age. Thus, two college students who are the same age (or two 90-year-old persons, for that matter) could be at different points in the development of their ethnic identity.

Among the expected reasons for individual differences in ethnic identity are differences in cognitive complexity and cognitive structure. Individuals vary in their thinking processes and in the organization of their thoughts across subject domains. They vary in their tendency to differentiate stimuli (i.e., to make a number of distinctions when analyzing stimuli and to understand phenomena in terms of many dimensions) and in their tendency to integrate their thoughts (i.e., to synthesize the differentiated elements in the cognitive structure). The cognitive structure in which thoughts are integrated can take various forms. One way to conceptualize these various cognitive structures is to imagine ethnic identity embedded in hierarchical, lateral, or centripetal organizations (Uba, 1981): Some people can be viewed as having hierarchical cognitive structures (in which concepts, built from a careful weighing of information, are integrated into a flexible structure so that new ideas can evoke reorganizations of thoughts and old ideas or bits of information can form new connections with other cognitive elements, permitting wider degrees of freedom in thinking than in other cognitive structures); others can be viewed as having lateral organizations (in which disparate thoughts are not fully integrated but are maintained as parallel, independent sets of thoughts); still others can be viewed as having centripetal organiza-

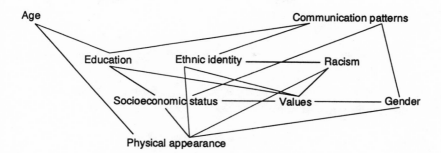

FIGURE 5.1. Ethnic identity in hierarchical cognitive organization.

tions (in which they try to assimilate and integrate everything into one or a few quickly established themes, even if this requires perceptual and cognitive distortions). These individual differences in how thoughts are differentiated and organized may affect how ethnic consciousness is differentiated and organized (and, thus, when it is adhibited) and may also affect individual differences in how broadly Asian American ideological and behavioral ethnicity are understood, how sophisticated the understanding about both one's own Asian American group and other Asian American groups is, and how ethnicity is organized within a person's cognitive structure. The degree of a person's awareness of these matters affects the breadth of his or her ethnic consciousness. It also affects a person's ability to see the relevance of ethnicity in various situations—a condition that is a necessary precursor to adhibition of identity.

For example, Figure 5.1 presents a way in which ethnic identity could be placed in a hierarchical cognitive structure. Ethnic identity is directly or indirectly related to a number of other constructs. Thinking about ethnic identity may lead to a range of thoughts or issues. A hierarchical cognitive structure is very dynamic; therefore, when new information is added, connections between elements can be added: Cognitive elements that were at one time subordinate in one constellation of ideas can become superordinate in another organization of thoughts and vice versa.

In a lateral organization, shown in Figure 5.2, thinking about ethnic identity would only lead to a few dimensions and simple evaluations of good and bad. If a schema for racism exists, very limited connections are made to that schema. The integration of thoughts is localized. It is as though a thought or bit of information has to be put into a box—and that box is not connected to any other boxes.

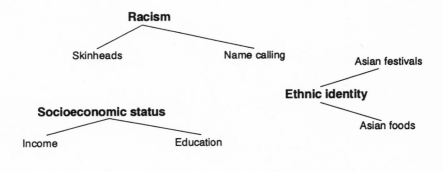

FIGURE 5.2. Ethnic identity in lateral cognitive organization.

Furthermore, the role of the thoughts in the cognitive structure is static.

Figure 5.3 depicts two centripetal structures. In centripetal organization #1, ethnic identity is at the hub and is a filter through which other thoughts and perceptions are understood. Ethnic identity would be invoked very often. In centripetal organization #2, ethnic identity would be understood only in terms of racism. Discussions of ethnic identity would always turn to thinking about racism. In both centripetal organizations, ethnic identity has a static role in a relatively rigid cognitive structure. These differences in cognitive structure would make a difference in the breadth of understanding of ethnic identity and in the adhibition of ethnic identity.

Unfortunately, current ethnic-identity scales for Asian Americans do not measure cognitive structure. High scores on ethnic-identity scales could indicate that ethnic identity is important to the individuals, but these high scores do not elucidate the cognitive sophistication of these ethnic identities.

Achievement of Ethnic Identity

One way to examine individual differences in the cognitive sophistication of a person's ethnic identity would be to look at how that ethnic identity was reached. Marcia (1966, 1980) identified four stages or ways in which individuals form an ethnic identity: the Diffuse Stage (at which individuals have neither explored nor committed themselves to an identity), the Foreclosure Stage (at which individuals have committed themselves to an identity but have done so by adopting

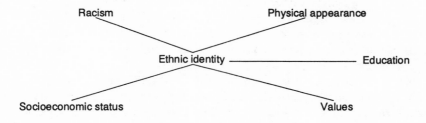

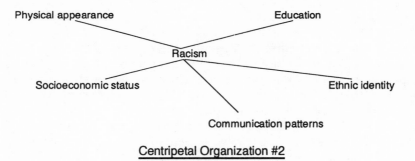

FIGURE 5.3. Ethnic identity in two centripetal cognitive organizations.

parental values without independently exploring their own identities), the Moratorium Stage (at which individuals, because of a significant experience that forced them to become aware of their ethnicity, are in the process of exploring their own identities but have not yet settled on or committed themselves to an identity), and the Achieved Identity Stage (at which individuals have explored their identities and have firmly committed themselves to an ethnic identity).

This model raises many questions. For instance, might not many people start to explore their ethnic identities owing to curiosity rather than a particular, significant experience? What happens when people cannot handle the ambiguity of the Moratorium Stage once they have reached that stage? (In particular, people with centripetal cognitive organizations would find this stage uncomfortable.) Do they deny, suppress, or repress the significance of their ethnicity to minimize the ambiguity, or do they rush back to another stage? Personality research on conceptual and beliefs systems has suggested that some people would move from a diffuse identity to whatever identity runs counter to that of their parents or the establishment (Harvey et al., 1961). To individuals with this personality tendency (which is not something that is simply outgrown), what is important is not whether they become strongly committed to or vehemently reject an ethnic identity; what is important is that they develop an identity that is contrary to that of their parents. Furthermore, is it not possible that after people reach the Achieved Identity Stage they continue to grow and explore their ethnic identities?

The questions it raises notwithstanding, this model shows that there can be individual differences in the consciousness and adoption of ethnic identity because people are at different stages of identity development. For instance, individuals at the Moratorium Stage would probably be more conscious of their ethnicity than would people at the Diffuse Stage; people at the Achieved Identity Stage have adopted more of an ethnic identity than people at the Moratorium Stage have. This model also demonstrates how different people could superficially appear to have the same form of ethnic identity although the process by which they arrived at that identity and the cognitive significance of that identity could vary. For example, some people might have a strong sense of ethnic identity because they worked at achieving that identity, whereas other people might have an equally strong sense of ethnic identity—but are just rubber-stamping the identity of their parents. Similarly, of two Asian Americans who may not have made a commitment to an ethnic identity, one may never have thought about it, whereas another still may be in the process of exploring an ethnic identity (Phinney, 1990).

Attitudes Toward Ethnicity

Individual differences in attitudes toward ethnicity will affect individual differences in the consciousness, adoption, and adhibition of ethnic identity. While some Asian Americans take pride in their ethnicity, others do not.

The results of one study suggest that many Asian Americans do not have an ethnic consciousness or that their ethnic consciousness is more negative than positive: This study found that more Asian Americans than African Americans or Latino Americans report that they would prefer to be Euro-American (Phinney, 1989). Among the reasons that their ethnic consciousness could be absent or negative are (1) they associate stereotypes of "orientals" with their own ethnicity; (2) they feel threatened by racists who dislike Asians or Asian Americans; (3) they have had limited experience with familial or

nonfamilial gatherings for ethnic holidays, which could have contributed to an identification with the ethnic group; (4) they are unaware of
the relevance of their ethnicity to their identity. Or, more specifically, as
suggested by ethnic-identity-formation models (see, e.g., Atkinson et
al., 1989; J. Kim, 1981), they are not motivated to move beyond an
elementary level of ethnic-identity development because they recognize neither how racism in the dominant culture oppresses ethnic
minorities nor how their ethnic culture influences their lives. Among
the other factors that may affect attitudes toward ethnic identity are (1)
exposure to Asian customs (Stephan & Stephan, 1989), (2) the amount
of political and economic power at hand for Asian Americans
(Matsumoto, Meredith, & Masuda, 1970), and (3) the degree of
occupational and residential mobility available (Makabe, 1979).

Attitudes toward ethnicity are neither all positive nor all negative.
An individual may have negative attitudes toward certain aspects of
ethnicity and positive attitudes toward other aspects; different people
will value different aspects of their ethnicity. Suppose an Asian
American female was raised in a traditional Asian American family
and was taught that females should always be subordinate and
obedient to males. Embracing such a subservient attitude, however,
conflicts with the feminist or egalitarian ideas that she has (Fong &
Peskin, 1969; D. W. Sue & Kirk, 1975). Her attitudes toward this
seemingly sexist aspect of her ethnicity could be negative; therefore,
adoption of an ethnic identity might not include this aspect. Someone
else, however, might not reject these sexist attitudes but might, in fact,
embrace them. Because people have different global attitudes toward
ethnicity as well as varying attitudes toward aspects of their ethnicity,
there will be individual differences in consciousness of ethnic identity.
People with a positive attitude toward many aspects of their ethnic
identity are likely to be motivated to discover more about those
aspects, and there is a greater likelihood that they will adopt their
ethnic identity.

Salience of Ethnicity

There are individual differences in the salience of ethnic identity (i.e., in
the importance of ethnic identity within a conglomeration of identities)
which, in turn, can affect how often ethnic identity is adhibited. If
ethnic identity is a salient identity for an individual, the individual's
threshold for invoking that identity will be low and the identity will be
adhibited more quickly than less salient identities will be (White &
Burke, 1987). Some people will manifest their ethnic identity only in
very specific situations—such as holiday festivals with the family—

and, at other times, will regard their ethnicity as irrelevant; others will be more committed to their ethnic identity and will manifest that identity across a broad spectrum of situations.

Having a salient ethnic identity does not necessarily indicate little acculturation (Nicassio, 1985). Many factors could affect the salience of ethnicity. One such factor could be attitude toward ethnicity. It has been suggested that those who feel positive about their ethnicity are likely to have a highly salient ethnic identity (White & Burke, 1987). Feeling positive about ethnicity may be related to factors such as media portrayals of Asian Americans and parental attitudes toward ethnicity.

A second factor that could affect the salience of ethnic identity is the concordance between the behaviors of other members of the ethnic group and a person's own behavior. Behaving in a way that is congruent with how one sees one's own ethnic group may increase the salience of ethnic identity. Individuals' evaluations of themselves are related to their particular identities (White & Burke, 1987). If they negatively evaluate their performance in a particular identity, that identity is likely to lose its salience. If man is a fabulous skier but a so-so tennis player, his identity as a skier probably would be more salient than his identity as a tennis player because he is more successful as a skier than as a tennis player. In order to maintain self-esteem, the activity at which he is proficient becomes more salient than the activity at which he is only mediocre. In the same way, if part of the ethnic identity for Asian Americans is the belief that they earn good grades but some Asian Americans find that they receive low grades, ethnic identity could lose some of its salience for the Asian Americans with low grades—and they may be less likely to invoke an ethnic identity.

A third factor that could influence variability in the salience of ethnic identity is the area in which a person resides or has attended school (Mass, 1992; Suinn, Rickard-Figueroa, Lew, & Vigil, 1987; Ting-Toomey, 1980). This factor could be influential because these areas would have a bearing on the effect of ethnicity on a person's life. Asian Americans who grow up in neighborhoods predominated by other minorities and who have had generally positive experiences with them probably tend to identify with other minorities more than people who have had little association with other minorities. If an Asian American is living in an area in which his family is the only Asian American family, he might feel either that he stands out from the crowd or that he blends in completely. The salience of his ethnic identity probably depends, in large part, on how his ethnicity affects the way that he is treated. Ethnic identity may become salient when Asian Americans are asked about their ethnicity, particularly if they feel positive about their ethnicity. Alternatively, such questions might cause other Asian Americans who do not have positive feelings about their ethnicity to feel that they are not blending in with their peers and defensively to make ethnic identity less salient to them.

The following provides a concrete example of how a residential area may affect ethnic identity. A Korean immigrant reported that when her family moved from a Euro-American, middle-class neighborhood to Los Angeles' Koreatown, life in Koreatown

> was a lot easier because there was the Korean markets and many Korean shops. We found people who looked like us and who was going through the same emotions. Now, I started to get the sense of belonging. . . . [At school] I did not feel strange any more because everybody was an immigrant also. I felt like I finally found a place where I could identify myself but still not as an American. Living in isolated Koreatown . . . made me feel more like a Korean than an American. The acculturation process was lot slower for me comparing to other Asian Americans who [were] living in a white neighborhood. I found myself having only Korean friends isolating myself from anything non-Korean. This in turn led me to believe how I was non-American. (Student term paper, 1992)

A residential area could also influence the salience of ethnicity insofar as it affects the amount of support that is provided for the three aspects of ethnic identity. Ethnic identity in general might be more salient for those who are geographically or psychologically close to the centers of the Asian American community than for those who are isolated from other Asian Americans (Hayano, 1981). For some people adhibition of an Asian American ethnic identity depends in part on the social context (i.e., whether there will be social support or understanding if they invoke their Asian American ethnic identity).

A fourth factor which can account for variation in the salience of ethnic identity is the perception that Asian Americans have of other Asian American groups and of the dominant group. In particular, perceptions that Asian Americans have of other Asian Americans could affect *which* ethnic identity is salient. In the case of Asian American ethnic identity, three types of ethnic identity could be adhibited in addition to an identity as simply an American: (1) identification with Asian Americans as a group; (2) identification with one's specific Asian American group (e.g., Chinese Americans or Filipino Americans); and, (3) in the case of the foreign born, identification with people in a specific Asian country. For instance, a Thai American could identify herself simply as an Asian American, as a Thai American, or as a Thai. *Which* ethnic identity is salient probably varies across situations.

The degree to which many Asian Americans identify themselves with other Asian American groups depends, in part, on their perceptions of those other Asian American groups. Many of those whose ancestors have been Americans for generations—or who have simply been Americans for a long time—want to distinguish themselves from those Asians in the United States whose nationality is not American (Shibutani & Kwan, 1965) or who are recent Asian immigrants (Phinney, 1989). The former do not identify with the immigrant experience and probably feel more American than do the latter. On the other hand, many Asians who have immigrated to the United States since 1965 do not identify with Asian Americans who are as American as third- or fourth-generation Asian Americans and who seem to have lost many Asian cultural characteristics. While other Americans may make no distinction between American-born Asian Americans and foreign-born Asian Americans—and between Asians in the United States who are not citizens and those who are—Asians and Asian Americans often make those distinctions in their ethnic identities. A Chinese American who reads about the problems that some Korean shopkeepers have in African American communities or about the high rate of welfare dependency among Southeast Asians may feel that Koreans and Southeast Asians have a negative public image and may shy away from identifying with groups that are under attack. At other times, different Asian American groups may not identify with each other because of different perspectives, values, and needs. For example, media coverage of the 1992 Los Angeles riot highlighted the antagonism between African Americans and Korean Americans. Some other Asian Americans adhibited identities that stressed their commonalities with Korean Americans, while others adhibited identities that stressed their differences from Korean Americans.

The extent to which Asian Americans perceive that the larger American society homogenizes Asian Americans from different cultural backgrounds could increase the salience of specific-group ethnic identification. Asian Americans might maintain separate ethnic identities as a defense against such homogenization (Hayano, 1981).

On the other hand, perceptions of shared vulnerability vis-à-vis non-Asian American groups can have the opposite effect. In an attempt to protect themselves from conflict with and oppression by the powerful and dominant and to make themselves feel less helpless and isolated (K. Smith, 1983), minority members who recognize the oppression affecting all minorities sometimes form coalitions with other minority members. Thus, at times, Asian Americans will stress an

"Asian American"—rather than, for example, a Korean American, Chinese American, or Filipino American—identity. Asian Americans, at times, will adhibit an identity as people of color, thereby linking them with a broader range of people including African Americans, Latino Americans, and Indigenous Americans.

Which ethnic identity is adhibited has implications for behavior. This multiplicity of ethnic identifications means that Asian Americans have multiple reference groups. For example, as a reference group for sexual behavior, a Chinese American college student could use Americans in general, Chinese, or Chinese Americans—all of whom have different standards of sexual behavior (D. Chan, 1990; K. Huang & Uba, 1992). The behavior that results from conformity to a reference group will vary widely depending on the reference group chosen. Furthermore, the reference group adopted for one type of behavior (e.g., sexual behavior) might not be the same reference group adopted for another type of behavior (e.g., grades in school).

Thus, there are individual differences in the three aspects of ethnic identity because of individual differences in the salience of ethnic identity. In turn, the salience of ethnic identity appears to be linked to perceptions, attitudes, and the area of residence.

Experiences with Racism

Another factor that may be at the root of individual differences in ethnic identity is the degree to which individuals have experienced racism and the ways in which they have responded to that racism. If attempts to develop an ethnic identity are criticized by others as anti-American or politically correct, this criticism may affect the degree to which some individuals adopt an ethnic identity as well as the circumstances under which they will publicly adhibit their ethnic identity. On the one hand, experiences with racism can cause some people to employ the defense mechanisms denial and identification to dissociate themselves from an ethnic identity. On the other hand, such experiences can lead to a sensitivity that picks up on even subtle forms of racism (K. Chan, in press), which, in turn, could lead to an increase in the salience of ethnic identity and cause individuals to increase their predilection toward all three aspects of ethnic identity—consciousness, adoption, and adhibition.

Racist trauma experienced by parents may also be associated with differences in ethnic identity. A study (Nagata, 1991) found that *Sansei* whose parents were put into American concentration camps during World War II were more likely to feel that their rights might be violated, more likely to feel vulnerable because of their minority status, and less likely to feel capable of being completely assimilated than were *Sansei* whose parents had not been interned. Another measure of ethnic identity—affiliation pattern—also demonstrates how the racism experienced by parents can affect their children: *Sansei* whose parents were put into concentration camps also preferred associating with Japanese Americans more than with Euro-Americans and preferred associating with Japanese Americans more than did *Sansei* whose parents were not interned (Nagata, 1989b, 1990, 1991). Finally, in part as a result of their experiences during World War II, *Nisei* parents encouraged their *Sansei* children to become very Americanized and did not provide much encouragement for them to feel ties to Japan (Nagata, 1991). In turn, these *Nisei* attitudes could also have placed limits on the ethnic identity of subsequent generations of Japanese Americans.

Foreign Born or American Born

Whether Asian Americans are American born or foreign born is a basis for individual differences in the adoption of different forms of ethnic identification. Those Asian Americans whose ancestors have been citizens of the United States for generations and are presumably more acculturated (e.g., Japanese Americans), are more likely to identify with the United States than are those who generally have not been in the United States as long (e.g., Southeast Asians). Because of their identification with the United States the former may prefer to identify themselves as a type of American (e.g., as Asian Americans or Japanese Americans rather than as Japanese). In contrast, a study of Southeast Asians in California found that they tend to define themselves in ethnic terms and not as Americans (Baldwin, 1982): Undoubtedly, this is in part because many Southeast Asians are not American citizens. Not being a native-born U.S. citizen could affect a person's sense of identity and sense of belonging. As an immigrant Korean college student said: "I think the image of an American portrayed in society and [on] television left a lasting image in my head [leading] me to believe I could never become an American." Becoming a citizen can precipitate changes in identity that, in turn, can cause concomitant changes in the nature of identity conflicts.

The development of ethnic identity can also differ for American-born and foreign-born Asian Americans. Gay (1985) proposed a model of ethnic identity for African Americans that may apply to American-born Asian Americans more than to foreign-born Asian Americans.

Similar to the Minority Identity Development model developed by Atkinson et al. (1989) is the 3-stage model of the formation of ethnic identity developed by Gay (1985), which consists of the following: (1) the Pre-Encounter Stage (at which Euro-American values dominate and individuals have either little sense of ethnic identity or have negative attitudes toward their ethnicity), (2) the Encounter Stage (at which an experience or event destroys the existing ethnic identity, and individuals—torn by ambivalence—struggle to establish new identities, immerse themselves in their ethnic cultures, reject everything representing Euro-American standards, and finally begin to establish a balance between embracing ethnic culture and rejecting Euro-American-based American culture), and (3) the Post-Encounter Stage (at which identity conflicts are resolved). If at all relevant, these models seem to be more relevant to American-born Asian Americans than to foreign-born Asian Americans because many of the latter do not start with the stage described in these models: As D. W. Sue (1989b) has pointed out, many foreign-born Asian Americans, especially those who were raised for a number of years in Asia, do not start with Euro-American values and negative attitudes toward their ethnic group.

Generational Differences

There appear to be generational differences in consciousness and adhibition of ethnic identity, but the results of studies on generational differences in ethnic identity do not present a simple picture. For example, one study found that while second-generation Chinese Americans had less of an ethnic identity than did first-generation Chinese immigrants,[2] there was a revival of ethnic identity in

---

[2]"Had" more or less ethnic identity is an abbreviated way of saying that they scored high or low on ethnic-identity scales. Most of the studies on Asian American ethnic identity have used the Ethnic Identity Questionnaire, which primarily examines the adoption aspect of ethnic identity and focuses on values and attitudes toward the ethnic community (e.g., Connor, 1977; Masuda et al., 1970; Matsumoto et al., 1970; Meredith, 1967; Newton et al., 1988; Ting-Toomey, 1980). The Suinn–Lew Self Identity Acculturation Scale (Suinn et al., 1987) and other scales (Makabe, 1979; Phinney & Alipuria, 1990) have examined such variables as the use of an Asian language; friendship patterns; involvement in ethnic organizations; preferences for Asian food, music, and reading material; and the search for ethnic identity. Apparently there have been few comparisons between the ethnic-identity scores of subjects on the two types of scales. An exception is the study by Mass (1992) that found consistency: Biracial Japanese Americans identified less with being Japanese than did other Japanese Americans on the Ethnic Identity Questionnaire and were more acculturated on the Suinn–Lew scale than other Japanese Americans were.

subsequent generations (Phinney, 1990). This is reminiscent of Hansen's Third Generation Return Thesis. Other research has found parallel results among Japanese Americans: *Nisei* in Washington and Hawaii had more ethnic identity than did *Sansei* (Masuda, Matsumoto, & Meredith, 1970; Meredith, 1967; Newton et al., 1988). However, still other research has found no difference between *Nisei* and *Sansei* in ethnic identity (Connor, 1977; Matsumoto, Meredith, & Masuda, 1970). The fact that all of the studies of Japanese Americans used the same test of ethnic identity eliminates some possible explanations for these discrepant findings.

Among the possible reasons for these conflicting findings could be that the samples were taken from different areas at different times. For example, Connor (1977) conducted his study in Sacramento, Meredith (1967) and Masuda et al. (1970) gathered their samples from Seattle, and Matsumoto et al. (1970) combined samples from Honolulu and Seattle. Japanese Americans constitute different proportions of the population in different states and are under different acculturative and racial pressures. This could affect their ethnic identity. Furthermore, Newton et al. (1988) conducted their study in the year that Hawaii celebrated the centennial of the arrival of Japanese there; and, therefore, these celebrations could have temporarily altered the ethnic identity of that sample of Japanese Americans in Hawaii. In this study conducted by Newton et al. (1988) *Sansei* in the sample were older than they were in the study by Matsumoto et al. (1970). Ambiguity about generations (Matsumoto et al., 1970) is another possible reason for these conflicting findings. For example, if an *Issei* and a *Nisei* married, in what generation are their children? If a number of subjects straddle the generations, the generation the researchers ultimately classify them in can have significant effects on the findings. Most *Issei* immigrated to Hawaii between 1885 and 1924; an *Issei* who immigrated to Hawaii in 1960 would be included as an *Issei* but would probably have a very different ethnic identity from most other *Issei* when tested in 1970. When samples are not large, the presence of such individuals could account for results which, while in the expected direction, fail to reach statistical significance (see, e.g., Matsumoto et al., 1970). The discrepancies in these findings cannot be resolved without additional research.

PROBLEMS WITH ETHNIC IDENTITY

That some Asian Americans have conflicts over their ethnic identities should not be surprising since a positive ethnic identity is not automatically conferred on a person (Gay, 1985). Having discussed various aspects of ethnic identity and factors that are at the root of individual differences in ethnic identity, consider the problems that some Asian Americans have with ethnic identity and the research that pertains to those problems.

Manifestation of Problems with Ethnic Identity

Ethnic-identity problems are sometimes manifested in people's stated preferences to belong to another group. Direct evidence of such an attitude among Asian Americans is limited: A study has found that 5- to 7-year-old Chinese Americans reported less preference for their own race than their African American or Euro-American peers did (Fox & Jordan, 1973). In fact, 21% of Chinese American and 13% of African American children identified with their own race but did not prefer their own race.

A slightly less direct and obvious manifestation of negative evaluations of racial and ethnic characteristics is dissatisfaction with ethnically related physical characteristics, as discussed in the preceding chapter. The case (described by Nagata, 1989b) of a 7-year-old, fourth-generation Japanese American illustrates such feelings.

> The girl frequently did not want to go to school and was withdrawn at home and at school. When she was at school, she avoided playing with the other children, did not participate in class, and sought to go home early. Her family sent her to therapy. During play therapy, she would select a doll with dark hair and another with blonde hair. The two dolls would battle. The blonde doll would always be victorious and the dark-haired doll would be knocked to the ground. When the girl picked stuffed animals, the light-colored animals always won. She "eventually revealed that children at school made fun of her 'tiny eyes' and black hair and did not pick her for sports teams. [Her play in therapy] sessions indicated that she wished she were not Japanese and felt anger toward her parents, blaming them for the differences in her eyes. [She reasoned that] if her parents were not Japanese, she would not be experiencing the ostracism she now faced." (Nagata, 1989b, p. 103)

Such negative feelings about ethnically related physical character- istics may be manifested in other ways. A female Vietnamese college student recalled her own attitudes when she was in high school:

> I considered myself as a Caucasian because all my friends were Caucasian and we grew up with all the same values ranging from favorite foods to dating habits. I never identified myself as an Asian, nor did I know what

being an Asian really stood for. Throughout my life I was influenced by my Caucasian friends, and believed in the same negative stereotypes about Asians being skinny, short, ugly, and old-fashioned. I developed a negative feeling about my own race. . . . I dreamed of getting breast-implants, nose surgery, and taking medicine to make my skin lighter in order to fit more in with my Caucasian friends. (Student term paper, 1992)[3]

Another manifestation of difficulties with ethnic identity can come in the form of "disidentification." Ethnic disidentification occurs when a person attempts to deny membership in his or her ethnic group by (1) disavowing that ethnic group, (2) maintaining ignorance about his or her ethnic culture, (3) professing to believe stereotypes of Asian Americans, or (4) denigrating his or her Asian American cultural background in an attempt to be treated superficially as an honorary Euro-American (Hayano, 1981).

A positive ethnic identity is not always stable across time and situations (S. Sue & Morishima, 1982). Asian immigrants may be especially vulnerable to identity crises when there is (1) constant association with people who do not share their particular Asian ethnicity (Palinkas, 1982); (2) no large, local, ethnic community with which to identify; and (3) a lack of traditional support systems. An identity crisis can lead to marginality, characterized by a person's (1) feelings of isolation and alienation from both cultures (D. W. Sue, 1989b); (2) inability to base his or her behavior on—or judge the behavior in terms of—stable standards (Okano & Spilka, 1971); (3) loss of deeply held world views (Westermeyer, 1984); (4) sense of meaninglessness (Okano & Spilka, 1971; Westermeyer, 1984), power-lessness, and helplessness; (5) lack of understanding of moral standards and norms; (6) lack of perceived control over his or her behavior; (7) failure to understand the consequences of his or her behavior (Okano & Spilka, 1971); and (8) delinquency and crime (Munoz, 1979).

For instance, the case (described by Lee & Cynn, 1991) of Jack, a 17-year-old Korean American illustrates an identity problem.

The eldest son of three children, Jack immigrated to the United States with his family when he was 8 years old. There were few ethnic minorities at

---

[3]Incidentally, it has been suggested (Pang et al., 1985) that insecurity about appearance may be one of the many reasons that Japanese Americans steer away from high-visibility careers such as politics and journalism and go into less visible careers such as laboratory or computer science and engineering. Racism probably has something to do with this pattern as well.

the high school where Jack was a senior and he was the only Korean American. There were two issues facing Jack. The first issue was that although his parents tried to teach him to be proud to be Korean and to learn about Korean culture, Jack did not identify with Koreans as much as his parents wanted. He felt guilty for that yet in several confrontations with his father, Jack stated that he would have preferred not to be Korean. Jack's father had threatened to disown him for being so disrespectful and attributed Jack's behavior to his being too Americanized. The second issue was that he was anxious about living up to the occupational aspirations that his parents had for him, feeling torn between wanting to please his parents but simultaneously feeling unmotivated to do his school work and feeling his parents cared only about his academic success and not about him personally. Jack's symptoms included being withdrawn, depressed, having a poor appetite, and having difficulty sleeping.

Basis for Ethnic-Identity Problems

Racism

One basis for ethnic-identity problems is racism. Asian Americans are influenced by schools and media, which are run by the dominant group and which propagate the racist, deprecatory, and colonialist attitudes that some members of the dominant group have about Asian Americans. Coming from the media and the schools, these racist assumptions may be perceived as having the imprimatur of authority, and, therefore, some Asian American children incorporate these racist assumptions into their ethnic identities. Negative stereotypes and membership in a devalued group can impede the ability of minorities to acquire positive identities (Spencer & Markstrom-Adams, 1990).

Sometimes Asian Americans will express their anger by trying to demonstrate that they do not fit the stereotype of quiet "orientals." But this can lead to parent–child conflicts if parents consider these behaviors to be shameful, disobedient, and nonconformist (Ford, 1987).

Instead of expressing hostility toward racists, sometimes Asian Americans suppress these feelings. The following experience is not uncommon.

> Sometimes I would walk home with a group of [non-Asian American] children behind me shouting "Ching Chong Chinaman" or "Jap." I was really angry but there was nothing I could do about it. I wanted to fight them but there were far too many children against me and no one would help me. So, all I could do whenever it happened was to ignore the entire incident. That didn't help much either. When they saw that I wasn't going to fight them they would yell at me all the louder. Life was torment. (M. Maruyama, 1971, p. 388)

Instead of expressing their anger outwardly, some Asian Americans will turn that anger on themselves (D. W. Sue, 1989b). This anger can take the form of self-hatred or hatred toward other members of the ethnic group.

> My sister got married to a white. I had naturally expected her to turn white and abandon the Chinese ways. What happened instead was that her husband took on the Chinese ways. I thought to myself, "if a white can be proud of being Chinese, why can't I?" (Maruyama, 1971, p. 385)

Some Asian Americans will try to enhance their status by acculturating or behaviorally "passing" as a member of another group (De Vos, 1976) and will thus define their success in terms of the degree to which other, non-Asian Americans accept them. Another Asian American recounted:

> By the sixth grade I had developed a philosophy. "There are only two groups of people in the world, blacks and whites, and if you're gonna make it in this world you'd better be part of one or the other." Because I grew up in a black neighborhood and that most of my buddies or friends were black, I chose to become a member of the black group. When I entered junior high school I soon found out that fitting into the group is to feel and act black. . . . I was more accepted because I was not the classic Chinaman any more. . . ."Happiness was being cool and black (Maruyama, 1971, p. 384–385)

Identity conflicts can arise when different sources simultaneously reinforce individuals for identifying with the ethnic group and not identifying with the ethnic group (De Vos, 1976). This contradictory reinforcement may result, on the one hand, in Asian Americans being torn between feeling connected to a minority, or ethnic, group while recognizing the implications of being a member of a minority in a racist society (Arredondo, 1984), and, on the other hand, feeling pride in their ethnic culture while seeing that culture denigrated in America. The identity conflicts faced by American-born Asian Americans who are taught some pride in their Asian culture by their parents while being brought up in the context of a dominant culture that often disparages or disregards non-European-based cultures can be quite different from the identity conflicts faced by foreign-born Asian Americans who are brought up with largely unchallenged, positive views of their Asian culture and then encounter an American culture that regards their Asian culture as inferior, exotic, or deviant.

Immigrant/Refugee Experiences

Immigrant experiences and subsequent attempts to live in a new country can also cause identity problems. Migration sometimes involves radical changes in social roles, statuses (Palinkas, 1982), and the effectiveness of familiar behavior patterns in bringing about expected results (Palinkas, 1982). As a consequence of their move to the United States, immigrant Asian Americans can simultaneously feel alienated from American society, on the one hand, and from the heritage of their original country or culture, on the other—and not know with which country or culture to identify (Yu & Kim, 1983). Oftentimes, recent immigrants feel that they do not belong in the United States, but they also feel that they would no longer fit in their native countries because of their acculturation to American ways.

Some refugees want to move back to Southeast Asia, but that is not only politically and economically impractical—their increasingly Americanized children often do not want to leave the United States. The result for some Southeast Asians is an identity limbo: Should they hold steadfastly to their Southeast Asian cultural identity, biding their time until they return to Southeast Asia, or should they adopt a bicultural identity, figuring that they will stay in the United States? Identity conflicts can be fed by differing perspectives, held by some Americans and Vietnamese, regarding the actions of Americans and Vietnamese during the Vietnam War (Carlin & Sokoloff, 1985). Based on their experiences during the Vietnam War, some Southeast Asians feared or hated Americans (Carlin & Sokoloff, 1985). An identity conflict can arise in a person when he or she tries to deal with the need to fit in with, or to become like, the people who were feared or hated just a few years ago. Clinging to their ethnic identity allows Southeast Asians to have a sense of stability and identity that was undermined by their refugee experience (Nidorf, 1985). But failure to acculturate can increase hostility toward Southeast Asians and make financial advancement more difficult. If Southeast Asians choose to take the other position and adopt a bicultural identity, they (especially older refugees) may be left with the gnawing feeling that their bicultural identity is a facade.

Compounding this identity problem for Southeast Asians is the stigma some feel about their status as refugees (Bliatout et al., 1985). Consider the feelings (in a case cited by Nidorf, 1985) of a 13-year-old Vietnamese girl who came to the United States in the 1980s and who had been in the United States for a couple of years.

This girl felt uncomfortable with American friends and feared rejection from Vietnamese peers who came in 1975 whom she saw as a superior group to those who came afterward. She concealed her ability to read and write Vietnamese flawlessly and tried to erase her accent. Her desire to belong with the Vietnamese who came in 1975 conflicted with both her negative perceptions of some of their behavior and with who she was. The result was self-loathing and somatic complaints such as headaches, poor appetite, and tension.

Integrating Identity

Other sources of identity problems for Asian Americans include confusion about how to integrate their cultures so that they do not categorize or divide their behavior into either "Asian" or "American." A Chinese-Vietnamese college student described the dilemma this way:

> I can't decide which culture I can relate myself to. There are some situations that I ran into, I don't know if I listen to the American voice or the Chinese voice inside my head. I do not know which culture [is] suitable for me. Being caught between two cultures is not a good place to be in. When you approach a problem or situation that needs to be solved, there are two voices in your head one tells you to do the American way and the other tells you to do it the Chinese way. (Student term paper, 1992)

A Chinese-Thai American college student described how she was integrating her identity:

> I'm only part Thai. I have some Chinese in me and the rest of me is American. I don't think I can ever be fully Thai as my parents would like, because almost everything I do I do using some parts of each culture. I eat some American food with chopsticks and a spoon. When I pray to the Buddha, I speak to him in English. When I speak to my sisters or Thai friends, I blend the two languages together (but they still understand me). I mix both cultures so much, sometimes I think I've started my own new culture. (Student term paper, 1992)

Misidentification by Others

As mentioned in the beginning of this chapter, ethnic identity is based both on how individuals identify themselves and on how others identify them. But sometimes there is a discrepancy between what H. Wong (1985a) labeled "ethnic self-identity" (i.e., how individuals identify themselves) and "ascribed ethnic identity" (i.e., how others categorize a person's ethnicity). For example, most Japanese Americans probably identify themselves as Japanese Americans, but many non-Asian Americans view them as Japanese; Filipinos might identify themselves as Filipino Americans, but other Americans often misidentify them as Mexicans. These Asian Americans face not only rejection from different groups but also a lack of validation for their own identities. When others misidentify Asian Americans' ethnic groups, when others assume that Asian Americans are foreigners when in fact they are Americans, or when Asian Americans are rejected by other Asian Americans for being too foreign or too American, identity problems may result.

Furthermore, if a person finds that his or her ethnic group is considered by others to be a secondary group, this discovery can be a source of identity problems. For instance, when Korean Americans are asked, "Are you Chinese or Japanese, or what?", the Korean Americans may feel that they do not belong to an ethnic group that counts. When Korean Americans are then asked, "Well, what's the difference between Chinese, Japanese, and Korean?", they not only have to cope with an ignoramus but also with a feeling that their ethnic identity has not been validated. Similarly, Thai Americans who repeatedly have to describe where Thailand is or must constantly deny that they are from Taiwan might feel put down.

Individuality

Finally, for some people identification with their ethnic group can conflict with their sense of individuality. Most people simultaneously want to belong to a group and be distinct from that group (K. Smith, 1983). The desire for individuality triggers fears of exclusion and isolation from a group (K. Smith, 1983), whereas the desire to belong to a group can trigger fears of loss of individuality. Those who fear that identification with an ethnic group might undermine their individuality may either have stereotypes about Asian Americans or may fear that such stereotypes would overshadow their individuality. Whatever the reason, some Asian Americans have tried to ignore or dismiss their ethnic background in an effort to develop and understand their own identities as individuals (Root, 1989).[4]

---

[4]Ethnic-identity conflicts also can arise from alcohol or drug abuse because such abuse can conflict with and undermine ethnic attitudes, values, preferred behaviors, and affiliations as the drug culture substitutes for the ethnic culture (Westermeyer, 1984).

CONCLUSION

There are no data on the percentage of Asian Americans who have ethnic-identity problems. Additional research is needed to determine why some people develop prolonged ethnic-identity problems and others do not, why some people manifest their identity problems in one way while others manifest their identity problems in another way, and what role cultural conflicts may play in the development of ethnic identity. Ethnic-identity conflicts are one form of stress Asian Americans face but that most other (Euro-)Americans do not face. In the next two chapters, attention will turn directly to the issue of stressors facing Asian Americans.

6

Stress

The diathesis–stress model of psychopathology maintains that psychopathology arises from a combination of biological predispositions and psychosocial stressors (i.e., psychological and social sources of stress). But no published research could be found on whether there are differences between Asian Americans and non-Asian Americans or differences among Asian American groups in the biochemical processes by which mental disorders arise; and there has been no research examining the confluence of biological predispositions and psychosocial stressors in the development of psychopathology in Asian Americans. One reason for this lack of research is that studying biological predispositions adds a tremendous amount to the expense of doing such research. Instead, the research in this area has focused on psychosocial stressors.

There is a vast array of psychological studies addressing the relationship between stress and psychological well-being, happiness, and physical health (Ader, 1981; Holmes & Rahe, 1967; Kobasa, 1979; Lazarus, 1966; Paykel, 1979; Rabkin & Struening, 1976; Rahe, 1975). Stress can contribute to unhappiness, coping and adjustment difficulties, and mental disorders in Asian Americans just as it can in others. For example, in Chinese Americans stress is positively correlated to the incidence of psychiatric symptoms (Lin, Simeone, Ensel, & Kuo, 1979).

Asian Americans apparently have stressors facing them that most Americans do not, and these stressors could contribute to the development of mental disorders in Asian Americans. Since this book is concerned with what distinguishes the mental health of Asian Americans from that of other Americans, the emphasis in this chapter and the next chapter is on those sources of stress for Asian Americans that are distinct from the sources of stress facing most other Americans: minority status/racism, cultural conflicts, immigrant status, and refugee experiences. The first three sources of stress are discussed in this chapter and the last source (refugee experiences) is covered in Chapter 7.

MINORITY STATUS/RACISM

There are a number of ways in which minority status can lead to psychosocial stress for Asian Americans as well as for other people of color. Minority status can make a person vulnerable to being cast as an interloper or scapegoat by other Americans (Lin, 1986; E. Smith, 1985). For example, some minority students at universities feel as if they are guests or do not truly belong at that university.

Minority status can also be a reason that many members of the dominant group implicitly relegate members of minorities to the role of audience rather than participant (E. Smith, 1985). For instance, because of their minority status, members of a minority at a business meeting might be ignored and patronized by many members of the dominant group who might not ask them for their ideas or might not even expect them to participate (E. Smith, 1985). In effect, many members of the dominant group may adopt a colonialist attitude toward people of color. As a result, the minority members may feel alienated, marginal, and socially isolated (E. Smith, 1985).

Members of minorities may be regarded as "tokens." Stress can be created, on the one hand, by the high visibility and lack of anonymity that comes with being a token "representative" of the minority group and, on the other, by the accentuation of differences between the characteristics of the minority and the dominant culture (E. Smith, 1985). For instance, they may find themselves in situations in which they feel that they are sticking out from the crowd because of their race or because they are expected to be a great fount of knowledge about Asia.

It is difficult to ignore the widespread Japan-bashing, by the media, politicians, and corporate businessmen, which provides psychological support and delusions of justification for taunting, disrespect, and violence against Asian Americans. These actions are directed against all Asian Americans because most Americans make no effort to distinguish Japanese from Japanese *Americans*, Chinese, Chinese Americans, or any other Asian or Asian American group. Similarly, antagonism toward Vietnamese based on the experiences of some Americans during the Vietnam War is generalized toward all Asian Americans. Hostility toward Korean merchants based on experiences with a few Koreans or on negative depictions of Korean shopkeepers in the news and movies is directed toward other Asian Americans. Thus, there is a confluence of factors that lead to racism against Asian Americans, and this confluence is compounded by the tendency of many people to form stereotypes based on limited association with Asian Americans.

Stress is generated and Asian Americans are made aware of the racism directed against them when police follow Asian Americans who are driving through tony residential areas but ignore Euro-Americans who drive through the same neighborhood or when Asian Americans hear reports of police harassing young Asian American men (e.g., stopping them under trumped-up pretexts and then taking their pictures to add to a mug book of "gang members" with no proof of such affiliation or probable cause to suspect they are gang members).

Racism is a source of stress because it is a source of oppression. For example, racism can restrict Asian Americans' equal access to economic resources (e.g., promotions), which, in turn, can be a source of stress. Even those Asian Americans with high socioeconomic status should not be considered immune to the effects of racism. A high socioeconomic status does not necessarily indicate that individuals have not experienced racial discrimination. For instance, an upper middle-class, Asian American engineer may find that he has been stereotyped as a competent technician but nothing more. Consequently, he is ignored when his peers are being promoted to positions with increased responsibility. Suppose he has two children. The child in grammar school may be taunted as a "Jap," a "Chino," or a "Gook." His other child in high school may not be accepted by the college of her choice because the university admits Asian Americans at a lower rate than it admits other applicants. Whatever the socioeconomic status, experiences with discrimination can cause suffering and leave scars.

Stereotypes of Asian American women as hard-working, unasser- tive, uncomplaining (True, 1990; D. Wong, 1980), and sexually available, as well as stereotypes of Asian American men as hard- working and asexual with no personality, set up Asian Americans for exploitation and oppression. For instance, based on these stereotypes of Asian American women, some men may assume that Asian American women are sexually available to anyone and are erotically and exotically satisfying, thus allowing these men to feel free to sexually harass Asian American women and to assume that the women will not complain or hurt them. Asian Americans might have extra work dumped on them by employers, with no added remuneration, because the employers think that they do not have a life anyway and will work hard without complaining.

It has been suggested (Blustein, 1982; Thein, 1980) that many of the problems faced by minority mental health clients are due to oppression. Oppression can cause fear and a sense of powerlessness (Thein, 1980) if it impedes a person's ability to control his or her own fate. Learned helplessness and an external locus of control can develop under such circumstances.

Racism can undermine a person's self-concept. For instance, it is not unusual for Asian American college students to refer offhandedly to their eyes as slanted or small. Where did these students get this notion? Considering the number of people in China alone, there may be more people in the world with Asian eyes than with European eyes. Then whose eyes are slanted? The eyes are just different. But many Asian Americans feel negative about some of their physical traits because of the racist input they have received from others.

The effects of racism and oppression can last for generations. For example, evidence has pointed to cross-generational effects of the largely racist-motivated internment of Japanese Americans during World War II (Commission on Wartime Relocation and Internment of Civilians, 1982). This internment not only affected the self-concepts and ideals about America held by some *Nisei*, but also affected their children, who generally were born after the war (Mass, 1986; Nagata, 1991): Many *Nisei* parents, trying to protect their children from the harsher realities of the concentration camps, raised their children to be as inconspicuous as possible. The general reticence of *Nisei* to talk with their children about the internment has sometimes caused *Sansei* to feel angry, rejected, excluded, confused, and sad (Nagata, 1991).

If parents can help their children become aware of the existence of racism, the children might be able to develop adaptive strategies and an increased sense of community with other victims of racism (S. Sue & Chin, 1983). But evidently there have been no empirical studies focusing on attempts by Asian American parents to teach their children how to cope with this particular source of stress.

As K. Chan (in press) has noted, an accumulation of experiences with racial discrimination, slurs, and rejection can lead to a sense of powerlessness and low self-esteem. In turn, a sense of powerlessness and low self-esteem can limit a person's perception of possible adaptive responses. There is an increased likelihood that individuals who do not have a wide range of adaptive responses will encounter stressors that they cannot deal with effectively.

If a person acknowledges the existence of racism, that person might have a sense of powerlessness, anger, and frustration. An Asian

American who has a schema that there is racism directed against Asian Americans will probably be more aware of racism than will a person who does not consciously recognize the racism; and this recognition of racism, whether overt or as an underlying trend, is stressful. Alienation and marginality can result. On the other hand, if a person tries to protect himself or herself from racist stressors by denying their existence, the stress does not necessarily go away. On the contrary, the unconscious sense of helplessness and anger might be expressed in somatic complaints such as headaches or stomachaches. The anger and frustration could also be displaced into self-hatred or into uncontrolled, angry explosions at family members (K. Chan, in press).

CULTURAL CONFLICTS

There are many values (such as politeness, importance of family, and hard work) that are shared by Asian Americans and by Americans in general. (Note that the values of the American mainstream, or "American" values, are largely Euro-American. "American" culture generally has not incorporated the values of American minorities into its values, the melting-pot myth notwithstanding.) But there are also some American values (such as spontaneity, assertiveness, and individualism) that, at times, conflict with Asian American values based on Asian philosophies or on the experiences of Asian Americans in the United States. Cultural conflict arises whenever the norms, values, and behavior of one culture clash with those of another culture (S. Sue & Chin, 1983). Individuals caught in a cultural conflict have difficulty reconciling the two cultural influences to which they are subject.

Research in this area of cultural conflicts suggests that such conflicts can be sources of psychological stress. Although cultural conflicts can lead to personality problems and intergenerational conflicts (S. Sue & Chin, 1983), people often are not aware of the degree to which their cultural background and cultural conflicts can create problems for them (Carlin & Sokoloff, 1985). In order to increase awareness of such sources of stress, therefore, it is important to consider some examples of areas of cultural conflict.

Cultural conflicts can exist between American culture and an Asian American individual, between members of an Asian American family, and within an individual. Consider first the cultural conflicts between American culture and the Asian American individual.

The parents of Southeast Asian children usually teach their children to respect their Southeast Asian culture and to be obedient, deferential, quiet, and respectful to parents. Children generally internalize these standards. But if Asian American children attend a Eurocentric American school that degrades Asian cultures or that emphasizes values antithetical to the values that Asian American parents are teaching their children (JWK International, 1978), the children may grow ambivalent and feel an inner conflict. Under pressure from teachers and peers to conform to such American norms as independence, assertiveness, and expressiveness (Carlin & Sokoloff, 1985; E. Lee, 1988), the children may experience a conflict with the values they have been taught by their parents. There are many other examples: American culture encourages open, straight-forward communication, whereas Asian American cultures generally encourage more oblique styles of communication. American culture values truthfulness, but Southeast Asians are often taught at home that being honest is secondary to avoiding the embarrassment of oneself or others (Carlin & Sokoloff, 1985). Euro-American culture encourages and considers healthy the open expression of emotions, but Asian American cultures, whether owing to Asian values or the experiences of Asian Americans in the United States, encourage Asian Americans to hide any feelings that could disrupt the harmony of the family (Kikumura & Kitano, 1976; D. W. Sue, 1989a) and discourage Asian Americans from openly challenging the views of others (M-K. Ho, 1976). Indeed, the direct communication of attitudes and sentiments in Asian cultures can be considered boorish. For instance, Southeast Asians children are often expected to comply quietly with parental demands without voicing their feelings or objections (Nidorf, 1985).

A Chinese-Thai American college student described her conflict this way:

> I wish I could be open and just let out what is bothering me, to say what I feel and not keep it bottled up inside. I'm an American so I should stand up for what I believe instead, I keep quiet and let it pass because that is what I am taught. . . . I don't always agree with [Asian values] in theory but I generally use [them] in my actions. (Student term paper, 1992)

Many foreign-born Asian Americans are ridiculed by their schoolmates if they do not mirror Americanized behavior but are also criticized by their parents if they behave "too much" like other Americans. As one Thai student put it,

> If I were at school . . . with my friends, I would speak English and use the American side of me. I think if I spoke Thai and behaved in a Thai manner

at school, most people would not see me as an American, but probably as a "FOB" [fresh off the boat]. In contrast, if I were at home with my family and relatives, I would speak Thai and use my Asian side. If I don't, my family would feel that I am losing my ethnicity as a Thai person and would feel that I do not have respect. (Student term paper, 1992)

Even expectations about body language can be different at school and at home (Carlin & Sokoloff, 1985). For example, teachers may instruct students that it is polite to look at authority figures when the latter are talking to them, whereas some Asian American parents teach their children that it is polite and deferential not to make eye contact with authority figures.

A subtle cultural conflict over assertiveness can arise when American corporate culture sometimes reinforces individuals who step forward at work to take credit for a job well done (and, thus, perhaps come to the attention of the employer and receive a raise); but Asian cultures reinforce quiet modesty, the subordination of the individual to the group (M-K. Ho, 1976), and the belief that others will recognize that a person is doing his or her job well without being told. An Asian American who is working for a large corporation run by non-Asian Americans may be torn between these two cultures and not know how to behave.

Regarding cultural conflicts between parents and children, for-eign-born children adopt Western ways more quickly than their parents because the former are more exposed to Americanizing pressures and have a greater need for acceptance from their age-mates than their parents do; thus, there are sometimes intergenerational conflicts that reflect cultural conflicts: Typically, the children prefer a more American way of behaving, and the parents prefer a more Asian way of behaving.

Many foreign-born Asian American parents lecture their children not to become too Americanized. They think their children should not lose their ethnic roots. The children are torn between wanting to fit in with their American peers and the American culture that they see on television and wanting to please their parents. For example, a Chinese-Vietnamese student said that her parents emphasized the need to retain her Chinese cultural values. She thought that this emphasis was racist. She would become very upset with her parents, but her Chinese values dictated that she restrain herself and not talk back to her parents. She recognized that the cultural gap between herself and her family was growing each year, resulting in increasing anguish and tension.

One area in which many foreign-born Asian Americans have

cultural conflicts is dating (JWK International, 1978; Weiss, 1973). Many immigrant Chinese American parents had no dating experience but had arranged marriages instead (Sung, 1985). Not surprisingly, then, these parents are often not sympathetic to the desires of their Americanized children to date; instead they see dating (as well as sports) as a distracting waste of time and effort (Sung, 1985) and are more restrictive about allowing their children to date than are other American parents (Reglin & Adams, 1990). Consider the case of a Chinese-Vietnamese college student who was told by his family that he could not date until he finished college. He was told that women would interfere with his studies—but that there would be plenty of women later when he was successful in his career. This familial ruling presented a conflict for him. He did not want to be different from his friends—and, therefore, he dated without telling his family. Similarly, a female Thai American student recounted:

> When I was sixteen, I felt I was ready [to start dating], but my parents didn't think so. They told me that it wasn't time yet and that if I had a boyfriend, it would interfere with my education. I fought with my parents telling them all my friends are dating and I didn't see how it could interfere with school. This only made matters worse and then my mom would start with her life story of how she wasn't even allowed to talk to boys when she was my age. I would argue back, telling her that it is different in Thailand than in America, and then she would really get furious leaving the problem unsolved. That was how most of our arguments ended. (Student term paper, 1992)

Another cultural conflict arises when children become more Americanized than their foreign-born parents and then raise children of their own. The grandparents, expecting obedience and filial piety from their grown offspring, want traditional Asian values taught to the grandchildren. The Americanized parents balk at rearing their children as traditionally as the grandparents would like because they fear that if their children were reared in accordance with the grandparents' wishes, their children would experience the same rejection and embarrassment that they did as children. At the same time, though, the parents want to be respectful of the grandparents.

Consistent with the hypothesis that cultural conflicts can be stressful, one study found that the more Chinese that was spoken between immigrant Chinese parents and their fifth- and sixth-grade sons, the more anxious the boys were; and the study found that the more favorable the parents' attitudes toward Chinese culture, the lower the self-esteem of the sons (Ou & McAdoo, 1980, cited in L. N. Huang & Ying, 1989). These results suggest that in the short run,

biculturality can create cultural conflicts and stress for Asian
children who are trying to forge an identity. A study of Vie~
Chinese-Vietnamese families in Canada has also subst~   ~s-
ing intergenerational conflict based on cultural con~   1986).

Similarly, an examination of Chinese America~   ~ a mental
health clinic revealed that the clients were anxious ab~ ~eir inability
to reconcile parental values concerning conformity to family roles, on
the one hand, with mainstream American values and roles, on the
other (Bourne, 1975). Similarly, the finding that Vietnamese adolescents who had strong English skills reported having frequent problems
with their parents (Charron & Ness, 1983) suggests that the acculturation of Vietnamese adolescents puts these adolescents at risk for
additional conflicts with their parents. Providing further evidence of
the psychological effects of cultural conflicts, a study (Aldwin &
Greenberger, 1987) of a nonclinical[1] sample of Korean American
college students found that when the college students personally
endorsed "modern" values (the researchers evidently equated modern
values with American values) but thought that their parents adhered to
traditional values, they were more likely to be depressed than students
who perceived intergenerational concurrence of values. Indeed, the
degree to which Korean American parents were perceived by their
children to be holding traditional values was the strongest predictor of
depression in the Korean American college students.

Finally, regarding cultural conflicts within the individual, a
Chinese-Vietnamese student posed the dilemma clearly: "Should I try
to be completely American and lose my Asian identity or risk not being
in the group and keeping my Asian culture?" Another Chinese-
Vietnamese student said that she identified with both Chinese and
American values but that she could not decide which was proper or
right for her.

Oftentimes Asian American adolescents have cultural conflicts
about how physically demonstrative to be with their girlfriends or
boyfriends. According to Chinese customs, and contrary to American
customs, public demonstrations of affection are discouraged (Union of
Pan Asian Communities, 1978), and sexuality is expressed subtly
(Sung, 1985). Thus, some Asian Americans are torn between American
and Asian norms.

---

[1]A nonclinical sample is a sample that has been drawn from a pool of people who
are not receiving mental health services (or, at least, who are not known to be receiving
mental health services). For example, a nonclinical sample might be drawn from a pool
of college students taking a psychology course or from names picked at random out of a
phone book.

Immigrant and refugee Asian Americans in particular may receive conflicting messages from their parents: Become successful in America but do so without becoming Americanized (Nidorf, 1985). Asian American parents want their children to succeed; but succeeding in America often calls for behaviors that some Asian American parents do not like. For example, if an Asian American who works at a large corporation wants to be successful, a willingness to move away from the family may be required. Thus, raising one's job status at the corporation could bring honor to the family, but to do so would require moving away from the family, and this could be interpreted as a sign of disrespect and ingratitude to the parents (Nidorf, 1985). Cultural conflicts arise when children want to respect their parents' wishes but find that their parents' advice is sometimes counterproductive or irrelevant to finding happiness and success in America (Nidorf, 1985). Such cultural conflicts can generate a growing psychological distance between how some Asian Americans see themselves or choose to behave, on the one hand, and what behaviors are expected of them, on the other (Yang, 1991).

There is a great deal of variability in the amount of cultural conflict experienced across Asian American ethnic groups and within Asian American ethnic groups. For example, Asian Americans in Hawaii, who are subject to less intense acculturation to Euro-American standards and less racism, might not experience cultural conflicts in the same way that mainland Asian Americans would. Many American-born Asian Americans are not experiencing a lot of these cultural conflicts: Some are very acculturated to American ways and, therefore, are not aware of many conflicts; and others have achieved a balance between cultures, so that potential cultural conflicts are minimized. In addition, different types of cultural conflicts can arise for Southeast Asian refugees, immigrant Asians, and American-born Asian Americans because of differences in acculturation. For example, conflicts involving dating are much more likely among Southeast Asians than among Japanese Americans.

IMMIGRANT STATUS

Stress arises when a person's ability to cope with stressors is taxed. Experiencing many changes in a short amount of time is stressful (B. S. Dohrenwend & Dohrenwend, 1974; S. Sue & Chin, 1983). This is true even if the changes are pleasant (e.g., marrying, moving into a new home), evidently because both pleasant and unpleasant changes challenge individuals to adjust their established behaviors and coping styles to new circumstances. This pattern apparently holds for Asian Americans as well as other Americans. For example, Southeast Asians who have experienced many significant changes in their lives tend to have more physical and psychological symptoms than those who have experienced fewer changes (Masuda, Lin, & Tazuma, 1980).

Clearly, immigrants experience numerous changes in their lives; and the majority of Asians in the United States from every Asian group, except Japanese Americans, are foreign-born. Asian immigrants to America have to adjust to a new culture (E. Lee & Lu, 1989): They need to adjust to the reality that many of the cultural values and behavior patterns that were useful and comprehensible in Asia are irrelevant, misconstrued, or ineffective in America (Yu & Kim, 1983) and must learn to deal with what is for them a foreign culture with unfamiliar language, social norms, values, and expectations (Abe & Zane, 1990; Munoz, 1979).

For instance, as a Korean student—who had been enrolled in the second grade in an American school and separated from the rest of the class, at the back of the room with a male, Euro-American teacher's aide who was trying to help her learn English—noted:

> It was hard for me to understand the directions he was giving me let alone learn anything from him. I felt so secluded from the other children. As days went by I felt more like a foreigner. I just wished everyday that someone would just come up to me and just explain what was going on in my life. (Student term paper, 1992)

Sometimes immigrants who do not speak English are sent to classes for the mentally retarded when schools do not have adequate, alternative resources for teaching English to non-English speakers. Even Filipino immigrants or Chinese immigrants from Hong Kong, who may already know English, can have linguistic difficulties adjusting to the United States. If English is a second language, the first language of these immigrants can affect their "accent, intonation, vocabulary, syntax, and idiomatic expressions" in English (Santos, 1983, p. 134). As a result, their English might not sound like that of a native-born American, and they may be embarrassed by their English. Without demonstrating a causal relationship between linguistic difficulties and stress, some research (S. P. Kim, 1983) has shown that Korean immigrant children with low self-concepts were significantly less proficient in English than Korean immigrant children with average or strong self-concepts.

Not only do immigrants encounter new social norms in America but they are also subject to changing social norms within their families.

Family members do not become Americanized at the same pace. When some members of the family become Americanized more quickly than other members, the behavior norms and relationships within the family change (E. Lee, 1988).

For instance, the relationship between husband and wife can change. According to traditional Asian values, women are expected to stay home and be passive and subservient (True, 1990; Westermeyer, Neider, & Vang, 1984). However, many foreign-born Asians discover that both husband and wife must work. Some wives then become more vocal about their perspectives, and husbands feel that their status has been lowered by their inability to support the family alone ("Mental health," 1985). If a Korean American wife were to work outside the home (a pattern contrary to that found in Korea) and become increasingly Americanized and assertive, her husband might have difficulty coping with the changes in his wife, and the wife might resent her husband for sticking to the traditional Korean notion that domestic tasks and child-rearing were her responsibility (Light & Bonacich, 1988; Shon & Ja, 1982). Marital tension due to changing spousal roles is a major reason that Korean clients have sought counseling (Yu & Kim, 1983).

In addition to differences between spouses in rates of Americanization, there usually are intrafamilial, generational differences in the rate of Americanization. Through school, children are immersed in American ways and, if their parents are foreign-born, tend to acculturate more quickly than their parents. Asian American children of foreign-born parents may find that their parents are unable to help them adjust culturally to life in the United States (Yu & Kim, 1983). One Korean American student noted, with a tinge of remorse and loneliness, that he was becoming Americanized more quickly than his parents, and with every passing year he could feel the widening cultural gap between his parents and himself.

Siblings might also acculturate at different rates. If an eldest son is the last member of the family to immigrate, he is likely to be the least acculturated. Although, traditionally, he should have a higher status than his younger siblings do, his lack of acculturation could undermine his status. The changing structure of the family and the roles that family members expect each other to fulfill cause stress for all concerned.

Generally, immigrant Asian American families are more traditionally Asian in structure than Asian American families that have been in the United States for generations. The eldest son in a traditional Asian American family faces particular stress because of the responsibilities that he has (L. N. Huang & Ying, 1989). The youngest daughter in a traditional, immigrant family also encounters a lot of stress arising from sexist treatment in the family and—since she is likely to be the most acculturated member of the family—more cultural conflicts with her parents than the other siblings have (L. N. Huang & Ying, 1989).

The employment opportunities of many foreign-born Asian Americans have been limited by their lack of proficiency in English. These Asian Americans are frequently in low-paying, menial jobs. Consequently, many find little reward or fulfillment in their work and feel pessimistic about their prospects for the future (Munoz, 1979; Okamura & Agbayani, 1991). This feeling is compounded by the fact that many immigrant Asians were highly educated professionals in Asia but are unable to transfer their skills into the American economy because their Asian education and employment history are devalued in the United States (Okamura & Agbayani, 1991). For instance, Filipinos from families which were privileged in the Philippines may have become accustomed to having servants and being of high status. When they come to the United States, they experience a sharp decline in lifestyle and status. Therefore, the jobs held by many Asian American immigrants not only are minimally rewarding but also represent a loss of status.

Korean immigrants often experience downward occupational mobility when they leave Korea and move to the United States (Yu, 1983). Although many Korean immigrants have taken the risk of becoming small-business owners, most have had no experience with such lines of work (Min, 1984). They usually open their businesses in high-crime areas where rent is affordable (Min, 1990). Once they become successful entrepreneurs, landlords quickly raise their rent (Min, 1990). Although immigrant Korean entrepreneurs tend to make more money than their wage-earning counterparts, they do not assimilate as quickly as immigrant Koreans who work in the general labor market (Min, 1990). Thus, making choices to mitigate one source of stress (e.g., low income) can result in the exacerbation of another source of stress (e.g., isolation, alienation, and stressful work conditions).

Compounding these stresses is the fact that many immigrants had grand dreams of what life would be in the United States. They have to adjust to the disparity between what they expected of life in the United States and what they actually experience in the United States (Shon & Ja, 1982). Owing to their losses and these adjustment burdens, many recent immigrants feel that they belong neither in the United States nor in Asia—and feel guilty for having immigrated.

Another source of stress for immigrants comes from changes in family composition, because some family members may have stayed in

Asia. Concomitant with this change in family composition is a loss of social support. Immigrants have to deal with many stressors without social support systems that would have expedited their adjustment (Kuo & Tsui, 1986) because these sources of support were left behind in Asia (Munoz, 1979). A study of Chinese Americans has highlighted the importance of social-support systems: It found that the effect of stressors was negligible when there was a great deal of social support (N. Lin et al., 1979). While it is not clear whether social support functions as an antecedent factor that lessens the likelihood of undesirable events or as a buffering factor that affects how individuals interpret and respond to undesirable life events, "social support . . . explained more than twice as much of the [psychiatric] illness variance as the stressful events and the demographic variables combined" (N. Lin et al., 1979, p. 116). Yet, because of U.S. immigration laws, many immigrant Asians have not been able to immigrate with their extended families. For example, if Filipinos do not have immediate family members in the United States, they must sometimes wait for years before they can emigrate. Because of sponsorship rules, Vietnamese who have settled in the United States frequently had their families and ethnic community split up, thereby weakening their support systems (Atkinson, Ponterotto, & Sanchez, 1984).

Immigrant Asian families often bear all of these losses and struggle with these difficulties largely for the sake of the children. The families make enormous sacrifices so that the children can be college educated. In turn, they generally expect that a college education in the United States will enable their children to achieve financial success. Cognizant of the sacrifices that their parents have made for them (e.g., leaving their friends and family in Asia, struggling to learn English, feeling embarrassed when they do not understand American ways, working long hours at low-paying jobs), the children experience a great deal of pressure to succeed in school. As a Korean college student wrote:

> My parents say that they [sacrificed] their lives for us because they want us to get a better education and to give us more opportunities. This kind of situation put more stress on my siblings and I. . . . Knowing that your parents had given up everything for you so, that you would have better of everything only leads you space to succeed and no room for failure. (Student term paper, 1992)

When the parents' high expectations cannot be met by the children, the children may feel isolated or may blame themselves (Shon & Ja, 1982).

Research (Aldwin & Greenberger, 1987) suggests that Korean American college students feel more pressure from parents to achieve good grades than their Euro-American counterparts do. That these high parental expectations for academic success in college were positively associated with depression among this sample of Korean American college students but not among their Euro-American counterparts suggests that Korean American students experience expectations of and pressure for high academic achievement in a way that Euro-American college students do not.

This pressure evidently starts early. One study involved questioning the parents of children in the fifth through eleventh grade who scored above the 90th percentile on achievement tests (Yao, 1985). When the sample of primarily immigrant Asian American groups (i.e., Chinese, East Indians, Filipinos, Korean, and Vietnamese) was compared with Euro-Americans, all the Asian American parents had higher expectations for their children's grades than the Euro-American parents did. In fact, 46% of these Asian American parents hoped that their children would enter a medical field, compared to 29% of the Euro-American parents studied.

Compounding this pressure, Korean American parents tend to be unwilling to listen to their children's expressions of fear and anxiety (Strom et al., 1987). The communication gap is exacerbated by the fact that many "1.5" Koreans are not fluent in Korean at a sophisticated level and that their parents are only fluent in Korean (J. Lee & Cynn, 1991).

Also adding to the pressure is the fact that many Asian Americans tend to view success or failure as more dependent on effort than ability (Mizokawa & Ryckman, 1990). This is particularly true of Korean Americans; to a lesser extent true of Chinese Americans, Filipino Americans, and Japanese Americans; and to an even lesser extent of Southeast Asians (Mizokawa & Ryckman, 1990). The increased pressure may be especially strong among immigrant Asian Americans: This would account for Korean Americans—a group with a higher percentage of immigrants than most other Asian American groups— feeling more pressure to achieve than other Asian Americans feel. For Southeast Asian refugees, of whom a higher percentage are foreign born than are Korean Americans, the primary motivation for coming to the United States was more often basic survival than just the education of their children; therefore, the pressure to achieve academically may be less severe for Southeast Asians than it is for Korean Americans. This increased pressure on immigrants also might explain why another study, not limited to sampling immigrant Asian Americans, found no difference between Asian American and Euro-American preadolescents and early adolescents in the amount of pressure they felt from their parents (Pang, 1991).

Because of the sacrifices made by parents to immigrate to the United States so that their children could be college-educated and have a better life than they had; because of traditional Asian values stressing obedience, filial piety, respect for authority, and suppression of individual desires for the good of the family; and because of parental expectations that the children will seek jobs that will reflect well on the family and will enable the children to support their parents when the parents become elderly, many immigrant Asian parents select, and feel justified in selecting, their children's college majors and career goals. Therefore, some Asian American students who may be more interested in art, music, or social sciences will, for example, major in business because their parents think that that major would be best. Some of these students do not even like business or math. The children may be torn between wanting to select their own fields, like most of their American peers, and acceding to their parents' wishes, out of filial piety and gratitude for their parents' sacrifices. The resulting conflict could cause the children to feel depressed (Bourne, 1975), resentful, or guilty (K. Huang, 1991).

Thus, immigrant Asian Americans face unique stressors. In the next chapter, consideration turns to the stressors faced by Southeast Asian refugees.

7

Stress and Refugees

S outheast Asian refugees have the same problems that other immigrant Asian Americans do—and a lot more. Before discussing some of their sources of stress, it would be helpful to review what they had to undergo to escape Southeast Asia and come to the United States. (Although the experiences of the different Southeast Asian groups were not identical, there were many similarities. For the present purposes, it is sufficient to discuss these common experiences.)

The first wave of Southeast Asian refugees arrived in 1975, when about 130,000 refugees, mostly Vietnamese, came to the United States. By and large these refugees were urban, educated, and relatively well-to-do (Zaharlick & Brainard, 1987). The second wave of Southeast Asian refugees has arrived in the United States primarily since the end of 1978. These refugees have been more likely to be rural, less educated and less proficient in English than their first-wave counterparts, and lacking the skills adaptable to the American economy that the first-wave had. This second wave has included Cambodians, Chinese-Vietnamese, Laotians, and Vietnamese. Chinese-Vietnamese and Laotians were more likely to have emigrated as families than Vietnamese were; frequently among Vietnamese, not all family members were able to leave Vietnam (Beiser, 1988). Members of this second wave initially sought refuge in camps in Thailand and elsewhere in Asia and the Philippines.

The U.S. government, which before 1975 had no experience dealing with the settlement of so many refugees in so short a time (Zaharlick & Brainard, 1987), developed policies that were not always beneficial to the refugees. For instance, the U.S. government restricted

135

the number of extended-family members who could emigrate and settle together in the United States (Westermeyer, 1987), thus compounding the adjustment problems and the loneliness of Southeast Asians by depriving many Southeast Asians of their support systems. The results for the Hmong have been studied: Hmong families who were placed in areas that were far away from their relatives had more conflicts between parents and adolescents and more marital discord than those who lived near relatives (Westermeyer, 1987).

The voluntary organizations that oversaw the sponsorship of refugees were largely independent from U.S. government regulation. Although sponsors generally were helpful in finding housing and jobs for refugees and in teaching them American ways, some refugees experienced a number of problems with sponsors. Among the problems experienced by the refugees were (1) feeling that their private sponsors were overprotective or overintrusive (Beiser, Turner, & Ganesan, 1989), (2) dealing with church sponsors who were trying to convert them to the sponsors' religion (Beiser et al., 1989; Westermeyer, 1987), (3) finding that their housing was close to their sponsors but far from the ethnic community, and (4) dealing with the resentment of sponsors when the refugees, who had previously accepted help from the sponsors, subsequently rejected the sponsors' help and went to live with relatives (Mortland & Ledgerwood, 1987). States did not have adequate resources to deal with the refugees (Westermeyer, 1987), and secondary migration[1] exacerbated the problems that the states experienced in their attempts to anticipate the refugees' service needs (Mortland & Ledgerwood, 1987).

The following are some of the sources of stress for Southeast Asians: traumatic experiences, separation, ambivalence/antagonism from Americans, culture shock, financial problems, health problems, and intergenerational conflicts. These sources of stress were often even more intense for Southeast Asian children.

TRAUMAS EXPERIENCED

Southeast Asian refugees experienced a number of traumas in Southeast Asia before they were able to flee (August & Gianola, 1987; Kinzie et al., 1990; Kinzie, Sack, Angell, Clarke, & Ben, 1989). Many witnessed the wounding or killing of family members and friends in war-related shootings, bombings, burnings, and land-mine explosions.

---

[1]After initially settling in one place in the United States, many refugees moved to other locations (e.g., where there were family and job opportunities or where the climate was not too harsh). This is what is called secondary migration.

Even after the Vietnam War ended, ordnance that did not explode during the war later killed unsuspecting thousands. Refugees often witnessed the execution, starvation, and rape of family members and friends by political terrorists and brigands. The refugees were frequently at risk of personal injury, death, or capture. Some were forced to kill or injure people who were their enemies. Many were tortured and starved in labor camps. In the process of fleeing, they frequently spent long periods with inadequate food, supplies, and shelter. In Thailand, Malaysia, or Indonesia, if the refugees' boats were allowed to land or if those trekking over land were not forced at gunpoint to walk across mine fields (Rumbaut, 1990), the refugees usually lived in crowded, unsanitary, rat-filled, disease- and crime-ridden camps.[2] Cambodians and Laotians lived an average of almost 3 years in the resettlement camps (General Accounting Office, 1990).

There were differences in the traumatic experiences of the various Southeast Asian groups. A brief review of these differences will give some idea of the nature of these traumas.

The Vietnamese who fled South Vietnam in 1975 generally had only a few days to prepare for departure because, until the last moment, the United States officially denied that its pullout from Vietnam was imminent. Many of the Vietnamese who fled in 1975 did so because they had ties to Americans, were in the South Vietnamese military, or were members of the elite of South Vietnam and feared that the North Vietnamese communists would target them for death or labor camps. Aside from the minority who were able to fly out of Vietnam or escape by land, most of the Vietnamese refugees fled in small, overcrowded, dilapidated boats to first-asylum countries such as Thailand and the Philippines or to places such as Hong Kong. To obtain a space on the boats, the refugees would pay a great deal of money to boat owners or others of influence. They would hide on their persons any remaining valuables in the form of thin gold wafers or jewelry. Because the boats were typically overcrowded or attacked by thieving pirates, the supplies of food and water often were depleted before land was reached. Some boat people had to spend all of the boat trip standing, often without food or water. Others had to stay below deck for days in smelly, tightly packed conditions. On occasion, boat people were forced by hunger to eat the remains of other people on the boat,

---

[2]The age of the refugees when they were in the camps seems to have made a difference in the refugees' perceptions of their experiences. Young children sometimes remember playing with branches or anything else they could find; adolescents often remember being bored and feeling remote; adults remember feeling relatively safe in camps or associate the camps with their realization of all that they had lost (L-N. Huang, 1989).

resulting in "guilt, anxiety, suicidal ideation, intrusive thoughts, and fear of revenge by relatives of those" who were eaten (Cravens & Bornemann, 1990, p. 42).

Most of the Chinese-Vietnamese in the United States left Vietnam in the second wave. The communist government, distrustful of the Chinese and of capitalists, and seeking the assets of businesses in Vietnam (which were disproportionately run by Chinese-Vietnamese), confiscated the assets of Chinese-Vietnamese, closed their businesses, and reduced their food rations (S. Chan, 1991): This forced many Chinese-Vietnamese—who had been discriminated against in Vietnam for generations—to leave Vietnam. They left primarily as boat people. The boats of most of the Chinese-Vietnamese boat people were attacked by pirates who raped, robbed, kidnapped, and killed many of the refugees. It has been estimated that more than half of the boat people died before reaching a refugee camp (Liem, 1980).

In Laos, the Pathet Lao took power in 1975 and began a campaign of repression by killing, torturing, or sending opponents to labor camps. For instance, there was the case (cited by Mollica & Lavelle, 1988) of a 40-year-old, single, Laotian daughter of a rich family in Laos. Her parents were killed by communists in 1974. Before being sent to a labor camp and escaping to Thailand, she was a prisoner for 5 years, during which time she was given mind-altering drugs, tortured, and raped by 20 to 30 guards daily. Most of those Lao who fled trekked to asylum in refugee camps in Thailand. They were often stuck in those camps for years because potential second-asylum countries (such as the United States) would not admit them.

Two Laotian minorities, the Hmong and the Mien, faced particular traumas at the hands of the Pathet Lao. During the Vietnam War, both the Hmong and Mien were used by the U.S. Central Intelligence Agency to fight the communists. The U.S. government promised to help the Hmong and Mien after the war. But the U.S. government abandoned most of the Hmong and Mien; and when the United States pulled out of Southeast Asia, the communists sought revenge against these two minorities. The Pathet Lao attempted to exterminate them by bombing and burning their villages or by executing them (Downing & Olney, 1982; Meredith & Rowe, 1986). These persecuted minorities tried to flee by sneaking to refugee camps in Thailand. About half of those who made this journey died (Kroll, 1982): They either starved, drowned trying to cross the Mekong River by holding on to stalks of bamboo, or were ambushed by Pathet Lao patrols (Downing & Olney, 1982). About half of the Hmong who were in Laos in 1974 died; almost every family had at least one family member who died during this Pathet Lao period (Meredith & Rowe, 1986).

In Cambodia the Khmer Rouge, led by Pol Pot, took power in 1975. Within days of the seizure of Phnom Penh, the capital of Cambodia, the Khmer Rouge cast most of the nearly 2 million residents of Phnom Penh into labor camps and collective farms. Pol Pot wanted to rid the country (then renamed Kampuchea) of bourgeois, Western influences and return it to its agrarian roots. Because they were thought to represent the old form of government and Western influence Buddhist monks and educated people were the first to be targeted for death by the Khmer Rouge (Rozée & Van Boemel, 1989). To increase their chances of surviving, Cambodians destroyed their symbols of education: They destroyed their books and their eyeglasses and stopped using French and proper Khmer grammar (Rozée & Van Boemel, 1989). Cambodian society and values were undermined with the splitting up of families and the murders of religious and political leaders (Kinzie, 1989). Few monks, leaders, or intellectuals escaped the killing (Rozée & Van Boemel, 1989).

Between 1975 and 1979, an estimated 1 to 3 million of Kampuchea's 7 million people died (Kinzie et al., 1989). Almost two thirds of the Cambodians had at least one close relative who died (General Accounting Office, 1990). About one third of the Cambodians were political prisoners and an additional one third suffered assaults (E. Lee & Lu, 1989). Untold numbers were sent to labor camps.

The Khmer Rouge separated families because it feared that family loyalty could undermine loyalty to the Khmer Rouge. Some Cambodian children were conscripted into armies of children (Nidorf, 1985), sent to work camps after their parents were killed, or sent to different labor camps from the ones their parents were in (Bromley, 1988). Consequently, children sometimes lost touch with their parents (Kinzie et al., 1989). Some children who had been separated from their families were returned to their villages to spy on their families for the Khmer Rouge (Rozée & Van Boemel, 1989). Neighbors also spied on each other in order to save their own lives, causing people to mistrust each other (Rozée & Van Boemel, 1989).

Sanctioned by the Khmer Rouge, the anonymous national police, comprised of young boys with automatic rifles, buried people alive for disobeying them or asking questions, tore children limb from limb, and beat people for no reason (Rozée & Van Boemel, 1989). It has been suggested (by Rozée & Van Boemel, 1989) that this treatment may have been especially traumatic for Cambodian women because they were frequently beaten on the head (where Cambodians believe the soul resides) by youngsters (who, according to Cambodian culture, are not supposed to touch elder people).

At the end of 1978, Vietnam invaded Kampuchea and pushed the

Khmer Rouge from power. Various factions fought for control of Cambodia until a tenuous peace was established in 1991. Meanwhile, hundreds of thousands of Cambodians sought asylum in refugee camps in Thailand. Many of those who fled had to leave behind loved ones who had died en route to Thailand.

The trauma Cambodians have suffered has been widespread. For example, about 95% of the Cambodian women seen in therapy at a Boston clinic had been sexually abused or raped (Mollica, 1986). Most of these women did not discuss the assaults until after three years of therapy (Mollica, Wyshak, & Lavelle, 1987).

Researchers examining the average number of traumatic experiences suffered by Southeast Asians have found that Cambodians suffered the most (Mollica et al., 1990). Not surprisingly, given these histories, war memories are more of a problem for Cambodians than for Vietnamese, Lao, or Hmong (Jones & Strand, 1986); also not surprisingly, a comparison of different Southeast Asian groups has revealed that the Hmong and Cambodian refugees were the unhappiest (Rumbaut, 1985).

Thus, Southeast Asian refugees have endured great trauma. The psychological effects of such traumatic experiences are often delayed and recurrent (K-M. Lin, 1986). Not only might they relive these traumatic experiences but they also might experience guilt for having survived when so many others died (Nidorf, 1985). Moreover, what they experienced contradicted the world views that they formerly held: The torture, execution, and accidental killing of innocent people, the inability of authority figures to protect them, and the absence of expected responses to stimuli (Muecke, 1987) contradicted their world views and caused confusion, alienation, anger, and frustration (Mortland & Ledgerwood, 1987).

Compounding these traumatic experiences is the belief that relatives are still in desperate straits in Southeast Asia. Many refugees in the United States worry and grieve about loved ones in Asia and feel guilty for their own relatively good and safe life (Mortland & Ledgerwood, 1987). In 1992 and 1993, Cambodians in Thai refugee camps were forced back into Cambodia, where they faced starvation, land mines, unabated malaria and tuberculosis, and internecine conflicts among warring factions.

Further compounding these traumatic experiences, Southeast Asians received inadequate mental health care in the refugee camps where one mental health worker could have a case load of over 1200 (Cravens & Bornemann, 1990). If a refugee with a mental disorder were not officially diagnosed, his or her chances of coming to the United

States were increased because U.S. statutes excluded refugees with mental disorders (Cravens & Bornemann, 1990). Indeed, there were refugees with mental disorders who were not officially diagnosed, much less treated. Furthermore, there was no concerted effort to follow up specifically on those who had received mental health services in the camps once they settled in the United States (Cravens & Bornemann, 1990). Therefore, many refugees have experienced traumas and have gone for years without adequate mental health treatment.

SEPARATION/SOCIAL ISOLATION

Unlike immigrants, refugees did not choose to come to the United States; they had no choice but to come, or else they would die (by being tortured, worked, or starved to death). Not surprisingly, one study found homesickness to be a problem for these somewhat reluctant arrivals: 75% of the Cambodians, 83% of the Chinese-Vietnamese, 86% of the Hmong and 91% of the Vietnamese reported feeling homesick (Moon & Tashima, 1982). Similarly, another study of 285 Southeast Asians found that homesickness was a problem for 80% (L. Nguyen & Henkin, 1983).

Refugees are separated from their familiar surroundings and from the possessions that they had to abandon when they fled. Not living in their native countries can be a bigger problem for Southeast Asians than for most Americans because Cambodians, for example, believe that their reincarnation can be adversely affected if they no longer live in Cambodia (Boehnlein, 1987). Other Southeast Asians are concerned that when they die, they will be buried next to Americans in an American cemetery—and, therefore, that there would be no one with whom they could talk (Kroll, 1982).

Refugees frequently have been separated from family members and friends who died or were taken away by military forces and never seen again, or they were sent to different forced-labor camps and made their way to different refugee camps, or they were assigned sponsors in different U.S. cities (E. Lee, 1988; K-M. Lin, 1986; Williams & Westermeyer, 1983). Many Southeast Asian refugees in the United States have family members who never left Southeast Asia; and the refugees may not know if their family members are safe or alive—or, if they are alive, where they are. Refugees have reported that the last time they heard from or saw their fathers was 15 years ago, when their fathers were in labor camps.

A number of studies have confirmed this estrangement. For

example, between 50% and 88% of one study's sample of Southeast Asians was separated from family members (S. Nguyen, 1982). Another study found that of Cambodians requesting disability benefits for blindness, 90% had lost at least one close family member and 79% lost from several to all of their extended family and close friends (Rozée & Van Boemel, 1989). Separation from the family is more of a problem for Cambodians than for Lao or Hmong (Jones & Strand, 1986, see Table 7.3). A study of nearly 40,000 Southeast Asians revealed that 5% of the Vietnamese, 21% of the Chinese, and almost 30% of the Hmong had lost contact with family members in Southeast Asia but that almost 80% of the Cambodians had lost contact with some family members in Cambodia (Rumbaut, 1985). Roughly 40% of all the refugees reported that one or two of their family members died while trying to flee Southeast Asia.

Because they are separated from their families and their homelands, many Southeast Asians are lonely. Loneliness was a problem for 77% of the Vietnamese in one study (Moon & Tashima, 1982) and for 55% of the Southeast Asians in another study (L. Nguyen & Henkin, 1983). Anger and guilt about what they have experienced can cause refugees to displace or project their anger and guilt on to other people (K-M. Lin, 1986), and this projection can compound the social isolation that these refugees feel.

As a result of this separation from their families, many Southeast Asian refugees in the United States are also without their social-support systems. The support system that they customarily relied on (i.e., the extended family, spiritual leaders, and herbal practitioners) might not be near where the refugees live, and little that is culturally appropriate exists in its place in the United States (J. Wong, 1980). The U.S. government compounded the problem with its dispersal program. Southeast Asian refugees are left in a quandary: Integration with and emotional support from American society is not coming quickly, and many refugees feel isolated from American society; yet some fear that a reliance on other Southeast Asians for support, security, a sense of belonging, and a positive sense of identity can result in further rejection by the larger American society (Lin, 1986; Zaharlick & Brainard, 1987).

A fear of antagonism from Americans, a distrust of Americans because of experiences with American military forces and the unkept promises of the U.S. government (D. Le, 1983), and a belief among some Southeast Asians that Americans are cannibals discourage some Southeast Asians from associating with Americans. This reluctance or fear can, in turn, lead to more social isolation and, undoubtedly, more stress (E. Lee, 1988).

AMBIVALENCE/ANTAGONISM FROM OTHERS

Another source of stress for Southeast Asians in the United States is the ambivalence or outright hostility some Americans feel toward Asians in general and Vietnamese in particular (Starr & Roberts, 1981, 1982). This antagonism can be rooted in racism, economic competition, negative sentiments about the Vietnam War, or xenophobic reactions to the Southeast Asians' lack of familiarity with American customs and language. Some examples of negative comments about refugees are, "I don't like the idea of them living in close surroundings with normal people" (Starr & Roberts, 1982, p. 174), "Why help our enemy, these Viet Cong . . . ?" (Starr & Roberts, 1982, p. 174), and "Taking these people is just a waste of taxpayers money. All these government programs penalize people who work and make it" (Starr & Roberts, 1982, p. 182). Acceptance of refugees seems to have been especially slow in rural America where newcomers of any background are accepted slowly, where there is little cultural heterogeneity, where there have been no previously resettled Southeast Asians, and where there are limited resources (Ballard, 1985). Because of this real and perceived rejection by some Americans, the self-esteem of refugees is lowered (Nicassio, 1985), and the sense of vulnerability and fear is raised.

CULTURE SHOCK

As mentioned earlier, any change in a person's life can be experienced as stress. Southeast Asian refugees have experienced many changes in their lives. For example, one study reported that Southeast Asian refugees in 1975 experienced a fourfold increase in changes in their lives (as measured by the well-established Holmes and Rahe Social Readjustment Rating Scale) compared to the 3 years before they emigrated (K-M. Lin, Masuda, & Tazuma, 1982).

One of the principle changes in the lives of Southeast Asian refugees is in cultural environment. The task of adjusting to a new culture is a major source of stress for Southeast Asians. Refugees from Southeast Asia are living in an American society whose norms and values often contradict the norms and values that they learned in Southeast Asia (Williams & Westermeyer, 1983). American behavior patterns frequently do not make sense to Southeast Asians, and some feel uncertain that they will ever understand American culture (Bemak, 1989). They often do not speak or read English well. In fact, a lack of proficiency in English is among the four most pressing problems reported by Vietnamese, Cambodian, Lao, and Hmong refugees (Jones

& Strand, 1986). Compounding the difficulty in learning English is the fact that there are also large differences in educational level among Southeast Asian refugees: A lack of education—and, perhaps, illiteracy in their native language—can make learning English especially difficult. Table 7.1 presents the results of two studies demonstrating difficulties with English for different refugee groups.

An illiterate Hmong from a rural background has described the stress that arises from a lack of proficiency in English.

> I'm so worried that I am a dumb/ignorant person who came to live in [the United States] and still didn't get a word of English. . . . It remains in the heart always for every single day. . . . None of these problems (language, jobs, etc.) can be solved unless there is no me on this earth. I don't think [these problems] can be solved if my life is not ended, because not the problems came to me, but I am the one who cause to have the problems. . . . No one would feel in need of a dumb person like me now. Nothing I can help anyone with. . . . Don't know the language, have no knowledge how to help others, I even can't drive. . . . So I really feel helpless. (Rumbaut, 1985, p. 473)

Another source of stress arising from culture shock is the fear among Southeast Asians that they will embarrass themselves by not behaving in accordance with American norms (Kroll, 1982; K-M. Lin, 1986). For example, because two men holding hands does not indicate homosexuality where they come from, recent arrivals might be embarrassed to learn that this behavior signifies something different in the United States (Kroll, 1982). They might also be embarrassed when they do not know the purpose of various household materials such as refrigerators or blankets and sheets (Kroll, 1982) or when they do not know how to pay bills (Bemak, 1989) or use public transportation.

A lack of awareness of their rights and obligations in American society (D. Le, 1983) and the functions of government agencies can also lead to misunderstandings, confusion, and insecurity among Southeast Asian refugees. For example, many Southeast Asians have distorted impressions of what constitutes legal police behavior (Kroll, 1982) or how the court system works. As a result, they may misinterpret the release of criminal suspects on bail as evidence that the courts have been bribed. In addition, based on their experiences with governments in Southeast Asia and with the failure of the U.S. government to fulfill all of its promises while they were in Southeast Asia, some are suspicious of government agencies that try to help them. Exacerbating their culture shock and their difficulties in coping with grief is the refugees' inability to perform culturally prescribed rituals not only

TABLE 7.1. Differences in English Proficiency Among Southeast Asian
Refugee Groups

	Problems with lack of English proficiency	Percentage literate in English
Cambodians	77%	28%
Chinese-Vietnamese	90%	53%
Hmong	90%	34%
Lao	—	49%
Vietnamese	79%	70%

Note. Percentages in the first column are from Moon and Tashima (1982) and percentages in the second column are from Gong-Guy (1987).

because in fleeing they did not have time to bury their dead family members and compatriots (and Buddhist monks who could perform the rituals were killed), but also because they were separated from their family and from their homeland (Kinzie, 1989). The inability to venerate ancestors who are buried in Asia causes concerns (Kroll, 1982) because it is believed that failing to perform traditional funeral rituals can cause spirits to generate bad events for the family (Boehnlein, 1987).

Most Southeast Asians came as refugees fleeing for their lives. As they struggle to survive and adjust to the United States, many Southeast Asians regret ever coming. At the same time, though, they recognize that they could not have stayed in Southeast Asia or in the refugee camps.

A Khmer woman in her mid-40s summarized her life:

> I lost my husband, I lost my country, I lost every property/fortune we owned. After coming over here, I can't learn to speak English and the way of life here is different; my mother and oldest son are very sick; I feel crippled, I can do nothing. I can't control what's going on. I don't know what I'm going to do once my public assistance expires. I may feel safe in a way—there is no war here, no communist to kill or to torture you—but deep down inside me, I still don't feel safe or secure. I feel scared. (Rumbaut, 1985, p. 475)

FINANCIAL PROBLEMS

A lack of money is the number one problem for Hmong and Vietnamese refugees (Jones & Strand, 1986). Of those whose first year in the United States was fiscal year 1991, about 45% of Vietnamese, 44% of Laotians, and almost 100% of Cambodians depended on welfare (N. Le, 1993).[3]

The adverse effects of poverty are not limited to adults: When children perceive economic problems in the family, there are adverse emotional and behavioral effects for the children (Takeuchi, Williams, & Adair, 1991). Sometimes Southeast Asian children have to help their parents earn a living. For instance, young children of Southeast Asian seamstresses, who are paid on a piecework basis, sometimes have to help their mothers with the work that the mothers bring home. The children, of course, are not paid and still have to keep up with their schoolwork.

Southeast Asian refugees frequently have low incomes because they are unemployed. This unemployment is often due to a lack of formal education, difficulties with English, and a lack of jobs skills that are of use in the American economy. Unemployment among Southeast Asians for the first few months after settling in the United States has been almost 90%, and after more than three years in the United States, about one third are still unemployed (Caplan, Whitmore, & Bui, 1985). Research has found unemployment to be a problem for 68% of the Cambodians and 85% of the Chinese-Vietnamese who were studied, and finances in general were found to be a problem for 97% of the Hmong studied (Moon & Tashima, 1982). Gong-Guy (1987) conducted a survey of 2,773 Southeast Asians between 18 and 64 years of age in California. Her results, which exemplify the nature of the economic problems, are shown in Table 7.2.

Table 7.3, based on Jones and Strand's (1986) study, also shows interethnic differences in how difficulties in finding work compare with other problems faced. The table shows that a lack of help in finding jobs and a lack of job skills are relatively more pressing problems for Lao and Hmong than for Vietnamese and Cambodians (Jones & Strand, 1986): This is not surprising since the Lao and Hmong were less likely than, for example, Vietnamese to bring to the United States urban job skills appropriate to the American economy. It is also

---

[3]Obtaining welfare also presents difficulties because of some refugees' inability to read English notices about what welfare is available, their lack of knowledge about how to apply for assistance, and their lack of familiarity with some of the documents that they need in order to receive welfare (General Accounting Office, 1990). In addition, refugees are sometimes hesitant to ask for welfare because they distrust governments, consider welfare disgraceful, or are afraid that accepting welfare "will jeopardize . . . their . . . ability to sponsor the immigration of additional family members" (General Accounting Office, 1990, p. 45).

TABLE 7.2. Difficulties of Southeast Asian Refugees

	Average family income	Percentage completely dependent on public assistance	Percentage who have experienced death of close family members
Cambodians	$11,698	79.3%	63.2%
Chinese-Vietnamese	$14,392	76.3%	6.9%
Hmong	$ 9,000	81.1%	18.2%
Lao	$15,500	81.1%	13.4%
Vietnamese	$15,000	49.7%	16.5%

Note. Data are from Gong-Guy (1987).

not surprising that the Cambodians rated job difficulties as less pressing than did Lao and Hmong because the Cambodians, having experienced so much trauma, rated other issues, directly related to their traumas, as more pressing problems.

In fact, unemployment and low income are related to the traumas experienced by Cambodians: Using Gong-Guy's data, researchers have found that traumatic experiences among Cambodians predicted their employment status and income in the United States years after the traumatic experiences, apparently independently of the effects of psychopathology (Uba & Chung, 1991). Evidently, dealing with their traumatic past impedes the economic advancement of Cambodians.

Sometimes refugees are dissatisfied with their jobs for the same reasons that immigrants are (L. Nguyen & Henkin, 1983): They frequently have jobs that are very different from the jobs they had in Asia; the jobs involve menial labor with little compensation and have lower status than the jobs the refugees had in Asia (Kelly, 1986; K-M. Lin, 1986). The psychological consequences for refugees are much the same as they are for the immigrants discussed earlier: Lowered self-esteem (Nicassio, 1985) and increased stress (K-M. Lin, 1986) are produced as a consequence of the loss of the refugees' former social status and the discrepancy between their self-concept and their actual social position. In addition, a loss of self-respect and a disorganization of identity can be engendered when the refugees find that their existing knowledge and skills are not adequate to meet their needs in the United States (Mortland & Ledgerwood, 1987). These financial difficulties have been exacerbated by the inflated, unrealistic expectations of many Southeast Asians about how good life would be in the United States.

TABLE 7.3. Rank Order of Problems Among Different Southeast Asian Refugee Groups

Cambodians	*Hmong*
War memories	Insufficient funds
Separation from family	Lack of job skills
Difficulties with English	Difficulties with English/lack
Difficulties with American agencies	of help finding a job (tied for third)
Lack of job skills	Difficulties with American agencies
Lack of help finding a job	Separation from family
Understanding American life	Lack of child care
Transportation problems	Transportation problems
Insufficient funds	Problems understanding American life
Lack of child care	War memories
Laotian	*Vietnamese*
Difficulties with English	Insufficient funds
Lack of job skills	Separation from family
Lack of help finding job	War memories
Insufficient funds	Difficulties with English
Separation from family	Lack of help finding job
Transportation problems	Lack of job skills
Problems understanding American life	Lack of child care
Difficulties with American agencies	Transportation problems
Lack of child care	Problems understanding American life
War memories	Difficulties with American agencies

Note. Adapted from Jones and Strand (1986). Copyright 1986 by Woodrow Jones, Jr., and Paul J. Strand. Adapted by permission.

HEALTH PROBLEMS

Health problems also create stress for Southeast Asians (Mollica, Wyshak, & Lavelle, 1987). Many of the health problems arise from inadequate nutrition, a lack of health care, and wounds sustained in Southeast Asia during the wars, while trying to escape, or from torture. Indeed, the traumas experienced by Cambodian refugees were related to their physical health years later in the United States (Uba & Chung, 1991). Health problems have also arisen from psychosocial stressors (E. Lee, 1988), poor nutrition, poor sanitation, and inadequate health care during the war years in Southeast Asia, in the refugee camps, and even in the United States.

Many Southeast Asians have not received effective health care in the United States because of their cultural beliefs about the sources and treatment of physical maladies, because of their fear of Western medicine, and because of a lack of health insurance, which often has not been included with their minimum-wage jobs (Uba, 1992). As a result, there is a high incidence of tuberculosis, hepatitis, malnutrition, malaria, intestinal parasites, and so forth among Southeast Asian refugees (General Accounting Office, 1990; Lin-Fu, 1988; Peters, Hershfield, Fish, & Manfreda, 1987; Sokoloff, Carlin, & Pham, 1984; Stehr-Green & Schantz, 1986). These illnesses can be sources of stress and can exacerbate the effects of other stressors facing Southeast Asian refugees. In addition, exposure to viral encephalitis or cerebral malaria coupled with inadequate or delayed treatment could cause intellectual deficits in some Southeast Asians who are already facing intellectually trying circumstances in the United States (Williams & Westermeyer, 1983). Compounding these problems is the lack of health care available to poor Asian Americans who need bilingual services: Of more than 400 federally funded community health centers, only eight provide comprehensive, primary care to such Asian Americans (Guillermo, 1993).

INTERGENERATIONAL CONFLICTS

Intergenerational conflicts also are stressors for Southeast Asians (S. Nguyen, 1982). In Southeast Asia, age confers status. But elderly Southeast Asians find that in the United States being old makes it more difficult to learn English and American ways. Younger members of the family generally assimilate more quickly than elder members do. Thus, the former are assigned roles with more power than they would ordinarily have. For example, younger family members might be called upon to mediate problems and misunderstandings that the parents have with non-family members. But this elevation of the children's role can generate tension within the family. Elderly Southeast Asians who feel that their authority is diminishing might displace their anxiety onto their families and become autocratic toward them (Timberlake & Cook, 1984).

When adolescents are forced to adopt the role of an adult in the family (E. Lee, 1988) (1) because their parents are still in Southeast Asia or have died, (2) because their parents have been so traumatized that they cannot function effectively, or (3) because the parents have not acculturated as quickly as the adolescents have, the role reversal can make the children feel insecure and confused (D. Le, 1983) and can make the parents feel despondent. By being thrust into adult roles while their American peers lead relatively insouciant lives, some Southeast Asian adolescents develop a sense of competence and importance (L. N. Huang, 1989), whereas others feel anger and resentment toward their parents (E. Lee, 1988) and estrangement from American peers (E. Lee, 1988). The adolescents may see their parents as poor role models and even as pitiful sources of shame because of the parents' poor English skills, low socioeconomic status, and ignorance of American culture (E. Lee, 1988). When the Southeast Asian adolescents detect their parents' self-doubts and self-hatred, they may blame or pity their parents ("Mental health," 1985), or they may feel a need to do something to help their parents overcome their helplessness and sorrow (E. Lee, 1988; Nidorf, 1985). Thus, confusion, resentment, anger, and frustration can grow from intergenerational conflicts concerning the social roles and expectations that family members have of each other (K-M. Lin, 1986).

Intergenerational conflict can also arise from the traumas experienced. Parents who have had to cope with many traumas might not be sympathetic if their children have relatively minor difficulties with school, friends, or the like. Instead, the parents may minimize the children's problems as being insignificant compared to what the parents have experienced.

Given the presence of all of the stressors faced by Southeast Asians, it is not surprising that in one study it was found that 72% of the 285 Southeast Asian heads of households were worried about the future and 40% were sad most of the time (S. Nguyen & Henkin, 1983).

SOURCES OF STRESS FOR CHILDREN

Traumas Experienced

Southeast Asian adults are not the only ones who have experienced traumas and adjustment problems. About half of the Southeast Asian refugees are children or adolescents (E. Lee, 1988). Many of the refugees were born and raised while their country was at war; therefore, war was the only reality that they knew before coming to the United States (D. Le, 1983). Thus, their feelings, behaviors, and personalities developed to some extent in the context of war, trauma, and starvation.

Among the traumas experienced by children were torture and rape by pirates and soldiers. They also often helplessly witnessed the starvation, execution, rape, and torture of family members (Nidorf, 1985). These traumas have made Southeast Asian refugee children aware of dangers in life that most people never know. This awareness of the possible dangers in life is compounded by their awareness that adults may not be able to protect them. Although the effect of these circumstances on personality development have not been studied empirically, the experiences of clinical psychologists have suggested possible effects: Adolescent females who experienced physical and sexual assaults by the pirates might become suicidal, withdrawn, celibate, or promiscuous, while adolescent males experiencing the same traumas might become anxious, impotent, or apathetic (Nidorf, 1985). It has been posited (L. N. Huang, 1989) that all of the uncontrollable traumas that were experienced by the refugees could cause these individuals to adopt the role of victim in other situations, develop a poor self-concept, and become very passive.

Nidorf (1985) recalled the story of Thu, a 12-year-old Vietnamese girl, who fled Vietnam with her parents and seven siblings. At the beginning of the escape, her father told her that they were just going to visit relatives. During the escape the family was separated and only she, her father, and one developmentally delayed brother made it to the United States.

> It was at sea that she awakened to the reality that she would probably never see her [beloved] mother again. Thai pirates attacked the boat, but spared Thu. Nevertheless, she blamed her father for his inability to protect her from this experience, and for having lied to her about their destination and the inevitable separation from her mother. On the boat she became enraged with him and she has never trusted him fully since. Sometimes now she invents stories to outsiders about his deficiencies, as a means to humiliate him. Her longing for her mother has been sharpened by a nagging sense of shame that she and her incompetent father and imperfect brother have made it to the land of freedom while her capable and cherished mother languishes at home without food or money. (Nidorf, 1985, p. 404)

Education

Despite the impression the popular media gives of the academic success of select Southeast Asians, many Southeast Asians have problems with school. Refugee children and adolescents have academic and social problems because of language difficulties, an absence of schooling while in Southeast Asia, and a lack of familiarity with American customs. They have to adjust to a new school system even though they may have never gone to school before or, because of the disruptions in Southeast Asia, may not have gone to school for years. Because of media stereotypes, Southeast Asians might be expected to learn English immediately (Williams & Westermeyer, 1983) and excel academically. Those Southeast Asians who cannot learn so quickly are placed under particular stress. Additionally, a study in Canada demonstrated that members of the older Vietnamese generations transfer their aspirations to members of the younger generation

(Woon, 1986), and this transfer compounds the pressure on the younger generation.

An illustration of what can happen when an adolescent is unable to succeed academically and meet the expectations of a parent is the case (cited by Nidorf, 1985) of Tam, a Vietnamese 16-year-old who was living with his uncle while his immediate family remained in Southeast Asia.

> His inability to meet his mother's expectations evoked feelings of anxiety and frustration. In despair, Tam dropped out of school and lost himself in television, believing if he could just absorb popular culture in appearance and manner, as taught by television, he would still have a chance to "make it" and bring honor to his mother. He began to affiliate with other dropouts, confusing their "hip" flashiness with success and adjustment. Enraged, his uncle requested him to leave his home. To support himself, Tam started doing petty theft. (Nidorf, 1985, p. 402)

According to the U.S. Commission on Civil Rights (1992), refugee children sometimes are placed in classes for those with learning disabilities so that academic failures can be attributed to personal characteristics of the children. It cited the case of Hmong students in California who were tested in English by a school psychologist even though the children did not understand English. The superior performance of these students in such areas as art and mathematics (which did not require English proficiency) was ignored, and the students were labeled "handicapped." With this label, some of the children "have stopped trying to learn and have accepted and internalized their 'disabilities' as their own personal attributes. . . . [Meanwhile the students' teachers and peers consider the children] academically incompetent because they have an inferior intelligence or an inferior culture" (U.S. Commission on Civil Rights, 1992, p. 80).

Social Relationships

Due to the racism, xenophobia, and their own or their classmates' insecurity, Southeast Asian youth may have difficulties with their classmates. A study of 51 nonclinical Southeast Asian refugee children has revealed that almost one third of the respondents said that fighting with schoolmates was a significant problem (L. N. Huang, 1989). This fighting was most frequently cited as the worst problem that refugee children have to face.

Another significant problem for refugee children, second only to fighting in the frequency it was cited, was social interactions with peers. This problem most likely is a result, on the one hand, of the racism and intolerance directed against the refugee children by their American peers and, on the other, of the refugee children's own difficulties learning American communication styles and interpersonal styles (Goldstein, 1988). In addition, because a child may lack formal education or because a child's officially listed age may not be correct, children are sometimes placed in classes with younger children. This placement can hurt the self-esteem of the child and can create social difficulties owing to the age discrepancy.

Compounding the stress associated with acculturation to American life is the treatment that refugees may receive from earlier arrivals, who sometimes look down upon or avoid the refugees who arrived later (Nidorf, 1985). Differences between the former and the latter are exacerbated by differences in their background in Vietnam, by their socioeconomic status in the United States, and by the desire of some refugees who arrived earlier to dissociate themselves from refugees who arrived later because the former do not want other Americans to associate them with the later arrivals and thereby ignore their own hard-earned acculturation (Matsuoka, 1991).

Identity

Refugee adolescents could face an especially acute identity crisis. The loss of their old culture, the seeming irrelevance or frequent failure of their old culture to help them adjust to life in the United States, and their failure to be completely identified with American culture have exacerbated the normal identity conflicts that arise for other adolescents (E. Lee, 1988).

Lack of Support

Many Southeast Asian children and adolescents need help in adjusting to the stressors that they are facing, but their parents are not able to help them because they are having their own difficulties dealing with traumatic experiences, losses, and current survival needs. Fathers, in particular, are often overburdened with guilt because they were not able to protect their families from the traumas encountered in Southeast Asia, or they are acutely stressed because they are not able to fulfill obligations either to family members whom they might have left in Southeast Asia or to their children in the United States (E. Lee, 1988). These parents might not be aware of the difficulties faced by their children and may not have the time or emotional resources to help their children adapt (D. Le, 1983; Williams & Westermeyer, 1983).

Unaccompanied Minors

Among the Southeast Asians who fled to the United States were children who came without families. These so-called unaccompanied minors have constituted 1% of the Southeast Asian refugees (Baker, 1982). On occasion, a Southeast Asian child has come to the United States because he or she had been separated from his or her family by the action of a Southeast Asian government or by some accident that took place before or during the escape. Sometimes Vietnamese, Cambodian, or Laotian families intentionally sent a child alone to the United States (Bromley, 1988): The families could not afford to pay for the whole family to leave Southeast Asia but wanted their child to have a better life than the child could be expected to have in Southeast Asia. Families hoped that the child would eventually be able to arrange for the family to join him or her (usually him) in the United States. On other occasions, the child's parents died in Southeast Asia, and the child escaped to a refugee camp with another family. That family would then turn the child over to authorities in the refugee camp when they discovered that smaller families were sponsored more quickly than larger families (L. N. Huang, 1989). The prolonged stays of unaccompanied minors in refugee camps has exacerbated their psychological vulnerability (L. N. Huang, 1989).

Unaccompanied minors face a number of stressors not typically experienced by other Americans or by other Southeast Asian children. Frequently, these minors went through many of the traumas experienced by other Southeast Asian refugees (Bromley, 1988) but without their parents there to help them. In the United States unaccompanied minors often live with elder siblings or distant relatives who do not provide the guidance, nurturing, and attention that the minors need (Chung & Okazaki, 1991; Nidorf, 1985). Distant relatives may consider the care of the minor to be an onerous familial duty or a chance to accrue additional money from welfare agencies (Chung & Okazaki, 1991).

Unaccompanied Southeast Asian minors are usually very aware of the sacrifices that their families have made for them (Nidorf, 1985). These minors often feel guilty about surviving (Baker, 1982), and they often feel responsible for and obligated to their parents in Southeast Asia. A major preoccupation of these minors is to send money and medical supplies to their families in Southeast Asia and eventually to sponsor their parents to come to the United States (Nidorf, 1985). The minors are afraid to disappoint their families (Nidorf, 1985) and are overcome with a sense of failure when they are unable to arrange for their families to join them in the United States (Baker, 1982).

At the same time, many unaccompanied minors feel depressed, agitated, lonely, homesick, rootless, humiliated, outcast, abandoned, unloved, and unprotected (L. N. Huang, 1989; E. Lee, 1988; Nidorf, 1985; Williams & Westermeyer, 1983). They may resent their parents or the world for their situation while longing for nurturing from their parents (Nidorf, 1985). Some will engage in antisocial behavior and join gangs to gain a sense of family and identity (Nidorf, 1985).

A number of problems have arisen with the sponsoring or foster families. On occasion, unaccompanied minors have reportedly been sexually molested by their American sponsors and foster families because the latter were not adequately screened (Williams & Westermeyer, 1983). Sometimes unaccompanied minors balk at accepting their foster family because they feel that by doing so they would be disloyal to their family in Southeast Asia (Baker, 1982). They sometimes displace their anger toward life and toward their biological parents on to their foster parents (L. N. Huang, 1989). Some of the minors have power struggles with their foster parents: Unaccompanied minors often had to learn to take care of themselves in the refugee camps but find that their foster parents usurp many of those responsibilities and roles (Bromley, 1988). Confused about why foster families take care of them (Baker, 1982), some minors think that since the foster family receives financial support to take care of them, they are in the position to give orders to the foster family. Other minors see themselves as "charity cases"; therefore, they feel ashamed and try to prove that they can take care of themselves. Still others, unaccustomed to doing household chores (Redick & Wood, 1982), think they are being used like slaves when the foster family delegates chores to them (Baker, 1982). When foster families do not understand Southeast Asian cultures, the successful adaptation of unaccompanied minors can be undermined. Those unaccompanied adolescents placed in ethnic foster families tend to be less depressed and more academically successful than those placed in Euro-American foster families (Union of Pan Asian Communities, 1978).

In addition to these problems, unaccompanied minors frequently are confused and anxious about what will happen to them in the United States (Baker, 1982). They often have difficulty understanding life in America and making friends; feel isolated, unliked, and pessimistic about their future in the United States; feel their Southeast Asian culture is useless in the United States; and struggle with feeling different (Bromley, 1988). Some try to hide their feelings of uncertainty, isolation, and shame "through exaggerated modeling of American teenage behaviors, for at least this way they will have an 'identity' with a clearly recognized subculture" (Nidorf, 1985, p. 414).

INTERGROUP AND INTRAGROUP DIFFERENCES

Heretofore, the discussion has focused on problems shared by various Southeast Asian refugee groups. But different Southeast Asian refugee groups are likely to experience these problems in varying degrees. Vietnamese, Cambodians, Lao, and Hmong rank the same problems in different orders of importance (Jones & Strand, 1986), as is shown in Table 7.3.

Furthermore, the amount of adjustment required varies among Southeast Asian ethnic groups because of their different educational backgrounds, exposure to Western ways while in their native countries, fluency in English before coming to the United States, job skills, traumas experienced, and so on. The amount of adjustment required also varies within Southeast Asian groups. For example, a study in Canada found that the adjustment of Vietnamese and Chinese-Vietnamese from northern and southern Vietnam begins at different starting points (Woon, 1986). That is, the attitudes and skills that members of these ethnic groups bring to the task of adjusting are not the same. Chinese-Vietnamese from southern Vietnam are more willing to adjust to Canada's norms than either their counterparts from northern Vietnam or ethnic Vietnamese. Vietnamese and Chinese-Vietnamese from northern Vietnam had less exposure to Western ways than Chinese-Vietnamese from southern Vietnam and, thus, are less fluent in English. They have to depend more on their children to deal with life in Canada than Chinese-Vietnamese from southern Vietnam do. Chinese-Vietnamese who were middle class in Vietnam face different stressors than are faced by those who were from the lower class in Vietnam: The former have suffered more downward mobility than the latter have, and Chinese from southern Vietnam have suffered more downward mobility than ethnic Vietnamese have. Chinese-Vietnamese from northern Vietnam have much higher levels of intergenerational conflict than are experienced by Chinese-Vietnamese from southern Vietnam. Thus, there is variation in the amount and type of adjustment that Vietnamese and Chinese-Vietnamese have to make in America.

CONCLUSION

This and the previous chapter have offered evidence that Asian Americans encounter many sources of stress that are not experienced by other Americans. The common sources of this stress, as has been shown, are quite significant.

While objectively many Asian Americans share these sources of stress, they do not all respond in the same way. The effects of these stressors vary because of external factors (such as the social-support systems available, the presence of racism, and social-class differences) and internal factors (such as the way in which situations are perceived, personality characteristics, temperament, coping methods learned, learning history, and intelligence). There is a need to study the factors that can mediate stress in Asian Americans. Unfortunately, little of the research on the stress faced by Asian Americans has included a theoretical conceptualization of the factors that mediate the relationship between stressors and adjustment. Because there is usually only a moderate relationship between stressors and psychological problems, intervening variables should be examined (Nicassio, 1985). The role of social-support systems in the prevention of mental disorders among Asian Americans has been barely touched. In fact, there has been very little research on the prevention of mental disorders among Asian Americans in general.

8

Psychopathology in the "Model Minority"

As previously mentioned, Asian Americans have been depicted as a model minority. Implicit in this stereotype is the notion that they do not have many problems. The last two chapters have provided evidence refuting that idea. Also implicit in the model minority stereotype is the notion that even when Asian Americans do have problems, they effectively deal with those problems. There is a belief that close-knit Asian American families and ethnic communities quietly and effectively prevent psychosocial stressors from leading to the development of mental disorders. In an attempt to expose the erroneousness of this aspect of the stereotype, this chapter looks at (1) rates of mental disorders among Asian Americans and the difficulties in assessing these rates, (2) interethnic and intraethnic differences in rates of psychopathology, (3) predictors of mental disorders among Asian Americans, and (4) types of mental disorders commonly found among Asian Americans.

RATES OF PSYCHOPATHOLOGY

Rates of psychopathology among Asian Americans are usually compared to rates among Euro-Americans. Information on the rates of psychopathology customarily come from three sources: subjective reports of psychological distress (i.e., the responses of people to diagnostic questionnaires), rates at which mental health services are sought, and clinical diagnoses of psychopathology. These methods of

158

assessing rates of mental disorder among Asian Americans can produce misleading results. Before reviewing the research on the purported rates of psychopathology among Asian Americans it is necessary to examine the ways in which estimations of these rates can be tenuous.

Assessing Psychopathology Rates

There are many difficulties in assessing the rates of mental disorder among Asian Americans. First, in both clinical and nonclinical populations, assessing rates of psychopathology by relying on subjective, self-reports of mental disturbance can produce biased results because in different cultures people have different criteria for what constitutes troubling behavior, and they have different ideas about which problems are psychologically based. That is, insofar as sociocultural factors define what is mental health or mental illness (Eisenbruch, 1991), what is judged to be maladaptive behavior in one culture might not be maladaptive in another (Marsella, Kinzie & Gordon, 1973). Inasmuch as Asian Americans and non-Asian Americans sometimes use different standards for judging whether a behavior is problematical or indicates psychological disturbance (as is demonstrated in the next chapter), comparisons between groups in subjective reports of psychological dysfunction might not be based on truly comparable grounds. For instance, some people might regard a behavior as a reflection of family cohesiveness while others might regard the same behavior as a reflection of overdependence on the family. Assessing rates of psychopathology by relying on the subjective perceptions of the friends and family of the potential client might not be reliable or valid either because they, too, would have cultural biases in their criteria for judging psychopathology.

Furthermore, in the case of some mental disorders, the people who have these disorders do not know that they have them; using subjective, self-reports to compare rates of psychopathology between groups could be biased *if* there are differences between the groups in the incidence of such mental disorders. For example, paranoid schizophrenics with delusions of persecution will mistakenly report that they do not have a mental disturbance because they believe their delusions and think that the problem lies in other people who are supposedly spying on them, trying to poison them, and so forth. If Asian Americans and non-Asian Americans do not have the same incidence of paranoid schizophrenia, the group that has a higher rate of paranoid schizophrenia might have its overall rate of psychopathology underestimated since the paranoid schizophrenics might not report that they have any mental disorder.

Second, judging rates of psychopathology based on the rates at which groups seek mental health services can be very misleading because Euro-Americans and Asian Americans who have the same underlying psychopathology may seek services at different rates. Some people might be anxious and seek help for those feelings, while others might be equally anxious but not see it as a condition noteworthy enough to report. In addition, this approach includes those who are receiving psychological services but who do not have any psychopathology (S. Sue & Morishima, 1982). For example, just as there are people who are in poor health (because of inadequate diet or lack of physical exercise) but have no diseases, likewise there are people who have low self-esteem and see therapists but have no mental disorders (S. Sue & Morishima, 1982). Assessing psychopathology rates simply by counting how many people go to therapists assumes that all of those receiving therapy have mental disorders—but this is not the case.

This approach also presumes that those with mental disorders will seek mental health services rather than other kinds of services. In the case of Asian Americans, this may not be a valid presumption. For instance, Asian American college students are reportedly more likely to focus on academic and career problems than their Euro-American counterparts, who are more likely to focus on emotional or interpersonal problems (Gim, Atkinson, & Whiteley, 1990; Tracey, Leong, & Glidden, 1986). Not surprisingly, then, Asian American college students tend to use campus vocational and academic counseling centers more than would be expected, based on their proportion of the student population, but use psychiatric services less than would be expected (Tracey et al., 1986). Sometimes Asian Americans invoke academic and vocational problems as a way of opening the discussion to other, more personal problems (D. W. Sue & S. Sue, 1972a; Tracey et al., 1986). But if the rate at which Asian Americans seek mental health services is the only behavior that is assessed, the incidence of psychopathology among Asian Americans will be undercounted.

Third, it is difficult to compare Asian American and non-Asian American rates of specific disorders because Asian American samples are usually small. The small samples make valid statistical analyses difficult. It is especially difficult to assess rates of mental disorder among specific Asian American ethnic groups because of small sample sizes.

Fourth, rates of psychopathology among Asian Americans are sometimes assessed either by identifying what proportion of a nonclinical sample of Asian Americans shows evidence of some psychological disorder or by counting the number of Asian Americans in a clinical sample that have been diagnosed as having a psychological problem. These methods assume that the diagnoses of psychopathology are accurate. But misdiagnoses, arising from culturally biased criteria for expressions of psychopathology, can undermine the validity of the data on which assessments of rates of psychopathology are based. What follows are some bases for misdiagnosis.

Manifestations of Problems

Asian Americans and non-Asian Americans with similar underlying problems frequently define and express their problems differently because of cultural behavior patterns and communication styles. For example, in keeping with evidence that the communication styles of Asian Americans tend to be more indirect than those of Euro-Americans, the problems of Asian Americans could be expressed in a more subtle and indirect way than they are expressed by other Americans. A therapist who is unfamiliar with these patterns of expression may misdiagnose Asian American clients. (A more detailed discussion of this issue appears in Chapter 10.)

There has also been evidence of interethnic differences in the forms that psychopathology takes. A study of Japanese American and Filipino American patients who had the same psychiatric diagnosis demonstrated clear group differences in symptoms: Japanese Americans showed more depression, more withdrawal, more disturbed thinking, and more inhibition, whereas Filipino Americans had more delusions of persecution and more overtly disturbed behavior (Enright & Jaeckle, 1963). Similarly, a factor analysis has shown that Chinese Americans, Japanese Americans, and Euro-Americans differ in which symptoms, complaints, and emotions tend to form syndromes (Marsella et al., 1973). Cross-cultural differences in symptom expression also have been found by others (e.g., Marsella, Sanborn, Kameoka, Shizuru, & Brennan, 1975). It is even possible that there are different types of psychopathology in Asian American cultures (B. P. Dohrenwend & Dohrenwend, 1974). Misdiagnosis can result if the diagnostician has a narrow and rigid way of defining what disorders exist and how they are manifested. Such a misdiagnosis adds spurious results to the data base on which assessments of rates of mental disorders are founded.

The manifestations of mental disorders among Asian Americans might be different from those of non-Asian Americans because, to some extent, sociocultural factors (such as interpersonal styles of relating; philosophical ideas; cultural beliefs, values, and practices; and economic and political circumstances) determine the pattern of personality development and the content of mental disorders (Eisenbruch, 1991; Singer, 1976). For example, "cross-national comparisons by WHO [the World Health Organization] suggest that, despite core features of depression resembling Western criteria, each culture has its own specific depressive symptoms" (Mollica et al., 1992, p. 111).

DSM-IV is the fourth edition of the *Diagnostic and Statistical Manual of Mental Disorders*. Published by the American Psychiatric Association, it is the basic diagnostic guide for psychotherapists. (Appendix A contains a simple, classificatory summary of presumably cross-cultural manifestations of some mental disorders.) This fourth edition marks initial concerted attempts to portray in DSM some of the cultural differences in the manifestations of mental disorders: It indicates that some behaviors, which might have been misinterpreted as psychopathological in the past, may reflect cultural variations (Cynthia Jones, American Psychiatric Association Draft Criteria group member, personal communication). However, since it has been derived primarily from psychotherapy with and research on non-Asian Americans, on occasion DSM-IV may not be as useful for diagnosing psychological problems in Asian Americans as it is for other Americans. There is little information on symptomatic distinctions for Asian Americans in particular. Moreover, since these new guidelines were not provided until 1994, many psychotherapists, unfamiliar with the experiences, behavior, and symptom patterns of Asian Americans and also unfamiliar with the research on this population may not yet be as sophisticated in recognizing the psychological characteristics of Asian Americans as they would like to be. Additional criteria that are relevant to the experiences of Asian Americans are needed in order to obtain reliable diagnoses of Asian Americans.[1]

Symptom Context

Misdiagnoses arise when symptoms and behaviors are not examined in their proper developmental context. Appropriate behavior for a 17-year-old is not the same as appropriate behavior for a 14-year-old. On occasion, young Southeast Asians are older than their official papers indicate. Children and their families in refugee camps sometimes claimed that the children were 2 or 3 years younger than they really were because doing so could give the children higher priority for receiving food and shelter. Maintaining this charade in the

---

[1]Despite these lapses in the cross-cultural sensitivity of DSM-IV, there are cultural, social, and economic pressures on therapists to use it. For example, insurance companies require that therapists use the standard, newest edition of DSM as a basis for their fees.

United States not only meant that the child would be eligible for welfare benefits longer—until he or she would officially reach the age of 18—but also maximized the chances for the child to become educated (Nidorf, 1985). If therapists are not sufficiently knowledgeable of the refugee experience, they may not know that a child's official age may not be his or her actual age. If therapists do not confirm a client's true age, misdiagnosis and age-inappropriate treatment can result.

For instance, there was a case (described by Nidorf, 1985) of a purportedly 11-year-old Laotian who was depressed. He blamed an old scar, from a minor burn, for causing him so much pain that he could not continue to go to school. A medical exam revealed he was actually 16 years old. Becoming more conscious of his appearance because he was well into puberty, his scarring had begun to embarrass him. This teenager wanted to date and felt uncomfortable in a class of 11-year-old children. His parents did not want him to discuss his personal problems because they were afraid their welfare benefits would end once he was no longer officially a minor. If the therapist had regarded him as an 11-year-old, misdiagnosis would have resulted.

Unless behaviors are also judged in their appropriate cultural context, misdiagnosis can result. Western values characteristically stress autonomy, self-determination, and independence. When Western patients do not strive for independence and decision-making, they might be labeled dependent personalities or passive personalities (Carlin & Sokoloff, 1985), a diagnosis which reflects a cultural bias. If some Asian Americans are largely oriented toward their families rather than toward being autonomous, they might merely be reflecting Asian cultural values rather than psychopathology. Western values stress individual expressiveness but, in the context of Southeast Asian values, emotional outbursts by Southeast Asian women could indicate a severe personality disorder (Tung, 1985). To prevent inaccurate assessments of rates of psychopathology, diagnosticians must be able to distinguish psychopathology from cultural variations in beliefs and normative behavior.

Ignorance of the cultural beliefs of some Asian Americans can be a source of misdiagnosis. For example, when a Southeast Asian client talks about seeing or talking with deceased relatives, it could reflect a cultural belief in the supernatural rather than a delusion or psychosis (Tung, 1985). When therapists are ignorant of the fact that in Southeast Asian cultures there is widespread acceptance of the notion that supernatural spirits have rights, needs, and feelings and that these forces intercede into people's lives for ill or good (Egawa & Tashima, 1982), they may erroneously conclude that these clients are delusional.

Only a therapist aware of such beliefs can determine whether a person's ideation is a reflection of culture or a sign of psychopathology. Similarly, some Southeast Asians assume that evil forces underlie psychological problems and will try to exorcise those evil forces through such methods as cupping or coining (Boehnlein, 1987). If therapists are ignorant of these methods, they may misdiagnose the physical bruising that results from cupping or coining as an indication that a child has been beaten by parents.

Yet therapists who indiscriminately apply cultural explanations may, for example, mistakenly think that a quiet Asian American is reserved for cultural reasons or is just not proficient in English, thereby failing to recognize that the client is actually depressed and withdrawn (August & Gianola, 1987). Therapists must "avoid 'over-diagnosing' (i.e., misinterpreting culturally sanctioned behavior as pathological) and 'under-diagnosing' (i.e., attributing psychiatric symptoms to cultural differences)" (K-M. Lin, 1990, p. 199).

Differences between Asian Americans and Euro-Americans in their standards of behavior could be mistaken by therapists as indicating abnormal behavior in Asian Americans. For example, studies (Cochran, Mays, & Leung, 1991; K. Huang & Uba, 1992) have found that fewer Asian American than non-Asian American college students have had sexual experience. To judge the degree of sexual experience that an Asian American adolescent has had as pathological just because it does not mirror a Euro-American norm would be an overdiagnosis. Behaviors sometimes need to be evaluated in the context of the cultural and gender norms of Asian Americans (Fugita & Crittendon, 1990). Unfortunately, the empirical data on behavioral norms among psychologically healthy Asian Americans have been too limited.

Accurately diagnosing psychopathology and assessing rates of psychopathology among Asian Americans also requires that behaviors be judged in their racial context. A therapist who is ignorant or naive about racism directed against Asian Americans might misinterpret as paranoia an Asian American client's recognition of socioeconomic injustice (Minrath, 1985). What appears to be pathological behavior or ideation could, indeed, be pathological, but it could also be an adaptive response to a racist environment (Minrath, 1985). In an individualistic society such as that found in the United States, some therapists have a bias toward seeing the sources of clients' problems as being within the person rather than being within the conditions and constraints of society (D. W. Sue, 1990). This bias is compounded by the "philosophical belief that clients should solve their own problems [and] that they are ultimately responsible for the outcomes in their lives" (D. W. Sue,

1990, p. 430). These biases toward seeing the intrapsychic causes of mental disorders can affect diagnoses and, therefore, the base of data on which assessments of rates of psychopathology are built. On the other hand, viewing clients simply as members of a minority—and overgeneralizing on the basis of their minority status—can interfere with the therapist's ability to recognize intrapsychic sources of psychological problems (Minrath, 1985). Therefore, if the racial context is not accurately perceived, misdiagnosis in one direction or the other can occur, and that misdiagnosis will affect assessments of rates of psychopathology.

Psychological-Testing Instruments

Therapists sometimes use psychological tests to help them understand their clients. But some psychological tests can lend credence to incorrect diagnoses by providing culturally biased pictures of Asian American clients.

When psychological, paper-and-pencil tests are being developed, generally the psychometricians write presumably valid questions; try out the questions on (primarily Euro-American) subjects; rewrite questions to correct any that are ambiguous, unreliable, or invalid; and give the questions to more subjects in order to establish the reliability of the results derived from the test. To establish the validity of the test, the test results will be compared to other measures (again, mostly validated with Euro-American subjects) that purport to address the same construct.[2] For most personality inventories there is no empirical evidence that they are valid for Asian Americans.

Just as there are few normative data on the behaviors of Asian Americans, there often are not data on normative responses of Asian Americans to various tests. For instance, the widely used Minnesota Multiphasic Personality Inventory (MMPI) was standardized on Euro-Americans and does not have norms for different Asian American groups (S. Sue & Morishima, 1982). Studies of other tests have demonstrated that Asian American and Euro-American norms are different: Nonclinical Asian American samples have scores higher than the American norm on the Symptom Check List 90-R (SCL-90-R) (Yamamoto, 1986); Euro-Americans and Asians (in Asian countries and in the United States) differ in their responses to the Zung Self-Rating

---

[2]Psychometricians try to devise tests that are both reliable and valid. A reliable test is one that will produce similar results when the test is retaken. A valid test is one that measures what it purports to measure.

Depression Scale (Fugita & Crittendon, 1990). Therefore, comparing the responses of an Asian American client to Euro-American norms could skew diagnoses of psychopathology. In effect, if such results were accepted on face value, ways in which Asian Americans are different from Euro-Americans would be equated with psychopathology, thereby over-diagnosing psychopathology in Asian Americans.[3] For instance, use of the Family Assessment Device can lead to misinterpretations of some Asian American behaviors as being pathological when actually the behaviors simply reflect cultural differences in family functioning among Asian Americans (Morris, 1990). Culturally sensitive therapists recognize this trap, but of course not all therapists are culturally sensitive to Asian Americans. Researchers and clinicians (e.g., Kinzie et al., 1989) have recognized the need to validate psychological tests and to establish standards based on the responses of nonclinical samples of Asian Americans; nevertheless, they have had to use these measures when there exist no relevant measures that have been validated with Asian Americans.

Some psychological tests are more valid for Asian Americans than other tests. One study (Marsella et al., 1975) comparing the responses of Chinese Americans, Japanese Americans, and Euro-Americans on five self-report measures of depression revealed some variation in the rankings of males and females from the three ethnic groups as a function of the depression measures used. That different tests provided some divergent results with Asian Americans suggests that not all psychological tests are equally valid for Asian Americans.

Some scales have cultural biases that make them invalid for Asian Americans (Young, 1972b). For example, one can imagine the differences in the responses of a sixth-generation Euro-American and a foreign-born Asian American to this statement that appears in the MMPI: "My way of doing things is apt to be misunderstood by others." If two people responded affirmatively to the MMPI statement, "Terrible thoughts about my family come to me at times," one of whom was a Euro-American male living in the suburbs with his family, and the other a traumatized Vietnamese male who saw his father executed, his mother starved to death, and his sister kidnapped by

---

[3]On the other hand, failure to have Asian American norms also can cause pathology to be underdiagnosed. Saeki, Clark, and Azen (1985) compared Japanese American and Euro-American children on a developmental sensory integration test. Japanese American children on average did better than Euro-American children on this test. However, since the norms for the test are based only on Euro-American children, Japanese American children whose performances are not up to Japanese American standards but rather to the standards of Euro-Americans might have undetected perceptual difficulties (Nagata, 1989a).

pirates, then clearly, these affirmative responses cannot have the same meaning. Some questions might not be applicable to Asian American clients or might not make sense to them (D. Le, 1983), especially to Southeast Asian clients who have no experience with such tests (Williams & Westermeyer, 1983): This could detract from the validity of psychological tests on these Asian Americans.

Most psychological tests have not been translated into a number of Asian languages. Administering psychological tests in English to those who are not fluent in English can yield spurious results.

Tests are developed in a way that takes into account response biases. Questions are designed in such a way that, for example, to get a high score the respondent sometimes must agree and sometimes must disagree with the question asked; in that way, a high score would not be an artifact of "response sets" (i.e., the response tendencies people bring to a test). Since most paper-and-pencil psychological tests are developed on primarily Euro-American subjects, psychometricians in effect take into account the response sets of Euro-Americans when developing the tests. But there are differences in the response sets of Asian Americans: Asian Americans respond with neutral or acquiescent answers more than other Americans do (Arkoff, Thaver, & Elkind, 1966).

Furthermore, sometimes when people answer psychological tests, rather than respond in a way that accurately reflects their behavior, they unconsciously choose responses that make them look good. Because psychometricians are interested in the respondents' actual behavior rather than in what the respondents think would sound good, the test-designers try to avoid eliciting this social desirability bias by wording their questions in particular ways. However, most psychological tests are not developed with the social desirability biases of Asian Americans in mind, and different responses might be considered more socially desirable by Asian Americans than by Euro-Americans. In addition, some Asian Americans have response sets to socially desirable test items that are different from the response sets of Euro-Americans. For example, possibly because of Asian cultural values emphasizing modesty, foreign-born Asian Americans are less likely than Euro-Americans to claim that they possess socially desirable traits or to deny that they have socially undesirable traits (Abe & Zane, 1990). These differences in response set call into question the validity of some paper-and-pencil tests.

There also appear to be culturally based differences in response sets to tests that clinicians use to explore their clients' conflicts. The Thematic Apperception Test is such a test. It involves looking at a picture and making up a story about what is seen in the picture.

Presumably, clients unconsciously project their desires and conflicts into their stories. Differences exist in Thematic Apperception Test themes for some Asian Americans compared to Euro-Americans: Chinese Americans more frequently invoke themes dealing with shame and authority figures than others do (J. Chin, 1983). These differences in themes, ideals, and solutions might partially reflect differences between Chinese fairy tales, which frequently emphasize the importance of filial piety and hard work, and Western fairy tales, which frequently emphasize children's aggressive and sexual impulses, on the one hand, and victories over bad people, on the other (J. Chin, 1983).

There might be cultural differences that affect responses to another projective test, the Rorschach Inkblot Test. Rorschach inkblots have been found to be less meaningful for Filipinos than for Euro-Americans (Rabin & Limuaco, 1967). The Chinese value placed on a holistic approach and the differences between Chinese and Westerners regarding the meaning of various colors (e.g., red indicates happiness and prosperity in Chinese culture but danger, aggression, and sexual impulse in American culture) could affect the responses of Chinese Americans to Rorschach Inkblots and how those responses should be interpreted (J. Chin, 1983). This is not to say that such tests are always inappropriate for Asian Americans. For example, when therapists encounter refugees who are uncommunicative or when they want to check on the accuracy of their clinical impressions, projective tests may be used—and have been used successfully—with many Asian Americans, including Vietnamese and Hmong clients (D. Le, 1983).[4] Nevertheless, such culturally based differences in the meaning of responses can lead to misdiagnosis by a therapist who is not knowledgeable about these differences.

Therapists sometimes explore, along with the client, the meaning of the client's dreams. But again, there appear to be some differences in the content of the dreams of Asian Americans and non-Asian Americans. Research comparing nonclinical samples of Asian Ameri-

---

[4]There are other useful clinical tools. For example, traumatized Southeast Asians are sometimes instructed to write their life stories, compose scrapbooks about themselves (Bromley, 1988), draw pictures of their lives (Canda, 1989), or perform dramas, traditional songs, or dances (Canda, 1989). In so doing, they indirectly can reveal their traumatic experiences, reflect on those experiences, express their deep feelings, resolve feelings of guilt and loss, and establish stronger identities (Canda, 1989). Quilting and needlework are traditional Hmong crafts, which are sold to supplement family income (Canda, 1989). Because the crafts frequently depict the refugees' experiences, therapists might discuss the crafts with their clients to learn about the client's personal history and to enable the client to express feelings regarding those experiences (Canda, 1989).

can and non-Asian American female college students has found no difference between the two groups in types of characters, emotions, friendliness, and sexuality expressed in their dream diaries (Tonay, 1991). However, that same study found that Asian American females described more unfamiliar settings in their dreams than non-Asian American women did and were less often aggressors and more often victims of male dream characters than the non-Asian American females were. Dreams of Cambodian women were often found to contain protracted violence, communication with spirits or dead relatives, and messages of impending good or bad luck (Thompson, 1991). These findings suggest that the notions that some therapists have about standard dream content might not constitute valid norms for Asian American females.[5] Apparently, no empirical research has been done either on differences in the content of the dreams of Asian American males and Euro-American males or on gender differences in the dreams of Asian Americans.

Some psychological tests have been translated into Asian languages and have been used successfully with Asian Americans. For example, the Diagnostic Interview Schedule, designed to diagnose posttraumatic stress disorder (PTSD), has been translated into several Asian languages such as Chinese, Japanese, and Korean (E. Lee & Lu, 1989; Yamamoto, 1986) and the SCL 90-R has been translated into Chinese, Japanese, Korean, Tagalog, Vietnamese, and Samoan (Yamamoto, 1982). Moreover, there are data on the responses of non-clinical populations of Chinese, Koreans, and Samoans on the SCL 90-R (Yamamoto, 1986). Other psychological tests that have been found (Yamamoto, 1986) to be useful in diagnosing some Asian Americans are the Psychiatric Status Schedule (which has been translated into Chinese, Japanese, Korean, Tagalog, Vietnamese, and Samoan and also comes in an audio-visual version) and the MMPI (which has been translated into Chinese, Japanese, and Korean). The results of both the Zung Scale for Depression and the SCL-90 distinguish between depressed and non-depressed Hmong (Westermeyer, 1986). In addition, the Zung Depression Scale has been translated into Hmong, Khmer, Lao, and other languages (Yamamoto, 1986). The Lao Depression Inventory has demonstrated its validity (Muskin-Davidson & Golden, 1989).

Many of the refugees who experienced traumas are too emotion-

---

[5]The difficulty in analyzing differences in dream content is compounded by the reluctance of Mien to discuss their dreams. Mien commonly consider dreams to be prophetic and think that neither talking about dreams nor trying to understand them will change the course of events prophesied in the dreams. Thus, Mien may not see any point in discussing their dreams (Moore & Boehnlein, 1991).

ally overwhelmed to articulate directly to the therapist the psychiatric symptoms they are experiencing (Mollica, 1986). Therefore, there is a particularly great need for appropriate psychological tests for these refugees. A diagnostic scale designed to measure panic, depression, somatization, and well- being has been found (Beiser & Fleming, 1986) to have satisfactory to excellent reliability, and the first three measures have demonstrated criterion validity.[6] Because it resembles a medical test, the Hopkins Symptom Checklist 25 (HSCL-25) has been readily accepted by Southeast Asians (Mollica & Lavelle, 1988). Versions of the HSCL-25 have been validated on Cambodians, Lao, and Vietnamese (Mollica, Wyshak, de Marneffe, Khuon, & Lavelle, 1987). The HSCL-25 has been proven effective in detecting symptoms universally associated with anxiety and depression (Mollica et al., 1987). In particular, it has reportedly been very helpful in evaluating Southeast Asians who have suffered traumas: The questionnaire is brief, it is written in simple language that can be understood by people with limited education, and it can be self-administered by literate Southeast Asians (Mollica et al., 1987). While some other diagnostic tests are so comprehensive or so emotionally intrusive that they can trigger strong emotional reactions and flashbacks, the HSCL-25 does not provoke intense emotional reactions (Mollica et al., 1987). Modeled after the HSCL-25, the Harvard Trauma Questionnaire (designed specifically for Cambodian, Laotian, and Vietnamese victims of trauma) has been proven reliable and valid and has not elicited negative side effects in the respondents (Mollica et al., 1992).

It could be argued that it is difficult, if not impossible, to demonstrate differences in the rate and distribution of mental disorders that result from both methodological problems in assessing rates of psychopathology and the paucity of research on differences between Asian Americans and Euro-Americans. Nevertheless, the existing findings will be discussed below, and the reader can evaluate those findings, noting the inherent limitations of this research.

Interracial Differences

The previous two chapters have demonstrated that Asian Americans often have to deal with psychosocial stressors in addition to those faced by all people. This suggests that Asian Americans might have higher rates of psychopathology than other Americans. What follows is a

---

[6]Criterion validity refers to the test's ability to predict other criteria of a construct or attribute.

discussion of the research on rates of psychopathology among Asian Americans.

There are indications that nonclinical samples of Asian Americans have more psychological manifestations of difficulties with life than similar samples of Euro-Americans do. For example, a study of Japanese Americans in Hawaii revealed that Japanese Americans (as a group) were more tense, apprehensive, and suspicious than their Euro-American counterparts (Meredith, 1966). Research (D. W. Sue & Frank, 1973; D. W. Sue & Kirk, 1972, 1973) on American-born Chinese and Japanese college students has found that Chinese American and Japanese American males as well as Chinese American females were more anxious, more lonely, less socially extroverted, and more isolated than the non-Asian control group.

Since these studies were conducted before many immigrant and refugee Asians arrived in the United States, the findings of more psychological distress among primarily American-born Asian Americans than among Euro-Americans probably do not reflect immigrant or refugee experiences. Unfortunately, theories about the causes of these differences in psychological well-being between Asian Americans and Euro-Americans have not been tested.

More recently, depression has been found to be at least as prevalent among Asian Americans (from a variety of ethnic groups) as it is among Euro-Americans (Kuo, 1984) and to be more common among a nonclinical sample of Korean Americans than among Euro-Americans (Aldwin & Greenberger, 1987). The different results of these two studies may reflect the probability that the first study included more American-born Asian Americans than the second study, which was limited to Korean Americans, primarily an immigrant group. It is expected that immigrants would be more likely to be depressed than both Euro-Americans and American-born Asian Americans because of the number and type of psychosocial stressors that immigrants face. The presence of American-born Asian Americans in the first study may have washed out significant differences between the Asian American and Euro-American samples. In support of this hypothesis, that study (Kuo, 1984) found that foreign-born Asian Americans tend to be more depressed than American-born Asian Americans (although American-born Chinese were an exception). Also lending credence to that hypothesis, another study found no differences in the psychological maladjustment of American-born Asian Americans and Euro-Americans but found foreign-born Asian Americans had more psychological maladjustment problems than Euro-Americans (Abe & Zane, 1990).

The tentative picture that emerges is that in the early 1970s American-born Asian American college students (who were most often the

Asian American subjects studied) experienced more psychological distress than Euro-Americans experienced. This increased distress may have been related to the fact that many of the Asian American college students were members of the first generation in their families to go to college and thus felt very pressured to do well academically. Alternatively, it could have been that the radical changes in America's standards of decorum at the time presented more conflicts in Asian American families than in other American families. This discrepancy then disappeared, so that by the 1980s, American-born Asian Americans were no longer more psychologically distressed than Euro-Americans, although foreign-born Asian Americans still had more psychological problems than Euro-Americans.

Interethnic Differences

There are interethnic differences in rates of mental disorders among Asian Americans. A study (Kuo, 1984) comparing Chinese Americans, Filipino Americans, Japanese Americans, and Korean Americans in Seattle found that Korean Americans had the highest incidence of depression, followed by (in order) Filipino Americans, Japanese Americans, and Chinese Americans. Again, probable reasons Korean Americans had a higher incidence of depression than Chinese Americans, Filipino Americans, or Japanese Americans include the fact that Korean immigrants on average have been in the United States for a shorter period of time, that they have lower-status jobs, and that they have more difficulty adjusting to America (Kuo, 1984).

Southeast Asian refugees have particularly high rates of psychopathology. In various studies the number of Southeast Asians with psychological problems has ranged from 10% (Erickson & Hoang, 1979) to 50% among newly arrived Southeast Asian refugees (General Accounting Office, 1990). A sample of Hmong refugees found "the highest recorded 1-year incidence rate of psychiatric disorders yet observed in any group of adults" (Westermeyer, Vang, & Neider, 1984, p. 173). This finding is not altogether surprising in light of the traumas experienced by many Southeast Asians.

For example, consider the case (described by Kinzie & Fleck, 1987) of a 40-year-old Cambodian woman who was referred for mental health services because of her depression and posttraumatic stress disorder. She was from a financially comfortable family in Cambodia. During the years the Khmer Rouge ruled Kampuchea, her husband and one of her children were executed, and her parents and another of her children died of starvation. She was beaten, tortured, and threatened with death. Later, she was homeless and had little food to eat. Among her psychological symptoms were headaches, little appetite, difficulty concentrating, sleep problems, lack of energy, irritability with her children, and disinterest in her environment. Every night she had nightmares about her experiences being tortured and the deaths of family members there. Reminders of her past, causing her to cry profusely, increased her symptoms, so she tried to avoid reminders of her past. She was also preoccupied by the fact that her dead children had not received proper Buddhist burials. (Drug therapy, presumably in combination with talk therapy, alleviated many of the symptoms of depression, but she continued to have some symptoms of PTSD.)

Even years after coming to the United States, Southeast Asian refugees have high rates of psychiatric disorders (Westermeyer, 1988). In fact, for the first 6 months after arriving in the United States, psychological problems among Southeast Asians are often suppressed (Timberlake & Cook, 1984). But 6 to 12 months after settling in the United States, because they have begun to feel safe enough to spend time thinking about their circumstances and because they have become increasingly aware of their personal, social, and material losses and the disruption of their life pattern, Southeast Asian refugees begin to allow themselves to feel sad and discouraged, grieve over their losses, and idealize the past (Timberlake & Cook, 1984). Even though there is a decrease in PTSD and depression over time, these disorders persist in roughly 50% to 85% of the Cambodians who were traumatized as children (Kinzie et al., 1989; Kinzie, Sack, Angell, Manson, & Rath, 1986).

There are also differences in the rates of psychopathology among Southeast Asian groups. Table 8.1 provides a summary of data from Gong-Guy's (1987) large study of Southeast Asians in California. The psychosocial dysfunction score in Table 8.1 refers to the degree to which individuals cannot attend to normal, daily tasks.

Intraethnic Differences

There is evidence that foreign-born Asian Americans have more mental disorders than American-born Asian Americans. Research has found that (1) foreign-born Asian Americans generally have more psychological adjustment problems (Abe & Zane, 1990) and are more depressed (Kuo, 1984) than American-born Asian Americans; (2) the higher the level of acculturation, the happier people are (Padilla et al., 1985); and (3) the longer that Southeast Asians are in the United States, the more their mental health improves (Beiser, 1988; Westermeyer et al., 1984). These findings are understandable since length of time in the United States and acculturation are associated with learning English,

TABLE 8.1. Ethnic Differences in High Psychopathology Scores Among Southeast Asians

	Percentage with high depression scores	Percentage with high anxiety scores	Percentage with high psychosocial dysfunction scores
Cambodians	36%	96%	36%
Chinese-Vietnamese	20%	96%	15%
Hmong	55%	86%	50%
Lao	39%	93%	43%
Vietnamese	30%	95%	22%

Note. Percentages are based on data from Gong-Guy (1987).

having a job, being able to afford material goods, making new friends, experiencing less cultural shock, and so on. For example, the mental health of Hmong is positively correlated with job training, learning English, and acquiring material goods (Westermeyer et al., 1984).

However, this pattern might not simply reflect the salubrious effects of acculturation. A study of admissions to California state mental hospitals from 1855 to 1955 found an increase in admissions among Chinese Americans (Berk & Hirata, 1973). That the Chinese American population became increasingly acculturated from the mid-19th to the mid-20th century suggests that the presently higher rates of psychopathology among foreign-born, rather than American-born, Asian Americans are not simply due to the increased acculturation of the latter. Other research suggests that acculturation is not a reliable predictor of satisfaction with life or mental health problems: As an indication of how unreliable acculturation is as a predictor, researchers have found higher levels of stress among acculturated Chinese Americans than among immigrant Chinese (Yu & Harburg, 1980) and have found no relationship between acculturation and levels of psychological stress in Chinese Americans (Yu & Harburg, 1981). Additional research is needed to clarify the role of acculturation.

PREDICTORS OF MENTAL HEALTH PROBLEMS

Research on rates of mental disorder among Asian Americans has a number of implications: It debunks part of the model minority myth, contributes to an understanding of the development of mental disorders, and on a very practical level has consequences for public policy: It tells providers in the mental health service system—including policy analysts, officials in government departments of mental health, and therapists—that there is a need for mental health services in Asian American communities. This means that there is a rational basis for funding mental health education and outreach programs for Asian Americans and for training therapists to provide services to Asian Americans.

But scholars and providers of mental health services also want to know what client characteristics are useful in predicting which Asian Americans will develop mental disorders. Such information helps social scientists to better explain why some people develop mental disorders. It indicates to government departments of mental health which Asian Americans are most at risk for developing mental disorders, thus helping service providers to decide where funding for prevention and treatment programs might be most judiciously spent.

Variables are deemed predictors when they distinguish between those who have mental disorders and those who do not. In the context of psychological research, a variable can be a predictor of mental disorders, but that does not mean that everyone with that predictor-characteristic will develop a mental disorder. Rather, it is a statistical predictor. For instance, poverty is a predictor of mental disorders. Not everyone who is poor has a mental disorder. But if you look at a *group* of poor people and a *group* of upper middle-class people, the former would have a higher rate of psychopathology perhaps because they have more stressors and fewer resources than the latter.

Research has revealed a few predictors of mental health problems among Asian Americans. Six in particular are reviewed below: (1) employment/financial status, (2) gender, (3) old age, (4) social isolation, (5) relatively recent immigration, and (6) refugee premigration experience and postmigration adjustment. There are other predictors, but these are among those which have been found most consistently in studies of Asian Americans. The first four variables are predictors of mental disorders for both Asian Americans and the general population of the United States. In general, those who have low incomes or are unemployed have more mental disorders than those who have higher incomes, females report having more psychological distress than males, the elderly more often have psychological problems than younger individuals do, and those who are socially isolated are more at risk for having a mental disorder than those who are not isolated. Although this pattern holds for both Asian Americans and the general population, the underlying reasons for their circumstances might be different. For instance, social isolation for foreign-born Asian Americans may stem from a lack of familiarity with

American culture, a lack of proficiency in English, or separation from the rest of a family that remains in Asia, but these are different from the reasons that other Americans generally feel socially isolated. Yet social isolation is a shared predictor of psychopathology. As predictors of mental disorders, the fifth and sixth variables (mentioned above) distinguish Asian Americans from other Americans.

Employment/Financial Status

Underemployment and low income are predictors of mental disorders in Asian Americans, as they are for the general population. For example, Chinese Americans with a higher socioeconomic status have been found to be more satisfied with life than those with lower socioeconomic status (Ying, 1992). A study of Chinese Americans, Filipino Americans, Japanese Americans, and Korean Americans found that the most depressed of these Asian Americans were those who were unemployed or only employed part-time and who had annual family incomes of less than $25,000; the least depressed were those Asian Americans who were retired and had family incomes over $40,000 (Kuo, 1984). Financial difficulties are sources of particular stress for Southeast Asians. Studies have shown that unemployment is correlated with depression in Chinese-Vietnamese (Yamamoto, Lam, Fung, Tan, & Iga, 1977) and with psychological distress among Southeast Asian men (Rumbaut, 1990) and that welfare status is associated with elevated levels of psychiatric symptoms, especially depression and anxiety, among Hmong (Westermeyer, 1987; Westermeyer, Callies, & Neider, 1990) and other Southeast Asians (Westermeyer et al., 1984; Westermeyer et al., 1983).

It is quite understandable that people who are unemployed or poor would be more depressed than fully employed, financially comfortable people. The former do not have as much disposable income to spend on entertainment, and they tend to live in areas with more crime, which also adds to the stress in their lives. Some have poor health because of a lack of adequate nutrition or health care. Frequently the unemployed feel that they have no social role or purpose in life or, if they do have a social role, that they are not fulfilling it. Additionally, the poor or unemployed are more likely than those who are working or well-to-do to feel that they cannot afford psychotherapy for their problems. Also contributing to the relationship between unemployment and poor mental health is the difficulty people with severe mental disorders would have keeping a job.

Gender

There often are gender differences in reported psychological problems among the general population of Americans. It is more socially acceptable for women than for men to acknowledge their fears, unhappiness, and difficulties with coping. Not surprisingly, then, research has found that Asian American women report having more problems than Asian American men do (Charron & Ness, 1983; Tracey et al., 1986). Southeast Asian women claim to be significantly less happy than Southeast Asian men do (Rumbaut, 1985). Questioning of a nonclinical sample of Cambodian, Chinese, and Vietnamese refugees has confirmed that, in the United States, Southeast Asian mothers are perceived to be the least happy member of the family by their children (L. N. Huang, 1989). Chinese American men are reportedly more satisfied with their marriages than Chinese American women are (Ying, 1992). It is not clear whether Asian American women report more problems than Asian American men because (1) men often underreport their problems, complying with the sexist stigma that denigrates men who admit emotional distress; (2) Asian American women face the double jeopardy of being targets of oppression on the basis of both their sex and their race; or (3) in a sexist society and in the traditional Asian American family structure, men have more freedom and, therefore, fewer sources of psychosocial stress.

Interestingly, Asian American women report having more problems than Euro-American women report having (consistent with the double jeopardy hypothesis), but Euro-American men admit to having more problems than Asian American men do (Tracey et al., 1986). It cannot be assumed that Asian Americans are more sex-typed than Euro-Americans in their willingness to acknowledge difficulties, because the personality research on sex roles has not consistently shown that Asian Americans exhibit more sex-typed behavior than Euro-Americans (see Chapter 4). Thus, while there are readily available, reasonable hypotheses (e.g., the double jeopardy hypothesis) to account for the reporting of more problems by Asian American women than Asian American men and Euro-American women, it is still unclear why Asian American men report fewer problems than Euro-American men do.

Complicating this picture are ethnic differences in the relationship between gender and psychological well-being. For example, although Southeast Asian men, in general, have been found to be happier than Southeast Asian women, Hmong and Khmer men, in particular, have been found to be more depressed than Hmong and Khmer women

(Rumbaut, 1985). An interethnic comparison found that Chinese American and Filipina American women were more depressed than their male counterparts but that Japanese American and Korean American women were less depressed than their male counterparts (Kuo, 1984). A study of Korean Americans found no relationship between gender and feelings of alienation, powerlessness, and social isolation (Moon & Pearl, 1991). Among the reasons for these discrepant findings could be the different measures of psychological well-being that were used: This suggests that gender may not be a simple predictor of a wide range of psychological problems.

Old Age

Among Americans in general, the elderly are at more risk than the young for developing mental disorders such as depression. This greater risk is understandable in light of the loneliness that can occur when a spouse dies and children no longer live at home, the increasing number of health problems that can come as one grows older, the financial insecurity that can accompany old age, and the loss of a sense of social role or purpose that can accompany retirement.

Similarly, there is evidence that Asian American elderly are particularly at risk for psychological difficulties. For example, elderly Southeast Asians are more at risk than younger Southeast Asians for feeling alienated (Nicassio & Pate, 1984) and unhappy (Rumbaut, 1985), older Korean Americans are more at risk than younger Korean Americans for feeling alienated and powerless (Moon & Pearl, 1991), and elderly Chinese immigrants in Canada report less psychological well-being than their Euro-Canadian counterparts report (Wong & Reker, 1985).

Social Isolation

Social isolation is positively associated with mental disorders among Americans in general. Various measures of social isolation (e.g., the size of the local ethnic community, marital status, separation from family, and cultural isolation) suggest that it also is a predictor of mental health among Asian Americans.

Mental illness rates among Asian Americans increase when the relative size of their population in the community decreases (Moritsugu & S. Sue, 1983). Among Southeast Asians, the larger the local Southeast Asian population, the lower the psychopathology rates (Van Deusen, 1982). In the absence of a sizable community of Southeast

Asians from the same ethnic group, Southeast Asians are at a high risk for depression (Beiser, 1988); and in the absence of a sizable Korean American community, Koreans are at increased risk of alienation (Moon & Pearl, 1991). For example, research has found that Korean Americans living in Oklahoma (where there are relatively few Korean Americans) felt more alienated and powerless than Korean Americans living in Los Angeles (where there are many Korean Americans) (Moon & Pearl, 1991). The direction of causality in these studies is not clear. It is possible that a lack of an ethnic community deprives people of a support system and causes social isolation, alienation, and mental disorders. Alternatively, more alienated people might move to areas where there are few people and, in particular, few Asian Americans.

Insofar as being single entails more social isolation than being married, research on marital status rather consistently suggests a relationship between social isolation and mental health. Unmarried Japanese Americans report more psychological distress than their married counterparts (E. Lee, 1988); Koreans in the United States living without a spouse are more alienated than those living with a spouse (Moon & Pearl, 1991); and widowed Southeast Asians are at higher risk for mental disorders than their married counterparts (Rumbaut, 1985). For example, a study of over 400 Southeast Asians at a Southeast Asian mental health clinic revealed that widowed Southeast Asians had more symptoms of depression and anxiety than women who were not widows (Kroll et al., 1989). Widowed, separated, and divorced Filipino Americans and Korean Americans (ethnic groups with a high percentage of immigrants) are much more depressed than their Chinese American and Japanese American counterparts (Kuo, 1984).

Exceptions to the pattern of these studies were E. Lee's (1988) report that for Filipino Americans marriage is not related to lower levels of psychological distress and Ying's (1992) finding that there were no significant differences in satisfaction with life for never-married and once-married Chinese Americans. Additional research is needed to clarify the reasons for these discrepant findings, but it is possible that the Filipino Americans in E. Lee's sample had more alternative sources of social support (e.g., extended family or ethnic community) to mitigate the isolation than the other samples had. There was a sample bias in Ying's study: The respondents were all listed in the San Francisco public telephone directory. People with phones are probably less socially isolated than those without phones—but the latter were excluded from the sample. Moreover, because the study was conducted in San Francisco, with its large Chinese American population, the increased social isolation that can accompany being unmarried may have been mitigated.

Research on loss of familial ties also suggests that social isolation is associated with psychological stress. Loss of and separation from family have been found to be strong determinants of psychological distress among Southeast Asians (Rumbaut, 1990). Adolescent refugees who commit suicide usually have experienced alienation (as well as survivor guilt) due to the loss of family connections (Nidorf, 1985).

Finally, cultural isolation is associated with depression. Among Southeast Asian refugees, a lack of proficiency in English is correlated with depression (E. Lee, 1988; Westermeyer et al., 1984; Westermeyer et al., 1983), alienation (Nicassio, 1983, 1985), emotional distress (Charron & Ness, 1983), and other mental disorders (Rumbaut, 1985). A study of Chinese Americans, Filipino Americans, Japanese Americans, and Korean Americans reported that the highest depression scores were found among those having religious beliefs that made them a minority within their ethnic group and that the lowest depression scores were found among those Asian Americans who practiced the dominant religion of their ethnic group (Kuo, 1984).

A study (Charron & Ness, 1983) of Vietnamese adolescents illustrated the situation facing some adolescent refugees: Vietnamese adolescents who failed to form friendships with Americans were at increased susceptibility for developing emotional problems. At the same time, having American friends also increased the chances that Vietnamese adolescents would have conflicts with their parents, and difficulty in getting along with parents was another predictor of emotional distress. In effect, social isolation from American peers increased susceptibility to developing emotional problems; social involvement with American peers increased the chances for conflict with parents. Not getting along with either their parents or American classmates also predicted high levels of emotional distress. Poor English skills and a lack of American education can exacerbate the problem of receiving support from American peers (Charron & Ness, 1983), but acculturation that is too rapid can undermine support from parents. Another study confirmed that participation in American organizations was positively related to alienation in Southeast Asians (Nicassio, 1983). But it was also suggested that belonging to American social groups could exacerbate feelings of isolation and discomfort if Southeast Asians could not speak or understand English well.

Recency of Immigration

Their relatively recent arrival in the United States sets foreign-born Asian Americans apart from the general U.S. population and is a predictor of mental disorders. The stress of emigration, isolation, and life-disruption apparently increases the risk for mental disorders. For example, a comparison of Koreans who immigrated recently with those who immigrated a number of years ago found that recent Korean immigrants feel more alienated, powerless, and socially isolated than Koreans who have been in the United States for a number of years (Moon & Pearl, 1991). The degree to which immigrant status is relevant to the mental health of immigrant Asian Americans probably depends, among other things, on their age at arrival in the United States, their current age, the skills they brought to the United States, their socioeconomic status, whether they were educated in the United States or in Asia, and the support system available in the United States.

Refugee Pre- and Post-Migration Experiences

Life Changes

The amount of life changes (K-M. Lin, Masuda, & Tazuma, 1982; Masuda et al., 1980) experienced by Southeast Asians are related to the presence of physical and psychological problems. Migration experiences in particular predict mental disorders (E. Lee, 1988; Nicassio, Solomon, Guest, & McCullough, 1986), especially for Southeast Asian women (Rumbaut, 1990).

Traumas

Traumatic histories seem to predict the Southeast Asians at highest risk for mental health problems. Trauma victims are more likely than those who have not experienced traumas to have multiple mental disorders (Carlson & Rosser-Hogan, 1991). Those who were traumatized had symptoms of depression, anxiety, and somatization more than those who were not traumatized (Kroll et al., 1989). Traumatic experiences are associated with recurrent nightmares, hypervigilence, numbing, memory difficulties, disorientation, conversion disorders, such dissociative disorders as psychogenic amnesia and psychogenic fugue (K-M. Lin, 1986), and increased rates of PTSD.

The severity of symptoms among Southeast Asians correlates with the amount of trauma (Carlson & Rosser-Hogan, 1991) and with the experience of specific traumas (Kroll et al., 1989). Young Southeast Asian males who were powerless to protect their family members from victimization or to prevent their own torture are subject to tremendous fear, guilt, shame, anger, apathy, uncertainty about their abilities, obsessiveness in making plans, and impulsivity (Cravens & Bornemann, 1990; Nidorf, 1985). Southeast Asian sexual-assault victims have symptoms such as "sleeping/eating disturbances, mood swings, phobias, school/work avoidance, sexual impotence/acting out, body pains, or depression" (Kanuha, 1987, p. 5). In a study of Cambodian women with nonorganically based blindness, the amount of blindness reported was associated with the number of years spent in labor camps, where traumas were experienced (Rozée & Van Boemel, 1989).

The age at which the refugees experienced the traumas also may predict the types of mental health problems that develop. One study found that half of the Cambodians who experienced traumas as children had PTSD (Kinzie et al., 1989). According to D. Le (1983), Southeast Asian children who experienced traumas before the age of two could be susceptible to the most serious psychological problems, because their terrorizing experiences took place before they developed the language to help them process and cope with memories of those experiences. There may be some validity to this proposition. If so, these memories would probably be difficult to access. But it is also possible that the lack of language disrupted the cognitive encoding and processing of what occurred or interferes with the ability to remember. Additional information is needed in this area.

Adjustment Difficulties

In a study of Hmong, the following were found to be risk factors for psychiatric disorders: inability to resume their premigration vocation, unrealistically optimistic expectations about America, a lack of proficiency in English while in Southeast Asia, and sponsorship by religious organizations seeking converts (Westermeyer, 1987). The following did not significantly affect the mental health of the Hmong: their level of education, the amount of English learned after coming to the United States, occupation in Laos, or the size of the community in Laos from which they emigrated (Westermeyer et al., 1984).

MANIFESTATIONS OF PSYCHOPATHOLOGY

As with other Americans, Asian Americans manifest mental disorders in some forms more frequently than in others. The following section outlines these manifestations of psychopathology and how commonly they are seen in Asian Americans.

Types

Somatization

Although there is some controversy about whether Asian Americans tend to somatize their psychological problems, the preponderance of research, over decades, indicates that Asian Americans frequently somatize their mental health problems (Abbott, 1976; Duff & Arthur, 1967; Gaw, 1982; Moore & Boehnlein, 1991; Nguyen, 1982; Nicassio, 1985)—that is, they often manifest their psychological problems as physical complaints. Such psychosomatic disorders as hypertension and peptic ulcers have been reported (Mass, 1976) to be prevalent problems among *Nisei,* and "Sanseis are more likely to complain of vague somatic disorders such as headaches, digestive troubles, insomnia, and backaches" than their Euro-American counterparts (Onoda, 1977, p. 183). Chinese Americans and Japanese Americans have reported more somatic complaints than Euro-Americans on the MMPI, even when Asian Americans and Euro-Americans have mental disturbances of equal severity (S. Sue & D. W. Sue, 1974). Chinese American students who have been deemed very depressed also are more likely to have concomitant somatic symptoms than their Euro-American counterparts (Marsella et al., 1973). Similarly, there is a high incidence of somatic problems among Vietnamese (Aylesworth, Ossorio, & Osaki, 1980) and Amerasian refugees in the United States (Nicassio, LaBarbera, Coburn, & Finley, 1988).

The tendency to somatize mental health problems—possibly just another way to express psychological distress rather than a distorted expression of it (Beiser & Fleming, 1986)—may be a reflection of Asian American cultural values that emphasize avoiding shame and maintaining the honor of the family. Somatic problems do not carry the stigma or negative social consequences that psychological problems do. It is possible that Asian Americans present their problems as somatic rather than emotional problems because they are more comfortable talking about physical problems than psychological ones. They (perhaps unconsciously) can use somatic complaints as an indirect way to seek help for psychological problems ("Mental health," 1985; D. W. Sue & S. Sue, 1972a). Alternatively, in some cases somatization may be an unconscious reflection of the holistic view of the mind and body adopted in Asian cultures (Nishio & Bilmes, 1987; S. Sue & Morishima, 1982).

Substance Abuse

A large study found lower rates of substance abuse among Asian Americans than among Euro-Americans, African Americans, or Latino Americans (Flaskerud & Hu, 1992). Drug abuse rarely has been encountered in the clinical experiences of some (e.g., Nicassio, 1985) who work with Southeast Asians. In contrast, a survey of Japanese American junior and senior high-school students in Seattle (Nakagawa

& Watanabe, 1973, cited in Nagata, 1989), at a time when drug use was relatively common among adolescents, found that 29% of the Japanese American students reported that they had tried drugs. Other clinical evidence (Zane & Sasao, 1992) suggesting the existence of serious substance abuse problems among some Asian Americans points to the need for additional empirical research.

Suicide

The rates of suicide among Japanese Americans and Chinese Americans are generally lower than among Euro-Americans (Committee on Cultural Psychiatry, 1989; Yamamoto, 1976); however, the suicide rate is higher than that of Euro-Americans for Chinese Americans after the age of 64 and for Japanese Americans after the age of 74 (Yu, Chang, Liu, & Fernandez, 1989). And suicide accounts for a larger proportion of the deaths of 15- to 24-year-old Chinese Americans and Japanese Americans than that of Euro-Americans in that age range (see Table 8.2.) because, in the latter group, accident, illness, and murder figure more prominently.

That foreign-born Chinese Americans and Japanese Americans have higher suicide rates than American-born Chinese Americans and Japanese Americans is an indication that the process of acculturation is stressful for some Asian Americans (Yu et al., 1989). Unaccompanied Southeast Asian minors may be at a much higher risk for committing suicide than their age-mates, in part because of the presumed Asian cultural acceptability of suicide (Nidorf, 1985). Moreover, many Southeast Asians believe no one has business interfering with their suicidal thoughts (Tung, 1985).

Conduct Disorders

A comparison of Euro-American children and children of foreign-born Chinese, Japanese, and Southeast Asians in kindergarten through eighth grade found that Asian Americans exhibited fewer conduct problems and less inadequacy/immaturity than the Euro-Americans exhibited (Touliatos & Lindholm, 1980). However, that study relied on teachers filling out a checklist of behavior problems for their students. Stereotypes of Asian Americans could have skewed these results.

Deserving more credibility is an analysis of Japanese Americans 21 years old or younger, using the Los Angeles County Department of Mental Health Services from 1985 to 1986 (Nagata, 1989b). It revealed that adjustment disorders and conduct disorders (along with affective

TABLE 8.2. Percentage of All Deaths Attributed to Suicide, 15- to 24-Year-Olds

	Chinese Americans	Japanese Americans	Euro-Americans
Males	15.1%	21.3%	12.9%
Females	20.8%	14.0%	8.8%
Total	16.8%	19.0%	11.9%

Note. Percentages are based on an analysis by Yu, Chang, Liu, and Fernandez (1989).

disorders and schizoid disorders) were the most commonly diagnosed problems of this group.

Other Common Problems

A survey (Matsushima & Tashima, 1982) of Asian American therapists revealed that depression, low self-concept, and relationship conflicts affected at least 50% of their Asian American clients. Between 40% and 50% of the clients were affected by problems with parent–child relationships, acculturation, somatic complaints, and isolation.

An analysis (Dubanoski & Snyder, 1980) of cases of child abuse and neglect reported to the Hawaii Department of Social Services and Housing revealed that while Japanese Americans had lower rates of child abuse than would be expected, based on the size of their ethnic group relative to the total population, Samoan Americans had higher rates of child abuse and neglect than would be expected, based on the size of their population. In both groups most of the cases of neglect and abuse were in the category of moderate neglect and abuse, entailing cuts, bruises, and welts that did not require medical treatment. Among the possible flaws in this analysis were culturally biased and gender-biased definitions of neglect as well as an unknown number of cases of neglect and abuse that did not come to the attention of the Department of Social Services and Housing. Nevertheless, other research, conducted in Hawaii 10 years later, confirmed the high rate of child abuse and neglect among Samoans (Blaisdell & Mokuau, 1991; Furuto, 1991). Among the reasons for this pattern may be poverty, lack of education, and a belief that physical discipline is more effective than teaching internalized self-control (Mokuau & Chang, 1991).

Interracial Differences

Many studies—testing a variety of different Asian American ethnic groups and using a variety of measures of psychopathology, including the MMPI, behavioral scales, and psychiatric diagnoses—have found that Asian Americans who use mental health services are more severely disturbed than their non-Asian American counterparts (Brown, Stein, Huang, & Harris, 1973; S. Sue & McKinney, 1975; S. Sue & D.W. Sue, 1974). For example, one study of Asian American and non-Asian American students at a campus psychiatric clinic compared each group's responses to the MMPI (S. Sue & D. W. Sue, 1974). Based on these responses, the Asian American students were judged to be more severely disturbed than the non-Asian Americans. Over 20 years ago, Chinese inpatients were found to be more psychologically disturbed than a Euro-American control group (Brown et al., 1973). Thirteen years later, research confirmed that Filipino Americans and Vietnamese Americans receiving public mental health services had more severe diagnoses than Euro-American, Latino American, or African American patients (Flaskerud, 1986a).

Asian American clients have been diagnosed as psychotic[7] more often than other Americans have. Table 8.3 presents some racial differences in the diagnosis of psychoses. A large study (Flaskerud & Hu, 1992) of the Los Angeles County mental health system found that the proportion of Asian Americans diagnosed as psychotic was larger than that of Euro-American clients; Asian Americans were also diagnosed as having major affective disorders at a proportionally higher rate than African Americans or Latino Americans. Among the reasons for these differences may be that there were cultural biases in the measures of psychopathology or that Asian Americans with mental disorders hesitate longer than other Americans before seeking mental health services, and, thus, their disorders become more severe.

Interethnic Differences

Severity

There is some evidence of interethnic differences among Asian Americans in the severity of psychological problems. As a group, Southeast Asians apparently have the most severe problems, whereas Japanese American have the least severe problems (Gim et al., 1990). This is not surprising since Southeast Asians experienced so many traumas and arrived here relatively recently, while Japanese Ameri-

---

[7]Mental disorders have been classified as psychoses (characterized by severe perceptual and cognitive distortions and a loss of contact with important aspects of reality) or neuroses (characterized by relatively long-term, nonorganically caused, unacceptable and distressing symptoms that do not involve a major loss of contact with reality).

TABLE 8.3. Percentage with Intake Diagnosis of Psychosis

Euro-American	12.7%
African American	13.8%
Latino American	14.5%
Indigenous American	17.6%
Asian American	22.4%

Note. Percentages are based on S. Sue's (1977) summary of a series of studies. Copyright 1977 by the American Psychological Association. Adapted by permission.

cans are the most acculturated Asian American group and, as a group, may have more resources available to them.

Among different Southeast Asian groups, there are also differences in the severity of mental health problems. Table 8.4 presents the results of a study of differences in severity of mental disorders found among a nonclinical sample of over 2,000 Southeast Asians in California. These findings can be understood in light of the differences among these groups in number, duration, and types of traumas experienced.

Types

There are interethnic differences in the types of psychological disorders manifested by Chinese Americans, Filipino Americans, Hawaiian Americans, and Japanese Americans (Finney, 1963). A survey of Asian American therapists treating Asian American clients asked the therapists what types of problems their clients most often presented (Matsushima & Tashima, 1982). Table 8.5 presents the types of problems most often presented to therapists serving Filipino Ameri-

TABLE 8.4. Estimated Percentage of Nonclinical Sample of Southeast Asians Needing Mental Health Services

	Needing Inpatient Services	Needing Outpatient Services
Chinese-Vietnamese	6.5%	13.7%
Vietnamese	7.5%	23.5%
Lao	18.7%	31.2%
Cambodians	19.9%	28.2%
Hmong	20.2%	34.7%

Note. Percentages are based on data from Gong-Guy (1987).

**TABLE 8.5. Client Ethnic Groups and
Types of Problems**

Intrapsychic problems (such as identity conflicts)
Japanese Americans
Filipino Americans

Employment difficulties
Southeast Asians

Alcohol and drug abuse problems
Hawaiian Americans
Filipino Americans
Japanese Americans
Samoan Americans

Note. Results are from Matsushima and Tashima (1982).

cans, Hawaiian Americans, Japanese Americans, Samoan Americans, and Southeast Asians (which included Thais, who came as immigrants rather than as refugees).

Intraethnic Differences

There is a very limited amount of research suggesting intraethnic differences in types of mental disorders. Acculturation seems to be related to the symptoms manifested. Hospitalized schizophrenic Japanese in Hawaii, Los Angeles, and Okinawa have manifested different types and degrees of symptoms (Kitano, 1970).

Southeast Asian Refugees: A Special Population

As would be expected given the traumas and hardships experienced by many refugees, Southeast Asians have displayed a variety of disorders. The most common mental health problems found among Southeast Asians are depression and anxiety (Flaskerud, 1988; Kinzie & Manson, 1983; Kinzie, Tran, Breckenridge, & Bloom, 1980; Kroll et al., 1989; E. Lee, 1988; S. Nguyen, 1982; Nicassio, 1985; Rozée & Van Boemel, 1989; Tung, 1985; Westermeyer et al., 1983).

Affective Disorders

Depression has been widely found among Southeast Asian refugees. For example, a study of two Los Angeles County mental health centers found that Vietnamese refugees tend to have higher rates of depression than other patients (Flaskerud & Anh, 1988). Similarly, a study of Amerasian refugees found they have higher rates of depression than their peers (Nicassio et al., 1988).

The case of a middle-aged, illiterate Hmong from a rural background illustrates how adjusting to life in the United States can contribute to depression.

> We are so afraid and worried that there will be one day that we will not have anything for eating or paying the rent, and these days these things are always in our minds. Some nights the sleep hardly comes to me at all. . . . I myself am too dumb/ignorant; any jobs they have require a literate person to get. We have the arms and legs but we can't see what they see, because everything is connected to letters and numbers. . . . We are not born to earth to have somebody give us feed; we are so ashamed to depend on somebody like this. When we were in our country, we never ask anybody for help like this. . . . I've been trying very hard to learn English and at the same time looking for a job. No matter what kind of job, even the job to clean people's toilets; but still people don't even trust you or offer you such work. I'm looking at me that I'm not even worth as much as a dog's stool. Talking about this, I want to die right here so I won't see my future. How am I going to make my life better? . . . Don't know how to read and write. Don't know how to speak the language. . . . Language, jobs, money, living and so on are always big problems to me and I don't think they can be solved in my generation. So I really don't know what to tell you. My life is only to live day to day until the last day I live, and maybe that is the time when my problems will be solved. (Rumbaut, 1985, pp. 471–472)

Depression among Southeast Asians may, in part, be a result of social isolation, lowered status, grief (K-M. Lin, 1986), a trauma-filled history, difficulty acculturating, financial problems, and the other stressors cited in Chapter 6. When Cambodian women were asked why they were depressed, their answers were rational, seemingly nonpathological, reasons: remembering beatings, mourning the death of spouse and children, and so forth (Rozée & Van Boemel, 1989). Not surprisingly, Hmong (Westermeyer et al., 1984) and Cambodians (Rumbaut, 1985) are the most depressed of the Southeast Asian refugees and the most pessimistic about their work, finances, children's future, and health. Depression can reemerge many years after immigrating (K-M. Lin, 1990) and often lasts many years (E. Lee, 1988). However, Southeast Asians are more willing to accept a diagnosis of anxiety over a diagnosis of depression. This is because they see stressors in their lives that account for their anxiety, but, because many are Buddhists and believe sadness to be a normal part of life and a natural reaction to unhappy situations (Tung, 1985), they do not think their depressive reactions indicate a mental disorder.[8]

Anxiety Disorders

Anxiety disorders, the other of the two most common mental disorders among Southeast Asians, can be the result of attempts to adjust to life in the United States (K-M. Lin, 1986), concern about relatives in Southeast Asia, financial difficulties, and the other psychosocial stressors described in Chapter 6. In addition to the typical ways that anxiety is expressed, anxiety can be manifested in shoplifting, burglary, difficulties at school, and difficulties at work (K-M. Lin, 1986).

Posttraumatic stress disorder, an anxiety disorder sometimes coexisting with adjustment disorders, is exhibited relatively frequently by Southeast Asian refugees and can persist for decades (Carlin & Sokoloff, 1985; Kinzie et al., 1990; Kroll et al., 1989; Moon & Tashima, 1982; Owan, 1985). Rates of PTSD among nonclinical samples of Southeast Asians have ranged from 10% (Gong-Guy, 1987) to close to 90% (Carlson & Rosser-Hogan, 1991).[9] PTSD is persistent among Mien (Moore & Boehnlein, 1991) and Cambodian patients (Kinzie, 1985), particularly Cambodians who were traumatized as children (Kinzie et al., 1989). It is not always easy to diagnose because of the hesitancy of refugees to disclose the traumas they have experienced.

Among the symptoms of PTSD in Cambodians are recurrent thoughts and nightmares about past experiences (Kinzie, 1985, 1989; Kinzie, Frederickson, Ben, Fleck, & Karls, 1984), avoidance of reminders of the past (Kinzie, 1985; Kinzie et al., 1984), homesickness (Kinzie et al., 1984), behaving as if death were possible at any time (Kinzie et al., 1984), and depression (Kinzie, 1989). By the time Cambodians with PTSD seek psychiatric services, they generally have difficulty concentrating, feel helpless, experience severe sleep disturbances and a loss of energy, have suicidal thoughts, and function at a severely impaired level (Kinzie, 1989). Many of the symptoms of PTSD are similar to the symptoms of chronic, unresolved grief (Boehnlein, 1987) and have not significantly diminished after 3 years in the United States (Kinzie et al., 1984). Rather than being reflections of intrapsychic psychopathology, these responses seem to be normal, considering the traumatic situations that caused them (Rozée & Van Boemel, 1989).

---

[8]Treatment for depression among Cambodians, Hmong, and Vietnamese tends to be more effective than treatment for anxiety and somatic problems (Mollica et al., 1990).

[9]These assessments of PTSD were, on occasion, based on questionnaires of symptoms rather than on diagnoses by therapists.

For example, the case (described by Kinzie, 1985) of a 34- year-old Cambodian illustrates how PTSD may be manifested. The patient's original complaint was of a chronic cough. He initially made little note of his difficulty concentrating, memory lapses, and lack of interests. Returning to the therapist 3 months later because he was feeling worse, he described his poor sleep, appetite, concentration, and energy level. He said he was irritable, had intrusive thoughts and nightmares about his past in Cambodia, was startled easily, and thought about dying. His father and three brothers were killed during the Pol Pot regime. He had endured threats, starvation, separation from his family, and long labor. He was diagnosed as having PTSD and being depressed. (After being given imipramine, an antidepressant, he was able to sleep longer, had fewer nightmares and startle reactions, had improved appetite, and turned to the task of finding a job.)

In general, these patients remain vulnerable to stress that could trigger the whole PTSD syndrome (Kinzie, 1989). PTSD can be the distal cause of marital and family problems (August & Gianola, 1987).

Conversion Disorders

It has been reported that conversion disorders (i.e., somatoform disorders that appear to be neurological disorders such as paralysis or blindness) are relatively common among Southeast Asian refugee patients (K-M. Lin, 1986). Consider an example (described by Freimer, Lu, and Chen, 1989) of a single, non-English-speaking, 23-year-old Laotian with a conversion disorder. He had been treated for physical injuries sustained during combat in Laos. Subsequently, he was examined for intermittent leg pain and weakness and a possible seizure disorder but the medical examination results were negative. One day he was found at home in a state which appeared to indicate a sudden stroke or fit. At the hospital his senses returned and he complained of pain in his hands and feet but physical examinations could find nothing wrong. His fine manual dexterity was somewhat inconsistent with the amount of motor dysfunction he apparently had. Given the inconsistency in his physical ailments and evidence that he was depressed, doctors tested whether hypnotic suggestion would have an effect. He was given amobarbital, a barbiturate with hypnotic effects, and then interviewed in that state. During and after the amobarbital session, both his mood and motor ability improved. He was transferred to a psychiatric, inpatient unit where he had difficulty walking, complained of leg and back pain, was sad, anxious, and had difficulty concentrating and remembering. During a second amobarbital inter-view, he indicated that he had been an anti-communist soldier as a teenager and was having a difficult time learning English and finding a job, was no longer receiving welfare, and was living with distant relatives from whom he felt alienated. Under the effects of amobarbital, frequent suggestions were made to him that he would quickly become more mobile and experience less pain. Although the pain continued, these suggestions were successful in allowing him to walk without aids and move his arms and legs freely after the amobarbital session. During a third amobarbital interview he openly, emotionally, and graphically told of an incident in Laos when he was shot and felt helpless as he was unable to move to aid a dying friend. He told of the loneliness and guilt he felt for leaving Laos without his family. His mood and mobility improved after this interview. The presence of depression and various physical complaints without evidence of physical causes for these complaints led to a diagnosis of conversion disorder. An additional diagnosis of PTSD was obtained only after several amobarbital interviews.

Dissociative Disorders

Dissociative disorders also have been reported to be fairly common among Southeast Asian refugees. According to one report, when the refugees first settle in the United States, almost all of them experience some amnesia and often feel that what they are experiencing is not real (K-M. Lin, 1986). Subsequent stress may result in psychogenic amnesia or psychogenic fugue (K-M. Lin, 1986).

Paranoia

Southeast Asian refugees have higher rates of brief reactive psychosis[10] and paranoid psychosis than other Americans experience (Nicassio, 1985; Westermeyer, 1989). Sometimes paranoia develops among Southeast Asians when they are under the stress of dealing with a new environment and are experiencing "varying degrees of miscommunication, fear of rejection, and . . . feeling . . . mistreated, slighted or discriminated against" (K-M. Lin, 1986, p. 69). Psychosis among Southeast Asians can take the form found in many ethnic groups, *viz*, "Aliens' paranoid psychosis" (Tung, 1985). This syndrome is characterized by a usually short-lived xenophobia and by feelings of persecution because one belongs to an ethnic minority (Tung, 1985).

---

[10]A brief reactive psychosis is a short-term psychosis that arises in response to stress.

Schizophrenia

Research (Flaskerud, 1988; Kinzie & Manson, 1980; Kinzie et al., 1980; Nicassio, 1985) and clinical experience (Tung, 1985) have revealed a higher rate of schizophrenia among Southeast Asian refugees than among nonrefugee patients.

Organic Brain Syndromes

Because of relatively high rates of (1) infections that could cause mental dysfunction, (2) starvation that could lead to nutritional and vitamin deficiencies, and (3) war-related or escape-related head injuries that could cause mental abnormalities, the chances are increased for Southeast Asian refugees to develop various organic brain disorders (K-M. Lin, 1986). However, there is as yet no evidence corroborating high rates of organic brain disorders among Southeast Asian refugees.

Somatization

As with other Asian Americans, Southeast Asian refugees often manifest their psychological stress through somatic complaints (Aylesworth et al., 1980; Flaskerud & Anh, 1988; E. Lee, 1988; S. Nguyen, 1982; Nicassio et al., 1988; Rahe et al., 1978; Rozée & Van Boemel, 1989; Timberlake & Cook, 1984). In addition to the reasons other Asian Americans tend to somatize, it is possible that refugees are preoccupied with their bodies and somatize because of the prolonged and extensive physical abuse that they have suffered (S. Nguyen, 1982). Among the most common somatic complaints of Southeast Asian refugees are sleep difficulties (such as insomnia and recurring nightmares), anorexia and weight loss, and headaches (Flaskerud, 1988; Flaskerud & Anh, 1988; Kinzie & Fleck, 1987; Kroll et al., 1989; E. Lee, 1988; S. Nguyen, 1982). Somatic problems frequently are explained by Southeast Asians as being due to weak kidneys, hot intestines, hormonal imbalances, or malnutrition (Grizell, Savale, Scott, & Nguyen, 1980; Nishio & Bilmes, 1987).

Other Psychological Problems

Other common manifestations of psychological problems among Southeast Asians include hypersensitivity (Timberlake & Cook, 1984), mood fluctuations (Timberlake & Cook, 1984), withdrawal (E. Lee, 1988), impaired interpersonal skills (Timberlake & Cook, 1984), tension (Timberlake & Cook, 1984), fatigue (Timberlake & Cook, 1984), feelings of inadequacy (Bromley, 1988), insecurity (J. Wong, 1980), low self-confidence (Timberlake & Cook, 1984; J. Wong, 1980), flat affect (Flaskerud & Anh, 1988), frustration (J. Wong, 1980), gambling (Tung, 1985), and difficulties adjusting to school (E. Lee, 1988; S. Nguyen, 1982). Alienation also is a problem for many Southeast Asians. Among Southeast Asians, the Hmong feel the most alienated, followed by Cambodians, Laotians, and Vietnamese (Nicassio, 1983). Many of these symptoms could be due to acculturative difficulties, racism, and overwork.

Irritability (Flaskerud, 1988), anger (Flaskerud, 1988; Flaskerud & Anh, 1988; J. Wong, 1980), tantrums (Flaskerud, 1988; Flaskerud & Anh, 1988; E. Lee, 1988), and violent antisocial behavior (Flaskerud, 1988; Flaskerud & Anh, 1988; E. Lee, 1988) are also common manifestations of psychological problems among Southeast Asians. Anger and violence may arise from frustration over acculturation difficulties, memories of traumas experienced, and grief (K-M. Lin, 1986). Problems dealing with anger are exacerbated because some spouses cannot be nurturing and give support to their troubled spouses. Because many have their own difficulties in dealing with their own traumatic pasts and trying to adapt to America, they are too physically and emotionally tired and too psychologically vulnerable to provide emotional support for their spouses (K-M. Lin, 1986).

Anger (e.g., about what has happened in their lives and about their inability to learn English quickly) is sometimes displaced on to family members because they are convenient targets, resulting in spousal and child abuse (E. Lee, 1988). A focus-group examination of Southeast Asians in Seattle (C. Ho, 1990) found that Vietnamese men generally considered their wives to be their property and that spousal abuse was often tolerated by Vietnamese, Cambodian, and Laotian wives. Marital and family problems are common manifestations of psychological distress among Southeast Asians (Flaskerud, 1988; Flaskerud & Anh, 1988; Timberlake & Cook, 1984).[11]

Rather than direct their anger toward others, some Vietnamese suppress their emotions, socially withdraw, and turn their frustration and anger on themselves in the form of suicidal behavior or running away (Brower, 1989; Flaskerud & Anh, 1988; E. Lee, 1988; S. Nguyen,

---

[11]A number of factors inhibit Southeast Asian women who are victims of spousal abuse from getting help or leaving their husbands, including the financial problems and cultural conflicts presented by such a response, the belief that children belong to the husband—and, therefore, that if the wife leaves her husband, she would have to leave her children—and the lack of shelters that are prepared to provide culturally and linguistically appropriate services to abused Southeast Asian women (C. Ho, 1990).

1982). Shame, guilt about having survived, and alienation can be precursors to suicide among unaccompanied, adolescent refugees (Nidorf, 1985).

Feelings of guilt are common (Timberlake & Cook, 1984; J. Wong, 1980). In unaccompanied Southeast Asian minors, feelings of guilt often stem from the "failed mission syndrome": These unaccompanied minors worry about the welfare of their family in Southeast Asia and feel guilty about their inability to arrange for their families to join them in the United States (Bromley, 1988).

CONCLUSION

The available research suggests that Asian Americans have a rate of psychopathology equal to or higher than that of Euro-Americans. This conclusion is tentative, however, given the difficulties in assessing rates of psychopathology among Asian Americans. In the absence of evidence that there are physical reasons for these differences in rates of mental disorders (if indeed Asian Americans do have higher rates of psychopathology than other Americans), it is reasonable to conclude that such differences are probably due largely to the psychosocial stressors facing them. The predictors of mental disorders among Asian Americans are consistent with the discussion in earlier chapters of the sources of stress facing Asian American groups. Differences between Asian American and Euro-American rates of psychopathology are also consistent with the previously discussed implication that there are stressors facing Asian Americans in addition to those facing everyone else. Interethnic and intraethnic differences in rates of mental disorders and in severity of psychopathology are generally in accord with what one would expect based on differences in acculturative stresses and traumas experienced, as discussed in Chapters 6 and 7. Most of the existing research has compared Asian American and Euro-American rates of psychopathology. But a comparison of Asian American rates of mental disorders with those of other minorities and a comparison of the rates and types of mental disorders among different Asian American groups would help to illuminate the role of different stressors in the development of mental disorders.

9

Underuse of Mental Health Services

Having examined the psychosocial stressors that potentially contribute to the development of mental disorders and the types of psychopathology found among Asian Americans, an issue that must be addressed is the frequency with which Asian Americans utilize mental health services and the barriers to mental health services that exist for Asian Americans. Research (Hatanaka, Watanabe, & Ono, 1975; Kitano, 1969; Leong, 1986; S. Sue, 1977; S. Sue & McKinney, 1975; S. Sue & D. W. Sue, 1974) rather consistently has indicated that Asian Americans underuse mental health services—that is, they do not use mental health services as much as would be expected based on the size of the Asian American population.

This pattern of underutilization has been found in a variety of Asian American groups (Chinese, Japanese, and a mix of Asian Americans), with both students and adults, in both inpatient and outpatient facilities, at numerous mental health facilities (Loo, Tong, & True, 1989; S. Sue & Morishima, 1982), and over decades. A classic study (S. Sue & McKinney, 1975) of 17 Seattle-area community mental health centers over a 3-year period found that Asian Americans constituted 2.4% of the total population in the area but only 0.7% of the patient population in the mental health centers. Asian American university students have used mental health clinic services at 50% of their expected rate (S. Sue & D. W. Sue, 1974). Studies of admittance rates to mental hospitals mirror this result: Chinese Americans, Filipino Americans, Hawaiian Americans, and Japanese Americans had lower admission rates to Hawaii State (Mental) Hospitals in fiscal year 1969–1970 than would be expected from their relative size in the total population (S. Sue & Morishima, 1982). A few years later, another study of Filipino Americans and Japanese Americans confirmed these findings (Kinzie & Tseng, 1978). More recently, a large study of the use of the services of the Los Angeles County Department of Mental Health over a 5-year period found that Asian Americans underused services: Asian Americans constituted 3.1% of the clients while they constituted about 8.7% of Los Angeles County (S. Sue, Fujino, Hu, Takeuchi, & Zane, 1991). (Only one study [O'Sullivan, Peterson, Cox, & Kirkeby, 1989] has not found that Asian Americans underuse mental health services. But, as S. Sue [1993] noted, in that study utilization figures from 1983 were compared to 1980 census figures. Given the large increase in the Asian American population at that time, such a comparison might not have yielded accurate utilization rates.[1])

In the case of the refugees, comparing their use of mental health services to the size of their population may seriously underestimate the degree to which they do not avail themselves of such services because an unusually high percentage of Southeast Asian refugees need mental health care. Based on assessments of a large, nonclinical sample of Southeast Asians in California (Gong-Guy, 1987), it has been estimated that 14.4% of Southeast Asians need inpatient mental health care and 53.7% need outpatient services, compared to only 3% and 12%, respectively, of the general population.

Further suggesting underuse of services, one study at a Hawaiian psychiatric clinic revealed that even when Japanese Americans had more severe diagnoses than the Euro-American patients, the Japanese Americans did not go to the clinic more than the Euro-Americans did (Kinzie & Tseng, 1978). Evidently, the relatively infrequent usage of mental health services by Asian Americans does not reflect a lack of need for services.

The pattern that emerges is that Asian Americans tend not to use inpatient and outpatient mental health services as much as would be expected from their size in the general population or their need for mental health services. Perhaps because they have not sought mental health services early in the development of their problems or because (in the case of refugees particularly) they have experienced such severe

---

[1]The results of that study conflict also with the general tenor of studies along other dimensions, such as the rate at which Asian Americans prematurely drop out of therapy and the differences between Asian American and Euro-American clients in the severity of psychological impairment. Follow-up studies are needed to determine whether these findings indicate a new trend in the use of mental health services or are just artifacts of the sample.

traumas, when Asian Americans do finally seek therapy, their disorders tend to be more severe than those of other clients. Looked at another way, compared to Euro-Americans, more severe levels of disturbance must be present before Asian Americans seek treatment from mental health professionals. In the case of Asian Americans who are hospitalized in mental institutions, the result may be that their stays in mental hospitals are longer than those of other patients (Kitano, 1969). Evidently, Asian Americans have low rates of utilization of mental health services, not because they do not need services but because they are reluctant to seek them out.

BARRIERS TO THE USE OF MENTAL HEALTH SERVICES

There are a number of reasons why Asian Americans underuse mental health services. Some of these reasons are based on the cultural beliefs, attitudes, and values held by many Asian Americans, and some of these reasons reflect shortcomings in the mental health service delivery system.

The following barriers will be considered: (1) cultural inhibitions about seeking mental health services (including the stigma associated with mental health problems, the ways in which mental health problems are identified, notions of the best ways to deal with psychological problems, and language difficulties), (2) patient suspiciousness, (3) consumer ignorance of available services, (4) lack of financial resources, (5) geographic inaccessibility of services, and (6) shortages of culturally sensitive personnel.

Cultural Inhibitions Concerning Mental Health Services

There are a number of Asian cultural values and attitudes that inhibit self-referral for mental health services. Among the reasons for these inhibitions about seeking mental health services are the stigma attached to mental health problems, the ways in which mental disorders are defined, views of how to deal with psychological problems, and language difficulties.

Stigma of Mental Health Problems

For most Americans, there is a stigma associated with mental health problems. But some Asian Americans feel stigmatized by mental health problems even more than other Americans do. Vietnamese, for example, have been reported to be even more sensitive to the stigma than Euro-Americans are (Atkinson et al., 1984). Many Asian Americans believe that having psychological problems is shameful and disgraceful (Duff & Arthur, 1967; Kitano, 1970; E. Lee, 1982; T-J. Lin & Lin, 1978; Mass, 1976; Tung, 1985). In particular, less acculturated Chinese Americans, Japanese Americans, and Korean Americans tend to feel more stigmatized when seeking mental health services than their more acculturated counterparts do (Atkinson & Gim, 1989).

There are a number of bases for this stigmatization. Many Asian Americans attach a stigma to mental disorders because they think that revealing problems or dealing with problems by seeking professional help are signs of personal immaturity (President's Commission on Mental Health, 1978), weakness (Narikiyo & Kameoka, 1991; Tung, 1985), and a lack of self-discipline (Tung, 1985).

Not only the client but also the client's family might attach a stigma to the seeking of mental health services. Some Asian Americans (e.g., traditional Filipinos, Chinese, and Southeast Asians) are ashamed of and deny the existence of their mental health problems because they think that mental disorders are penalties meted out either by God or malevolent spirits for the immoral behavior or foibles of the clients or their families (Araneta, 1982; Ganesan, Fine, & Lin, 1989; E. Lee, 1982; T-J. Lin & Lin, 1978; Muecke, 1983; S. Nguyen, 1982; Shon & Ja, 1982; Tung, 1985; Westermeyer, 1979). They may also be ashamed of and deny their mental health problems because they think that the problems reflect hereditary flaws that shame the family (Araneta, 1982; Flaskerud & Liu, 1990; Kitano, 1970; E. Lee, 1982; T-J. Lin & Lin, 1978; Shon & Ja, 1982). In addition, parents feel guilty when an offspring has a mental disorder because the parents reason that child-rearing practices contribute a great deal to personality development and psychological weaknesses (Araneta, 1982; Shon & Ja, 1982).

Asian Americans traditionally are supposed to deal with problems by themselves and, if that fails, to seek help from family members. Consequently, some Asian Americans consider it especially shameful to need extrafamilial intervention for the resolution of personal problems. Clients are therefore embarrassed about seeking help, reluctant to admit to outsiders that they have psychological problems (T-J. Lin & Lin, 1978), and apprehensive about the reaction of their families to the fact that they are seeking help (K. Huang, 1991). P. W. Chen (1977), for example, found that 77% of his Chinese American respondents reported being embarrassed about having to ask for any of the social services they need.

Because of this stigma, in many cases Asian Americans do not even let their families know that they are receiving mental health services, much less seek support from them. They are afraid that revealing this information will cause their families to feel ashamed or to castigate them for seeking help outside the family. When some Asian American families discover that a family member is going to therapy, the family members refer to the individual's psychotherapy sessions as "secret meetings" (E. Lee, 1982), clearly implying a lack of acceptance for such activity. This negative feedback from the family can cause clients to feel guilty and isolated from the family (E. Lee, 1982). Despite the research on family cohesiveness cited in Chapter 3, Asian Americans who seek therapy often do not have the support of their families to do so. Even in the area of academic problems, Korean American families reportedly do not provide more support for their children's academic problems than Euro-American families do (Aldwin & Greenberger, 1987). Thus, the lack of utilization of mental health services may be due in part to the reticence of some Asian Americans to admit to themselves, to their family, and to mental health service providers that mental health problems exist.[2]

Identification of Mental Health Problems

Cultural differences exist in conceptions of mental health (S. Sue, Wagner, Ja, Margullis, & Lew, 1976). Sometimes, in defining mental disturbance, Asian Americans use criteria different from those used by non-Asian Americans and therapists. For example, whereas therapists frequently define mental health in terms of psychological understanding, quality of life, and the ability to share feelings, Japanese Americans sometimes define mental health in terms of the ability to work hard and provide for the family (Fugita et al., 1991). Japanese Americans are more likely than Euro-Americans to consider negative personal characteristics, poor interpersonal relations, and a lack of trustworthiness to be indicators of poor mental health (Suan & Tyler, 1990). Similarly, Chinese living in Canada associated mental illness with deviating from socially sanctioned behavior (T-J. Lin & Lin, 1978).

Southeast Asians often consider behaviors a sign of mental disorders only if the behaviors upset the group (Tung, 1985). They generally will seek professional help only for psychotic or dangerous

---

[2]To overcome this stigma, help-seeking might be recast in terms of culturally approved values (S. Kim, 1983): Seeking therapy can be interpreted as a sign of willpower, courage, and an effort to do something good for family honor. Disabusing Southeast Asians of the notion that a person is either crazy or normal (Kam, 1989) can also help to mitigate the stigma.

behavior (Moon & Tashima, 1982; Van Deusen, 1982). Coming from cultures in which people do not seek psychological help for unhappiness, they customarily do not consider negative feelings and emotional problems to be reasons for seeking professional help (Tung, 1985).

Many Asian Americans will not seek mental health services because of the way in which their symptoms are manifested. As mentioned in the previous chapter, Asian Americans tend to express their psychological problems in the form of psychosomatic symptoms (Owan, 1985). Instead of seeking the services of mental health specialists, many Asian Americans may look at their somatic symptoms, conclude that their problems are physical, and seek the services of physicians, acupuncturists, herbalists, spiritualists, or—if they do not make a sharp distinction between mind and body in the way that most people in the West do—providers of holistic medicine.

The belief that mental disorders are caused by organic factors further encourages Asian Americans to define their disorders in physical terms. For example, Chinese Americans and Filipino Americans are more likely than Euro-Americans to believe that mental disorders are caused by organic factors (S. Sue et al., 1976). Similarly, many Southeast Asians do not see the relevance of mental health services to their problems because they do not explain the causes of their mental disorders in psychological terms (E. Lee, 1988; Nishio & Bilmes, 1987; S. Sue & Zane, 1987; Van Deusen, 1982).

Indeed, Southeast Asians rarely invoke intrapsychic explanations for mental disorders (H. Wong, 1985b). Psychiatric disorders (including behavioral abnormalities and psychological suffering) are often viewed by Southeast Asians and Chinese Americans as manifestations of medical dysfunctions, hereditary weaknesses, imbalances of yin and yang, having been born under an unlucky star, or supernatural punishment requiring the services of priests and shamans rather than mental health workers (Ganesan et al., 1989; L. N. Huang & Ying, 1989; E. Lee, 1982, 1988; E. Lee & Lu, 1989; K-M. Lin, Inui, Kleinman, & Womack, 1982; Moon & Tashima, 1982; Owan, 1985; Tung, 1985).

Among Southeast Asians, supernatural curses or retribution tend to be viewed as the causes of psychoses, whereas a physical problem, a yin–yang imbalance, or stress tend to be viewed as the causes of nonpsychotic disorders (Tung, 1985). When stress is believed to be the source of psychological problems, Southeast Asians often externalize the source of their distress. That is, they emphasize external factors to account for their stress rather than focus on their own intrapsychic conflicts, personality characteristics, or perceptual and cognitive distortions. Their perspective on their problems is frequently at odds with Western, psychological perspectives and therapies: They think that if their environmental circumstances were simply changed, they would no longer feel distressed (Tung, 1985).

Thus, because of their conceptions of mental health, some Asian Americans do not use the same criteria that other Americans use for determining whether a behavior is problematic, indicative of mental disorder, or amenable to psychotherapy. As a result, some Asian Americans are less likely than other Americans to feel a need for mental health services.

Dealing with Psychological Problems

Most Asian Americans try to deal with their psychological problems without seeking professional mental health services. As with other Americans, Asian Americans tend to choose self-reliance or reliance on the family as a means of dealing with their problems (Suan & Tyler, 1990). Asian Americans customarily seek help from friends, family, physicians, and clergy before turning to mental health professionals (Atkinson et al., 1984; Bourne, 1975; JWK International, 1976; Kitano, 1969; E. Lee, 1988; Moon & Tashima, 1982; Owan, 1985; Van Deusen, 1982; H. Wong, 1985b).

Southeast Asians have a tradition of seeking help from family or friends because in Southeast Asia there is an absence of psychologists, psychiatrists, and social workers (Brower, 1989; Tung, 1985). Inasmuch as mental illness shames the whole family in Southeast Asian cultures, it is considered the collective responsibility of the family to take care of the disturbed family member as long as possible (S. Nguyen, 1982). Southeast Asians are taught to use personal and familial resources for dealing with their problems and not to burden other people with their problems (S. Nguyen, 1982). Thus, minor psychological problems are handled by family and perhaps friends. To some Southeast Asians, the thought of talking about intimate problems with a stranger (i.e., a therapist) is absurd (Brown, 1987).

Traditional Asian American families will often try to treat mental disorders by exhorting or reasoning with the disturbed family members to "correct" their behavior (T-J. Lin & Lin, 1978). Each family member might contribute his or her own proposal for treatment, and that treatment will be tried until the family has exhausted its tolerance and resources (T-J. Lin & Lin, 1978). The result can be that the family intensively tries to solve the problem on its own for 20 years or more, during which time the disturbed person does not receive professional psychological help (T-J. Lin & Lin, 1978; S. Nguyen, 1982).

When the troubled person and his or her family are not able to resolve the problem, they often turn to organizations or healers within the ethnic community, such as churches, physicians, elders, clan associations, and other ethnic organizations (S. Sue & Morishima, 1982). Southeast Asians, for example, usually do not seek help outside their ethnic community (Moon & Tashima, 1982). Southeast Asians come from traditions in which problems that cannot be managed within the family are addressed by the ethnic community support system: community elders, monks, or spiritual healers are consulted (Bemak, 1989).

The case (cited by L. N. Huang & Ying, 1989) of Rose, an 18-year-old Chinese immigrant, illustrates this pattern of help-seeking. After graduating from high school about one and a half years previously, Rose had become sullen, withdrawn, and friendless. She started wearing garish make-up, stayed out late, and verbally abused her mother. When Rose's behavior began to deteriorate, her mother sought treatment for her from an *acupuncturist, relatives, a physician, and a minister*. As it turned out, Rose did not improve so her embarrassed and confused family would lock her in her room. At night she sometimes managed to escape and wander the streets until her brother would find her and take her home. It was not until she physically assaulted her mother that the family took Rose to seek services from a professional in mental health.

Relying on members of the ethnic community for help has been the historical pattern for Asian Americans. For instance, family members, family associations, and churches historically have helped Chinese Americans deal with psychological problems and provided social services (R. Chin 1982, cited in S. Sue & Morishima, 1982). In many ways, this general pattern of dealing with psychological problems is similar to that of other Americans.

In the case of the most acculturated Asian American group, Japanese Americans, although both *Nisei* and *Sansei* exclude professional mental health services from their first or second choice of ways to resolve psychological problems, they both tend to have a positive attitude toward professional mental health care when that option is explicitly presented (Uomoto & Gorsuch, 1984). *Sansei* think that seeking mental health services is more socially acceptable than *Nisei* do (Uomoto & Gorsuch, 1984). *Sansei* and *Yonsei* are as likely as Euro-Americans to advocate usage of mental health services to other people (Narikiyo & Kameoka, 1992). However, there are reportedly (Narikiyo & Kameoka, 1992) significant differences between where *Sansei* and *Yonsei* think that *other* people should obtain help and where *they* would seek help for themselves. They are much more likely to rely on themselves, their family, or friends—and less likely to rely on professional mental health care providers—for their own mental health needs.

What Asian Americans consider to be appropriate ways of dealing with problems depends largely on what they perceive to be the sources of their problems. Japanese Americans consider interpersonal problems a more likely cause of psychological problems than Euro-Americans do (Narikiyo & Kameoka, 1992); therefore, it is not surprising that the former consider talking with family or friends to be more useful in resolving problems than the latter do. When traditional Filipinos think that a psychological problem is caused by unrequited love, sexual frustration, or sexual excess, they are likely to seek some sexual remedy (Araneta, 1982). When the source of a psychological problem is believed to be the arousal of the ire of spirits, rituals such as prayer and exorcism are considered to be more appropriate treatments than psychotherapy. Some Southeast Asians balk at Western psychotherapy because it lacks a spiritual orientation, which they think is important in dealing with mental problems (Kam, 1989). A major reason that Southeast Asian refugees do not keep their follow-up appointments is their feeling that the therapist "did not understand their problem and did not meet their expectations" (S. Nguyen, 1982, p. 170).[3]

Many Asian Americans think that it is detrimental to dwell on and deeply analyze gloomy, disturbing, or embarrassing thoughts (S. Sue et al., 1976): Chinese Americans, Filipino Americans, and Japanese Americans are more likely than Euro-Americans to believe that one should not dwell on such thoughts if one wishes to maintain mental health (E. Lee, 1982; S. Sue & Morishima, 1982; S. Sue et al., 1976). This attitude may be related to the value placed on self-control, the belief that perseverance through adversity without complaining is a sign of dignity, and the idea that complaining indicates a small spirit (C. Ho, 1990).

Talking about problems is frequently not seen as an appropriate way to deal with problems. Among Southeast Asians, feelings are considered essentially private matters, and lamenting and talking about one's problems is considered indiscreet (Tung, 1985). Chinese culture promotes the idea that talking does not help resolve problems, and that individuals should avoid revealing their private concerns to outsiders (K. Huang, 1991).

Therefore, even when Asian Americans seek help for psychological problems, they may not seek psychotherapy, which regards the recognition of emotions and the sharing of feelings as a beneficial, cathartic release, or as a means of legitimating those feelings and uncovering the sources of unhappiness and psychological conflict. Some Asian Ameri-

---

[3]It has been claimed that when therapists provide biofeedback, acupuncture, and relaxation training as an adjunct to psychotherapy, some Asian Americans are not so reluctant to seek mental health services (Yamamoto, 1986).

cans think that professional mental health services per se are not helpful (Atkinson et al., 1984). The case (cited by S. Sue & Zane, 1987) of Mae illustrates this point. Mae, an immigrant from Hong Kong, was seeking mental health services because of problems with her demanding in-laws. She talked with her close friend about her problem but together they could not come up with a way to solve her problems. She was ambivalent about seeing a therapist: She felt hopeless and could not think of any other approaches to take but questioned whether therapy would help, doubting that talking would be helpful, and doubting that the therapist, an American-born Chinese man, would understand or be able to generate a solution that she and her close friend had not already considered and rejected. Similarly, Vietnamese college students have been found to be less confident than Euro-American students in the ability of mental health professionals to be helpful (Atkinson et al., 1984).

As means of resolving psychological problems, Asian cultures have traditionally promoted coping strategies such as becoming involved in activities and trying not to think too much about problems rather than talk therapy (K. Huang, 1991).[4] For instance, Asian Americans who are feeling frustrated, angry, depressed, or anxious are sometimes instructed by family elders to be more family-oriented and less self-absorbed, to keep busy, and not to think about their personal problems (D. W. Sue & D. Sue, 1990). In particular, foreign-born Asians tend to believe that self-control, willpower, determination, and avoidance of unpleasant thoughts can prevent people from having "inappropriate" emotions and can help them deal with their troubles (Arkoff et al., 1966; Kaneshige, 1973; Root, 1985; Tung, 1985).

Another coping strategy that is often promoted is to accept and endure one's problems. Traditionally oriented Asian Americans who are not able to overcome their psychological difficulties through the application of willpower alone tend to respond by being fatalistic and stoically bear their pain and unhappiness (M-K. Ho, 1984; Kaneshige, 1973). "In Eastern philosophy [e.g., Taoism], it is important to accept that a situation is as fate intended, and not to challenge it" (C. Ho, 1990). Buddhism holds that life is full of suffering, that stress and suffering are

---

[4]It has been argued that Southeast Asian cultures, because of the value that they often place on harmony in interpersonal relations, promote the use of suppression, repression, and denial as a way of dealing with negative feelings (S. Nguyen, 1982). However, suppression, repression, and denial are common defense mechanisms for other Americans as well, so it is not clear to what extent these defense mechanisms are culturally circumscribed. Finney (1963) found interethnic and intraethnic differences in the types of defense mechanisms most often used, but not much empirical research has focused on this issue.

normal parts of life for everyone, and that people should persevere (Kanuha, 1987; S. Nguyen, 1982).[5] Thus, for example, Southeast Asian cultures emphasize patient, stoic, and resigned endurance of personal suffering (Tung, 1985). Most Southeast Asians think that they should deal stoically with adversities and not reveal their personal weaknesses, particularly minor mental disorders (S. Nguyen, 1982). One seeks help only as a last resort. Even third- and fourth-generation Japanese Americans are more likely than Euro-Americans to advocate endurance and adjustment as coping strategies for mental disorders (Narikiyo & Kameoka, 1992).

Again, differences among Asian American groups must be kept in mind. Although members of many Asian American groups think that emotional control is important in mental health, members of some Asian American groups do not. For instance, no difference has been found between Japanese Americans and Euro-Americans in the degree to which they see emotional control as important in determining mental health (Suan & Tyler, 1990). The belief that mental disorders are punishments from supernatural forces can be a barrier to a belief in the efficacy of mental health services for Southeast Asians but not so for Japanese Americans (and not all Southeast Asians hold such beliefs). Some researchers (Atkinson & Gim, 1989; Atkinson, Whiteley, & Gim, 1990) have speculated that those Asian Americans who identify with Asian cultures more than with American culture may be reluctant to seek services for mental health problems; but once they decide that help is needed, they prefer professional help from "authorities." Those Asian Americans who identify with American culture more than with Asian cultures may more quickly recognize when psychological help is needed but feel less inclination to seek such help from professionals. Generally consistent with this interpretation, a study of third- and fourth-generation Japanese Americans revealed that those who scored at the very high range (i.e., very acculturated) on the Suinn–Lew Self-Identity Acculturation Scale thought that therapists were less attractive sources of help than did those who scored in the middle range on the test (Atkinson & Matsushita, 1991).

Language Difficulties

Language barriers also contribute to the underuse of mental health services by some Asian Americans. Studies of non-English-speaking

---

[5]A therapist might incorporate Buddhist and spiritual beliefs into therapy as a way to relieve the anxiety of Southeast Asian clients (Kam, 1989), to motivate the clients, and to help them cope. For instance, survivor guilt and feelings of shame might be mollified by invoking the Buddhist concept of karma (Kinzie, 1989).

patients have shown that the language barrier affects patient attitudes, accessibility to a range of patient services, and treatment effectiveness (e.g., Marcos & Alpert, 1976; Marcos, Alpert, Urcuyo, & Kesselman, 1973). For example, difficulties with English could impede the ability of some Asian Americans to learn about available services, fill out forms, and interact with personnel.

Many non-English-speaking Asian Americans are afraid to seek services from people who do not speak their native language (Shu & Satele, 1977). They balk at the thought of having to labor at speaking English in order to obtain services; they feel apprehensive about their ability to communicate or understand an English-speaking therapist; and they dread the resulting feelings of frustration, fatigue, guilt, or anger (Tung, 1985). Therapists, too, become frustrated and discouraged by the language gap (Larsen, 1979). A potential solution would be for clients to supply an interpreter, but this is problematic because they are likely to be reluctant to disclose private information in front of the neighbor or child whom they have enlisted to translate for them (Office of Civil Rights, 1973).

Research has found that when therapists and clients speak the same language, Asian American clients have more therapy sessions, drop out less, feel more rapport with their therapist, and believe therapists are more effective and more empathic than when the therapists and clients do not share a common language (Flaskerud, 1986b; Flaskerud & Liu, 1990, 1991; Leong, 1986). Similarly, the presence of a bilingual staff has been found to be one of the most important characteristics of mental health facilities that sucessfully serve Chinese Americans, Filipino Americans, Japanese Americans, and Korean Americans (B-L. Kim, 1978). Not surprisingly, the presence of a bilingual staff is more important to immigrant Asians than to American-born Asians. Such research clearly demonstrates that a language gap between therapists and clients can be a barrier to mental health services.

Client Suspiciousness

Asian American clients often enter treatment feeling unwelcome, fearful, and suspicious of non-Asian American therapists (P. Chen, 1977; Shu & Satele, 1977). This suspiciousness, in turn, can constitute a barrier to service utilization. Perhaps, as a reaction to having been the victim of institutional and personal discrimination, a client may be suspicious of Euro-American therapists or mental health clinics or hospitals run by Euro-Americans (Nagata, 1989a). Experiences that

Asian Americans may have had with discrimination can make them acutely aware of the social consequences of being different. As a result, they may shy away from mental health services because they fear another label which would make them seem different—namely, that of being a person with a mental disorder.

Some Asian American clients fear that therapists have different conceptions of mental health and different treatment goals than the former have. For instance, some clients are concerned that therapists will try to force them to adapt to Euro-American, middle-class standards of behavior (S. Sue, 1973).

Asian American clients may also be suspicious that services will not be confidential. Unfamiliar with the role of a mental health service professional, Southeast Asian clients might not know about confidentiality standards in American psychotherapy (Ishisaka, Nguyen, & Okimoto, 1985). Suspecting a lack of confidentiality, immigrants and Southeast Asian refugees sometimes fear that using mental health services can increase the chance that they will be deported ("Mental Health," 1985). They also fear that it could be seen as a lack of appreciation for what American sponsors or social service providers have done for them ("Mental Health," 1985) or that it might jeopardize their ability to sponsor relatives for emigration to the United States.

Ignorance of Available Services

Another reason that mental health services have not been sought by Asian Americans is ignorance of the availability of such services (P. Chen, 1977; Office of Special Concerns, 1977; Tung, 1985; Van Deusen, 1982). Ignorance of where to find mental health services is a particular problem for immigrants (B-L. Kim, 1978). Mental health systems often limit funding for outreach and public education programs for Asian Americans that are in appropriate languages, that address Asian American inhibitions and conceptions of mental health, and that reach out to Asian Americans through meaningful channels (such as ethnic newspapers, ethnic churches, and television shows in Asian languages). A study of Chinese Americans, Filipino Americans, Japanese Americans, Korean Americans, and Samoan Americans found that only 4% of these Asian Americans learned of social services through a combination of outreach and ethnic media (Asian American Field Survey, 1977). This lack of information on available services has apparently been due largely to the lack of much culturally appropriate outreach to Asian American communities as well as a lack of coordination between mental health service systems and those religious, health, and social services within the ethnic communities that could act as referral resources for mental health care. Research is needed to update these findings.

Lack of Financial Resources

Often self-employed or in low-paying jobs with minimal benefits, recent immigrants and refugees in particular have been intimidated by the cost of mental health services either because they lacked health insurance or because their health insurance was inadequate (H. Wong, 1985).[6] Prospective Asian American clients usually do not know that most therapists charge on a sliding scale and that, therefore, affordable psychotherapy can be found.

Services geared toward those who cannot afford private care can carry welfare (and thus shame-inducing) connotations for some prospective recipients. Receiving mental health services at less than full cost can conflict with Asian American cultural values that emphasize the need to repay obligations (H. Wong, 1985b). Since many are not convinced that mental health services can even help, they will avoid potentially shame-inducing public mental health care and eschew more expensive private mental health care.

Geographic Inaccessibility of Services

Where mental health services are located can be a barrier to their use. The rate at which clients prematurely drop out of therapy is related to the location of the service (Flaskerud, 1986b).

However, there is some controversy regarding where facilities should be located. Some argue that mental health facilities should be located within Asian American communities—highly visible, accessible, and integrated into the community. Mental health facilities that are far from Asian American communities may be inaccessible to those who rely on public transportation (Lum, 1985). Providing mental health services in the clients' homes, churches, or community centers can increase rapport between clients and therapists (E. Lee, 1982; True,

---

[6]In the early 1970s when free mental health services were provided in Los Angeles' Chinatown, there was no significant increase in the number of people receiving mental health services (Brown et al., 1973), which suggested other barriers more salient than the financial one. With the increased number of financially struggling Asian Americans, cost may have become a greater barrier since then.

1976; H. Wong, 1985b; Yamamoto, 1986) and, therefore, might increase utilization rates. In contrast, others think that mental health facilities should be located near but not in the ethnic community because some Asian Americans feel ashamed and embarrassed by their need for services; they do not want others in their ethnic group to see them going to a place that provides mental health services (and the chances of this occurring are increased when the facilities are located in areas where many Asian Americans live). Still others have recommended incorporating mental health services into a multiservice center that provides legal and social services as well as language programs (Murase, Egawa, & Tashima, 1985; S. Sue & Zane, 1987). This multiservice-center option can lessen embarrassment about receiving mental health services because it can be seen as just one more service which is available, thus providing a socially acceptable reason for clients to be at a place that offers mental health services. This in turn increases the awareness of the existence of mental health services, and helps in coordinating mental health services with other social service needs (Murase et al., 1985).

There is a need both for mental health services that are integrated into mainstream mental health services and for free-standing mental health services for Asian Americans because of intraethnic and interethnic differences in levels of acculturation and mobility (S. Sue & Zane, 1987; Uba, 1980, 1982). Such an approach minimizes the chances that some group of Asian Americans will be underserved or receive culturally inappropriate mental health services. (For further discussion of mental health delivery systems see Appendix B.)

Shortages of Culturally Sensitive Personnel

When therapists have world views that are different from those held by their clients, are unaware of those differences or the bases for those differences, and encounter cultural practices and behaviors that are difficult for them to understand, the therapists are apt to misinterpret their clients' behaviors as indicating psychopathology (Kitano, 1970). That is, biases in the therapists' world views can blur their ability to distinguish between psychopathology and sociocultural variance (Kranz, 1973; Scheff, 1972; Sechrest, 1969; Singer, 1976; Tseng & Hsu, 1969/1970).

Asian American clients often sense when therapists do not recognize or understand Asian American values and styles of interacting and when therapists misinterpret the culturally influenced behaviors of Asian Americans. When that happens, Asian Americans are discouraged from seeking mental health services from those therapists. Similarly, when therapists are aware that they are not communicating clearly with their clients, they sometimes become anxious, lose confidence in their ability to help their Asian American clients, and seek to end therapy as soon as possible (Tung, 1985).

Mental health service providers need to understand the history, traditions, parental roles, language styles, sex-role differences, familial functions and responsibilities, belief and value systems, and religious practices of Asian Americans (Sanders, 1975). That shortages of culturally knowledgeable and culturally sensitive therapists can be a barrier to Asian Americans' receiving mental health services is revealed by a great deal of research that indicates that bilingual, bicultural, or culturally sensitive mental health service providers and staff are preferred by Asian Americans in general and are judged to be more effective by Asian American clients.

It has also been demonstrated repeatedly that there is a dramatic increase in the use of mental health services by Asian Americans when there are culturally relevant mental health facilities. For example, San Francisco's Richmond-Maxi Center was specifically designed to serve Asian Americans. More patients were treated at the Richmond-Maxi Center in the first 3 months after it was established than were seen in the previous 5 to 6 years in that catchment area[7] (Murase, no date; N. Wong, 1977). Similarly, Asians Americans used an Asian American counseling and referral service in Seattle more in 1 year than they used 17 other community mental health centers over a 3-year period (S. Sue & McKinney, 1975). Findings consistent with the above have been found for Asian American mental health facilities in Los Angeles (Hatanaka et al., 1975) and Oakland (True, 1975). Asian Americans are more likely to use the services of a mental health service center when that facility employs bilingual, bicultural personnel (H. Wong, 1982). Substance abusers are also more likely to go to treatment facilities that are staffed with members of their ethnic group because they feel they can trust, relate to, and communicate and identify with the staff in such facilities (Westermeyer, 1984).

Although some Asian Americans prefer Euro-American therapists because they ascribe higher status to Euro-Americans or cling to historical grudges against members of other Asian groups (L. N.

---

[7]Mental health service delivery systems, usually state or county departments of mental health, divide the areas in which they oversee services into what are called "catchment areas." A large city, for example, might be divided into several catchment areas so that the Department of Mental Health can effectively manage and can provide services that best meet the needs of the people in a specific area.

Huang, 1989), Asian Americans generally increase their use of mental health services when therapists are Asian American (Atkinson & Matsushita, 1991; Atkinson, Poston, Furlong, & Mercado, 1989; Wu & Windle, 1980). When Asian American clients share the same ethnicity as the therapist, they are less likely to drop out of therapy, and therefore care is likely to be more effective than when client and therapist are not of the same ethnic group (Flaskerud & Liu, 1990; E. Lee, 1985; S. Sue et al., 1991). This finding is consistent with the notion that Asian American clients prefer culturally similar or culturally sensitive therapists and that the absence of such therapists results in lower rates of usage of mental health services by Asian Americans.[8]

The increased availability of culturally sensitive personnel might account for a change, over the decades, in the apparent rate at which Asian Americans drop out of therapy prematurely. Research in the 1970s found that Asian Americans were more likely than Euro-Americans to drop out of therapy quickly (S. Sue, 1977; S. Sue & McKinney, 1975). For example, one study found that over 50% of the Asian Americans dropped out of therapy after one session compared to about 30% of the Euro-Americans (S. Sue, 1977). More recently, however, there has been evidence that Asian Americans do not drop out as much as they did when studied earlier and are more likely than Euro-Americans to return after one therapy session (O'Sullivan et al., 1989; S. Sue et al., 1991). While the discrepancy between the results of this research and earlier research may be due to differences in the age and socioeconomic status of the people studied and to inclusion of more post-1965 immigrants and refugees in recent studies than in earlier studies, the discrepancy also may be due to the availability of more culturally sensitive services now than there were two decades ago.

Although there has probably been an increase in the number of culturally sensitive mental health professionals, there is often still a shortage of personnel who are bilingual, bicultural, and sensitive to cultural characteristics found among many Asian Americans (President's Commission on Mental Health, 1978; Sanders, 1975; S. Sue & Morishima, 1982). The failure to recruit, train, and distribute adequate numbers of such personnel has been a barrier to service utilization.

---

[8]However, an ethnic match is not enough. More important to many Asian Americans than sharing ethnicity with the therapist is that the therapist be more educated and older than the client; that he or she have similar attitudes, personality, and socioeconomic status as the client (Atkinson, et al., 1989); and that he or she be empathic.

CONCLUSION

The research presented in this chapter has demonstrated that Asian American populations need mental health services but that their cultural values, beliefs, and experiences often deter them from seeking services. Increasing the effort to provide mental health services to Asian Americans by training more therapists to provide culturally sensitive services for the growing Asian American population and by focusing more on outreach to Asian Americans can help to mitigate some of these barriers.

Mental health delivery systems have begun to recognize these barriers, but when it comes to breaking them down, some locales have fared better better than others. A number of factors—including the cost of establishing culturally sensitive outreach and services—dissuade some in the mental health delivery system from dealing appropriately with these barriers. The expense of establishing culturally sensitive mental health services appears even more imposing because Asian Americans make up only a small percentage of the total population in most areas of the country; they may live scattered sporadically throughout a state's different (mental health delivery system) catch-ment areas, and they may be a heterogeneous population. However, failing to provide culturally sensitive mental health services in the long run can be more expensive for society than providing such services.

10

Psychotherapy

Many people who would bene-
fit from psychotherapy balk at the idea of seeking the services of a
psychotherapist. Sometimes people are afraid that seeing a therapist
will mark them as "crazy," or they are afraid of the therapeutic situation
simply because it is unfamiliar to them; they become apprehensive—
concerned that the therapist will instantly know every dark secret that
they have—and reticent about revealing their vulnerabilities to the
therapist. To defend themselves against anxiety about these matters,
many people do not go to therapy. Some people, unconsciously trying
to protect themselves from acknowledging that fear is preventing them
from seeking therapy, rationalize their decision by belittling psychotherapy, telling themselves that they cannot afford it.

Other people are reluctant to become involved in therapy simply
because they do not think it will do any good. They overgeneralize
from the experiences of their friends, or even their own, with therapists
who were not particularly skilled. Based on experiences with one
therapist who was not noticeably helpful, they conclude that the reason
psychotherapy was ineffective is that psychotherapy per se is not
useful, rather than that a particular therapist was not helpful.

Many Asian Americans share this hesitation about therapy and
have other, culturally based misgivings as well. This chapter focuses on
the ways in which therapy can conflict with the culturally based
expectations and social interaction styles of Asian Americans and on
potential areas of misunderstanding between therapists and Asian
American clients. To have a context for understanding some of these
conflicts and misunderstandings, a brief overview of Western psychotherapy is warranted.

WESTERN PSYCHOTHERAPY

There are basically two forms of Western psychotherapy. One form, non-insight-oriented therapy, tries to alleviate symptoms without helping clients understand why they have the problems they do. The other form, insight-oriented therapy, tries to alleviate symptoms and problems by helping clients uncover and gain insight into the underlying causes of their problems. Whichever form of therapy is used, a trusting relationship between the client and the therapist is needed. No matter which type of therapy is used, the ethics of psychotherapy (e.g., client confidentiality) are the same.

Non-Insight-Oriented Psychotherapies

Behavior Therapy

One of the most common non-insight-oriented therapies is behavior therapy. Based on behaviorism and social-learning theory, behavior therapy assumes that problematic behaviors have been learned, just like all other behaviors—that is, they are behaviors that have been reinforced in the past, observed, or classically conditioned. The assumption underlying behavior therapy is that problematic or maladaptive behaviors can be unlearned, using instrumental or classical conditioning—that is the focus of this type of therapy. A behavioral approach to therapy would involve treating symptoms and not looking for underlying, intrapsychic causes of behavior.

Psychopharmacological Therapy

Another common form of non-insight-oriented therapy is based on the biological or medical model of psychopathology. This model assumes that at least some mental disorders are either physically caused or analogous to physical illness. Indeed, genetic factors and inappropriate amounts of neurotransmitters have been implicated in a number of forms of psychopathology, such as affective disorders and schizophrenia. This form of therapy, involving the administration of medicines to address neurochemical imbalances or symptoms, frequently is used in conjunction with other forms of therapy. For example, antidepressants have been well received and effective in treating depression and in reducing (but not always eliminating) the intrusive thoughts, nightmares, and hyperarousal among Cambodians with PTSD (Boehnlein, Kinzie, Rath, & Fleck, 1985; Kinzie, 1989; Kinzie & Leung, 1989); these drugs are sometimes given in conjunction with talk therapy.

The effectiveness of this type of therapy can be seen in the case (described by K-M. Lin & Poland, 1989) of a 38-year-old, Chinese American computer programmer who frequently directed hostile outbursts against neighbors and people in his office building. For several years he had delusions of persecution and auditory hallucinations (e.g, hearing voices which ridiculed or threatened him and voices which made comments about his behavior). He concluded that the voices were those of his neighbors. Because he thought his co-workers were spying on him and talking about him, he quit his job. He had difficulty sleeping and was irritable and agitated. Diagnosed as a paranoid schizophrenic, he received haloperidol (a tranquilizer). Although he initially complained about side-effects such as palpitations, restlessness, and pains, within two weeks he no longer had hallucinations and he later became less preoccupied with his delusions.

Insight-Oriented Therapies

Most people who have never participated in psychotherapy expect the therapist to tell them what they are doing wrong with their lives. In effect, they expect the therapist to give advice, recommend courses of action, and tell them how to resolve their problems. Just so, Asian Americans tend to view therapy as an authoritarian process in which the therapist acts like a parent or omniscient expert and tells the client what to do (Arkoff et al., 1966). But therapists are human beings; they are neither sages nor prognosticators. Instead of imposing their values on the clients and telling them how to live their lives, insight-oriented therapists, who constitute the majority of therapists, focus on helping clients to understand themselves and their problems. It is believed that once clients have this understanding, they will be able to generate solutions to their own problems (Tseng & McDermott, 1975), based on their values.

Consider the case of a 38-year-old, married, and depressed *Nisei* (described by Yamamoto & Acosta, 1982), whose father had died after a long illness. While he was ailing, she had taken very good care of him at home until, unable to care for him at home any longer, she put him into a convalescent home. She visited daily and did all she could to comfort and care for him but he complained about living there. After his death at age 75, she became depressed, could not sleep, became anorexic, and had severely critical thoughts about herself (e.g., ruminating about what she could have done for him, but did not do). She would no longer enter her father's bedroom or watch television because she would be reminded of her father watching television.

The therapist suggested that the reason she was so self-critical was not that she had neglected her father but that she secretly resented having to do so much to take care of him. She had felt guilty over having those thoughts and criticized and punished herself. That insight could help her focus on the actual reason for her guilt and self-criticism. Such an understanding of her feelings would be a basis for her, with the help of the therapist, to resolve her problem.

Psychodynamic Therapies

Psychodynamic therapies are insight-oriented and focus on intrapsychic and interpersonal conflicts, with special emphasis on the role of a person's unconscious motives. Presumably, these motives are frequently based on childhood experiences, unresolved fears and conflicts, and defense mechanisms. Psychoanalytic therapy, also known as Freudian therapy, is the form of psychodynamic therapy that most people associate with psychotherapy, but it is not typical of the forms of psychotherapy practiced nowadays.

Cognitive Therapies

The basic premise of cognitive therapies, which also are insight-oriented, is that psychological problems stem from misinterpretations and cognitive distortions of people (including oneself) and situations. Rather than concentrate on the unconscious, cognitive therapies focus on changing the way people feel and behave by helping them recognize how their thinking processes and assumptions cause them to misinterpret people (including themselves) and situations.

There are many cognitive therapies, including combinations of cognitive and behavioral therapy. A survey of Asian American therapists working with Asian American clients (Matsushima & Tashima, 1982) showed that cognitive/behavioral techniques were used usually or almost always by 46% of these Asian American therapists whereas a psychodynamic approach was used by 32% and a pharmacotherapeutic approach was used by 18% of the therapists.

Psychotherapy with Asian Americans

Although most therapists have personally preferred forms of therapy, they are not blindly attached to a particular approach: They have some flexibility in the type of therapy they use depending on the nature of a client's problem. For example, the survey of Asian American therapists found that somatic problems were most often treated with pharmaco-therapy, adjustment problems (e.g., work, acculturation) were most often treated with cognitive/behavioral methods, and intrapsychic problems (e.g., low self-concept, identity conflicts, relationship problems, depression) were most often treated with psychodynamic and related techniques emphasizing self-exploration (Matsushima & Tashima, 1982). Many forms of therapy are effective with Asian Americans: Therapists have reported that behavioral (Ford, 1981; M. K. Ho, 1984), psychopharmacological, and various insight-oriented therapies (M. K. Ho, 1984; Matsuoka, 1990; Tung, 1991; Yamamoto & Acosta, 1982) have been successfully used with Asian American clients.

If an immigrant Asian American or refugee were having difficulties adjusting to life in the United States, even a therapist who customarily is insight-oriented might treat the client with techniques that are not particularly insight-oriented.[1] Most therapists are not going to insist that poverty-stricken clients gain insight into their poverty. Some therapists vary their techniques (along such dimensions as authoritativeness and structure imposed on the therapeutic situation) depending on the level of acculturation of their Asian American clients (Matsushima & Tashima, 1982). Since Asian Americans in general prefer therapies that emphasize external sources of stress over intrapsychic conflicts and immediate techniques to manage practical problems over in-depth discussions of the problem (Brown et al., 1973; S. Kim, 1983; E. Lee, 1988; S. Sue & Zane, 1987; Yamamoto & Acosta, 1982), therapists with experience treating Asian American clients will often focus on the immediate problem.

---

[1]For example, therapists might organize groups of Southeast Asians and provide them instructions on how to speak English, shop, use computers, and use public transportation; might explain American culture and Western perspectives about mental illness and physical illness; might support recreational and cultural celebrations; or might sponsor guest speakers who discuss dental care or common herbs found in the United States. Therapists might enlist the help of monks, herbalists, and ethnic mutual-aid organizations (Bemak, 1989; Canda, 1989; Canda & Phaobtong, 1992; Irby & Pon, 1988; Kanuha, 1987; E. Lee, 1988; E. Lee & Lu, 1989; K-M. Lin et al., 1982; Boehnlein, 1987) that can provide information and emotional support, perform bereavement rituals, teach mediation, counsel, alleviate loneliness, renew social networks, reinforce traditional values, help clients strengthen pride in their culture and a sense of ethnic identity, and reestablish feelings of security (C. Ho, 1990; Kinzie, 1989; Moore & Boehnlein, 1991; S. Nguyen, 1982; Owan, 1985; Rozée & Van Boemel, 1989), thereby helping individuals cope with their problems (Owan, 1985; Silverman, 1985) and ameliorating the risk of becoming depressed (Beiser et al., 1989).

DISCREPANT EXPECTATIONS AND POTENTIAL AREAS OF MISUNDERSTANDING

Since Asian Americans, like other Americans, sometimes are unfamiliar with therapeutic processes and since therapy runs counter to some cultural expectations that Asian Americans have, a good therapist will explain the nature of psychotherapy (e.g., what happens in therapy, the role of the therapist, and the rationale behind various therapeutic activities) to naive clients (Ishisaka et al., 1985).[2] For now, consider some ways in which therapy can conflict with the cultural expectations and interaction styles of many Asian Americans as well as ways in which lack of familiarity with psychotherapy, racism, and language difficulties can contribute to misunderstandings between therapists and Asian American clients.

Rapidity of Diagnosis

The psychological evaluation of a client does not take place instantaneously, but many foreign-born Asian Americans expect a rapid diagnosis without the need for intrusive questions (K. Huang, 1991). Traditional Chinese, for example, do not understand the reason for lengthy evaluation sessions because traditional Chinese healing practices do not require protracted evaluations for diagnoses (E. Lee, 1982). But as one can infer from the discussion of different types of therapy, it can take time to uncover the maladaptive, learned behaviors, the pharmacological needs, the unconscious motives, or the errors in thinking that underlie a problem.

Brevity of Therapy

Just as they expect diagnosis to take place quickly, many Asian Americans expect therapy to be brief. Southeast Asians, for example,

---

[2]When misconceptions that clients have about therapy are corrected and when the therapeutic process, the need for verbal self-disclosure, and the importance of clients' regular attendance at therapy sessions are explained, clients hold more appropriate expectations about therapy, are more satisfied with therapy and their therapist, are less likely to leave therapy prematurely, become less dependent on their therapist, perceive their therapist as being more respectful and accepting of the client, perceive more change in themselves, and are more satisfied with their adjustment than when these matters are not explained (Lambert & Lambert, 1984).

are accustomed to brief therapeutic interventions (such as the one-time performance of a ritual) by monks, shamans, or elders for other problems (Bemak, 1986; Kinzie et al., 1980) and frequently expect their psychological symptoms to be reduced quickly by the therapist (Kinzie, 1989; Lin & Shen, 1991).

Moreover, people usually assume that the superficial problems that they present to a therapist represent their basic problems. Consequently, they think that if they just tell the therapist what their problems are, the therapist will tell them how to fix the problems. But sometimes the ostensible problems are just symptoms of underlying intrapsychic, learned, or biochemical problems. For the therapist to comprehend the underlying problem and for clients to gain insight into their problems, extended discussions may have to take place. This can be a time-consuming process. Many foreign-born Asian Americans, unfamiliar with the conceptual underpinnings of Western psychother-apy, feel frustrated by the questions, balk at a therapy that apparently involves only talking (S. Nguyen, 1982), and dismiss as ineffectual therapists who rely only on talk (Kam, 1989; Yamamoto & Acosta, 1982).

Those who want therapy to be completed quickly might suppose that they should seek non-insight-oriented therapies because those would not take as much time. However, the type of therapy employed depends, at least in part, on the nature of the problems. In many cases, if the underlying problems are not addressed, a client simply will develop new symptoms for the same underlying problems when the immediate, ostensible problems pass.[3]

In addition, some disorders (e.g., those stemming from massive traumas) have waxing and waning symptoms that require long-term therapy (Kinzie, 1989). Time-limited therapy with Cambodians who have PTSD as a result of massive traumas (rather than the single stressor that causes many cases of PTSD among other Americans) has produced poor results (Kinzie, 1989; Kinzie & Fleck, 1987) and has left the clients feeling anxious and abandoned (Kinzie, 1989).

---

[3]But to help clients and encourage them to stay in therapy long enough to address more deeply rooted issues, therapists might focus initially on solving immediate problems or on helping clients to receive social services (Fugita et al., 1991; M-K. Ho, 1984; S. Nguyen, 1982) and later move toward more psychologically threatening, underlying issues (D. W. Sue & S. Sue, 1972). One advantage to focusing on concrete needs first is that it provides a context for clients to see therapy as just another way to help them deal with unfortunate or uncontrollable events and free them from feeling shamed (M-K. Ho, 1984).

Scheduling Appointments

Many Southeast Asians do not know what expectations therapists have about appointments. Since punctuality often is not stressed in Southeast Asian cultures, Southeast Asian clients might be late for appointments. Some Southeast Asian clients do not consider follow-up therapy appointments to be binding (Tung, 1985), or they frequently show up without an appointment (D. W. Sue & D. Sue, 1977; Tung, 1985). The resulting confusion can embarrass the client.

Perceived Sources of Problems

Like other Americans, Asian American clients often differ from therapists in their assumptions about the causes of psychological problems. Since some Asian American clients have divergent views on the causes of the problems, they also have correspondingly different views on how to resolve those problems. Therapists tend to focus on the clients' feelings, past experiences, unconscious motives and conflicts, cognitive distortions, or biochemical imbalances in order to find the source of psychological problems, whereas Asian American clients often look to a lack of willpower and self-discipline to find the source of psychological problems (Root, 1985). Insight-oriented therapists believe that insight into problems provides new perspectives that can bring about change, whereas Asian American clients often believe that change is derived from learning to have increased willpower and self-discipline (Root, 1985; S. Sue & Morishima, 1982). Therapists and Asian American clients sometimes hold different expectations regarding the clients' responsibility for their current plight (Singer, 1976; D. W. Sue, 1978) and their ability to initiate change (Singer, 1976). Misunderstandings can arise, the rapport between therapist and client can be compromised, and therapy may be deemed unhelpful if the therapist and client have different conceptualizations of therapy and of the client's problem (S. Sue & Zane, 1987), if the criteria for successful therapy are not jointly agreed upon by the therapist and the client, or if the therapeutic goals are not consistent with cultural expectations (Fugita et al., 1991) or clearly discussed so as to prevent premature withdrawal from therapy.

Communication Styles

Since therapists do not have crystal balls, to uncover unconscious motives and conflicts and to understand the cognitive distortions taking place, therapists usually want clients to discuss openly their thoughts and feelings. In fact, oftentimes therapists find that it is helpful simply to give clients free reign to talk about their problems to an empathic listener. In contrast, many Asian American clients, reared to listen quietly to authority figures out of respect, expect the therapist, as an authority figure, to do most of the talking (Kinzie, 1985; S. Sue & Morishima, 1982). Some clients (e.g., Mien) believe that verbally taking the lead in therapy would be disrespectful (Moore & Boehnlein, 1991). Therefore, there are sometimes discrepancies between the expectations of therapists and Asian American clients. It is necessary to consider the reasons behind the potential communication gap between therapists and their Asian American clients.

Reluctance to Discuss Problems

Many Asian Americans are hesitant to discuss their feelings and problems openly. Some of the same attitudes that discourage Asian Americans from seeking mental health services discourage them, once they are in therapy, from discussing their problems.

For example, in the case of Southeast Asians, inasmuch as feelings (e.g., depression, regrets, guilt, and shame) are considered essentially private matters, discussing them would be considered indiscreet and an indication of a lack of character (Kinzie, 1989; E. Lee, 1988; Owan, 1985; Tung, 1985). Thus, Southeast Asian clients seldom report psychological symptoms spontaneously (Kinzie et al., 1990). If asked about such feelings, Southeast Asian clients may try to avoid discussing these issues by talking around the subject or by not talking during the rest of the therapy session (Tung, 1985).

Fear of shaming the family not only discourages Asian Americans from seeking therapy but also causes some Asian Americans, once in therapy, to hesitate to discuss their problems openly. Even in a therapeutic situation, some Asian Americans will not want to discuss family relationships, nor will they explicitly criticize their parents or make any comments that might reflect poorly on themselves, their family, or their ethnic community (Tung, 1985). In turn, such a style can interfere with the therapists' diagnoses and effectiveness.

Many Asians think that there is no purpose in complaining about problems since they are natural, unavoidable aspects of life (Kinzie et al., 1990). Just as this perspective discourages Asian Americans from seeking mental health services, it also discourages Asian Americans from discussing their problems once they are in therapy ("Mental Health," 1985; Tung, 1985). Although this belief is based at least in part on Buddhist perspectives, even non-Buddhist Asian American clients hold such beliefs because many Buddhist beliefs have become incorporated into Asian American culture.

Attendant with a discussion of feelings could be the arousal of strong, uncontrollable emotions, but Asian cultural values stressing interpersonal harmony and self-control reinforce restraint of emotional expressiveness and silent endurance of suffering (E. Lee & Lu, 1989). The display of strong emotions is considered another sign of weakness (Kinzie, 1989; E. Lee & Lu, 1989). For example, Japanese culture holds that the ability to control one's strong emotions is necessary for mental health and reflects maturity and wisdom (Fugita et al., 1991). Thus, some Asian Americans will hide their distress out of a sense of stoicism and pride (Brower, 1989; Kinzie et al., 1990). A therapist unfamiliar with the reasons for this behavior could misinterpret such restraint as indicating a lack of affect, the client's lack of awareness of his or her own feelings, or "confirmation" of stereotypes of Asians as inscrutable or deceptive people (D. W. Sue, 1990).

In addition to concerns about stigma and traditional coping strategies, there are other reasons that Asian Americans are reluctant to discuss their problems. Many Asian Americans are reared to think that talking a lot about themselves or quickly disclosing personal information and emotions to a stranger is immodest, boring, dominating, and indicative of a lack of self-control (Johnson & Johnson, 1975; S. Kim, 1983; Leong, 1986; Owan, 1985; Tung, 1985). Rather than being inclined to blurt out their life story to a therapist, Asian Americans generally are accustomed to having others find out about them indirectly, gently, and over a relatively extended period (Johnson & Johnson, 1975).

Experiences with racism also may have reinforced silence in some minority group members. Some Asian Americans are reticent about discussing their problems because they have seen hostility directed toward minorities when they mention their problems.

Cambodians have a special reason to be uncommunicative. Many have expanded the notion of individual karma to national karma: To account for the atrocities suffered during Pol Pot's reign, some Cambodians assume that the atrocities were a punishment for something bad done by Cambodians in the past (Kinzie, 1989; Kinzie et al., 1984). Because of this sense of group shame as well as cultural values stressing the importance of accepting life as it is, Cambodians generally find it difficult to talk about their experiences in Cambodia (Kinzie, 1989; Kinzie et al., 1984).

Furthermore, knowing that the Khmer Rouge tortured or killed people who appeared intelligent, many refugees physically and emotionally survived the torture and rape in Southeast Asia by not expressing themselves and by acting as if they were confused or stupid

(Chung & Okazaki, 1991). Many continue that coping style in the United States: They hide their feelings, do not ask questions, and do not complain about their circumstances (Chung & Okazaki, 1991).

Some Southeast Asians are hesitant about revealing their problems because they find it difficult to trust therapists. Many Southeast Asian clients have had their trust betrayed by others in the past (Rozée & Van Boemel, 1989): When the Khmer Rouge tortured and murdered innocent people, many Cambodians lost confidence in authority figures; when the Khmer Rouge forced children to spy on parents and forced neighbors to spy on neighbors, many Cambodians developed a generalized feeling that they could not trust others (Rozée & Van Boemel, 1989); when the Vietnamese government seized the assets of Chinese-Vietnamese, denied them jobs, and reduced their food rations, the distrust that many Chinese-Vietnamese felt toward the Vietnamese government grew; when the Pathet Lao attacked the Hmong and Mien and when the United States reneged on its promises to them, many Hmong and Mien lost their trust in others. When a lack of trust is carried over into the therapeutic relationship, effective treatment is impeded.

Even the setting in which therapy takes place can inhibit self-disclosure. Southeast Asians sometimes feel uncomfortable in formal office settings because the room elicits traumatic memories (Bemak, 1989). For example, asking Cambodian patients benign questions (such as their names) in a small room with no women present can remind Cambodians of interrogations in Kampuchea and may result in their becoming blocked (Kinzie, 1989). If a therapist takes notes on nondemographic information during therapy sessions, clients who are reminded of the way information was used against them in Southeast Asia might become fearful and wonder why the information is being recorded (Ishisaka et al., 1985).

Many Southeast Asians have suffered traumas faced by few Americans. Most American therapists, then, have not had a great deal of experience diagnosing the problems of clients who have faced perhaps years of the types of traumas experienced by Southeast Asians. The therapists can be helped in their efforts if they know what traumas were experienced (Mollica, Wyshak, de Marneffe, et al., 1987; Rozée & Van Boemel, 1987). However, psychological numbing and amnesia can be consequences of experiencing traumas and can be reasons that Cambodians do not talk spontaneously about their traumatic past (Kinzie, 1989; Kinzie et al., 1990). Similarly, Mien reportedly (Moore & Boehnlein, 1991) rarely discuss their PTSD symptoms because of psychological numbing, a sense of shame, or the view that these symptoms are just more inconveniences in their difficult lives. This avoidant behavior seems to be resilient: Even after other PTSD symptoms have been eliminated, the avoidant symptoms remain (Kinzie, 1989; Kinzie & Leung, 1989).

A client's family might encourage the client's denial of and reluctance to discuss traumas in order to protect both the client and family members from memories of their traumas (E. Lee & Lu, 1989). Southeast Asian clients are often deeply involved with their families, who may have also had to deal with traumas and adjustment problems. Families often do not want their familial harmony disrupted by confrontations with psychological problems, and family members may think that the client would be better off not thinking about his or her traumatic past. To that end, family members may indicate to clients that the traumatic past should not be dredged up and that the display of emotions regarding that past are not acceptable (E. Lee & Lu, 1989).

In fact, initial discussions of symptoms and personal histories with therapists can temporarily exacerbate a client's condition because they represent a breach in the client's behavior pattern of avoidance (Kinzie, 1989). Cambodians, for instance, generally do not find it cathartic to discuss their traumatic past (McQuaide, 1989). Indeed, repeatedly re-calling traumatic experiences can increase the occurrence of PTSD symptoms, such as intrusive thoughts, depression, and psychological numbing (Kinzie & Fleck, 1987). Thus, it is not surprising that some traumatized Southeast Asians would say that therapy made them feel worse than they did before. However, like going through purgatory, sometimes it is necessary to delve into unpleasantness in order to reach resolution.

Another reason that some Asian Americans hesitate to discuss their personal problems is that they are confused by the demeanor of the therapist. Therapists generally hope their clients will be low self-monitors; that is, that they will express their attitudes and feelings with little regard for cues from others, situational constraints, or the potential for disrupting social harmony. But many Asian Americans are high self-monitors; that is, they tend to monitor situations, to look for cues about how to behave, and then to try to behave accordingly (K. Huang, 1991). If they receive no cues from a therapist about how to behave, they will be anxious and quiet, fearing that they will behave in a socially inappropriate way and embarrass themselves (Shon & Ja, 1982).[4]

Whereas American psychotherapists tend to adopt democratic and egalitarian roles with their clients (E. Lee, 1982; Yamamoto & Acosta,

---

[4]Note how this relates to the discussion in Chapter 3 about the possibility that Asian Americans are more concerned than Euro-Americans about fulfilling the needs of videotaping experimenters.

1982), many Asian Americans, seeing their therapists as authority figures, do not expect or want their therapists to take such egalitarian roles (S. Kim, 1983; S. Sue & Zane, 1987). Traditional Asian Americans—unaccustomed to horizontal, democratic relationships—can feel insecure or anxious if their therapist's behavior is egalitarian (Yamamoto & Acosta, 1982). Thus, when a therapist attempts to establish rapport with clients with excessive and irrelevant small talk, resistance and hostility can be aroused in Asian American clients (Ford, 1987).

In Asian cultures one's behavior toward another traditionally depends on one's relationship to that person. Therefore, traditional Asian Americans might try to judge the status of therapists, asking therapists about such matters as their marital status, background, salary, personal belongings, and so forth, looking for "areas of mutual compatibility . . . [and] to 'evaluate' the clinician's background" (E. Lee, 1982, p. 545; Union of Pan Asian Communities, 1978). If therapists, unaccustomed to responding to such questions, balk at answering, the rapport and credibility needed in therapeutic relationships could be undercut (M-K. Ho, 1984; E. Lee, 1982; Shon & Ja, 1982). Furthermore, the potential discrepancy between a therapist's ascribed status (e.g., being young, being female) and achieved status as an expert could erode a therapist's credibility to some Asian Americans (S. Sue & Zane, 1987) and, therefore, cause them to feel uncertain how to behave toward that therapist. For example, the discomfort that Filipinos feel when discussing their personal problems is sometimes exacerbated if a therapist has less education, is younger, or is of the opposite sex (Okamura & Agbayani, 1991).

Vietnamese generally expect authority figures, such as therapists, to "appear calm, quiet, and unhurried, thus conveying the impression of maturity, wisdom, and dignity" (Ishisaka et al., 1985, p. 49). They consider a "loud voice and warm, hearty greeting [to be] rude and unseemly in a person of authority" (Brower, 1989, p. 134). If they encounter a therapist who is loud and hearty, Vietnamese clients might respond with embarrassed silence (Brower, 1989). On the other hand, since Filipino cultures emphasize the importance of social acceptance and emotional closeness, therapists may need to be more personable when working with Filipino Americans than with some other Asian American groups (Okamura & Agbayani, 1991), lest the clients feel unwelcome and not talk much in therapy.

If therapy sessions are unstructured (i.e., the client is expected to take the initiative in the conversation) and if the therapist does not tell the client who should start talking, how much the client should talk, what should be discussed, and that the disclosure of a great deal of information is appropriate (Fugita et al., 1991), many Asian American clients do not know how to behave—and they retreat into silence. Exacerbating the confusion, Asian American clients will often hesitate to ask a therapist questions because they fear that asking questions would make them appear distrustful and critical of the therapist (Tsui & Schultz, 1988). Unstructured therapeutic settings can arouse discomfort, anxiety, and confusion for Asian Americans brought up in traditional Asian American family environments that have highly structured social roles and patterns of social interaction (D. W. Sue & D. Sue, 1977). In response to these feelings, such clients respond by remaining silent because silence is considered the safest way to avoid embarrassment and to maintain harmony.

Directive, structured, and unambiguous therapeutic strategies are preferred by most Asian American clients because such approaches are consonant with their expectations, values, and interaction styles (Atkinson, Maruyama, & Matsui, 1978; E. Lee, 1988; Matsushima & Tashima, 1982; Mokuau, 1987; S. Nguyen, 1982; Okamura & Agbayani, 1991; Root, 1985; Rozée & Van Boemel, 1989; D. W. Sue, 1989b, 1990). If a therapist is not directive or maintains a neutral, nonjudgmental demeanor in the initial session, Asian American clients might misinterpret that as indicating disinterest or incompetence (Fugita, et al., 1991; E. Lee, 1982; Yamamoto & Acosta, 1982). Reluctant to bore the therapist or talk to a therapist whom they believe to be incompetent, these Asian Americans might simply not discuss their feelings or experiences.

The confusion that can arise when the therapist behaves in a way that the client does not expect can disrupt the rapport between them, undermine the therapist's credibility in the client's eyes, frustrate the client, cause the client to be taciturn, or motivate the client to drop out of therapy prematurely. Therapists who have had a great deal of experience with Asian American clients will usually both explain the therapeutic process and accommodate some of their therapeutic styles to meet the expectations and needs of clients.

Finally, sometimes a multidisciplinary, team approach is adopted in therapy—that is, individuals from different backgrounds (e.g., a psychologist, a physician, a social worker, and a psychiatric nurse) work together to help the patient. This approach, while helpful, also can be confusing to some Asian Americans (E. Lee, 1982) if the roles of the various professionals are not explained. If the patients are unfamiliar with the roles of various professional mental health service providers, they, understandably, do not know how to behave toward them. If the primary therapist does not provide cues indicating how they should behave, Chinese or Southeast Asian patients, for instance, may feel anxious and respond with only polite silence (K. Huang, 1991; Ishisaka, et al., 1985).

This discussion of the reasons that Asian Americans are frequently taciturn in therapy notwithstanding, their tendency to be reticent about discussing problems should not be overgeneralized. Clinical experience has demonstrated that Asian Americans can readily discuss their feelings of "hopelessness, worthlessness, sadness, loneliness, and low energy" (Mollica & Lavelle, 1988, p. 276; Beiser & Fleming, 1986).

But insofar as clients are reticent about talking frankly about their problems, a therapist is hampered in his or her ability to obtain a thorough history of the client, make a proper diagnosis, and effectively treat an Asian American client. Consequently, clients, not realizing how important it is to speak their mind in therapy, might not derive as much benefit as is possible from therapy sessions.

Miscommunication

Miscommunication between therapist and client can undermine the mutual trust and rapport needed between them as well as the therapist's credibility, and the effectiveness of therapy (Flaskerud, 1986b; D. W. Sue, 1990). The communication styles of many Asian Americans are likely to be misinterpreted by culturally insensitive therapists who do not have experience with Asian American clients. For example, Asian Americans sometimes make self-deprecating remarks because of cultural values such as modesty rather than because they actually believe those statements and have low self-esteem (Tung, 1985); a therapist who is unfamiliar with such cultural values and interaction styles might tend to assume the latter. Many Asian Americans are hesitant to disclose a great deal of information about themselves because of cultural values and experiences with racism; a therapist who is ignorant of Asian American cultural styles of communicating might misinterpret this as indicating that the clients are shy, repressed, in denial, inhibited, resistant (i.e., unconsciously trying to avoid addressing their problems), defensive, nonverbal, unperceptive, simple-minded, negative, uncooperative, or sullen (Mokuau & Shimizu, 1991; Root, 1985; D. W. Sue & D. Sue, 1977).

The case of Dave (described by D. Sue & D. W. Sue, 1991) illustrates what can happen when the therapist is not attuned to an Asian American client's communication style or cultural values. Dave, a 21-year-old, Chinese American majoring in electrical engineering, was having academic problems, headaches, indigestion, and insomnia. A medical exam revealed no organic disorder. At the first therapy session, he appeared depressed and anxious, responded to questions with brief, polite statements, rarely offered unsolicited information about himself, avoided discussing his feelings, and expressed his concern about his academic problems in an indirect manner. After a number of sessions, it was revealed that Dave did not like engineering but that his parents wanted him to become an engineer. The therapist interpreted the situation as indicating that Dave was not taking responsibility for his life, was too dependent on his parents, and feared letting his parents know how angry he was. The therapist instructed Dave to imagine that his parents were seated opposite him and to express his true feelings as though they were present. Although expressing his feelings was very difficult for Dave, under constant pressure from the therapist, Dave did so eventually. Subsequently, Dave appeared to become even more withdrawn and guilt-ridden than he was initially. The therapist evidently did not recognize that Dave's truncated statements could have reflected attempts to be respectful toward the therapist or perhaps a confusion about the therapeutic process. The therapist also failed to recognize that Dave's desire to avoid criticizing his mother and father could have reflected efforts to speak respectfully about them. When the therapist told Dave to imagine telling his parents how he felt, it was the therapist's own values (e.g., openness and expression of feelings) that were being imposed on Dave. Such behavior might have conflicted with the value that Dave placed on respect for his parents (D. Sue & D. W. Sue, 1991). The therapist's ethnocentric perspective may also have biased the diagnosis.

On occasion, Asian Americans feel that they are being bumptious when they are forced by circumstances to speak directly. To ensure that they are not being bumptious, some Asian American clients will not discuss their problems without repeated prodding. An analogy has been drawn (Fugita et al., 1991) between Japanese American cultural values that call for repeated offers of food before such an offer is accepted and the need to ask clients questions more than once. Failure to encourage the clients to discuss their problems can limit the information the therapist can obtain and can make diagnosis and treatment more difficult.

The following instance (described by Toupin, 1980) illustrates what can happen when a therapist is not aware that Asian Americans often look for social cues encouraging them to speak up about their problems and may misinterpret the intentions of a therapist who is not sensitive to their style of communication. An Asian American client who had been seeing a therapist three times a week was going to be away for a month during the Christmas season. The therapist told the client to call if he needed to talk. Like other Asian Americans who tend to try to avoid imposing on others (Union of Pan Asian Communities, 1978), the client did not call because he did not want to impose on the therapist's holiday and because he did not consider the therapist's offer to be sincere since the therapist did not insist that he call. His anxieties built and he soon had to be placed in a mental hospital. The therapist had not employed a culturally appropriate way to encourage the client to call.

When personal information is revealed, it is not disclosed as directly by many Asian American clients as most therapists expect and prefer. Euro-American, middle-class rules and conventions of speaking and listening, emotional tones, interpretations of speaking patterns, notions of personal space, readings of facial expressions, and expectations concerning eye contact sometimes do not coincide with those of many minorities, including Asian Americans (Fong, 1965; Johnson & Johnson, 1975; D.W. Sue, 1990; D. W. Sue & D. Sue, 1977).

While Euro-Americans generally try to speak directly to a point, many Asian Americans think that such a speaking style can disrupt interpersonal harmony and alienate other people. Such directness is considered to be too blunt and a sign of immaturity, rudeness, and a lack of finesse (D. W. Sue & D. Sue, 1977). Instead, Asian Americans traditionally have been taught to employ indirect styles of communicating, to avoid direct confrontations, and to deflect unpleasantness that can lead to disagreements and embarrassment (Hong, 1989; JWK International, 1978; Kalish & Reynolds, 1976; S. Kim, 1983; Liem, 1980). For example, direct verbal confrontation, which could lead to irreconcilable conflicts, are frequently parried by Japanese Americans (Kitano & Kikumura, 1980). Similarly, Vietnamese styles of interacting call for expressing desires and feelings indirectly and avoiding confrontations (Union of Pan Asian Communities, 1978). Therefore, Vietnamese sometimes will not answer a question if answering the question could disrupt interpersonal harmony (Liem, 1980), will indicate that they agree with a speaker simply because disagreement might be considered rude or might conflict with the answer that the speaker may want to hear (Brower, 1989), or will be vague to avoid confrontation. If a therapist is too blunt and too direct, some Asian American clients, particularly those who are not so acculturated, will be put off.

If emotional difficulties are discussed by Southeast Asians, they will often be expressed in an oblique, understated way with little obvious emotion, implying that the problem is more mild than it really is (Hong, 1989; Owan, 1985; Tung, 1985). Negative emotions such as anger, grief, and depression may be expressed in an indirect, muted way (Tung, 1985). Such an interaction style makes it easier to sustain interpersonal harmony. If the therapist does not recognize this style of interaction, misdiagnosis can result: A culturally naive therapist may mistake this style for denial, lack of affect, lack of awareness of his or her own feelings, deceptiveness, or resistance on the part of the client (D. W. Sue, 1990).

Asian Americans commonly are taught to be especially sensitive to nonverbal and indirect communication (JWK International, 1978) because in Asian cultures more than in American culture the speaker relies on the social sensitivity of the listener. The listener is supposed to be sensitive to indirect verbal and nonverbal social cues, read between the lines, and infer the attitudes and sentiments of the speaker (Shon & Ja, 1982) so that speakers do not have to make blunt statements that could be socially disruptive, embarrassing, or hurtful. Spurred on by cultural values and racism, many Asian Americans will speak euphemistically and ambiguously (D. W. Sue, 1990). Vietnamese clients, for instance, might hint at their desires or might talk around the subject and wait for the listener to catch on (Liem, 1980; Morrow, 1987). Yet, Asian Americans sometimes find that a therapist is not sensitive to this style of communication and, thus, does not notice the social cues the Asian Americans are providing. The result can be frustration and ineffective therapy if Asian American clients seek services from such an inexperienced or insensitive therapist.

Without being conscious of it, some Asian Americans expect that their therapist will be able to pick up on subtle cues, which they may prefer over direct and open communication; if the therapist demands the latter, they might will think the therapist is too blunt and insensitive (Shon & Ja, 1982). Culturally insensitive therapists who do not notice the indirect cues that Asian American clients are giving might misdiagnose the clients as being deceptive or resistant to therapy. But clients who provide hints about their feelings are not being deceptive and are not resisting therapy if they expect the listeners to understand those cues (Lam, 1980; Morrow, 1987).

If a therapist is not sensitive to indirect modes of communication such as suggestions, examples, pauses, and nonverbal behavior, he or she will misunderstand what his or her clients mean (Fugita et al., 1991; E. Lee, 1982). If some Asian Americans are silent or speak softly, the reason is probably that they are being polite and respectful; it is not necessarily that they are shy or weak, or want to yield the floor, or do not want to speak (Rozée & Van Boemel, 1989; D. W. Sue & D. Sue, 1977). Among Vietnamese it is not unusual for conversation to be punctuated by long periods of silence (Liem, 1980). When a therapist does not understand why an Asian American client might be silent and is uncomfortable with the person's silence, the therapist might misinterpret the silence (Root, Ho, & S. Sue, 1986) and speak prematurely, thus preventing the client from fully revealing what he or she wanted to discuss (D. W. Sue & D. Sue, 1977).

On the one hand, a therapist who is not aware that many Asian Americans will understate their emotional condition could mistakenly underestimate the severity of his or her client's problems. On the other hand, a naive therapist might overestimate a problem by assuming that something that is simply a manifestation of a general difference between Asian Americans and Euro-Americans (e.g., in verbal expressiveness and the tendency to dominate) indicates that a particular Asian American is maladjusted (J. Chin, 1983). In support of this proposition, a study found that Euro-American therapists (who in general are probably less aware of Asian American communication patterns than are Asian American therapists) diagnosed their Chinese American clients as being more depressed and inhibited, less socially poised, and poorer in interpersonal skills than Chinese American therapists did (Li-Repac, 1980).

Sometimes clients and therapists make inaccurate inferences based on the volume of the others' speaking voices. People born in Asian countries, where denizens often speak more softly than people in the United States, sometimes interpret loud speech as indicative of aggressiveness or poor self-control (D. W. Sue & D. Sue, 1990). In contrast, a culturally insensitive therapist might mistake the quiet speech of Asian American clients as indicating that the clients are distant and unemotional (Kikumura & Kitano, 1976).

Another source of misunderstanding is in the meaning of body language. For example, Asian cultural values that stress respect for and deference to authority cause Asian Americans to avoid extended eye contact with a person of purportedly superior status. Some Asian Americans consider direct, sustained eye contact to be challenging or confrontational (M-K. Ho, 1984; E. Lee, 1982). However, a culturally naive therapist could misconstrue such avoidance of eye contact as an indication of shyness, depression, or disinterest (D. W. Sue, 1990). When Vietnamese clients nod, that does not necessarily mean that the clients agree with or understand what the therapist has said (Union of Pan Asian Communities, 1978). The clients might just be trying to maintain harmony in the relationship and avoid embarrassment. A culturally naive therapist might assume that if Vietnamese, Cambodian, or Laotian clients smile, the clients are happy or embarrassed. In fact, the smiles also could indicate anger, sorrow, agreement, disagreement, stoicism, understanding, not understanding, or rejection (Brower, 1989; Morrow, 1987).

Being sensitive to Asian American interaction styles includes behaving with the graciousness that Asian Americans expect in respect-ful interpersonal relationships. If therapists do not behave with the expected graciousness (e.g., warmly welcoming the clients through verbal and nonverbal communications, offering tea or soft drinks, encouraging the clients to remove their coat to be more comfortable, or offering a comfortable chair), clients might feel unwelcome (M-K. Ho, 1984). A therapist inadvertently could insult clients and their families by not greeting family members in the proper order: Among Vietnamese, Cambodians, and Laotians, the head of the family or the eldest person is supposed to be greeted first (Morrow, 1987). Therapists might intend to establish warm relationships by using nicknames when referring to clients or by Anglicizing the pronunciation of their clients' names but find, instead, that they have offended the clients (Brower, 1989).

Furthermore, Mien believe that calling attention to or publicly praising children can cause evil spirits to pay attention to the children—which increases the chances that the children will become ill or die (Moore & Boehnlein, 1991). Therefore, if a therapist innocently remarks on how pretty a child is, the parents may become angry or distrustful of the therapist (Moore & Boehnlein, 1991). Such unintentional offenses can drive clients away from therapy and lead them to conclude that psychotherapy is not appropriate for them or that therapists in general do not understand their perspectives.

Given the value placed on interpersonal harmony, the desire to be respectful of authority figures (Kinzie et al., 1988), the reluctance to speak up, and the indirect style of communicating found among many Asian Americans, it is not surprising that many Asian American clients will hesitate to disagree directly with a therapist, or let a therapist know when they are confused, or tell a therapist that they are dissatisfied with the therapy—even though the therapist would like them to do so (E. Lee, 1982; Root, 1985, 1989). Instead, most Asian Americans who feel dissatisfied or confused will simply and without explanation stop seeing the therapist. For example, because they do not want to be disrespectful to authority figures, Southeast Asians usually cope with a conflict with an authority figure by suppressing and refusing to ac-knowledge their anger, resentment, or frustration, and so might drop out of therapy rather than confront these feelings (Brower, 1989). Similarly, if a psychiatrist prescribes a medicine that is ineffectual for a particular patient or a psychologist prescribes a treatment that does not help, a Mien client might not mention that the treatment did not work, in order to protect the therapist's honor (Moore & Boehnlein, 1991). But by dropping out of therapy prematurely, the clients can form inaccurate impressions of the effectiveness of psychotherapy.

Therapists sometimes are limited in how much they can comfortably change their communication styles. "The difficulty in shifting styles may be a function of inadequate practice, inability to understand the other person's world view, [theoretical orientation,] and/or personal biases or racist attitudes that have not been adequately resolved" (D. W. Sue & D. Sue, 1990, p. 72). In keeping with American Psychological Association Guidelines (American Psychological Association, 1990), therapists who have such problems should consult with other therapists who have more experience working with Asian Americans or might refer clients to such therapists (D. W. Sue & D. Sue, 1990). However, if a therapist knows that he or she cannot provide effective therapy to some individuals and refers them to another therapist, the clients might misinterpret this as a sign of rejection or think that they are "so messed up" that the therapist had to send for "reinforcements." Even if a therapist acknowledges to a client the reason for such a referral, the Asian American client may think that the therapist is not revealing the true reason and is just trying to protect his or her feelings. Given this misinterpretation, the client might not follow up on the referral but, instead, might drop out of therapy, concluding that psychotherapy cannot help.

Group Therapy

Asian American clients generally expect individual therapy (i.e., a one-to-one relationship in therapy). Sometimes, though, a therapist thinks that a client would be helped by group therapy (which involves gathering a number of clients together and discussing their problems under the guidance of a therapist) because this type of therapy can help clients see that others share their problems, see how others are trying to deal with their problems, and so forth. There are a number of ways in which group therapy can conflict with the expectations of many Asian Americans and, thus, generate confusion and anxiety.

First, Asian American immigrants and refugees usually are not receptive to group therapy (M-K. Ho, 1984) because such therapy is culturally foreign (Kinzie, 1989), confusing, intimidating, and contrary to cultural values emphasizing that feelings are private matters. Asian American immigrants and refugees also commonly fear that there will be a lack of confidentiality in such group settings (Kinzie et al., 1988).

Second, there are cultural differences in interaction styles that can create apprehension and confusion for some Asian American clients. Asian American and non-Asian American clients tend to have different perspectives on the importance of verbally participating in group therapy. For example, many Euro-American clients think that it is necessary to speak up in order for anything to be accomplished in group therapy, whereas Asian American clients frequently think that loquacious people are just seeking attention (Kaneshige, 1973). Additionally, participants in group therapy often challenge the statements of other members of the group. But directly confronting people and putting them on the spot is considered rude by most Asian Americans (M-K. Ho, 1984).

Non-Asian American participants in group therapy probably will be unaware of Asian American cultural patterns of communicating. They may be more accustomed to verbal openness and might interpret some Asian American communication patterns as an indication of abstruseness or lack of emotion (Johnson & Johnson, 1975). Research has found that Euro-Americans are likely to interpret reticence in Japanese Americans as aloofness, modesty as ineptitude, and "excessive" agreeableness as insincerity (Johnson & Johnson, 1975).

Asian Americans have varying degrees of flexibility in their communication styles; that is, most can somewhat tailor their communication styles to the situation. But this flexibility is not unlimited. How much flexibility Asian Americans have is related in part to their level of acculturation.

If an Asian American does not verbally participate much in group therapy, the other members of the group may start to ignore him or her or make inaccurate interpretations of his or her silence, perhaps projecting their own hostility onto the person. They might make statements on behalf of the Asian American or claim that he or she is more dysfunctional than they are, and otherwise dehumanize and alienate the Asian American (Tsui & Schultz, 1988). These problems are exacerbated when the therapist is not familiar with Asian American values and communication styles. As a consequence, when Asian Americans expect others to attack them for no apparent reason (Tsui & Schultz, 1988), they may become increasingly taciturn or drop out of therapy (Leong, 1986).

Third, the racism of members of the group could cause them to patronize and stereotype an Asian American member, perhaps ridicule the person's Asian language, or assume the need to translate or interpret what he or she has said (Tsui & Schultz, 1988). Alternatively, as a manifestation of their own awkwardness in a situation with a person of a different background, group members might focus on asking about impersonal matters like Asian food or language, under the specious guise of trying to understand the Asian American client (Tsui & Schultz, 1988). The result could be wasted therapy sessions.

Fourth, differences in the structure of some Asian American

families and that of their non-Asian Americans peers can make it difficult for group members to identify or empathize with each other. For example, Chinese Americans and Filipino Americans often have a great deal of contact with their extended family and pseudo-family. These Asian Americans may have difficulty relating to the experiences and values of non-Asian American group members whose families are not so structured or whose lives center around friends or nuclear families (Kuo & Tsui, 1986).

This is not to say that group therapy is always ineffectual for Asian American clients. Group therapy has been found to be useful with American-born Asian Americans; and group therapy for immigrant Asian Americans has been found to be useful if it includes a number of Asian American clients, addresses concrete tasks, or focuses on providing information, referral, advocacy, legal aid, and English classes rather than on sharing personal feelings and opinions (M-K. Ho, 1984; E. Lee, 1988). If there are a number of Asian Americans in a group, there might be a shared familiarity with Asian American communication styles and a diminution of the isolation they might feel.[5]

Family Therapy

Another form of therapy that therapists sometimes think would be helpful is family therapy. This involves including the whole family in the therapy so that family dynamics can be explored, feelings can be expressed, and conflicts can be resolved. However, family therapy, too, can create a number of difficulties. This type of therapy can arouse apprehension in Asian American clients because it involves disclosing to the clients' families that personal problems have been discussed with an outsider, and this could arouse feelings of shame. Moreover, in this type of therapy, families might not be forthcoming or concede that the sources of the problems are in the family because the family members want to protect family's honor (Tung, 1985).

---

[5]It has been suggested that if therapists want to conduct group therapy with Asian American clients, the group should be homogeneous in terms of country of origin, dialect, language fluency, sex, problems, social background, ethnic background, and so on (M-K. Ho, 1984; E. Lee, 1988; E. Lee & Lu, 1989; Tung, 1985). If there is a mix, females may defer to men and the young may defer to the old (Kinzie et al., 1988) because in Asian societies men and the old traditionally do most of the talking. This social hierarchy also can restrict the participation of group members, limit the topics discussed in the groups, and inhibit group members from voicing their conflicts (Kinzie et al., 1988).

In addition, Asian Americans from traditional, hierarchical families are not accustomed to sharing their feelings with each other (E. Lee, 1982). Parents in such families may feel that expressing their fears or sadness can undercut their authoritative roles and may shame them, and children may balk at the thought of seeing vulnerability in their parents (E. Lee, 1982). Even if family members argue at home, they might not express their disagreements in front of the therapist out of respect for the therapist (Hong, 1989).

Despite these difficulties in conducting family therapy with traditional Asian Americans, family therapy has been found to be more appropriate for Asian Americans who identify a great deal with an Asian culture than it is for acculturated Asian Americans (Yamamoto & Acosta, 1982). Like most Americans, third and subsequent generations of Asian Americans tend to prefer individual therapy (Yamamoto & Acosta, 1982).

Lack of Drug Therapy

Since many Asian Americans believe there is a connection between their mental and physical state, they expect their psychological problems to be treated with something that will alter their physical being. For example, when Southeast Asian spiritual healers treat psychological problems, they frequently prescribe herbs, particular foods, or physical manipulations such as coining (Bemak, 1989). Thus, Southeast Asians often expect therapists to prescribe medicine or to do something more than talk. Perhaps in part because they expect medicines to work, Southeast Asians tend to respond more quickly and more frequently to psychotropic drugs than Euro-Americans do (Tung, 1985). If they do not receive something other than talk, they might feel neglected, might drop out of treatment, and might decide that psychotherapy does not have much to offer them.

Poor Compliance with Drug Therapy

Sometimes drug therapy is a part of psychotherapy but the fact that Southeast Asians often do not comply with the medication regimen handicaps the effectiveness of psychotropic medicines that may be prescribed to them. One study found that 61% of 41 depressed Southeast Asian patients who were supposed to be taking antidepressants did not have detectable levels of the medicine in their blood; only 15% of the patients who were supposed to be taking the antidepressants had therapeutic levels in them (Kinzie, Leung, Boehnlein, & Fleck, 1987).

Similarly, a study of Cambodian, Hmong, and Laotian mental health patients reported no medication could be found in 53% of those who claimed to be taking the medication regularly; another 31% had detectable levels of medication in their blood, but the amount of medication was too low to serve a therapeutic function (Kroll et al., 1990).

There are a number of reasons that Southeast Asians in particular may not comply with medication regimens. This first reason, however, applies to Asian Americans in general: It is possible that Asian Americans sometimes receive dosages of psychotropic drugs that are too high for them. Although there is some controversy, a great deal of research indicates that the effective range of dosages of neuroleptic drugs is lower for Asian Americans than for Euro-Americans, even when standardized for body weight (Committee on Cultural Psychiatry, 1989; Ishisaka et al., 1985; K-M. Lin & Finder, 1983;K-M. Lin et al., 1989; K-M. Lin & Shen, 1991; T-J. Lin & Lin, 1978; Muecke, 1983; Rosenblatt & Tang, 1987; Sramek, Sayles, & Simpson, 1986; Yamamoto, 1982). This pattern has been reported for Chinese Americans (Committee on Cultural Psychiatry, 1989; T-J. Lin & Lin, 1978), Japanese Americans (T-J. Lin & Lin, 1978), and Southeast Asians (Tung, 1985). Southeast Asians, for instance, usually require psychotropic medications with half to two thirds of the dosage given to most Americans (S. Nguyen, 1982; Tung, 1985).[6]

Second, Southeast Asians are more likely to develop side effects (Mollica & Lavelle, 1988) and experience more intense side effects than Euro-Americans (Tung, 1985).[7] However, Southeast Asians generally do not expect unpleasant side effects from medications; indeed, they tend to assume that unpleasant side effects indicate that the treatment is neither safe nor effective (Kroll et al., 1990) or that Western medicine is too strong for Southeast Asians (K-M. Lin & Shen, 1991). The side effects of antidepressants can arouse fear that the medication will harm them by causing their body to lose its natural balance (Kroll et al., 1990). Furthermore, clinical experience with Southeast Asians (Tung, 1972) has shown that if the patients have any side effects that families

---

[6]There are individual differences among Asian Americans in response to these drugs. For example, Chinese schizophrenics on average need half as much haloperidol (a tranquilizer) as Euro-American schizophrenics (Committee on Cultural Psychiatry, 1989). "A fourth of the Chinese, however, require dosages as high as or higher than white Americans" (Committee on Cultural Psychiatry, 1989, p. 312; K-M. Lin & Poland, 1989). There are large (up to 40-fold) differences in dosage requirements within ethnic groups (K-M. Lin & Shen, 1991).

[7]There are reportedly (Kroll et al., 1990) no differences among Cambodians, Hmong, and Laotians in the side effects experienced from antidepressants, but men reported more autonomic side effects than did women.

do not expect and if the therapist fails to reassure the families, the relatives of Southeast Asian patients are likely to encourage the patients to alter or discontinue their ingestion of tranquilizers.

Southeast Asian clients sometimes attribute their depression and anxiety to their antidepressant medication, denying "that these symptoms were present, or present as severely, before using the medication" (Kroll et al., 1990, p. 281). There is another way in which medication is sometimes considered potentially harmful. Southeast Asian patients sometimes fear that antidepressant medication will make them sleep too deeply or will make them too drowsy to be able to wake up and defend themselves and their families in case of home burglary or assault in the high-crime areas in which many of them live (Kroll et al., 1990). The sedative side effects can make them anxious and cause them to question the safety of the medication (Kroll et al., 1990).

One potential reason for the side effects is that Asian herbal treatments and diets influence the metabolism of some psychotropic medicines (K-M. Lin & Shen, 1991). Asian diets include soy and fish sauces as well as fermented and pickled foods that interact with the monoamine oxidase inhibitors used to treat depression, panic disorders, and PTSD (K-M. Lin & Shen, 1991). When monoamine oxidase inhibitors are combined with such foods, serious side effects may result. For example, using soy sauce when taking monoamine oxidase inhibitors can lead to severe hypertension.

A third reason for noncompliance is that the drugs do not eliminate some of the problems that Asian American clients experience. "For many patients, antidepressant medications are of limited value in addressing the traumas, hardships, and losses which they had experienced in their homelands and are continuing to experience in the United States" (Kroll et al., 1990, p. 282).

A fourth reason for noncompliance is that in "Southeast Asia, medications are given on a short-term basis with the expectation that they will provide rapid symptomatic relief" (Kroll et al., 1990, p. 281). Therefore, many Southeast Asians do not understand why they continually need to take medication for chronic conditions or why that medication may have to be taken for quite a while before therapeutic effects become apparent (Moore & Boehnlein, 1991). In addition, many Southeast Asian patients, unaware of the importance of their drug therapy dosage and schedule (K-M. Lin & Shen, 1991) or the purpose of the drugs prescribed, will reduce or discontinue their medicinal regimen without telling the therapist (Kroll et al., 1990; Tung, 1985), because they either fear that all medicines are addictive, think the medicines are too expensive, or feel cultural conflict over accepting Western medical treatment (Moore & Boehnlein, 1991).

There appear to be interethnic differences in compliance with drug regimens among Southeast Asians, with Cambodians more likely to comply with drug regimens than Hmong, Lao, Mien, or Vietnamese (Kinzie et al., 1987; Kroll et al., 1990) and Hmong more likely to comply than Lao (Kroll et al., 1990). It is not clear whether this pattern reflects differences in the pharmaceutical dynamics of psychotropic drugs in different Southeast Asian groups (Kroll et al., 1990). Explaining the problems and benefits of medication does not improve compliance for all Southeast Asians (Kinzie et al., 1987; Kroll, et al., 1990).

Language Problems

S. Sue and Morishima (1982) cited the case of a non-English-speaking Chinese immigrant who was hospitalized for 27 years. A subsequent lawsuit claimed that

> the Illinois Department of Mental Health had never treated the patient, identified only as David T., for any mental disorders and had found a Chinese-speaking psychologist to talk to him only after twenty-five years. The suit said that David, who was in his fifties, was put in [a hospital] in 1952. He was transferred to a state mental hospital where doctors conceded they could not give him a mental exam because he spoke little English. But they diagnosed him as psychotic anyway. . . . [In] 1971 a doctor who spoke no Chinese said David answered questions in an "incoherent and unintelligible manner." It was charged also that David was quiet and caused little trouble but was placed in restraints because he would wander to a nearby ward that housed the only Chinese-speaking patient. (p. 4)[8]

Although most language and insensitivity problems are not as severe as this, a number of difficulties can arise when the clients and therapists are not proficient in the same languages. Clients who are not proficient in English sometimes have difficulty expressing their problems in English (Carlin & Sokoloff, 1985) and are limited to using simple English words to convey complex thoughts, feelings, and experiences (D. W. Sue & D. Sue, 1990). Several studies (Marcos & Alpert, 1976; Marcos et al., 1973) of foreign-language-speaking clients have suggested that a language barrier between therapists and clients adversely affects diagnosis, frequency of misinterpretations, and treatment effectiveness. Due to apprehensions about being misunder-

---

[8]The $5 million lawsuit was eventually won, but the size of the award was reduced (Stanley Sue, personal communication).

stood, clients might not say much at all, thus leaving them vulnerable to the previously described misinterpretations which arise from inhibited speech.

Bilingual clients can present a more complicated clinical challenge than monolingual clients. If the therapist cannot switch languages with clients, important information can be lost, the therapist can be manipulated, and clients can unconsciously obfuscate issues (Romero, 1985), thereby detracting from the effectiveness of therapy. For example, different associations are elicited when bilingual people are presented with semantically identical words in different languages (Marcos & Alpert, 1976). Because people usually dream in their first or primary language, some foreign-born bilingual clients may have difficulty relaying their dreams to a therapist who only understands English (Carlin & Sokoloff, 1985). Asian American clients who have forgotten their first language when awake but still dream in that language may be unable to describe their dreams when they awaken (Carlin & Sokoloff, 1985).

There are variations in what clients say in two languages (Romero, 1985), what stories they tell (Marcos & Alpert, 1976), and what emotions they express (Marcos & Alpert, 1976). Clients who are bilingual sometimes switch away from English when dealing with emotional issues (Romero, 1985). In fact, sometimes anxiety-provoking memories can only be verbalized in one language (Marcos & Alpert, 1976). Since a person's first language tends to be more emotionally charged than the second language (Marcos & Alpert, 1976), English is sometimes used by foreign-born people to avoid the language in which their most important fantasies, memories, and traumas are stored (Marcos & Alpert, 1976). If clients switch away from their first language, it could indicate that the clients are (perhaps unconsciously) trying to resist dredging up emotion-ladened thoughts. To the therapist this is potentially important information which, if lost, would impede the therapeutic process.

The use of translators also presents problems, one of which is that it can cause therapy to take two to three times longer than usual (Larsen, 1979; E. Lee, 1982).

A second problem is that untrained translators sometimes lose subtle nuances in what is said (H. Wong, 1985b) and often make what they consider to be small changes and embellishments in translation. Translators might try to explain the client's statements when they consider them too ambiguous; they might try to improve the client's image—and, by association, that of the ethnic group (Tung, 1985); and they might offer their own opinions rather than translate the therapist's questions (C. Ho, 1990). Translators might distort what is said in order to compensate for their own feelings of discomfort when the client makes painful disclosures or reveals intimate emotions (Kinzie, 1989). Meanwhile, clients may feel resentful if they are aware that a translator has made changes in their statements; but the clients may feel unable to object to the changes made (Tung, 1985). Clients may also feel embarrassed or rejected if they notice that the interpreter is reacting to what is being said (Kinzie, 1989). These disadvantages inherent in using a translator can cause therapists to feel uncertain of the accuracy of the therapist–client communication and unsure of their own adequacy in the therapeutic situation. The interpreter needs to be knowledgeable about mental health, as well as linguistically accomplished, tactful, and detached, and it is not easy to find such skilled interpreters (Citizen's Advisory Council Report, 1979; Tung, 1985).

A third problem with the use of interpreters is that sometimes a term or phrase can be translated in different ways. For example, if a therapist asks a Vietnamese client if he or she has marital problems, the interpreter could translate "marital problems" as "*tro ngai hon nhan*," meaning marital obstacles such as religious differences between spouses or incompatible horoscopes, or as "*bat hoa giua vo chong*," meaning spousal discord (Yu, 1985). When relying on translators, the therapist would not know exactly which question was asked and answered.

A fourth problem is that a client might feel uncomfortable because of a particular translator's age, sex, level of education (Kinzie, 1989), relationship to the client, or mere presence (Hong, 1989). If the interpreter is a family member, for instance, the client might not want to discuss his or her problems in front of that family member. Such an interpreter may distort questions or answers that arouse his or her own discomfort or may make unwarranted assumptions (Hong, 1989).

A fifth problem is that the presence of an interpreter means that a triad is involved in the therapeutic situation and dyadic coalitions could shift (Tung, 1985). The presence of this third person also increases psychological distance between the therapist and client (Kinzie, 1989).

Stereotypes

If the client and therapist are of different races, they might stereotype each other based on previous experiences with people of these racial or ethnic groups (J. Chin, 1983; Leong, 1986). Stereotyping can function as a defense mechanism to help the individuals cope "with the anxiety aroused by the interracial nature of the relationship" (Minrath, 1985, p. 20) and can therefore complicate the therapeutic relationship.

A therapist with a superficial or stereotypical understanding of Asian American cultural values might overemphasize cultural similarities in all people of a particular ethnic group. Such a therapist might unconsciously assume that the cultural values and behavior patterns of a client's ethnic group coincide with the values and behaviors of a particular Asian American client (S. Sue & Zane, 1987) or might assume that an Asian American client cannot speak English well (Mokuau & Shimizu, 1991). Asian American clients, finding this assumption incorrect, insulting, and culturally insensitive, would be wary of such a therapist. Such stereotyping can disrupt the trust needed in an effective therapist–client relationship.

To avoid being stereotyped, some Asian American clients may try to appear "white" (for a Euro-American therapist), may discontinue the therapy, or may conspicuously avoid discussing their ethnicity, their minority status, and their experiences with racism (Minrath, 1985). This, too, can detract from the therapeutic relationship.[9]

CONCLUSION

This chapter has focused on some areas of misunderstanding between therapists and Asian American clients and on ways in which therapy can conflict with the expectations and communication styles of Asian Americans. From this discussion it should not be concluded that psychotherapy is inappropriate for Asian Americans. Rather, this

---

[9]On the other hand, a therapist–client match in ethnicity could lead to a problem such as countertransference (which can occur regardless of whether there is an ethnic match) which is what happens when a therapist loses objectivity because of identification with clients. It can be manifested as a denial by the therapist that there is identification with the client or as an overidentification with a client whom the therapist sees as an extension of him- or herself (Kinzie, 1989; E. Lee, 1982; Maki, 1990; "Mental Health," 1985). In the former case, the therapist might refuse to acknowledge the similarities that he or she shares with the client out of fear of losing professional distance (Maki, 1990). In the latter case, the therapist identifies so much with the client that he or she tries to work out his or her own problems through the client rather than focus on the client's problems. A therapist also might assume to know the client's cultural perspectives when in fact he or she is unconsciously overgeneralizing from personal experience (Maki, 1990). For example, a therapist might have inhibitions and might encourage the client to act out those inhibitions. Or, if a client rejects his or her ethnic identity and the therapist does not, the "halo effect" could lead the therapist to a value-driven and incorrect diagnosis that the client has poor self-esteem or is racist (Maki, 1990). Because of these potential dangers, therapists try to be cognizant of the potential for countertransference.

overview points to the need to inform Asian American clients about the nature of psychotherapy and the need for therapists to be culturally sensitive.

While American Psychological Association Guidelines (American Psychological Association, 1990) encourage therapists to try to be culturally sensitive, that does not mean that all therapists are equally successful at it. A question that arises is whether Asian Americans should only seek mental health services from Asian American therapists.

Asian Americans tend to judge "their therapists as more credible and competent if they are Asian-Americans" than if they are not (Leong, 1986, p. 198). One reason could be that Asian American clients communicate differently with Asian American therapists than they do with non-Asian American therapists. The differences in communication are not just because the therapists and clients speak the same language: Ethnic match and language match between Asian American clients and therapists each contribute separately to the length of time that clients stay in therapy (E. Lee, 1985; S. Sue et al., 1991).

There is empirical evidence (Dinges & Lieberman, 1989) that just as Euro-Americans as a group behave differently when they are interacting with other Euro-Americans than when interacting with Japanese Americans, Japanese Americans behave differently when, in the same situation, they are interacting with other Japanese Americans rather than with Euro-Americans. Some Asian Americans apparently are more able to relax, more willing to disclose certain types of information, feel more intimate, and feel they understand another person and are better understood by that person when the person is of their own ethnic group (Shibutani & Kwan, 1965). The openness of an Asian American client may in part be a function of the therapist's ethnicity and not simply a reflection of the client's personality and resistance or a reflection of the therapist's cultural sensitivity. Therefore, insofar as clients feel more rapport with a therapist and are more willing to be open when a therapist is Asian American than when the therapist is not, it is beneficial for such clients to have Asian American therapists.

Nevertheless, what is more important than the ethnicity of the therapist is whether the therapist has strong clinical skills (e.g., knowledge of therapeutic techniques as well as the ability to listen carefully, empathize, communicate clearly, and establish rapport) and how culturally sensitive the therapist is. Whether or not the therapist is Asian American, culturally sensitive therapists—generally preferred by Asian Americans over therapists who are not culturally sensitive (Gim, Atkinson, & Kim, 1991)—need to know about the cultural and racial context in which the clients live and need experiences interacting with Asian Americans: This includes being adept at using and understanding Asian American communication styles; having familiarity with Asian American values, variations in family structure, and the experiences that some Asian Americans have had with traditional healers; having knowledge of traumas experienced by refugees; and having an understanding of other sources of stress facing Asian Americans.[10]

When Asian American therapists with Asian American clients were asked what areas of knowledge they considered most important in treating Asian American clients, they emphasized knowledge of Asian American cultural values and understanding of the problems facing Asian Americans (Matsushima & Tashima, 1982). For example, if a therapist is not knowledgeable about the experiences of Southeast Asian refugees and has not had much experience with traumatized Southeast Asian refugees, he or she will be less able than a therapist with such knowledge to explain to the clients how their experiences relate to the experiences of other refugees and to help them recognize that their responses to traumatic experiences are frequently seen, expected, and normal—thereby decreasing the fear and shame felt by the clients (Kinzie, 1989; E. Lee & Lu, 1989; Moore & Boehnlein, 1991). Such an inexperienced therapist would also not be in a position to assure clients that he or she knows other refugees with similar problems who have been treated successfully and thereby help the clients to feel less alone and more hopeful than they would otherwise feel (Ishisaka et al., 1985).

When Asian American therapists were asked which cultural values therapists most need to know about when conducting therapy with Asian Americans, the therapists identified (in descending order of importance) the values shown in Table 10.1; when they were asked which ethnic-specific problems and concerns were important for therapists to know about, they mentioned the concerns listed in Table 10.2. These results emphasize the importance of a therapist's cultural sensitivity and his or her knowledge of the experiences of those in Asian American communities.

The case (described by Westcott, 1985) of a Japanese American graduate student at the University of Hawaii demonstrates how cultural sensitivity in a therapist can make a difference. The graduate student was seeking permission to drop his courses, noting that his

---

[10]It may be that statistically Asian American therapists are more likely than non-Asian American therapists to have the knowledge and experience needed to be culturally sensitive.

TABLE 10.1. Most Important Cultural Values for Therapists to Know About

Importance of family
Shame and guilt
Respect for people based on their status and roles
Styles of interpersonal behavior
Stigma associated with mental illness
Restraint of self-expression
Orientation toward group
Achievement
Sense of duty and obligation
Expectations that follow from different roles

Note. Data in table are based on Matsushima and Tashima (1982).

father had become mute and partially paralyzed due to an auto accident. He did not know how much longer his father would live. He said that when he visited his father in the hospital, he felt there was a lot to say (i.e., about his love and admiration for his father) but that he did not know what to say and thought it would be bad form to state his feelings directly. The student told the therapist of many good times he had with his father. The therapist suggested that the student talk about those good experiences with his father the next time he went to the hospital to visit him. The student realized that doing so would enable him to talk about his relationship with his father and his feelings for him without embarrassing his father.

In this case, the counselor's cultural sensitivity gave rise to a

TABLE 10.2. Important Ethnic-Specific Problems Therapists Need to Know About

Immigration experiences (presumably including traumas experienced prior to leaving Asia)
Cultural conflicts in lifestyle and values
Importance of family issues
Racism
Conceptualizations of mental health and attitudes toward mental health services
Behavioral styles and norms
Language
Ethnic identity
Intergenerational problems

Note. Data in table are based on Matsushima and Tashima (1982).

culturally appropriate solution. Such a solution might not have occurred to someone who did not understand what the student was saying about the communication styles in his family.

The degree of cultural sensitivity needed from a therapist will vary depending on factors such as how acculturated an Asian American client is and the nature of the problem. Because of the diversity in Asian American populations, there will be wide variances in the needs of Asian Americans for culturally sensitive services.

11

Conclusion

The intent of this book has been to provide an overview of psychological research on Asian Americans. The perspective taken here emphasizes cultural and minority-based explanations for this research. Such an approach will hopefully increase appreciation for multicultural psychological perspectives.

This perspective has revealed several major points. Among them is that there are sources of psychosocial stress facing Asian Americans in general, and foreign-born Asian Americans in particular, that are not faced by most other Americans. Consistent with that, psychological problems appear to be more prevalent among foreign-born than among American-born Asian Americans. Especially in the case of the Southeast Asian refugees, the evidence strongly suggests that these sources of psychosocial stress contribute to a relatively high incidence of mental disorders.

Despite the need for mental health services in Asian American communities, Asian Americans do not use mental health services as much as would be expected based on their proportion of the total population in the United States. Moreover, Southeast Asian refugees, who, as a group have experienced numerous traumas, do not use mental health services in proportion to estimates of their need for mental health services. The striking finding (Gong-Guy, 1987) that 14.4% of a large, nonclinical sample of Southeast Asians were judged to need inpatient mental health services (compared to 3% of the general population in the United States) and that 26.7% of that sample were thought to need outpatient mental health services (compared to 12% of the general population) indicates a great need for mental health services in this population.

One reason that Asian Americans do not seek mental health services in proportion to their size in their community or to their needs is that many have had experiences or hold cultural values and beliefs that deter them from seeking mental health services. Unfortunately, an insufficient amount of outreach by mental health service systems and the lack of cultural sensitivity in mental health service providers working with Asian Americans also deters them from seeking mental health services.

When mental health service delivery systems provide identical services to everyone, in practice what is most often offered are mental health services designed to meet the needs of the majority. Since Asian Americans are rarely the majority, services designed to meet the needs of the majority would not be oriented toward meeting the special mental health service needs of Asian Americans. But in many cases, in order for Asian Americans to receive equally effective care, they need services that are different from those provided to other Americans— that is, they need services that are culturally sensitive to Asian Americans.

One factor that undermines the availability of culturally sensitive mental health services is that all too often when government agencies collect data that would be relevant to mental health services (as well as other social services), their reports refer only to "white," "black," "Hispanic," and "other." When Asian Americans are categorized as "other," in practical terms, they become lost in the bureaucracy. Those who want mental health service delivery systems and funding agencies to pay attention to the mental health needs of Asian Americans and to provide culturally sensitive services find that they have to prove the need for such services without readily available data to back them up. Most government officials will hesitate to support the call for additional services if they do not have numbers to substantiate the claim that more services are needed.

Another factor that impedes the availability of culturally sensitive mental health professionals is the lack of adequate institutional support for Asian Americans who would become therapists. For instance, the supply of Asian American psychiatrists is potentially limited by the fact that Asian Americans applying to medical school, a prerequisite to becoming a psychiatrist, are not considered minorities (Uba, 1994). Consequently, Asian Americans are excluded from apprenticeships and grants designed to encourage minorities to enter or stay in medical school.

While this book emphasized a cultural and racial perspective on the psychological research on Asian Americans, this is not the only approach that could have been taken. Other people might adopt different, although equally valid, perspectives to this research. For example, a person could examine the research by focusing on generational or gender differences. Such an approach could provide different understandings of the same research and alternative ways of thinking about that research. Since this divergence of perspectives can help to illuminate our understanding, simply accepting the interpretations presented in this book could stifle the expansion of our knowledge.

Also limiting our understanding of Asian American psychology are the large gaps in the research. Among the many areas which have received scant attention are the differences between Asian American and Asian cultural values and beliefs.

There is a need to broaden perspectives. More studies comparing Asian Americans and other minority groups would be helpful, particularly if they have samples that are larger than those usually found. Such comparisons would help to explicate the role of minority status in the psychological functioning of Asian Americans. A wider variety of Asian American groups need to be studied. Between-group and within-group differences need to be looked at in such areas as family dynamics, varieties of nontraditional family structures, identity issues, rates and types of mental disorders, and so forth. The broadening of our theoretical perspectives (e.g., beyond the trait approach to studying personality) could provide insight into the relationships between personality, on the one hand, and cultural values and experiences as a minority, on the other.

For practical reasons, it would probably be helpful to establish more Asian American behavior-pattern norms in nonclinical samples and to develop psychological tests that are more culturally appropriate than most of those that exist now. All too often researchers have to use tests that have not demonstrated their validity with Asian Americans or have to create their own ad hoc measures that have not been well established.

Finally, examinations of factors that mediate stress for Asian Americans would fill a large gap in the research. Such research could provide rationales for intervention strategies.

Appendix A
Types of Mental Disorders

Psychiatric disorders are most often defined by their symptoms in the *Diagnostic and Statistical Manual of Mental Disorders* (DSM). The following brief summary of the types of mental disorders includes those that were mentioned in Chapter 8.

AFFECTIVE DISORDERS

The primary characteristic of affective disorders is a disturbance in the individual's mood. Broadly speaking, there are three types of affective disorders.

Depression

Clinical depression is not synonymous with simply feeling unhappy or overwhelmed. It is characterized by sadness, feelings of failure and worthlessness, listlessness, indifference to activities that used to be pleasurable, change in appetite, sleep problems, agitation or slowed movement and speech, decrease in energy, difficulty concentrating, anxiety, tearfulness, irritability, and thoughts about death. It is also called a unipolar disorder.

Mania

Mania is characterized by excessive euphoria, unbounded enthusiasm, loquaciousness, restlessness, and quick shifts in thoughts. It is also a unipolar disorder.

Manic-Depressive Disorder

A person with manic-depression (also known as bipolar disorder) alternately experiences mania and depression.

ANXIETY DISORDERS

Not surprisingly, the predominant symptom in anxiety disorders is anxiety, generally experienced as diffuse feelings of apprehension. In this category are the phobic disorders, wherein a person is so afraid of particular, identifiable objects, activities, or situations that avoiding these frightening things interferes with that person's ability to lead a normal life. Also in this category is posttraumatic stress disorder (PTSD) which is caused by especially traumatic experiences such as assault, torture, rape, military combat, and bombings. People with PTSD often feel detached from other people, experience psychic numbing (i.e., a reduced responsiveness to the world), lose interest in activities that they enjoyed before the traumatic event(s) took place, are hyperalert, have insomnia, and have intrusive thoughts about their traumatic experiences.

SOMATOFORM DISORDERS

This group of disorders is characterized by psychological problems that manifest themselves as physical complaints. Symptoms such as paralysis, blindness, or chronic pain suggest a physical disease or injury but no organic cause can be found. For example, one study cited in this book was based on Cambodian women who had experienced traumas in Southeast Asia and were now blind even though no physical reason for their blindness could be found. People with somatic disorders do not voluntarily control their symptoms: They are not faking them. Somatization disorder and conversion disorder are two types of somatoform disorders (mentioned earlier, in Chapter 8).

DISSOCIATIVE DISORDERS

These disorders are characterized by a sudden, temporary change in a person's sense of identity. Among the types of dissociative disorders are psychogenic amnesia and psychogenic fugue. The former is characterized by a sudden inability to remember important personal information (such as one's name and address) following a severe psychosocial stress; the latter is characterized by both amnesia (whereby one's previous identity cannot be recalled) and a sudden and unexpected move away from home and work to a new place where a new identity is assumed.

SCHIZOPHRENIA

Schizophrenia is characterized by such symptoms as a deterioration in level of functioning at work or school, in social relations, and in personal hygiene; delusions (i.e., false beliefs); hallucinations (i.e., sensory distortions such as hearing voices); incoherent shifts in ideas from topic to topic; inappropriate or flat affect; withdrawal from social contact; bizarre ideas; and apathy. In effect, the individual has split from reality. Not all schizophrenics have all of the aforementioned symptoms. Paranoid schizophrenia, a relatively common form of schizophrenia, is characterized by delusions.

PARANOID DISORDER

People who are paranoid have delusions that convincingly fit together around an identifiable theme. In this disorder, delusions are not as fragmentary as they are in paranoid schizophrenia. People with a paranoid disorder do not have the hallucinations, inappropriate affect, and personality disintegration characteristic of people with paranoid schizophrenia. Paranoid people often have delusions that they are powerful, that others have designs to hurt them, or that they are receiving special messages about what others think of them or how others think they should behave.

ADJUSTMENT DISORDERS

This disorder is characterized by maladaptive responses to such environmental stressors as marital problems, acculturation, chronic illness, residence in a deteriorating neighborhood, and persecution because of race or religion. People with this disorder may become withdrawn, depressed, and anxious, or they may violate behavior norms (e.g., commit vandalism).

SUBSTANCE USE DISORDER

This disorder is characterized by the pathological use of such substances as alcohol, barbiturates, and amphetamines for at least one month. This use results in impairment in social relations or in functioning at work or school.

ORGANIC BRAIN DISORDERS

This is a heterogeneous group of disorders caused by physical damage to the brain. Accidents, illnesses, chemical imbalances, and toxic agents can cause organic brain disorders. For example, a Southeast Asian refugee who experienced head trauma as a result of bombings, beatings, or torture could have such common organic brain disorder symptoms as impairment of thinking and memory, emotional disturbance, and personality changes.

PERSONALITY DISORDERS

These disorders are characterized by long-lasting, maladaptive personality patterns and excessive and rigid personality traits that cause unhappiness or that interfere with social relations and with functioning at work or school. A person with a personality disorder has particular personality traits in an excessive and rigid way.

CONDUCT DISORDERS

These disorders are characterized by repeated and persistent violations of the rights of others and age-appropriate norms. The conduct may or may not be associated with aggressive, antisocial behavior and affection or empathy with others.

Appendix B
Mental Health
Delivery Systems

There are a number of policy options available to the mental health service delivery systems that are trying to meet the needs of Asian Americans. A mental health service delivery system may try to provide such services in (1) the same (i.e., mainstream) facilities as and with the same personnel who provide mental health services to everyone else in the catchment area, (2) the same (mainstream) facilities but with a few therapists who are specially trained to provide culturally sensitive services to Asian Americans, or (3) facilities that are physically segregated from mainstream facilities and that specialize in providing culturally sensitive services to Asian Americans.

Mainstream Facilities, General Personnel

Sometimes mental health service delivery systems simply provide care to Asian Americans in the same facilities and with the same personnel who treat all other clients. This approach to the delivery of services assumes that care for Asian Americans can be provided by mainstream facilities and by any competent therapist.

Behind this policy option are two quite distinct rationales which are based on very different values. One rationale is that Asian Americans need to accommodate themselves to the standard, American, mental health service delivery system and that such adaptation by individuals is part of the assimilation that is required of all groups in the United States. Underlying this rationale is the belief that minorities "need" to "overcome" ways in which they are different from Euro-Americans. Moreover, it would be argued, the mental health system should not try to accommodate itself when there are relatively few Asian Americans in any given catchment area, only a small proportion of them need mental health services, and an even smaller proportion need public mental health services (since others can afford to see therapists in private practice). The other rationale is that Asian Americans should receive culturally sensitive services but that those services can be provided in mainstream facilities with the personnel presently at hand.

Disadvantages

1. Even when the intent is to provide culturally sensitive services in mainstream facilities, the result of adopting this option may not be culturally sensitive mental health services for Asian Americans: Most mental health systems have not demonstrated strong responsiveness to the needs of Asian Americans when services are provided in mainstream facilities. The studies of underutilization of mainstream facilities do not support the expectation that culturally sensitive services can be consistently provided by the general personnel at mainstream facilities. Most therapists do not have sufficient training to provide culturally sensitive mental health services to Asian Americans. A major revamping of the training of mental health service providers would be required for all therapists at mainstream facilities to be able to provide culturally sensitive services. The curricula for therapists-in-training would need to address numerous Asian American cultures. There is nothing inherently wrong with such revision of curricula but professors who do not know much about Asian American mental health and students who do not anticipate working with Asian American clients or who do not want to prolong the completion of their training would probably resist major changes in curricula and training (Crompton, 1974; Kuramoto, 1971), thereby rendering such changes less likely. In all likelihood, therefore, most therapists in mainstream facilities will not be sufficiently exposed to curricula and training that would enable them to provide culturally sensitive services to a range of Asian American clients.

2. Rather than acculturate so that they can receive the same services that are delivered to other Americans, many Asian Americans with mental disorders simply would not seek help. Therefore, the option of mainstream services with general personnel could exacerbate the underutilization problem and prolong people's suffering.

3. Since the mainstream services most likely would not be located in or near Asian American communities, this option may not help Asian Americans become more aware of the availability of services.

Advantages

1. Adopting this mainstream option might enable Asian Americans to have sustained services that are not as vulnerable to budgetary cuts as services at separate facilities might be.

2. When mental health services for Asian Americans are provided within the same governmental bureaucracy that deals with other social services, services can be coordinated because people working in the mental health field would know to whom the client should be referred for additional help (for instance, with welfare and vice versa). Also, when services are coordinated rather than fragmented, clients are less likely to be forced to go to one place for services and then be left adrift, not knowing where to go for other needed services.

3. This option of mainstream facilities might provide culturally appropriate services to Asian Americans who are sufficiently acculturated to eschew bilingual services but who need a minimal level of cultural sensitivity from their therapist.

Mainstream Facilities, Specially Trained Personnel

A second policy option entails establishing separate, culturally sensitive teams of mental health service providers but housing these services within mainstream facilities, perhaps as a separate wing or unit of workers in the mainstream facilities. The chief assumption behind this option is that services for Asian Americans do not need to be physically separate and autonomous in order to be culturally responsive.

Disadvantages

1. When services for Asian Americans are provided in semiautonomous units alongside mainstream services, the result can be power struggles between the different staffs, administrative confusion, and unnecessary duplication of mental health services provided (Anders, Parlade, Chatel, & Peele, 1977).

2. Therapists who are not part of the special unit may not expect to encounter many Asian American clients. Consequently they may not put much effort into learning how to provide culturally sensitive services for them. Nevertheless, even therapists who do not focus their practice on Asian American clients may occasionally have such clients. These clients can then suffer owing to the inexperience of a therapist who does not have much training for or experience in working with Asian Americans.

3. This mainstream option probably will not help Asian Americans become more aware of available mental health services. It is quite likely that most Asian

Americans in the community would not know that the mainstream facilities have personnel who are specially trained to be culturally sensitive to Asian American clients.

4. Since these services would be located wherever the mainstream facilities existed rather than in locations easily accessible to Asian American communities, this option could render services inaccessible to those Asian Americans who need to rely on public transportation.

Advantages

1. Since both mainstream and culturally specialized services would be available at the same location, potential clients would have a clear choice of services. The presence of these choices could deter workers in the mental health service delivery system from automatically and indiscriminately sending all Asian Americans to separate facilities or to specialized services for Asian Americans without considering the appropriateness of such services for the individual client. When there is a clear choice of services, an effective matching of needs and services and an increased use of services by Asian Americans might result.

2. An advantage that this particular mainstream option has over the previous option is that widespread changes in mental health service training would not be required; special training would only be required of those who worked with Asian American clients.

3. Therapists who want to specialize in working with Asian Americans but do not want to limit their practice exclusively to Asian Americans, would prefer such a setting to the other two options.

4. Adopting this option can increase the cultural sensitivity of the personnel at the mainstream services who are not part of the separate wing or unit because the personnel in the separate wing or unit would presumably interact with the former, thus increasing the former's awareness and understanding.

Segregated, Free-Standing Facilities, Special Personnel

Mental health services for Asian Americans can be provided in facilities that are physically segregated from mainstream services and staffed by personnel who are culturally sensitive to Asian Americans. Underlying this option is the belief that the bureaucracies in mainstream facilities cannot provide sufficiently sensitive services. These separate facilities would presumably focus on Asian Americans who most need culturally sensitive and multilingual services—viz., immigrants and refugees.

Disadvantages

1. A separate facility for Asian American clients might attract many mental health service providers who are trained to work with Asian Americans. But concentrating such therapists in these segregated facilities could limit the opportunities for a wide range of service providers to learn about therapy for Asian Americans: An opportunity to promote understanding of Asian Americans could be lost. Such a concentration of therapists who are culturally sensitive to Asian Americans also could result in the presence of fewer qualified therapists to treat Asian Americans in mainstream facilities. As a consequence, acculturated Asian Americans who might regard mental health facilities specifically for Asian Americans as, in fact, being for Asian Americans who need bilingual therapy and who might not think their problems are related to their ethnicity may go to mainstream services where few therapists have culturally relevant training. These Asian Americans might not need bicultural and bilingual therapists, but they still might benefit from having therapists who are sensitive to their cultural backgrounds and their experiences as minorities. If this option is the only one adopted in the mental health service delivery system, the more acculturated Asian Americans could fall between the cracks in the service delivery system.

2. Separate facilities can be more expensive to maintain than the other two options. As a result, they may be more vulnerable to budgetary cutbacks.

3. It can be financially difficult for a mental health system to have enough facilities at different locations that would be accessible to the wide range of Asian Americans. If there are separate facilities for Asian Americans, they are likely to be limited in number. Most likely the separate facilities would be placed where many Asian Americans live. But Filipino Americans, for example, often are scattered through a city rather than residentially clustered, and often do not live in areas where other Asian Americans live. These Asian Americans, therefore, might find that culturally sensitive mental health services are no closer to them than mainstream services.

4. Separate facilities might deter Asian Americans who think that services for Asian Americans would provide less confidentiality than mainstream facilities where they could be lost in the crowd. Some Asian Americans would fear that if they went to a separate mental health facility for Asian Americans, there would be an increased chance that someone whom they know would see them seeking mental health services.

Advantages

1. This option affords institutional flexibility to meet the needs of Asian Americans. For example, intake personnel who are multilingual in a variety of Asian languages could be hired. Clients might perceive such a facility as being

compatible with their needs and orientations. Separate facilities staffed by Asian American personnel could increase the use of mental health services by some Asian Americans because they would feel that they were welcome and "belonged" there.

2. Separate facilities could function simultaneously as service delivery centers and as training centers for therapists who want to learn how to provide culturally sensitive services to Asian Americans. The facilities could also serve an advocacy role, providing experience-based, coherent input into governmental policy decisions about Asian American mental health issues. It is more difficult politically to minimize or ignore the mental health care needs of Asian Americans when there are free-standing facilities, staffed by service providers who can serve as advocates for such services; otherwise specialists in providing mental health services to Asian Americans are scattered around and effectively lost in the mental health system.

3. These separate facilities could be reconfigured into multiservice centers that provide legal aid, English classes, help in finding jobs, and so on. Such multiservice centers could decrease the stigma associated with seeking mental health services and make mental health services more accessible (Murase et al., 1985).

4. By concentrating the often limited number of therapists who are culturally sensitive to Asian Americans in separate facilities for Asian Americans, those therapists who are culturally sensitive can be deployed effectively.

5. Such facilities might have increased visibility to the Asian American public. For instance, potential Asian American clients could look in the phone book for mental health services and find a listing such as "Asian/Pacific Islander American Mental Health Services." Furthermore, because these facilities would probably be located in or near Asian American communities, the facilities would be more geographically accessible than mainstream services. The high visibility afforded by separate facilities could increase awareness of these services in the Asian American community. In addition, the high visibility of such facilities might cause some Asian Americans to think about becoming involved in the mental health field.

References

Abbott, Kenneth. (1976). Culture change and the persistence of the Chinese personality. In George DeVos (Ed.), *Responses to change: Society, culture and personality* (pp. 74–104). New York: Van Nostrand.

Abe, Jennifer, & Nolan Zane. (1990). Psychological maladjustment among Asian and White American college students. *Journal of Counseling Psychology, 37,* 437–444.

Ablon, Joan. (1976). The social organization of an urban Samoan community. In Emma Gee (Ed.), *Counterpoint: Perspectives on Asian America* (pp. 401–412) Los Angeles: Regents of the University of California.

Aboud, Frances E. (1984). Social and cognitive bases of ethnic identity consistency. *Journal of Genetic Psychology, 145*(2), 217–230.

Ader, Robert. (1981). *Psychoneuroimmunology.* New York: Academic Press.

Aldwin, Carolyn, & Ellen Greenberger. (1987). Cultural differences in the predictors of depression. *American Journal of Community Psychology, 15,* 789–813.

American Psychological Association, Board of Ethnic Minority Affairs, Task Force on the Delivery of Service to Ethnic Minority Populations (1990). *Guidelines for providers of psychological services to ethnic, linguistic, and culturally diverse populations.* Washington, DC: Author.

Anders, Ana, Rafael Parlade, John Chatel, & Roger Peele. (1977). Why we did not establish a separate complete program for Spanish speaking patients. In Eligio R. Padilla & Amado M. Padilla (Eds.), *Transcultural psychiatry: An Hispanic perspective* (pp. 63–66). Los Angeles: Spanish Speaking Mental Health Research Center.

Anderson, James N. (1983). Health and illness in Pilipino immigrants. *Western Journal of Medicine, 139,* 811–819.

Araneta, Enrique, Jr. (1982). Filipino Americans. In Albert Gaw (Ed.), *Cross-Cultural Psychiatry* (pp. 55–68). Boston: John Wright.

Arkoff, Abe. (1964). Deference—East, West, mid-Pacific: Observations concerning Japanese, American, and Japanese-American women. *Psychologia, 7,* 159–164.

Arkoff, Abe, Falak Thaver, & Leonard Elkind. (1966). Mental health and counseling ideas of Asian and American students. *Journal of Counseling Psychology, 13,* 219–223.

261

Arkoff, Abe, & Herbert Weaver. (1966). Body image and body dissatisfaction in Japanese-Americans. *Journal of Social Psychology, 68,* 323–330.

Arredondo, Patricia. (1984). Identity themes for immigrant young adults. *Adolescence, 19,* 977–993.

Asian American Community Mental Health Training Center. (1976). *Asian and Pacific American curriculum on social work education.* Unpublished manuscript. Los Angeles: Asian American Community Mental Health Training Center.

Asian Pacific American Education Advisory Committee. (1990). *Enriching California's future: Asian Pacific Americans in the CSU.* Office of the Chancellor: California State University.

Atkinson, Donald, & Ruth Gim. (1989). Asian American cultural identity and attitudes toward mental health services. *Journal of Counseling Psychology, 36*(2), 209–212.

Atkinson, Donald, Mervin Maruyama, & Sandi Matsui. (1978). The effects of counselor race and counseling approach on Asian Americans' perceptions of counselor credibility and utility. *Journal of Counseling Psychology, 25,* 76–83.

Atkinson, Donald, & Yoshiko Matsushita. (1991). Japanese-American acculturation, counseling style, counselor ethnicity, and perceived counselor credibility. *Journal of Counseling Psychology, 38*(4), 473–478.

Atkinson, Donald, George Morten, & Derald W. Sue. (1989). A minority identity development model. In Donald Atkinson, George Morten, & Derald W. Sue (Eds.), *Counseling American minorities* (pp. 35–52). Dubuque, IA: William C. Brown.

Atkinson, Donald, Joseph Ponterotto, & Arthur Sanchez. (1984). Attitudes of Vietnamese and Anglo-American students toward counseling. *Journal of College Student Personnel, 25,* 448–452.

Atkinson, Donald, W. Carlos Poston, Michael Furlong, & Pauline Mercado. (1989). Ethnic group preferences for counselor characteristics. *Journal of Counseling Psychology, 36,* 68–72.

Atkinson, Donald, Scott Whiteley, & Ruth Gim. (1990). Asian American acculturation and preference for help providers. *Journal of College Student Development, 31*(2), 155–161.

August, Lynn, & Barbara Gianola. (1987). Symptoms of war trauma induced psychiatric disorders. *International Migration Review, 21,* 820–832.

Ayabe, Harold. (1971). Deference and ethnic difference in voice levels. *Journal of Social Psychology, 85,* 181–185.

Aylesworth, Lawrence S., Peter G. Ossorio, & Larry T. Osaki. (1980). Stress and mental health among Vietnamese in the United States. In Russell Endo, Stanley Sue, & Nathaniel Wagner (Eds.), *Asian Americans: Social and psychological perspectives* (pp. 64–80). Palo Alto, CA: Science and Behavior Books.

Baker, Nicholas. (1982). Substitute care for unaccompanied refugee minors. *Child Welfare, 61,* 353–363.

Baldwin, B. C. (1982). *Capturing the change.* Santa Ana, CA: Immigrant and Refugee Planning Center.

Ballard, Chester. (1985). A resettlement attempt that failed: But important lessons were learned. *Public Welfare, 43,* 41, 45.

Barringer, Herbert R., David Takeuchi, & Peter Xenos. (1990). Education, occupational prestige, and income of Asian Americans. *Sociology of Education, 63,* 27–43.

Beiser, Morton. (1988). Influences of time, ethnicity and attachment on depression in Southeast Asian refugees. *American Journal of Psychiatry, 145,* 46–51.

Beiser, Morton, & Jonathan Fleming. (1986). Measuring psychiatric disorders among Southeast Asian refugees. *Psychological Medicine, 16,* 627–639.

Beiser, Morton, Jay Turner, & Soma Ganesan. (1989). Catastrophic stress and factors affecting its consequences among Southeast Asian refugees. *Social Science and Medicine, 28*(3), 183–195.

Bemak, Fred. (1989). Cross-cultural family therapy with Southeast Asian refugees. *Journal of Strategic and Systemic Therapies, 8,* 22–27.

Berk, Bernard, & Lucie Cheng Hirata. (1973). Mental illness among the Chinese: Myth or reality? *Journal of Social Issues, 29,* 149–166.

Berrien, F. K., Abe Arkoff, & Shinkuro Iwahara. (1967). Generational differences in values: Americans, Japanese Americans, and Japanese. *Journal of Social Psychology, 71,* 169–175.

Blaisdell, Kekuni, & Noreen Mokuau. (1991). *Kānaka Maoli:* Indigenous Hawaiians. In Noreen Mokuau (Ed.), *Handbook of social services for Asian and Pacific Islanders* (pp. 131–154). New York: Greenwood Press.

Blane, Howard T. & Kazuo Yamamoto. (1970). Sexual role identity among Japanese and Japanese-American high school students. *Journal of Cross-Cultural Psychology, 1,* 345–354.

Bliatout, Bruce, Ben Rath, Vinh The Do, Kham One Keopraseuth, Hollis Bliatout, & David Tsanh-Tsing Lee. (1985). Mental health and prevention activities targeted to Southeast Asian refugees. In Tom Owan (Ed.), *Southeast Asian mental health: Treatment, prevention, services, training, and research* (pp. 183–208). Washington, DC: U.S. Dept. of Health and Human Services.

Blustein, David. (1982). Using informal groups in cross-cultural counseling. *Journal for Specialists in Group Work, 7,* 260–265.

Boehnlein, James. (1987). Clinical relevance of grief and mourning among Cambodian refugees. *Social Science and Medicine, 25,* 765–772.

Boehnlein, James, J. David Kinzie, Ben Rath, & Jenelle Fleck. (1985). One-year follow-up study of post-traumatic stress disorder among survivors of Cambodian concentration camps. *American Journal of Psychiatry, 142,* 956–959.

Bourne, Peter G. (1975). The Chinese student—acculturation and mental illness. *Psychiatry, 38,* 269–277.

Bromley, Mary. (1988). Identity as a central adjustment issue for the Southeast Asian unaccompanied refugee minor. *Child and Youth Care Quarterly, 17*(2), 104–114.

Brower, Imogene C. (1989). Counseling Vietnamese. In Donald R. Atkinson, George Morten, & Derald W. Sue (Eds.), *Counseling American minorities: A Cross-cultural perspective* (pp. 129–147). Dubuque, IA: William C. Brown.

Brown, Foster. (1987). Counseling Vietnamese refugees: The new challenge. *International Journal for the Advancement of Counseling, 10*, 259–268.

Brown, Timothy R., Kenneth M. Stein, Katherine Huang, & Darrel E. Harris. (1973). Mental illness and the role of mental health facilities in Chinatown. In Stanley Sue & Nathaniel Wagner (Eds.), *Asian-Americans: Psychological perspectives* (pp. 212–231). Palo Alto: Science and Behavior Books.

Bunzel, John, & Jeffrey Au. (1987). Diversity or discrimination? Asian Americans in college. *The Public Interest, 87*, 49–62.

Canda, Edward. (1989). Therapeutic use of writing and other media with Southeast Asian refugees. *Journal of Independent Social Work, 4*, 47–60.

Canda, Edward, & Thitiya Phaobtong. (1992). Buddhism as a support system for Southeast Asian refugees. *Social Work, 37*(1), 61–67.

Caplan, Nathan, Marcella Choy, & John Whitmore. (1992, February). Indochinese refugee families and academic achievement. *Scientific American,* 36–42.

Caplan, Nathan, John Whitmore, & Quang Bui. (1985). Economic self-sufficiency among recently arrived refugees from Southeast Asia. *Economic Outlook USA, 12*(3), 60–63.

Caplan, Nathan, John Whitmore, & Marcella Choy. (1989). *The boat people and achievement in America: A Study of family life, hard work, and cultural values.* Ann Arbor: University of Michigan Press.

Carlin, Jean, & Burton Sokoloff. (1985). Mental health treatment issues for Southeast Asian refugee children. In Tom Owan (Ed.), *Southeast Asian mental health: Treatment, prevention, services, training, and research* (pp. 91–112). Washington, DC: U.S. Dept. of Health and Human Services.

Carlson, Eve, & Rhonda Rosser-Hogan. (1991). Trauma experiences, posttraumatic stress, dissociation, and depression in Cambodian refugees. *American Journal of Psychiatry, 148*(11), 1548–1551.

Cauce, Ana Mari, Yumi Hiraga, Craig Mason, Tanya Aguilar, Nydia Ordonez, & Nancy Gonzales. (1992). Between a rock and a hard place: Social adjustment of biracial youth. In Maria Root (Ed.), *Racially mixed people in America* (pp. 207–223). Newbury Park, CA: Sage.

Caudill, William, & Lois Frost. (1974). A comparison of maternal care and infant behavior in Japanese-American, American, and Japanese families. In William Lebra (Ed.), *Mental health research in Asia and the Pacific: Vol. 3. Youth, socialization, and mental health* (pp. 3–15). Honolulu: University Press of Hawaii.

Chan, David W. (1990). Sex knowledge, attitudes, and experiences of Chinese medical students in Hong Kong. *Archives of Sexual Behavior, 19*, 73–93.

Chan, Kenyon. (in press). Sociocultural aspects of anger: Impact on minority children. In Michael Furlong & Douglas Smith (Eds.), *Anger, hostility, and aggression in children and adolescents: Assessment, prevention, and intervention strategies in schools.* Brandon, Vermont: Clinical Psychology Publishing.

Chan, Kenyon, Ruby Takanishi, & Margie Kitano. (1975). Asian American

Education Project Preliminary Report. Los Angeles: UCLA Asian American Studies Center.

Chan, Sucheng. (1991). *Asian Americans: An interpretive history.* Boston: Twayne.

Chang, Theresa S. (1975). The self-concept of children in ethnic groups: Black Americans and Asian Americans. *Elementary School Journal, 76,* 52–58.

Charron, Donald, & Robert Ness. (1983). Emotional distress among Vietnamese adolescents: A statewide survey. *Journal of Refugee Resettlement, 1,* 7–15.

Chen, Clarence L. & Dorothy C. Yang. (1986). The self image of Chinese-American adolescents: A cross-cultural comparison. *International Journal of Social Psychiatry, 32,* 19–26.

Chen, Pei-Ngor. (1982). Eroding filial piety and its implications for social work practice. *Journal of Sociology and Social Welfare, 9*(3), 511–523.

Chen, Peter W. (1977). *Chinese-Americans view their mental health.* San Francisco: R and E Research Associates.

Chew, Charlene A. & Dorothy C. Ogi. (1987). Asian American college student perspectives. *New Directions for Student Services, 38,* 39–48.

Chia, Rosina. (1989). Pilot study: Family values of American versus Chinese-American parents. *Journal of the Asian American Psychological Association, 13*(1), 8–11.

Chin, Jean Lau. (1983). Diagnostic considerations in working with Asian-Americans. *American Journal of Orthopsychiatry, 53,* 100–109.

Chin, Robert. (1982). Conceptual paradigm for a racial-ethnic community: The case of the Chinese American community. In Stanley Sue & Thom Moore (Eds.), *The pluralistic society: A community mental health perspective* (pp. 222–236). New York: Human Sciences Press.

Chiu, Lian-Hwang. (1987). Child-rearing attitudes of Chinese, Chinese American, and Anglo-American mothers. *International Journal of Psychology, 22*(4), 409–419.

Chiu, Lian-Hwang. (1988). Locus of control differences between American and Chinese adolescents. *Journal of Social Psychology, 128,* 411–413.

Chow, Esther N. (1987). The influence of sex-role identity and occupational attainment on the psychological well-being of Asian American women. *Psychology of Women Quarterly, 11*(1), 69–82.

Chun-Hoon, Lowell. (1973). Jade Snow Wong and the fate of Chinese American identity. In Stanley Sue & Nathaniel Wagner (Eds.), *Asian Americans: Psychological perspectives* (pp. 125–135). Palo Alto, CA: Science and Behavior Books.

Chung, Rita, & Sumie Okazaki. (1991). Counseling Americans of Southeast Asian descent: The impact of the refugee experience. In Courtland Lee & Bernard Richardson (Eds.), *Multicultural issues in counseling: New approaches to diversity* (pp. 107–126). Alexandria, VA: American Association for Counseling and Development.

Citizen's Advisory Council, State of California Health and Welfare Agency, Department of Mental Health Services (1979). *Multi-cultural issues in mental health services: Strategies toward equity.* Sacramento: Author.

Cochran, Susan, Vickie Mays, & Laurie Leung. (1991). Sexual practices of heterosexual Asian-American young adults: Implications for risk of HIV infection. *Archives of Sexual Behavior, 20*(4), 381–391.

Commission on Wartime Relocation and Internment of Civilians. (1982). *Personal justice denied.* Washington, DC: U.S. Government Printing Office.

Committee on Cultural Psychiatry. (1989). Suicide among the Chinese and Japanese. In Committee on Cultural Psychiatry (Ed.), *Suicide and ethnicity in the United States* (pp. 58–71). New York: Brunner/Mazel.

Connor, John. (1974a). Acculturation and changing need patterns in Japanese-American and Caucasian-American college students. *Journal of Social Psychology, 93,* 293–294.

Connor, John. (1974b). Acculturation and family continuities in three generations of Japanese Americans. *Journal of Marriage and the Family, 36,* 159–165.

Connor, John. (1974c). Value continuities and change in three generations of Japanese Americans. *Ethos, 2*(3), 232–264.

Connor, John. (1975). Value changes in third-generation Japanese Americans. *Journal of Personality Assessment, 39,* 597–600.

Connor, John. (1977). *Tradition and change in three generations of Japanese Americans.* Chicago: Nelson-Hall.

Cook, Harold, & Chris Chi. (1984). Cooperative behavior and locus of control among American and Chinese-American boys. *Journal of Psychology, 118*(2), 169–177.

Cravens, Richard B. & Thomas Bornemann. (1990). Refugee camps in countries of first asylum and the North American resettlement process. In Wayne Holtzman & Thomas Bornemann (Eds.), *Mental health of immigrants and refugees* (pp. 38–50). Austin, TX: Hogg Foundation for Mental Health.

Crompton, Don W. (1974). Minority content in social work education. *Journal of Education for Social Work, 10,* 9–18.

Daniels, Roger. (1988). *Asian America: Chinese and Japanese in the United States since 1850.* Seattle: University of Washington Press.

DeVos, George. (1976). Responses to change: Recurrent patterns. In George DeVos (Ed.), *Responses to change: Society, culture, and personality* (pp. 342–359). New York: Nostrand.

Diamond, Michael J. & Michael H. Bond. (1974). The acceptance of "Barnum" personality interpretations by Japanese, Japanese-American, and Caucasian-American students. *Journal of Cross-Cultural Psychology, 5,* 228–235.

Dinges, Norman, & Devorah A. Lieberman. (1989). Intercultural communication competence: Coping with stressful work situations. *International Journal of Intercultural Relations, 13,* 371–385.

Dohrenwend, Barbara S. & Bruce P. Dohrenwend. (1974). *Stressful life events: Their nature and effects.* New York: Wiley.

Dohrenwend, Bruce P. & Barbara S. Dohrenwend. (1974). Social and cultural influences on psychopathology. *Annual Review of Psychology, 25,* 417–452.

Downing, Bruce, & Douglas Olney. (1982). *The Hmong in the West.* Papers of the 1981 Hmong Research Conference, University of Minnesota, Southeast Asian Refugee Studies Project.

Dubanoski, Richard, & Karen Snyder. (1980). Patterns of child abuse and neglect in Japanese- and Samoan-Americans. *Child Abuse and Neglect, 4,* 217–225.

Duff, Donald F. & Ransom J. Arthur. (1967). Between two worlds: Filipinos in the U.S. Navy. *American Journal of Psychiatry, 123,* 836–843.

Egawa, Janey, & Nathaniel Tashima. (1982). *Indigenous healers in Southeast Asian refugee communities.* San Francisco: Pacific Asian Mental Health Research Project.

Eisenbruch, Maurice. (1984). Cross-cultural aspects of bereavement. II: Ethnic and cultural variations in the development of bereavement practices. *Culture, Medicine, and Psychiatry, 8,* 315–347.

Eisenbruch, Maurice. (1991). From post-traumatic stress disorder to cultural bereavement: 2. Diagnosis of Southeast Asian refugees. *Social Science and Medicine, 33*(6), 673–680.

Endo, Russell. (1980). Asian Americans and higher education. *Phylon, 41*(4), 367–378.

Enright, John B. & Walter R. Jaeckle. (1963). Psychiatric symptoms and diagnosis in two subcultures. *International Journal of Social Psychiatry, 9,* 12–17.

Erickson, Roy V. & Giao Ngoc Hoang. (1980). Health problems among Indochinese refugees. *American Journal of Public Health, 70,* 1003–1005.

Fenz, Walter, & Abe Arkoff. (1962). Comparative need patterns of five ancestry groups in Hawaii. *Journal of Social Psychology, 58,* 67–89.

Finney, Joseph C. (1963). Psychiatry and multi-culturality in Hawaii. *International Journal of Social Psychiatry, 9,* 5–11.

Flaskerud, Jacquelyn. (1986a). Diagnostic and treatment differences among five ethnic groups. *Psychological Reports, 58,* 219–235.

Flaskerud, Jacquelyn. (1986b). The effects of cultural-compatible intervention on the utilization of mental health services by minority clients. *Community Mental Health Journal, 22*(2), 127–141.

Flaskerud, Jacquelyn. (1988). Mental health needs of Vietnamese refugees. *Hospital and Community Psychiatry, 39*(4), 435–437.

Flaskerud, Jacquelyn, & Nguyen Thi Anh. (1988). Mental health needs of Vietnamese refugees. *Hospital and Community Psychiatry, 39,* 435–437.

Flaskerud, Jacquelyn, & Li-tze Hu. (1992). Relationship of ethnicity to psychiatric diagnosis. *Journal of Nervous and Mental Disease, 180*(5), 296–303.

Flaskerud, Jacquelyn, & P. Y. Liu. (1990). Influence of therapist ethnicity and language on therapy outcomes of Southeast Asian clients. *The International Journal of Social Psychiatry, 36,* 18–29.

Flaskerud, Jacquelyn, & P. Y. Liu. (1991). Effects of an Asian client–therapist language, ethnicity, and gender match on client outcomes. *Community Mental Health Journal, 27,* 31–42.

Fong, Stanley. (1965). Assimilation of Chinese in America: Changes in orientation and social perception. *American Journal of Sociology, 71,* 265–273.

Fong, Stanley. (1973). Assimilation and changing social roles of Chinese Americans. *Journal of Social Issues, 29,* 115–127.

Fong, Stanley, & Harry Peskin. (1973). Sex-role strain and personality adjustment of China-born students in America: A pilot study. In Stanley

Sue & Nathaniel Wagner (Eds.), *Asian Americans: Psychological perspectives* (pp. 79–85). Palo Alto, CA: Science and Behavior Books. (Originally published in *Journal of Abnormal Psychology, 74*, 563–567, 1969.)

Ford, Robert. (1981). *Counseling strategies for ethnic minority students.* Olympia, WA: Office of the Superintendent of Public Instruction.

Ford, Robert. (1987). Cultural awareness and cross-cultural counseling. *International Journal for the Advancement of Counselling, 10,* 71–78.

Fort, Jane G., Jean C. Watts, & Gerald S. Lesser. (1969). Cultural background and learning in young children. *Phi Delta Kappan, 50,* 386–388.

Fox, David J. & Valerie B. Jordan. (1973). Racial preference and identification of black, American Chinese, and white children. *Genetic Psychological Monographs, 88,* 229–286.

Freimer, Nelson, Francis Lu, & Joseph Chen. (1989). Posttraumatic stress and conversion disorders in a Laotian refugee veteran: Use of amobarbital interviews. *Journal of Nervous and Mental Disease, 177*(7), 432–433.

Fugita, Stephen, & Kathleen Crittenden. (1990). Towards cultural- and population-specific norms for self-reported depressive symptomatology. *International Journal of Social Psychiatry, 36*(2), 83–92.

Fugita, Stephen, Karen Ito, Jennifer Abe, & David Takeuchi. (1991). Japanese Americans. In Noreen Mokuau (Ed.), *Handbook of social services for Asian and Pacific Islanders* (pp. 61–77). New York: Greenwood Press.

Fukuyama, Mary A. & Tom K. Greenfield. (1983). Dimensions of assertiveness in an Asian American student population. *Journal of Counseling Psychology, 30*(3), 429–432.

Furuto, Sharlene Maeda. (1991). Family violence among Pacific Islanders. In Noreen Mokuau (Ed.), *Handbook of social services for Asian and Pacific Islanders* (pp. 203–215). New York: Greenwood Press.

Ganesan, Soma, Stuart Fine, & Tsung-Yi Lin. (1989). Psychiatric symptoms in refugee families from Southeast Asia: Therapeutic challenges. *American Journal of Psychotherapy, 43*(2), 218–228.

Gaw, Albert. (1982). Chinese Americans. In Albert Gaw (Ed.), *Cross-cultural psychiatry* (pp. 1–29). Boston: John Wright.

Gay, Geneva. (1985). Implications of selected models of ethnic identity development for educators. *Journal of Negro Education, 54*(1), 43–55.

General Accounting Office. (1990). *Asian Americans: A status report.* Washington, DC: U.S. Government Printing Office.

Gibbs, Jewelle Taylor, & Larke Nahme Huang. (1989). A conceptual framework for assessing and training minority youth. In Jewelle Taylor Gibbs, Larke N. Huang, & Associates (Eds.), *Children of color: Psychological interventions with minority youth* (pp. 1–29). San Francisco: Jossey-Bass.

Gim, Ruth, Donald Atkinson, & Soo Kim. (1991). Asian-American acculturation, counselor ethnicity and cultural sensitivity, and ratings of counselors. *Journal of Counseling Psychology, 38,* 57–62.

Gim, Ruth, Donald Atkinson, & Scott Whiteley. (1990). Asian American acculturation, severity of concerns, and willingness to see a counselor. *Journal of Counseling Psychology, 37*(3), 281–285.

Goldstein, Beth. (1988). In search of survival: The education and integration of Hmong refugee girls. *Journal of Ethnic Studies, 16*, 1–27.

Gong-Guy, Elizabeth. (1987). *California Southeast Asian mental health needs assessment*. Oakland, CA: Asian Community Mental Health Services.

Grizzell, Steve, Joyce Savale, Phil Scott, & Detroit Nguyen. (1980). Indochinese refugees have vastly different views and use of medical care system. *Michigan Medicine, 79*, 624–628.

Gudykunst, William, Lori Sodetani, & Kevin Sonoda. (1987). Uncertainty reduction in Japanese-American/Caucasian relationships in Hawaii. *Western Journal of Speech Communication, 51*(3), 256–278.

Guillermo, Tessie. (1993). Health care needs and service delivery for Asian and Pacific Islander Americans: Health policy. In J. D. Hokoyama and Don Nakanishi (Eds.), *The state of Asian Pacific America: A public policy report. Policy issues to the year 2020* (pp. 61–78). Los Angeles: LEAP Asian Pacific Public Policy Institute and UCLA Asian American Studies Center.

Harvey, O. J., David E. Hunt, & Harold M. Schroder. (1961). *Conceptual systems and personality organization*. New York: Wiley & Sons.

Hatanaka, Herbert K., William Y. Watanabe, & Shinya Ono. (1975). The utilization of mental health services by Asian Americans in Los Angeles. In Wesley H. Ishikawa & Nikki Hayashi Archer (Eds.), *Delivery of services in Pan Asian communities* (pp. 33–39). San Diego: San Diego Pacific Asian Coalition Mental Health Training Center, San Diego State University.

Hayano, David. (1981). Ethnic identification and disidentification: Japanese-American views of Chinese Americans. *Ethnic Groups, 3*, 157–171.

Hess, Robert D., Chih-Mei Chang, & Teresa M. McDevitt. (1987). Cultural variations in family beliefs about children's performance in mathematics: Comparisons among People's Republic of China, Chinese-American, and Caucasian-American families. *Journal of Educational Psychology, 79*, 179–188.

Higa, Masanori. (1974). A comparative study of three groups of "Japanese" mothers: Attitudes toward child rearing. In William Lebra (Ed.), *Mental health research in Asia and the Pacific: Vol. 3. Youth, socialization, and mental health* (pp. 16–25). Honolulu: University Press of Hawaii.

Ho, Christine K. (1990). An analysis of domestic violence in Asian American communities: A multicultural approach to counseling. *Women and Therapy, 9*, 129–150.

Ho, Man-Keung. (1976). Social work with Asian Americans. *Social Casework, 57*(3), 195–201.

Ho, Man-Keung. (1984). Social group work with Asian/Pacific-Americans. *Ethnicity in Group Work Practice, 7*, 49–61.

Holmes, Thomas, & Richard Rahe. (1967). The social readjustment rating scale. *Journal of Psychosomatic Research, 11*, 213–218.

Hong, George. (1989). Application of cultural and environmental issues in family therapy with immigrant Chinese Americans. *Journal of Strategic and Systemic Therapies, 8*, 14–21.

Hsieh, Theodore, John Shybut, & Erwin Lotsof. (1969). Internal versus external control and ethnic group membership: A cross-cultural comparison. *Journal of Consulting and Clinical Psychology, 33,* 122–124.

Hsu, Jing, Wen-Shing Tseng, Geoffrey Ashton, John Jr. McDermott, & Walter Char. (1985). Family interaction patterns among Japanese-American and Caucasian families in Hawaii. *American Journal of Psychiatry, 142*(5), 577–581.

Huang, Karen. (1991). Chinese Americans. In Noreen Mokuau (Ed.), *Handbook of social services for Asian and Pacific Islanders* (pp. 79–96). New York: Greenwood Press.

Huang, Karen, & Laura Uba. (1992). Chinese American sexual attitudes and behaviors. *Archives of Sexual Behavior, 21*(3), 227–240.

Huang, Larke Nahme. (1989). Southeast Asian refugee children and adolescents. In Jewelle Taylor Gibbs, Larke N. Huang, & Associates (Eds.), *Children of color: Psychological interventions with minority children* (pp. 278–321). San Francisco: Jossey-Bass.

Huang, Larke Nahme, & Yu-Wen Ying. (1989). Chinese American children and adolescents. In Jewelle Taylor Gibbs, Larke N. Huang, & Associates (Eds.), *Children of color: Psychological interventions with minority children* (pp. 30–66). San Francisco: Jossey-Bass.

Huang, Lucy Jen. (1981). The Chinese American family. In Charles Mindel & Robert Habenstein (Eds.), *Ethnic families in America: Patterns and variations* (2nd ed.) (pp. 115–141). New York: Elsevier.

Ibrahim, Farah. (1984). Cross-cultural counseling and psychotherapy: An existential-psychological approach. *International Journal for the Advancement of Counselling, 7,* 159–169.

Irby, Charles, & Ernest Pon. (1988). Confronting new mountains: Mental health problems among male Hmong and Mien refugees. *Amerasia Journal, 14,* 109–118.

Ishisaka, Hideki, Quynh Nguyen, & Joseph Okimoto. (1985). The role of culture in the mental health treatment of Indochinese refugees. In Tom Owan (Ed.), *Southeast Asian mental health: Treatment, prevention, services, training, and research* (pp. 41–63). Washington, DC: U.S. Department of Health and Human Services.

Jeffres, Leo W. (1983). Communication, social class, and culture. *Communication Research, 10*(2), 219–246.

Jiobu, Robert. (1988). *Ethnicity and assimilation: Blacks, Chinese, Filipinos, Japanese, Koreans, Mexicans, Vietnamese, and Whites.* Albany: State University of New York Press.

Johnson, Colleen L. (1977). Interdependence, reciprocity and indebtedness: An analysis of Japanese American kinship relations. *Journal of Marriage and the Family, 39,* 351–363.

Johnson, Colleen L. & Frank A. Johnson. (1975). Interaction rules and ethnicity: The Japanese and Caucasians in Honolulu. *Social Forces, 54,* 452–466.

Johnson, Frank A. & Anthony Marsella. (1978). Differential attitudes toward verbal behavior in students of Japanese and European ancestry. *Genetic Psychology Monographs, 975,* 43–76.

Johnson, Frank A., Anthony J. Marsella, & Colleen L. Johnson. (1974). Social and psychological aspects of verbal behavior in Japanese-Americans. *American Journal of Psychiatry, 131,* 580–583.

Jones, Woodrow Jr. & Paul Strand. (1986). Adaptation and adjustment problems among Indochinese refugees. *Sociology and Social Research, 71,* 42–46.

JWK International Corporation. (1976). *Identification of problems in access to health care services and health careers for Asian Americans.* Annandale, VA: Author.

JWK International Corporation. (1978). *Summary and recommendations of conference on Pacific and Asian American families and HEW-related issues.* Annandale, VA: Author.

Kalish, Richard, & Sharon Moriwaki. (1973). The world of the elderly Asian American. *Journal of Social Issues, 29,* 187–209.

Kalish, Richard, & David Reynolds. (1976). *Death and ethnicity: A psychocultural study.* Farmingdale, NY: Baywood Publishing.

Kam, Katherine. (1989). A false and shattered peace. *California Tomorrow: Our Changing State, 4,* 8–21.

Kaneshige, Edward. (1973). Cultural factors in group counseling and interaction. *Personnel and Guidance Journal, 51,* 407–412.

Kanuha, Valli. (1987). Sexual assault in Southeast Asian communities: Issues in intervention. *Response to the Victimization of Women and Children: Journal of the Center for Women Policy Studies, 10,* 4–6.

Kelly, Gail. (1986). Coping with America: Refugees from Vietnam, Cambodia, and Laos in the 1970s and 1980s. *Annals of the American Academy of Political and Social Science, 489,* 138–149.

Kikumura, Akemi, & Harry Kitano. (1976). The Japanese American family. In Charles H. Mindel & Robert W. Habenstein (Eds.), *Ethnic families in America: Patterns and variations* (pp. 43–60). New York: Elsevier.

Kim, Bok-Lim. (1978). *The Asian Americans: Changing patterns, changing needs.* Montclair, NJ: Association of Korean Christian Scholars in North America.

Kim, Bok-Lim. (1980). *Korean American child at school and at home.* Technical report to the Administration for Children, Youth, and Families. Washington, DC.

Kim, Jean. (1981). *The process of Asian-American identity development: A study of Japanese American women's perceptions of their struggle to achieve positive identities.* Unpublished doctoral dissertation, University of Massachusetts.

Kim, S. Peter. (1983). Self-concept, English language acquisition, and school adaptation in recently immigrated Asian children. *Journal of Children in Contemporary Society, 15*(3), 71–79.

Kim, Sung. (1983). Eriksonian hypnosis framework for Asian Americans. *American Journal of Clinical Hypnosis, 25,* 235–241.

Kim, Sung. (1991). Cultural and other factors in assessing Asian- Americans. *The California Psychologist, 24*(4), 14, 22.

Kinzie, J. David. (1985). Overview of clinical issues in the treatment of Southeast Asian refugees. In Tom Owan (Ed.), *Southeast Asian mental health:*

Treatment, prevention, services, training, and research (pp. 113–135). Washington, DC: U.S. Department of Health and Human Services.

Kinzie, J. David. (1989). Therapeutic approaches to traumatized Cambodian refugees. *Journal of Traumatic Stress, 2,* 75–91.

Kinzie, J. David, James Boehnlein, Paul Leung, Laurie Moore, Crystal Riley, & Debra Smith. (1990). The prevalence of post-traumatic stress disorder and its clinical significance among Southeast Asian refugees. *American Journal of Psychiatry, 147,* 913–917.

Kinzie, J. David, & Jenelle Fleck. (1987). Psychotherapy with severely traumatized refugees. *American Journal of Psychotherapy, 41,* 82–94.

Kinzie, J. David, R. H. Frederickson, Ben Rath, Jenelle Fleck, & William Karls. (1984). Post-traumatic stress disorder among survivors of Cambodian concentration camps. *American Journal of Psychiatry, 141*(5), 645–650.

Kinzie, J. David, & Paul Leung. (1989). Clonidine in Cambodian patients with posttraumatic stress disorder. *Journal of Nervous and Mental Disease, 177*(9), 546–550.

Kinzie, J. David, Paul Leung, James K. Boehnlein, & Jennelle Fleck. (1987). Antidepressant blood levels in Southeast Asians: Clinical and cultural implications. *Journal of Nervous and Mental Disease, 175*(8), 480–485.

Kinzie, J. David, Paul Leung, Ahn Bui, Ben Rath, Kham One Keopraseuth, Crystal Riley, Jenelle Fleck, & Marie Ades. (1988). Group therapy with Southeast Asian refugees. *Community Mental Health Journal, 24,* 157–166.

Kinzie, J. David, & Spero Manson. (1983). Five-years' experience with Indochinese refugee psychiatric patients. *Journal of Operational Psychiatry, 14,* 105–111.

Kinzie, J. David, William Sack, Richard Angell, Greg Clarke, & Rath Ben. (1989). A three-year follow-up of Cambodian young people traumatized as children. *Journal of the American Academy of Child and Adolescent Psychiatry, 28*(4), 501–504.

Kinzie, J. David, William Sack, Richard Angell, Spero Manson, & Ben Rath. (1986). The psychiatric effects of massive trauma on Cambodian children: 1. The children. *Journal of American Academy of Child Psychiatry, 25,* 377–383.

Kinzie, J. David, Kiet Anh Tran, Agatha Breckenridge, & Joseph Bloom. (1980). An Indochinese refugee psychiatric clinic: Culturally accepted treatment approaches. *American Journal of Psychiatry, 137,* 1429–1432.

Kinzie, J. David, & Wen-Shing Tseng. (1978). Cultural aspects of psychiatric clinic utilization: A cross-cultural study in Hawaii. *International Journal of Social Psychiatry, 24*(3), 177–188.

Kitano, Harry. (1969). Japanese-American mental illness. In Stanley Plog & Robert Edgerton (Eds.), *Changing perspectives on mental illness* (pp. 256–284). New York: Holt, Rinehart & Winston.

Kitano, Harry. (1970). Mental illness in four cultures. *Journal of Social Psychology, 80,* 121–134.

Kitano, Harry, & Roger Daniels. (1988). *Asian Americans: Emerging minorities.* Englewood Cliffs, NJ: Prentice-Hall.

Kitano, Harry, & Akemi Kikumura. (1980). The Japanese American family. In

Russell Endo, Stanley Sue, & Nathaniel Wagner (Eds.), *Asian-Americans: Social and psychological perspectives* (pp. 3–16). Palo Alto, CA: Science and Behavior Books.

Knoll, Tricia. (1982). *Becoming Americans: Asian sojourners, immigrants, and refugees in the western United States.* Portland, OR: Coast to Coast Books.

Kobasa, Suzanne. (1979). Stressful life events, personality, and health: An inquiry into hardiness. *Journal of Personality and Social Psychology, 37*(1), 1–11.

Kobata, Fran. (1979). The influence of culture on family relations: The Asian American experience. In Pauline K. Ragan (Ed.), *Aging parents* (pp. 94–106). Los Angeles: University of Southern California Press.

Kranz, Peter. (1973). Toward achieving more meaningful encounters with minority group clients. *Hospital and Community Psychiatry, 24,* 343–344.

Kriger, Sara F. & William H. Kroes. (1972). Child-rearing attitudes of Chinese, Jewish, and Protestant mothers. *Journal of Social Psychology, 86,* 205–210.

Kroll, Jerome, Marjorie Habenicht, Thomas Mackenzie, Meo Yang, Sokha Chan, Tong Vang, Tam Nguyen, Mayjoua Ly, Banlang Phommasouvanh, Hung Nguyen, Yer Vang, Langsanh Souvannasoth, & Roberto Cabugao. (1989). Depression and post-traumatic stress disorder in Southeast Asian refugees. *American Journal of Psychiatry, 146,* 1592–1597.

Kroll, Jerome, Paul Linde, Marjorie Habenicht, Sokha Chan, Mee Yang, Tong Vang, Langsanh Souvannasoth, Tam Nguyen, Mayjoria Ly, Hung Nguyen, & Yer Vang. (1990). Medication compliance, antidepressant blood levels, and side effects in Southeast Asian patients. *Journal of Clinical Psychopharmacology, 10*(4), 279–283.

Kuo, Wen. (1984). Prevalence of depression among Asian- Americans. *Journal of Nervous and Mental Disease, 172*(8), 449–457.

Kuo, W., R. Gary, & N. Lin. (1975, August). *Locus of control and symptoms of psychological distress among Chinese-Americans.* Paper presented at the meeting of the Society for the Study of Social Problems, San Francisco.

Kuo, Wen, & Yung-mei Tsui. (1986). Social networking, hardiness, and immigrant's mental health. *Journal of Health and Social Behavior, 27,* 133–149.

Kuramoto, Ford. (1971). What do Asians want? *Journal of Social Work Education, 7*(3), 7–17.

Kurokawa, Minako. (1969). Acculturation and childhood accidents among Chinese and Japanese Americans. *Genetic Psychology Monographs, 79,* 89–159.

Lambert, Riki G. & Michael J. Lambert. (1984). The effects of role preparation for psychotherapy on immigrant clients seeking mental health services in Hawaii. *Journal of Community Psychology, 12,* 263–275.

Larsen, J. K. (1979). Innovations. *American Institutes for Research, 6*(2).

Lazarus, Richard. (1966). *Psychological stress and the coping process.* New York: McGraw-Hill.

Le, Daniel. (1983). Mental health and Vietnamese children. In Gloria Powell (Ed.), *The psychosocial development of minority group children* (pp. 373–384). New York: Brunner/Mazel.

Le, Ngoan. (1993). The case of the Southeast Asian refugees: Policy for a community "at risk." In J. D. Hokoyama & Don Nakanishi (Eds.), *The state of Asian Pacific America, a public policy report. Policy issues to the year 2020* (pp. 167–188). Los Angeles: LEAP Asian Pacific Public Policy Institute and UCLA Asian American Studies Center.

Lee, Evelyn. (1982). A social systems approach to assessment and treatment of Chinese American families. In Monica McGoldrick, John Pearce, & Joseph Giordano (Eds.), *Ethnicity and family therapy* (pp. 527–551). New York: Guilford Press.

Lee, Evelyn. (1985). Inpatient psychiatric services for Southeast Asian refugees. In Tom Owan (Ed.), *Southeast Asian mental health: Treatment, prevention, services, training, and research* (pp. 307–327). Washington, DC: U.S. Department of Health and Human Services.

Lee, Evelyn. (1988). Cultural factors in working with Southeast Asian refugee adolescents. *Journal of Adolescence, 11,* 167–179.

Lee, Evelyn, & Francis Lu. (1989). Assessment and treatment of Asian-American survivors of mass violence. *Journal of Traumatic Stress, 2,* 93–120.

Lee, Julie, & Virginia Cynn. (1991). Issues in counseling 1.5 generation Korean Americans. In Courtland Lee & Bernard Richardson (Eds.), *Multicultural issues in counseling: New approaches to diversity* (pp. 127–140). Alexandria, VA: American Association for Counseling and Development.

Leonetti, Donna. (1983). *Nisei aging project report.* Seattle: University of Washington.

Leong, Frederick. (1985). Career development of Asian Americans. *Journal of College Student Personnel, 26*(6), 539–546.

Leong, Frederick. (1986). Counseling and psychotherapy with Asian-Americans: Review of the literature. *Journal of Counseling Psychology, 33,* 196–206.

Leong, Frederick, & Shiroz Piroshaw Tata. (1990). Sex and acculturation differences in occupational values among Chinese American children. *Journal of Counseling Psychology, 37,* 208–212.

Liem, Nguyen. (1980). The resettlement of Vietnamese refugees. *Journal of Asian-Pacific and World Perspectives, 4,* 39–50.

Light, Ivan, & Edna Bonacich. (1988). *Immigrant entrepreneurs: Koreans in Los Angeles, 1965–1982.* Berkeley: University of California Press.

Lin, Chin-Yau, & Victoria Fu. (1990). A comparison of child-rearing practices among Chinese, immigrant Chinese, and Caucasian-American parents. *Child Development, 61*(1), 429–433.

Lin, Keh-Ming. (1986). Psychopathology and social disruption in refugees. In Carolyn Williams and Joseph Westermeyer (Eds.), *Refugee mental health in resettlement countries* (pp. 61–73). Washington, DC: Hemisphere Publishing.

Lin, Keh-Ming. (1990). Assessment and diagnostic issues in the psychiatric care of refugee patients. In Wayne Holtzman & Thomas Bornemann (Eds.), *Mental health of immigrants and refugees* (pp. 198–206). Austin, TX: Hogg Foundation for Mental Health.

Lin, Keh-Ming, & Ellen Finder. (1983). Neuroleptic dosage in Asians. *American Journal of Psychiatry, 140,* 490–491.

Lin, Keh-Ming, Thomas Inui, Arthur Kleinman, & William Womack. (1982). Sociocultural determinants of the help-seeking behavior of patients with mental illness. *Journal of Nervous and Mental Disease, 170,* 78–85.

Lin, Keh-Ming, Minoru Masuda, & Laurie Tazuma. (1982). Adaptational problems of Vietnamese refugees: 3. Case studies in clinic and field: Adaptive and maladaptive. *The Psychiatric Journal of the University of Ottawa, 7,* 173–183.

Lin, Keh-Ming, & Russell Poland. (1989). Pharmacotherapy of Asian psychiatric patients. *Psychiatric Annals, 19,* 659–663.

Lin, Keh-Ming, Russell E. Poland, Inocencia Nuccio, Kazuko Matsuda, Nhuhy Hathuc, Tung-Ping Su, & Paul Fu. (1989). A longitudinal assessment of haloperidol doses and serum concentrations in Asian and Caucasian schizophrenic patients. *American Journal of Psychiatry, 146,* 1307–1311.

Lin, Keh-Ming, & Winston Shen. (1991). Pharmacotherapy for Southeast Asian psychiatric patients. *Journal of Nervous and Mental Disease, 179,* 346–350.

Lin, Nan, Ronald Simeone, Walter Ensel, & Wen Kuo. (1979). Social support, stressful life events, and illness: A model and an empirical test. *Journal of Health and Social Behavior, 20*(2), 108–119.

Lin, Tsung-ji, & Mei-Chin Lin. (1978). Service delivery issues in Asian-North American communities. *American Journal of Psychiatry, 135,* 454–456.

Lin-Fu, Jane. (1988). Population characteristics and health care needs of Asian Pacific Americans. *Public Health Reports, 103,* 18–27.

Li-Repac, Diana. (1980). Cultural influences on clinical perception: A comparison between Caucasian and Chinese-American therapists. *Journal of Cross-Cultural Psychology, 11,* 327–342.

Loo, Chalsa, Ben Tong, & Reiko True. (1989). A bitter bean: Mental health status and attitudes in Chinatown. *Journal of Community Psychology, 17*(4), 283–296.

Lott, Juanita Tamayo. (1976). Migration of a mentality: The Pilipino community. *Social Casework, 57,* 165–172.

Lum, Roger. (1985). A community-based mental health service to Southeast Asians refugees. In Tom Owan (Ed.), *Southeast Asian mental health: Treatment, prevention, services, training, and research* (pp. 283–306). Washington, DC: U.S. Department of Health and Human Services.

Lyman, Stanford. (1974). *Chinese Americans.* New York: Random House.

Makabe, Tomoko. (1979). Ethnic identity scale and social mobility: The case of Nisei in Toronto, *The Canadian Review of Sociology and Anthropology, 16,* 136–145.

Maki, Mitchell. (1990). Countertransference with adolescent clients of the same ethnicity. *Child and Adolescent Social Work Journal, 7*(2), 135–145.

Marcia, James. (1966). Development and validation of ego-identity status. *Journal of Personality and Social Psychology, 3,* 551–558.

Marcia, James. (1980). Identity in adolescence. In Joseph Adelson (Ed.), *Handbook of adolescent psychology* (pp. 159–187). New York: Wiley.

Marcos, Luis, & Murray Alpert. (1976). Strategies and risks in psychotherapy with bilingual patients: The phenomenon of language independence. *American Journal of Psychiatry, 133,* 1275–1278.

Marcos, Luis, Murray Alpert, Leonel Urcuyo, & Martin Kesselman. (1973). The effect of interview language on the evaluation of psychopathology in Spanish-American schizophrenic patients. *American Journal of Psychiatry, 130,* 549–553.

Marsella, Anthony, David Kinzie, & Paul Gordon. (1973). Ethnic variations in the expression of depression. *Journal of Cross-Cultural Psychology, 4,* 435–458.

Marsella, Anthony, Kenneth Sanborn, Velma Kameoka, Lanette Shizuru, & Jerry Brennan. (1975). Cross-validation of self-report measures of depression among normal populations of Japanese, Chinese, and Caucasian ancestry. *Journal of Clinical Psychology, 31,* 281–287.

Maruyama, Magoroh. (1971). Yellow youth's psychological struggle. *Mental Hygiene, 55,* 382–390.

Mass, Amy Iwasaki. (1976). Asians as individuals: The Japanese community. *Social Casework, 57,* 160–164.

Mass, Amy Iwasaki. (1986). Psychological effects of the camps on Japanese Americans. In Roger Daniels, Sandra Taylor, & Harry Kitano (Eds.), *Japanese Americans: From relocation to redress* (pp. 159–162). Salt Lake City: University of Utah Press.

Mass, Amy Iwasaki. (1992). Interracial Japanese Americans: The best of both worlds or the end of the Japanese American community? In Maria Root (Ed.), *Racially mixed people in America: Within, between and beyond race* (pp. 265–279). Newbury Park, CA: Sage.

Masuda, Minoru, Keh-Ming Lin, & Laurie Tazuma. (1980). Adaptation problems of Vietnamese refugees. II: Life changes and perception of life events. *Archives of General Psychiatry, 37,* 447–450.

Masuda, Minoru, Gary Matsumoto, & Gerald Meredith. (1970). Ethnic identity in three generations of Japanese-Americans. *Journal of Social Psychology, 81,* 199–207.

Matsumoto, Gary, Gerald Meredith, & Minoru Masuda. (1970). Ethnic identification: Honolulu and Seattle Japanese-Americans. *Journal of Cross-Cultural Psychology, 1,* 63–76.

Matsunaga-Nishi, Setsuko. (1980). Presentation. In U.S. Commission on Civil Rights Conference (Ed.), *Civil rights issues of Asian and Pacific Americans: Myths and realities* (pp. 397–399). Washington, DC: U.S. Government Printing Office.

Matsuoka, Jon. (1990). Differential acculturation among Vietnamese refugees. *Social Work, 35*(4), 341–345.

Matsuoka, Jon. (1991). Vietnamese Americans. In Noreen Mokuau (Ed.), *Handbook of social services for Asian and Pacific Islanders* (pp. 117–130). New York: Greenwood Press.

Matsushima, Noreen Mokuau, & Nathaniel Tashima. (1982). *Mental health treatment modalities of Pacific/Asian-American practitioners.* San Francisco: Pacific Asian Mental Health Research Project.

McDermott, John F., Walter Char, Albert Robillard, Jing Hsu, Wen-Shing Tseng, & Geoffrey Ashton. (1984). Cultural variations in family attitudes and their implications for therapy. In Stella Chess & Alexander Thomas (Eds.), *Annual Progress in Child Psychiatry and Child Development* (pp. 145–154). New York: Brunner/Mazel.

McQuaide, Sharon. (1989). Working with Southeast Asian refugees. *Clinical Social Work Journal, 17,* 165–176.

Mental health care system works to meet needs of Southeast Asian refugees. (1985). *Refugee Reports, 6*(6), 1–5.

Meredith, Gerald. (1966). Amae and acculturation among Japanese-American college students in Hawaii. *Journal of Social Psychology, 70,* 171–180.

Meredith, Gerald. (1967). Ethnic identity scale: A study in transgenerational communication patterns. *Pacific Speech Quarterly, 2,* 57–67.

Meredith, Gerald. (1969). Sex temperament among Japanese-American college students in Hawaii. *Journal of Social Psychology, 77,* 149–156.

Meredith, Gerald, & Connie W. Meredith. (1966). Acculturation and personality among Japanese-American college students in Hawaii. *Journal of Social Psychology, 68,* 175–182.

Meredith, William, & George Rowe. (1986). Changes in Lao Hmong marital attitudes after immigrating to the United States. *Journal of Comparative Family Studies, 17,* 117–126.

Miller, Michael D., Rodney A. Reynolds, & Ronald E. Cambra. (1987). The influence of gender and culture on language intensity. *Communication Monographs, 54*(1), 101–105.

Min, Pyong Gap. (1984). A structural analysis of Korean business in the United States. *Ethnic Groups, 6* (1), 1–25.

Min, Pyong Gap. (1990). Problems of Korean immigrant entrepreneurs. *International Migration Review, 24,* 436–455.

Minatoya, Lydia, & William Sedlacek. (1979). *Another look at the melting pot: Asian-American undergraduates at the University of Maryland, College Park.* College Center Research Report #14–79. College Park: University of Maryland.

Minrath, Marilyn. (1985). Breaking the race barrier: The white therapist in interracial psychotherapy. *Journal of Psychosocial Nursing and Mental Health Services, 23*(8), 19–24.

Mizokawa, Donald, & David Ryckman. (1990). Attributions of academic success and failure: A comparison of six Asian-American ethnic groups. *Journal of Cross-Cultural Psychology, 21,* 434–451.

Mokuau, Noreen. (1987). Social workers' perceptions of counseling effectiveness for Asian American clients. *Social Work, 32,* 331–335.

Mokuau, Noreen, & Nathan Chang. (1991). Samoans. In Noreen Mokuau (Ed.), *Handbook of social services for Asian and Pacific Islanders* (pp. 151–169). New York: Greenwood Press.

Mokuau, Noreen, & Debbie Shimizu. (1991). Conceptual framework for social services for Asian and Pacific Islander Americans. In Noreen Mokuau (Ed)., *Handbook of social services for Asian and Pacific Islanders* (pp. 21–36). New York: Greenwood Press.

Mollica, Richard. (1986). *Cambodian refugee women at risk.* Paper presented at the American Psychological Association annual meeting, Washington, DC.

Mollica, Richard, Yael Caspi-Yavin, Paola Bollini, Toan Truong, Svang Tor, & James Lavelle. (1992). The Harvard Trauma Questionnaire: Validating a cross-cultural instrument for measuring torture, trauma, and posttraumatic stress disorder in Indochinese refugees. *Journal of Nervous and Mental Disease, 180*(2), 111–116.

Mollica, Richard, & James Lavelle. (1988). Southeast Asian refugees. In Lillian Comas-Diaz & Ezra Griffith (Eds.), *Clinical guidelines in cross-cultural mental health* (pp. 262–293). New York: Wiley & Sons.

Mollica, Richard F., Grace Wyshak, & James Lavelle. (1987). The psychosocial impact of war trauma and torture on Southeast Asian refugees. *American Journal of Psychiatry, 144,* 1567–1571.

Mollica, Richard, Grace Wyshak, James Lavelle, Toan Truong, Svang Tor, & Ter Yang. (1990). Assessing symptom change in Southeast Asian refugee survivors of mass violence and torture. *American Journal of Psychiatry, 147*(1), 83–88.

Mollica, Richard F., Grace Wyshak, Daphne de Marneffe, Franlinette Khuon, & James Lavelle. (1987). Indochinese versions of the Hopkins Symptom Checklist-25. *American Journal of Psychiatry, 144*(4), 497–500.

Moon, Anson, & Nathaniel Tashima. (1982). *Help seeking behavior and attitudes of Southeast Asian refugees.* San Francisco: Pacific Asian Mental Health Research Project.

Moon, Jeong-Hwa, & Joseph Pearl. (1991). Alienation of elderly Korean American immigrants as related to place of residence, gender, age, years of education, time in the U.S., living with or without children, and living with or without spouse. *International Journal of Aging and Human Development, 32*(2), 115–124.

Moore, Charles A. (1967). *The Chinese mind: Essentials of Chinese philosophy and culture.* Honolulu: East-West Center Press.

Moore, Laurie, & James Boehnlein. (1991). Treating psychiatric disorders among Mien refugees from highland Laos. *Social Science and Medicine, 32*(9), 1029–1036.

Moritsugu, John, & Stanley Sue. (1983). Minority status as a stressor. In Robert Feldner, Leonard Jason, John Moritsugu, & Stephanie Farber (Eds.), *Preventive psychology: Theory, research, and practice* (pp. 162–174). New York: Pergamon.

Morris, Teresa. (1990). Culturally sensitive family assessment. *Family Process, 29*(1), 105–116.

Morrow, Robert. (1987). Cultural differences—be aware. *Academic Therapy, 23*(2), 143–149.

Morrow, Robert. (1989). Southeast Asian child rearing practices: Implications for child and youth care workers. *Child and Youth Care Quarterly, 18*(4), 273–287.

Mortland, Carol, & Judy Ledgerwood. (1987). Secondary migration among

Southeast Asian refugees in the United States. *Urban Anthropology and Studies of Cultural Systems and World Economic Development, 16,* 291–326.

Muecke, Marjorie. (1983). In search of healers—Southeast Asian refugees in the American health system. *Western Journal of Medicine, 139,* 835–840.

Muecke, Marjorie. (1987). Resettled refugees' reconstructions of identity: Lao in Seattle. *Urban Anthropology, 16*(3–4), 273–289.

Munoz, Faye Untalan. (1979). Pacific Islanders: An overview. In U.S. Commission on Civil Rights Conference (Ed.), *Civil rights issues of Asian and Pacific Americans: Myths and realities* (pp. 342–348). Washington, DC: U.S. Government Printing Office.

Murase, Kenji. (n.d.). *Summary of report of Subpanel on Mental Health of Asian/Pacific Americans.* Unpublished manuscript. President's Commissions on Mental Health. Washington, DC.

Murase, Kenji, Janey Egawa, & Nathaniel Tashima. (1985). Alternative mental health service models in Asian/Pacific communities. In Tom Owan (Ed.), *Southeast Asian mental health: Treatment, prevention, services, training, and research* (pp. 229–259). Washington, DC: National Institute of Mental Health.

Muskin-Davidson, Mary Beth, & Charles Golden. (1989). Lao Depression Inventory. *Journal of Personality Assessment, 53*(1), 161–168.

Nagata, Donna. (1989a). Japanese American children and adolescents. In Jewelle T. Gibbs, Larke N. Huang, & Associates (Eds.), *Children of color: Psychological interventions with minority children* (pp. 67–113). San Francisco: Jossey-Bass.

Nagata, Donna. (1989b). Long-term effects of the Japanese American internment camps: Impact upon the children of the internees. *Journal of the Asian American Psychological Association, 13,* 48–55.

Nagata, Donna. (1990). The Japanese American internment: Exploring the transgenerational consequences of traumatic stress. *Journal of Traumatic Stress, 3*(1), 47–69.

Nagata, Donna. (1991). Transgenerational impact of the Japanese American internment: Clinical issues in working with children of former internees. *Psychotherapy, 28,* 121–128.

Nakagawa, B. & R. Watanabe. (1973). *A study of the use of drugs among the Asian American youth of Seattle.* Seattle: Demonstration Project of Asian Americans.

Narikiyo, Trudy, & Velma Kameoka. (1992). Attributions of mental illness and judgments about help seeking among Japanese-American and White American students. *Journal of Counseling Psychology, 39*(3), 363–369.

Newton, Barbara, Elizabeth Buck, Don Kunimura, Carol Colfer, & Deborah Scholsberg. (1988). Ethnic identity among Japanese Americans in Hawaii. *International Journal of Intercultural Relations, 12*(4), 305–315.

Nguyen, Liem Thanh, & Alan B. Henkin. (1983). Perceived sociocultural change among Indochinese refugees: Implications for education. In Ronald J. Samada & Sandra L. Woods (Eds.), *Perspectives in immigrant and minority education* (pp. 156–171). New York: University Press of America.

Nguyen, San Duy. (1982). Psychiatric and psychosomatic problems among South East Asian refugees. *The Psychiatric Journal of the University of Ottawa, 7,* 163–172.

Nicassio, Perry. (1983). Psychosocial correlates of alienation: Study of a sample of Indochinese refugees. *Journal of Cross-Cultural Psychology, 14*(3), 337–351.

Nicassio, Perry. (1985). The psychosocial adjustment of the Southeast Asian refugee: An overview of empirical findings and theoretical models. *Journal of Cross-Cultural Psychology, 16*(2), 153–173.

Nicassio, Perry, Joseph D. LaBarbera, Paulette Coburn, & Rose Finley. (1986). The psychosocial adjustment of the Amerasian refugees: Findings from the Personality Inventory for Children. *Journal of Nervous and Mental Disease, 174,* 541–544.

Nicassio, Perry, & J. Kirby Pate. (1984). An analysis of problems of resettlement of the Indochinese refugees in the United States. *Social Psychiatry, 19,* 135–141.

Nicassio, Perry, Gary S. Solomon, Steven Guest, & Joel E. McCullough. (1986). Emigration stress and language proficiency as correlates of depression in a sample of Southeast Asian refugees. *International Journal of Social Psychiatry, 32,* 22–28.

Nidorf, Jeanne. (1985). Mental health and refugee youths: A model for diagnostic training. In Tom Owan (Ed.), *Southeast Asian mental health: Treatment, prevention, services, training, and research* (pp. 391–429). Washington, DC: U.S. Dept. of Health and Human Services.

Nihira, Kazuo, Iris Mink, & Carol Shapiro. (1991, April). *Home environment of developmentally disabled children: A comparison between Euro-American and Asian-American families.* Paper presented at the biennial meeting of the Society for Research in Child Development, Seattle.

Nishio, Kazumi, & Murray Bilmes. (1987). Psychotherapy with Southeast Asian American clients. *Professional Psychology Research and Practice, 18*(4), 342–346.

Office of Civil Rights. (1973). Untitled report. Washington, DC: Department of Health, Education, and Welfare.

Office of Special Concerns. (1977). *Asian American field survey: Summary of the data.* Division of Asian American Affairs, Department of Health, Education, and Welfare. Washington, DC: U.S. Government Printing Office.

Ogawa, Dennis, & Terry Welden. (1972). Cross-cultural analysis of feedback behavior within Japanese American and Caucasian American small groups. *Journal of Communication, 22,* 189–195.

Okamura, Jonathan, & Amefil Agbayani. (1991). Filipino Americans. In Noreen Mokuau (Ed.), *Handbook of social services for Asian and Pacific Islanders* (pp. 97–115). New York: Greenwood Press.

Okano, Yukio, & Bernard Spilka. (1971). Ethnic identity, alienation and achievement orientation in Japanese-American families. *Journal of Cross-Cultural Psychology, 2,* 273–282.

Olmedo, Esteban L. (1979). Acculturation: A psychometric perspective. *American Psychologist, 34,* 1061–1070.

Onoda, Lawrence. (1977). Neurotic-stable tendencies among Japanese American Sanseis and Caucasian students. *Journal of Non-White Concerns, 5,* 180–185.

O'Reilly, Joseph, Kenneth Tokuno, & Aaron Ebata. (1986). Cultural differences between Americans of Japanese and European ancestry in parental valuing of social competence. *Journal of Comparative Family Studies, 17*(1), 87–97.

Osako, Masako. (1976). Intergenerational relations as an aspect of assimilation: The case of Japanese Americans. *Sociological Inquiry, 46,* 67–72.

O'Sullivan, Michael, Paul Peterson, Gary Cox, & Judith Kirkeby. (1989). Ethnic populations: Community mental health services ten years later. *American Journal of Community Psychology, 17,* 17–30.

Ou, Y. S. & H. McAdoo. (1980). *Ethnic identity and self-esteem in Chinese children.* Unpublished report, Columbia Research Systems, Columbia, Maryland.

Owan, Tom. (1985). Southeast Asian mental health: Transition from treatment to prevention—A new direction. In Tom Owan (Ed.), *Southeast Asian mental health: Treatment, prevention, services, training, and research* (pp. 141–167). Washington, DC: U.S. Department of Health and Human Services.

Padilla, Amado M., Yuria Wagatsuma, & Kathryn J. Lindholm. (1985). Acculturation and personality as predictors of stress in Japanese and Japanese-Americans. *Journal of Social Psychology, 125*(3), 295–305.

Pak, Anita W., Kenneth L. Dion, & Karen K. Dion. (1985). Correlates of self-confidence with English among Chinese students in Toronto. *Canadian Journal of Behavioral Science, 17*(4), 369–378.

Palinkas, Lawrence. (1982). Ethnicity, identity and mental health: The use of rhetoric in an immigrant Chinese church. *The Journal of Psychoanalytic Anthropology, 5*(3), 235–258.

Pang, Valerie O. (1981). *The self-concept of Japanese American and White American children in the fourth through sixth grade as measured by a modified Piers–Harris Children's Self Concept Scale.* Unpublished doctoral dissertation, University of Washington.

Pang, Valerie O. (1991). The relationship of test anxiety and math achievement to parental values in Asian-American and European-American middle school students. *Journal of Research and Development, 24*(4), 1–10.

Pang, Valerie O., Donald T. Mizokawa, James K. Morishima, & Roger G. Olstad. (1985). Self-concepts of Japanese-American children. *Journal of Cross-Cultural Psychology, 16*(1), 99–109.

Paykel, Eugene. (1979). Causal relationships between clinical depression and life events. In James Barrett, Robert Rose, & Gerald Klerman (Eds.), *Stress and Mental Disorder.* New York: Raven Press.

Payton, Carolyn. (1985). Addressing the special needs of minority women. *New Directions for Student Services, 29,* 75–90.

Pedersen, Paul. (1991). Balance as a criterion for social services for Asian and Pacific Islander Americans. In Noreen Mokuau (Ed)., *Handbook of social services for Asian and Pacific Islanders* (pp. 37–57). New York: Greenwood Press.

Peters, David, Earl Hershfield, David Fish, & Jure Manfreda. (1987). Tuberculosis status and social adaptation of Indochinese refugees. *International
Migration Review, 21,* 845–856.

Phinney, Jean. (1989). Stages of ethnic identity development in minority group
adolescents. *Journal of Early Adolescence, 9,* 34–49.

Phinney, Jean. (1990). Ethnic identity in adolescents and adults: Review of
research. *Psychological Bulletin, 108,* 499–514.

Phinney, Jean S. & Linda Line Alipuria. (1990). Ethnic identity in college
students from four ethnic groups. *Journal of Adolescence, 13,* 171–183.

Plummer, Davenport. (1971). Verbal interaction and verbal ability: Research
and practice. *The English Record, 21,* 168–174.

Powers, Stephen, Melisa Choroszy, & Peggy Douglas. (1987). Attributions for
success and failure of Japanese-American and Anglo-American university
students. *Psychology, A Quarterly Journal of Human Behavior, 24*(3), 17–23.

President's Commission on Mental Health. (1978). *Report of the President's
Commission on Mental Health.* Washington, DC: U.S. Government Printing
Office.

Rabin, A. I. & J. A. Limuaco. (1967). A comparison of connotative meaning of
Rorschach's inkblots for American and Filipino college students. *Journal of
Social Psychology, 72,* 197–203.

Rabkin, Judith, & Elmer Struening. (1976). Life events, stress and illness.
Science, 194, 1013–1020.

Rahe, Richard. (1975). Epidemiologic studies of life change and illness.
International Journal of Psychiatric Medicine, 6, 133–146.

Redick, Liang-Tien, & Beverly Wood. (1982). Cross-cultural problems for
Southeast Asian refugee minors. *Child Welfare, 61,* 365–373.

Reglin, Gary, & Dale Adams. (1990). Why Asian American high school students
have higher grade point averages and SAT scores than other high school
students. *High School Journal, 73*(3), 143–149.

Rohner, Ronald, & Sandra Pettengill. (1985). Perceived parental acceptance—
rejection and parental control among Korean adolescents. *Child Development, 56,* 524–528.

Romero, Dan. (1985). Cross-cultural counseling: Brief reactions for the
practitioner. *Counseling Psychologist, 13*(4), 665–671.

Root, Maria. (1989). Guidelines for facilitating therapy with Asian American
clients. In Donald Atkinson, George Morten, & Derald Sue (Eds.),
Counseling American minorities: A cross-cultural perspective (pp. 116–128).
Dubuque, IA: William C. Brown. (Originally published in *Psychotherapy, 22,*
349–356, 1985).

Root, Maria P., Christine Ho, & Stanley Sue. (1986). Issues in the training of
counselors for Asian Americans. In Harriet Letley & Paul Pedersen (Eds.),
Cross-cultural training for mental health professionals (pp. 199–209). Spring-
field, IL: Charles Thomas.

Rosenblatt, Rebecca, & Siu Wa Tang. (1987). Do Oriental psychiatric patients
receive different dosages of psychotropic medication when compared with
Occidentals? *Canadian Journal of Psychiatry, 32,* 270–274.

Rotter, Julian. (1966). Generalized expectancies for internal versus external control of reinforcement. *Psychological Monographs, 80.*

Rozée, Patricia, & Van Gretchen Boemel. (1989). The psychological effects of war trauma and abuse on older Cambodian refugee women. *Women and Therapy, 8*(4), 23–50.

Rumbaut, Ruben. (1985). Mental health and the refugee experience: A comparative study of Southeast Asian refugees. In Tom Owan (Ed.), *Southeast Asian mental health: Treatment, prevention, services, training, and research* (pp. 433–456). Washington, DC: U.S. Dept. of Health and Human Services.

Rumbaut, Ruben. (1990). The agony of exile: A study of the migration and adaptation of Indochinese refugee adults and children. In Frederick L. Ahearn, Jr., & Jean Athey Garrison (Eds.), *Refugee children: Theory, research, and practice* (pp. 53–91). Baltimore: Johns Hopkins University Press.

Ryan, Angela, & Michael Smith. (1989). Parental reactions to developmental disabilities in Chinese American families. *Child and Adolescent Social Work Journal, 6*(4), 283–299.

Saeki, Kaeko, Florence Clark, & Stanley Azen. (1985). Performance of Japanese and Japanese-American children on Motor Accuracy-Revised and Design Copying Tests of the Southern California Sensory Integration Tests. *American Journal of Occupational Therapy, 39,* 103–109.

Sanders, Daniel. (1975). Dynamics of ethnic and cultural pluralism: Implications for social work education and curriculum innovations. *Journal of Education for Social Work, 11,* 95–100.

Santos, Rolando. (1983). The social and emotional development of Filipino-American children. In Gloria Powell (Ed.), *The psychosocial development of minority group children* (pp. 131–146). New York: Brunner/Mazel.

Scheff, Thomas. (1972). On research and sanity: Political dimensions of psychiatric thought. In William P. Lebra (Ed.), *Mental health research in Asia and the Pacific: Vol. 2. Transcultural research in mental health* (pp. 400–406). Honolulu: University Press of Hawaii.

Sechrest, Lee. (1969). Philippine culture, stress, and psychopathology. In William A. Caudill & Tsung-Yi Lin (Eds.), *Mental health research in Asia and the Pacific* (pp. 306–334). Honolulu: East-West Center Press, University of Hawaii.

Seipel, Michael. (1988). Locus of control as related to life experiences of Korean immigrants. *International Journal of Intercultural Relations, 12,* 61–71.

Seligman, Martin. (1975). *Helplessness: On depression, development, and death.* San Francisco: Freeman.

Shibutani, Tamotsu, & Kian Kwan. (1965). *Ethnic stratification: A comparative approach.* London: Macmillan.

Shon, Steven, & Davis Ja. (1982). Asian families. In Monica McGoldrick, John Pearce, & Joseph Giordano (Eds.), *Ethnicity and family therapy* (pp. 208–229). New York: Guilford Press.

Shu, Ramsay, & Adele Satele. (1977). *The Samoan community in Southern*

California: Conditions and needs. Chicago: Asian American Mental Health Training Center.

Silverman, Morton. (1985). Preventive intervention research: A new beginning. In Tom Owan (Ed.), *Southeast Asian mental health: Treatment, prevention, services, training, and research* (pp. 169–181). Washington, DC: U.S. Department of Health and Human Services.

Singer, K. (1976). Cross-cultural dynamics in psychotherapy. In Jules Masserman (Ed.), *Social psychiatry: Vol 2. The range of normal in human behavior* (pp. 115–147). New York: Grune & Stratton.

Slaughter-Defoe, Diana, Kathryn Nakagawa, Ruby Takanishi, & Deborah Johnson. (1990). Toward cultural/ecological perspectives on schooling and achievement in African- and Asian-American children. *Child Development, 61,* 363–383.

Slote, Walter. (1972). Psychodynamic structures in Vietnamese personality. In William Lebra (Ed.), *Mental health research in Asia and the Pacific: Vol. 2. Transcultural research in mental health* (pp. 114–133). Honolulu: University Press of Hawaii.

Smith, Elsie M. (1985). Ethnic minorities: Life stress, social support, and mental health issues. *Counseling Psychologist, 13*(4), 537–579.

Smith, Elsie M. (1989). Black racial identity development. *Counseling Psychologist, 17,* 277–288.

Smith, Ken K. (1983). Social comparison processes and dynamic conservatism in intergroup relations. *Research in Organizational Behavior, 5,* 199–233.

Sokoloff, Burton, Jean Carlin, & Hien Pham. (1984). Five-year follow-up of Vietnamese refugee children in the United States (Pt. 1). *Clinical Pediatrics, 23,* 565–570.

Sollenberger, Richard T. (1968). Chinese American child-rearing practices and juvenile delinquency. *Journal of Social Psychology, 74,* 13–23.

Solomon, Irvin D. (1985). Minority status, pluralistic education and the Asian-American: A teacher's perspective and agenda. *Education, 106*(1), 88–93.

Spencer, Margaret, & Carol Markstrom-Adams. (1990). Identity processes among racial and ethnic minority children in America. *Child Development, 61,* 290–310.

Sramek, John J., Marsha A. Sayles, & George M. Simpson. (1986). Neuroleptic dosage for Asians: A failure to replicate. *American Journal of Psychiatry, 143*(4), 535–536.

Starr, Paul, & Alden Roberts. (1981). Attitudes toward Indochinese refugees: An empirical study. *Journal of Refugee Resettlement, 1*(4), 51–61.

Starr, Paul, & Alden Roberts. (1982). Attitudes toward new Americans: Perceptions of Indo-Chinese in nine cities. *Research in Race and Ethnic Relations, 3,* 165–186.

Stehr-Green, Jeanette, & Peter Schantz. (1986). Trichinosis in Southeast Asian refugees in the United States. *American Journal of Public Health, 76,* 1238–1239.

Stephan, Cookie W. & Walter G. Stephan. (1989). After intermarriage: Ethnic identity among mixed-heritage Japanese-Americans and Hispanics. *Journal of Marriage and the Family, 51,* 507–519.

Stephan, Walter G. & Cookie W. Stephan. (1985). Intergroup anxiety. *Journal of Social Issues, 41*(3), 157–175.

Steward, Margaret, & David Steward. (1973). The observation of Anglo-, Mexican-, and Chinese-American mothers teaching their young sons. *Child Development, 44,* 329–337.

Strom, Robert, S. H. Park, & S. Daniels. (1987). Child rearing dilemmas of Korean immigrants to the United States. *International Journal of Experimental Research in Education, 24,* 91–102.

Suan, Lance, & John Tyler. (1990). Mental health values and preference for mental health resources of Japanese-American and Caucasian-American students. *Professional Psychology: Research and Practice, 21,* 291–296.

Sue, David, Steve Ino, & Diane Sue. (1983). Nonassertiveness of Asian Americans: An inaccurate assumption? *Journal of Counseling Psychology, 30,* 581–588.

Sue, David, & Derald W. Sue. (1991). Counseling strategies for Chinese Americans. In Courtland Lee & Bernard Richardson (Eds.), *Multicultural Issues in Counseling: New Approaches to Diversity* (pp. 79–87). Alexandria, VA: American Association for Counseling and Development.

Sue, David, Derald W. Sue, & Diane Sue. (1983). Psychological development of Chinese-American children. In Gloria Powell (Ed.), *The psychosocial development of minority group children* (pp. 159–166). New York: Brunner/Mazel.

Sue, David, Diane M. Sue, & Steve Ino. (1990). Assertiveness and social anxiety in Chinese-American women. *Journal of Psychology, 124*(2), 155–163.

Sue, David, & Stanley Sue. (1987). Cultural factors in the clinical assessment of Asian Americans. *Journal of Consulting and Clinical Psychology, 55,* 479–487.

Sue, Derald W. (1975). Asian Americans: Social psychological factors affecting their life-styles. In J. Steven Picou & Robert E. Campbell (Eds.), *Career behavior of special groups: Theory, research, and practice* (pp. 97–121). Columbus, Ohio: Merrill.

Sue, Derald W. (1978). World views and counseling. *Personnel and Guidance Journal, 56,* 458–462.

Sue, Derald W. (1989a). Ethnic identity: The impact of two cultures on the psychological development of Asians in America. In Donald Atkinson, George Morten, & Derald W. Sue (Eds.), *Counseling American minorities: A cross-cultural perspective* (pp. 103–115). Dubuque, IA: W. C. Brown. (Originally published in 1973, in Stanley Sue & Nathaniel Wagner [Eds.], *Asian-Americans: Psychological perspectives* [pp. 146–149]. Palo Alto, CA: Science and Behavior Books.)

Sue, Derald W. (1989b). Racial/cultural identity development among Asian Americans: Counseling/therapy implications. *Journal of the Asian American Psychological Association, 13*(1), 80–86.

Sue, Derald W. (1990). Culture-specific strategies in counseling: A conceptual framework. *Professional Psychology: Research and Practice, 21*(6), 424–433.

Sue, Derald W. & Austin Frank. (1973). A typological approach to the psychological study of Chinese and Japanese American college males. *Journal of Social Issues, 29,* 129–148.

Sue, Derald W. & Barbara Kirk. (1972). Psychological characteristics of Chinese American students. *Journal of Counseling Psychology, 19,* 471–478.

Sue, Derald W. & Barbara Kirk. (1973). Differential characteristics of Japanese-American and Chinese-American college students. *Journal of Counseling Psychology, 20,* 142–148.

Sue, Derald W. & Barbara Kirk. (1975). Asian Americans: Uses of counseling and psychiatric services on a college campus. *Journal of Counseling Psychology, 22,* 84–86.

Sue, Derald W. & David Sue. (1977). Barriers to effective cross-cultural counseling. *Journal of Counseling Psychology, 24,* 420–429.

Sue, Derald W. & David Sue. (1990). *Counseling the culturally different: Theory and practice* (2nd ed.). New York: Wiley & Sons.

Sue, Derald W. & Stanley Sue. (1972a). Counseling Chinese-Americans. *Personnel and Guidance Journal, 50,* 637–644.

Sue, Derald W. & Stanley Sue. (1972b). Ethnic minorities: Resistance to being researched. *Professional Psychology, 3,* 11–17.

Sue, Stanley. (1973). Training of "third-world" students to function as counselors. *Journal of Counseling Psychology, 20,* 73–78.

Sue, Stanley. (1977). Community mental health services to minority groups: Some optimism, some pessimism. *American Psychologist, 32,* 616–624.

Sue, Stanley. (1980). Psychological theory and implications for Asian Americans. In Russell Endo, Stanley Sue, & Nathaniel Wagner (Eds.), *Asian-Americans: Social and psychological perspectives* (pp. 288–303). Palo Alto, CA: Science and Behavior Books.

Sue, Stanley. (1993). The changing Asian American population: Mental health policy. In J. D. Hokoyama & Don Nakanishi (Eds.), *The state of Asian Pacific America: A public policy report. Policy issues to the year 2020* (pp. 79–93). Los Angeles: LEAP Asian Pacific Public Policy Institute and UCLA Asian American Studies Center.

Sue, Stanley, & Robert Chin. (1983). The mental health of Chinese-American children: Stressors and resources. In Gloria Powell (Ed.), *The psychosocial development of minority group children* (pp. 385–397). New York: Brunner/Mazel.

Sue, Stanley, Diane Fujino, Li-tze Hu, David Takeuchi, & Nolan Zane. (1991). Community mental health services for ethnic minority groups: A test of the cultural responsiveness hypothesis. *Journal of Consulting and Clinical Psychology, 59*(4), 533–540.

Sue, Stanley, & Harry Kitano. (1973). Stereotypes as a measure of success. *Journal of Social Issues, 29,* 83–98.

Sue, Stanley, & Herman McKinney. (1975). Asian Americans in the community mental health care system. *American Journal of Orthopsychiatry, 45,* 111–118.

Sue, Stanley, & James Morishima. (1982). *The mental health of Asian Americans.* San Francisco: Jossey-Bass.

Sue, Stanley, & Derald W. Sue. (1971). Chinese American personality and mental health. *Amerasia Journal, 1,* 36–49.

Sue, Stanley, & Derald W. Sue. (1973). Chinese-American personality and mental health. In Stanley Sue & Nathaniel Wagner (Eds.), *Asian Americans: Psychological perspectives* (pp. 111–124). Palo Alto, CA: Science and Behavior Books.

Sue, Stanley, & Derald W. Sue. (1974). MMPI comparisons between Asian American and non-Asian students utilizing a student health psychiatric clinic. *Journal of Counseling Psychology, 21,* 423–427.

Sue, Stanley, Nathaniel Wagner, Davis Ja, Charlene Margullis, & Louise Lew. (1976). Conceptions of mental illness among Asian and Caucasian American students. *Psychological Reports, 38,* 703–708.

Sue, Stanley, & Nolan Zane. (1985). Academic achievement and socioemotional adjustment among Chinese university students. *Journal of Counseling Psychology, 32*(4), 570–579.

Sue, Stanley, & Nolan Zane. (1987). The role of culture and cultural techniques in psychotherapy: A critique and reformulation. *American Psychologist, 42*(1), 37–45.

Suinn, Richard, Kathryn Rickard-Figueroa, Sandra Lew, & Patricia Vigil. (1987). The Suinn–Lew Self-Identity Acculturation Scale: An Initial Report. *Educational and Psychological Measurement, 47,* 401–407.

Sung, Betty. (1985). Bicultural conflicts in Chinese immigrant children. *Journal of Comparative Family Studies, 16,* 244–269.

Suzuki, Bob H. (1977). Education and the socialization of Asian Americans: A revisionist analysis of the "model minority" thesis. *Amerasia Journal, 4,* 23–52.

Takaki, Ronald. (1989). *Strangers from a different shore.* Boston: Little, Brown.

Takamura, Jeanette C. (1991). Asian and Pacific Islander elderly. In Noreen Mokuau (Ed)., *Handbook of social services for Asian and Pacific Islanders* (pp. 185–202). New York: Greenwood Press.

Takeuchi, David, David Williams, & Russell Adair. (1991). Economic stress and children's emotional and behavioral problems. *Journal of Marriage and the Family, 53,* 1031–1041.

Tashima, Eugene, & Karen Ito. (1982). *Asian American self-concept: Preliminary thoughts on illness expression and the role of women.* Los Angeles: UCLA Asian American Studies Center.

Thein, Tin Myaing. (1980). Health issues affecting Asian/Pacific American women. In U.S. Commission on Civil Rights (Ed.), *Civil rights issues of Asian and Pacific Americans: Myths and realities* (pp. 153–164). Washington, DC: U.S. Government Printing Office.

Thompson, Janice. (1991). Exploring gender and culture with Khmer refugee women: Reflections on participatory feminist research. *Advances in Nursing Science, 13*(3), 30–48.

√Timberlake, Elizabeth, & Kim Cook. (1984). Social work and the Vietnamese refugee. *Social Work, 29,* 108–113.

Ting-Toomey, Stella. (1980, May). *Ethnic identity and close friendships in Chinese-American college students.* Paper presented at the annual meeting of the International Communication Association, Acapulco, Mexico.

Ting-Toomey, Stella. (1980). Ethnic identity and close friendships in Chinese-American college students. *International Journal of Intercultural Relations, 5,* 383–406.

Tomine, Satsuki. (1985). Jan Ken Po Gakko: A Japanese-American cultural education program. *Journal of Multicultural Counseling and Development, 13*(4), 164–169.

Tonay, Veronica. (1991). California women and their dreams: A historical and sub-cultural comparison of dream content. *Imagination, Cognition, and Personality, 10*(1), 85–99.

Tong, Ben. (1971). The ghetto of the mind: Notes on the historical psychology of Chinese America. *Amerasia Journal, 1,* 1–31.

Touliatos, John, & Byron Lindholm. (1980). Behavior disturbance of children of native-born and immigrant parents. *Journal of Community Psychology, 8*(1), 28–33.

Toupin, Elizabeth Ahn. (1980). Counseling Asians: Psychotherapy in the context of racism and Asian-American history. *American Journal of Orthopsychiatry, 50*(1), 76–86.

Tracey, Terence, Frederick Leong, & Cynthia Glidden. (1986). Help seeking and problem perception among Asian Americans. *Journal of Counseling Psychology, 33*(3), 331–336.

True, Reiko Homma. (1975). Mental health services in a Chinese American community. In Wesley Ishikawa & Nikki Hayashi Archer (Eds.), *Service delivery in Pan Asian communities.* San Diego: Pacific Asian Coalition.

True, Reiko Homma. (1976, October). *Mental health service delivery in the Asian American community.* Paper presented at the annual conference of the American Public Health Association, Miami Beach, Florida.

True, Reiko Homma. (1990). Psychotherapeutic issues with Asian American women. *Sex Roles, 22,* 477–486.

Tseng, Wen-Shing, & Jing Hsu. (1969/1970). Chinese culture, personality formation and mental illness. *International Journal of Social Psychiatry, 16,* 5–14.

Tseng, Wen-Shing, & John T. McDermott. (1975). Psychotherapy: Historical roots, universal elements and cultural variations. *American Journal of Psychiatry, 132*(2), 378–384.

Tsui, Philip, & Gail Schultz. (1988). Ethnic factors in group process: Cultural dynamics in multi-ethnic therapy groups. *American Journal of Orthopsychiatry, 58,* 136–142.

Tung, May. (1991). Insight-oriented psychotherapy for the Chinese patient. *American Journal of Orthopsychiatry, 61*(2), 186–194.

Tung, Tran Minh. (1985). Psychiatric care for Southeast Asians: How different is different? In Tom Owan (Ed.), *Southeast Asian mental health: Treatment, prevention, services, training, and research* (pp. 5–40). Washington, DC: U.S. Department of Health and Human Services.

Tung, Tran-Minh. (1972). The family and the management of mental health problems in Vietnam. In William Lebra (Ed.), *Mental health research in Asia and the Pacific: Vol. 2. Transcultural research in mental health* (pp. 107–113). Honolulu: University Press of Hawaii.

Uba, Laura. (1980). *Approaches to mental health service delivery for Asian Americans in Los Angeles county.* Nashville, TN: Vanderbilt Institute for Public Policy Studies.

Uba, Laura. (1981). Ascribing meaning to single, molecular measures: A question of methodological adequacy. *Journal of Personality and Social Psychology, 40,* 1090–1094.

Uba, Laura. (1982). Meeting the mental health needs of Asian Americans: Mainstream or segregated services. *Professional Psychology, 13,* 215–222.

Uba, Laura. (1992). Cultural barriers to American health care among Southeast Asian refugees. *Public Health Reports, 107*(5), 544–548.

Uba, Laura. (1994). Supply of health care professionals. In Nolan Zane, David T. Takeuchi, & Kathleen N. J. Young (Eds.), *Confronting critical health issues of Asian and Pacific Islanders* (pp. 376–396). Newbury Park, CA: Sage.

Uba, Laura, & Rita Chung. (1991). The relationship between trauma and financial and physical well-being among Cambodians in the United States. *Journal of General Psychology, 118,* 215–225.

Union of Pan Asian Communities. (1978). *Understanding the pan Asian client: A handbook for helping professionals.* San Diego: Author.

United States Commission on Civil Rights. (1992). *Civil rights issues facing Asian Americans in the 1990s.* Washington, DC: Author.

Uomoto, Jay. (1986). Examination of psychological stress in ethnic minorities from a learned helplessness framework. *Professional Psychology: Research and Practice, 17,* 448–453.

Uomoto, Jay, & Richard Gorsuch. (1984). Japanese American response to psychological disorder: Referral patterns, attitudes, and subjective norms. *American Journal of Community Psychology, 12,* 537–550.

Van Deusen, John. (1982). Health/mental health studies of Indochinese refugees: A critical overview. *Medical Anthropology, 6,* 231–252.

Watanabe, Colin. (1973). Self-expression and the Asian-American experience. *Personnel and Guidance Journal, 51,* 390–396.

Watts, Alan. (1951). *The wisdom of insecurity.* New York: Vintage Books.

Weiss, Melford. (1973). Selective acculturation and the dating process: The pattern of Chinese-Caucasian inter-racial dating. In Stanley Sue & Nathaniel Wagner (Eds.), *Asian Americans: Psychological perspectives* (pp. 75–78). Palo Alto, CA: Science and Behavior Books.

Welty, Paul T. (1985). *The Asians: Their evolving heritage.* New York: Harper & Row.

Westcott, Nina. (1985). A cross-cultural adaptation of the structured life-review technique. *Techniques: A Journal for Remedial Education and Counseling, 1,* 364–366.

Westermeyer, Joseph. (1979). Folk concepts of mental disorder among the Lao: Continuities with similar concepts in other cultures and in psychiatry. *Culture, Medicine, and Psychiatry, 3,* 301–317.

Westermeyer, Joseph. (1984). Advances in alcohol and substance abuse. *Cultural and Sociological Aspects of Alcoholism and Substance Abuse, 4*(1), 9–18.

Westermeyer, Joseph. (1986). Two self-rating scales for depression in Hmong refugees. *Journal of Psychiatric Research, 20,* 103–113.

Westermeyer, Joseph. (1987). Prevention of mental disorder among Hmong refugees in the United States. *Social Science and Medicine, 25*(8), 941–947.

Westermeyer, Joseph. (1988). DSM-III psychiatric disorders among Hmong refugees in the United States. *American Journal of Psychiatry, 145,* 197–202.

Westermeyer, Joseph. (1989). Paranoid symptoms and disorders among 100 Hmong refugees: A longitudinal study. *Acta Psychiatrica Scandinavica, 80,* 47–59.

Westermeyer, Joseph, Allan Callies, & John Neider. (1990). Welfare status and psychosocial adjustment among 100 Hmong refugees. *Journal of Nervous and Mental Disease, 178*(5), 300–306.

Westermeyer, Joseph, John Neider, & Tou-Fu Vang. (1984). Acculturation and mental health: A study of Hmong refugees at 1.5 and 3.5 years post-migration. *Social Science and Medicine, 18,* 87–93.

Westermeyer, Joseph, Tou-Fu Vang, & John Neider. (1983). A comparison of refugees using and not using a psychiatric service: An analysis of DSM III criteria and self-rating scales in cross-cultural context. *Journal of Operational Psychiatry, 14,* 36–40.

Westermeyer, Joseph, Tou-Fu Vang, & John Neider. (1984). Symptom change over time among Hmong refugees: Psychiatric patients versus nonpatients. *Psychopathology, 17,* 168–177.

White, Clovis L., & Peter J. Burke. (1987). Ethnic role identity among Black and White college students: An interactionist approach. *Sociological Perspectives, 30*(3), 310–331.

White, W. Glenn, & Edith Chan. (1983). A comparison of self-concept scores of Chinese and White graduate students and professionals. *Journal of Non-White Concerns, 19,* 138–141.

Williams, Carolyn, & Joseph Westermeyer. (1983). Psychiatric problems among adolescent Southeast Asian refugees. *Journal of Nervous and Mental Disease, 171,* 79–85.

Wong, Diane. (1980). Asian/Pacific American women: Legal issues. In U.S. Commission on Civil Rights (Ed.), *Civil rights issues of Asian and Pacific Americans: Myths and realities* (pp. 140–148). Washington, DC: U.S. Government Printing Office.

Wong, Herbert Z. (1985a). Asian and Pacific Americans. In Lonnie R. Snowden (Ed.), *Reaching the underserved: Mental health needs of neglected populations.* Beverly Hills, CA: Sage.

Wong, Herbert Z. (1985b). Training for mental health service providers to Southeast Asian refugees: Models, strategies, and curricula. In Tom Owan (Ed.), *Southeast Asian mental Health: Treatment, prevention, services, training, and research* (pp. 345–390). Washington, DC: U.S. Department of Health and Human Services.

Wong, Janlee. (1980). Indochinese refugees: The mental health perspective. In

U.S. Commission on Civil Rights (Ed.), *Civil rights issues of Asian and Pacific Americans: Myths and realities* (pp. 222–233). Washington, DC: U.S. Government Printing Office.

Wong, Normund. (1977). *Psychiatric education and training of Asian American psychiatrists.* Paper presented at annual meeting of the American Psychiatric Association, Toronto, Ontario, Canada.

Wong, Paul, & Gary Reker. (1985). Stress, coping, and well-being in Anglo and Chinese elderly. *Canadian Journal of Aging, 4*(1), 29–37.

✓ Woon, Yuen-Fong. (1986). Some adjustment aspects of Vietnamese and Sino-Vietnamese families in Victoria, Canada. *Journal of Comparative Family Studies, 17,* 349–370.

Wu, I-hsin, & Charles Windle. (1980). Ethnic specificity in the relative minority use and staffing of community mental health centers. *Community Mental Health Journal, 16,* 156–168.

Yamamoto, Joe. (1976). Japanese-American suicides in Los Angeles. In Joseph Westermeyer (Ed.), *Anthropology and mental health: setting a new course* (pp. 29–36). The Hague: Mouton Publishers.

Yamamoto, Joe. (1982). Japanese Americans. In Albert Gaw (Ed.), *Cross-Cultural Psychiatry* (pp. 31–54). Boston: John Wright.

Yamamoto, Joe. (1986). Therapy for Asian Americans and Pacific Islanders. In Charles B. Wilkinson (Ed.), *Ethnic Psychiatry* (pp. 89–142). New York: Plenum Medical Book Co.

Yamamoto, Joe, & Frank Acosta. (1982). Treatment of Asian Americans and Hispanic Americans: Similarities and differences. *Journal of the American Academy of Psychoanalysis, 10,* 585–607.

Yamamoto, Joe, Julia Lam, Desmond Fung, Frank Tan, & Mamoru Iga. (1977). Chinese-speaking Vietnamese refugees in Los Angeles: A preliminary investigation. In Edward F. Foulks, Ronald M. Wintrob, Joseph Westermeyer, & Armando R. Favazza (Eds.), *Current perspectives in cultural psychiatry* (pp. 113–118). New York: Spectrum.

Yang, Julia. (1991). Career counseling of Chinese American women: Are they in limbo? *Career Development Quarterly, 39*(4), 350–359.

Yao, Esther. (1985). A comparison of family characteristics of Asian-American and Anglo-American high achievers. *International Journal of Comparative Sociology, 26,* 198–208.

Yi, Kris, Nolan Zane, & Stanley Sue. (1986). Cognitive appraisal of assertion responses among Asian and Caucasian Americans. *Asian American Psychological Association Journal,* 65–68.

Ying, Yu-Wen. (1992). Life satisfaction among San Francisco Chinese-Americans. *Social Indicators Research, 26,* 1–22.

Young, Nancy F. (1972a). Changes in values and strategies among Chinese in Hawaii. *Sociology and Social Research, 56,* 228–241.

Young, Nancy F. (1972b). Independence training from a cross-cultural perspective. *American Anthropologist, 74,* 629–638.

Yu, Elena. (1985). Studying Vietnamese refugees: Methodological lessons in transcultural research. In Tom Owan (Ed.), *Southeast Asian mental health:*

Treatment, prevention, services, training, and research (pp. 517–541). Washington, DC: U.S. Department of Health and Human Services.

Yu, Elena, Ching-Fu Chang, William Liu, & Marilyn Fernandez. (1989). Suicide among Asian American youth. In Marcia Feinleib (Ed.), *Report of the Secretary's Task Force on youth suicide* (pp. 157–176). Washington, DC: U.S. Department of Health and Human Services.

Yu, Eui-Young. (1983). Korean communities in America: Past, present, and future. *Amerasia Journal, 10*(2), 23–51.

Yu, Kuen, & Luke Kim. (1983). The growth and development of Korean-American children. In Gloria Powell (Ed.), *The psychosocial development of minority group children* (pp. 147–158). New York: Brunner/Mazel.

Yu, Lucy C., & Ernest Harburg. (1980). Acculturation and stress among Chinese Americans in a university town. *International Journal of Group Tensions, 10*(1–4), 99–119.

Yu, Lucy C., & Ernest Harburg. (1981). Filial responsibility to aged parent: Stress of Chinese Americans. *International Journal of Group Tensions, 11*(1–4), 47–58.

Zaharlick, Amy, & Jean Brainard. (1987). Demographic characteristics, ethnicity, and the resettlement of Southeast Asian refugees in the U.S. *Urban Anthropology and the Studies of Cultural Systems and World Economic Development, 16,* 327–373.

Zane, Nolan, & Toshi Sasao. (1992). Research on drug abuse among Asian Pacific Americans. *Drugs and Society, 6*(3–4), 181–209.

Zane, Nolan, Stanley Sue, Li-Tze Hu, & Jung-Hye Kwon. (1991). Asian-American assertion: A social learning analysis of cultural differences. *Journal of Counseling Psychology, 38,* 63–70.

Index

Achievement orientation, 18, 44–46, 68, 132–133, 152
Acculturation, differences in 13
  and attitudes toward mental health services, 32, 199, 206
  and cultural conflicts, 30, 127
  and ethnic identity, 104, 108, 110, 115–116
  intraethnic differences in, 31
  as factor in the way mental health services are delivered, 207, 210, 218, 237, 256
  and parental restrictiveness, 40
  and personality, 82, 86–87
  and psychopathology rates, 173–175, 180–182
Affiliation, 64–66
Age, as predictor of mental health problems, 175, 178
Alienation
  and age, 178
  and ethnic identity, 91, 112
  gender differences in, 178
  in Korean Americans, 181
  and racism, 83, 120, 123
  in Southeast Asians, 180, 194
  and stress, 47, 131
  and therapy, 235
  and traumas, 140
Amerasians, 183, 189
American born (see Foreign born compared to American born)

Anger (see Hostility)
Anxiety, 66–68, 251–253
  and acculturation, 126, 155
  in Cambodians, traumatized, 173
  in Chinese Americans, 171
  gender differences in, 67
  in Hmong, 176
  intergroup and social types of, 78–79
  in Japanese Americans, 171
  and locus of control, 83
  and psychopathology, rates of, 160
  in Southeast Asians, 179, 188, 190–191, 170, 206
  and traumas, 181
  in Vietnamese, 152
  (see also Posttraumatic stress disorder)
Appearance physical, 83–84, 111–112 (see also Self-concept)
Asian Americans, differing from non-Asian Americans
  in academic pressure, 132–133
  in academic support, 200
  in attitudes toward mental health services, 214
  in attitudes toward own race, 102, 111
  in classification of abnormal or problematic behavior, 11, 159
  in communication styles, 34–38, 230, 232, 244

293